'SUFFER THE LITTLE CHILDREN':

NATIONAL AND INTERNATIONAL DIMENSIONS OF CHILD POVERTY AND PUBLIC POLICY

ADVANCES IN EDUCATION IN DIVERSE COMMUNITIES: RESEARCH, POLICY AND PRAXIS

Series Editor: Carol Camp Yeakey

ADVANCES IN EDUCATION IN DIVERSE COMMUNITIES:
RESEARCH, POLICY AND PRAXIS   VOLUME 4

'SUFFER THE LITTLE CHILDREN':
NATIONAL AND INTERNATIONAL DIMENSIONS OF CHILD POVERTY AND PUBLIC POLICY

EDITED BY

CAROL CAMP YEAKEY
Washington University in St. Louis, St. Louis, MO, USA

JEANITA W. RICHARDSON
Virginia State University, Petersburg, VA, USA

JUDITH BROOKS BUCK
Hampton University, Hampton, VA, USA

ELSEVIER
JAI

Amsterdam – Boston – Heidelberg – London – New York – Oxford
Paris – San Diego – San Francisco – Singapore – Sydney – Tokyo

1-31-7

ELSEVIER B.V.
Sara Burgerhartstraat 25
P.O. Box 211
1000 AE Amsterdam
The Netherlands

ELSEVIER Inc.
525 B Street, Suite 1900
San Diego
CA 92101-4495
USA

**ELSEVIER Ltd
The Boulevard, Langford
Lane, Kidlington
Oxford OX5 1GB
UK**

ELSEVIER Ltd
84 Theobalds Road
London
WC1X 8RR
UK

First edition 2006

British Library Cataloguing in Publication Data
A catalogue record is available from the British Library.

ISBN-10: 0-7623-0831-1
ISBN-13: 978-0-7623-0831-6
ISSN: 1479-358X (Series)

⊗ The paper used in this publication meets the requirements of ANSI/NISO Z39.48-1992 (Permanence of Paper). Printed in The Netherlands.

CONTENTS

LIST OF CONTRIBUTORS

Kingsley Banya	Florida International University, Miami, FL, USA
Ximena de la Barra	United Nations Children's Fund (UNICEF), Panama, Republica de Panama
Francis Musa Boakari	University of the Incarnate Word, San Antonio, TX, USA and Federal Universidad de Piaui, Teresina, Piaui, Brazil
Judith Brooks Buck	Hampton University, Hampton, VA, USA
Juliet Elu	Spelman College, Atlanta, GA, USA
Kassie Freeman	Dillard University, New Orleans, LA, USA
Samuel Hinton	Eastern Kentucky University, Richmond, KY, USA
Rodney K. Hopson	Duquesne University, Pittsburgh, PA, USA
Sesha Kethineni	Illinois State University, Normal, IL, USA
Tricia Klosky	Saint Mary's University of Minnesota, Winona, MN, USA
Tamás Kozma	University of Debrecen, Debrecen, Hungary
David Matheson	University College of Northampton, United Kingdom
Rob McBride	United Kingdom
Elavie Ndura	University of Nevada-Reno, Reno, NV, USA
Gabriella Pusztai	University of Debrecen, Debrecen, Hungary
Jeanita W. Richardson	Virginia State University, Petersburg, VA, USA
Jamil Salmi	The World Bank, Washington, D.C., USA

Maria Teresa Tatto	Michigan State University, East Lansing, MI, USA
Katalin Torkos	University of Debrecen, Debrecen, Hungary
Margot Wilson	University of Victoria, British Columbia, Canada
Frank C. Worrell	University of California at Berkeley, Berkeley, CA, USA
Carol Camp Yeakey	Washington University in St. Louis, St. Louis, MO, USA

DEDICATION

To the children of the world, who must endure the sufferings of which we write.

PROLOGUE

As the 21st century begins, the overwhelming majority of the people in the world who live in poverty are women and children. Humanity has seen stunning advances and has made enormous strides for children, many of them in the last decade, many others in just over the span of a generation. Children's lives have been saved and their suffering prevented (UNICEF, 2000). For example, polio, once a global epidemic, is on the verge of eradication in some countries, and deaths from two remorseless child killers, measles and neonatal tetanus, have been reduced over the past 10 years by 85% and more than 25%, respectively. Some 12 million children are now free from the risk of mental retardation due to iodine deficiency. Blindness from vitamin A deficiency has been significantly reduced. More children are in school today than at any previous time.

Despite the many stunning steps forward, a number of goals remain out of reach for hundreds of millions of children throughout the world. In researching the lives of children around the world, one finds that their status is inextricably interwoven with the lives and status of women. Their lives and futures are threatened in a world marked by deeper and more intractable poverty, greater inequality between the rich and poor, proliferating conflict and violence, the deadly spread of HIV/AIDS, and the interminable issues of discrimination and exploitation of women and children (UNICEF, 2000).

These problems are not new, but they are more widespread and profoundly entrenched than they were even a decade ago. Interwoven and reinforcing, they feed off one another and abrogate the rights of women and children in compounding ways. In some countries and regions, these issues threaten to undo much of what has been accomplished. Intergenerational patterns of poverty, violence and conflict, discrimination and disease are not unconquerable. These problems-like other challenges before them-can be met. Given the resources that the world has at hand, these deadly cycles can be broken within a single generation.

Some of the most dramatic and compelling stories of our times are of the significant gains in social development when the ideals of human dignity, justice and equality became reality through the actions of governments, organizations and individuals. Millions of people who might have died from communicable diseases and preventable illnesses in the past 50 years were saved because of public health measures such as immunization, improved access to safe water and sanitation facilities, and mass information campaigns. Hundreds of thousands of women are alive today because of well-spaced and healthy pregnancies. Millions of children, born of healthy mothers, well-nourished and immunized against childhood diseases, have survived whereas others, born before the child survival and development revolution of the 1980s and its life-saving programs, did not. Thousands of children and adolescents are now in school rather than trapped in exploitative and hazardous labor, or living on the streets and train platforms, or being trafficked for prostitution.

But there are also sober accounts of the 20th century and early 21st century about actions and inaction and times when not even the slightest shadow of the ideals of human rights could be seen. Clearly, not all societies have enjoyed the fruits of progress – and women and children especially have been denied. Over the past 20 years, at the same time that the world economy increased exponentially, the number of people living in poverty grew to more than 1.2 billion, or one in every five persons, including more than 600 million children (Rainwater & Smeeding, 2003; UNICEF, 2000). Even polio, a virus largely conquered decades ago, is resurfacing in Asia and ten African nations. In the last 15 years, denial and an unconscionable silence have allowed the HIV/AIDS pandemic to kill millions and decimate societies, especially in Sub-Saharan Africa. Yet while Sub-Saharan Africa continues to have the world's highest incidence of AIDS, Eastern Europe and Central Asia are suffering from the fastest rate of grown in HIV infections (Nakashima, 2004). And in the last 10 years, the rape of women and girls and the systematic slaughter of civilians, including children, have become conventional weapons of war in every region of the world where conflicts rage. One has only to witness the great humanitarian catastrophe in Darfur, the western Sudanese province where more than one million people have been chased out of their homes by government-backed militia force called Janjaweed. Human rights and aid groups accuse the Sudanese government of carrying out an ethnic cleansing campaign through brutal rape and sexual exploitation, targeting three tribes: the Fur, Massaleit and Zaghawa (Wax, 2004).

The question becomes how can our contemporary era hold such disparate and conflicting realities? Why has progress been possible in some countries and not in others? And what distinguishes countries where the rights of women and children are protected and promoted from those where women and children languish in poverty because the commitment to their rights was and is a hollow promise? Answers to these questions turn on the point of leadership. Where leadership for children and for women is just, their rights are protected. Where leadership is abdicated, abuses and human rights violations follow. We now know that where women's rights are at risk, children's rights are also. Poverty is the immutable overlay which traps injustice.

The number of people living in poverty continues to grow as globalization – one of the most powerful economic phenomena of our time – proceeds along its inherently asymmetrical course: expanding markets across national boundaries and increasing the incomes of a relative few while further strangling the lives of those without the resources to be investors or the capabilities to benefit from the global culture (Barber, 1996). The majority of the poor are women and children. While poor before, they are even poorer now, as the two tiered world economy widens the gaps between rich and poor countries and between rich and poor people.

Slave-like conditions also describe the lives of millions of other children throughout the world. There is no way to precisely calculate the exact number of young boys and girls whose lives are endangered by their sale and trafficking, by debt bondage, serfdom, forced or compulsory labor, forced or compulsory recruitment into armed conflict, prostitution, pornography or by the production and trafficking of drugs. Efforts to eliminate these gross violations have been ongoing and have been energized by the 1999 Worse Forms of Child Labor Convention. But according to estimates by the International Labor Organization (ILO), some 250 million children between the ages of 5 and 14 work in developing countries and some 50 million to 60 million children between the ages of 5 and 11 work in hazardous circumstances. The challenge of preventing and eradicating extreme violations of children's rights illustrate the layers of want, discrimination and exploitation that drive humanity's poorest children into obscure and dangerous worlds. Further, the developed countries of the world are far from innocent of the plagues of exploitative child labor and human trafficking (Cockburn, 2003; UNICEF, 2000).

Women and children are among the first to suffer when crises remove the veneer from seemingly prosperous nations to reveal the poverty and discrimination that exists. Even in countries that have robust economic growth, poverty is paralyzing ever greater numbers, as in parts of the United States, the United Kingdom and Canada (Rainwater & Smeeding, 2003). Natural disasters contribute to shredding the veneer of prosperity and human suffering, with women and children in poverty suffering disproportionately. One has only to revisit the recent devastation wrought by Hurricane Katrina in the Gulf Coast in the U.S. and the initial governmental response to it, to understand the disadvantages wrought by poverty, racial discrimination and the geography of opportunity (Alter, 2005). It is not only that America neglected her poor in the Gulf Coast region following Hurricane Katrina, but that this population has been neglected for decades, often suffering generational poverty. In Latin America, the poorest 20% of people share less than 3% of national income. In contrast, countries such as Costa Rica, Cuba, Sri Lanka and Vietnam have shown, that even against international political odds, consistent policies aimed at providing a solid foundation of social services pay off in better health conditions and higher literacy rather than those found in countries with greater economic resources (Rainwater & Smeeding, 2003).

In other countries, deepening pockets of poverty are masked in average national statistics. Only by disaggregating the national averages can the poor, who are huddled in the margins, be located. In the U.S., in New York City, for example, the percentage of children born into poverty rose from 44 to 52% from 1990 to 1996, a 20% increase, and the number of homeless children rose 21% during the same period. And, after years of decline, the child poverty rate in America is once again, on the increase (Crosson-Tower, 2004), at the very time when the U.S. government curtails its network of social safety programs for its most vulnerable citizens.

With the breakdown of many official nation-states and an unbridled international trade in weapons, the armed conflicts of the past decades are arenas of chronic human insecurity and flagrant atrocities, with increasingly large populations governed and terrorized by rogue groups. Consider the conflicts of the past decade, among them those in Afghanistan, Iraq, Angola, Bosnia and Herzegovina, the Democratic Republic of the Congo, Eritrea, Ethiopia, Rwanda, Sierra Leone, Somalia, Sri Lanka and the Sudan, and the brutalities that enveloped Kosovo and East Timor. Moreover, the inestimable humanitarian toll has yet to be calculated for women and children of the Middle East, for not only the present generation, but future generations. These and other flash points, noted earlier, challenge over burdened relief and development efforts, undermine the rights of children and women and, pose grave risks on a daily basis to humanitarian workers. Like the ravages of poverty, the festering conflicts of today, many masked as political instability as opposed to rank expansionism, threaten the achievements in health and education that governments, the international community and local citizens have labored for decades to attain. What makes the ruthless conflicts that tear at the world so sustainable? The fact is that poverty, protracted instability, rank expansionism, greed and a vacuum of political leadership set the stage for many of the global conflicts and the human devastation they spawn.

At the same time, there is pervasive violence in both the industrialized and developing worlds, as well, that runs through the lives of children and women – sometimes a subtle subtext, other times a pattern of explosive moments – in their families and communities, in mass media and entertainment. In the United States, the incidence of violence within the family and the larger society, once hidden from public sight and statistics, is ubiquitous, sparing no ethnic group or culture as it trickles down from one generation to the next. Children reared on violence often turn into violent adults. In the richest nation in the world, the United States, small arms and light weapons used by children have found their way from manufacturers to schoolrooms with tragic results. Culpablity must accrue not only to those who use weapons, but to those who provide weapons for financial gain. They too must be considered "partners to the crime." Unfortunately, state budget priorities reveal that in the U.S., states have spent more on incarceration and punishment of youth, than on their re-education and rehabilitation (Children's Defense Fund, 2002; Yeakey, 2003).

For all the gains made, the story of the 20th and the early years of the 21st century is about failed political leadership – a lack of vision, an absence of courage, a passive neglect. The number of violations of children's rights that occur around the globe every day are staggering. They range from acts of omission – such as the failure to register births or provide access to health care services and primary school – to the deliberate abuses of armed conflict, forced labor and sexual exploitation. Clearly, any nation's focus of "guns over butter," of military spending over investments in job creation, environmental protection, family planning, and the health, education and nutrition of all of her children is a serious issue.

Suffer the Little Children: National and International Dimensions of Child Poverty and Public Policy could not be published at a more propitious time. With international conflicts serving to envelop not only the world's financial resources, but human resources as well, as concerned citizens, our focus must be on creating a world, for ourselves and our children, where we can all live in peace and harmony, despite ethnic or religious differences. Democracy's challenge throughout the world is to rethink her own definitions of progress in order to improve the quality of life, not only for the rich, but for the poor who live in our midst, as well. In June of 1947, General George Marshall outlined a plan which stands to this day as one of the most outstanding examples in human history of visionary leadership, generosity of spirit, far-sighted practicality, and the willingness to dream and to act on the grand scale. All are fundamental prerequisites for successfully managing the transition which must now be made to serve humanity and to address the sufferings of women and children, throughout the world. The wisdom offered in *Suffer the Little Children: National and International Dimensions of Child Poverty and Public Policy* may help us find our way.

REFERENCES

Alter, J. (2005). Poverty, Race & Katrina, Lessons of A National Shame. (Special Report). **Newsweek**, September 19, 2005, Volume CXLVI, No. 12., 26–53.

Barber, B. R. (1996). *Jihad vs. McWorld*. New York: Ballantine.

Children's Defense Fund (2002). The state of children in America's union: A 2002 action guide to leave no child behind. Washington, DC: Children's Defense Fund.

Cockburn, A. (2003, September). 21st century slaves. *National Geographic, 204*(3), 2–25.

Crosson-Tower, C. (2004). *Exploring child welfare*. Boston, MA: Pearson/Allyn & Bacon.

Nakashima, E. (2004). Record numbers infected with HIV: U.N. cites rapid rise in Asia and Eastern Europe. *Washington Post* (July 7), A1, A14.

Rainwater, L., & Smeeding, T. M. (2003). *Poor kids in a rich country, America's children in comparative perspective*. New York, NY: Russell Sage Foundation.

United Nations Children's Fund (2000). *The state of the world's children 2000*. New York, NY: UNICEF.

Wax, E. (2004). In Sudan, death and denial: Officials charged with concealing crisis as thousands starve. *Washington Post* (June 27), A1, A22.

Yeakey, C.C. (2003). From classrooms to cellblocks. In: C. C. Yeakey & R. D. Henderson (Eds), *Surmounting All Odds: Education, Opportunity and Society in the New Millennium* (Vols 1 and 2). Greenwich, CT: Information Age.

Carol Camp Yeakey
Jeanita W. Richardson
Judith Brooks Buck
Editors

INTRODUCTION

Women and children compose the overwhelming majority of the people of the world in poverty across the globe. *Suffer the LittleChildren: National and International Dimensions of Child Poverty and Public Policy*, examines the burden of poverty on children, and the implications of that poverty upon the lives and future mobility of generations of children. One of the best aspects of this body of work is that it places the problem of child poverty in international context. In essence, the universality of child poverty is illuminated as well as the relationship between women's status and child poverty and, the greater likelihood that children of color, in particular, across the globe will live in poverty.

Suffer the Little Children: National and International Dimensions of Child Poverty and Public Policy, the fourth volume in the series, Advances in Education in Diverse Communities: Research, Policy and Praxis, examines some of the profound societal issues that serve to inhibit the life chances of children and young adults. But going beyond mere data analysis, the volume examines the social, political and economic contexts in which poverty occurs utilizing a critical perspective by which to view issues in developed, emerging and transitional societies which impact children. Implicit throughout the volume are the decisions and non-decisions of governments as they confront issues of growing child poverty and the repercussions of that poverty for future generations. Lessons learned and unlearned as "developed" countries deal with mounting child poverty, in an era of prosperity, provide an important contrast to other articles in the volume.

The conditions of which we write are representative of various regions of the world. As such, we deem it appropriate to begin the volume with an examination of the state of the children in the United States, unarguably the wealthiest and most developed nation in the world. In "America's Shame: Children Living in the Shadows of America's Prosperity," Camp Yeakey, Richardson and Brooks Buck, provide the rich data and analysis in a telling portrayal of the plight of children in America. Matheson, in "Talking Poverty: Urban Scots and Social Deprivation," writes about language hegemony in Scotland and issues of social advancement. "Fenced Into Cycles of Deprivation: Orphans, Their Female Carers and Education in Malawi" by Rob McBride focuses on the rise in HIV/AIDS and the subsequent increase in the number of orphans in Malawi. In "Roma Childhood in Eastern Europe" Tamas Kozma, Gabriella Pusztai and Katalin Torkos illustrate the problems of Roma (gypsy) children through the life of a particular group of emigrants, and looks for the answers behind their decisions to emigrate as well as their adaptation to a new social environment. Elavie Ndura's "African Refugees' Acculturation in the United States: Uncertain Paths to the American Dream" critically examines the plight of African refugees in the United States and their pursuit of the elusive American dream. Speaking to the issue of cultural assimilation or alienation and its effect of Black children's educational opportunities across the globe is the focus of Kassie Freeman's chapter entitled, "The Loss of Identity and the Underutilization of Black Children's Educational Potential: Rethinking Assimilation Globally." Representing the southernmost islands in the Caribbean chain, Frank C. Worrell writes eloquently of children in poverty in his chapter "Children and Youth in Poverty in Trinidad and Tobago: A Lack of Commitment in the Midst of Plenty." Kingsley Banya and Juliet Elu write of the plight of children used as child soldiers in Sub-Saharan Africa in "The Dilemma of Child Soldiering in Sub-Saharan Africa." In an attempt to reconcile the triumph of Western liberalism with the chaos of war, crime, terror and poverty, Jamil Salmi's "Violence, Democracy and Education: An Analytic Framework" attempts to understand how violence coexists, in a significant fashion, with capitalism and democracy. Salmi goes further by questioning what role education plays in this context. Maria Teresa Tatto's "The Reach and Possibilities of Educational Reform for the Rural Poor in Mexico" examines the goal of providing "education for all" and the assumptions framing educational policy toward the rural and indigenous poor in Mexico. Francis Musa Boakari examines why neo-liberal government policies and the pressures of globalization have failed to improve pervasive social inequality in Brazil, in "Poverty and Education: Brazil's Search for Viable Solutions?" In the absence of political leadership across the globe, Carol Camp Yeakey and Judith Brooks Buck, in "Small Hands: International Dimensions of Child Labor and Exploitation," address the deplorable exploitation of children around the world, including the United States, in the interest of profit and greed. While on a Fulbright Fellowship in Namibia, Rodney K. Hopson compiled the data for his chapter entitled "Child Protection and Survival in Southern Africa: Focus on Child Welfare Policy in Namibia." Jeanita W. Richardson reminds us that despite the medical and public health gains of recent decades, benefits have not been equitably dispersed through the world, leaving in their wake the sufferings of poor children. How delinquent, dependent/neglected, and abused children are treated by criminal justice agencies is a concern that crosses geographical boundaries and is the topic of Sesha Ketheneni and Tricia Klosky's chapter, "Juvenile Instutitonalization Practices in India: A Study of Two Institutions in Madras." Samuel Hinton, discusses the specific issues related to poor and destitute children in Sierra Leone in his research "Child Poverty in Sierra Leone: Vignettes from the Leonenet Street Children's Project." Margot Wilson writes of very young teenagers

(15 years of age and under) who have sustained unmarried and therefore unwanted pregnancies in her research entitled "Stolen Childhood: Cultural Constructions of "Unmarried" Pregnancy in Bangladesh." Kingsley Banya in "The World Bank, NGOs and the State of Development in Sub-Saharan Africa: Implications for Alleviating Poverty and Advancing Societal Reform," examines the critical role of assistance agencies in alleviating poverty and advancing societal reform. Finally, Ximena de la Barra points us toward the future in her forward looking article "Defeating the Trends: In Search of a Better Future."

In a real sense, the conclusion to these chapters is still being written. It would appear that governments are enveloped even more in international conflagrations and the controversies surrounding involvement in a global economy. As citizens of the world, we await the enlightened political leadership and will to turn the devastation and sufferings articulated in the ensuing chapters, into a cause to end the problems of poverty and human degradation for the betterment of our children, as well as ourselves.

Carol Camp Yeakey
Jeanita W. Richardson
Judith Brooks Buck
Editors

1. AMERICA'S SHAME: CHILDREN LIVING IN THE SHADOWS OF AMERICA'S PROSPERITY

Carol Camp Yeakey, Jeanita W. Richardson
and Judith Brooks Buck

> In this part of the world, a child is born into poverty every 34 seconds and 30 million people suffer chronic hunger. It's Africa, you might guess. But you would be wrong: It's the United States.
>
> D. L. Toler (January 21, 2000).

A time of need is upon us. America, the wealthiest nation in the world and the most developed, presents a Dickensian dichotomy before our eyes: poverty and homelessness are on the rise even as our streets hum with ambitious newcomers. In our major cities, we have a clash of opulence and opportunity, hard labor and raw daily indigence have rarely been so palpable. Now it is poverty, not simply having a black or brown skin, that prevents millions of children from sharing in the American dream. But, as one will see in succeeding pages, all too often, skin color and poverty are so interrelated in America, as to be intellectually indistinguishable.

Children continue to represent the largest group of poor in the United States. According to data from the Children's Defense Fund (CDF), 11.6 million children under 18 years of age, or one out of every six American children, lived below the poverty level in 2000 (Children's Defense Fund, 2002). Although this number reflects a gradual decrease in the number of poor children for the last seven years, more children live in poverty today than thirty years ago. Unfortunately

'Suffer the Little Children': National and International Dimensions of Child Poverty and Public Policy
Advances in Education in Diverse Communities: Research, Policy and Praxis, Volume 4, 1–38
Copyright © 2006 by Elsevier Ltd.
All rights of reproduction in any form reserved
ISSN: 1479-358X/doi:10.1016/S1479-358X(04)04001-X

the decrease in child poverty has been rather short-lived. The U.S. Census reports that in 2002, the ranks of the poor rose as economic hardship hit individuals and families alike (Clemetson, 2003). Also, the proportion of children living in families where at least one parent worked is at an all-time high (Crosson-Tower, 2004). Data indicate that the total percentage of people in poverty in the United States increased to 12.4% and totaled 34.8 million. At the same time, the number of families living in poverty increased to seven million. The number of children in poverty rose, as well to 12.2 million. Worse still, the rate of increase of children in poverty under age 5 jumped a full percentage point to 19.8% living below the poverty line. These numbers provide a moving economic picture of poverty in America.

This chapter examines the face of child poverty in America. In so doing, we compare America with other nations of the world and examine the consequences of child poverty in our global economy. Although all of the information contained in the ensuing pages is important in order to understand the complexity of child poverty in America, words alone, cannot humanize the issue. As one reviews the facts, it is vital that you imagine how the lives of real children are affected by bearing the enormous burden of living in poverty, with diminished opportunities to succeed, in the richest nation in the world.

CONCEPTUALIZATIONS OF POVERTY

Concern with the size of poverty in any nation leads to a broader question: What does it mean to be poor in a rich society? More specifically, what does it mean for a family, and particularly its children, to live in a state of poverty within a prosperous society? To begin to answer these questions, we must look at poverty in the context of its opposite, plenty. As members of modern societies, we use a wide range of goods and services to effect our participation in social relations and to create and sustain our sense of social identity. The mainstream standard of living defines the average American's family resources that fall sufficiently short of the mainstream as deprivation, precarious subsistence, exclusion – in short, poverty. Our common cultural understanding is that we cannot play our social roles or participate meaningfully in our communities without the basic material resources necessary to carry out our activities. One way or another, each of us has to "make a living" in order to "have a life." The roles and activities that define participation are age-graded – child, teenager, young adult, mature adult, senior citizen. For any one age, these common cultural understandings allow people to pass judgment on their own rank and that of others in a continuum from destitution to unseemly affluence, based on what kind of participation they can effect.

As members of modern society, we develop a lively sense of the implications of different levels of resources-that is, we see that experiences of plenty or of deprivation often seem to be critical in determining which other members of society we choose to interact with and the kinds of social participation that are feasible for us. In short, if we do not look at poverty as one aspect of socioeconomic inequality in modern societies, we are missing its essential nature.

Whatever perspective we choose, any correct study of poverty must proceed from a sociologically grounded understanding of the interpenetration of material and social well-being in modern societies (Rainwater & Smeeding, 2003). It must also recognize the particular degree of socioeconomic inequality in the social stratification system of each society. European Union (EU) member countries now ground their approaches to poverty in an understanding of the nature of social stratification in prosperous and postindustrial societies such as their own: "The poor shall be taken to mean persons, families and groups of persons whose resources (material, cultural and societal), are so limited as to exclude them from the minimum acceptable way of life in the member state in which they live" (European Commission, 1985, p. 35).

By contrast, writings about poverty in the United States tend not to focus so sharply on social exclusion, but rather on the characteristics of the poor themselves. As Michael Katz (1989) argues, Americans have always been deeply preoccupied with the distinction between the undeserving and the deserving poor, historical concepts borrowed from the Elizabethan Poor Laws in the 1600s. Two perspectives inform the American characterization of poverty. The first perspective sees economic status – that is, people's command over goods and services – as the defining and sufficient indicator of being poor. The second perspective, more sociological in nature, is more broadly concerned with people's socioeconomic situation. It was the second perspective that dominated the elite interest in poverty in the 1960s and launched the War on Poverty. Michael Harrington's *The Other America: Poverty in the United States*, first published in 1962, is generally credited with putting poverty on the agenda in the administrations of Presidents John F. Kennedy and Lyndon Baines Johnson. Harrington combined his own experience as a writer about the American working class with much sociological research during the 1950s on the inner city, juvenile delinquency and slums. For Harrington (1962), there was:

... a language of the poor, a psychology of the poor, a worldview of the poor.

To be impoverished is to be an internal alien, to grow up in a culture that

is radically different from the one that dominates society . . . . (The poor) need an American Dickens to record the smell and texture and quality of their lives. The cycles and trends, the massive forces, must be seen as affecting persons who talk and think differently (p. 18).

The debate on the merits of absolute versus relative definitions of poverty has obscured the more fundamental difference between economic and social definitions of poverty (Rainwater & Smeeding, 2003). An economic measure of poverty determines the income needed to provide a minimum level of consumption of goods and services and implicitly assigns a given level of utility or satisfaction to the output of consumption. A social measure of poverty is concerned ultimately not with consumption but with social activities and participation. Researchers of the latter orientation do not look at the problem of poverty in relatively affluent societies as one of low consumption per se, but focus instead on the social and personal consequences of poor individuals' inability to consume at more than an extremely modest level. Without a prerequisite level of goods and services, individuals cannot act and participate as full members of their society, and it is this participation in social activities that confers utility, not consumption. While such a view is mainly identified with sociological and anthropological traditions, a few economists have adopted its insights by focusing on consumption as an intermediate activity-that is, as an input to social activities that in turn confer utility.

Perhaps it is Denton Vaughan (1993) who provides the most compelling description of the social meaning of poverty in contemporary societies:

> In the complex, largely urban, and industrial and service societies of the post-World War II United States, Canada, and Western Europe, the poverty problem stems from the existence of substantial population subgroups whose members lack the material resources required to perform – except with the greatest difficulty – roles in the central societal domains of family work, and citizenship as defined by the mainstream members of society and as generally accepted by members of the low income groups themselves. (Members) have a relatively well-developed sense of the material resources associated with different levels in the material status hierarchy. It is this sense that permits the individual to judge the difference between a good salary and a poor one, a nice car and a bare bones econo-box, or a decent apartment and a slum tenement, and more generally to assess his or her location in the overall stratification system (Vaughan, 1993, pp. 22–23).

INTERNATIONAL COMPARISONS

How does America compare with other industrialized countries? Utilizing data from the 2003 Luxembourg Income Study (LIS), we find that the United States had an extremely high poverty rate in 1997 of 20.3% (Rainwater & Smeeding, 2003). See Table 1. Somewhat fortuitously, the official poverty rate of children was 19.9% in 1997. In other words, 20.3% of all American children lived in families with equivalent incomes below one-half of the median equivalent income. These are incomes so low that these children and others in their family were not able to

Table 1.   Child Poverty by Country.

Note: Adapted from: Rainwater and Smeeding (2003, p. 21).

participate enough in community activities to be perceived, by both themselves and others, as regular members of society. Italy had the second-highest child poverty rate at just below 20%, followed closely by the United Kingdom at 16.3%. The two Commonwealth nations, Canada and Australia, have rather hgh rates at more than 13.9 and 13.5% respectively. At 11.9%, Spain's child poverty rate is almost as high. The child poverty rates in the rest of the countries, starting with Germany, are all below 10%. France has a rate of approximately 7%, as does the Netherlands. Switzerland follows at 6.4%. The rest of the countries have very low rates of around 5% or less. Very low rates of child poverty prevail in the four Nordic countries.

In short, the poverty rate of American children is over four times as high as that of children in northern Europe. The contrast with the rate in the United Kingdom is almost as dramatic. British children suffer a poverty rate over three times as high as that of the northern European countries. What are the odds of escaping poverty in these developed countries? By answering that question, we see even starker contrasts. An American child has a slightly less than four-to-one chance of escaping poverty, and the odds are about the same for an Italian or British child (Rainwater & Smeeding, 2003). In contrast, a Nordic child has a twenty-five-to-one chance or better of escaping poverty.

If we broaden our analysis to all countries for which LIS data exist, we find no wider range of poverty rates. Interesting possibilities for comparison do emerge when we consider the child poverty rate for the most recent years for each country, as demonstrated in Table 2.

Two Western European countries-Austria and Luxembourg-fit neatly into the group of northern continental countries with rates under 5%. Ireland's high child poverty rate of 12%, on the other hand, is about the same as Spain's, Australia's and Canada's, but not as high as the 16.3% rate in the United Kingdom.

The most interesting observation to be made about the five Eastern European countries is that the range of child poverty in these countries is as great as it is in the countries of Western Europe. In fact, of all the twenty-five countries, the two with the very lowest child poverty rates are the Czech Republic and Slovakia. Their rates are even about the same as those of Sweden and Finland. Hungary and Poland appear in the middle of the range with rates somewhat higher than France's, but lower than Spain's. At 23.2%, the child poverty rate in Russia is higher even than in the United States. (Of course, the situation in Eastern European countries has been unstable in the post-Communist period, and many suspect that poverty has increased in some of these countries). For Israel and Taiwan, their rates are not too different from the German poverty rate, but lower than those of the two Commonwealth nations, the United Kingdom and the United States.

Thus, broadening our scope from fifteen to twenty-five countries tells us that, with the range of economic development that these countries represent, there is little relationship between a country's prosperity and its child poverty rate. The Western European countries with very low poverty rates have Gross Domestic Products (GDP) close to three times those of the Czech Republic and Slovakia, yet their poverty rates are not very different. Spain and Ireland have twice the real GDP of Poland, but the three countries have very similar poverty rates. The United Kingdom, Italy, the United States, and Russia represent an enormous range of GDP, yet these four all have very high child poverty rates.

Further, as evidenced in Table 3, a child's chance of being poor in the United States differs dramatically depending on whether he or she lives in a one- or two-parent family. An American child in a two-parent family has only about an 11% chance of being poor as compared to a 60% chance if the child lives with a lone parent who is a mother. In fact, in all countries studied, one's chance of being poor in a one-parent mother family is much higher than in two-parent families.

Because so few children in most countries live in solo-mother families, the difference across countries in the percent of children living in solo-mother families has little to do with the difference in total child poverty rates. Only in the cases of Australia, Canada and the United States would total poverty rates be noticeably lower if the proportion of solo-mother families was the average for these 17

Table 2. Level and Trend in Child Poverty Rates: 1970–1997.

Nation	Year of Survey	Before 1971	1972–1975	1976–1981	1982–1985	1986–1988	1989–1993	1994–1997
United States	1969, 1974, 1979,1986,1991, 1997	13.10%	17.30%	18.50%		22.90%	21.50%	22.7% ≥ 20.3%
Western Europe								
Austria	1987	–	–	–	–	4.8	–	–
Belgium	1985, 1988, 1992, 1997	–	–	–	3.4	3.1	3.8	5.1
Denmark	1987, 1992	–	–	–	–	5.3	4	–
Finland	1987, 1991, 1995	–	–	–	–	2.9	2.5	3.2
France	1979, 1984a, 1984b, 1989, 1994	–	–	6.3	6.5/8.6c	–	7.5	7.2
Germany (West)	1973, 1978, 1983/1984, 1989,1994	–	4.0	3.2	4.8/6.4d	–	4.4	8.7
Ireland	1987	–	–	–	–	12.0	–	–
Italy	1986, 1991, 1995	–	–	–	–	10.8	9.6	19.5
Luxembourg	1985, 1991, 1994	–	–	–	4.1	–	3.6	4.6
The Netherlands	1983, 1987, 1991, 1994	–	–	3.8	2.5	3.6	4.1	7.0
Norway	1979, 1986, 1991, 1995	–	–	–	–	3.8	4.6	3.7
Spain	1980, 1990	–	–	12.3	–	–	11.9	–
Sweden	1967, 1975, 1981, 1987, 1992, 1995	3.5	1.9	3.9	–	3.0	2.7	2.4
Switzerland	1982, 1992	–	–	–	3.3	–	6.4	6.7
United Kingdom	1969, 1974, 1979, 1986, 1991, 1995	5.3	7.0	8.5	–	9.9	16.7	16.3

Table 2. (*Continued*)

Nation	Year of Survey	Before 1971	1972–1975	1976–1981	1982–1985	1986–1988	1989–1993	1994–1997
Eastern Europe								
Czech Republic	1992	–	–	–	–	–	3.4	–
Hungary	1991, 1994	–	–	–	–	–	9.5	10.1
Poland	1986, 1992, 1995	–	–	–	–	10.6	9.0	12.7
Russia	1992, 1995	–	–	–	–	–	19.9	23.2
Slovakia	1992	–	–	–	–	–	3.2	–
Other								
Australia	1981, 1985, 1989, 1994	–	–	14.0	13.1	–	14.0	13.5
Canada	1971, 1975, 1981, 1987, 1991, 1994, 1997	15.2	14.6	13.9	–	13.6	13.5	13.1 > 13.9
Israel	1979, 1986, 1992, 1997	–	–	8.2	–	11.1	10.6	11.3
Taiwan	1986, 1991	–	–	–	–	5.8	9.9	–

Note: Adapted from: Rainwater and Smeeding (2003, pp. 24, 25).

Source: Authors' calculations, using data from the Luxembourg Income Study (http://www.lisproject.org).

Notes: LIS has annual data for the United States from 1994 to 1997. The child poverty rates for these years are as follows: 1994, 22.7; 1995, 20.1; 1996, 19.9; 1997, 20.3.

(a) For comparison the 1994 rate for West Germany is given in this table. Elsewhere in the text the rates are for all of Germany. There is a survey change in Germany from 1983 to 1984 and after.

(b) There are significant changes in the Dutch data that are likely to affect the comparability from year to year.

(c) The two figures represent poverty rates in the 1984a and 1984b surveys.

(d) The two figures represent poverty rates in the 1983 and 1984 surveys.

Table 3. Poverty Rates for Children by Family Type (a).

Country (Year)	All Children (in %)	Children in Two-Parent Family (in %)	Children in Single Parent/Solo Mother Family (c) (in %)	Percent of Children in Solo mother Families (c,d) (in %)
United States (1991)	21.50%	11.10%	59.50%	21.20%
Australia (1990)	14.00	7.70	56.20	12.40
Belgium (1992)	3.80	3.20	10.00	8.10
Canada (1991)	13.50	7.40	50.20	13.40
Denmark (1991)	3.30	2.50	7.30	14.30
Finland (1991)	2.50	1.90	7.50	9.50
France (1984)	6.50	5.40	22.60	6.50
Germany (1989)	6.80	2.90	42.70	9.90
Ireland (1997)	12.00	10.50	40.50	5.30
Israel (1986)	11.10	10.30	27.50	5.10
Italy (1991)	9.60	9.50	13.90	4.40
Luxembourg (1985)	4.10	3.60	10.00	6.80
The Netherlands (1991)	6.20	3.10	39.50	8.40
Norway (1991)	4.60	1.90	18.40	15.40
Sweden (1992)	2.70	2.20	5.20	14.60
Switzerland (1982)	3.30	1.00	25.60	6.90
United Kingdom (1986)	9.90	8.40	18.70	13.00

Note: Adapted from: Luxembourg Income Study as cited in Skolnick and Currie (2004, p. 108).

(a) Poverty is defined as percentage of children living in households with adjusted disposable income minus less than 50 percent of median adjusted disposable income for all persons. Income includes all transfers and tax benefits.

(b) Child poverty rates in two-parent families are for those children living in situations where there are only two adults who are married, or are living together as married.

(c) Single parent/solo-mother families are children living in those situations where one female adult resides in the household. Other adults (e.g. older children) may also occupy the residence.

(d) Because some children live in other types of situations, e.g. in multiple family unit households or in lone-father units, the weighted averages of children in solo-mother and two-parent households do not add to the "all children" total.

countries. In other countries with greater than 10% of children in solo-mother families (Denmark, Norway, Sweden, United Kingdom), the poverty rates for single parent children are close enough to two parent rates to not make a great deal of difference in the overall poverty rate. Demography is clearly not destiny for children in solo-mother families in Denmark and Finland (7% poverty rate), and Sweden (5% poverty rate) do better than children in two-parent families in many of the nations studied.

The combination of difference in the poverty rates of children in two-parent as compared to solo-mother families and the smaller differences in the percentage of children who live in solo-mother families has an important effect on the family type composition of the poor. In five countries, more than half of poor children live in solo-mother families – the United States, Australia, Germany, Switzerland, and Norway, with Canada coming close at around 40%. At the other extreme, fewer than 15% of poor children are in solo-mother families in the Netherlands, Belgium, Italy and Israel. Children in solo-mother families make up between 15 and 30% of the poor in Luxembourg, Ireland, France, the United Kingdom and Sweden. Thus, the rate of feminization of poverty varies dramatically across these countries based on both the poverty rate for children in single parent units and on the percentage of children living in each type of unit.

The phenomenon, most noted in the U.S., termed the feminization of poverty becomes crystal clear when we realize that one of every eight American children is a poor child living with a solo mother. Fewer than 1 in 100 children are in the same situation in Sweden, the Netherlands, Luxembourg, Italy, Finland and Belgium. In the United States 1 of every 10 children is a poor child living in a two-parent family. This ratio is not too different in three other countries – Ireland, Israel and Italy. In contrast, the ratio is about 1 in 50 in Finland, Germany, Norway, Sweden and Switzerland.

The results of the recently released LIS (2003) study are striking. United States low-income children have a lower real standard of living than do their counterparts in almost every other nation studied. However, in contrast to her low income children, America's high income children are better off than their counterparts in every nation studied. The wide variance in child well-being found in the U.S. mirrors the high level of overall income inequality in our nation.

CHARACTERISTICS OF POOR
CHILDREN IN AMERICA

Children are poor as a result of living in poor families. Just as all families are unique, with their own individual characteristics and histories, poor families have diverse backgrounds and life circumstances that cause them to live in poverty. Despite a commonly help perception that the heaviest concentrations of poor people live in large cities, more poor children actually live in suburban or rural areas.

Officially, poverty is defined by the U.S. government in its index of poverty. A poverty line is established as a means of separating those who are considered poor from those who are not. This measurement is important because it is used to compute whether people are eligible for government assistance programs. To arrive at this estimate of a poverty line, the food budget thought to be minimally adequate for a family's subsistence is "multiplied by 3 on the assumption that food should constitute one-third of a family's budget" (Karger & Stoesz, 2002, p. 118). This method for defining poverty was first developed in 1963, as a baseline, for the minimal diet necessary to survive. In 2001, a family of three (one parent and two children) had to make less than the poverty threshold of $14,269 in order to be considered poor by the Census Bureau (U.S. Census Bureau, 2002). While there is great debate as to how poverty is to be computed, the reality is that the numbers indicate a large number of children living in families unable to afford adequate food, shelter, medical care and other basic necessities. The burden of poverty reduces a child's chances to grow up to be a healthy, well-adjusted, contributing adult in our society. At the same time, poverty increases a child's chances of suffering the negative outcomes associated with poverty. It is important to note that most poor families' incomes are usually far below the poverty threshold. Approximately 42% of American children subsist in one of three low-income categories: extremely poor, quite poor or near poor. Extremely poor families report income below 50% of the federally determined poverty level. Quite Poor children's household income ranges between 50-100% of the poverty threshold. Near Poor children reside in homes reporting 100–185% of the poverty threshold (Bennett et al., 1999).

Minority children are disproportionately at risk of growing up in poverty. Although minorities represent only one-third of all children under 6 years old, they represent the vast majority of poor children. In 2000, 28.0% of Hispanic children, 30.9% of Black children, 13.0% of White children, and 14.5% of Asian and Pacific Islander children were poor. Even so, in terms of numbers, poor, non-Hispanic Caucasian children still outnumber poor African American and Hispanic children (CDF, 2002).

State of the Children in the United States

Over the past several years, states have enjoyed tremendous prosperity and, for many, significant budget surpluses. During this period states had a choice, that is, to invest in children. Unfortunately, many states did not. Instead states passed tax cuts for the past seven consecutive years totaling approximately $36 billion. The fiscal reality of states now has changed. Forty three states and the District of Columbia report revenues below forecasted levels, and 21 states and the District of Columbia already are spending above budgeted levels. Total budget shortfalls, before the end of 2001, already equaled $40 billion. States once again have choices about how they will address their budget crises. Will they balance their budgets

Table 4.   10 Best and Worst States on Key Child Indicators.

Best States			Worst States		
Rank	State	Rate (%)	Rank	State	Rate (%)
Children living in poverty					
1	New Hampshire	7.10	51	District of Columbia	30.90
2	Minnesota	9.30	50	West Virginia	27.70
3	Colorado	9.80	49	Louisiana	27.60
4	Utah	10.70	48	Mississippi	25.80
5	New Jersey	10.80	46	Arkansas	25.50
6	Kansas	11.10	46	New Mexico	25.50
7	Connecticut	11.30	45	Arizona	22.50
8	Nebraska	11.40	44	Kentucky	21.80
9	Delaware	11.60	43	Texas	21.60
10	Maine	11.90	42	Alabama	21.40
Preschool children living in poverty					
1	New Hampshire	8.60	51	District of Columbia	32.10
2	Colorado	11.00	50	Arkansas	31.20
3	Hawaii	11.00	49	Louisiana	30.80
4	New Jersey	11.40	48	West Virginia	30.50
5	Minnesota	11.50	47	Mississippi	28.80
6	Connecticut	11.90	46	New Mexico	27.40
7	Maine	13.90	45	Alabama	25.60
8	Nebraska	14.00	43	Arizona	25.00
9	Nevada	14.60	43	Tennessee	25.00
9	Virginia	14.60	42	Oklahoma	24.80

Note: Adapted from: Children's Defense Fund (2002, p. 42).

on the backs of children and families or protect children and families from budget cuts?

Table 4 provides a ranking of the ten best and worst states on key child indicators. Key child indicators include: children living in poverty; preschool children living in poverty; cash assistance for working poor families; maxmum cash welfare benefits as a percent of poverty, affordability of rent, children with no health insurance, early prenatal care, low birth weight babies, births to unmarried parents; teen birth rates, infant morality; and two-year olds who are fully immunized.

Table 4 reveals that the best states for children living in poverty are New Hampshire and Minnesota, while Alabama, Texas, Kentucky, Arizona, New Mexico, Arkansas, Mississippi, Louisiana, West Virginia. and the District of Columbia, are among the worst states based on the aforementioned key child indicators. Similarly, with respect to preschool children living in poverty, New Hampshire, Colorado and Hawaii rank among the best states, while the states in the

Table 5. Family Income and Poverty (Child Poverty, 1999–2000).

State	Under Age 18			Under Age 6			Unemployment Rate	
	Number Poor	Percent Poor (%)	Rank	Number Poor	Percent Poor (%)	Rank	2000 (%)	2001 (%)
Alabama	235,195	21.4	42	90,808	25.6	45	4.6	5.3
Alaska	23,337	12.7	15	8,628	16.4	19	6.6	6.3
Arizona	298,525	22.5	45	106,945	25.0	43	3.9	4.7
Arkansas	171,163	25.5	46	64,173	31.2	50	4.4	5.1
California	1,798,162	19.9	39	651,788	21.9	37	4.9	5.3
Colorado	105,875	9.8	3	39,431	11.0	2	2.7	3.7
Connecticut	93,971	11.3	7	30,925	11.9	6	2.3	3.3
Delaware	21,915	11.6	9	9,622	16.5	21	4.0	3.5
District of Columbia	35,095	30.9	51	12,595	32.1	51	5.8	6.5
Florida	703,297	19.8	38	231,567	21.0	36	3.6	4.8
Georgia	392,504	18.5	33	136,538	19.3	32	3.7	4.0
Hawaii	35,254	12.1	11	9,859	11.0	2	4.3	4.6
Idaho	47,465	13.7	18	17,114	16.1	17	4.9	5.0
Illinois	509,689	16.0	28	188,304	18.4	30	4.4	5.4
Indiana	225,305	14.6	23	82,008	16.5	21	3.2	4.4
Iowa	99,155	13.9	20	33,541	15.8	16	2.6	3.3
Kansas	78,138	11.1	6	33,954	15.7	15	3.7	4.3
Kentucky	210,909	21.8	44	72,919	23.7	41	4.1	5.5
Louisiana	330,967	27.6	49	114,333	30.8	49	5.5	6.0
Maine	35,341	11.9	10	11,581	13.9	7	3.5	4.0
Maryland	176,637	13.5	16	64,383	15.5	14	3.9	4.1
Massachusetts	210,235	14.2	21	69,789	14.8	11	2.6	3.7
Michigan	367,235	14.5	22	142,093	18.0	28	3.6	5.3
Minnesota	116,225	9.3	2	45,635	11.5	5	3.3	3.7
Mississippi	194,241	25.8	48	66,553	28.8	47	5.7	5.5
Missouri	223,088	15.9	27	81,293	18.2	29	3.5	4.7
Montana	42,623	19.0	34	12,075	19.7	33	4.9	4.6

Table 5. (Continued)

State	Under Age 18			Under Age 6			Unemployment Rate	
	Number Poor	Percent Poor (%)	Rank	Number Poor	Percent Poor (%)	Rank	2000 (%)	2001 (%)
Nebraska	49,675	11.4	8	18,976	14.0	8	3.0	3.1
Nevada	62,412	12.6	14	23,582	14.6	9	4.1	5.3
New Hampshire	21,083	7.1	1	7,842	8.6	1	2.8	3.5
New Jersey	220,409	10.8	5	76,729	11.4	4	3.8	4.2
New Mexico	125,657	25.5	46	41,872	27.4	46	4.9	4.8
New York	902,469	19.6	37	302,182	20.4	35	4.6	4.9
North Carolina	365,653	19.0	34	115,243	18.7	31	3.6	5.5
North Dakota	24,084	15.1	24	7,374	16.4	19	3.0	2.8
Ohio	454,561	16.0	28	153,620	17.4	26	4.1	4.3
Oklahoma	168,244	19.4	36	66,222	24.8	42	3.0	3.8
Oregon	147,091	18.0	32	61,261	23.5	40	4.9	6.3
Pennsylvania	436,895	15.2	26	153,781	17.9	27	4.2	4.7
Rhode Island	42,589	17.2	31	13,073	17.3	24	4.1	4.7
South Carolina	199,222	20.0	40	60,498	20.0	34	3.9	5.4
South Dakota	27,670	13.8	19	10,222	17.3	24	2.3	3.3
Tennessee	278,806	20.3	41	110,818	25.0	43	3.9	4.5
Texas	1,251,606	21.6	43	435,223	23.2	39	4.2	4.9
Utah	75,189	10.7	4	35,973	15.0	13	3.2	4.4
Vermont	17,704	12.4	13	6,637	16.1	17	2.9	3.6
Virginia	230,765	13.5	16	80,671	14.6	9	2.2	3.5
Washington	251,270	16.7	30	100,482	21.9	37	5.2	6.4
West Virginia	109,821	27.7	50	35,514	30.5	48	5.5	4.9
Wisconsin	159,913	12.1	11	59,600	14.9	12	3.5	4.6
Wyoming	19,056	15.1	24	6,109	17.2	23	3.9	3.9
United States	12,423,390	17.5		4,411,958	19.6		4.0	4.8

Note: Adapted from: Children's Defense Fund (2002, p. 50).

Table 6. Infant Mortality, 1999.

State	All Races		White		Black	
	Rate	Rank	Rate	Rank	Rate	Rank
Alabama	9.80	48	6.90	42	16.0	21
Alaska	5.70	6	4.70	2	0.0	0
Arizona	6.80	22	6.20	32	19.1	33
Arkansas	8.00	37	7.00	44	12.0	4
California	5.40	5	5.00	7	12.9	7
Colorado	6.70	17	6.30	33	16.2	23
Connecticut	6.10	12	5.70	18	10.6	2
Delaware	7.40	31	3.90	1	18.0	29
District of Columbia	15.00	51	0.00	0	19.0	32
Florida	7.40	31	5.60	16	13.6	9
Georgia	8.20	40	5.40	12	13.8	10
Hawaii	7.00	27	0.00	0	0.0	0
Idaho	6.70	17	6.60	36	0.0	0
Illinois	8.50	43	6.30	33	18.4	30
Indiana	8.00	37	7.00	44	17.0	26
Iowa	5.70	6	5.30	11	0.0	0
Kansas	7.30	28	6.80	39	14.4	14
Kentucky	7.60	34	7.10	46	12.7	6
Louisiana	9.20	47	5.90	26	14.2	12
Maine	4.80	1	4.70	2	0.0	0
Maryland	8.40	42	5.10	9	14.6	15
Massachusetts	5.20	4	4.80	5	9.8	1
Michigan	8.10	39	6.00	30	17.9	28
Minnesota	6.20	13	5.40	12	15.4	18
Mississippi	10.10	49	6.80	39	14.2	12
Missouri	7.80	36	5.80	22	18.9	31
Montana	6.70	17	5.90	26	0.0	0
Nebraska	6.80	22	5.90	26	0.0	0
Nevada	6.60	16	6.10	31	0.0	0
New Hampshire	5.80	9	5.70	18	0.0	0
New Jersey	6.70	17	5.20	10	14.1	11
New Mexico	6.90	25	6.50	35	0.0	0
New York	6.40	15	5.50	14	10.6	2
North Carolina	9.10	46	6.90	42	15.5	19
North Dakota	6.80	22	5.80	22	0.0	0
Ohio	8.20	40	6.60	36	17.6	27
Oklahoma	8.50	43	8.00	49	15.6	20
Oregon	5.80	9	5.70	18	0.0	0
Pennsylvania	7.30	28	5.80	22	16.8	24
Rhode Island	5.70	6	5.00	7	0.0	0
South Carolina	10.20	50	6.70	38	16.9	25
South Dakota	8.90	45	7.70	48	0.0	0

Table 6.   (*Continued*)

State	All Races		White		Black	
	Rate	Rank	Rate	Rank	Rate	Rank
Tennessee	7.70	35	5.70	18	15.2	17
Texas	6.20	13	5.50	14	12.5	5
Utah	4.80	1	4.80	5	0.0	0
Vermont	5.80	9	5.90	26	0.0	0
Virginia	7.30	28	5.60	16	13.0	8
Washington	5.00	3	4.70	2	15.0	16
West Virginia	7.40	31	7.30	47	0.0	0
Wisconsin	6.70	17	5.80	22	16.0	21
Wyoming	6.90	25	6.80	39	0.0	0
United States	7.10		5.80		14.6	

Note: Adapted from: Children's Defense Fund (2002, p. 61).

south or southwest portion of the U.S., rank among the worst states. What becomes clear on the basis of the data is the significant concentrations of poverty in Black and Hispanic children and the geographic distribution of that poverty. Aggregate data fails to reveal the disproportionate poverty rates of children of color in rural, urban and suburban settings. Though the African American population is dispersed through the United States, it is concentrated in urban centers and the southeast region of the country, which is also the region with significant concentrations of rural poverty (Office of Minority Health, 2000). Rural Blacks, Hispanics and Native Americans are three times more apt to be poor as rural Whites. Rural minority residents tend to be poorer in terms of real income than either their White rural counterparts or minority urban counterparts.

Table 5 examines family income and poverty. In the richest nation on earth, there are poor children in every state. The youngest children are the most likely to be poor nearly everywhere. As we can see, New Hampshire, Minnesota, Colorado, and Utah rank as the best states in terms of family income and poverty for children under age 18, and under age 6. The worst rankings in this category are the District of Columbia and the states of West Virginia, Louisiana, Mississippi, again, the southeast region of the country.

Black babies are between two and three times as likely as White babies to die before their first birthday. Table 6 provides the combined infant mortality for all races, by state, as well as the breakdown of infant mortality for Whites and for Blacks.

In 48 states, the cost of child care for a four-year old in an urban child care center is more than the cost of public college tuition, as revealed by data in Table 7. As

Table 7. Center-Based Child Care Costs vs. Public College Tuition Costs, 2000.

State	Center-Based Child Care Costs for a 4-Year Old (in Dollars)	Tuition at a 4-Year Public College (in Dollars)	College Tuition as a Percent of Child Care Costs (%)
Alabama	$3,672	$2,833	77.2
Alaska	6,019	2,855	47.4
Arizona	4,352	2,252	51.7
Arkansas	3,640	2,785	76.5
California	4,858	2,559	52.7
Colorado	5,096	2,775	54.5
Connecticut	6,405	4,435	69.2
Delaware	5,510	4,642	84.2
District of Columbia	0	2,070	0.0
Florida	4,255	2,244	52.7
Georgia	4,992	2,524	50.6
Hawaii	5,505	2,965	53.9
Idaho	4,814	2,458	51.1
Illinois	5,304	4,038	76.1
Indiana	4,732	3,646	77.0
Iowa	6,198	2,998	48.4
Kansas	4,889	2,439	49.9
Kentucky	4,368	2,723	62.3
Louisiana	4,160	2,430	58.4
Maine	5,790	4,122	71.2
Maryland	4,774	4,552	95.3
Massachusetts	8,121	4,105	50.5
Michigan	4,830	4,538	94.0
Minnesota	7,436	3,800	51.1
Mississippi	3,380	2,872	85.0
Missouri	4,784	3,701	77.4
Montana	4,680	3,011	64.3
Nebraska	4,680	2,930	62.6
Nevada	4,862	2,034	41.8
New Hampshire	6,520	6,083	93.3
New Jersey	5,252	5,255	100.1
New Mexico	4,801	2,340	48.7
New York	8,060	3,983	49.4
North Carolina	5,876	2,054	35.0
North Dakota	4,627	2,990	64.6
Ohio	5,672	4,495	79.2
Oklahoma	4,108	2,183	53.1
Oregon	5,580	3,582	64.2
Pennsylvania	6,188	5,610	90.7
Rhode Island	6,365	4,318	67.8
South Carolina	3,900	3,638	93.3

Table 7.   (*Continued*)

State	Center-Based Child Care Costs for a 4-Year Old (in Dollars)	Tuition at a 4-Year Public College (in Dollars)	College Tuition as a Percent of Child Care Costs (%)
South Dakota	4,243	3,210	75.7
Tennessee	4,420	2,698	61.0
Texas	4,160	2,644	63.6
Utah	4,550	2,147	47.2
Vermont	5,980	6,913	115.6
Virginia	4,857	3,733	76.9
Washington	6,604	3,357	50.8
West Virginia	4,238	2,549	60.1
Wisconsin	6,104	3,313	54.3
Wyoming	4,056	2,416	59.6

Note: Adapted from: Children's Defense Fund (2002, p. 52).

indicated, center based child care costs for a four-year-old, often surpass the tuition of a four-year public college. In some instances, in states such as Alaska, Colorado, and Iowa, the cost of child care for a four year old is double the cost of tuition at a 4-year public college. In New Hampshire, the cost for child care and tuition at a four year college are quite similar. As a result, parents with young children can look forward to similar costs whether their children are in infancy or young adulthood.

Table 8 provides data which details how states spend on average three times more money, per prisoner than per public school pupil in the United States. Table 8 not only provides the expenditures per pupil, and the expenditures per prisoner, but also provides the pupil/teacher ratio and the high school completion rate by state. Expending as much as three times more funds on incarceration, as opposed to public school education, raises serious questions about America's national priorities in preparing our youth to assume responsible positions in the larger society. What is most glaring about this data set is the fact that not one state in the world's weathiest and most developed country expends more on public education, than incarceration (Yeakey, 2003).

As a result of the data depicted in Table 8, the data in Tables 9, 10 and 11, should come as no surprise, for they speak to the extreme violence endemic to American society. Table 9 examines child abuse and neglect in America, by race. In 1999, there were more than 800,000 children reported, to be abused and neglected. Table 10 examines firearm deaths of children and teens, by manner. In 1999, 3,385 children and teens, or nine a day, were killed by firearms in 1999. Three out of five were victims of homicide, and one third were suicides. Table 11 provides data on youth who are at risk in America, in a state by state breakdown. As depicted in

Table 8.   Public School Education.

State	Pupil/ Teacher Ratio, 1998	High School Completion Rate, 1997–1999 (%)	Expenditures Per Pupil, 1997–1998 (in Dollars)	Expenditures Per Prisoner, 1997 (in Dollars)	Ratio of Per Prisoner Expenditures to Per Pupil Expenditures
Alabama	15.7	83.1	$4,849	$7,600	1.6
Alaska	16.7	90.8	8,271	31,953	3.9
Arizona	20.0	75.0	4,595	16,884	3.7
Arkansas	16.2	82.9	4,708	14,964	3.2
California	21.0	81.5	5,644	20,654	3.7
Colorado	17.7	83.3	5,656	14,652	2.6
Connecticut	14.0	90.1	8,904	21,677	2.4
Delaware	16.0	89.1	7,420	16,378	2.2
District of Columbia	13.9	87.2	8,393	n/a	n/a
Florida	18.4	84.8	5,552	17,988	3.2
Georgia	15.8	83.7	5,647	15,925	2.8
Hawaii	17.7	90.7	5,858	18,964	3.2
Idaho	18.2	85.5	4,721	21,269	4.5
Illinois	16.5	86.2	6,242	18,032	2.9
Indiana	17.0	88.6	6,318	19,664	3.1
Iowa	15.2	88.2	5,998	21,291	3.5
Kansas	14.8	91.6	5,727	18,490	3.2
Kentucky	16.1	86.6	5,213	11,752	2.3
Louisiana	16.6	82.1	5,188	8,705	1.7
Maine	13.2	92.9	6,742	30,656	4.5
Maryland	16.9	90.1	7,034	18,334	2.6
Massachusetts	13.8	90.1	7,778	34,055	4.4
Michigan	18.5	90.1	7,050	23,956	3.4
Minnesota	16.9	90.4	6,388	33,677	5.3
Mississippi	16.1	82.1	4,288	10,783	2.5
Missouri	14.7	91.6	5,565	11,972	2.2
Montana	15.7	91.0	5,724	14,226	2.5
Nebraska	14.3	91.5	5,958	15,964	2.7
Nevada	18.9	74.5	5,295	14,335	2.7
New Hampshire	15.4	87.3	6,156	21,967	3.6
New Jersey	13.8	90.2	9,643	21,326	2.2
New Mexico	16.5	82.7	5,005	28,400	5.7
New York	14.6	85.2	8,852	22,845	2.6
North Carolina	15.8	86.1	5,257	21,880	4.2
North Dakota	14.4	93.6	5,056	20,863	4.1
Ohio	16.2	89.3	6,198	17,572	2.8
Oklahoma	15.4	85.4	5,033	8,845	1.8
Oregon	20.0	78.5	6,419	24,527	3.8
Pennsylvania	16.4	87.6	7,209	25,832	3.6

Table 8.   (*Continued*)

State	Pupil/ Teacher Ratio, 1998	High School Completion Rate, 1997–1999 (%)	Expenditures Per Pupil, 1997–1998 (in Dollars)	Expenditures Per Prisoner, 1997 (in Dollars)	Ratio of Per Prisoner Expenditures to Per Pupil Expenditures
Rhode Island	13.9	86.7	7,928	31,874	4.0
South Carolina	15.2	86.9	5,320	16,340	3.1
South Dakota	14.3	91.5	4,669	12,869	2.8
Tennessee	15.3	89.5	4,937	17,664	3.6
Texas	15.2	79.2	5,444	13,283	2.4
Utah	22.4	89.7	3,969	27,533	6.9
Vermont	12.8	95.3	7,075	29,723	4.2
Virginia	14.2	87.0	6,067	20,288	3.3
Washington	20.1	87.0	6,040	26,481	4.4
West Virginia	14.2	89.2	6,323	23,227	3.7
Wisconsin	14.4	90.6	7,123	22,223	3.1
Wyoming	14.2	87.8	6,218	17,021	2.7
United States	16.5	85.5	6,189	18,428	3.0

Note: n/a – not applicable (The state did not participate in the assessment).
Adapted from: Children's Defense Fund (2002, p. 65).

Table 11, one in seven youths in America is a high school dropout and one in eight is unemployed. More than 1.7 million youths were arrested in 2000, and almost one in five of the youths incarcerated were in adult facilities (Yeakey, 2003).

WHY CHILDREN LIVE IN POVERTY

The key question becomes, why are such a large number of children living in poverty in the United States? Why does almost one of every three American children experience at least one year of poverty before turning age 16? The reasons are complex and interrelated involving changes in our economic structure, the reconfiguration of society as well as factors, such as the individual characteristics of parents.

A major reason why so many children are living in poverty today is because real wages have been falling for most Americans since 1973 (Coontz, 1995). This means that the value of wages in terms of buying power, what a family can actually purchase with a paycheck, has declined steadily for 30 years. This speaks to the long-term trend of income inequality in our country. As Coontz relates:

Table 9. Child Abuse and Neglect, 1999.

State	Percent by Race					
	Number (1)	Rate (2)	Black (%)	American Indian, Alaska Native (%)	Asian/ Pacific Islander (%)	White (%)	Other and Unknown (%)
Alabama	13,773	12.9	38.0	0.2	0.2	60.0	1.6
Alaska	6,032	30.7	6.5	42.5	2.4	37.8	10.8
Arizona	9,205	6.9	9.2	5.7	1.0	78.3	5.9
Arkansas	7,564	11.5	19.1	0.2	0.1	56.6	23.9
California	130,510	14.6	18.0	1.0	1.0	33.0	44.0
Colorado	6,989	6.6	8.4	1.3	0.8	62.8	26.8
Connecticut	14,514	17.5	23.1	0.0	0.8	37.8	38.4
Delaware	2,111	11.6	45.2	0.1	0.5	53.1	1.0
District of Columbia	2,308	24.2	63.0	0.0	1.0	1.6	34.4
Florida	67,530	18.9	31.9	0.1	0.4	66.6	1.0
Georgia	26,888	13.1	47.4	0.1	0.4	45.9	6.2
Hawaii	2,669	9.2	2.5	0.9	61.9	12.1	22.6
Idaho	2,928	8.4	0.4	1.6	0.1	55.7	42.2
Illinois	33,125	10.4	39.1	0.0	0.4	48.6	11.9
Indiana	21,608	14.1	17.6	1.4	0.2	71.3	9.4
Iowa	9,763	13.6	8.0	0.9	0.7	74.2	16.2
Kansas	8,452	12.1	14.3	0.7	0.1	76.0	8.8
Kentucky	18,650	19.3	13.9	0.1	0.2	78.3	7.5
Louisiana	12,614	10.6	51.9	0.1	0.4	46.6	0.9
Maine	4,154	14.3	0.6	0.5	0.2	97.4	1.3
Maryland (3)	15,451	11.8	n/r	n/r	n/r	n/r	n/r
Massachusetts	29,633	20.2	n/r	n/r	n/r	n/r	n/r
Michigan	24,505	9.6	40.7	0.7	0.4	55.8	2.4
Minnesota	11,113	8.7	26.3	9.4	3.8	58.7	1.8
Mississippi	6,523	8.7	52.8	0.2	0.5	46.3	0.2
Missouri	9,079	6.5	26.0	0.2	0.3	72.0	1.4
Montana	3,414	15.3	0.8	24.9	0.3	57.1	16.8
Nebraska	3,474	7.8	12.4	4.6	0.8	66.1	16.1
Nevada	8,238	16.8	20.2	1.3	1.0	65.3	12.1
New Hampshire	926	3	n/r	n/r	n/r	n/r	n/r
New Jersey	9,222	4.6	47.2	0.3	0.7	33.6	18.2
New Mexico	3,730	7.5	3.7	8.6	0.7	75.7	11.2
New York	64,045	14.4	31.0	0.2	0.1	38.0	30.7
North Carolina	36,976	19.1	37.9	2.4	1.1	57.1	1.5
North Dakota	1,284	8	3.5	26.2	0.2	68.8	1.2
Ohio	53,311	18.7	30.7	0.3	0.1	61.0	8.0
Oklahoma	16,210	18.4	13.5	14.4	0.5	69.1	2.6
Oregon	11,241	13.6	4.9	2.3	1.2	56.5	35.2

Table 9.   (*Continued*)

State	Percent by Race						
	Number (1)	Rate (2)	Black (%)	American Indian, Alaska Native (%)	Asian/ Pacific Islander (%)	White (%)	Other and Unknown (%)
Pennsylvania	5,076	1.8	n/r	n/r	n/r	n/r	n/r
Rhode Island	3,485	14.5	16.3	1.0	2.1	72.6	8.0
South Carolina	9,580	10	45.8	0.3	0.6	52.5	0.7
South Dakota	2,561	12.9	n/r	n/r	n/r	n/r	n/r
Tennessee	10,611	7.9	31.6	0.0	0.3	62.5	5.6
Texas	39,488	6.9	24.5	0.3	0.7	73.2	1.4
Utah	8,660	12.2	1.9	2.0	1.2	49.7	45.3
Vermont	1,080	7.8	0.6	0.1	0.6	97.9	0.8
Virginia	8,199	4.9	39.3	0.1	1.1	51.6	7.9
Washington	8,039	5.4	9.9	8.6	2.4	71.0	8.0
West Virginia	8,609	21.3	5.1	0.1	0.1	84.0	10.7
Wisconsin	9,791	7.3	30.0	3.0	2.0	58.5	6.5
Wyoming	1,221	9.6	1.8	5.7	0.3	75.9	16.2
United States	826,162	11.8	26.4%	1.8%	1.4%	54.3%	16.2%

Note: Adapted from: Children's Defense Fund (2002, p. 62).

(1)   Number of child victims where abuse or neglect is "substantiated" or "indicated." North Dakota reported no victims in either of these categories but did report child victims In need of services."
(2)   Number of child victims/1000 children.
(3)   n/r data not reported.

> Most poverty . . . comes from our changing earnings structure, not from our changing family structure. Between 1969 and 1989 the number of young white men earning less than the poverty figure for a family of four rose from one in ten to almost one in four. For African American men the comparable figure rose from 26% to 37%; for Hispanics, from 25% to 40% (Coontz, 1995, p. 9).

The number of low wage workers, or the working poor continues to expand proving that work alone will not necessarily keep an individual or family out of poverty.

A second factor in the explanation of high rates of poverty among children is that, as the real value of wages shrink, more resources are going to a smaller number of people in our country.

> Even after taxes, the top 20% rake in 44% of total income (not counting capital gains from the sale of homes, wares, stocks and bonds); the bottom 20% must get by on 3.9%. And this astonishingly small share includes the cash value of food stamps and other benefits for the poor! In fact, the top 1% of the population has as much income as the entire bottom 40% (Coontz, 1995, p. 11).

Table 10.   Firearm Deaths of Children and Teens, by Manner[a], 1999.

State	Total	Homicide	Suicide	Accident	Unknown Intent
Alabama	83	44	26	10	3
Alaska	23	9	11	1	2
Arizona	86	55	30	0	1
Arkansas	40	15	20	3	2
California	402	320	66	8	8
Colorado	63	34	24	3	2
Connecticut	18	13	5	0	0
Delaware	5	1	3	1	0
District of Columbia	45	41	3	1	0
Florida	137	86	43	4	4
Georgia	117	67	41	5	4
Hawaii	0	0	0	0	0
Idaho	23	7	13	3	0
Illinois	228	182	37	7	2
Indiana	91	57	27	6	1
Iowa	23	2	17	2	2
Kansas	31	12	14	3	2
Kentucky	39	21	11	5	2
Louisiana	93	52	27	11	3
Maine	9	2	5	1	1
Maryland	98	78	16	0	4
Massachusetts	20	10	9	0	1
Michigan	116	66	40	7	3
Minnesota	45	15	27	3	0
Mississippi	72	37	17	11	7
Missouri	92	47	34	7	4
Montana	19	2	12	5	0
Nebraska	18	6	11	1	0
Nevada	26	15	10	1	0
New Hampshire	4	1	3	0	0
New Jersey	32	25	6	0	1
New Mexico	45	24	17	4	0
New York	132	101	25	5	1
North Carolina	93	54	33	4	2
North Dakota	9	2	6	0	1
Ohio	81	38	30	10	3
Oklahoma	62	28	21	12	1
Oregon	33	7	21	5	0
Pennsylvania	124	77	39	5	3
Rhode Island	8	6	2	0	0
South Carolina	51	22	20	8	1
South Dakota	14	1	9	3	1
Tennessee	85	47	22	12	4

Table 10.   (*Continued*)

State	Total	Homicide	Suicide	Accident	Unknown Intent
Texas	254	141	89	21	3
Utah	21	3	17	0	1
Vermont	3	0	2	1	0
Virginia	86	48	35	3	0
Washington	62	20	34	6	2
West Virginia	19	8	10	0	1
Wisconsin	74	41	27	6	0
Wyoming	11	0	11	0	0
United States	3365	1990	1078	214	83

Note: Adapted from: Children's Defense Fund. (2002, p. 66).
[a] Ages 0–19.

A third factor for the high number of children living in poverty is that there has been a decline in the real value of government assistance to families. Until 1996, Aid to Families with Dependent Children (AFDC) was the major cash benefit for poor families. (In 1996, it was replaced by Temporary Assistance for Needy Families (TANF). When AFDC was replaced with TANF, benefits from AFDC were worth less than 1975 benefits for every state, and the annual cost-of-living increases in food stamp benefits did not offset the loss. Even so, many eligible families do not use all services available to them. Failure to utilize services may be due to the fact that families do not know they are eligible for assistance, because the administrative barriers are too cumbersome to overcome, or for other reasons, such as the placement of welfare offices in locations difficult to reach.

The reconfiguration of families in U.S. society, also called the feminization of poverty, has contributed to the increase in childhood poverty. As the number of one-parent, female headed households grows, so does the chance that children will grow up in poverty. As we have shown from data in the Luxembourg Study, in Table 3, the U.S. leads the world in the number of single parent/solo mother families. In addition, according to U.S. Census data for 2000, 39.8% or two of five children living in single-parent female headed families were living in poverty, compared to 8.2% of children living in two parent families in 2000. Further, the poverty rates for children of color, living in minority, single-parent female-headed households are higher compared to their white counterparts (Di Nitto, 2000), a factor often referred to as institutionalized racism. This growing number of single-parent families is attributable both to increased divorce rates and to the tenfold increase since 1950 in the number of births outside marriage (Children's Defense Fund, "Census 2000 Supplementary Survey").

Table 11. Youth at Risk.

State	Dropout Rate, 1997–1999 (in %) (1)	Unemployment Rate, 16–19-Year-Olds, 2000 (in %) (2)	Number of Juveniles Arrested, 2000 (3)	Number of Juveniles in Corrections Facilities, 2000	
				Juvenile Facilities	Adult Facilities
Alabama	16.9%	18.6%	10,721	1,731	236
Alaska	9.2	16.7	5,530	357	37
Arizona	25.0	8.3	52,674	1,872	898
Arkansas	17.1	14.7	16,336	898	353
California	18.5	17.0	242,492	14,644	1,604
Colorado	16.7	12.3	45,641	2,013	159
Connecticut	9.9	n/r	19,101	894	452
Delaware	10.9	16.3	6,765	91	14
District of Columbia	12.8	33.1	n/r	46	39
Florida	15.2	12.9	124,845	6,320	1,455
Georgia	16.3	9.7	25,984	4,125	910
Hawaii	9.3	16.5	10,915	193	10
Idaho	14.5	13.2	18,692	597	72
Illinois	13.8	11.9	45,896	3,903	868
Indiana	11.4	11.9	34,789	2,895	571
Iowa	11.8	8.8	21,814	1,215	74
Kansas	8.4	13.3	n/r	1,159	111
Kentucky	13.4	15.8	1,668	1,531	186
Louisiana	17.9	15.6	32,334	2,396	632
Maine	7.1	12.0	9,990	389	4
Maryland	9.9	14.8	40,030	1,782	295
Massachusetts	9.9	9.4	17,819	2,250	195
Michigan	9.9	10.3	43,776	4,364	778
Minnesota	9.6	8.9	69,270	1,819	112
Mississippi	17.9	18.1	14,652	1,431	369
Missouri	8.4	11.9	28,912	2,434	372
Montana	9.0	16.0	4,550	365	69
Nebraska	8.5	9.7	18,190	1,405	49
Nevada	25.5	12.9	25,349	889	218
New Hampshire	12.7	9.6	6,303	417	27
New Jersey	9.8	12.7	65,777	2,189	110
New Mexico	17.3	17.0	9,748	553	312
New York	14.8	13.3	45,380	6,896	1,739
North Carolina	13.9	13.3	45,388	2,172	743
North Dakota	6.4	8.5	7,839	285	· 6
Ohio	10.7	11.3	54,059	3,954	606
Oklahoma	14.6	10.4	25,618	1,480	89
Oregon	21.5	12.7	32,016	1,497	207
Pennsylvania	12.4	13.9	89,033	6,219	440

Table 11.   (*Continued*)

State	Dropout Rate, 1997–1999 (in %) (1)	Unemployment Rate, 16–19-Year-Olds, 2000 (in %) (2)	Number of Juveniles Arrested, 2000 (3)	Number of Juveniles in Corrections Facilities, 2000	
				Juvenile Facilities	Adult Facilities
Rhode Island	13.3	16.6	6,616	365	6
South Carolina	13.1	15.0	8,281	1,705	527
South Dakota	8.5	6.5	8,593	965	126
Tennessee	10.5	13.4	18,027	2,548	142
Texas	20.8	15.4	187,494	7,811	3,420
Utah	10.3	8.8	24,616	1,202	168
Vermont	4.7	7.7	2,163	120	18
Virginia	13.0	7.7	30,524	3,107	405
Washington	13.0	18.6	44,535	2,280	198
West Virginia	10.8	18.9	2,337	477	25
Wisconsin	9.4	9.2	n/r	1,837	618
Wyoming	12.2	10.7	7,670	392	56
United States	14.5%	13.1%	1,710,752	112,479	21,130

Note: Adapted from: Children's Defense Fund. (2002, p. 67).

(1) Percent of 18–24 year olds who are not enrolled in school and are not high school graduates
(2) n/r data not report
(3) Number of arrests reported to the Federal Bureau of Investigation (FBI). Not all jurisdictions in a state report to the FBI.

Coupled with institutionalized racism is the fact that the failure of absent parents to financially contribute to the support of their children is seen as another major cause of child poverty today. This gender-segregated division of labor is often referred to as institutionalized sexism (Heffernan et al., 1997). Today, the vast majority of single-parent families (about 90%) are headed by women. Female headed families often receive little or no financial help from the child's father. In 1999, only 35% of female-headed families received any child support or alimony during the year (Nelson, 2002).

The difficulties of a single mother family are often compounded when the mother is a teen. In fact, we know that children born to unmarried teen mothers are more likely to drop out of school, give birth out of wedlock, divorce or separate, and be dependent on welfare. And, when the mothers of these families do not complete high school, their children are 10 times more likely to be living in poverty by the ages of 8 to 12 than children born to non-adolescent, married mothers with at least a high school education (Nelson, 2002).

Family poverty is linked to the level of education of the parents, as well. People without high school diplomas will earn only about 75% as much as high school graduates, and earn less than half of what college graduates are likely to make during their lifetimes (O'Hare, 1995). During the twenty-first century, economists believe that it will be increasingly more important for adults to have skills and technical knowledge in order to hold jobs that can support a family. Other personal characteristics of parents such as mental retardation, emotional illness, those involved with substance abuse and illegal activities also increase the likelihood that families will live in poverty.

In far too many cases, grandparents are now becoming the primary care givers for their grandchildren. Today, more and more grandparents are raising their children's children. Parental substance abuse – along with divorce, and teenage pregnancy, and the increased incarceration of women – are the leading reasons that grandparents take over the care of their grandchildren. No matter how much they love their grandchildren, seniors often have trouble coping, when a retired lifestyle is suddenly replaced with diapers and play groups. The problems grandparents face include finding enough money, on a fixed retired income, adequate health care and, in some cases, the physical strength and energy to keep up with young children.

The fact that children are too young to vote and have no effective advocacy group or lobby in the federal government serves to perpetuate child poverty and the conditions which cause it. In comparison, senior citizens or elders in the U.S. have a very effective lobby, the American Association of Retired Persons, for improving living conditions for seniors. While there are advocacy groups who work on behalf of children, they have not yet established the power base necessary to force policymakers to make the necessary changes required to lift children out of poverty.

Consequences of Growing Up in Poverty

Regardless of the causes of poverty, increasing numbers of American children are growing up in environments that put them at high risk of adverse outcomes. Figure 1 provides a telling portrayal of a child life, each day in America.

As the aforementioned depicts, growing up in poverty places a child at a profound disadvantage and greatly lowers the chance that the child will mature into a well-adjusted, productive, and contributing member of society. Research today reveals that just about every part of a child's life is affected by poverty. Further, growing up in the adverse conditions created by poverty increases the chance that such children will cost taxpayers more money as they will require more expensive publicly funded services throughout their lives.

5	children or teens commit suicide.
9	children or teens are homicide victims.
9	children or teens are killed by firearms.
34	children or teens die from accidents.
77	babies die.
180	children are arrested for violent crimes.
367	children are arrested for drug abuse.
401	babies are born to mothers who received late or no prenatal care.
825	babies are born at low birthweight.
1310	babies are born without health insurance.
1329	babies are born to teen mothers.
2016	babies are born into poverty.
2319	babies are born to mothers who are not high school graduates.
2543	public school students are corporally punished.
2861	high school students drop out.
3585	babies are born to unmarried mothers.
4248	children are arrested.
7883	children are reported abused or neglected.
17,297	public school students are suspended from school.

Fig. 1. Each Day in America. *Source:* Adapted from Children's Defense Fund (2002, p. 14.).

The stress of living in poverty is greatly magnified as risk factors, in Fig. 1, interact. Basic life stressor factors caused by living in poverty, can lead to isolation, tension, anger and hopelessness. Fighting to attain the basic necessities – food, clothing, medical care and shelter-, that other Americans take for granted, poverty often forces one **to**: live in inadequate and crowded housing; **send their children to inferior schools; and to be** exposed to more crime and violence than non-poor families.

In addition, a growing body of scientific evidence reveals that early brain development of the child is negatively affected by stressors often inherent with poverty and that these deficits may not be reversible. Over the past twenty years, researchers have documented the effect of malnutrition on brain development. The Carnegie Corporation (1994) emphasized this point:

We have long understood that factors other than genetic programming affect brain development. Nutrition is perhaps the most obvious example: we know that inadequate nutrition before birth and in the first years of life can so seriously interfere with brain development that it may lead to a host of neurological and behavioral disorders, including learning disabilities and mental retardation (p. 20).

There are approximately 31 million people in this country who are food insecure, defined as either hungry or not sure of when they will eat their next meal (Karger & Stoesz, 2002). Of these, 75% are women and children. A hungry child is 2 to 11 times more likely to experience fatigue, concentration problems, dizziness, irritability, frequent headaches and ear infections, unwanted weight loss, and frequent colds. Inadequate food supply also causes other health problems, such as stunted growth (defined as being in the shortest 10% of children for their age), low birth weight, and iron deficiency anemia (Sherman, 1994). Anemia is the most common consequence of inadequate nutrition and manifests itself with slow development in infants, inattentiveness, and conduct disorders.

Other life stressors that place poor children at risk include health and health care factors. Poor children are more likely to begin life at a disadvantage, as they are 1.2–2.2 times more likely to be born with a low birth weight, (less than 2500 grams or 5.5 pounds) (Nelson, 2002). Low birth weight babies are more likely to die in infancy, have a doubled risk of learning problems (such as learning disabilities, hyperactivity, emotional problems, and mental illness), have a significantly greater risk of neurodevelopmental problems (seizures, epilepsy, water on the brain, cerebral palsy, and mental retardation), and, are at a higher risk of losing their eyesight and hearing. Overall, poor children are three times more likely to suffer from fair or poor health and are much more likely to have health problems than non-poor children (Nelson, 2002).

Another reason why poor children are at greater risk of poor health is that many poor families do not have health insurance. Employer-based insurance is the major source of insurance for children, yet the number of children covered by this benefit has decreased over the past two decades. Employers are dropping coverage, ending coverage, or asking more from employee premiums for dependent coverage. This trend will greatly impact children in the future. Children of color are disproportionately represented among the uninsured, although the numbers are highest for White children.

Relative to the intersect between poverty and environmental factors, lead poisoning is one of the most serious environmental heath hazards threatening children today (Crosson-Tower, 2004). Although all children are at risk, those living in low-income or minority families are at an increased risk. For example, African American children are five times more likely to be exposed to lead poisoning compared with White children. Lead contamination generally comes from lead-based paint found in older, inadequately maintained houses. Children living in these houses breathe the dust that forms after the paint deteriorates, and may eat the sweet-tasting paint chips. Repeated exposure may cause kidney damage, learning disabilities, developmental delays and behavioral problems. Very high levels of lead in blood can cause seizures, coma and even death.

Poor children are more than three times as likely to live in inadequate and/or crowded housing, move around about twice as much as non-poor children, and are more likely to go without heat or other utilities (Ellwood, 1988; Sherman, 1994; Sidel, 1986). In the past decade, homelessness has increased more among families with children than any other group. In fact, a 1997 survey conducted by the U.S. Conference of Mayors showed that families with children represent 35% of those in homeless shelters (Dahl, 1994).

Poverty further restricts a family's choices of neighborhoods where they can raise their children. Poor children are more likely to live in crowded, noisy and crime-ridden neighborhoods. The lower quality of life in these neighborhoods means that poorer families have less access to good jobs, safe play areas and parks, and positive role models for their children (Sidel, 1986).

All of the foregoing factors contribute to increased life stressors for families raising their children in poverty. These stressors and inequalities can breed violence, and its ultimate consequence, assaults, criminality and ultimately, incarceration (Table 8). As Sherman so aptly notes:

> Many social science disciplines, in addition to psychology, have firmly established that poverty and its contextual life circumstance are major determinants of violence . . . Violence is most prevalent among the poor, regardless of race . . . Few differences among the races are found in the rates of violence when people at the same income level are compared.

> But beyond mere income level, it is the socioeconomic inequality of the poor – their sense of relative deprivation and their lack of opportunity to ameliorate their life circumstances – that facilitates higher rates of violence . . . . Not only do the poor in America lack basic necessities, but they are aware that they do not have those things most other Americans have and that they lack other opportunities needed to obtain them in the future.

> Media depictions of other Americans, who are living the "good life" serve to compound the already untenable conditions of poverty with a heightened sense of deprivation (Sherman, 1994, p. 38).

As a result of the foregoing, the educational consequences of poverty should come as no surprise. Children brought up in poverty are much less likely to graduate from high school and receive additional education or training, thereby making it more difficult to earn wages high enough to live above the poverty level as adults. For every year a child lives in poverty, the chance that he or she will fall behind in school increases considerably (Kozol, 2000). Nor can poor children count on receiving a public education that will help them overcome the disadvantages they experience, because they live in poverty. The richest school districts in America spend 56% more per student than do the poorest. Although additional funding does not guarantee a quality education, it is a contributing factor. It is almost conventional wisdom that the poorest children attend the poorest schools, and school achievement is found to be significantly lower in poor schools.

Since many government relief programs were dismantled in the 1990s, homeless adults receive little help from the government. But a federal law that requires local school districts to seek out and enroll homeless students and provide services to them has forced public schools across the nation to become safety nets of last resort. With unemployment and spiraling housing costs pushing a growing number of families into homelessness, school systems across the country are seeing more and more children living in shelters, cars or motels. Some states are reporting a nearly 50% increase in homeless students over the year (Dillon, 2003). Schools have become the only safe haven when students' home lives disintegrate. Clearly job layoffs and surging housing prices, and the cessation of unemployment benefits, have caused the rise in the homeless population.

Despite evidence to the contrary, persistent myths have guided public policy decisions and continue to be pervasive, pejorative elements of the poverty/welfare discourse in America (Extra, 1995). A brief mention of some of these myths is important here. The first myth is that poor women have more children because of the financial incentives of welfare benefits. However, data reveals no significant rate of increase in child bearing in those states that pay higher benefits for additional children. And, real benefits have not kept pace with inflation, thereby diminishing welfare in real dollars. In addition, federal law presently refuses to pay for additional children born out of wedlock, rending this argument moot. Another myth is that America fails to subsidize middle class families. But, all taxpayers receive a stipend for additional children in the form of a tax credit from the federal government for $2450. State tax agencies provide even more in credits. Compared to monies that families receive from welfare, middle class taxpayers receive 2.3 times more than poor families. A third myth relates to the fact that the public is resistant to spending money for the poor. As McGrory noted "The suspicion that poorer people are getting something for nothing is much harder to bear than the visible good fortune of the richer" (Extra, 1995, p. 2). Yet, data examining America's public attitudes toward the poor revealed that 80% of respondents indicated that the government is responsible for extinguishing poverty. A fourth myth is that America has spent over $5 trillion dollars on welfare since the 1960s and it has not worked. However, upon close examination, analysis reveals that Aid to Families with Dependent Children consumed only 1.5% of the $5 trillion, for other programs consumed most of the money, including health care for the elderly and disabled. What is most important is the fact that in the thirty years since 1964 and 1994, alone, welfare payments equaled two years of military expenditures. A final debilitating myth is that anyone who wants to get off welfare can just get a job. The reality is that many welfare recipients are the working poor. And, as we will see in the next section, jobs that pay a low wage and have no benefits, simply do not sustain families.

In Consideration of Broader Economics

It makes sense in both humane and economic terms to make the changes necessary to raise children out of poverty and off of government welfare. Adults who have grown up in poverty are more likely to require costly public assistance and programs, and they also earn less and produce less economic output. In Table 1 we have seen that other industrialized nations with fewer resources and similar economic and social problems have put public policies in place that ensure that children are protected and have a better chance to reach their full potential. But in order to raise children out of poverty, we need to make attitudinal shifts toward children. First, America needs to value all of her our children. Whether they are poor children, or children of color from rural or urban areas, we must feel responsible for them all and not view them as "other people's children." Second, we need to value the role of the family and the job of parenting. This requires a two generational approach to reducing poverty. Finally, we need to value and fund prevention programs, and move away from our current crisis orientation that forces us to invest in more programs designed to deal with the problems of poverty after the damage has been done.

Because of increased joblessness, booming budget deficits and the wartime economy, the number of hungry families in America is rising (Nelson, 2003). About 12 million American families last year worried that they could not afford to buy food and 32% of them actually experienced someone going hungry at one time or another. It was the third year in a row that the Department of Agriculture has seen an increase in the number of households experiencing hunger and those worried about having enough money to pay for food (Number of Hungry Families, 2003). The prevalence of hunger and food insecurity in America is clearly tied to the poverty rate, because they fluctuate together. Some 34.6 million Americans were living in poverty last year – 1.7 million more than in 2001, according to the Census Bureau (Number of Hungry Families, 2003). It does not seem as if hunger would be a problem in this country since food is abundant. Supermarket shelves in the United States are filled with hundreds of different products and restaurants are practically on every corner. Plus, the country is struggling with obesity. Nearly 65% of adults and 13% of children are overweight to the point of obesity (Number of Hungry Families, 2003). But ironically, hunger and obesity often coexist because many hungry families struggle with their weight. They tend to buy high-calorie foods that are low in nutrients, but are filling. As a result, nutritious diets are compromised. Also, many families will spend their incomes on fixed expenses, like housing, before buying food.

Overall, requests for emergency food assistance jumped by 17% this year and requests for shelter increased by 13%, according to the 25 city survey conducted by the U.S. Conference of Mayors (Chan, 2003). The annual survey pointed to unemployment and lack of affordable housing as the leading causes of hunger and homelessness. The survey underscores the impact the economy has had on everyday Americans. People were turned away from food assistance agencies in 56% of the cities and from shelters in 84% of the cities. Those figures, the highest in six years – reflect budget deficits and belt-tightening in cities and states, which, in turn, has affected the availability of food banks and shelters. The report found that the homeless population consists of 41% single men, 40% families with children, 14% single women and 5% unaccompanied youth (Chan, 2003).

As noted earlier, in 1996, America experienced an overhaul in its welfare system from AFDC to TANF. Amidst the signs of the effects of the new law, because of stringent welfare requirements, is a decline in the welfare rolls, albeit not a decline in the overall poverty of poor Americans. Another trend is also emerging, an unwelcome trend: a rising share of children particularly black children in cities, are turning up in no-parent households, left with relatives, friends or foster families without either their mother or their father (Bernstein, 2002). The findings are reopening the debate on what shifting welfare rules are doing to families. The law now requires 50% of welfare recipients to work up to 30 hours a week, with some exceptions for hardship. Among those most affected by the new changes, African American children in central cities. Those living without their parents had more than doubled on average, to 16.1% from 7.5%, when researchers controlled for other factors (Bernstein, 2002). What is occurring is the complex relationship between welfare reform and its impact on families. In some cases, we see positive effects on family structures, and in other cases we see more children living in no-parent families. In earlier sections of this chapter, the trend of grandparents raising grandchildren, was noted as well as the many pressures such families faced. To be sure, an individual child is sometimes better off living with a grandmother, but as a societal matter, more children living with neither parent cannot be viewed in a positive fashion. Children who do not live with their parents do significantly worse on average than those in single-parent homes, as reflected in higher rates of school failure, mental health problems and delinquency.

The state of America's economy is cause for even more concern. The economy, and its alleged economic upturn is not just a jobless recovery, but is now being called a job loss recovery. The hemorrhaging of jobs in the aftermath of the recent "mild" recession is like nothing the U.S. has seen in more than half a century

(Herbert, 2003). Millions continue to look desperately for work, and millions more have given up in despair. The official jobless rate, now 6.2%, does not come close to reflecting the grim nature of the employment situation in the U.S. The official rate refers only to those actively seeking work. It does not count the discouraged workers who have looked for jobs within the last 12 months, but have given up because of the lack of offers. Then, there are the involuntary part-timers who would like full-time jobs, but cannot find them. Further, there are people who have had to settle for jobs that pay significantly less than jobs they once held. When one combines the unemployed and the underemployed, what remains is a percentage of the work force that is in double digits. That combination represents a tremendous loss of purchasing power for a society that needs broad-based wage growth among its consumers to remain economically viable. On the business side, corporate profits are up as increased productivity (based primarily on improvements in technology) is way up and outsourcing of U.S. jobs is increasing. Hiring, of course, of full time U.S. workers with benefits has decreased, while the employment of part time and temporary workers is more prevalent.

A word about the minimum wage is important here. The federal minimum wage rose in 1997 to $5.15 per hour. Although this increase in the minimum wage is a step in the right direction, it still leaves full-time, year-round minimum wage employment at only 82% of the 1998 poverty level for a family of three (Dahl, 1998). While advocates continue to lobby for further increases in the minimum wage and for automatic adjustment for inflation, given the influence of the corporate lobby in America, as well as the outsourcing of jobs overseas, it is doubtful that the minimum wage will be increased in the foreseeable future.

Furthermore, the average hourly wage increase for the 85 million Americans who work in non-supervisory positions in offices and factories is a flat 3 cents. Wages are up just 2.1% since November 2002 – the slowest wage growth America has experienced in 40 years. Economists are now suggesting that if the American economy has experienced a recovery at all, "... that it is a recovery for capital, not labor; indeed that it's a recovery for capital at the expense of labor (Meyerson, 2003, p. A14). ... In Bangalore, India, where American companies are on a huge hiring spree for the kind of talent they used to scoop up in Silicon Valley, the starting annual salary for top electrical engineering graduates is $10,000 – compared with $80,000 here in the States" (Meyerson, 2003, p. A14). Not only is the current recovery the first to take place in an economy in which global wage rates are a factor, but the first since before the New Deal of the 1930s to take place in an economy in which the rate of private-sector unionization is in single digits – just 8.5% of the workforce.

For years, public and non-profit food assistance programs have been reporting a sharp rise in the number of working families using their services. But now, working families are becoming common visitors, similar to the indigent elderly, to the city's soup kitchens and food pantries. Driving the shift in strategy, experts and providers say, is a familiar social and economic phenomenon: the growing numbers of working poor turning up at the soup kitchens and pantries, in most cases, single mothers with children. It appears that "the face of poverty is a working woman with two children" (Kaufman, 2003, p. 1).

As previously noted, states across the country are experiencing billion dollar budget deficits that are crippling, for all Americans, but most particularly for the poor. Even in President Bush's home state of Texas, 54,000 children have been dropped from the federal state health insurance program under new regulations from Austin, Texas, the state capitol. As one commentator noted, this suggests that any celebrations of economy recovery in Washington may be as premature as that "... mission accomplished banner hung behind President Bush on the USS Abraham Lincoln to hail the end of major combat in Iraq" (Broder, 2003, p. B7). In Florida, tens of thousands of low-income youngsters who are eligible for a children's health insurance program are being placed on waiting lists. State officials say they cannot afford to insure the children now. In California, an estimated 300,000 eligible children are being shunted to similar waiting lists. No one knows when they might get coverage (Herbert, 2004). What this speaks to is a different view of "the other America," of the children being left behind.

The global economy has made its presence felt, first for low income workers, but now for high income workers in America. Offshoring and outsourcing are two of the favored euphemisms for shipping work overseas. Others call it global sourcing. Whatever term one utilizes, the expansion of this practice from manufacturing to the higher-paying technical and white collar occupations is the latest big threat to employment in the U.S. Years ago, when concern was being expressed about the shipment of factory jobs to places with slave wages, hideous working conditions and even prison labor, proponents said there was no cause for concern. Proponents suggested that exporting labor-intensive jobs would make U.S. companies more competitive, leading to increased growth and employment, and higher living standards. The government advised U.S. workers to adjust, to become better educated and skillful enough to thrive in a new world of employment, where technology and the ability to process information were crucial components. Unfortunately, white collar workers whose jobs are now threatened across the U.S. are well educated, but they are nevertheless in danger of following the well-trodden path of their factory brethren to lower wage work, or the unemployment line (Herbert, December 29, 2003). This development represents a frontal assault on the livelihood of solidly middle class Americans, some of whom may be required to train the foreign workers who will replace them. The outsourcing of good jobs has been underway for years and there is no dispute that the practice is speeding up. As one commentator related, "Anything that is not nailed to the floor is being considered for outsourcing" (Herbert, December 29, 2003, p. 2). An even greater irony is that millions of white collars workers who are and will be affected by this phenomenon over the next several years are clueless as to what they can do about it. They do not have organized representation in the workplace, and government policies overwhelmingly favor the corporations. These hardworking men and women and their families have little protection against the powerful forces of the global economy. The exacting social and economic consequences for their families have yet to be felt.

CONCLUSION

More economists are beginning to speak of America's 12% problem, that is, the fact that more than 12% of the population is steeped in poverty. Almost forty years ago President Lyndon B. Johnson in his State of the Union address declared a War on Poverty in America, a war that America has not won, and it appears a war that America has only begun to fight. The truth is that America tolerates even accepts persistent child poverty. Our education system reflects it, as do our tax policies, child care policies and child support policies. While the national slogan of our present government is to "leave no child behind," the fact is that we continue to pull millions of children behind each year. The reality is that poor children may never catch up and become fully participating or contributing members of society. The data from earlier portions of the paper suggest that poor children in France, Germany and the Nordic countries are six times more likely to escape poverty than their American counterparts. Given the increasing diversity in American society, spiraling divorce rates in America and the blatant race based and gender based nature of child poverty, we see that decades of economic growth have not lifted the poorest Americans to a higher standard of living.

In America it would appear, that for some, "it is the best of times," for others, "it is the worst of times" (Dickens, 1859). Our 12% problem is a tremendous challenge that will require the best of our efforts and the leadership of true statespersons, not mere politicians; men and women of social conscience, not mere elected officials who know the price of everything, yet the value of nothing. If we have learned anything from the past, we must learn the dire social and economic consequences that our policies have wrought as we have failed to enrich and make better the lives of our future generations. As the late anthropologist Margaret Mead once stated, "There is no greater insight into the future than to recognize that when we save our children, we save ourselves" (National Commission on Children, 1991, p. 2).

REFERENCES

Bennett, N. G., Li, J., Song, Y., & Yang, K. (1999, June). *Young children in poverty: A statistical update* (June 1999 ed.). National Center for Children in Poverty (2002, March 8).

Bernstein, N. (2002, July 29). Side effect of welfare law: The no-parent family. *The New York Times* (http://www.nytimes.com//2002/07/29/national/29WELF.html?todaysheadlines).

Broder, D. S. (2003, November 15). Budget gloom state by state. *Washington Post*, B7.

Carnegie Corporation (1994). *Starting points: Meeting the needs of our youngest children.* New York: Author.

Chan, S. (2003, December 10). Survey indicates more go hungry, homeless: Aid lacking as greater demands conflict with improving economy. *Washington Post*, A22.

The Children's Defense Fund (2002). *The state of children in America's union, A 2002 action guide to leave no child behind.* Washington, DC: Children's Defense Fund.

Children's Defense Fund (2000). Census 2000 supplementary survey: Poverty status during previous 12 months, by age. Every child deserves a fair start. Retrieved from the World Wide Web on June 28. http://childrensdefense.org/fs_poverty_statebystate.htm.

Clemetson, L. (2003, September 3). Census shows ranks of poor rose in 2002 by 1.3 million. *The New York Times* http://www.nytimes.com/2003/09/03/national/03CENS.html?th.

Coontz, S. (1995, March). The American family and the nostalgia trap. *Phi Beta Kappan.*

Crosson-Tower, C. (2004). *Exploring child welfare, a practice perspective.* Boston, MA: Pearson/Allyn & Bacon.

Dahl, K. (Ed.) (1998). *The state of America's children yearbook.* Washington, DC: Children's Defense Fund.

Dickens, C. (1859). *A tale of two cities.* Boston: Houghton Mifflin.

Dillon, S. (2003, November 27). School is Haven when children have no home. *New York Times* (http://www.nytimes.com/2003/11/27/education/27HOME.html?th).

Di Nitto, D. M. (2000). *Social welfare policy: Politics and public welfare.* Boston: Allyn & Bacon.

Ellwood, D. T. (1988). *Poor support: Poverty in the American family.* New York: Basic Books.

European Commission (1985). On specific community action to combat poverty (Council Decision of December 19, 1984) 85/8/EEC. *Official Journal of the European Communities,* 2(24).

Extra (1995, May/June). (pp. 1–3), Http://fair.org/extra/9505/welfare-myths.html.

Harrington, M. (1962). *The other America: Poverty in the United States.* New York, NY: Macmillan.

Heffernan, J., Shuttlesworth, G., & Ambrosino, R. (1997). *Social work and social welfare.* Minneapolis/St. Paul: West Publishing.

Herbert, B. (2003, December 26). Bracing for the blow. *The New York Times* (http://www.nytimes.com/2003/12/26/opinion/26HERB.html?th).

Herbert, B. (2003, August 7). Despair of the jobless. *The New York Times* (http://www.nytimes.com/2003/08/07/opinion/07HERB.html?th).

Herbert, B. (2004, January 23). The other America. *The New York Times* (http://www.nytimes.com/2004/01/23/opinion/23HERB.html?).

Karger, H. J., & Stoesz, D. (2002). *American social welfare policy: A pluralist approach.* Boston: Allyn & Bacon.

Kaufman, L. (2003, December 27). As face of poor changes, so do food baskets. *The New York Times* (http://www.nytimes.com/2003/12/27/nyregion/27PANT.html?).

Katz, M. B. (1989). The undeserving poor: From the war on poverty to the war on welfare. New York, NY: Pantheon.

Kozol, J. (2000). *Ordinary resurrections.* New York, NY: Crown.

National Commission on Children (1991). *Beyond rhetoric: A New American agenda for children and families*. Washington, DC: NCC.

Nelson, D. W. (2002). *Kids count data book*. Baltimore, MD: Annie C. Casey Foundation.

Nelson, D. W. (2003, November 1). Number of hungry families rising: Agriculture department report shows alarming trend. *Daily Progress*, A7.

Meyerson, H. (2003, December 24). Un-American recovery. *The Washington Post*, A14.

Office of Minority Health (2000). *Healthy people 2000 progress review for black Americans* (http://www.omhre.gov/inetpub/wwwroot/healthy2000book/tab5.html). Washington, DC.

O'Hare, W. P. (1995). *Kids count data book*. Baltimore, MD: Annie C. Casey Foundation.

Rainwater, L., & Smeeding, T. M. (2003). *Poor kids in a rich country, America's children in comparative perspective*. New York, NY: Russell Sage.

Sherman, A. (1994). *Wasting America's future: The children's defense fund report on the costs of child poverty*. Boston: Beacon Press.

Sidel, R. (1986). *Women and children last: The plight of poor women in affluent America*. New York, NY: Penguin Books.

Skolnick, J. H., & Currie, E. (Eds) (2004). *Crisis in American institutions*. Boston, MA: Pearson/Allyn & Bacon.

Toler, D. L. (January 1, 2000). Secrets and lies: Debunking the myths about Africa. *Essence* (http://web.lexis.com/universe . . . 214c0b26c6dce0e989f4ed9).

U.S. Census Bureau (2002, January). Poverty 2001: January 22, 2002. Retrieved from the World Wide Web June 30, 2002; http://www.census.gov/jjes/poverty/threshld/thresh01.html.

Vaughan, D. R. (1993). Exploring the use of the public's views to set income poverty thresholds and adjust them over time. *Social Security Bulletin*, 56(2), 22–46.

Yeakey, C. C. (2003). From cellblocks to classrooms. In: C. C. Yeakey & R. D. Henderson (Eds), *Surmounting All Odds: Education, Opportunity and Society in the New Millennium*. Greenwich, CT: Information Age.

2. TALKING POVERTY: URBAN SCOTS AND SOCIAL DEPRIVATION

David Matheson

One of the most abiding memories I have is of being told not to drop my ts, to say butter and not bu'er, to say water and not wa'er. I was given this message at home and at school. My own ts dropped only rarely but those of many of my peers fell more frequently. We were bombarded with cries of speak properly, we grew up with notions such being well-spoken ringing in our ears. The ultimate, mind you, was the assertion by my teacher in the last year of primary school (I was eleven years of age) that any girl who said whit or wa'er or used any other recognisable Glaswegian pronunciation would never find a man! Noticeable was that teachers never used a glottal stop, except for comic effect. Nothing serious ever appeared in the Mither Tongue. Glaswegian usage, we were told again and again, was for the "dim wits."

INTRODUCTION

Hardly surprisingly, like many fellow Glaswegians, I grew up believing that the language of the majority of my fellow citizens was slang[1] and hence to be disparaged, if not altogether despised. The fact that we were all equally able to express ourselves in Glaswegian or varying degrees of "Standard" English was conveniently overlooked. The hegemonical dominance of the "Standard" was total. Our native tongue was to be extirpated as rapidly as possible if we wanted any social advancement at all and in working class Glasgow in the 1960s and 1970s social

'Suffer the Little Children': National and International Dimensions of Child Poverty and Public Policy
Advances in Education in Diverse Communities: Research, Policy and Praxis, Volume 4, 39–55
ISSN: 1479-358X/doi:10.1016/S1479-358X(04)04002-1

advancement was a major item on many a personal agenda. The multilingualism now so much *à la mode* was never an issue. Implicitly we were indoctrinated with notions of transient bilingualism whose goal, like that of the 19th and 20th century social missionaries in the Celtic areas of Scotland (and elsewhere), was to teach us the English in order that we forget the Glaswegian.

The sense of linguistic inferiority which such treatment fosters is neatly summed up by Nigel Grant who writes: "The cannie Scot is weill-cryit: he cannie think, he cannie speik, he cannie express hissel" (Grant, 1997, p. 30).[2]

This apparent inarticulateness is said to be endemic in the Scottish urban working class. It is based on the notion of linguistic insecurity of speakers of Glaswegian:

> The Glasgow working-class have been diagnosed, on the evidence of teachers and employers, as suffering from 'linguistic insecurity', becoming self-conscious and tongue-tied in the presence of authority figures . . . . Working-class Glaswegians can find it difficult to get themselves taken seriously or treated with respect outside of their own milieu (Macafee, 1988, p. 90).

This is reiterated in Macauley (1977) on the basis of comments from employers, university lecturers and training college lecturers that a major criticism of school-leavers is their lack of confidence in speaking. However, as Macafee (1988) also discovered, those same people who may feel tongue-tied in some circumstances are, in their own social milieu, often fluent on every topic bar education, social status and Standard English.[3] The goal of this paper is to examine the situations which have engendered this and to question whether there is any light on that particular horizon.

THE VERNACULAR

A basic problem concerns that of the vernacular and the value one attaches to it. One can simply note the existence of the vernacular as being a language form or speech pattern of varying distance from the "Standard" (Macafee, 1988). One can, as Illich does, consider that "vernacular speech is made up of the words and patterns grown on the speaker's own ground, as opposed to what is grown elsewhere and then transported" (Illich, 1980, pp. 26, 27). Illich is quite vitriolic (for a change!) on the value of the vernacular and its relation to the "Standard." He argues that the notion of the "Standard" as something to be learnt and insisted upon arose in late 15th century Spain, fostered by Queen Isabella's counsellor Nebrija, as a means of creating a nation. "Henceforth people will have to rely on the language they receive from above, rather than develop a tongue in common with one another" (Illich, 1980, p. 21). It is the notion of relying on others to set the "Standard" which renders the whole process political rather than social.

Clearly a situation where children are scolded (or even gently corrected) for using one lexicon rather than another, for using one grammar rather than another, is a negation of the home-grown speech in favour of one imposed from elsewhere. The question as to whether this *ought* to happen is one I shall return to later.

Whether a speech pattern is defined as colloquial, slang, dialect or language is clearly a question of power politics. Indeed the relation between what is deemed acceptable and unacceptable language is one well-established but often fluid over time. Power shifts and consequently one could argue, as does Montgomery (1995), that "a language is a dialect with an army and a navy" (p. 186). From this we quickly deduce that where the "army and navy" are lacking then the speech pattern will more be more likely to assume a lower status. This is echoed by MacLeod (1989) when he writes that "what separates minority languages from other languages is not the numerical disparity but the absence of real power" (p. 37).

What concerns me here is the language of those of the lowest status in a particular society. I intend to concentrate on Glasgow and its speech since it is with these that I am most familiar. However much of what I have to say is applicable, perhaps with modifications, to the speech of the poor in many other areas.

INFERIOR LANGUAGE IN INFERIOR MINDS?

The generalised inferiorist attitude of the Scots is well documented. Even its bourgeoisie feel insecure. As Young puts it, Scotland in much its modern history was:

> a total culture in which an insecure and authoritarian élite articulated an obsessive awareness
> of its own provincial inferiority and backwardness (Young, 1979, p. 21).

Catherine Matheson and I have discussed elsewhere the extent to which this remains true for the mass of the Scottish people, especially in the light of the cultural renaissance which has been happening in the country since the 1950s (Matheson & Matheson, 1998, 1999, 2000a, b). It remains that the Scots do not have an elevated sense of self. Arguably it is higher than it was in the past but it still has much room for development. The sheer sense of gloom and morbid nostalgia in much Scottish popular culture is fortunately giving way to offerings much more focussed on the present. Even if that present is ugly in parts, the focus on it is at least tending towards being forward-looking.

However, the Scots are still regaled with a persistent marginalisation by the London-based media, their speech patterns are mocked and their media representations are all too frequently stereotypes.[4] Nonetheless, after centuries of defining themselves in opposition to the English, the Scots *are* finding a sense of definition of themselves per se. However the feeling of being on the edge, and a precarious edge at that, persists.

Breitenbach et al. (1998) discuss the double marginalisation of Scottish women. This, they say, is down to being both Scottish and women. Consider then the marginalisation of the Scottish urban poor. If Scottish women as a group are hard done by, the poor are in just as weak a position and poor women even more so. The argument of Breitenbach *et al.* considers general social factors and general cultural hegemony. How more depressing the situation becomes when we add in the specific ingredient of socially marginalised language which, not at all coincidentally, is the language of the poor.

"The accent of the lowest state of Glaswegians is the ugliest one can encounter" (University lecturer quoted in Macauley, 1975, p. 94, cited in Menzies, 1991, p. 1) This is a very prevalent feeling among the inhabitants of Glasgow *including* those who use this speech pattern. It is a feeling which is so prevalent that it is difficult, if not impossible, to grow up in that city without becoming infected by it. Indeed one of the first things the average upwardly mobile Glaswegian tries to do is to diminish the accent. Strenuous efforts are made not to "talk Glesga," to dissociate oneself from this part of one's heritage. The object is forcibly *not* in order to improve communications with non-Glesga speakers. Such might be achieved by simply becoming bilingual or bidialectical. One could become diglossic in the manner of the Swiss Germans who use their local dialect of *Schwytzertütsch* among family and friends but switch to High German for business, education, literature and so on. But diglossia is not presented as an option. The Glesga speech is deemed impoverished. It is relegated to the depths of the uncouth, the great unwashed, the scum of the earth, the *Lumpenproletariat*. Yet just what is an ugly accent is clearly a value-judgement, an imposition of norms perceived as superior.

The denigration of Glaswegian can even extend to judges in courts of law refusing to hear a plaintiff who insists on using that tongue. In the late 1980s we had a long-running civil action brought by some demented neighbours who objected to our garbage cans being where they (or their material ancestors) had sat for over 60 years. This resulted in innumerable visits to Glasgow Sheriff Court. On one memorable occasion, whilst waiting for our case to come up, I witnessed the following exchange between a Sheriff and a Plaintiff who had brought a very simple Small Claims Case to recover what he had paid for some faulty goods which the retailer had refused to take back. I have transliterated the Plaintiff's dialogue but rather than use a plethora of apostrophes to indicate glottal stops I have written in the letters which would be dropped. A general rule of thumb is to glottally stop any *t*s at the end of words and most *t*s in the middle of words.

> JUDGE: Please state your case.
> PLAINTIFF: Yer Honour,[5] iss very simel. Ah boat...*(Your Honour, it's very simple. I bought...)*

JUDGE: Excuse me, would you mind repeating what you just said?

PLAINTIFF: As Ah wis sayen, yer Honour, Ah boat... (*As I was saying, your Honour, I bought...*)

JUDGE: Look, my good man, would it be too much for you to address this court in the Queen's English?

PLAINTIFF: Yer Honour, Ah'm daein ma bes but ye've goat tae gie us a chance. (*Your Honour, I'm doing my best but you've got to give me a chance.*)

JUDGE: I am giving your every chance but you are wasting the Court's time. Now speak properly or I shall fine you for contempt.

PLAINTIFF: But, yer Honour, Ah cannae help the wey Ah speak. Ah'm ur tryin tae talk clear an at. (*But, your Honour, I can't help the way I speak. I'm really trying to be clear.*)

JUDGE: Don't say I didn't warn you. £50 fine for contempt and don't disgrace this court again with such incomprehensible gibberish.

PLAINTIFF: But, whit huv Ah done? Ah'm ony tryin tae say ma piece. (*But, what have I done? I'm only trying to say my piece.*)

JUDGE: If you don't leave this courtroom immediately I shall have the Court Officers take you down.

The Plaintiff left, head shaking. I looked at the assorted lawyers in the courtroom. None showed the slightest reaction at this blatant racism. It was however perpetrated by one Scot against another so perhaps social discrimination would be a more appropriate term.

It is depressing to remark that the incident I observed is not unique. Crowther and Tett (1997) recount a similar tale, this time in Edinburgh where a young man was jailed for contempt of court in 1993 for saying *aye* instead of *yes*. It is doubly ironical that, as Billy Kay (1986) tells us, it was the courts of law which were the last bastion of spoken Scots among the *Establishment*.

Referring to minority (in power terms) language as gibberish was and still is quite common. In various of his writings Nigel Grant (see for example Grant, 1988) tells us how peoples have often called the "Other's" speech stuttering, mumbo-jumbo and so on. Catherine Matheson (1999) reminds us that in Quebec in 1967 Canadian French was reported in the Scottish press as having been referred by English Canadians as "dog's jabber" and how persons using Canadian French would suffer discrimination even in their own towns and cities. Indeed the parallels between the case of Canadian French prior to De Gaulle's memorable visit in 1967 and situation of the dialects of urban Scots are many but space requires that we leave examining it for another moment.

GLASGOW, GLASWEGIAN AND EDUCATION

It is clear that the low status of Glaswegian is such that children who use this speech form are at a distinct disadvantage from the moment they start school, a disadvantage whose impact of course depends much on the sensitivity (and good sense) of the teacher. Put another way, the children's cultural capital, at least in linguistic terms, does not match that in the school. As language is a key marker of identity then this point is critical in educational attainment. If the Sapir-Whorf hypothesis is even *partially* correct, and language exerts any influence on thinking, then beginning (and perhaps continuing) school with a culture clash based on language can only be detrimental to the learner. If the Sapir-Whorf hypothesis is correct and thinking is actually determined by language then the learner's experience is that not only is her/his speech found wanting but the very thoughts that stimulated that speech are also.

It is worth noting in passing that my own experience of plurilingualism tends to support Sapir-Whorf. I find that there are some things which I cannot think about in the same way in different languages. Whether it be due to the structure of the language, (French for example being much more structured and formalised than English or Scots), or due to the words that are available, (Scots has many more terms relating to the weather and to mood than does English), my very thinking changes with the language I am thinking in. Indeed, in my personal experience, I could go further and say that what I am capable of thinking changes with the language I use.

The impact of this clash of cultural capital is potentially disastrous for the learner. Lacking the basic "knowing how" to speak "properly" goes far beyond simply not knowing the appropriate terms to employ. It means that the learner who might wish to succeed is faced with a stark choice: to choose to fail, to become diglossic, to lose the home speech pattern in favour of what is literally the dominant discourse. Such a choice is bad enough when social and material success is presented as a credible possibility. When we descend the economic scale to the real *have-nots*, where unemployment is the norm, where substance abuse is rife and deadly, and life expectancy somewhat shorter than the average, the choice is tough indeed. In the event those who do succeed may well adopt transient diglossia which in time gives way to monolingual Scottish Standard English (SSE). Few go so far as to adopt Received Pronunciation (RP) English (though it is notable that until the 1960s this was quite common, especially for those in public arenas[6]). A possible reason for this is given by Menzies (1991):

> Even if the English dialect speaker takes lessons to perfect an RP accent, [s/]he will still be English. If the Scot does this, [s/]he may throw away more in the loss of an outward, recognisable national identity. If the two hypothetical speakers are to talk together, both may disguise their regional origins but only one belies his[/her] national identity (p. 3).

The trend is rather to lose the Glesga speech in favour of SSE. SSE does not aspirate the letter *r* as does RP English and admits a few Scotticisms. These can amount to nothing more than the use of the past participle in some cases where an English person would use the present participle. For example, a Scots person's hair needs *washed* while an English person's hair needs *washing*. This is an example of covert Scotticisms as most Scottish people do not recognise them as being specifically Scottish. Scottish Standard English also admits the occasional Scots term such as *outwith* (instead of *outside of*), *dreich* (roughly meaning *miserable* in a weather sense but much more emotive than is *miserable*), *kirk* (church), *creil* (lobster pot), *ceilidh* (dance).

It is well established that in terms of results in external examinations in schools there exists a sort of halo around Glasgow. As a whole the city performs well below average in comparison to the rest of Scotland. When we look in detail at the figures we find that, not unexpectedly, there is a range to the results within the city with the poorest areas performing the worst, mixed areas filling the middle ground and basically the more bourgeois an area then the higher the external examination results (Scottish Office, 1998).

It would be crass to ascribe all of this to the speech patterns prevalent in each of the areas but, given the argument above, it would be short-sighted to ignore this factor although it is certainly one among many. Is it however coincidental that Glaswegian just happens to be most associated with poor areas and that schools in poor areas perform significantly less well than those in mixed or middle class areas? It is well established that the urban poor tend to do less well at school and there is no end of theories to explain this. But if we compare the schools in poor areas of Glasgow with poor areas adjacent to Glasgow we only find replication of the Glasgow results in Cumbernauld which an overspill town from Glasgow and hence Glaswegian is a common speech form there. Could it be that the persistent attempts at extirpating Glaswegian from the school have acted as van Ploeg (1998) says that education can: "to repress and frustrate children's ability to think and judge for themselves, instead of developing it and enhancing it" (p. 178).

RESTRICTED CODE AND GLASWEGIAN

As a speech pattern of the poor, Glaswegian is almost inevitably associated with restricted language code. Indeed such was the case when I trained as a teacher in Jordanhill College in Glasgow in the late 1970s that it was held up as a typical form of context-specific language. As Illich puts it: "The modernized poor are those whose vernacular domain, in speech and action, is most restricted" (Illich, 1980, p. 36).

The originator of the theory of elaborated and restricted language code, Basil Bernstein, recounts that

Children socialised within middle-class and associated strata can be expected to possess *both* an elaborated and restricted code, whilst children socialised within some sections of the working-class strata, particularly the lower working-class, can be expected to be *limited* to a restricted code (emphasis in original) (Bernstein, 1971, p. 136).

I have problems with the whole notion of restricted code and its alleged use by working class children and adults. My problems stem from having grown up with these folk, worked with them, played with them and, as a child, on occasion fought with them. In all this, I have never known two interlocutors using restricted code be any more confused by each other's dialogue than two persons using a more elaborated language code. If you know the context that I am discussing with you and there is no real room for confusion, or any possible confusion can quickly be corrected, then restricted code actually allows you to say more in a shorter time. It allows for "punchier" dialogue. Its use is limited to shared experience where there is no need for grandiose description.[7] Nonetheless equating Glaswegian with restricted code gives a perfect legitimisation to efforts to destroy it by lending an aspect of social philanthropy to the endeavours.

REINVENTING LITERARY SCOTS

Much has been made of the current attempts to revive literary Scots. The great literary tradition of Scots ground to an effective halt with the departure in 1603 of James VI and I to London though it did have a few upturns in the form of Robert Burns in the 18th century and the renaissance of Scots poetry from the 1920s on. A major problem for the revivalists was that the orthographic conventions associated with a "Standard" simply did not exist and, arguably, "one of the marks of a language which separates it from a dialect is the presence of a standard form" (MacLeod, 1989, p. 42). There was an attempt by MacDiarmid and others to create synthetic Scots, known as *Lallans*, but this never caught on. It used words which had not been heard since the time of the great Medieval poets, the Makars. The latest attempt tries to make a modern written language for modern usage. For our present purposes let us consider two majors aspects of the current revival:

(a) what is considered as *richt Scots*;
(b) the role of the urban dialects of Scots in the development of "Standard" Scots.

The revival was marked by an early attempt to codify the Scots language by that most traditional of methods, a dictionary. Dictionaries are certainly helpful in getting everyone writing a language to use more or less consistent spelling. Whether they are actually necessary for communication in that language is another question. Few parents really struggle to understand their children's first attempts at writing.

Once the child can form letters and make the sounds associated with them as singlets, doublets and so on, then s/he can write in an understandable manner, albeit a probably unorthodox one. What dictionaries do achieve is the codification of what counts as acceptable language and spelling.

The first volume of the Scottish National Dictionary appeared in 1931 when Lallans was still being actively promoted. As Lallans is based not just on Old Scots but on rural Scots, it is little surprise that the first edition banned Glaswegian (Whyte, 1995, p. xiv). According to Macafee, this was because the language of the mass of the people of Scotland's largest city was deemed "hopelessly corrupt because of the influx of Irish and foreign immigrants" (Macafee, 1988, p. 38).

This negative attitude to Glaswegian has continued more or less unabated ever since. The tone is sometimes little short of racist:

> Glaswegians, in their native habitat, have succeeded in debasing both the English language and the guid Scots tongue. What is left is city slang at its worst, without an ounce of linguistic beauty to glean amongst the dross of Scottish-English-Irish-American verbiage (Purdie, 1983, p. 60 in Macafee, 1988, p. 41).

This implies that there is such a thing as "Standard" Scots which makes us ask why there are such attempts to create it. The contradiction seems to escape writers such as Purdie. What these people do is to hark back to an age of rurality. Effectively they are returning to the myth of the Kailyard,[8] that literary cabbage patch which spawned so much unmitigated nostalgia for a golden age which, like most golden ages, never existed. The Kailyard gave us such works as *The Little Minister* and *Dr Findlay's Casebook*. With Tartanry and Clydesidism, Kailyard is one of the major backward-looking iconic constructions in Scottish writing and mythology. Kailyard, Tartanry and, to a lesser extent, Clydesidism are stereotypes, or rather the mythical structures, which form Scottish kitsch and many of the means by which Scotland and things Scottish are identified both within and outwith Scotland.

> Kailyard focuses on a quaint vision of Lowland rural Scotland marked by bucolic intrigues. Tartanry is similarly rural but focussed on a romantic vision of Highland Scotland. Clydesidism harks back to an urban, industrial past where the honest workers are oppressed by tyrannical bosses but keep their self-esteem intact. An important point in each of these constructions is that they are essentially backward-looking (Matheson & Matheson, 2000b, p. 29).

It might be hoped that in this age of relativism and plurality that space might be found for Glaswegian as a variety of this emerging "Standard" Scots. Not so. As Horsbroch (personal communication, August 8, 1999) puts it:

> The . . . problem is wi cities lyke Glesca whaur Scots is affa erodit amang monie fowk nou; naebodie fae the citie says ken, nicht or awa an thay say know, night, away. But the'r nae gettin awa fae the fact that know, night an away is Inglis, an isna Scots. Tae speak Scots ye hae tae

learn tae uise sic wurds or whit ye en up speakin is a mixter-maxter that isna ane thing or anither.[9]

For Horsbroch, the fact that the Glaswegians say *night* instead of *nicht* and so on is of fundamental importance. But Glaswegian is not a written language and so while the Glaswegians might say *night*, there is nothing that stops them writing *nicht* in Scots. Simply to dismiss Glaswegian as "eroded" somehow seems to miss the point. It is the language of a large mass of people who are in Scotland and who are most definitely not speaking "Standard" English. What then are they speaking?

Horsbroch's comment is somewhat undermined by Douglas, whose article appears on the website of the Scottish Language Resource Centre (SLRC) (one of the principle sources of information on Scots language revival). For Douglas:

> Present day Scots is often described as 'eroded' or 'diluted', as if there were something unnatural about this. But it is part of a natural process, akin to that which affects the landscape (Douglas, n.d., p. 3).

Clearly if Scots, however defined, can still be Scots when it is apparently diluted or eroded, then surely Glaswegian has as much right to be considered a proper dialect of Scots even if it is "eroded." The exclusion of Glaswegian on the grounds that it contains words of Irish, English or American origin as does Purdie strikes me as more than a little daft, it is simply hypocritical. Douglas (n.d.), inter alia, waxes lyrical about the quantity of Scandinavian, French and Gaelic words in Scots (whatever that may be). Why should Scots (which appears in the revived form to be very much an amalgam of the dialects of Aberdeen and the Lowland rural areas) be so proud of its importations and yet revivalists such as Horsbroch exclude Glaswegian on apparently those very same grounds? A possibly significant difference lies in the fact that the dialect of Aberdeen and those of the Lowland and Southern Upland rural areas are the dialects of the mass of the people in these areas. They are not specific to a particular class. In much the same way as any individual, *Schwytzertütsch* is the dialect of the area concerned so it is for these "real" Scots dialects. This viewpoint is shared by the European Bureau of Lesser-Used Languages (1999) whose web entry on Scots excludes Glaswegian. The essential point about Glaswegian is that it is the language of the poor (Hornberger, 1998). The upwardly mobile divest themselves of it as rapidly as possible.

THE IRONY OF CULTURAL RELATIVISM

There is in the end a terrible irony in this scenario, if not several ironies. The first concerns the declamations by Scots revivalists that the Scots should be proud of the unique expressiveness of their native tongue. Yet, many of these same revivalists seemingly wanting to exclude from the ranks of Scots speakers that large mass formed by the speakers of Glaswegian.

It will be ironical, as well as dangerously divisive, if middle-class liberal opinion in Britain is able to appreciate and respect the Eastern and Caribbean heritage, but not that of the urban working class (Macafee, 1988, p. 42).

The bottom line is that if Glaswegian remains marginalised in Scots revivalism, then Scots revivalism itself becomes of marginal interest to the speaker of Glaswegian. This in itself will substantially weaken the attempts to revive Scots as a written language and may indeed prove fatal. Lallans did not survive beyond the bounds of poetry. This present effort has gone somewhat further and is producing some serious discourse in the language. What it has not succeeded in doing is popularising itself. There are hundreds of thousands of Glaswegian speakers (both in and around the city) who might welcome validation of their speech. As Menzie (1991) found in her work in the East End of Glasgow, for pupils in school, Scots is synonymous with slang and yet all it took to dispel this notion was for her to have some discussions with the pupils in her study about just what they were speaking. In many cases she found that to learn that their "slang" was in fact Scots became a source of pride. As she puts it:

They now described those words as 'my dialect' or 'the Scots language'. The abolition of that quintessentially negative term 'slang', which taints attitudes towards any speech form to which it is applied or misapplied, might contribute to the saving of Lowland Scots (Menzies, 1991, p. 12).

Unfortunately, Lowland Scots, as defined by the revivalists, may not want to be saved in this way. It makes me wonder just what the revivalist movement, if such it is, is actually driving at. The establishment of Scots as a national language is, in my mind, a non-starter. The grip of English is just too strong. Scotland is not in the position that Norway found itself in after splitting with Denmark. Danish is not a world language, English is. A role that Scots might usefully play is in helping people who feel linguistically marginalised (if not also marginalised in other ways) to be validated in their speech pattern. In order to do this, Scots must be inclusive. It cannot afford to leave out people on the spurious grounds of their language being "eroded." Glaswegian speakers have suffered enough from being told to speak "good English." It would be ridiculous for all these efforts at reviving Scots to end up with the Glaswegians being told to speak "guid Scots." It is heartening that this is the subject of at least some debate in the Scottish Languages Resource Centre (SLRC) as witnessed by Law and McHardy whose text *Threapin on Scots* appears on the SLRC website:

We should not be indifferent to the issues of anti-working class and anti-rural discrimination that arise, because in ignoring the needs of our Scots speakers we may be ignoring the language

development needs of as many as 1.5 million fellow-citizens, and given this neglect, it should
be no surprise that Scotland has acquired a reputation for dourness and inarticulateness (Law
& McHardy, 1997, p. 3).

Maybe there is hope, if only a little, that the revival of literary Scots will not
continue to suffer from anti-working class discrimination. There again it may be
another case of *plus ça change, plus ça reste la même chose*.

EVOLUTION IN EDUCATION?

Possession of a second language learned in early childhood, if positively supported by
the education system, seems to confer predilection to learn further languages. In Scotland
we cannot attest this, because Scots has not until very recent time been so supported,
but made the subject of suppression, so that those pupils slow to learn English perhaps
because Scots was strong in their homes have been marked out as educational failures
(Law & McHardy, 1997, p. 4).

Since all speakers of Scots are in some measure bidialectical, if not in fact bilingual,
it seems at first odd that the Scots as a whole are so poor at learning other languages.
It is, after all, well established that fluency in a second language facilitates learning
a third. Peering below the surface however yields some potential explanation. Scots
speakers, as we have seen, all too frequently do not recognise their mother tongue
as a language. Couple this with the scant regard that the education system has for
that tongue and we see how easily one might arrive at a mindset which is set against
learning another language. When one is all too accustomed to hearing just how
often one makes mistakes in what one thinks of as one's first language, English,
which is in fact one's second, how can one develop the confidence to learn what
is in effect a third language?

Law and McHardy go on:

Failure to build education on mother tongue leaves some of the Scots-speaking part of the
population badly equipped both in English and in Scots, poor in vocabulary, and stunted in
writing and reading.

Problems of social self-esteem are also exacerbated by the situation, with Scots seen as a low-
status language fit only for comedy, a cause and sign of depravity, practically on a level with
slang and swearing (Law & McHardy, 1997, p. 5).

Encouragement to incorporate at least a recognition of Scots has come from the
Scottish Culture Group (SCG) in a report to the Scottish Consultative Committee
on the Curriculum (SCCC). The SCCC is the closest the Scots come to the English
Qualifications and Curriculum Authority (QCA) which lays down the English

National Curriculum which all public schools in that country are required to follow. Unlike the QCA, the SCCC merely advises, it does not mandate.

> For generations the use of Scots was discouraged in schools on the grounds that it interfered with the learning of correct English. Over the last 25 years there has been increased but spasmodic attention to the potential contribution of Scots language and literature to the curriculum. It remains true however that Scots in its varieties has never won the coherent practical support which . . . it merits (SCG, n.d., Part 4).

The Scottish Office Education and Industry Department (now superseded by the Scottish Executive Education Department), whose role was also advisory on the curriculum but whose "suggestions" could always be backed up by Her Majesty's Inspectors of Schools, took note of the growing demands for recognition of minority cultures and set forth its opinion in the documents associated with the revision of the curriculum for pupils aged 5–14.

> Teachers should . . . build on the diversity of culture and language in their schools by:
>
> fostering respect for and interest in each pupil's mother tongue and its literature, whether English, Scots, Gaelic, Urdu, Punjabi, Cantonese or any other;
>
> developing each pupil's proficiency in the written and spoken forms of Standard English as the language of national and international communication and also, as far as resources allow, in any other language thought by the parents to be important in the pupil's community; . . .
>
> creating awareness of bias and prejudice and challenging these in their own use of language and in the language use by others (*English 5–14*, 1991, p. 59).

The statement is pretty weak, especially in its lumping together indigenous and non-indigenous minority languages, and its authors deciding to put all these definitely non-English matters under the banner of *English* smacks almost of cultural imperialism. It brings back to mind the argument which surrounded the original development of the document. It was held that the document should bear the name *Communication*. One cannot but feel that perhaps the writers lost the argument over the title but were determined to keep its spirit in the contents. In any case, simply listing Scots alongside other speech patterns recognised as languages is very much a step forward. Of course, it leaves open to question just what is meant by *Scots* but that is another matter.

Nonetheless developments have occurred since the publication of *English 5–14* and the latest development in external examinations in Scotland, the *Higher Still* programme for upper secondary pupils, allows oral work to be done in Scots, and this is explicitly stated time and again throughout the 348 pages of the documentation on *Arrangements for English and Communication* (Scottish Qualifications Authority (SQA) 1998). However, the SQA has not seen fit to require that candidates read any work in Scots except under one of the optional parts of Advanced Higher where candidates "students who have developed particular interests in Scottish language and literature are catered for" (SQA, 1998, Introduction, p. 8). There is, however, at all but the most elementary level the requirement that candidates will study at least one Scottish text (SQA, 1998). Problems of course arise as to how one defines a "Scottish text" and the arguments about this persist.[10]

CONCLUSION

Glaswegian speakers have a little to comfort them in the developments which have occurred in education and in Scots language revivalism. The dust has yet to settle on the debate over whether Glaswegian is authentic Scots, but, at least, the authority that sets the syllabi for external examinations, the SQA, is continuing to open its eyes to the existence of Scots, albeit still under the umbrella of English. At least it is there in print. Whether teachers will take much heed of this in the manner they regard their pupils" speech patterns is yet to be seen. However, given that pupils can do oral presentations in Scots at any of the various levels of the Higher Still programme, teachers will have little real option but to put communication first and accent and lexicon second. But should they do this?

It is all well and good to argue that Glaswegian and other dialects of Scots are part of the learner's heritage but that same learner still has to go forth into the world and earn a living. It is all too smug of those who are already in jobs (especially in academia) to argue that all that is needed is some patience on the part of an anglophone interlocutor for any dialect of Scots to be just about comprehensible (and vice versa). If only the world were so simple. As the case with the Sheriff cited above shows, patience is not always the hallmark even of the Scots when dealing with one another, never mind when dealing and being dealt with by non-Scots. Teachers are therefore in a quandary. Just how do you validate your learner's speech patterns *and* prepare him/her for the world of work where, frankly, *Hullaw rer. Hows it gaun?* given down a phone line will rarely result in other than bemusement. Perhaps an incremental approach is needed whereby we aim firstly for learners to feel validated in their daily speech, then we endeavour to make them diglossic in a manner in which each speech pattern is equally valid but our learners use whichever is appropriate to the circumstances. Just as it is not generally appropriate for me to speak French to an anglophone audience, then neither is it generally appropriate to speak Scots to one. Janet Menzies makes an interesting point which could hold the key to the dilemma:

> I feel it to be significant that the informants have a very poor knowledge of Scottish literary figures and their work (whether in Scots or English). In my opinion, a vital factor in cultivating a

> healthy attitude towards a language within the language community is that it must be perceived
> as having enough status to be an acceptable medium for creative art. Scots literature must be
> a contributory factor towards the survival of the Scots language. In addition, if schools took a
> little time to highlight the history, status and use of Scots, the effects could only be beneficial.
> Perhaps the result would be a greater confidence in the use both of the vernacular and of English
> (Menzies, 1991, p. 12).

Perhaps this greater confidence would result in adults wishing to transmit more of Glaswegian to their offspring than is often currently the case. Seeing that your language actually has status helps enormously in reversing the language shift which Fishman (1991) argues cannot be successful without intergenerational language transmission. Seeing that one's language has status makes one less reluctant to open one's mouth and speak when outside of one's social milieu. It helps raise one's head and see beyond the horizons of the social deprivation of which one's language has previously been a hallmark. It enables one to become diglossic and to maintain both speech patterns as resources to be drawn on as the need arises. An wi this new confidence a buddy kin staun up fur his/her lexicon and reassert its right tae exist as an authentic voice o the cuntrie the Scoats caw ther ain, an if aw thon goes at ge'ing Scoats intae a stannar form ur jis anurra try at cultural imperialism bie middle class boarne-agin Scoats speakers that wan to rediscover thur roots, then that voice will be eble tae weedel them oot an pit thum stret.[11]

NOTES

1. Slang items are colloquial neologisms coined in certain semantic fields where there tends to be rapid turnover of fashionable terminology (Macafee, 1988, p. 40).

2. The cannie Scot is well named: he can't think, he can't speak, he can't express himself.

3. This is neatly exemplified in that British televisual icon of all that is depressing in Scottish working-class urban life, *Rab C Nesbitt*. The eponymous Rab was a degenerate who postulated (regularly) on the human condition. He was also lazy, drunken, devoid of any moral rectitude and so on. *Rab C Nesbitt* ran on U.K. TV for most of the 1990s and is still occasionally revived for one-off *specials*.

4. See for example the character of Calum in *Brookside* on the U.K.'s Channel 4. Put simply, Calum is a thug, probably psychopathic and is presented with no positive Scottish character to balance him.

5. A Sheriff is usually to be addressed as "My Lord" though few bat an eye at "M'Lud" "Your Honour" demonstrates just how much this Plaintiff (and his appellation of the Sheriff was the one most laypersons used) had internalised American TV courtroom drama rather than the British variety. Clearly a victory of Perry Mason over Kavanagh QC!

6. A case in point is Marie McLaughlin who went from the East End of Glasgow to pop stardom in the 1960s as *Lulu* and in doing so lost every trace of her original Glesga speech, except notably when she got angry.

7. I observed a neat example of this occurred one Monday morning in a school where I worked which was in an economically deprived peripheral housing scheme in Glasgow.

The Terminator had been on TV the night before and in the afternoon a soccer match between Glasgow Rangers and Glasgow Celtic had been shown live on TV. Two lads whom I witnessed discussing *The Terminator* simply described every character as either *he* or *she*. Each had effectively the film running in his head and so needed very few cues to get the other's drift. To an outside listener, their conversation sounded like total gibberish but then again it was not intended for an outside listener. Eaves-droppers beware. When they moved on to discuss the match they named every player in their oral re-run of the highlights of the match. To the outside listener (i.e. me) it was clear what they were describing and the range of imagery employed was quite impressive even to an avoider of soccer such as myself.

8. Kail is a form of cabbage.

9. The ... problem is with cities like Glasgow where Scots is now very eroded among many people now; nobody from the city says *ken, nicht* or *awa* and they say *know, night* and *away*. But there's no getting away from the fact that *know, night* and *away* is [*sic*] English and isn't Scots. To speak Scots you have to learn to use such words or what you end up speaking is a hotch-potch that is neither one thing or another.

10. Under the new Higher Still Arrangements for English and Communication (being introduced in Scottish schools from the start of the new session) teachers and students are encouraged, where appropriate, to take advantage of the opportunity of choosing Scottish texts as the focus of their literary study in any of the units of the course, but this is entirely optional. There are no texts specified for study. Teachers are free to make their own choice of literature. However, there is a compulsory element in Unit 2, Literary Study, where at least *one* of the texts studied must be Scottish. Any text studied may be judged to be a Scottish text if it meets one or both of the following requirements:

- it deals with issues of life or experience in Scotland
- it is the work of a Scottish writer, whether or not resident in Scotland (Press statement by SCCC 5/8/99).

11. And with this new confidence one can stand up for one's own lexicon and reassert its right to exist as an authentic voice of the country the Scots call their own, and if all those attempts at getting Scots into a standard form are just another example of cultural imperialism by middle class born-again Scots speakers who want to rediscover their roots then that voice will be able to weed them out and set them straight.

REFERENCES

Bernstein, B. (1971) *Class, codes and control* (Vol. 1). Theoretical Studies towards a Sociology of Language. London: Routledge & Kegan Paul.

Breitenbach, E., Brown, A., & Myers, F. (1998). Understanding women in Scotland. *Feminist Review* (Spring).

Crowther, J., & Tett, L. (1997). Inferiorism in Scotland: The politics of literacy north of the border. Paper presented to the 27th Annual SCUTREA Conference. Available from http://www.leeds.ac.uk/educol.

Douglas, S. (no date). *The Scots language: Its European roots and Scottish destiny.* http://www.pkc.gov.uk/slrc/tocher/euroroot/euroot-1.htm, *English 5–14* (1991) Edinburgh: Scottish Office Education Department.

European Bureau of Lesser Used Languages SCOTS (1999). http://www.eblul.org/minor-gb.htm.

Fishman, J. (1991). *Reversing language shift: Theoretical and empirical foundations of assistance to threatened languages.* Philadelphia, Multilingual Matters.

Grant, N. (1988). The education of minority and peripheral cultures: Introduction. *Comparative Education, 24*(2).

Grant, N. (1997). The Scots leid an ither wee toungs: Hou kin Scots haud up in Europe? *Chapman* (p. 86).

Hornberger, N. (1998). Language policy, language education, language rights: Indigenous, immigrant, and international perspectives. *Language in Society*, 27.

Illich, I. (1980). *Vernacular values.* http://www.oikos.org/ecology/illichvernacular.htm.

Kay, B. (1986). *Scots – the Mither tongue.* Edinburgh: Mainstream.

Law, J., & McHardy, S. (1997). *Threapin on Scots.* http://www.pkc.gov.uk/slrc/threaps/threape.htm.

Macafee, C. (1988). *Some studies in the Glasgow vernacular.* Glasgow University, Unpublished Ph.D. Thesis.

Macauley, R. K. S. (1975). Linguistic insecurity. In: J. D. McClure (Ed.), *The Scots Language in Education* (ASLS Occasional Papers No. 3). Aberdeen: Waverley Press.

MacLeod, S. (1989). *Language death in Scotland.* University of Aberdeen Unpublished Ph.D. Thesis.

Matheson, C. (1999). Vive le Québec libre! De Gaulle as street theatre and psychodrama. In: V. Best & P. Collier (Eds), *Powerful Bodies.* London: Peter Lang.

Matheson, C., & Matheson, D. (1998). Problématiques régionales et questions linguistiques en Ecosse. In: S. Perez (Ed.), *La Mosaïque Linguistique: Regards éducatifs sur les pays industrialisés.* Paris: L'Harmattan.

Matheson, C., & Matheson, D. (1999). At the centre and the edge: The evolving nature of Scottish and French Swiss Identity and the Response from Education. Presented to the Conference on Citizenship, Institute of Education, London, 6–7 July.

Matheson, C., & Matheson, D. (2000a). Languages of Scotland: Culture and the classroom. *Comparative Education 36*(3). Special Issue in Honour of Professor Nigel Grant, edited by Professor Thyge Winter-Jensen.

Matheson, C., & Matheson, D. (2000b). Education and cultural identity. In: C. Matheson & D. Matheson (Eds), *Educational Issues in the Learning Age.* London: Continuum.

Menzies, J. (1991). An investigation of attitudes to Scots and Glasgow dialect among secondary school pupils. In: J. D. McClure (Ed.), *Scottish Language 10* (Aberdeen) available at http://www.ndirect.co.uk/~love/menzie1.htm.

Montgomery, M. (1995). *An introduction to language and society.* London: Routledge.

Purdie, H. (1983). Reviews. *Chapman 37. Scottish Culture and the Curriculum: A Report to Scottish CCC from the Review of Scottish Culture Group* (no date). http://www.ndirect.co. uk/~love/CCSERVED.htm.

Scottish Office (1998). *Examination results in Scottish schools 1996–1998* http://www.scotland.gov.uk/ library/documents-w4/erss-19.htm.

Scottish Qualifications Authority (1998). *Arrangements for English and communication.* Dalkeith and Glasgow: SQA.

Van der Ploeg, P. (1998). Minority rights and educational authority. *Journal of Philosophy of Education*, *32*, 2.

Whyte, C. (Ed.) (1995). *Gendering the nation: Studies in modern Scottish literature.* Edinburgh: Edinburgh University Press.

Young, J. (1979). *The rousing of the Scottish working class 1770–1933.* London: Croom Helm.

3. FENCED INTO CYCLES OF DEPRIVATION: ORPHANS, THEIR FEMALE CARERS AND EDUCATION IN MALAWI☆

Rob McBride

INTRODUCTION

Over the past decade, and coinciding with the rise in HIV/AIDS incidence, there has been a spectacular increase in the number of orphans in Malawi. Few orphans eat as many as two poor meals a day; most have few clothes, no shoes, bedding or soap. Hungry, poorly clothed children do not go to school or if they go, do not stay. Without completing at least primary school, job prospects are low. Without education or work orphans remain poor and become involve in casual sexual relationships. Orphans give birth to orphans. Those who are HIV positive give birth to those who are susceptible to HIV. Cycles of poverty, orphanhood and HIV/AIDS continue.

☆There are various definitions of what an orphan is. UNAIDS say an orphan is a child who has lost a mother (this is significant in Malawi where women are almost always the carers) or both parents (UNAIDS, 2001). In another publication UNAIDS adds that the child should be aged 15 or less (UNAIDS, 2000). We have come across other definitions where the age of 18 is seen as significant. In Malawi the government works with the (Malawian) legal definition that an orphan is "A child who has lost one or both parents because of death and is under the age of 18 years." (Ministry of Gender Youth and Community Services/UNICEF, 1999a, p. 1). As this last definition is widely accepted in practice, this paper will adhere to it.

'Suffer the Little Children': National and International Dimensions of Child
Poverty and Public Policy
Advances in Education in Diverse Communities: Research, Policy and Praxis, Volume 4, 57–71
Copyright © 2006 by Elsevier Ltd.
All rights of reproduction in any form reserved
ISSN: 1479-358X/doi:10.1016/S1479-358X(04)04003-3

Care systems for orphans in Malawi are overwhelmed. In almost all cases carers are women, very often elderly grandmothers who maybe infirm themselves. Indeed, it will be argued that the poverty of women more generally and the consequent relationships they have with men are at the hub of the cycles of deprivation described above. This is not to attribute blame but to seek to understand.

The research that underpins this paper was carried out in the Zomba area of Malawi during the first three months of 2001. It may be best described as in-depth research (McBride, 2002). That is to say, that it is primarily interested in ordinary people, their perceptions and investigating their decision-making. An interest in complexity has preceded generalisation; and local decision-making over national policy. I have sought to suspend the theories of academics; and those who have senior political position or privileged access to influence and power are treated much as ordinary people we have met in villages and schools. Some of these ideas are not far away from those of Robert Chambers when he asked whose reality counts (see Chambers, 1997)? We were determined to "put the last first" (Chambers, 1983; Hamilton, 1994) – if there were claims were being made by government, INGOs or other agencies we expected to see how they were operating at the grassroots level.

We[1] have spent numerous hours speaking to and interviewing people in and around the town of Zomba.[2] We have tried, above all, to develop an understanding of how and why people make decisions and subsequently act. Much time has been spent in second and third interviews with the same respondents in an effort to understand reasoning processes and the constraints that help mould decisions. We cannot claim that our conclusions are particularly unusual but we do have a strong evidential basis for *understanding*[3] the needs of orphans – this will be critical if effective policy is to emerge. This chapter will provide evidence to support the claims, tested with people and agencies that operate outside the geographical research area, made in the paragraphs above.

A significant technique was to concentrate on life histories, a method long used to give "voice to people long denied access" (Smith, 1994, p. 288). We believed, in addition, that it would enable ordinary people to talk at a time of the mass trauma of HIV/AIDS and that respondents, especially older carers, would be able to reflect upon their own circumstances and reveal their inner thoughts. Many of the older people we spoke to were very keen to, and could see significant reasons for, relating their experiences with orphans. Interviewing young children is not easy and it soon became readily apparent that older orphans, those aged 13 and above, were better sources of data. We could explore the lives of younger orphans by asking the older ones to reflect upon their younger years.

Some evidence presented will be in the forms of portrayals of individuals and in direct quotations from interviews. Many of the orphans and carers have argued that they are ignored and forgotten. This is not in relation to the occasional glimpse of world travelers in a post-modern, globalised age but by fellow Malawians. Our promise to them has been that we, as researchers, have no money but we will tell their stories in their own voices (as best we can, it must be vicarious (Denzin & Lincoln, 1994, pp. 10/11), and the "crisis of representation"). Hence there will be some "direct reporting" but we should first give a short introduction to the context.

THE IMPACT OF HIV/AIDS AND THE GROWTH IN ORPHAN NUMBERS

At the end of 1999, 16% of all Malawians between 15 and 49 years were HIV positive, according to the World Health Organisation (see UNAIDS, 2000, attachment). In the same year:

> UNAIDS estimated that approximately 390,000 children in Malawi were AIDS orphans (losing their mother or both parents) out of a total of approximately 600,000 orphans. By 2005, AIDS is expected to account for almost 75% of all orphaned children. The increasing number of orphans combined with the decreasing capacity of families and communities to cope and assist with the children, has made them a very vulnerable group (UNAIDS, 2001, p. 6).

It is very clear that the "number of AIDS cases will get worse before it gets better" (World Bank, n/d) and that one of the outcomes of the impact of HIV/AIDS in Malawi and surrounding countries has been the enormous and continuing growth of orphans. Extrapolating from National Aids Control Programme figures (NACP, 1995, quoted in MOGYCS/UNICEF, 1999b, p. viii), the number of orphans in Malawi has more than quadrupled by the end of 2001, from 140,000 to 600,000. Most orphans in Malawi are fortunate in that the formation of the National Orphan Care Task Force (UNAIDS, 2000, p. 28) in 1991 has led to the emergence, with support from INGOs such as UNICEF, Action Aid and Save the Children, of registered Orphan Care Groups (OCGs) which do their best to monitor, support, counsel, provide some food from a small village "garden," buy clothes when possible and so on. These, along with the willingness of relatives, friends and others has resulted in the provision of rudimentary care for most orphans, yet, as we have seen, most carers cannot get beyond very basic levels of care.

THE LIVES OF ORPHANS

It is possible to classify orphans, so we have found different categories of:

circumstances that lead to orphanhood including: short illness of parent; long illness; sudden death e.g. car accident; orphanhood at very young age and no knowledge of one or both parents, in early childhood (7–11), in teenage years;

"double" orphanhood, i.e. loss of parents and of carers (uncle or grandparents etc.);

orphanhood and loss of relatives including loss of mother; father; both parents; one or both grandparents; some have, additionally, lost uncles and aunts who may have acted as carers. Male and female orphans experience different life chances;

care arrangements[4] (though most "carers" are women) including remaining parent; remarried parent; grandmother (frequent); grandfather; uncle or aunt; neighbour, family friend or "civic" figure e.g. teacher; elder sibling; large orphan group into small family, and other variations on size; orphaned family kept together or dispersed; individuals or small groups with no care arrangements; sometimes orphaned children are treated as servants to the adopting family; there are varying kinds of care and treatment.

Yet these are only indicators. Individual children have their own ways of adapting to events and contexts and are not always fruitfully stereotyped. Here are portrayals of some orphans to give the reader an insight into two cases[5] we have seen.[6] These are excerpts from audio-taped interviews, both were seen more than once in an effort to be as accurate as this process allows.

E is a male orphan of seventeen whose father is dead. He lives with his mother and three younger sisters.

> E: "My father died two years ago, from tuberculosis. When he was alive we had no problems. The problems began when he started falling sick. My father had a small business, working in the village making carvings and curios. I used to help him. We had clothes then, bedding and food. Of course there were some hard times because business is unpredictable, but basically it was much better than now."
>
> RM: "What sort of food and clothes do you want?"
>
> E: "I don't mind, any clothes not special clothes. During this cold season, it would be helpful to have a jacket. As for food, we eat porridge in the morning, sometimes tea, but we cannot afford tea very often. Usually we have nsima and green vegetables, like pumpkin leaves, for lunch and the same for supper."[7]
>
> RM: "What food is missing?"
>
> E: "Rice, sugar, meat or fish."
>
> RM: "You have just finished standard eight [primary school] will you go to secondary school next year?"
>
> E: "I want to go to secondary school but I cannot afford the fees. I may try and go to a private school and support myself through piece work but sometimes people do not pay me immediately or pay very little and it is difficult."

R is a female orphan whose father is dead. Even though she is twenty now, her life history goes back to when she was younger and is the sort of story we came across frequently. She lives with her mother, three sisters and three brothers.

R: "When I was ten years old my father died. Everything was going well until then but since my father has died we are poor with few clothes and so on. Also family affairs and relationships have been difficult. When I was young there was unity among the family, including between me and my mother. My mother has lost control as a result of her poverty, especially since I got married."

"I decided to get married when I was sixteen because home was not so good. My husband was 20. I moved away to my husband's family but had problems with his parents. I returned home but my husband came to fetch me and we moved to be near his new job but he did not treat me well – he was chasing other women. I returned home again without him but he followed. I was pregnant. Again in this village he began chasing women and eventually left. He was not giving me any financial or material support."

"I decided to forget my husband and then took a boy-friend. He did not support me enough so I broke with him last August [2000]. A woman friend was cooking beer and she gave me the idea to do the same, beginning in December. My brother made the still. I make a little money cooking beers, kachaso, and men come here to drink it."

[R had a still made from a large ceramic pot, copper piping and a wooden cooling trough. 'kachaso' is made from a mixture of sugar and maize husks. It is double distilled and sold for about fifty pence [forty cents US] a bottle. A small sip offered to me by a group of five men with half dipped eyes demonstrated that it was a fiery brew. All five had become much the worse for wear on less than a bottle].

RM: "Do the men only drink kachaso or do you sell sex?" [I apologise for such a difficult question].

R: "No I do not have sex with the customers. They are well known to me and are married people who do not 'try it on' [as translated]. I have had sex with three boyfriends since my husband left. I found myself in difficult financial problems. I have been back for four years now and much has been missing, particularly clothing, food and soap. I hoped to begin a permanent relationship that would help me live better. They gave me money but took sex and then decided to leave."

If I were to draw attention to issues arising from these two interviews (readers may have other thoughts), in the light of other interviews we conducted, I would note the following:

- both are very poor and are aware of their poverty;
- E sees his way forward through education;
- R would like a permanent relationship with a man who she would see as helping her out of poverty. She "tried out" three men with practically no concern or mention of HIV/AIDS. This is not unusual in this part of Africa and is sometimes called "transactional sex," it being considered neither prostitution nor part of a long term relationship. Her poverty was a critical issue in a series of decisions she had made – including getting married and trying to find a man;
- throughout, R, and many women like her (see below), showed very low self-esteem, especially when they could not afford clothes or soap for washing themselves and their clothes.

In another part of the interview we asked R about her perceived future and she replied that she was not thinking of the future just trying to get out of poverty now. Many others, males and females, saw education (in its broadest sense) as a way forward. Indeed, we did not encounter what we considered to be begging for relief, rather many interviewees believed they could help themselves if they were given an opportunity.

ORPHANS AND EDUCATION

There are a few INGO funded projects in Malawi that pay attention to the educational needs of orphans but we did not encounter one directly. In general there is no specialist provision for orphans in schools but all schools we visited saw the need, and, with support, are prepared to adapt. Some orphans, who were being successfully cared for were "doing well" at school but for the vast bulk there were problems which can be considered by phase as pre-schooling; primary schooling; secondary schooling; and vocational education.

Pre-schooling. This takes place within OCGs. They are highly regarded as a means of getting children introduced to each other, to schooling and also as an opportunity for carers to meet and discuss concerns and interests. Pre-school groups have practically no toys or equipment and are staffed by unpaid volunteers who usually have no training.

Primary schooling. Many orphans do not go to school as they cannot afford breakfast. When in school they often feel uncomfortable if they have shabby clothes or if they have no soap and are unwashed (rural areas tend to be dusty and the dust clings to the skin) – they "do not feel at ease with themselves" . . . (a headteacher reported). Once they have missed a period of school it becomes less attractive to return.

Schools in our study suggested they would like to provide each child (all children) with a porridge breakfast every day. One school was asked to plan and budget for such a scheme. It provided a detailed and fairly sophisticated budget estimating that it would cost less than 2 U.K. pence or 3 U.S. cents[8] per meal. This would provide some food and encourage pupils and students to attend regularly. The school would also like to provide a bar of soap to every child who attended for a full week.

A number of schools also see the need for increased pastoral support, including counselling. Indeed the school seems the best place to provide such psycho-social support and efforts could be made to develop schooling that goes beyond delivery of knowledge. This suggests curricula changes which might include the introduction of civic education where the huge social changes associated with HIV/AIDS could be discussed and understood. We have concluded that in the same way that all educational debates and provision should be gendered, they cannot be properly understood now in countries like Malawi without being "HIVed."

Secondary schooling. Unlike primary schooling, secondary schooling is not free and we met many orphans who had the qualifications to go to secondary school but could not afford fees, uniforms or books. Some OCGs, with the help of well-wishers, were able to support some of these children but very few. Without a secondary education, employment hopes are weak.

Vocational education. As the orphans reach their late teens and beyond, craft work can help provide a valuable source of income.[9] OCGs provide limited facilities and tuition in local crafts such as mat making, tinsmithing, carpentry, sewing and knitting. It should be stressed that there is a need for a concerted push into vocational education, at a time when most large aid funders are encouraging investment in basic education. If orphan care groups are to provide vocational training more effectively there is a need for equipment, such as sewing machines and carpentry tools, and secure buildings to store them.

We have concluded, on the evidence collected, that cycles of deprivation dominate orphans' lives. Without opportunities for education and training outlined above, we and the Malawians we have spoken to, believe that these cycles will continue. The level at which people are living seems to place them below a threshold where they can help themselves beyond a hand to mouth existence. In a place where there are, notoriously, no fences between plots and chickens roam among the crops, people feel fenced in.

We have seen, above, the sorts of decisions women make in this situation. We further conclude that women's poverty is rather more critical than that of men.

WOMEN'S POVERTY AND ITS EFFECT

Let us consider another partial portrayal. The subject here is *L, a thirty-nine-year old widow with six children*, i.e. orphans, to care for.

L: "My husband passed away five years ago, leaving me with five children. I have had another baby since." [at the breast as we speak]

RM: "How come you have another baby?"

L: "I met a man at the local market. He was selling fish and twice he propositioned me but I refused to listen. Eventually he visited my house. He made promises, brought a few presents, some soap, a chitanje,[10] some relish[11] and one evening he stayed the night. We had intercourse only once and I found myself pregnant with this little one. The man has never returned to the market and I have not seen him again. I am angry and feel cheated to have another mouth to feed. If I do see him again I would not wish to talk to him, I feel so bitter. There is nothing I can do anyway."

RM: "Can you explain why you had sex with him?"

Up to this point the interview had been conducted in Chichewa with Martin Gulule translating. Her next response was clear and in English, we think, for greater effect.

L: "Poverty! I thought this man would help me feed my children. I cannot deny that I did feel like having a man – I had not had sex since my husband died - but if I had not been poor I would not have done anything."

RM: "Did you not think of using a condom and what about HIV/AIDS?"

L: "I do not think using a condom is an appropriate thing to do. I have never handled a condom and only heard about them on the radio. As for AIDS I did think about it but what could I do?"

RM: "Did the man force himself onto you?"

L: "No."

RM: "What about the future?"

L: "I would like to start a business and so avoid the people who come to cheat me. I miss my husband very much and can remember life when he was alive. He had a business and we lived well but now times are hard. I do not sleep well and am often stressed."

RM: "Would you like to marry again?"

L: "Not after what has happened. I am very frightened of sex not because of HIV/AIDS but because of the possibility of being pregnant."

A large percentage of women, carers and older orphans, stated that they would like the training needed to help start their own business. One NGO has provided funding to OCGs for a revolving fund[12] for business start-up. This seems to have worked well in some of the care groups but the money available is far below what is needed and more training on how best to use and account for the money was sought. As with orphans themselves, carers see education as a significant means of breaking out of poverty. Currently most people eligible for loans through this route are carers but some OCGs are beginning to consider the older orphans. Typical small businesses sell fish, vegetables, or second-hand clothes in local markets.

Another reality we observed was that women of all kinds felt they needed the support of a man, including his wages, to bring up children properly (this is a research conclusion and not an authorial criticism). Many of the men had gone to Zomba and other larger towns in search of work, leaving the women in the villages. From time to time, especially at weekends, men would return to the villages in search of what is called Chewerewere – a word associated with moving about at night or, translated literally, "moving here and there" or "moving aimlessly." The result is so often another mouth for the woman to feed, more hardship and stress. In this way women's poverty is at the hub of the cycles of poverty we have discerned and it is made all the worse by orphanhood and HIV/AIDS.

The Malawian government has policies on orphans and their care but as an extremely poor country, there are problems with implementation – the government is well aware of these problems (MOGYCS/UNICEF, 1999b, p. x). Policy is the subject of the next section.

NATIONAL POLICIES

Policy is rarely the same as practice and we might demonstrate this in more or less any country that exists (for example, Samoff, 1999, p. 417; Sarason, 1990). In 1991 the Malawian government, a number of NGOs and agencies, including UNICEF and the WHO, and religious organisations met to discuss the issue of orphans. This led to the production of guidelines on the care of orphans, a National Task Force on orphans and a National Orphan Care Programme (NOCP). The NOCP has core strategies as follows:

- IEC (Information, Education, Communication)
- Community participation
- Multi-sectoral Approach
- Co-ordination through the Ministry of Gender, Youth and Community Services (MOYGCS/UNICEF, 1999b, p. x).

This provision, however little implemented, has supported the creation and development of OCGs. In the Zomba area we found that nearly every village was covered in some way by an OCG and all the OCGs were active as best they could be. But OCGs had no budgets, other than what they could raise, which was very variable, and few ever had a visitor or advisor. In the brief of the local District Social Welfare Officer, OCGs were one of a number of responsibilities including community HIV/AIDS support, involvement in the Youth Probationary Service and more. His travel budget was simply not large enough for him to travel to the outlying areas and the OCG co-ordinators find it difficult to travel the other way. Indeed the OCGs rarely had contacts of any kind, including with each other.[13]

Some OCG coordinators were much more active than others and attracted some funding. One had, for example, a link with an English couple working in Malawi. They and some friends provided some support for secondary school fees, supported the development of some IGAs[14] and arranged for an overseas organisation to pay for some maize for orphans. Some others had a link with a local wealthy white farmer who provided some maize and one very active group persuaded an INGO to pay for two fulltime workers (this latter arrangement was a unique one). Plainly, none of this is directly related to policy but is a situation that has emerged from the NOCP policy.

We were told by a senior civil servant in Malawi that, in a sense, orphan care is "beyond policy" because so many ministries have a legitimate interest

– the Ministry of Education for schools; the Ministry of Gender, Youth and Community Services; the Ministry of Health for HIV/AIDS related matters, and so on. Complexity is added in that ministries work with donor representatives, NGOs, religious bodies and other interests, who perform an advocacy role and maybe active in the field. There is a case for a measure of co-ordination at the centre though not, in the view of OCGs, at the expense of periphery and local action.

Efforts to coordinate all government and donor activity in HIV/AIDS are being made through the National Aids Coordinating Programme (NACP) working with UNAIDS. Together they have formed the Technical Working Group (with other significant organisations) and developed a number of thematic sub-groups, one of which is concerned with orphans and widows. At the time of writing there were plans for this group to meet but some of the members were already saying that travel budgets were too small for many to attend regularly.

Policy development or planning is not significant as a starting point at this juncture. We might argue that focusing on what could be achieved in practice, i.e. policy implementation, based upon issues formed through research should be of greater concern to policy-makers.[15] In terms of more recent activity we found INGOs are more prominent than government so let us consider them next.

THE PRACTICE AND POLICIES OF INGOs AND AGENCIES

The evidence for this section came from a series of discussions with INGO and agency staff in Malawi and London. Most of those active in the field, or who had an interest, were invited to a day conference in Lilongwe in late March 2001. Our circulated description of the day meeting, to which interested ministries were also invited to send staff, included the statement:

> This is an opportunity for . . . (Rob McBride and Martin Gulule) . . . to listen to the agencies active in this field; for the agencies to comment on the outcomes of their research; and for all the participants to interact.

This was one of the meetings in which we tested our preliminary conclusions. There was widespread agreement about significant matters yet, in the field, not a great deal was happening at that time.[16] All agreed that there was much more to be done and this became the focus of debate, rather than on what was actually not happening.

It was decided that a list of "issues" generated on the day would probably become a useful starting point for the orphans and widows thematic sub-group of the NACP (see above). There was broad agreement that the work reported here presented an accurate picture, though some other issues were added. In particular there was a discussion about the growth of orphanages, usually funded by charitable groups from outside Malawi. They were criticised as undermining the community based approach that the Malawian government preferred – some it appeared were offering material conditions far above what village orphans could expect. There were also complaints that some groups were just turning up and building orphanages without consultation or efforts to fit into planned provision. It was acknowledged that for particular cases, where for example, there was extreme poverty or abuse or a child had no relatives at all, an orphanage might be helpful, especially if it were licensed and inspected.

This opened up a larger question of community versus no-community provision. Could OCGs continue to provide pre-school and vocational training, for example, using voluntary unpaid and untrained workers or should there be formal funded provision in the forms of playgroups and vocational centres. Could the existing OCGs be developed as community centres with more formal facilities? Certainly those involved in running the OCGs, as well as those served by them, i.e. the orphans, were keen for services to remain local and easy to get to.

Other "issues" raised are too numerous to discuss here but many have been referred to above.

TO CONCLUDE

Very little support, in practice, is going into orphan care and what is, comes from private charitable sources. Ministries, agencies and INGOs have not denied this. Budgets that are committed to Malawi, at the time of writing, allow operation in only a few small projects. It must also be said that widespread awareness of the whole issue of orphans is only just beginning to emerge.

Perhaps much of this chapter reads as unduly negative but the primary aim is to reflect the evidence collected. There were some success stories, we were told, of child headed households who were struggling but coping. We visited a small number. One such group comprised four sisters and the baby of the second eldest. The eldest, twenty years old had given birth but her baby had died. The living baby had a virulent skin rash covering its whole body and looked, to my untrained eye, very sickly.

We sat with the family on the mud veranda in front of their house and conducted a very pleasant interview, which featured some laughter. Their food came from what little they could grow in their garden but mostly from the local OCG. The three younger girls refused to go to school without breakfast, which was most of the time, or if they had no soap to wash. Here are some small excerpts from the interview:

> RM: "Where are the fathers of the babies."
> Eldest: "They have disappeared."
> RM: "What do you hope for?"
> Eldest: [Pause] "We cannot think of much. We concentrate on getting food. We live from day to day."
> RM: "Are you happy?"
> 2nd Eldest: "We are basically OK, especially when we have nsima or if we sell some kachaso and have some money."

I could not conclude that they were pleased with life nor that they were not but I suspect that there was an element of bravado in their talk which covered up a great deal of hardship.

At the Zomba conference for OCG committee members we provided a draft report, including nearly all the points in this paper and asked the forty attendees to tell us what was missing from our reconstruction of their stories. They split into groups and a spokesperson responded for each. Most of the comments stress the accuracy of the arguments we had presented and no major changes were asked for, though they had been invited.

Following these responses I feel justified in concluding, even if it is negative, that these communities are fenced into a mode of existence that prevents them lifting themselves out of poverty. With a little help, some focused on helping them to help themselves, they could certainly do better. In particular, we must consider supporting pre-schooling; free breakfasts in primary schools free secondary education; vocational education provision; start up funding for small businesses and business training, especially for women and older orphans; and, financial support for OCGs. Policy developed with a view to implementation will almost certainly require aid funding as the Malawian government is unlikely to be able to find sufficient funds.

It is not clear that this aid will be forthcoming and, if it is not, there is a real risk that there will be present in Malawian society a sizeable minority of adult orphans who feel deprived, cheated and ignored. Aside from the personal distress and waste of human potential, this could well be a seed bed for social disruption and, perhaps more seriously, the continual presence and growth of HIV/AIDS.

NOTES

1. My colleague, who also acted as translator was Martin Gulule of Chancellor College, University of Malawi, Zomba. The small research project, entitled "Understanding the

Educational Needs of Orphans in Malawi" was funded by the Department For International Development (U.K.), using ESCOR funding.

2. We interviewed thirty five orphans; twenty five carers; eight OCG coordinators up to three times each. Interviews were recorded by notes and/or audio-tape and varied in structure from open-ended to tightly structured depending upon the respondent and the data required. To go beyond this initial respondent set we used theoretical sampling (see Strauss & Corbin, 1990) by taking additional respondents and testing our emerging theories. We also tested our theories with OCG co-ordinators, the Social Welfare Office in Zomba and, perhaps most significantly with people active in the field, including at the Lilongwe conference (from NGOs, agencies and ministries). The eight OCGs cover some one hundred and seventy villages; the District Social Welfare Officer works with thirty OCGs and those present at the Lilongwe conference cover parts of the whole country and other countries. The Zomba conference was very much concerned with asking the attendees to consider the validity of our preliminary report which was circulated in both English and Chichewa.

3. By *understanding* I mean that I have sought to portray people as they portray themselves. To this end repeated interviews were used to try and establish "the native's point of view" (see Geertz, 1983) though still vicariously.

4. We have encountered fostering arrangements in Malawi, though mostly by more educated Malawians of the children of less educated relatives and friends. Fostering is fairly widespread in many parts of Africa (see Goody, 1982, for example) but a major study of fostering, which may have been valuable, was not possible in this case.

5. The term "cases" is significant (see Stake, 1995; Stenhouse, 1980/1987). After Stenhouse there is a distinction between cases that are studied to develop our understanding and "samples" that are meant to serve as a basis for generalisation. It could be argued that we can generalise "naturalistically" and softly from cases to give a broader, but not all inclusive, larger picture.

6. Descriptive portrayals are used as a form of "representation" (see comments above) but also as a means of creating an "active" text that the reader can question (see McBride, 2002; Stronach & MacLure, 1997); as a means of conveying complex data; and to provide access to readers beyond academics (see MacDonald, 1976).

7. Porridge is a watery form of maize meal with a little sugar. Nsima is the staple food of maize meal, a thicker mixture of maize meal.

8. Approximately £3.50, or US$5.60 per pupil per annum.

9. There is a tendency to seek incomes from a range of sources (see Ellis, 2000) but this is very difficult in much of Malawi as the economy is so depressed.

10. A chitanje is a colourful print cotton cloth that women wear over their clothes, like a skirt, as a form of modesty.

11. Meat or fish to eat with nsima, the maize meal staple.

12. Loans are repaid with interest and this is then loaned, in turn, to others.

13. As part of this research project a day conference was arranged in Zomba for committee members of OCGs to meet and discuss the outcomes of this work. All travel expenses were paid.

14. Income generating activities, usually small businesses as already described.

15. Grindle and Thomas (1991, pp. 193/194), for example, acknowledge that conditions in developing countries do not always provide sufficient scope for action. We feel that this is the case in Malawi.

16. One of the INGOs that seemed most informed about the situation claimed to have helped in the formation of some 250 youth clubs and supported 23,500 orphans.

REFERENCES

Chambers, R. (1983). *Rural development: Putting the last first*. London: Longman Scientific & Technical.

Chambers, R. (1997). *Whose reality counts? Putting the first last*. London: Intermediate Technology Publications.

Denzin, N. K., & Lincoln, Y. S. (Eds) (1994). *Handbook of qualitative research*. London: Sage.

Ellis, F. (2000). *Rural livelihoods and diversity in developing countries*. Oxford: Oxford University Press.

Goody, E. N. (1982). *Parenthood and social reproduction. Fostering and occupational roles in West Africa*. Cambridge: Cambridge University Press.

Grindle, M. S., & Thomas, J. W. (1991). *Public choices and policy change. The political economy of reform in developing countries*. London: John Hopkins University Press.

Hamilton, D. (1994). Traditions, preferences, and postures in applied qualitative research. In: N. K. Denzin & Y. S. Lincoln (Eds), *Handbook of Qualitative Research*. London: Sage.

MacDonald, B. (1976). The portrayal of persons as evaluation data. Paper presented at the Annual Meeting of the American Educational Research Association in San Francisco, as part of a symposium entitled "Issues and Methods in Qualitative Evaluation" (April 23).

McBride, R. (2002). The importance of in-depth research for education for development. Playing down presence. In: M. Schweisfurth, C. Harber & L. Davies (Eds), *Learning Democracy and Citizenship: International Experiences*. London: Symposium Publications.

Ministry of Gender Youth and Community Services/UNICEF (1999a). *Training manual on orphan care*. Lilongwe, MOGYCS/UNICEF.

Ministry of Gender Youth and Community Services/UNICEF (1999b). *Best practices on community-based care for orphans*. Lilongwe, MOGYCS/UNICEF.

Samoff, J. (1999). No teacher guide, no textbooks, no chairs: Contending with crisis in African education. In: R. F. Arnove & C. A. Torres (Eds), *Comparative Education. The Dialectic of the Global and the Local*. Oxford: Rowman & Littlefield Publishers.

Sarason, S. (1990). *The predictable failure of educational reform*. San Francisco: Josey-Bass.

Smith, L. M. (1994). Biographical method. In: N. Denzin & Y. Lincoln (Eds), *Handbook of Qualitative Research*. London: Sage.

Stake, R. E. (1995). *The art of case study research*. London: Sage.

Stenhouse, L. (1980/1987). The study of samples and the study of cases. Reprinted In: R. Murphy & H. Torrance (Eds.) (1987), *Evaluating Education: Issues and Methods*. London: Harper & Row.

Strauss, A., & Corbin, J. (1990). *Basics of qualitative research: Grounded theory procedures and techniques*. London: Sage.

Stronach, I., & MacLure, M. (1997). *Educational research undone. The postmodern embrace*. Buckingham: Open University Press.

UNAIDS (2000). REPORT on the global HIV/AIDS epidemic. Geneva, Joint United Nations Programme on HIV/AIDS, (UNAIDS).

UNAIDS (2001). The HIV/AIDS epidemic in Malawi. The situation and the response. Lilongwe, UNAIDS c/o Office of the UN Resident Coordinator.

UNICEF (1999). *Children orphaned by aids. Front-lines responses from eastern and southern Africa.* New York: UNICEF.

World Bank (no date). *The impact of AIDS on capacity building. The partnership for capacity building in Africa.* New York: World Bank.

4. ROMA CHILDHOOD IN EASTERN EUROPE

Tamás Kozma, Gabriella Pusztai and Katalin Torkos

INTRODUCTION

This paper illustrates the problems of Roma children through the life of a particular group of emigrants and aims to determine what is behind the decision to emigrate and what it takes to support adaptation to a new social environment. European literature has not dealt with the emigration of this ethnic group until now because during the period from the introduction of the Iron Curtain until 1990, emigration from East to West was minimal except during the major political upheavals.

Ongoing research has revealed a region called the "Partium," which is representative of the whole area because of its mixed ethnicity. This paper highlights the present situation of the gypsies in this region and the background of gypsy children's school failures, and presents a case study on an emerging class of gypsies and their problems. During the empirical analysis, network analysis methods are also used; these are useful in research dealing with social integration of immigrants according to the international literature (Kelly-Portes & Brenner, 1993).

MINORITY EDUCATION AS A UNIVERSAL PROBLEM

Minority education is a central problem nowadays in many countries throughout the world because gypsies' education and qualification levels are still very

'Suffer the Little Children': National and International Dimensions of Child
Poverty and Public Policy
Advances in Education in Diverse Communities: Research, Policy and Praxis, Volume 4, 73–95
Copyright © 2006 by Elsevier Ltd.
ISSN: 1479-358X/doi:10.1016/S1479-358X(04)04004-5

low compared to mainstream society. Therefore, labor-force participation in the case of minorities is also low, and the percentage below the poverty line is extremely high. Education can help to change the present situation because it can increase participants' chances of being active in the labor market (Hicks, 1995). Furthermore, there are positive social consequences for those in work, such as fewer financial problems, lower crime levels, fewer domestic conflicts, and probably lower levels of emigration. This important role of education, that is, to improve the social position of minorities, has already been achieved in many countries. For example, in the USA, the proportion of different ethnic groups in the population like Mexican, Latinos (Puerto Rican, Cuban), African-Americans, Asian-Americans, and Filipinos is high, and the average level of education differs among different groups. The educational level for Latinos is very low, thus explaining their high rates of unemployment, although nowadays, education is a more important explainer of their relative income gains (Carnoy, 1995). In Europe, there are also large numbers of ethnic groups in the Netherlands, France, U.K., Germany, Italy, among others, who are treated differentially. In many of these countries, minority education problems have also not been completely solved yet.

Many countries have realized that early childhood education is the basis of further education for ethnic groups. Deficiencies in basic education have a negative effect on the economic variability of people in the labor market. Without proper basic education, people cannot retrain for the labor market because of increased competition, and so attention should focus on children's education and socialization. In ethnic groups, the role of the family in education is very strong, and sometimes this makes school socialization rather difficult, usually resulting in low achievement and dropouts in school. According to Hinchliffe (1995), there are several roles of education in the labor markets. These include: improving cognitive abilities, e.g. from basic numeracy and literacy at one end of the scale to a greater capacity for logical and analytical reasoning at the other end; or personality traits, e.g. obedience, respect for authority, self-reliance, ability to make decisions, etc. There is also a third role of education, namely that school increases the potential productivity of individuals, and the education system acts as a selection mechanism to sort out those who possess non-school-related characteristics such as intelligence and motivation, which are associated with productivity.

Hill (1995) writes about the sources of school achievement among minority students. His work is interesting because he wrote about very similar school problems in the case of Indian and Black students as for gypsy/Roma students in Hungary. For example, Indian children in early elementary grades were eager and teacher-accommodating, but by upper-elementary grades, they were "silent Indians" and non-participants in classroom instructions; and later, the teacher became "the enemy" (Wolcott, 1967). In the case of Black minority children, the experiences were similar, and they also failed at school (McDermott, 1974). Bourdieu's (1972) theory of social reproduction approach can help us to understand the low school achievement of minority students. According to Bourdieu, the "cultural capital" can explain why upper-class (and mostly non-minority) children are most likely to enjoy high-status occupations. For the most part, modern schools teach the skills, knowledge, and world-view of an upper-class heritage. Upper-class students are already equipped with accumulated cultural capital of this cultural heritage by the time they enter school (Hill, 1995). This is why preschool education is becoming increasingly important in education in developed countries. Hill (1995) mentions that cultural differences are not a direct reason for problems experienced by minorities at school because cultural and language differences may be present; but whether or not they affect the minority students' academic work in the classroom depends on how the minority's cultural model, taking effect through the culture of peer groups, organizes the minority student's interpretations.

THE AREA OF THE "PARTIUM"

The area of the "Partium" today comprises three countries and is one of the researched areas of eastern and central Europe. This report is part of a long-term research investigation dealing with the present situation of the communities in this area.

The name "Partium" (Fig. 1) designates a kind of historical and geographical unit, in which expansion and political content have changed several times during the semi-millennial history of the Carpathian Basin. However, its latent intellectual and cultural unit can still be felt in several social manifestations. The historical heart of the area at present is Hungary, Ukraine, and Romania, including the counties of Bereg, Szatmar, Central-Szolnok, Kraszna, Bihar, Zarand, and Arad. Territorially, the "Partium" was initially part of the independent principality of Transylvania and then the Hungarian Monarchy for many centuries. After World War II, its area was divided into three parts, as a consequence of the Treaty of Trianon (two-thirds of the area of Hungary having been attached to neighboring countries). Its western part remained under the rule of Hungary, its large eastern part became part of Romania, and its northern part became the first part of Czechoslovakia, then part of the former Soviet Union, and finally part of Ukraine.

Owing to its good cultivable land, the "Partium" became a significant agricultural area, and because of its roads connecting different regions, it also transformed into an important commercial center. However, in the 20th century, it has changed into a periphery. In the area of the former Soviet Union, the "Partium" was the farthest southwestern part of the country, and its acquisition was nothing more

PARTIUM

Fig. 1.   The Partium: Hungary, Ukraine, and Romania.

than just a military matter. In Romania, this area was systematically neglected, partly because of its long distance from the capital and the nationally significant industrial areas, and partly because the national policy relied on the negative discrimination of Hungarian inhabitants. The small part of the "Partium" that remained in Hungary had to deal with the dramatic problems associated with the acquisition of territory: the industrial, economic, and cultural centers of the area (Arad, Nagyvarad, Munkacs), and the railways that connected these areas. This is why, on the one hand, this area broke away from the economic and social circulation that stimulated development and, on the other hand, Hungary also neglected this area for a long time. After the Treaty of Trianon in 1920, this previously economically rich area was divided by national boundaries into parts that stopped development there, even up to the present day. Today, because of such negative consequences, probably the most significant problem is poverty and the lack of qualifications among the inhabitants in this area.

The distinguishing feature of this region to date has been its remarkably rich ethnicity. There are not only Hungarians but also Romanians, Ukrainians, Ruthenians, gypsies, Jews, and Slovakians, among others. In spite of the economic disadvantages, it is characteristic of this area that ethnic groups successfully and traditionally live together without any conflicts (in contrast to other European countries in similar situations where there are tensions).

The high degree of religiosity of the "Partium," i.e. bordering between Western Christianity and Orthodoxy, together with the religious tolerance of inhabitants in this area, is remarkable. Often, different denominational churches are built close to each other in the centers of the settlements. This is no accident, because the "Partium" was an initial segment of the principality of Transylvania, where, in 1568, the religious freedom of the four established regions was enacted for the first time. After the Counter-Reformation, with the exception of Transylvania, reformation remained the strongest, and as a result, there was a higher rate of intermarriage among denominations.

In the 20th century, the three divided parts of this region notably drifted away from each other in terms of the level of economic development, degree of social security, and political culture. By the turn of the millennium, the situation had improved in the Hungarian areas but worsened in those parts belonging to Ukraine. This multifactorial difference in the aforementioned levels explains the remarkable level of migration from Ukraine, whose main emigrants were gypsies, who crossed the relaxed national borders (as a consequence of the eastern European political transformations).

This paper gives an overall picture of the aforementioned problems by presenting the most important data and literature concerning the gypsies.

GYPSIES IN THE "PARTIUM": PROBLEMS OF THE SOCIAL INTEGRATION OF THE GYPSIES

Gypsies originated as an ethnic group from north India and appeared in Europe in the 15th century. At present, most live in eastern and central Europe: Romania, Czech Republic, Slovakia, and Hungary. There was another large influx of gypsies into this area in the 18th century. There are data on the number of gypsies since 1721, but there has been great difficulty in determining who are gypsies. In 1990 in Hungary, in the national census, only 5% of the population identified themselves as gypsies, but the number of people who followed a gypsy-type lifestyle was much higher, almost 10%. This difference derives from the fact that a large number of people who can be categorised as gypsies (owing to their origin), do not acknowledge themselves as gypsies. However, very few speak gypsy language, and some non-gypsy people acknowledged themselves as having a gypsy lifestyle. The most characteristic features of the gypsy lifestyle are the following: an extremely low degree of qualification, disadvantaged situation in the labor market, segregation inside settlements, high rate of childbirth, and a propensity for behaving against accepted norms. Researchers dealing with gypsies usually use the definition that "a gypsy is a person who is acknowledged gypsy by its non-gypsy environment according to particular criteria, for example lifestyle, anthropological nature etc." (Kocsis & Kovacs, 2000, p. 13)

Among other ethnic groups in this region, the gypsies lost their ancestral language the most, but in spite of their continuing residence in the area for several centuries, their integration into European culture is still a large problem. Even in the 18th and 19th century, arrangements for settling the gypsies were introduced, with the aim of helping them become accustomed to farming and organizing their formal education. During the socialist period, to help eliminate segregation of gypsy communities, a housing-policy program was introduced to resettle them. Soon after, new gypsy communities arose. According to some researchers, this anomalous situation derives from a transitory state when the gypsies' traditional internal legal institution, the voivodeship, was canceled as a consequence of resettling, and the acceptance of the norms of the dominant society was very slow.

However, there is an ambitious and industrious class of gypsies who wish to change the circumstances of their lives. These people have regular wages, as they play a part in the labor market and want to live among Hungarian people. According to present research, they are gradually giving up their gypsy identities as a consequence of their social mobility.

The areas inhabited by gypsy groups are peripheral and border regions. As the map shows, most gypsies live in the north-east and the south-west areas of Hungary, but only 6% live in the north-west area. More than one-third live in the north-east part of Hungary. There are several settlements where the percentage of gypsies is well over 60%.

Because of the forced industrial policy, the countries of the eastern Europe had a characteristically one-sided urbanization that undervalued the importance of the traditionally agricultural areas and supported educated and ambitious people to move towards the industrial centers. The industrial policy sealed the fate of those regions where there were mostly small villages (with the average number of inhabitants being less than a thousand). This development caused a kind of succession in some regions replacing one community with another. Besides, it is important to emphasize that most of the gypsies live near the closed boundaries namely in the countries of the former Soviet bloc. In previous years, there was minimal border crossing in this bloc, and it was almost impossible to move toward the former Soviet Union. These borders were guarded very strictly, and the inhabitants of the different countries were largely cut off from each other.

This isolation further increased the poverty of these areas. The regions near the closed boundaries have not enjoyed economic relations with each other for many decades. The prospering black market in the second half of the 1980s that also involved the gypsies was due to the decline of the political system. In this area, near the borders, wages and education levels are low, and the local governments are poor and frequently deficient.

There are not only regional differences in the percentage of the gypsy students but also remarkable differences concerning the type of settlements in which they live. Gypsy children are significantly under-represented in the cities and over-represented in small villages. In the cities, the percentage of gypsy children is about 20%, but in the villages, it is 56%. Generally, the smaller a settlement, the higher the percentage of gypsy pupils (Kertesi & Kézdi, 1996). There are mostly small villages in the area of the "Partium," and with a high percentage of gypsies is very high.

In Hungary, the relative poverty has become greater and more visible for some years now. According to the Central Statistical Bureau of Hungary, the percentage of people living under the poverty line was about 10% of the population in the 1980s and became about 15% in the year of 1992 increasing to 50% in 1995 (Forster & Toth, 1997). In 1995, the standard of living decreased in about half of Hungarian society.

There are several indicators that can definitely forecast poverty, for example, low educational level, living in villages, unemployment, living on disability or a widow's pension, being dependent, being an agricultural worker, unqualified people, children and old people, large families, single mothers, parents under the age of 30, gypsies, etc. (Andorka, 1995). People who live in remote areas and those in families where the head of the family has only primary school education are twice as likely to be living in poverty. Labor-market participation also influences the rate of poverty. Households with an unemployed head of the family are twice as likely to be poorer than those whose head of the family is employed. Those most likely to be living in poverty have been unemployed for a long period of time and are not old enough to retire or not entitled to social insurance. Demographic factors that determine poverty are also very strong. Propensity to poverty is highest in families with at least three children; single mothers; those younger than 30; and those over 60 and living alone.

Based on the aforementioned criteria, gypsy families are the most threatened by poverty. The poverty rate of gypsies is about 70%. Longitudinal analyses have shown also that there is practically little chance for the gypsies at present to escape this poverty (Forster & Toth, 1997).

In highly developed industrial countries, labor-force participation is essential for working-aged people. In the decades of socialism, the labor-force participation of the gypsies was almost complete, but the proclaimed full employment covered a kind of latent unemployment, because gypsies were uneducated individuals who worked mostly for construction companies and in heavy industry. After the political transformation in Hungary in the beginning of the 1990s, the liquidation of large companies equaled the liquidation of workplaces that gave employment to uneducated people. This liquidation of jobs directly affected the gypsies (Fraser, 1995). By 1993, the unemployment rate had become 13.6% in Hungary. Although the increasing rate of unemployment can be partly regarded as a consequence of discharges and the liquidation of the companies, because the economy did not have sufficient capacity to provide jobs for all unemployed people. However, the percentage of long-term unemployed had increased as well. In 1995, 40% of the unemployed had not been working for more than a year, and by 1996, this percentage had increased further to about 50%. Social problems caused by the long-term unemployment increased further, and the rate was high for unemployed individuals who lived in households without any wage-earners. The risk of being unemployed was very different according to social classes. The most vulnerable classes were young people, uneducated people, and gypsies (Forster & Toth, 1997).

The extent of gypsy unemployment is demonstrated by the fact that in 1994, only 26% of the working-aged gypsies were employed. Most were compelled to find casual work, such as "wheeling and dealing." As a consequence of this process, it can be seen that the integration of the gypsies is waning again, even though the percentage of those gypsies who altered their lifestyle to an earlier expected rustic-civil lifestyle has increased (Szuhay, 2000, p. 36).

In the interests of overcoming social disadvantages, the importance of education is very high because education is a prerequisite for labor-force participation, and a good school performance is a very important indicator in terms of success in the world of work, prestige of workplaces and income. A poor school performance increases the chances of unemployment. In the case of people having only primary school education, the risk of being unemployed is 10 times greater than in those who have a higher education degree.

Programs that support increasing the educational level for gypsies derive from efforts that try to help their social integration, which is expected to improve the gypsy labor-force participation and by this improving their standard of living. Until this time, these programs were unsuccessful because the improvement in school performance for gypsy children was very low (Pártos, 1979). Nevertheless, there is some success in the sense that, today, there is notable improvement of their educational level, the increase in their qualification level and the support of school performance in the case of children (Forray & Hegedus, 1991).

As regards their school achievement, in previous decades there was a significant improvement in the rates of those who finished primary school. However, the index of advanced schooling and the drop out rate continued to decline. As present, gypsy children are 50 times less likely to finish secondary school and six times less likely to obtain a qualification than non-gypsy children.

DIFFERENT EDUCATION SYSTEMS IN THE "PARTIUM"

In the Hungarian education system, the school-leaving age is 16 years. The 8-year primary school period is followed by secondary school, either by 3 years of vocational training, grammar school, or technical school (vocational training and grammar school ending with a final examination, after which, the individual can apply for a 3- or 4-year college course or a 5- or 6-year university course.

Romania's school grades and school types differ from Hungarian types. The school leaving age is also 16 years but recently the new education act has reduced this to the end of the first eight classes. In Romania, compulsory education involves a 10-year old elementary school followed by secondary school, either a lyceum or a technical school. There are two kinds of lyceums, the 4-year general lyceum and the 4- or 5-year technical lyceum that can be divided into two equal periods. The higher vocational education can be after the technical lyceum that takes 1 or 2 years in specialized schools. The lower vocational education takes 1, 2, or 3 years in vocational schools after finishing the eight classes (Varga, 1996, p. 332).

In Ukraine, there is a 3-year elementary school, followed by a 5-year post-elementary school, which ends with exams in four basic subjects. This is then followed by 2 years of grammar school, 3 years of vocational school, or 4 years of technical secondary school. Upon finishing technical secondary school and grammar school, the individual can apply for college or university.

As regards the educational level of gypsies in Romania, according to the Romanian Census Bureau, the percentage of gypsies in the whole population under the age of 12 is 0.28%. The percentage of gypsies is negligible in higher education, lyceum, and technical secondary school, but 0.4% attend vocational school, 2.9% finish primary school, and 96.6% finish the 4-year elementary school or attend a course to learn how to read and write. Comparing the education level of the gypsies to other ethnic groups in Romania, gypsies fall behind. More than 20% of the gypsies are said to be illiterate, while in other ethnic groups (e.g. Hungarians or Germans), this rate is about 1% (Varga, 1996).

At present, we do not have all the data from Ukraine in relation to the educational level of the gypsies (ongoing research), but it can already be seen that their educational level is even lower than it was in case of the Romanian gypsies.

In the Hungarian part of the "Partium" in 1992, the percentage of gypsy people is 7.68%, i.e. an increase more than twice that in the 1960s. The percentage of gypsy pupils surpasses the percentage of the gypsy inhabitants that can be due to their high birth rate. In 1992, this percentage is 10.32% in the Hungarian area of the "Partium." In the Ukrainian part of the "Partium," the percentage of the gypsy population is 9.31%, and these live scattered throughout this area.

Because of school failures, most gypsy children cannot continue their studies in secondary school. One important indicator of their failure is the high rate of dropouts. The percentage of Hungarian gypsies who cannot finish the 8-year primary school in the capital is 15.5%, in the towns 23.7% and in the villages 27.3%. The percentage of Hungarian gypsies who are able to finish secondary school is 9.9% in the capital, 2.8% in the towns and 1.8% in the villages (Kemény, 2000).

The individual failures are consolidated, and generally there is a strong connection between the percentage of gypsy pupils and the schools' results. The higher the percentage of gypsy children in a school, the higher the percentage of those pupils who drop out in several subjects, or repeat the year. Research has proved that these disadvantages can be explained by the socialization of the gypsies at home and not in the type of settlement, type of the school they attend, school equipment, or the phenomenon of segregation (Kertesi & Kézdi, 1996).

Examining the schools visited by gypsy children, it becomes evident that the equipment and personal conditions of the school are closely related to the circumstances of a settlement. On the one hand, there are schools in the towns where no gypsy children attend, and the aforementioned conditions are poorer than those where gypsy children attend. On the other hand, as regards the settlement, the schools of small villages are very poor with respect to their equipment and facilities but this concerns both the gypsy and non-gypsy children. The disadvantage of the settlement in the case of the education system is independent of the rate of gypsy inhabitants, and this is almost the same everywhere in the country.

The education policy is not really able to emphasize a school's achievement because the family and contemporary influences play a more significant role in this respect. It is indicated as the main cause of the educational problems of the gypsies that they are cumulatively disadvantaged people, their education level is very low, the living circumstances and lifestyles are not suitable, and the rate of unemployment is very high. Gypsies live on the edge of the society, and their children should be taught basic skills of civilization and be supported financially. The traditions and culture of their families and communities are viewed negatively and used against them, to their disadvantage. From the 1960s, it seemed appropriate to create gypsy classes in the schools to meet these aims; originally this was not to support segregation and reduce costs, but to decrease cultural and civil disadvantages. Moreover, it was thought that later these children could adapt successfully to mixed classes. Today, we realize that this plan collapsed. In some places, student boarding schools were organized to support gypsy pupils to separate them from their cumulatively disadvantaged environment. Probably, the number of such boarding schools did not increase because of financial factors (Forray & Hegedus, 1991).

The disadvantages associated with the families are such that gypsy families traditionally have a bad relationship with schools. Parents' qualifications are also very low, and they cherish the memory of a school full of failures. They do not even know those behavioral patterns that would enable them to communicate with school in a proper way, they are not able to cooperate with school, their relationship with school is full of anxiety, and full of aggression. As a consequence, parents are generally unable to successfully manage their children at school, and moreover there is a great chance that they pass on their own negative attitudes about school to their children, thus guaranteeing their children's failure at school. Furthermore, gypsy children also have to face the consequences of the stereotypes of the majority in school communities. Failures deriving from learning problems and the rejection of a prejudicial environment can easily lead one to give up, difficulty avoidance and early dropout from school. Furthermore, the learning motivation of children from gypsy families is generally very low because, on the one hand, the educational level of their parents is also very low, and on the other hand, the special skills that can be found in gypsy families are not skills learned at school but "cultural artifacts" are learned from the family and the relatives. Finally, we should mention that education in Hungary is free; there is no tuition, but school equipment has to be bought by parents. Most gypsy families live below the poverty line, and school is a serious financial burden for them, e.g. clothes, books, school equipment, etc.). Most gypsy families are financially interested in their children's dropping out of school early to earn money as soon as possible (Lisko, 1996).

Most gypsy pupils attend a school where the percentage of gypsies is over 10%. In the case of non-gypsy children, two-thirds attend a school where the percentage of gypsy children is less than 2%. In one-fourth of Hungarian schools, there are no gypsy children. On the whole, this means that most of the non-gypsy children never see gypsy children at school. The segregation of gypsy and non-gypsy children was very high in the 1990s in Hungary, and the regional position of the gypsies does not explain such a high degree of segregation (Kertesi & Kézdi, 1996).

With knowledge of the crucial influence of the family socialization, it is important that in gypsy families, there has been a kind of change in their scale of values for some decades. In studies between 1971 and 1991, it can be seen that most of the gypsy families' opinions have changed very much in connection with the usefulness of schools. According to the gypsies in 1971, it was enough for only four or five classes to be finished, but by 1993, they preferred to finish the eight years of primary school (Kemény, 2000).

In considering the performance of schools where gypsy pupils attend, these are much worse than any other primary school in Hungary. In case of schools where a large number of gypsy children attend, the dropout rate is very high, there are many over-age pupils, and there are a high number of children who repeat school years. This extremely high degree of school failures can be attributed to the fact that in these schools, there are many gypsy children whose family socialization is unsuitable for successful academic achievement. It also plays an important role in the school failures of gypsy children that the number of children coming from families with a low status is surpassed, so contemporary relationships also mean for them a very homogeneous environment. This kind of segregation in previous years has even strengthened because many non-gypsy children "escape" to other schools from those which became homogeneous ethnically.

THE GYPSY EDUCATIONAL EXPERIENCE

From the axioms of psychological research, before entering school there is a need for a kind of preschool stage that helps children to adapt to the school and supports them in shaping a behavior that the school later can rely on. Children need kindergarten if they do not obtain sufficient support from the family in preparing for school; kindergarten is also a very important institution that supports equal opportunities. Thus, kindergarten plays a significant role in the socialization of gypsy children. One current problem is that in Hungary, the kindergarten is the least accessible for disadvantaged children because the kindergarten system is not completely extended to smaller villages where the majority of the gypsy families live. Kindergarten can be crucial in the life of gypsy children because at that point, gypsies consider their children to be at the age where it is the family's task to take care of their children. Moreover, gypsies do not have any great trust in formal educational at all (Forray & Hegedus, 1991).

There is a relatively strong connection between the rate of attending kindergarten and school failures. Those children who attended kindergarten and experienced the rule system of formal education are better socialized for school. This illustrates that children with poor parents have a lower educational and that there is a wide gap between habits, rules, norms of the school and family. This gap should be narrowed because it is a crucial point in school achievements. When both parents or even just the mother is unemployed, there is a higher probability that the child will not attend kindergarten. In other cases when there are several children in a family, the mother is most likely to stay at home and also does not let her children attend kindergarten. On the one hand, the more children in a family, the less the parents can spend on their children's schooling, and a high number of children is usually associated with a low income per head. On the other hand, in Hungary, often families with several children have a very low educational level. The lower the educational level of the parents, the less able they are to pass on those skills and norms (ambition, ability of concentration, attention, punctuality, persistence, etc.) to their children, which could influence their children's school achievements (Kezdi & Kertesi, 1996).

Kindergarten increases the chance of success because it can promote school readiness and reduce the gap between family socialization and the school norm system; in those families with children who do not attend kindergarten, often parents are unemployed, have a low educational level, have a large family, and are unable to socialize their children according to the accepted the school norm system (Kezdi & Kertesi, 1996).

The dispersion of gypsy children in the counties is very uneven. The rate of gypsy pupils in north-eastern Hungary is surpassed, about 15%, but in the south-west of the country, it is only about 2% (Kezdi & Kertesi, 1996). As regards the first 4 years of primary school, gypsy children are more successful in this stage than in the next 4 years of primary school. This former period is the period when children have to face most failures, and this is the stage when most give up studying. During the second half of primary school, there are an increasing number of behavioral problems, and teachers are unable to deal with these effectively. This chapter is not concerned with the analyses of the cultural and social-psychological background of disciplining problems, but it is important to mention that often the lifestyle of the gypsy families and the workshop-style operation of schools underlie the aforementioned problems.

The dropout rate in primary school is very high among those people who follow a gypsy lifestyle. For example, more than one-tenth of people between the age of 20 and 24, and almost one-fifth of people from 25 to 29 have not finished the eight years of primary school in Hungary.

Bearing in mind that, today, primary school is a prerequisite for almost all trades and careers, the youngest gypsy generation almost excludes itself from the possibility of getting any kind of qualification. Consequently, gypsies arise as an unqualified class, always struggling with the problems of labor-force participation.

The school admittance rate of gypsy children to grammar schools is 6% and for technical secondary school 10%. For non-gypsy children, almost 100% chose further education after primary school, but only half of the gypsy pupils do the same (which is a significant improvement over earlier decades; Kezdi & Kertesi, 1996). In Hungary, after the political transition, several new institutions were founded with the aim to support further education of gypsy pupils. The creation of ability-improvement courses, gypsy minority educational institutions and scholarships or other forms of support from different kind of funds contributed to the rate of further education. In terms of finishing primary school and applying for further education, the most important factor is the relationship between parents, children and school. Today, most gypsy families realize the advantages and disadvantages of further education as before – and its importance (Kemény, 2000).

The small number of gypsy pupils who undergo secondary education often never finish it. Sensitive young children who are separated from the home environment enter an unknown environment, have to adapt to the new environment, and have to aim for a good school results. Usually the school results in the first secondary year are worse than in the last primary school year but later can be overcome. In almost all gypsy children, except when the parents have a higher educational level, there are many external influences that complicate the situation in secondary school. Only a very small number of gypies attend secondary school, and even fewer finish it (Forray & Hegedus, 1991).

In the present system of secondary education, gypsy pupils take part mainly in vocational education. The concept of vocational education is made problematic by the fact that the vocational educational system that was earlier associated with large companies is in crisis.

In Hungary, finishing primary school is a prerequisite for applying for vocational schools. For gypsy pupils, qualifications are essential because they can improve their own labor-force participation, and this is the only type of school at secondary level that mostly can be achieved by gypsy children. Furthermore, gypsies often gradually lose touch with society and will not integrate. In the gypsy population, there are few qualified people who have attended vocational schools to ensure social mobility for themselves and succeeding generations (Lisko, 1996).

At present, there is another problem that hinders the successful vocational education of gypsy children: In previous years, pupils could find a apprenticeship training only if their parents bought such possibilities for their children by paying huge amounts of money to entrepreneurs. Since parents from the lower classes of society are unable to pay this money, the chances of their children attending vocational schools are almost nonexistent.

The participation of gypsy students in higher education is extremely low, less than 1%. There is now ongoing research on gypsies who have degrees, the aim being to identify those factors that support their successful school career, and we would like to put forward some suggestions in connection with such supporting programs that would help gypsies in their school achievements.

During the analysis of the interviews, we aimed to determine whether there is a kind of gypsy migration between the separate areas of the "Partium," because there was an intensive connection system and migration among the inhabitants according to our earlier experiences. The next objectives were to find the reasons for their emigration, to find out more about the culture of these families, and then to follow the progress of their children at school.

We adopted different approaches to certain stages of the research. We used both quantitative and qualitative methods, conducting interviews and observations of gypsy families, and we asking schoolmasters, the leaders of gypsy organizations, and students. This wide range of methods reflects the complexity of the problem. In this paper, only the initial results are summarized, and further steps in the research later will be presented.

During the research, we have found that the differences among of gypsies living in the area of the "Partium" is much greater than for any other ethnic groups in this area. They range from caravan-dwellers and lonely beggars with their children in the streets, to rich businessmen. Children from families with different lifestyles have different school achievements because children of wandering gypsies and beggars usually do not attend school.

Here, we concentrate on that group of gypsy children and youths whose parents try to break away from their position, even taking the risk of emigration. These people came from the Ukrainian and Romanian part of the "Partium" to Hungary. Using interviews and observations,we shall explore the world of the so-called "gypsy musicians." In this case, the adjective "musician" is not solely a profession for these people (most of them also have another profession) but also a subculture: a kind of lifestyle, a peculiar identity, a device to separate themselves from other groups of gypsies. This class is able to give up the gypsy lifestyle by having more effective norms, discipline, and ambition.

From interviews carried out with "gypsy musicians," the main reason for emigration is not to improve their financial status but to escape the experience of insults directed towards them as an ethnic group. One of the interviewees came from Romania in 1989 and considered themself a political emigrant. They gave an account of the regular interference of the Romanian secret police because they considered themself Hungarian, did not speak Romanian, sent their children to Hungarian schools, and did not want to join the Romanian Communist Party. One of the oldest of the interviewees said that the greatest indictment was against them in Romania when he played a patriotic Hungarian song in a public restaurant. Romania is a very young country (less than 100 years old in its present form) where the percentage of ethnic groups is very high. The ethnic groups of gypsies who consider themselves Hungarian and speak Hungarian, were severely oppressed. Physical violence was often used as a form of coercion in order that Hungarian gypsies would consider themselves Romanians as opposed to Hungarians. The intent of such coercion was to alter the statistics during the time of national census.

One of the interviewees (in their twenties and from Ukraine) said that at the end of the 1980s, in the former Soviet Union in her Ukrainian school, every Hungarian and gypsy student had to listen to the following reprimand: "What bread do you eat? Hungarian or Ukrainian? You will see that the time will come as in the case of the Jews." Thus, there appeared to be a strong solidarity between the Hungarians and the gypsies. It was also mentioned that they had jobs there, and their poor standard of living was no less than that of other people; these immigrant families did mention a certain increase in their standard of living in Hungary. One of them, for example, was a tailor who had several handymen and was considered a reliable and good worker. At present, they still think that they had made a good decision to migrate to Hungary, and this opinion was very attractive for other people considering the idea.

The first large wave of immigrants was at the end of the 1980s, but it was difficult then to obtain a passport or any kind of permission for the whole family because of strict border controls. Consequently, most immigrants from Romania bypassed legal routes and crossed established boundaries. This was fraught with danger: As one of the interviewees said, when he first attempted to cross borders illegally, he was caught by the frontier guards, beaten, and his head shaved (a huge insult to gypsies). Later, the laws on traveling or migrating abroad were relaxed in Romania, but in Ukraine, currently there are still very strict rules, and a very good financial background and good connections are needed to obtain a passport. For this reason, most of the immigrants in the area of "Partium" are from Romania and not from Ukraine. From the mid-1990s, the number of immigrants has been decreasing continuously as a result of a relaxation in anti-ethnic attitudes in Romanian and Ukranian politics. Certainly, in both countries, there are certain xenophobic parties but not with sufficient political strength to form their own governments. The decline in emigration can also be explained by the fact that the more mobile families had already left Romania and Ukraine, and those who remained at home knew that in spite of their poor environment at home, they would not progress in life without help from contacts abroad. Moreover, Hungary complicated the administrative conditions for transmigration under pressure from Hungarian organizations in Romania and Ukraine. The intellectual class who founded these Jungarian organizations feels that emigration will not solve the problem of the three million Hungarian people (also including gypsies) in Romania and Ukraine.

Before transmigration, most of the interviewees knew Hungary, as they had worked there illegally for several years. They were referring to families who, for example, still regularly came over to Hungary to work illegally as musicians when there was a wedding or any other important event. In preparing for the transmigration, contact with relatives abroad is important. One of the interviewees said that their godparents lived in Hungary, and they helped her during the first months upon arrival in Hungary. A housewife said that in spite of her large family, she let another family (with nine members) stay with her family for several months while they finalized arrangements. Of course, their knowledge of the Hungarian language facilitates the transmigration process.

In the first half of the 1990s, emigration was common among ambitious gypsy musicians, almost all of them taking advantage of this possibility, except those where a serious obstacle arose, e.g. having handicapped children, not having children, etc. These people consider emigration as an investment in the next generation, and when there is no following generation or a following generation seems unable to survive, they consider such investment unnecessary.

In the first stage of our research, we looked for immigrants in that part of the "Partium" where there are mostly poor, small villages with large numbers of gypsies. We realized that small villages were bypassed for bigger towns of this region, for settlement purposes. The interviewees said that during the last 10 years, most of the emigrants came to these bigger towns, then to the Hungarian capital, and after that abroad to countries such as Germany and Canada. The reason for going further from the "Partium" is probably that these emigrants found the Hungarian part of the "Partium" an economically disadvantaged area that does not have enough opportunities for them.

For those emigrants who came to the Hungarian Part of the "Partium," cheap living places were available only in the poor parts of the city centers. Their ruined lodging houses are rather large, which is good for large gypsy families who usually spend their days at home together because the children are at home, and the father works only in the evening and at night. Their houses are rather tidy, cleaner than in other gypsy houses, highly decorated, and very colorful, in line with the gypsy tradition. The domination and continuous operation of the high tech, for example, hi-fi sets, TV sets, mobile phones, etc., are characteristic of these homes, but the furniture is poor and probably second hand. Usually, there is a dog that lives with the family and is treated as part of the family. In their material environment, elements of traditional gypsy culture and modern consumerism coexist.

For those gypsy-musician families who want to break away from the gypsy environment, effective norms help them to achieve their goals. The family has strict and specific norms that differ from the norms of other gypsy groups. Our interviewees found deviant behavior, e.g. getting drunk, regular drinking, and staying out late, which are natural behavioral patterns in non-musician gypsy families. Besides following strict rules and sanctions, it is considered important for the adults in large families to be attentive to their children and present themselves as role models. In these groups, in contrast with other gypsy groups, it is unacceptable for girls in their teenage years to have partners and then children. According to researchers examining gypsy cultures, individuals begin their sexual lives early.

With gypsy male musicians, monogamy is practiced in the marriage. According to custom, it is very important for a girl to have a respectable life until marriage. The father of a 22-year-old girl emphasized that his daughter had not had a partner, before marriage. Social sexual behavior is based on culture and tradition, which in part influence opportunities available later in life. While some gypsy cultures discourage children before marriage, other gypsy cultures do not.

Although the older generation emphasized that they do not interfere in their children's choices, and they do respect old traditions (for example, deciding about marriage in childhood), they expect their children to marry children from other gypsy-musician families. They do not even like to marry Hungarian individuals. It appears from the aforementioned that the gypsy communities try to defend their financial status and their different culture by endogamy in their own group of gypsies. This endogamy, which, from our experience, is the principal of all kinds of relationships, prevents these people from becoming part of a multiplex group involving people with different social positions. This kind of closed system of relationships also prevents individuals from opening up to groups of a higher status, from acquiring knowledge to help ensure better results in schooling, or from learning special skills to land better jobs. When asked why this is the norm for them, it appeared that they were conscious of the characteristics and the importance of inherited family subculture, usually giving answers to explain their behavior such as, "We saw it this way," or "This is a habit in this family."

Religion plays an important role in the life of the immigrant gypsy musician families and the middle-aged generation. This generation became non-believers in Hungary during the years of socialism. Certainly, this religious life is supported by the state of being an ethnic group because belonging to a church or speaking a mother tongue are very important identifiers for them. It is also part of their upbringing to ensure that their children attend divinity classes and church. Otherwise, it has been a frequent phenomenon in the "Partium" for a long time that Catholic and Protestant gypsy communities support gypsy families in solving their problems. For example, in families of gypsy people of a low social position, these communities supported them in their everyday problems by motivating them (sometimes financially) to gain a qualification or to attain a higher standard of living. In this case, a low social position means closed communities, with limited contact with individuals different from oneself and limited opportunity to better one's station in life.

According to the interpretation of gender roles between the generations, there are differences. People in their fifties embody the model of a large family that is based on the prestige of the father, and the mother's role is to keep together and take care of the family in a way so as to soften the father's severity. A father said, for example, that his adult son is afraid to smoke when the father is present. For young women, identification with roles is somewhat uncertain because the traditional role of the mother is fading as a consequence of educational institutions, and because their low level of qualification means that they cannot be a part of the labor market. The situation for young men is much more stable because of the inherited musician trade and because they see a strong father model both inside and outside the house during their childhood. Furthermore, being a musician ensures income and financial stability which inculcates pride and self confidence. For example, they proudly show the articles and photos of their performances to other members of the family.

The differences in dressing of the generations are also remarkable but very similar to the dressing of non-gypsy people. Middle-aged people of gypsy musicians wear simple and tidy clothes of the low- and middle-class, but young gypsies have very fashionable and expensive sport clothes.

They consider their relationship between the generations ideal and exemplary, but there are differences in their attitudes to life. The older people are more frugal and less materialistic, while the young people are materially oriented, particularly in terms of clothes, technological items, and entertainment products. This is a widespread phenomenon not only in gypsy communities but also among Hungarian people.

The importance of the family relationship can be realized also in the everyday activities because the different generations are cooperating with each other continuously; for example, grandfathers go to the schools for their grandchildren. Helping in this way concerns not only people living in a single household but also larger families where there are several generations, and the relative relationships and emotional connections are very strong. In such cases, it is not unusual to accommodate relatives for extended periods of time. Relative relationships also influence the decisions of emigration or further migration.

There is a kind of advance in school attainment of gypsies, but this advance is negligible in comparison to the advance of non gypsy Hungarian populations in previous decades. Although the interviewed families of gypsy musicians are very ambitious and take definite steps on behalf of social progress, they also have a low level of education attainment and less social mobility in comparison to other gypsy communities. The foregoing is a consequence of having only a primary school education.

Although many from the generation of immigrant parents may not have finished their 8 years of primary school, along the scale of values having a good skill or business is better than having a high educational level. Even so, interestingly, the interviewees considered their children's education to be important.

Concerning preschool institutions, nursery was mentioned by an immigrant mother from Romania who had to go to work very early, because there was no child-care leave for mothers. She said that she let her son attend nursery with a very heavy heart, and her child did not enjoy himself there: He was always crying, so the mother left her job soon to be able to care for her child at home. Throughout our interviews, we found that most children were looked after at home until kindergarten age. These children lived in large families, where they are always around the adults; they did not have a separate children's environment, there were no playrooms or toys, and the children usually played with adults' belongings.

Parents in gypsy-musician families cherished the positive experiences of kindergarten. They were satisfied with the kindergarten teachers and proud of their children because they were better at singing and versification than other children. Compared with non-musician gypsy families, children from these families often coped much better with the new expectations and demands of beginning school. The parents supported their children at school and mentioned that their children achieved good marks at school. The teachers' relationship with their children was undoubtedly positive, and children could not mention any negative experience in connection with schooling. There are several reasons for this: Their children attended school in tidy and clean clothes; they prepared for their lessons; they had all the necessary equipment; and their behavior was always very polite. The parents mentioned that the teachers had liked their children very much.

In spite of all the aforementioned positive attitudes to schooling, children often dropped out of schools or finished primary school about 2 or 3 years later, and did not apply for secondary schools. This shows that the parents' will was no more effective in the teenage period of their children's life. One of the mothers said "I cannot study instead of my child." Parents often do not like talking about failures during this period of primary school. Families are happy for their children to gain a certificate after 8 years at school when their children finish primary school.

In terms of further education, the younger generation made a precise cost-benefit analysis of whether to study more or not, concentrating on the loss of income during that period and the expected expenses. They considered studying while working unimaginable, one interviewee saying: "I'm too tired for studying then." In these cost-benefit analyses, their social advance and the increase in their income through their studies were very minor. This experience accords with a statement from Boudon (1881) in terms of explaining the decision concerning further education of socially low-positioned young people. These families do not consider the lack of further education to be an impediment in life. Qualifications are considered important, however, for girls to become a singer. Parents prepare their daughters to become wives and mothers who do not need a high level of education or any kind of qualification.

Boys also did not learn their professions within formal education, but according to the traditions, they took after the model of their fathers – they "grew" into their profession. According to the family habits, the gypsy musician's children are given instruments at the age of 4 or 5 that to be revealed their talent ("I gave the instrument into the hand of my other son and he hold it as a gyppo, a non-musician gypsy, he did not become a violinist but later a concertina player").

Of all the elements of school, parents usually overvalue the school achievements of their children and describe them with better marks; their attitude to primary school changes after the first 4 years, their children often drop out, they are over age, and they attend night schools. Dropping out from lower secondary education was not a problem. Any apparent problems in connection with education were considered by parents to be related to adolescence. Although their children's behavior did not become deviant (because of strict upbringing) their interest in further schooling had diminished. However, it is promising that interviewees expressed a desire for their grandchildren to have a higher education.

The labor-force participation of immigrant gypsies is full of paradoxes. Although officially they may be on a minimum wage, they often earn much more from tips, thus avoiding paying taxes and contributions to the state.

The most disadvantaged individual is the completely unqualified young woman. Job centers can help to provide them with ongoing work, but the demand for uneducated labor force is decreasing. One young woman said that she worked at a tobacco company as a handygirl and had an accident, but while recovering from her injuries, her contract lapsed, and she was made redundant. This situation and her defenselessness made her suspicious and sad, and for this reason, many gypsies feel that they are stereotyped for their failures in looking for and finding jobs. Unsuccessful employment, and the powerlessness associated with this, can lead to a suspicion of discrimination felt by the interviewees. With respect to school achievement and social mobility through advanced schooling, the uncertainty or the lack of young women's prospects for the future figure prominently. This may be because the daughters of gypsy-musician families are part of a very strong unit of family or relative relationships, but they do not have any other external links to other social positions, with elevated social status. Yet, they expressed their bravest hopes in connection with further education of those children who are from mixed race families. There are those who will probably have the possibility later to use external networks of relationships. On the whole, the strong cultural and environmental separation of the families indeed can be the source of strong family community cohesion based on effective norms.

SUMMARY

In his paper, we have introduced the problematic points of gypsies' integration into the society of the "Partium." An extremely complex situation created according to the concurrence of the cultures was addressed to address acculturation as a consequence of political pressure. After the collapse of socialism, there was considerable transmigration among the gypsies. The movement of emigrants, their social position, and their changing lifestyle are important elements in the continuous social processes in this area.

During the research, it became clear that there is an extremely internal differentiation and a cultural variety in gypsy people living this area, and it appeared that a low level of education can be experienced in all groups of gypsies. This can be explained by unfavorable decisions concerning further studies, even with a supportive school and family. Students explained their decisions by using cost-benefit analysis considerations in connection with the values of education, the overvalued risk of investing in education, and the lack of future prospects.

A considerable number of studies on gypsies have focused on the conflicts between ethnic minorities and mainstream society, but there are few studies on the influence of environmental factors on school achievement in different groups of gypsies. Research investigations of this type could help in developing programs in the area of educational policy and social policy by actually promoting the life of gypsy people. A further purpose of our research is to explore in greater detail the educational statistics among the ethnic minorities in this area.

REFERENCES

Andorka, R. (1995). *Szegenyseg es szocialpolitika a 90-es evekben*. Budapest: Press publica.

Boudon, R. (1981). *The logic of social action*. London: Routledge & Kegan Paul.

Bourdieu, P. (1972). *Esquisse d'une theorie de la pratique, precede de trois etudes d'ethnologie kable*. Switzerland: Libraririe Dros.

Carnoy, M. (1995). Race earning differentials. In: M. Carnoy (Ed.), *International Encyclopedia of Economics of Education* (pp. 235–242). Oxford: Pergamon.

Forray, R. K., & Hegedus, T. A. (1991). *Tamogatas es integracio-Oktataspolitikai szempontok a ciganysag iskolazasahoz*. Budapest: Oktataskutato Intezet.

Forster, M. F., & Toth, I. G. (1997). *Szegenyseg es egyenlotlensegek Magyarorszagon es a tobbi visegradi orszagban*. Budapest: Press publica.

Fraser, A. (1995). *The gypsies*. Oxford: Blackwell.

Hicks, N. L. (1995). Education and economic growth. In: M. Carnoy (Ed.), *International Encyclopedia of Economics of Education* (pp. 192–198). Oxford: Pergamon.

Hill, J. (1995). School culture and peer groups. In: L. W. Anderson (Ed.), *International Encyclopedia of Teaching and Teacher Education* (pp. 332–335). Oxford: Pergamon.

Hinchliffe, K. (1995). Education and the labor market. In: M. Carnoy (Ed.), *International Encyclopedia of Economics of Education* (pp. 20–23). Oxford: Pergamon.

Kelly-Portes, A., & Brenner, J. (1993). Embeddedness and immigration: Notes on the social determinants of economics action. *American Journal of Society*, *99*, 1320–1350.

Kemény, I. (2000). *A magyarorszagi romak*. Budapest: Press Publica.

Kertesi, G., & Kézdi, G. (1996). Cigany tanulok az altalanos iskolaban. In: *Ciganyok es iskola*. Budapest: Oktataskutato Intezet (pp. 22–47).

Kocsis, K., & Kovacs, Z. (2000). A cigany nepesseg tarsakalomfoldrajza. In: *A ciganyak Magyarorszagon*. Budapest: MTA.

Lisko, I. (Ed.) (1996). *A cigany gyerekek szakkepzesenek tamagatas*. Budapest: Oktataskutato Intezet.

McDermott, R. (1974). Achieving school failure: An anthropological approach to illiteracy and social stratification. In: G. Spindler (Ed.), *Education and Cultural Process: Antropological Approaches*. New York: Holt, Rinehart & Winston.

Pártos, F. (1979). A cigany es nem cigany lakossag velemenye a fobb tarsadalompolitikai celkituzesekrol. In: H. T. Partos (Ed.), *A kozvelemeny a ciganyokrol*. Budapest: Tomegkommunikacios Kutaokozpont.

Szuhay, P. (2000). *Amit a ciganyokrol tudni kell*. MPI: Veszprem.

Varga, E. A. (1996). A nemzetisegek iskolazottsaga Romaniaban. *Statisztikai Szemle*, *LXXIV*(4), 332–351.

Wolcott, H. F. (1967). *A Kwakiutl village and school*. New York: Holt, Rinehart & Winston.

5. COMING TO AMERICA: DASHED HOPES AND UNCERTAIN FUTURES

Elavie Ndura

INTRODUCTION

According to the U.S. Committee for Refugees (2002) there were approximately 15 million refugees in the world in 2001, of which over three million were African. Refugees are persons who flee to a different country to escape persecution based on personal or group characteristics such as race, ethnicity, religion, nationality, social group, political opinion, or armed conflict, and lack of a durable solution (U.S. Committee for Refugees, 2001). For example, in Burundi, a small African country of about 6 million people, the civil war between the Tutsi and the Hutu has forced over half a million refugees to seek shelter in other African countries, Europe, and the United States (UNHCR, 2000).

Because refugees are uprooted from familiar surroundings and customs that give meaning to their everyday life, their survival and success in their host country are contingent upon how well they acculturate or adjust to the new society and the new culture. The adjustment process of refugees and all other immigrants, in general, is influenced by a host of individual and societal factors (Arthur, 2000; Haines, 1985; Kent, 1953; C. Suárez-Orozco & M. Suárez-Orozco, 2001). The process becomes even more complex for refugees who often have to deal with additional emotional issues resulting from their past experiences in their native countries. However, even though refugee groups may share some of the factors that affect their acculturation, it is important to acknowledge that their unique

'Suffer the Little Children': National and International Dimensions of Child
Poverty and Public Policy
Advances in Education in Diverse Communities: Research, Policy and Praxis, Volume 4, 97–120
Copyright © 2006 by Elsevier Ltd.
ISSN: 1479-358X/doi:10.1016/S1479-358X(04)04005-7

previous experiences and current circumstances shape their cultural adaptation in very special and unique ways. Therefore, examining the cultural adaptation process of particular refugee groups becomes an important goal and task in order to understand their cultural background and delineate the range of services that may be necessary to help the newcomers take full advantage of their newly found freedoms and opportunities.

This chapter reports on the findings from a study that examined the acculturation process of Burundi refugees who have been resettled in the United Stated, focusing on their dreams and challenges. Overall, the goals of the project were to: (1) develop awareness of the Burundi refugee experiences; (2) develop awareness of important aspects of Burundi culture that will help schools and social services providers better understand and serve Burundi clients; and (3) contribute to the knowledge about refugee populations while at the same time filling a void in existing literature about African refugees in general and Burundi refugees in particular. It is hoped that the findings presented in this chapter will be useful to educational institutions, as well as refugee resettlement, immigration, and social services agencies as they develop policies and programs to assist new African refugees in their acculturation process in the United States.

This chapter will evolve along five main components. After a brief review of relevant literature, the study design will be outlined, followed by a presentation and discussion of the findings. The chapter will close with some general conclusions and recommendations.

RELEVANT LITERATURE

The concept of immigrants' cultural adjustment has been previously explored and investigated by many scholars; however, most existing literature is about immigrants from Asia, Europe, and Latin America and very little has been written about African immigrants in the United States (Arthur, 2000). Nevertheless, every study contributes to our common understanding of the immigrant experience in general, and the refugee experience in particular. The studies reviewed below helped set the stage for the current study by highlighting the complexity of the immigrants' cultural adjustment process and therefore suggesting that acculturation is an important field of research, as it impacts the success of refugees in their new country.

Kent (1953) studied the assimilation process of intellectuals from Central Europe, noting the influence of a variety of personal factors such as the degree of similarity between the original and the new culture, and the availability of social services agencies on the process. M. Suárez-Orozco (1989) conducted a psychosocial study of motivation and achievement of Central American refugees in U.S. high schools. He pointed out how real life in the American inner city changed their initial idealistic perception of the opportunities that America has to offer, such as educational opportunities and financial stability. C. Suárez-Orozco and M. M. Suárez-Orozco (2001) investigated children of immigrants in the U.S. and how they were faring in American society. They discovered that immigrant children's success in schools is dependant upon the whole family's successful long-term cultural adaptation, which is in turn influenced by many factors like family cohesion, interpersonal relations, and socioeconomic and educational background. They raised an important question of whether immigrants who look, talk, dress, and move differently will be allowed to truly become members of their new societies.

Arthur (2000) conducted a study of 650 African immigrants residing in Atlanta, Minneapolis, the District of Columbia, and Charlotte, North Carolina. His study revealed important factors that influence cultural adjustment. He highlighted the lingering emotional attachment to the motherland, her culture and values, as potential obstacles to full acculturation for many African immigrants. His informants represented the major, larger groups of African immigrants from Nigeria, Cape Verde, Egypt, South Africa, Ghana, Liberia, Kenya, Ethiopia, and Somalia.

Burundi immigrants remain an invisible group in the literature on the immigrants' acculturation process. The research that has been conducted on Burundi refugees is limited to those in refugee camps in Tanzania (Mabuwa, 2000; Malkki, 1995; Sommers, 1998). The number of Burundi refugees, like all other African refugees living in the United States, has increased dramatically over the past ten years (UNHCR, 2000). However, they have remained unnoticed by educational researchers and policy makers mainly due to their unexplored national origin, language, and customs. This study, which was conducted by a fellow Burundi immigrant, is be the first attempt to explore the circumstances and experiences of Burundi refugees in the United States.

DESCRIPTION OF THE STUDY

Purpose Statement and Research Questions

The purpose of this qualitative, phenomenological case study was to describe the dreams and challenges that characterize the acculturation process of Burundi refugee families who have been resettled in a large metropolitan city in the South-Western United States. In this study, the acculturation process is defined as cultural adaptation or adjustment to American society and culture.

The overarching question that guided the study was: "What are the acculturation dreams and challenges of Burundi refugees in the United States?" In order to answer this central question, the following focus questions were addressed: (1) How do Burundi refugees describe their experiences with employment in the U.S.? (2) How do they describe their experiences with social services in the U.S.? (3) How do they negotiate the traits of their cultural identity in their social interactions within the American multicultural society? (4) How do parents perceive their children's schooling experiences in the U.S.? (5) How do children describe their schooling experiences in the U.S.? (6) In what ways do previous life experiences in Burundi and transitional host countries influence their adjustment process? (7) What expectations do they have for themselves and their families? This chapter will address focus questions 1, 2, 3, 6, and 7.

Design

A qualitative, phenomenological case study design (Creswell, 1998; Marshall & Rossman, 1999; Stake, 2000; Wolcott, 1994; Yin, 1994) was used as the framework for the study in order to maximize the collection of rich data. This conceptual framework allowed the researcher to collect data in a natural setting pertaining to the research questions; and it provided significant insight into the refugees' social and cultural universe. The study combined the phenomenological and case study traditions in order to maximize information about the refugees as a special case and to gain better understanding of their lived experiences in American society.

Participants

In 1997–1998 over 500 Burundi families were resettled in the United States from different refugee camps in Africa by Catholic Social Services (CSC) and the International Rescue Committee (IRC). About fifteen families were sent to the current research site, some of whom have already relocated to different cities throughout the country. The researcher, working as a volunteer, became actively involved in the acclimation process of the newcomers.

The participants consisted of a convenience criterion sample (Creswell, 1998) of 14 Burundi refugees (11 adults and three high school students) who had been resettled in a large metropolitan city in the South-Western United States since 1998. The convenience sample was limited to Burundi refugees who reside in the same metropolitan area, due to time and financial constraints. Nevertheless, since all the informants meet the criterion of being Burundi refugees who have been resettled in the United States from other African countries, quality assurance was maximized. This chapter will report on the findings from the interviews with the 11 adult participants.

The participants consisted of five married couples and one divorced male. Three of the couples had three children each; one had nine children; and another couple had one child and a baby on the way. The divorced participant did not have children. The participants ranged in age between 26 and 56 years old. Five were females and six were males. The participants represented different levels of education from their countries of origin. Seven had a college education; two had a secondary vocational education (grades 1–13); one had a general secondary education (grades 1–13); and one had a seventh grade education. Six of the participants (two females and four males) held professional positions in Burundi, mostly in education; two (both males) were college students; and three females were housewives. Three out of the five married couples already owned their home in the U.S.; two couples were still renting an apartment; and one participant was renting a room in one of the couple's home. The participants had been resettled from different African countries outside of their native Burundi into the U.S. between 1998 and 2002. All participants' names have been replaced with pseudonyms throughout this paper.

Procedures and Data Sources

The study was conducted over the course of one year in 2002–2003. Initially, the researcher called the adult participants on the telephone to request their participation in the study, as well as the participation of their school-aged children (7–17 years old). As the participants' culture dictates, she spoke with the male head of household, wherever applicable, in this initial recruitment telephone conversation in which she explained the project and requested the family's participation. She also gave each family a hospitality gift (a food/fruit basket and soft beverages) at the time of her initial visit, a practice that is very highly valued and appreciated in the participants' customs. These personal telephone calls and the researcher's sensitivity to the participants' culture helped develop the affinity that is required in order to conduct culturally responsive research. Being a fellow Burundi immigrant who speaks the participants' first language also helped establish a sense of sameness, which allowed for the development of a sense of trust (Vásquez-Montilla et al., 2000), another prerequisite for credible qualitative data collection. However, as a future publication will discuss, this affinity still did not guarantee access to all desired information from all target participants.

Data for the study were collected from three sources: interviews, document analysis, and direct observation in order to achieve triangulation – or to search for the convergence of information (Creswell, 1998; Marshall & Rossman, 1999; Stake, 2000; Yin, 1994). Most of the data were collected through semi-structured open-ended interviews, conducted in Kirundi, the participants' first and home language, or English (According to participants' preference) – often mixed with French. The participants were asked to share their experiences as refugees in the United States. They were prompted to talk about work, social services, social interactions, and schooling experiences. The researcher also recorded any information that the participants volunteered regarding their experiences before resettling in the United States. The interviews were scheduled to last one to two hours, however, they lasted at least 3–4 hours each. Six of the participants allowed the researcher to tape-record their interviews. The other five participants only allowed the researcher to write down notes during the interviews. All the interviews were conducted at the participants' homes. A Burundi immigrant, who is proficient in Kirundi, French, and English, transcribed the recorded interviews. The professional transcriptionist lives outside the U.S. and she does not know any of the participants personally. Field notes from the researcher's direct observation were collected. Direct observation generated data about the participants' physical environment, family/community interactions and the general atmosphere surrounding the interviews. Relevant documents were analyzed to help answer the research questions. The researcher also maintained a journal in which she recorded her data collection experiences.

Data analysis and Interpretation

All data from interviews, documents, and direct observation were analyzed separately during and after the data collection phase, identifying generated themes with different colors from the beginning. Data analysis and interpretation were done in five complementary stages. In the *initial stage*, the researcher coded for themes in the seven areas of emphasis outlined in the research questions: (1) work, (2) social services, (3) cultural identity, (4) schooling perceptions, (5) schooling experiences, (6) previous life experiences, and (7) expectations. Then, she analyzed the data again to generate additional themes within new areas of interest that had been created and expressed by the participants (Marshall & Rossman, 1999). All themes were color-coded and corresponding passages from the interview transcripts, documents, and field notes were marked with different colored highlighting pens, accordingly (Glesne, 1999; Marshall & Rossman, 1999). This was the *second stage* of data analysis and interpretation. In the *third stage*, the researcher made a detailed description of the case and its setting in order to provide a clear picture of the Burundi refugee phenomenon (Creswell,

1998). In the *fourth stage*, she examined and categorized the generated themes in order to establish patterns that helped generate a grounded theory (Strauss & Corbin, 1998)). *Finally*, she developed naturalistic generalizations that can inform policies and practices relevant to Burundi refugees in the United States (Creswell, 1998). The preliminary report reflecting the description and interpretation of the case was returned to select participants who read and verified its authenticity and accuracy (Asmussen & Creswell, 1995). The informants were asked three questions: Is the researcher's description and interpretation of your experiences as Burundi refugees in the United States accurate? Are the themes and constructs that the researcher identified consistent with your lived experiences? Are there any themes or constructs that she missed? The informants' comments and feedback were incorporated in the final reports about the study.

FINDINGS

The data revealed eight themes or concepts associated with the participants' acculturation challenges and dreams: (1) professional integration; (2) social relations; (3) family dynamics; (4) cross-cultural differences; (5) language issues; (6) nostalgic memories; (7) education; and (8) acclimation. This section will discuss each of the above themes or concepts. Themes one through six describe the participants' acculturation challenges, and themes seven and eight pertain to their acculturation dreams or expectations. All the participants' names used in this section and throughout the chapter are pseudonyms. Participants' quotes are used as they appeared in the transcribed data from interviews that were conducted in English. The researcher translated the quotations from the Kirundi and French data.

Professional Integration

The participants' apparent difficulty in obtaining adequate employment that matches their education and qualifications was a major source of disappointment and frustration. As the quotes below demonstrate, participants felt that there is no equity in employment since refugees are always given low-paying, manual labor jobs as soon as they arrive in the United States. They expressed a serious concern about their degrees from their countries of origin not being accepted or validated in the United States.

Bertha, who came to the U.S with an engineering degree and many years of experience as a professional educator, and who chose to do her interview in

English, stated, "I have noticed that . . . labor work is mostly . . . available, mostly offered to refugees . . . however, those who have careers . . . those who brought their own . . . diplomas, they are having trouble to find job which is suitable and they are called to work in hotels . . . to be dishwashers . . . they are taking any job, mostly labor, manual job. It was really hard for most of us to get something that, you know, can really fit with what we deserve because we are calling ourselves intellectual, and educated . . . but . . . it seems like . . . in the United States, it is not easy to have your own degree be accepted . . ."

Boniface, who worked as high school principal in his native country hinted in his own English words at the inequity in employment opportunity and elaborated on the challenge and frustration caused by the lack of inadequate professional integration, ". . . America is a great country . . . with opportunities, but these opportunities . . . are not dispatched as it should be . . . to me it was like just refugees . . . were assigned those jobs [minimum wage jobs] . . . this is a little bit frustrating . . . the principal of a high school he come to load and unload the truck . . . I was working for example 8 hours, waking up at 4 o'clock and going back home at 6–7 pm very tired and when you are waking up to go to work we were feeling you didn't have the trust to go . . . you were feeling scared of what is gonna happen the next day . . . this is the really bad experience I have in this country, beside you also could feel a kind of not discrimination but when people look at you and they think even that minimum salary job you have you don't know how to perform it." He added that when they are resettled in the United Sates, refugees expect to obtain the same kind of professional opportunities they had in their home countries, but that instead, they are forced to rebuild their lives from scratch.

Jerry explained in his own English words that even though the resettlement agencies provide assistance in finding employment, they do not care about the quality of the job that refugees get, "They can find anything for you . . . just to work. If you gonna work for $2.00, they don't care about that $2.00, they don't care how you are gonna do this for $2.00 . . . they don't care about that. So the important for them is just to find you anything to work . . ."

Angela believed that refugees are given jobs that other people do not want. In a comment translated from Kirundi she stated, "Concerning employment, it seems like the agencies help you find work, but often I think that they get you impossible jobs that people don't like to do; those are the jobs they find for refugees, for new comers to America." Most refugees share this difficult experience, regardless of their educational background, as Connie explained in her translated statement, ". . . whenever we receive those jobs, we work for the least wage possible, very low rates because they don't recognize our degrees here. This is a problem because you come here as a doctor, or with a Bachelor's degree, you start working in hotels, day care, where you work for $7.00 per hour, you work for $6.00, so they don't even give you the highest rate they have . . ." The participants complained that they are not given credit for their prior employment experiences. As Louis concluded, "They multiply your prior work experience with zero."

Social Relations

Most of the participants felt isolated within their community in the United States. Relating his experiences from his country of origin, Todd, who mixed French and Kirundi in his interview explained, "Where I lived, people are more sociable, sharing in the festivities, in the get-togethers, we feel like close friends. Families are very close, which makes it easy to resolve a number of problems." Louis expressed the same concern, "Ever since I started working, I worked in the field of agricultural research. The job was very nice, working five days a week. On my days off I went to visit with friends . . . what I miss the most is our custom . . . visiting with one another, visiting with anybody and feeling at home, even without having to prearrange the visit. There are even friends who tell you, "that is your room," and they tell you that if you arrive when they are not home, you can just go to the nearby convenience store, give their name so that the store owner can give you a drink (take care of you)."

Connie commented that she has felt a kind of racial kinship among Blacks-particularly Black African immigrants, but that she ambivalent about the attitudes of some people of other races. She said, "Blacks are very nice . . . when they meet outside more than when they meet in Africa . . . When you see a Black person, even when he doesn't know you, he greets you, even if he is far from you . . . He just notices that you have the same skin color, and greets you . . . He may not stop to have a conversation because everyone is busy, but you notice that he is happy to see you . . . in any case I feel a certain attraction, you feel that you come from the same place, and he sees that you have the same origin, you have something in common . . . But other people like Whites, Mexicans, and others . . . everybody is different. Some of them exchange greetings when you meet them, and others won't talk to you . . . But when I greet you and you do not respond, I feel shocked . . . I wonder what you think of me . . ."

Angela elaborated on the issue of social isolation in an articulate Kirundi statement, ". . . in our native country we are used to visiting with one another, but here . . . its is different because some people tell you that they have a sister or brother that they haven't seen for five years . . . and this is confusing . . . but on the other hand sometimes I understand because it is very difficult to live in this country . . . everybody works all the time because there are so many expenses to cover . . . but this is not how we live . . . you feel like you have done something wrong when you don't see somebody . . . we are used to visiting with one another and exchanging gifts regularly . . . and this feel really good . . ."

Social isolation causes culture shock for Boniface, who expected a warmer welcome upon his arrival in the United States. He shared in his own English words, ". . . that was a kind of expectation behind when we arrived. We thought it was a shock actually. We thought that . . . people we were going to meet were people who care. But actually, if you are not lucky, you will never meet with the person who cares . . . they really do care in such a way that they are sometimes . . . good work mates, good colleagues; they can help you in whatever you want at work, but you will never have a chance to sit down, socialize; there is no time . . . for nobody actually . . . if you have the chance that they ask you where you are from . . . that is the end . . . it looks like everybody is for himself [or] for herself . . . They don't show you that they really don't have time for you, but you cannot feel this warmth you have . . . we used to [have] over there in Africa . . ."

Family Dynamics

Several participants shared their concern about the changes in family dynamics brought about by life in the United States. Boniface explained, "The . . . challenge is in general in . . . everybody's family . . . It can happen among ourselves, parents themselves; it can be between parents and children because the system our children are growing in is kind of, I am sorry to say that, a non-value system because this country is loosing the family values we work on in Africa . . ." Jerry attributed his failed marriage to this changing family dynamics, which he believes empowers women beyond what he was accustomed to in his home country. He shared, ". . . I have three years in the country . . . I came with wife . . . When we just came in, you know America freedom, she said 'I don't need you no more'. Then, we decided to divorce."

English language acquisition is one of the main factors that negatively impact refugee family dynamics as Bertha explained, "First of all, language remains an issue. It is an important issue, because of its consequences . . . many consequences for not knowing the language. Parents have serious issues about how to communicate with their children concerning their upbringing. This is the first issue. Children's upbringing because once they arrive here, children acquire the language fast before their parents do, and then they adopt local [American] behaviors that they observe among native [American] children. They no longer listen to their parents, and they respond to them in English; they want to show that children are smarter than the parents, because they want to show that they understand legal issues better than the parents. When parents advise children not to go out without telling them or not dress in sagging pants that expose their body, children respond that they are free to do whatever they want. This causes parents who are quick to anger to slap the children. Then the children scream and call the police . . . this causes hatred between parents and children . . . Parents become confused because in their home land, parents are responsible for their children's upbringing, yet here [in the United States] it seems like the government assumes more responsibility towards the children."

Louis expanded on this issues in very concerned terms: "Problems with children [constitute a major challenge]. Children change when they arrive here. The way people tell them that here [in the United States] no one will ever again tell them what to do nor correct them; that parents have no right to punish their children . . . not even the right to pinch erring children nor to 'give them the look'." He added that he mainly talked about the problems with the children because they are the primary reason why parents chose to live in exile. He stated, "The reason why I chose to expound on the children's issues is because we choose to become refugees 80% of the time in order for our children to have a good future. We didn't come [to the U.S.] in order to obtain cars or houses, or to live in a place that has electricity. We came to make it possible for our children to live a good life." Connie reflected on similar family misunderstandings and summarized her thoughts about the changing family dynamics in a powerful Kirundi proverb "Amerika yokuvyarira ntiyokurerera" (It would be better to have America give birth to your children, but not raise them for you).

Cross-Cultural Differences

Todd summarized what it takes to adjust to a new culture and new ways of life in terms that translate into careful observation as well as conscious effort and strategies to acculturate. He explained, "We want to learn their customs, to take them as they are without laughing at them because in the end we have to behave like them in order to be allowed to live with them in their society-easily. This requires intelligence, looking without looking, talking without talking, without pointing fingers." Cross-cultural differences often cause misunderstandings as Heri noted, ". . . I don't have any problem about my work, but [the] problem I have is misunderstanding each other because I . . . work with different people. So, it is [a] different culture sometimes . . ."

Cross-cultural differences also often result in different communication styles, which can be a challenge for new comers in U.S. society. Angela explained this problem very clearly by stating, ". . . it is difficult for us who come from other countries because we have a way of showing respect for other people . . . you can't maintain eye contact with a person who is older than you . . . you have to get close to the person, looking down, in order to greet him . . . but in this country, they think that you have no manners [when you act like that]. They expect you to be boisterous in order to be heard . . ." She added that due to cross-cultural differences, children's plays are often misinterpreted. She noted, ". . . there are often problems with children playing. Because in our home country, we are accustomed to run as we play; children run, chat, hug each other, push each other; this is how we play where we come from . . . but it doesn't mean that they hate each other; but in this country . . . when you touch a child, they say that you have hit them . . . that you are a bad person . . . Even in school, when a child falls down when another child pushes him, they send a letter saying that your child was involved in a fight . . . even if this did not happen on purpose . . . so you see, cultural issues are difficult."

Veronique finds American different cultural practices isolating, She said, "Africans are really sociable; they get together, they help one another a lot. They are warm people. It's difficult to communicate with people who have different customs here. In this country, you can spend a long time without anyone visiting you-other than on the telephone . . ."

Dress style is another cross-cultural factor that can cause culture shock as Connie explained, "Another thing that has shocked me is the way people dress . . . when you look at the way an African woman dresses . . . and then you look at the way people here dress . . . especially in warm weather . . . they walk around almost naked . . . this really shocked me and still shocks me . . . to this day I don't understand . . . I would say that their body has no secret parts that they should hide . . . they expose [their body] . . . but we are not accustomed to this and I think that I will never get used to this." She also mentioned that the styles of greetings are different because Americans do not often shake hands even when they haven't seen each other for a long time.

Sometimes, these differences surface in the form of misinformed questions about Africa and the Africans as in Louis's example: "In this country, when people hear that you have an accent, they ask you 'where are you from.' You tell them 'Africa.' And then they ask you 'which part.' And you tell them. And then they ask you whether you lived with animals, 'snakes,' and they ask you how many lions you killed."

Language Issues

English language acquisition was seen by all participants to be key to successful acculturation. Referring to English as the "machine of communication," Boniface stated, "...Language is a barrier. We know English is a second language for us, but it looks like you are not given an opportunity to...I mean enough time to improve this machine of communication which would help us in the situation of jobs so that we can do better." English language acquisition is especially an issue for parents who did not have strong prior educational background because it causes family conflicts, as Angela explained, "Often children go to school to learn English...when they ask parents questions, they don't understand each other, and this is difficult because parents cannot communicate with them. Often children forget our language, and this causes a lot of problems due to misunderstandings between parents and children...This can drive parents to despair..."

Limited English language proficiency is an obstacle to successful employment. Bertha clarified, "...because of language problems, many of us...have difficulty maintaining our jobs...Many people loose their jobs because of language problems, and they remain unemployed for years...It's like the government brings us here without having planned enough on how we will survive...often those who have no educational background or who are moderately educated have serious problems with the language, and it takes them a long time to secure employment because being unable to make themselves understood remains a problem."

Jacques elaborated on this issue, "In reality, work is not easy...language difficulties are obvious because...we are not used to English, and here, you are nothing if you do not speak English; you are not worth anything when you don't speak English...English is a major handicap..." He added that even those who came to the United States with some knowledge of English have difficulties saying, "...When I had just arrived, before I started working, I used to think that I knew English. But when I started working, I realized that I was zero. When I arrived somewhere and repeated a word twice or three times without making myself understood, though I understood what was being said...I was deeply hurt." Todd expressed similar concerns, "...it is difficult to secure employment because of the language-communication-not knowing how to express oneself- not knowing how to explain what you know..."

Nostalgic Memories

The participants' comments revealed some degree of emotional attachment to their native land and a strong longing for the lifestyle they left behind. Bertha missed the interdependent aspect of African living the most, and shared in very nostalgic terms: "Life in Africa was easy...people live together socially...especially when you are working, you don't have to worry about day care when you have children, or who is gonna clean my house, how am I gonna handle cooking...or doing any other kind of house work . . . [This] was not a problem in Africa because family members and extended family members are very united and rely on each other. If you have a child, the child belongs to society; the child belongs to your family. And what you do is to take him or . . . her directly to your family member who is around, and the one who helps you today is gonna also have something to ask you . . . tomorrow . . . so it is like . . . helping . . . one another, and that system works very well and this reduces stress."

Bertha also missed the communal nature of African living, which encourages the sharing of resources as she explained, ". . . I really miss . . . the way of living in a family structure where . . . you depend on one another . . . where you share a lot. People in the village . . . grow rice, they grow beans, they grow potatoes and bananas, and you don't have to worry about . . . how much money . . . you need . . . for food. Family members will bring you food, or you go for the weekend, you pick up whatever you need, and that's all . . . The salary you have even if it is small, it is gonna be enough because you share the food [which is grown in the countryside]. So, that was really a good life."

Boniface longed for the relaxed nature of African living. He commented with a nostalgic laughter: ". . . In Africa . . . you had time to go say hello to a neighbor . . . We had time to sit down, time to rest, time to eat, time to do personal things that are not related to your job; this is really what I miss the most . . . We had time to see friends, to speak to friends . . . we had time for our family . . . time to waste actually . . ." He reiterated the fact that taking care of children was much easier in Africa: "I will give you an example of our children. When I wake up in the morning to go to work, I really worry . . . about this little guy, how I have to wake him up, to take him out in the rain, or . . . when it is freezing, taking him to . . . day care . . . This wasn't a problem in Africa because the child was for everybody; everybody's child was like a prince and everybody was running . . . to help . . ."

Heri missed family, friends, and the much simpler life he lived in Africa. He shared, ". . . I miss my family, I miss friends . . . We have easy life because we don't have a lot of things . . . like good house, new car . . . So whatever job you have, you can live; you don't have any job, you can live; and then you have peace in your mind . . . So over here is different . . . you need new car, you need new house . . . so you have to work hard . . . If you don't have any job, your life is gonna going down, you gonna be a homeless . . ." Jerry also felt the pain of being separated form his family. He laments, "I miss family because none [is] with me now; [I'm] just by myself right here in this country, so [it is] becoming hard to [for] me . . . I don't have any kind of family . . . it is very hard [for] somebody to live without his family . . ."

Angela finds American life tiring because it does not offer opportunities for assistance like was available in Africa. She shared, ". . . Things have changed a lot . . . because where we come from, we worked, but we had somebody to help us with house work . . . so even when you were tired, you didn't have to worry about house work, laundry . . . life was easier then . . . you still had to pay the person who helped you, but he didn't get tired either because you helped each other . . . But now it is very difficult . . . You come home from work and instead of taking a shower and resting, I have to cook . . . instead of resting, you have to continue working . . . so you see, my previous life was very easy, it is not the same as here [in the United States]."

Life was really good in Africa, the only thing that was missing was peace, Connie asserted with pride: ". . . Looking at the way we lived in Africa, the good life we had, the only thing we didn't have was peace; but when we arrive here [in the United States], because you have to work night and day, you break yourself trying to make a living and to support those that you left behind . . . "

Jacques, too, longed for the comfortable life he had in Africa. He explained, ". . . Life was very good . . . because we were in the equivalent of 'middle class' . . . we were really in the middle class . . . well, you worked and went home and got paid every month . . . you could build a house . . . we had built a beautiful house of a nice size . . . actually if the house had wheels so that we could bring it over here, we would be very comfortable . . . We didn't have to worry about high rent or think about mortgages that you have to spend thirty years paying . . . We paid off our house in three or four years . . . a five-bedroom house . . . we were really comfortable and life was really very good . . . we had no problems . . . we had friends, of course before things got messed up [referring to Burundi's political turmoil that forced the participants to live in exile] . . . You had time to rest and to take care of family matters . . . not like here where we are constantly running . . . life was really good . . . we had everything we needed . . . Of course if you compare [to the U.S.], our countries are poor, but they have the essentials . . ."

Jacques also misses the socializing that the flexible environment offers in Africa. He stated, ". . . The thing I miss the most, I miss the way we had time to sit down, to chat with family members, to exchange stories, to hang out, like on Sundays . . . but here there is no such time. Whenever I get a little time here, it is to rest my body so that I have enough energy to wake up early and go back to work . . . But over there, I could sit down, chat with friends, listen to their problems and try to assist them, like giving them advice . . . you had time to take care of more than just yourself . . ."

Connie nostalgically recalled the joyous celebrations that brought family and friends together in Africa: ". . . When I remember the way we celebrated Christmas or New Year's Day, we would gather the entire village together . . . we would cook lots of food, people would gather up and sing and dance . . . But here, where will we gather? Where will we hold the celebrations? Really, the difference is enormous . . . Here you may remember that it is Christmas day because you have to, but when we remember the way we celebrated it back home, the way you went to church, and met up with friends after church, stopping by each other's house one after another, we cannot do this here . . . there is no time, that is the problem." She drew a very perceptive conclusion, "I really feel that the only thing that makes them [Americans] better off than we are is that they have peace . . . If we had peace, our country [Burundi] would really be a land of milk and honey; no one would wish to live in exile if we had peace."

Education

The participants understand the importance and value of acquiring a good education, as a condition of social mobility in the United States. Most of their dreams and expectations for themselves and for their children hinge on education. Bertha shared, "I am dreaming for a better education, so I can provide for my family, I can have a better salary, where I don't have to worry about mortgage . . . if the mortgage is gonna be paid this month or not; and the dreams are also for our children to have a better education as well, to take advantage of the opportunities and peace that we have here in the United States, to learn and grow . . . So we wish there was a program to support refugees to go to school and pay their schooling . . ."

Boniface reiterated the need for a good education: ". . . education comes first because without education you cannot . . . expect to go anywhere or to do any big steps because I want to make big steps . . . so I [would like] to have the opportunity to fulfill my education and from there, I will make sure my children go further more than I did myself. I want them to be really educated. I want them to feel proud of themselves, so this will be a goal filled when I see them in college, at university, big in those big universities of America . . . So my goals, my expectations, and my dreams is to educate my children, to help them to be educated more than ourselves . . ."

The participants do not only believe that refugee resettlement agencies should provide them with the necessary assistance to get an education, but they expect it. Yvonne stated with insistence: "The first thing I would like to have, since I was not born here and I don't know English, the first thing I want is for those who brought me over here to send me to school because I don't have any way of paying for a college education myself; I don't have the means to pay for day care for my child and college. I need to go to school . . . because I can't live here in America If I don't know the language, if I can't read a book, if I can't fill out a check . . . I wouldn't be able to do anything. I am asking those who brought me over here to help me get an education . . . and to help me learn about American customs . . ." Yvonne also wants the American government to assist refugees in getting a good education. She specified, "I am asking the government to help us refugees learn local [American] customs ... and go to school for a long time to learn about their laws and customs ..."

Angela expected her resettlement into the United States to be an almost guaranteed opportunity to further her education. She explained with some disappointment that she would like the U.S. government to assist refugees to achieve their educational dreams. She shared, "... We thought that once we arrived here we would study in order to obtain well-paying jobs ... I wish I could go to school and get an education so that I can get a good job that pays well ... so that I can save money for my children's education ... I want my children to be well educated and live a better life so that they don't have to work as hard as we have had to ... Education is very expensive ... it is difficult to go to school, raise a family, and work, all at the same time ... That is why we pray for opportunities to go to school first ... if the [U.S.] government would help pay for the necessary tuition for the kind of education we want ... even if we would need to pay back the money ... The top priority for me is to get an education ... Getting the kind of education I want would help me a lot ..."

Jacques explained that it is impossible to become a part of the middle class without a good education: "We are educated, but we must continue to seek further educational opportunities ... in order to build a better future for our children and ourselves because nothing is possible without education ... everything comes through education ..."

Acclimation

The participants feel that they would have been better prepared for their lives and experiences in the United States if they had been allowed more time to adjust to their new environment before beginning to work. They feel that for the most part, they were rushed into the employment scene and into independence without an adequate understanding of U.S. society and available opportunities. Bertha explained, "... We whish there was a system ... to help refugee ... where refugees can use their own ... degree or where they can be accepted with some kind of training before they start job ... a system which could integrate the refugees who have careers ... to continue their dreams ..."

Louis explained that refugees should be allowed more time to recover emotionally and physically upon their arrival in the United States. He clarified, "You see, when refugees arrive, they are emotionally exhausted ... [tired] of everything ... but they are forced to seek employment without having rested. It would be better to give them some time to rest and to recover; then they would teach them [refugees] about life in the United States. You would ask them to help you find employment or school to get an education once you are emotionally well rested."

Heri, who wished for training in money management, also would have liked more information on living in the United States. He stated with insistence: ". . . The first thing I can ask . . . teach me to know how can I live in this country . . . [this is] the only thing I need in my life because until now, I don't know what is going on. Yeah, the only thing I need only."

Jerry reiterated the need for better preparation saying, ". . . They bring new people from there to here . . . I think there is something they have to teach them before [sending] them to work or . . . school because . . . some people . . . don't know what they are doing . . . [something] much better [than] what they did at IRC [International Rescue Committee] or Catholic Social Services. You just sit down like five to fifteen minutes; they teach you if you got emergency call 911, if you got this, do this. I think it is not enough because we still need some help; this is a new culture."

The lack of adequate preparation has severe consequences as Jerry went on to explain: ". . . I believe there is a lot of people [who are] in jail because they are doing something they don't know. Why they are doing that they don't know the reason because they don't teach them . . . the second thing, . . . when we teach somebody, we have to teach [him] in his best language, the one we understand because when we went to the bank to open the account, they just tell you . . . 'you wanna open an account just sign here'. You don't know all the papers [or] what they say [because] you are still new. 'Sign here' and you sign; you don't know what you sign for. So, I think it is better they change all this too. Everybody . . . before [they] sign [or] do anything, they can just understand what they sign for because later it [becomes] hard, it [becomes] a problem . . ."

Angela explained how her family was rushed into survival in an unfamiliar environment as they had to report to their resettlement agency for their first appointment on their second or third day in the country: ". . . It was very hard for us to wake up very early in the morning while we were still tired from the flight and before we became used to our surroundings . . . we had to get the children and ourselves ready early in the morning . . . and we had to catch a bus, but we did not yet know the bus schedule . . . one day we missed the bus . . . therefore, we had to walk with the children in the cold to another bus stop that was farther . . . it was very hard . . . we had sweaters, but they were not weather appropriate because it was very cold . . ."

Angela would have liked to have more time to adjust and identify employment opportunities of interest instead of being rushed into jobs they don't want. She stated, ". . . First, they should give newly arrived refugees time to rest and develop a clear mind . . . They should not rush us into employment without giving us a choice . . . Second, the American government should monitor refugee assistance across all the states in order to grant similar benefits to all refugees and to support them for a longer period of time because they [the U.S. government] bring them over here in order to help them, so they [refugees] are among those who qualify for government assistance . . ." Overall, as Bertha explained, the participants expected more assistance from the U.S. government than they actually received. She stated, ". . . Quite often, refugees expect to receive more things, for the most part because they know America has everything. So, when they arrive here, and realize that they have spent six months without adequate employment, it becomes a problem . . . They expect more, but resettlement agencies are responsible for many refugees. So what they do is to help them with housing and food and then help them find the first available jobs, cleaning hotels, working in restaurants, the lowest possible manual jobs."

Connie made a recommendation that would help with the acclimation of refugees. She suggested hiring a bilingual teacher for the community. She stated, ". . . looking at our community, for instance, it is not a small community . . . if they could give us a teacher who is bilingual in English, French . . . and Kirundi . . . He would teach the community because when you really want the people you teach to succeed, you explain things in a language that they understand . . . in their own Kirundi language, and teach them English as well. It may take some time for them to learn, but they will be more successful than they have been attending classes with people with whom they do not share the language. So, it would be nice if the government could accept to hire and pay such a teacher who would be in charge of teaching the adults . . . a teacher who understands their language, their needs, and what motivates them . . . this same teacher would also coordinate after school activities for the children . . ."

DISCUSSION

Five focus questions were asked in order to examine the acculturation dreams and challenges of Burundi refugees in the United States: (1) How do Burundi refugees describe their experiences with employment in the U.S.? (2) How do they describe their experiences with social services in the U.S.? (3) How do they negotiate the traits of their cultural identity in their social interactions within the American multicultural society? (4) In what ways do previous life experiences in Burundi and transitional host countries influence their adjustment process? (5) What expectations do they have for themselves and their families? This section will address each one of these questions in the light of the above findings.

The participants were very vocal in expressing their frustration with a system that welcomes them into the country, and yet fails to offer opportunities for professional integration. They recognized the fact that refugees' access to quality, well paying jobs is limited, which led them to suspect that the system may be discriminatory against refugees, particularly those of African descent.

They were aware of the importance of acquiring a good education, yet painfully realized that with their work and family responsibilities, getting an education was a dream out of their reach. They questioned the intentions of a system that rushes them into low- level manual labor and thus limits their chances to further their education and to acclimate to their new social and economic environment.

While the participants recognized and appreciated the efforts of the resettlement agencies to assist refugees meet their basic needs of food and shelter and to find employment, they felt like this support was short lived and was in some ways inadequate. They expressed the need for more time and opportunities to learn and understand how the American system works in order to function more effectively. They stressed the importance of allowing refugees enough time to recover from their emotional traumas before requiring them to enter the job market.

The participants related some conflicts resulting from cross-cultural misunderstandings and miscommunication. They felt that many people in the United States have a negative image of Africa and the Africans, and that these attitudes impacted the refugees' relationships with Americans, especially White Americans. They felt isolated within their American neighborhoods as if no one cared about them or their well-being.

They were concerned about the negative influences of American culture on their children. They felt that the children tended to lose their Burundian values as they learned the English language faster than the parents and began to socialize with children who were born or had lived longer in the United States.

They questioned the effects of the involvement of law enforcement officers in family conflicts, especially when they intervene to resolve disagreements between parents and their children. They believed that this practice is more destructive to the family unit as it does not encourage the type of communication and respect that form the foundation of a good Burundian family.

The participants had been resettled into the U.S. from different countries in Africa, but they all identified themselves as Burundian. The interviews related an almost overwhelming sense of nostalgia for the Burundian way of life that they had left behind. They did not talk about their war-related experiences, except when they mentioned in passing that the only thing Burundi was missing was peace.

It could be argued that their nostalgic dispositions impact their adjustment process in the U.S., as they tend to long more for what they left behind than for the opportunities that lie ahead. They portrayed their previous life in Burundi as the best that can ever be. They miss the social aspect of Burundi living. They miss the relaxed working environment that allowed plenty of time for rest, family, and friends. They miss the cultural celebrations that gathered people together without any concern for time. They miss the simplicity of Burundian living.

The study findings showed that Burundi refugees are very ambitious and hard working people. They are well aware of what it will take for them and their children to succeed in American society. They hold very high expectations of themselves and their families. They expressed dreams of building a strong educational basis, academically and socially. They want to work their way up into the U.S. middle class. They want their children to get as much education as possible.

The participants recognize that they cannot achieve their dreams on their own. They call on the U.S. government to assist them by facilitating their professional integration and by helping them achieve their educational goals. They want to live the American dream.

CONCLUSIONS AND RECOMMENDATIONS

Africans, like all other immigrants, experience a number of acculturation challenges as they encounter and are exposed to the traditions, values, norms, interactions and communication styles of the dominant society. Consequently, acculturation becomes a complex and challenging process for all immigrants in general, and refugees and other immigrants of African origin, in particular because they have to deal with additional societal forces that have traditionally disadvantaged people of color in the United States.

Welcoming immigrants in general, and refugees in particular, into the United States implies the assumption of federal, state, and local responsibilities to formulate and enact policies that give the new comers a fair chance to pursue and achieve the American dream. Shore (2002) identifies seven building blocks of the American Dream: economic security, food security, health care, early care and education, housing, transportation, as well as time and energy. In as much as most immigrant families have to rebuild their lives from scratch both socially and economically, education becomes the main route to success across generations. Becoming successful within the American system is dependent upon becoming familiar with the laws, cultural norms and values, as well as expectations that regulate the American way of life. Therefore, facilitating the educational and professional integration of Burundi refugees and of all other immigrants benefits their families, community, and the nation.

The following eight recommendations should be considered in order to facilitate the acculturation process of Burundi refugees and other immigrants in the United

States. First, policy makers and refugee resettlement agencies should work together to design policies and programs that motivate and empower refugee families and their children to seek and pursue solid educational opportunities that will help them better their lives in their new country. The absence of such efforts limits refugee families' and their children's mobility within the American competitive socio-economic landscape.

Second, special programs should be established to facilitate the accelerated professional integration of African refugees in order to minimize the sense of loss in occupational and social status that results from being forced to become menial workers due to the absence of an effective academic degree equivalency system. Third, refugees cannot be expected to function effectively within an unknown legal, social, and economic system. Therefore, sustainable acclimation programs should be developed and implemented in order to familiarize the refugees with their adoptive country's norms and expectations for success.

Fourth, cross-cultural programs and activities should be organized to allow local communities plenty of opportunities to interact with refugee communities and other new comers, thus fostering mutual respect and understanding. Cultural festivals, neighborhood barbeques, block parties, town hall meetings, joint holiday celebrations, are only a few examples. Fifth, existing refugee assistance programs should be expanded for longer periods of time, depending on the needs of individual refugee families because they do not acculturate equally at the same pace.

Sixth, language must be recognized as a major acculturation tool. Therefore, refugee families should be immersed in a three- to six- month intensive English language program in order to develop comfortable proficiency in the language before being required to work to support themselves and their families. Seventh, a special scholarship fund should be established to facilitate access to higher education for children from refugee families, particularly African refugees, in order to help them break the cycle of poverty that is often created by the social and economic hardships that are prevalent among first generation refugee families. Any individual's intergenerational mobility is impacted by the amount of opportunity available in society, and access to higher education represents an important vehicle for expanding the opportunity to move up the social and economic ladder (McMurrer et al., 1997).

The shift in family dynamics constituted a serious concern for the study participants. The magnitude of this issue can only be understood when placed within the African cultural context that regulates the relationships between husband and wife and between parents and children. These relationships are characterized by ultimate loyalty and respect. The eighth recommendation, therefore, would be to involve refugee families in joint communication activities or workshops that would empower them to acculturate in a way that will sustain their family units.

Family cohesion is a prime indicator of success in Burundi culture and most African cultures. Expecting Burundi and other African refugee families to prosper socially and economically within the American macro-culture without assuring them the tools they need to navigate the new system and sustain their family units is leading them through uncertain paths to the American Dream.

ACKNOWLEDGMENTS

This work was supported in full or in part by a grant from the University of Nevada Junior Faculty Research Grant Fund. This support does not necessarily imply endorsement by the University of the research conclusions.

REFERENCES

Arthur, J. A. (2000). *Invisible sojourners: African immigrant diaspora in the United States.*Wesport, Connecticut: Praeger.

Creswell. J. W. (1998). *Qualitative inquiry and research design: Choosing among five traditions.* Thousand Oaks: Sage.

Glesne, C. (1999). *Becoming qualitative researchers: An introduction* (2nd ed.). New York: Longman.

Haines, D. W. (Ed.) (1985). *Refugees in the United States: A reference book.* Westport, Connecticut: Greenwood Press.

Kent, D. P. (1953). *The refugee intellectual: The Americanization of the immigrants of 1933–1941.* New York: Columbia University Press.

Mabuwa, R. (2000). *Seeking protection: Addressing sexual and domestic violence in Tanzania's refugee camps.* New York: Human Rights Watch.

Malkki, L. (1995). *Purity and exile: Violence, memory, and national cosmology among Hutu refugees in Tanzania.* Chicago: University of Chicago Press.

Marshall, C., & Rossman, G. B. (1999). *Designing qualitative research* (3rd ed.). Thousand Oaks: Sage.

McMurrer, D. P., Condon, M., & Sawhill, I. V. (1997). Intergenerational mobility in the United States. Urban institute. Retrieved April 22, 2004, from http://www.urban.org/url.cfm?ID=406796.

Sommers, M. (1998). *A child's nightmare: Burundian children at risk. A field report assessing the protection and assistance needs of Burundian children and adolescents.* Womens Commission for Refugee Women and Children. Retrieved January 14, 2002, from http://www.theIRC.org/wcrwc/reports/wc_burundi.html.

Stake, R. E. (2000). Case studies. In: N. K. Denzin & Y. S. Lincoln (Eds), *Handbook of Qualitative Research* (2nd ed., pp. 435–454). Thousand Oaks: Sage.

Strauss, A., & Corbin, J. (1998). *Basics of qualitative research: Techniques and procedures for developing grounded theory* (2nd ed.). Thousand Oaks: Sage.

Suárez-Orozco, M. M. (1989). *Central American refugees and U.S. schools: A psychosocial study of motivation and achievement.* Stanford: Stanford University Press.

Suárez-Orozco, C., & Suárez-Orozco, M. M. (2001). *Children of immigration.* Cambridge, Massachusetts: Harvard University Press.

United Nations High Commissioner for Refugees (2000, July). *Refugees and others of concern to UNHCR: 1999 statistical overview*. Geneva: Author. Retrieved January 14, 2002 from http:/www.unhcr.ch.

U.S. Committee for Refugees (2001). *World refugee survey major findings*. Author, 2001. Retrieved January 14, 2002, from http://www.refugees.org.

U.S. Committee for Refugees (2002). *World refugee survey 2002*. Author, 2002. Retrieved January 8, 2003, from http://www.refugees.org.

Vásquez-Montilla, E., Reyes-Blanes, M. E., Hyun, E., & Brovelli, E. (2000). Practices for culturally responsive interviews and research with Hispanic families. *Multicultural Perspective*, *2*(3), 3–7.

Wolcott, H. F. (1994). Posturing in qualitative research. In: M. D. LeCompte, W. L. Millroy & J. Preissle (Eds), *The Handbook of Qualitative Research in Education* (pp. 3–52). San Diego: Academic Press.

Yin, R. K. (1994). *Case study research: Design and methods* (2nd ed.). Thousand Oaks: Sage.

6. THE LOSS OF IDENTITY AND THE UNDERUTILIZATION OF BLACK CHILDREN'S EDUCATIONAL POTENTIAL: RETHINKING ASSIMILATION GLOBALLY

Kassie Freeman

INTRODUCTION

In order for Black children to assimilate into the dominant culture in different countries, historically, their cultural values have been minimized or, in some cases, attempts have been made to altogether separate them from their cultural group. This process of cultural assimilation or alienation has had a devastating effect on Black children's educational opportunities around the globe, particularly as it relates to the loss of their identity and to the underutilization of their human potential. This chapter provides an overview of the similarities of the historical experiences of Black populations globally that have led to the assimilation process of Black children where the majority population is non-Black (e.g. Australia, Great Britain, and the U.S.A.) and discusses how Black children's loss of identity has led to the underutilization of their potential. The chapter concludes with the necessity of rethinking the assimilation paradigm as one way to impact on the poverty of Black populations.

'Suffer the Little Children': National and International Dimensions of Child
Poverty and Public Policy
Advances in Education in Diverse Communities: Research, Policy and Praxis, Volume 4, 121–144
Copyright © 2006 by Elsevier Ltd.
All rights of reproduction in any form reserved
ISSN: 1479-358X/doi:10.1016/S1479-358X(04)04006-9

In this chapter, Black populations are defined using the racial designation. That is, the physical characteristics that identify Blacks, e.g. color, hair, and/or other distinguishing physical features that define races. Although more recently ethnicity has been used to define groups' identity and experiences in educational research, I use race because in comparative and international research race more accurately describes the similarity of Black experiences.

DIFFERENT COUNTRIES, SIMILAR HISTORICAL EXPERIENCES

Understanding the historical experiences of any group of people is tremendously important for understanding the formation and/or loss of their identity. As James Anderson has so rightly indicated in numerous writings and speeches (e.g. 1988 and 1999), to understand the educational experiences of Blacks, it is necessary to examine the historical context of their existence. Although, as Lorde (1992) indicated, Blacks in different countries have experienced particular histories. Blacks across societies have had similar experiences relative to their humanity and their pursuit of education. The common historical linkage among Blacks in the Diaspora is captured by Opitz et al. (1992) who wrote in reference to Afro-Germans: "In the course of colonial exploitation, enslavement, and domination, 'Negro' (from Latin niger, i.e. black) became an especially negative epithet. The thinking underlying this label attempted to link physical characteristics with intellectual and cultural ones" (p. 7). Across cultures, being Black has historically been thought of as being intellectually inferior and being without a culture or having a primitive or uncivilized culture.

While often not recognized, Blacks have been a part of European societies longer, in most cases, than in America. For example, Fryer (1992), who wrote what would be considered the seminal work on Blacks in Britain, indicated that African descendants have been in Britain for centuries; as a group, they "have been living in Britain for close on 500 years. They have been born in Britain since about the year 1505" (p. ix). That would mean that, based on American history, Black Britons as a group were in England more than one hundred years before the arrival of Blacks in America in Jamestown, Virginia, in 1619 (Clarke, 1972). While Opitz, Oguntoye and Schultz (1992) indicated that "there is no precise method of determining when the first Africans came to Germany and when the first Afro-Germans were born," they indicated that "several paintings have survived from the twelfth century that depict Africans living in Germany" (p. 3). Although the exact arrival of Blacks across cultures may be unclear, what is certain is that by the mid-sixteenth and seventeenth centuries, Blacks were settled in countries around the globe. For example, "in the mid-sixteenth century, one-tenth of the population in the Portuguese capital were Black, and, as in France and England, it was probably also true in Germany" (Opitz et al., 1992, p. 3).

Blacks in different countries faced similar treatment in the portrayal of their culture. Blackness was associated with evilness, inferiority in every way, and sub-humanism. In Britain, for example, "Africans were said to be inherently inferior, mentally, morally, culturally, and spiritually, to Europeans" (Fryer, 1992, p. 7). Likewise, in Germany, Blacks were portrayed negatively. In general, "Africans were seen as the lowest human form, thought to be related to the highest animal form, the monkey" (Opitz et al., 1992, p. 8). At that time, "most Portuguese seem to have thought that blacks as a people were innately inferior to whites in physical beauty and mental ability and moreover, that they were temperamentally suited to a life in slavery" (Saunders, 1982, p. 166). Although on a different continent, Blacks in the U.S. were experiencing the same devaluation of their humanity. In the U.S., this statement about the use of Slave Codes best captures how Blacks were viewed: "There were variations from state to state, but the general point of view expressed in most of them [Slave Codes] was the same, that is: slaves are not persons but property, and laws should protect the ownership of such property, and should also protect the whites against any dangers that might arise from the presence of large numbers of Negroes" (Franklin & Moss, 1988, p. 114). This devaluation of the Black culture caused, according to Clarke (1972), Africans the world over to begin by the nineteenth century to search for a definition of themselves.

Another similar link in the historical experiences of Black populations was the exploitation of their labor. As Clarke (1972) indicated, "The story of the African slave trade is essentially the consequences of the second rise of Europe . . . . They were searching for new markets, new materials, new manpower, and new land to exploit. The slave trade was created to accommodate this expansion" (p. xvii). Just as Blacks in America were relegated to working the land and working as servants to increase the wealth of the majority population, so were Blacks in European countries. For example, according to Fryer (1992), "The majority of the 10,000 or so black people who lived in Britain in the eighteenth century were household servants – pages, valets, footmen, coachmen, cooks, and maids – much as their predecessors had been in the previous century" (p. 73). Although working menial jobs, Fryer conceded that as a Liverpool writer declared in 1893, "it was the capital made in the African slave trade that built some of our docks and the price of human flesh and blood that gave us a start" (p. 66). Similarly in Germany, Blacks were used for menial labor. For example, Blacks "were forced to cultivate export products or to work on the plantations and in the mines of whites" (Opitz et al., 1992, p. 25). The same was the case in Portugal. According to Saunders (1982),

"The nobility employed – or underemployed – large numbers of slaves solely as domestic servants" (p. 63).

Even when Blacks were interested in working higher status jobs, they were forbidden. For example, in London after 1731, Blacks were not allowed to learn a trade. In fact, on September 14 of that year the lord mayor of London issued the following proclamation prohibiting apprenticeships for Black people:

> It is Ordered by this Court, That for the future no Negroes or other Blacks be suffered to be bound Apprentices at any of the Companies of this City to any Freeman thereof; and that Copies of this Order be printed and sent to the Masters and Wardens of the several Companies of this City, who are required to see the same at all times hereafter duly observed (cited in Fryer, 1992, p. 75).

Although there were some Blacks in the U.S. who possessed some skills, especially the few slaves who lived in towns, the great majority of slaves' responsibilities were divided between two distinct groups, the house servants and the field hands (Franklin & Moss, 1988). According to these researchers, slaves had little opportunity to develop initiative because their responsibilities were proscribed for them. Therefore, the idea that Blacks did not want to work and thus played a role in having their skills underutilized was not the case.

Understandably, the exploitation of labor is and has always been intricately linked to lack of educational opportunities. To keep groups uneducated or undereducated has been, across societies, a formula across societies for the underutilization of their talents. Nkrumah, the son of the late African leader, describes it as a sort of worldwide formula by which African descendants everywhere have been relegated to the bottom educationally and economically. As such, the idea has been to prevent Blacks from being empowered intellectually, culturally, and economically.

As Anderson (1988) has indicated, it is through education that individuals begin to feel empowered, and African Americans were active agents in their right to be educated. From slavery until now, African Americans have had to struggle to have the opportunity to participate in any form of education. According to Anderson, "Blacks emerged from slavery with a strong belief in the desirability of learning to read and write" (p. 5). As an example of the intensity of anger that slaves held for keeping them illiterate, Anderson quoted a former slave: "There is one sin that slavery committed against me which I will never forgive. It robbed me of my education" (p. 5). Restrictive legislation had been passed to prohibit slaves from learning to read and write (Fleming, 1981). According to Fleming, from 1850 to 1856 less than 5% of African Americans out of a population of 4.5 million could read and write.

Just as Blacks in America were forbidden to learn to read and write, the same was true in other countries where the controlling population was non-Black. For example, Saunders (1982) indicated that in Portugal, very few Blacks were able to read and write.

As Opitz et al. (1992) indicated relative to Afro-Germans, "The limitations of educational opportunities concurrent with the favoring of some individuals led to hierarchical structures that undermined the solidarity of the community" (p. 33). In that sense, not only has lack of educational opportunities been utilized to limit the use of the talent and skills of Blacks but education has also been used as a force to destabilize communities. That is, education as a commodity has been used as a means to favor some intra-group members over others as a way to undermine community relationships. In Portugal, for example, mulattoes were thought to be more conversant "with Portuguese customs, were supposed to be more gifted intellectually than were blacks from Africa" (Saunder, 1982, p. 172).

Therefore, the commonality of the Black historical experience in countries where non-Blacks are the dominate populations has been the underutilization of the potential of Blacks by demeaning their humanity through enslaving them, destabilizing their communities, exploiting their labor, and/or limiting their educational opportunities. However, even when Blacks were allowed to participate in education, a process of cultural alienation and/or annihilation was implemented.

CULTURAL ALIENATION AND ANNIHILATION

A group's loss of identity occurs through cultural alienation and/or annihilation. According to C. Anderson (1994), one way that the use of power over a less powerful group takes form is "the group with the greater power annihilates the powerless group or drives them out of the territory" (p. 82). Thus, cultural alienation and annihilation can be defined as that process that controlling populations use to minimize or eradicate the culture of minority populations. Generally, this process is synonymous with assimilation, acculturation, or deracination (the term Mankiller (1993) used to describe the mission of boarding schools to annihilate the American Indian culture) – i.e. the uprooting or destruction of a race and its culture. More specifically, she stated, "The primary mission of Sequoyah and the other boarding schools was a full-scale attempt for the children to leave everything behind that related to their native culture, heritage, history, and language" (p. 8).

In order for Blacks to assimilate into the dominate culture in different countries, they were often separated (alienated) from their own cultural group or an attempt was made to eliminate (annihilate) their culture altogether. Clear examples of cultural alienation and annihilation can be found across Black populations. In

Australia, for example, "between 1910 and 1970 it [Australian Government] forcibly stole up to 100,000 aboriginal children from their families to live with whites in an attempt at forced integration – "to breed the black out," as politicians of the day expressed it (Evenson, 1998, p. A10). As in other countries, forcibly taken from their families were, particularly, the children who, because of rape, had White fathers. Doris Pilkington (1996), whose aboriginal name is Nugi Garimara, wrote an intriguing account of the assimilationist policy of Australia that took her mother and her mother's sisters, Daisy and Grace, away from their families. She wrote the following:

> Patrol officers travelled far and wide removing Aboriginal children from their families and transported them hundreds of kilometers down south. Every mother of a part-Aboriginal child was aware that their offspring could be taken away from them at any time and they were powerless to stop the abductors (p. 40).

The aboriginal experience was not unlike that of Black Britons and African Americans. As it related to the experience of Black Britons, Fryer (1992) indicated that most Black Londoners "had been torn from their parents and ethnic groups while still children. They were atomized in separate households, cut off from the cultural nourishment and reinforcement made possible by even the most inhumane plantation system" (p. 70). As a Black Briton recently stated in the popular press (1999, August 15): "I have done a lot of thinking about issues of assimilation and national identity. And I'm beginning to suspect that immigrants can only blend totally into their host environment if they are the same colour as the host or dominant population" (p. 58).

Similarly, African American families were divided. Franklin and Moss (1988) described the process of dividing Black slave families in the U.S.: "Since the domestic slave trade and slave breeding were essentially economic and not humanitarian activities, it is not surprising to find that in the sale of slaves there was the persistent practice of dividing families. Husbands were separated from their wives, and mothers were separated from their children" (pp. 106–107). Although the dividing of families might have been justified for economic reasons, it also served the function of cultural annihilation and/or alienation. That is, when families were divided, they had to reconstruct their social institutions into new forms.

Education has been used as one of the primary channels through which cultural alienation and annihilation have occurred. As Pilkington (1996) noted about the Aboriginal girls who were taken from their family, the belief was that "part-Aboriginal children were more intelligent than their darker relations and should be isolated and trained to be domestic servants and labourers" (p. 40). In a like manner, in America, Blacks were treated to educational opportunities differently by color. For example, according to Franklin and Moss (1988), mulattoes had more of a chance of schooling than others.

In addition to using education as a divisive tool based on color among Blacks, cultural alienation and annihilation have occurred through the transmission of education. That is, the way in which education has been transmitted (teaching style) and the content of educational materials (curriculum) have discounted the social and cultural capital of Black populations (consciously or subconsciously) and have therefore minimized the culture of Black populations. Researchers such as DiMaggio and Mohr (1985) have suggested that cultural capital is typically specialized social behaviors that make one accepted at different levels of society. Whereas some theorists (e.g. Coleman, 1990) have indicated that while social capital is related to cultural capital, social capital is more related to relations among persons. For example, Coleman (1988) explains social capital as the networks that provide information, social norms, and achievement support.

In simplest terms, the concepts of cultural and social capital mean assets, in the form of behaviors, on which individuals and/or families can draw to meet a certain set of established values in a society (Freeman, 1997). As Freeman noted, these societal values are generally established by majority groups in society and encompass behaviors such as the way individuals speak and the way they dress. The more individuals are able to meet these established standards, the more they are accepted by different institutions (e.g. schools) in society. There is no doubt that the cultural and social capital that students bring to the classroom has tremendous implications for how they will be accepted, treated, and provided with necessary information. According to Cicourel and Mehan (1985), students are provided different educational opportunities because students arrive in school with different types of culture capital. Black students typically arrive in school with different cultural capital, and schools therefore attempt to eradicate their cultural values in order to make them assimilate.

Who has taught, what has been taught, and how it has been taught over time have severely eroded the cultural identity and educational opportunities of Blacks. Although this has been the case historically, Black educators and researchers, particularly in the U.S., are currently extensively examining and discussing ways to undo the intellectual damage to Black children by demonstrating the importance of valuing the culture of Blacks rather than eradicating their culture. For example, several researchers and educators have written about the impact of the influence of the curriculum (what is being taught) on the education of Black children (e.g. Banks, 1988; Freeman, in press; Hollins, 1996; King, 1995).

The school curriculum, as defined by Hollins (1996), is "in fact that package of knowledge, skills, and perspectives that prepares us to develop the attributes of thought and behavior that comply with the prescribed norms" (p. 82). When there are inconsistencies in the compliance with these norms by different cultural groups, in this case Black populations, this can lead to various group members questioning their identity, being turned off to learning, and/or under-performing academically.

The curriculum validates individuals' culture, history, and sense of self – what is possible. Therefore, when Black populations' culture is not included in the very heart of school, this must create the feeling within students that something is missing. Banks (1988) says it best: "It is important for students to experience a curriculum that not only presents the experience of ethnic and cultural groups in accurate and sensitive ways, but that also enables them to see the experiences of both mainstream and minority groups from the perspectives of different cultural, racial, and ethnic groups" (p. 161). Searle (1994), a Black British educator, mirrors Banks' statement. In reference to the national curriculum of Britain, he stated: "The national curriculum, with its gradindian sequence of learning and testing, the narrow cultural chauvinism of its approach to knowledge and human experience and its blatantly racist exclusion of cultures, histories, languages and perspectives of Britain's black people, is already creating a tedium and uniformity which will do nothing to spark the interest and motivation of young people to learn" (p. 26).

It is as though the fact that many Black students have underachieved is completely divorced from the curriculum. Linkages have clearly been established between the curriculum and its effect on African American students' achievement (Hollins, 1996; King, 1995). As Hollins (1996) indicated, for African American children the "discontinuity between the home-culture and school learning ultimately disrupts the learning process for many children and the resulting failure may lead them to reject the Euro-American culture and school learning as well" (p. 84).

Aside from what has been taught (the curriculum), as a way to stem the tide of alienation and annihilation of the Black culture through education, Black educators have also more recently focused their research on who has taught and how Black children have been taught. For example, researchers/educators such as Foster (1997), Irvine (1994), Ladson-Billings (1994), and Siddle-Walker (1996) have examined the role of culturally relevant pedagogy and the relevance of the cultural perspective of Black teachers in Black students' achievement. More specifically, these researchers have suggested the importance of historically and currently understanding the role Black teachers have played in helping Black students achieve.

At the same time Black educators in the U.S. have focused their research on the inclusion of a Black perspective and valuing Black culture in the educational system, Black researchers in other countries have also begun to address these same issues. Searle (1994), about the British system, stated: "The ignorance of teachers and the school system generally about the communities whom they serve is still a vital factor which promotes conflict and misunderstanding between teachers and students" (p. 25). Bridges (1994), another British educator, supported Searle's assertion. He indicated that more Black teachers were employed as a way "of counter-balancing the underrepresentation of black teachers in the borough and, through this, to attack the real problems of underachievement among black children" (p. 4).

Cultural alienation and annihilation have had a devastating effect on Black students' participation in education. Over time, the process of trying "to breed the black out" (assimilation), whether through the devaluation of the cultural capital of Blacks or the what and who of the transmission of knowledge, has severely impacted the black students' sense of self and achievement. There should be little doubt that cultural alienation/annihilation has lead to a "culture of exclusion" for Black populations globally.

CULTURE OF EXCLUSION

Even when Blacks have had the opportunity to participate in education, relating to Black British, Searle (1994) indicated, a "culture of exclusion" has existed. Searle describes "culture of exclusion" as it relates to Black Britons in this way: "There is much mystification surrounding the word 'exclusion' in education parlance. Schools do not refer to 'expulsions' now, even though almost all parents would know what that means. The preferred term is 'permanent exclusion,' but it comes to the same thing" (p. 19). Searle reported that secondary schools "in Nottingham, Reading, Bristol and the north London borough of Brent showed that black students were up to six times more likely to be suspended from school than their white peers" (p. 24). Drawing on the research of Searle and Bridges (1994), a culture of exclusion, then, can be defined as that process whereby Black children are excluded from schooling, whether through suspension or expulsion or placement in the lower tracks of schooling – which would be referred to as "internal expulsion" (p. 11).

Educational expulsion (suspension) is a phenomenon that is similarly faced by Black populations globally. For example, the honorable Fernando Ka (1998), in a report on the conditions of Blacks in Portugal, indicated the following: "The black community in general – and the children and young people in particular – are victims of educational expulsion. The number of those that manage to complete compulsory education (up to the 9th grade) is frightfully low, and even worse if we consider the number of those who manage to complete secondary education (12th grade)" (p. 2).

In the U.S., as in Britain and Portugal, a greater number of Black children are subjected to suspension or expulsion. For example, a comprehensive study conducted by the Children's Defense Fund (1975) in the 1970s reported the following:

> No one is immune from suspension, but black children were suspended at twice the rate of any other ethnic group. Nationally, if they had been suspended at the same rate as whites, nearly 50% or 188,479 of the black children suspended would have remained in school. Although black children accounted for 27.1% of the enrollment in the districts reporting to OCR, they constituted 42.3% of the racially identified suspensions (p. 12).

In support of these earlier findings, in a more recent study, Morris and Goldring (1999) cited studies that concluded that "desegregation was often accompanied by an increase in the overall student suspension as well as a high disparity between black and white student suspension" (pp. 60–61).

However, the greatest numbers of African American students are subjected to "internal expulsion." A recent report (Klenbort, 1999) in the Southern Regional Council periodical presented, as an example, a statement from a high school sophomore who spent his schooling in the lower-level track: "You live in the basement, you die in the basement. You know what I mean?" Researchers, such as Oakes (1985), Wheelock (1992), and Braddock II and Slavin (1995), support this student's description of tracking or what can be referred as internal expulsion. Page and Page (1995) describe how tracking became the norm following desegregation: "Schools in the region [Southern region] became increasingly resegregated through the use of tracking, with the majority of African American students assigned to lower tracks and the majority of Caucasian students assigned to higher tracks" (p. 73).

The way in which tracking can best be thought of as "internal expulsion" is best captured by Oakes (1985) and Braddock II and Slavin (1995). For example, Braddock II and Slavin indicated that the effects of tracking on students were striking. They found that students in lower tracks performed significantly less well than similar low achievers in untracked schools and were much more likely to end up in non-college-preparatory programs by tenth grade. This effect, they suggested, "being in the low track in eighth grade slams the gate on any possibility that a student can take the courses leading to college" (p. 8). Oakes suggested that "lower-track students are more alienated from school and have higher drop-out rates" (p. 9). These researchers also found that tracking hurts students' self-esteem, causing them to feel inferior. Based on these researchers findings, then, the effects of tracking on students' life chances is tantamount to being excluded. That is, Black students who are in tracks are in school, but because they are more likely to drop out or to have limited opportunities beyond secondary school, the school has, in a sense, excluded them. Morris and Goldring (1999), in their study on disciplinary rates of African American and White students in Cincinnati magnet and nonmagnet schools, explained it in this way: "The overall effect of disciplining students, which involves removing them from the classroom, will drastically impact students' acquisition of educational materials presented by the teacher. Other long term effects might include African American students falling behind academically, or worse, dropping out of school altogether" (p. 64).

Whether internally excluded or suspended or expelled, Black students globally share similar experiences. At least, as described in Britain, Portugal, and the U.S., Black students comprise the majority of students facing a "culture of exclusion." This "culture of exclusion" has led to the underutilization of Blacks in education, which, in turn, has implications for societal and individual costs.

NONMONETARY COSTS OF UNDERUTILIZATION OF HUMAN POTENTIAL

Through the historical experiences of Black populations, the pattern of cultural alienation and annihilation and the culture of exclusion surrounding their schooling, a clear pattern emerges as to how Black children's human potential has been underutilized. The underutilization of Black population's human potential has not been without costs to individuals or societies. What is the underutilization of potential and how has it been manifested as it relates to Black populations?

The underutilization of human potential is defined as a too narrow definition of talents (what constitutes merit), the inappropriate matching of abilities with tasks (underemployment), or the lack of use of talents (unemployment) which prevents individuals or groups from maximizing their capabilities and/or productivity (Carnoy, Freeman, Findlay, Joiner, & Magyari-Beck, 1999). The understanding of the underutilization of human potential takes on many dimensions across cultures. For example, it can occur in the case of discrimination, differential educational opportunities among individuals and/or groups, the inappropriate training for the market, or a division in the distribution of technological knowledge-digital divide. Schultz (1961) commented on one aspect of this issue of the underutilization of human potential in the early 1960s when he stated: "Human capital deteriorates when it is idle because unemployment impairs the skills that workers have acquired" (p. 320). Additionally he remarked that there are many hindrances to the free choice of professions due to discrimination, whether ethnic, class, gender, or religious. Understanding the underutilization of human potential has merit because it can help to better understand educational inequality (especially for children), the underemployment and unemployment of different groups, the differences in roles in societies, and the economic division between the "haves" and "have-nots."

Farrell (1992) outlined a model in which he described four points where inequality as it relates to educational opportunities is likely to occur: (1) Access: the differences in children from different groups getting into the school system; (2) Survival: once in school the differences in children from various groups staying in the school system to some defined level, usually the end of a cycle (primary, secondary, higher); (3) Output: the differences in children from different groups learning the same things to the same level; and (4) Outcome: the differences in children from different groups living relatively similar lives subsequent to and as a result of schooling (having equal income, having jobs of the same status, having equal access to positions of political power, etc.).

Drawing on Farrell's (1992) research, other researchers (Freeman et al., 1999) found that there are four points at which underutilization of human potential typically occurs: (1) the transition of students into schooling; (2) the experiences of students within the educational setting; (3) the transition of students to the labor market; and (4) the experiences in the workplace. In a recently completed cross-cultural study, these researchers found that minority groups tended to be underutilized across societies at each point. At each of these points, underutilization of potential occurs for Black populations because of a too narrow definition of merit and because of who is defining merit for different groups. That is, at the point of entrance to schooling, as pointed out in this research, the culture of Black populations undergoes a process of being discounted, whether through alienation or annihilation. This in turn leads to a culture of exclusion, where students are turned off from schooling, which limits labor market opportunities. As demonstrated in this research, this cycle of underutilization has historically been and continues to be the case with Black populations globally. This cycle of underutilization of human potential understandably has costs for individuals and societies.

Economics of education theorists typically divide costs and benefits of education into monetary and nonmonetary (Johns et al., 1983; Merisotis, 1998; Schultz, 1961; Thurow, 1972). They generally assess monetary and nonmonetary costs by societal and private-individual factors (Johns et al., 1983).

The monetary costs (i.e. unemployment and underemployment which leads to lower productivity and reduced tax revenue) associated with the underutilization of the potential of Blacks have been generally well documented (Carnoy, 1994; Schultz, 1961; Thurow, 1972). In fact, Levitan et al. (1972) reported that "underutilization and underdevelopment not only deprive Blacks of opportunities to improve their material welfare but also cost the nation the economic contribution they could make if they had better employment and income opportunities" (p. 427). However, the current costs associated with unemployment and/or underemployment of Blacks continue to be extremely costly to societies. In Australia, for example, a recent article in the Daily Telegraph reported that the unemployment rate among Aborigines (23% unemployment rate) was three times the general rate and was growing twice as fast. Although the Australian government subsidizes approximately 70% of Aboriginals who work, the article concluded that instead of subsidies, "better education and training are needed" (Daily Telegraph, 1999, p. 10). These monetary costs associated with the underutilization of the potential of Aboriginals is not unlike the costs other countries, such as Portugal and the U.S., are facing with Black populations.

In Portugal, Ka (1998) stated concerning to Blacks' participation in the labor market: "It is not easy for a Black person to find a decent job in this country, even if s/he has good academic and/or professional qualifications. The colour of the skin is always a barrier, often difficult to transpose" (p. 7). Similarly, the latest labor report from the United States Department of Labor (1999) indicated that although the unemployment rates for African Americans and Hispanics have declined in the past two years, the "unemployment rate of African American men is still twice that of white men. For African American teens, unemployment has fallen dramatically over the past six years but remains around 25% or higher" (pp. 11–12).

Although the costs associated with the underutilization of the potential of Blacks have been documented, considerably less has been written about the nonmonetary costs associated with education, particularly as it relates to the underutilization of Black populations. This is particularly troubling given that nonmonetary costs to societies and individuals are much more difficult to penetrate and eradicate. What are nonmonetary costs associated with the underutilization of Blacks' human potential? Nonmonetary costs are usually those costs that are more indirect and are usually seen over time. Merisotis (1998) defines nonmonetary costs as costs that accrue to individuals, to groups of people, or to society broadly that are not directly related to economic, fiscal, or labor market effects. As with monetary costs, nonmonetary costs can be assessed by societal and individual costs.

SOCIETAL NONMONETARY COSTS

Societal nonmonetary costs would include such things as lack of benefits of intergenerational effect, increased crime, and decreased adaptability to lifelong learning and use of technology – i.e. mismatch between skill levels (Johns et al., 1983; Merisotis, 1998). By the very nature of nonmonetary costs, it is difficult to affix a price tag. Nonetheless, as Bowen (1977) has indicated, the importance of better understanding the nonmonetary benefits to societies and individuals is crucial:

The monetary returns alone, the forms of enhanced earnings of workers and improved technology, are probably sufficient to offset all the costs. But over and above the monetary returns are the personal development and life enrichment of millions of people, the preservation of the cultural heritage, the advancement of knowledge and the arts, a major contribution to the national prestige and power, and the direct satisfactions derived from college attendance and from living in a society where knowledge and the arts flourish. These nonmonetary benefits surely are far greater than the monetary benefits – so much greater, in fact, that individual and social decisions about the future of higher education should be made primarily on the basis of nonmonetary considerations and only secondarily on the basis of monetary factors (p. 458).

While there are clearly more costs associated with the underutilization of Black potential, these are highlighted because they are typically considered among the most important.

Intergenerational Effect

Intergenerational effect, according to Johns et al. (1983), can be understood as a process whereby the quality of life of children whose parents have attended college and value education is transmitted between generations. That is, the higher the level of education, the higher the value of education that parents instill in their children. For example, college choice theorists (e.g. Hearn, 1991; Hossler & Gallagher, 1987) have well-documented that the children of college-educated parents are more likely to choose higher education participation than those of parents who have not participated in higher education. Therefore, the fact that Black families have been undereducated is costly to societies because it causes generations of children to be underutilized primarily at the first and second points of underutilization (i.e. the transition of students into schooling and their experiences once in school). As Fig. 1 demonstrates, the transition into school and the experience in schooling have a reciprocal impact on the intergenerational effect. That is, because generations of Black populations have not been the beneficiaries of education, in many cases, they are unable to transmit education to their children which impacts students transition into school and their experiences once in school (e.g. different cultural capital and lack of information), which in turn impacts on the educational outcomes of future generations.

This would be considered a nonmonetary cost because what is hurt most is the ability of generations who are uneducated to instill the aspiration and motivation to continue schooling. In addition, Merisotis (1998) indicated that children whose parents are educated are more likely to have higher cognitive development and have a better quality of life in general. For example, daughters of college-educated mothers are "considerably less likely to become unmarried teen parents" (p. 3).

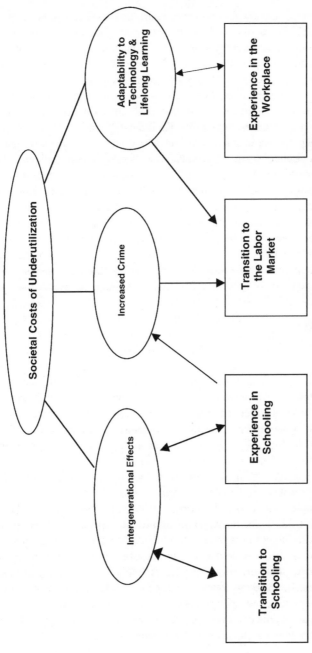

Fig. 1. Linkages Between Societal Costs of Underutilization and the Four Points of Underutilization.

As an example of how this process is currently working, in the U.S. the Labor Department (1999) reported: "African Americans continue to lag behind in college attendance. This means that these minority groups lack access to many of the skills that higher education provides" (p. 5). The same is the case in Portugal. Ka (1998) stated about the conditions of Blacks participation in education: "In Portugal, Black people have scarce means of access to education, particularly higher levels of education. It is distressing the number of Black students in Portuguese higher education" (p. 2). Related to families, Ka indicated that "families are subjected to enormous deprivation which determines a high rate of low achievement" (p. 3).

If, as college choice theorists (e.g. Hearn, 1991; Hossler & Gallagher, 1987) have asserted, parents have the biggest influence on students choosing or not choosing higher education participation, the costs associated with the historical system of undereducating Black populations, who are in turn unable to pass on the motivation and aspiration to participate in education to their children, are being realized at all levels of schooling across societies. Breaking such a cycle itself will include costs. To better understand across societies how to dramatically increase the number of Blacks participating in education at all levels so that future generations will not lose the effects (benefits) of education is a challenge, but a highly necessary challenge to undertake.

Increased Crime

Increases in crime rates in communities with less-educated populations are also associated with underutilization of human potential and therefore increased costs to society. For example, Merisotis (1998) suggested that "there are far fewer prisoners with at least some college education compared with those with high school or less" (p. 3). It should be no surprise that with a "culture of expulsion," more Blacks become disinterested in schooling. As Fig. 1 demonstrates, the schooling experience is directly linked to increases in crime, which impacts on students' inability to transition to the labor market.

For example, when *The Economist* (1999) discussed Tony Blair's (Prime Minister of Britain) war on poverty, the article indicated that the government's micro-initiative would be aimed at trouble spots such as "crime and educational failure" (p. 2). It is widely accepted across societies that increased crime among different segments of populations is associated with decreased educational opportunities. In speaking about social costs related to poverty and education, Carnoy (1994) summed up the linkage between costs, education, and crime in this way: "The middle class is a 'hostage to worry' about crime, and spends more and more each year on guns, self-defense courses, and other paraphernalia related to warding off assailants . . . . . All this means that whatever the costs of increasing crime, they are being privatized, and they are rising . . . The rising social costs of poverty should be convincing argument for the need to reduce racial inequality" (pp. 240–241).

Adaptability to Lifelong Learning and Technology

Individuals who are adaptable to changing skills and understanding of techniques of lifelong learning while being acutely aware of technology are what all societies will increasingly require. Because the potential of Black populations has been underutilized at all four points, societies face enormous costs associated with increasing Black students' motivation and aspiration to participate in higher levels of schooling at the same time that higher skills are already necessary. These societal costs have also had consequences for Black individuals across societies.

The report from the U.S. Labor Department (1999) sums of the importance of adaptability to lifelong learning and technology: "In the information-based, skills-intensive economy of the twenty-first, one thing is clear: knowing means growing . . . . While many workers will continue to be in occupations that do not require a bachelor's degree, the best jobs will be those requiring education and training . . . . Lifelong learning for workers will become more important as a result" (pp. 4–5). This report indicated that because African Americans lag behind Whites in college attendance, this group lacks access to many of the necessary skills that higher education provides. Similarly in Portugal, Ka (1998) stated, "Few are the Black persons that can benefit from adequate professional training, although Portugal has been one of the European Union countries that received the largest amounts in subsidies for that end" (p. 5). Therefore, it is easy to see how, relative to adaptability to lifelong learning and technology, the potential of Blacks has been and continues to be underutilized at the points of transition into the labor market and in the labor market itself (see Fig. 1).

INDIVIDUAL NONMONETARY COSTS

Relating to benefits of education to the individual, Bowen (1977) said: "Education should be directed toward the growth of the whole person through cultivation not only of the intellect and practical competence but also of the affective dispositions, including the moral, religious, emotional, and esthetic aspects of the personality" (p. 38). Unfortunately, as pointed out historically, education has not necessarily served Black individuals in this way. In fact, individual costs to Blacks would include psychological barriers – affective dispositions, as Bowen stated, such as decrease in motivation and aspiration to participate in education (Freeman, 1997) – and what Steele (1999) refers to as "stereotype threat." Having their talents underutilized over the centuries has impacted the psychological being (self-esteem and confidence) because the costs of underutilizing their potential has gone to the heart and soul of Blacks and overcoming this phenomenon will not be easy.

Aspiration and Motivation

In a qualitative study Freeman (1997) conducted among Black high school students to assess college choice (i.e. why some African Americans choose to participate in higher education and some do not), a student responded: "They lose hope" (p. 537). As Fig. 2 suggests, that sense of loss of hope impacts on students desire to transition to the next level of schooling. The experiences within school affect students' motivation and aspiration, which impacts on their acquiring the skills to transition to the labor market and also can impact on their experiences once in the labor market.

Aspiration and motivation are obviously tied to intergenerational effect, explained earlier, and are associated with academic achievement (Freeman, 1995). As Freeman stated, children who do not perform well academically are obviously more prone to disconnect from schooling. Also, motivation and aspiration are closely linked to cultural affinity. That is, the more individuals there are of the same culture who are not participating in education, the more unmotivated individuals from the same group will be. For example, individuals start to assume that if other individuals like me who have participated in the labor market have not obtained positions commensurate with their level of schooling, why should I bother.

The costs to societies of individuals who lose their motivation and aspiration to participate in schooling at any level, while difficult to assess, are high. The questions become, how do societies go about first impacting motivation and aspiration, and next, how do societies place a price tag on impacting the change of a process that has been historically implemented?

Stereotype Threat

In the same way that Black individuals' motivation and aspiration have been impacted by the underutilization of Blacks over time, Steele (1999) more recently has documented a process that he refers to as "stereotype threat" that can also influence the costs of the underutilization of the potential of Blacks. He describes

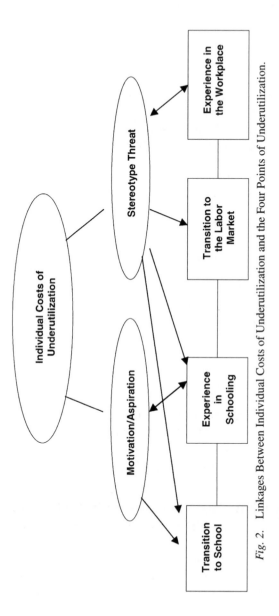

Fig. 2. Linkages Between Individual Costs of Underutilization and the Four Points of Underutilization.

"stereotype threat" as "the threat of being viewed through the lens of a negative stereotype, or the fear of doing something that would inadvertently confirm that stereotype – something external, the situational threat of being negatively stereotyped" (p. 45). Figure 2 depicts that "stereotype threat" influences students at the point of transition to schooling and their experiences in school and shows that students' experiences in school have a reciprocal impact on "stereotype threat." Through their research, Steele reported that Black students taking an experimental test "under 'stereotype threat' seemed to be trying to hard . . .. The threat made them inefficient on a test that, like most standardized tests, is set up so that thinking long often means thinking wrong, especially on difficult items like the ones we used" (p. 50). Steele's findings cut across social class, and in fact, he indicated that "what exposes students to the pressure of 'stereotype threat' is not weaker academic identity and skills but stronger academic and skills" (p. 50).

In addition to the academic costs to Blacks that accompany "stereotype threat," Steele (1999) stated: "Sadly, the effort that accompanies 'stereotype threat' exacts an additional price . . .. We found the blood pressure of black students performing a difficult cognitive task under 'stereotype threat' was elevated compared with blacks students who were not under 'stereotype threat' or white students in either situation" (pp. 50–51).

Unlike societal nonmonetary costs, individual costs are often ignored or underestimated. Certainly, there are enormous costs associated with the damage exacted on the individual psyche of Blacks by having their potential underutilized. Unless and/or until individual costs are addressed, programs or models will have a difficult time being effectuated. As Henry Levin in conversation stated, "Individuals act on what they perceive not necessarily on what others say is."

Through societies' underutilization of the human potential of Blacks, the nonmonetary costs have been high and the effects are still growing. How do all of these pieces tie together to demonstrate a composite of the costs associated with the underutilization of Black populations? How do these pieces fit together to make the case for an expanded research agenda?

BLACK CHILDREN'S EDUCATIONAL POTENTIAL: RETHINKING THE ASSIMILATION PARADIGM

As this chapter demonstrates, Black children globally are underachieving academically. Their educational potential is severely restricted due to the minimizing of their identity through the process of cultural assimilation and alienation. This loss of identity has led to the underutilization of Black children's potential thereby often leading to them being disinterested in school, underachieving academically, or dropping out of school. In order to fully value and capture the potential of Black children, a different paradigm is necessary.

First, it is important that schools and societies value the culture of all children. As pointed out, school curriculums must be reflective of the histories and heritage of all groups in society. All children bring cultural and social capital to schools and other settings that must be recognized and valued, not minimized or "bred out."

Next, the process of exclusion in school has to be factored into Black children's loss of identity and into their underutilization of their educational potential. What are the methods to prevent students from internal and external expulsion? Better still, what are the alternative ways of stimulating Black children's interest in school as opposed to expelling them? Each time, students are expelled from school, their potential is being underutilized.

To better understand the barriers constructed across cultures to underutilize the potential human potential of Blacks in countries where non-Blacks are the controlling populations, much more research needs to be conducted. In order to more fully understand this process, more research on each point where underutilization occurs has to be explored. This chapter demonstrates how each aspect of the Black experience impacts on each experience and level of schooling.

To understand the costs, particularly the nonmonetary costs as indicated by Bowen (1977), associated with the underutilization of Black potential is imperative so that countries better understand how everyone is losing. A quote from the Commission on Research in Black Education from Wendell Berry summarizes the imperative that countries assess the underutilization of the human potential of Black populations: "If the white man has inflicted the wound of racism upon Black men, the cost has been that he would receive the mirror image of that wound into himself."

Finally, though, it is not enough for countries to assess the costs associated with the underutilization of the potential of Black populations, for this research suggests that at each point Blacks have been underutilized. At the beginning of the twenty-first century, countries will find it necessary to develop strategies to address the societal and individual costs associated with Black populations' underutilization while simultaneously increasing the utilization of the potential of Blacks. Carnoy (1997) describes the way the process of increasing the spending on the underutilization of Blacks should work: "The vicious cycle of increasing social costs will gradually break. Down the road, as early-childhood investment reduces spending on adult social problems, more public funds will become available for general education and other activities that improve worker productivity and growth rates" (p. 241). However, countries have not yet been able to develop a formula for assessing the individual and societal costs and therefore to appropriately target their spending.

To fully utilize the potential of all people, must be the goal of all societies. To attempt to force all cultural groups to assimilate into one model inevitably will lead to the underutilization of a cultural group, in this case Black populations which creates social and economic problems which are detrimental to the whole of society. For globalization to be successful for individual countries and countries collectively, the potential of all of their citizens must be utilized. In order to balance this imperative, different paradigms and players have to be a part of the research agenda, particularly as it relates to Black children.

REFERENCES

Anderson, C. (1994). *Black labor White wealth: The search for power and economic justice*. Edgewood, MD: Duncan & Duncan.

Anderson, J. D. (1988). *The education of Blacks in the South, 1860–1935*. Chapel Hill, NC: University of North Carolina Press.

Banks, J. A. (1988). *Multiethnic education* (2nd ed.). Boston: Allyn & Bacon.

Braddock, J. M., II, & Slavin, R. E. (1995). Why ability grouping must end: Achieving excellence and equity in American education. In: H. Pool & J. A. Page (Eds), *Beyond Tracking: Finding Success in Inclusive Schools*. Bloomington, IA: Phi Delta Kappa Educational Foundation.

Bridges, L. (1994). Exclusions: How did we get here? In: J. Bourne, L. Bridges & C. Searle (Eds), *Outcast England: How Schools Exclude Black Children*. London: Institute of Race Relations.

Bowen, H. (1977). *Investment in learning*. San Francisco: Jossey-Bass.

Carnoy, M. (1994). *Faded dreams: The politics and economics of race in America*. Cambridge, England: Cambridge University Press.

Children's Defense Fund (1975). *School suspensions: Are they helping children?* Washington, DC: Author.

Cicourel, A. V., & Mehan, H. (1985). Universal development, stratifying practices, and status attainment. *Research in Social Stratification and Mobility*, 4(5), 728–734.

Clarke, J. H. (1972). Introduction. In: J. A. Rogers (Ed.), *World's Great Men of Color*. New York: Macmillan.

Coleman, J. S. (1988). Social capital in the creation of human capital. *American Journal of Sociology*, 94, 95–120.

Coleman, J. S. (1990). *Foundations of social theory*. Cambridge, MA: Belknap Press of Harvard University.

DiMaggio, P., & Mohr, J. (1985). Cultural capital, educational attainment, and marital selection. *American Journal of Sociology*, 90(6), 1231–1261.

Evenson, B. (1998, February 23). Land crisis brewing down under: A 1996 court ruling means aboriginals could claim 80% of Australia's land mass. *The Ottawa Citizen*, A10.

Farrell, J. (1992). Conceptualizing education and the drive for social equality. In: R. Arnove, P. Altbach & G. Kelly (Eds), *Emergent Issues in Education*. Albany, NY: State University of New York Press.

Foster, M. (1997). *Black teachers on teaching*. New York: New Press.

Franklin, J. H., & Moss, A. A., Jr. (1988). *From slavery to freedom: A history of Negro Americans* (6th ed.). New York: McGraw-Hill.

Freeman, K. (1997, September/October). Increasing African Americans' participation in higher education: African American high school students' perspective. *The Journal of Higher Education, 68*(5), 523–550.

Freeman, K., Carnoy, M., Findlay, H., Joiner, B., & Magyari-Beck, I. (1999). *Economic development and the utilization of human potential: Bridging the gap between higher education, economics, and culture.* Nashville, TN: Vanderbilt University, Department of Leadership and Organizations.

Freeman, K. (in press). My soul is missing: African American students' perceptions of the curriculum and the influence on college choice. *Review of African American Education, 1*(1).

Fryer, P. (1992). *Staying power: The history of Black people in Britain* (6th ed.). London: Pluto Press.

Hearn, J. C. (1991). Academic and nonacademic influences on the college destinations of 1980 high school graduates. *Sociology of Education, 64*, 158–171.

Hollins, E. R. (1996). *Culture in school: Revealing the deeper meaning.* Mahwah, NJ: Lawrence Erlbaum.

Hossler, D., & Gallagher, K. (1987). Studying student college choice: A three-phase model and the implications for policymakers. *College & University, 62*(3), 207–221.

Johns, R. L., Morphet, E. L., & Alexander, K. (1983). *The economics and financing of education* (4th ed.). Englewood Cliffs, NJ: Prentice-Hall.

Ka, F. (1998). Black people's situation in Portugal. Paper prepared for Fisk University Race Relations Institute Conference, Nashville, TN.

King, J. E. (1995). Culture-centered knowledge: Black studies, curriculum transformation, and social action. In: J. Banks & C. A. Banks (Eds), *Handbook of Research on Multicultural Education.* New York: Macmillan.

Ladson-Billings, G. (1994). *The dreamkeepers: Successful teachers of African American children.* San Francisco: Jossey-Bass.

Levitan, S., Mangum, G., & Marshall, R. (1972). *Human resources and labor markets: Labor and manpower in the American economy.* New York: Harper & Row.

Lorde, A. (1992). Foreword to the English Language Edition. In: M. Opitz, K. Oguntoye & D. Schultz (Eds), *Showing Our Colours: Afro-German Women Speak Out.* London: Open Letters.

Mankiller, W. (1993). *Mankiller: A chief and her people.* New York: St. Martin's Press.

Merisotis, J. P. (1998). Who benefits from education? An American perspective. *International Higher Education.* Chestnut Hill, MA: Boston College, Department of Higher Education.

Morris, J. E., & Goldring, E. (1999). Are magnet schools more equitable? An analysis of the disciplinary rates of African American and White students in Cincinnati magnet and nonmagnet schools. *Equity and Excellence in Education, 32*(3), 59–65.

Oakes, J. (1985). *Keeping track.* New Haven, CT: Yale University Press.

Opitz, M., Oguntoye, K., & Schultz, D. (Eds) (1992). *Showing our colours: Afro-German women speak out.* London: Open Letters.

Page, J. A., & Page, F. M., Jr. (1995). Tracking and its effects on African-Americans in the field of education. In: H. Pool & J. A. Page (Eds), *Beyond Tracking: Finding Success in Inclusive Schools.* Bloomington, IA: Phi Delta Kappa Educational Foundation.

Pilkington, D. (1996). *Follow the rabbit-proof fence.* Queensland, Australia: University of Queensland Press.

Saunders, A. C., & De, C. M. (1982). *A history of black slaves and freedmen in Portugal 1441–1555.* Cambridge, England: Cambridge University Press.

Schultz, T. W. (1961). Investment in human capital. *American Economic Review, 51*, 1–17.

Searle, C. (1994). The culture of exclusion. In: J. Bourne, L. Bridges & C. Searle (Eds), *Outcast England: How Schools Exclude Black Children.* London: Institute of Race Relations.

Steele, C. M. (1999, August). Thin ice: "Stereotype threat" and Black college students. *The Atlantic Monthly, 284*(2), 44–54.

Thurow, L. C. (1972). Education and economic equality. *Public Interest, 28,* 66–81.

Tony Blair's war on poverty. (1999, September 25). *The Economist, 352*(8138), 18–19.

The United States Department of Labor (1999). Labor Day 1999 executive summary. *Future work: Trends and challenges for work in the 21st century.* Washington, DC: U.S. Department of Labor.

Walker, V. S. (1996). *Their highest potential: An African American school community in the segregated south.* Chapel Hill, NC: University of North Carolina Press.

Wheelock, A. (1992). *Crossing the tracks: How "untracking" can save America's schools.* New York: New Press.

7. CHILDREN AND YOUTH IN POVERTY IN TRINIDAD AND TOBAGO: A LACK OF COMMITMENT IN THE MIDST OF PLENTY

Frank C. Worrell

INTRODUCTION

Located between 10 and 11 degrees north of the equator, and seven miles from the northeast corner of Venezuela, Trinidad and Tobago are a twin island republic and the southernmost islands in the Caribbean chain that begins off the coast of Florida. The islands have a tropical maritime climate with two seasons – a hot dry season from January to May and a hot rainy season from June to December. The daily temperature ranges from the low 70s to the high 80s year round, and for the 10-year period 1987–1996, Trinidad's mean low and high temperatures were 73 and 89 degrees Fahrenheit, respectively. As the islands are located south of the hurricane belt, neither has been hit by a hurricane since Hurricane Flora hit Tobago in 1963.

Often referred to as T & T by the inhabitants, this twin-island nation has a population of about 1.2 million people, and is one of the most cosmopolitan of the Caribbean islands, with a population that includes people of African (39.5%),

'Suffer the Little Children': National and International Dimensions of Child
Poverty and Public Policy
Advances in Education in Diverse Communities: Research, Policy and Praxis, Volume 4, 145–175
Copyright © 2006 by Elsevier Ltd.
All rights of reproduction in any form reserved
ISSN: 1479-358X/doi:10.1016/S1479-358X(04)04007-0

East Indian (40.3%), and mixed (18.4%) descent, as well as smaller numbers of Chinese, European, and Syrian descent. Trinidad and Tobago is known as the land where calypsos and steel drum music originated, and has one of the major annual carnivals of the world in the pre-Lenten period. In this chapter, I examine poverty in Trinidad and Tobago and its impact on children and youth in that country. The first section of the chapter provides the historical background of this Caribbean nation. Subsequent sections focus on the economy and how poverty affects the health, education, and criminal involvement of the country's children and youth. The chapter concludes with some recommendations for action. Data for this article are drawn from a variety of sources, including reports from the Central Statistical Office of Trinidad and Tobago (CSA, 1996, 1997, 1998a, b), as well as a report by a researcher at the University of the West Indies (e.g. Theodore, 1995) and a 2001 report published by the United Nations Development Program (UNDP, 2001).

A BRIEF HISTORY OF TRINIDAD AND TOBAGO

Trinidad pre-1797

Long before Columbus' arrival on the island, Trinidad was inhabited by the Siboney, a group of cave dwellers, and later on, an Amerindian group called the Arawaks, "a gentle, peace, agricultural people" (De Suze, 1966). The Arawak name for Trinidad was Iere which translates into *The Land of the Humming Bird*, and even today, bird watchers come from many parts of the world to watch the more than 40 species of humming birds that are native to Trinidad. Trinidad was also inhabited by the Caribs, a group whose name now graces the entire region, although there is some debate about how active a presence the Caribs had in Trinidad prior to the arrival of the Spaniards (De Suze).

On Columbus' third voyage in 1498, he took a more southerly route than on his previous voyages and came upon Iere from the southeast. As the southern range of the island has three peaks, Columbus claimed the island for Spain, and named it *La Ysla de la Trinidad* after the holy Trinity, a name that was eventually truncated to Trinidad. After Columbus laid claim to Trinidad, it remained uninhabited for about 30 years, and relatively neglected for about 200 years until the development of tobacco plantations in the late 1600s and early 1700s. From 1784 to 1797, Trinidad's population increased by about 270% from 6,503 to almost 18,000 people. The increase in population was greatest among the African slaves, and by 1797, 56.4% of Trinidad's population were slaves of African descent (Brereton, 1981).

Trinidad 1797–1888

In February of 1797, a British fleet captured Trinidad. Over the next 90 years, numerous events of import took place. Trinidad established itself as a major sugar colony and the influx of slaves of African descent continued. The slave trade was abolished in the British Empire in 1807, and slaves were declared free in 1834, and actually freed in 1838 after a four-year apprenticeship period. The freeing of the slaves resulted in a labor shortage that was solved when the British government began financing the immigration of indentured laborers from India in mid-1840. Trinidad continued to receive indentured laborers from India through 1917, and Chinese immigrants who began arriving in 1852 added to Trinidad's diversity. These influxes of people from the Far East gives Trinidad a unique population profile in the Caribbean region.

Tobago pre-1889

Caribs inhabited Tobago prior to European settlement of the island. Columbus never landed on the island and the first Europeans on Tobago were British explorers in 1530. When European interest in Tobago was finally aroused in the early 1600s, Tobago became one of the most sought-after prizes in the Caribbean, and changed colonial masters regularly. Between 1632 and 1814, Tobago was held by the Dutch four times, the Spanish once, the British six times, the Caribs twice, and the French four times. There were also two brief occupations of Tobago by Courlanders (present-day Latvians), a period when Tobago was declared neutral, and an ill-fated and unsuccessful attempt to capture Tobago by America in 1778 during the War of Independence. In 1814, the Treaty of Paris ceded Tobago to Britain, and in 1889, Britain amalgamated the island to Trinidad.

THE ECONOMIC BASE OF TRINIDAD AND TOBAGO

By 1970, Trinidad and Tobago had become the most prosperous nation in the Caribbean, due in large part to the discovery of oil and natural gas reserves in Trinidad. In 1901, the first oil well was drilled in Trinidad and the first oil refinery was built in 1913. The development of the internal combustion engine and the automobile in the 1989–1910 period increased the value of oil across the globe including Trinidad and Tobago. The First World War resulted in an oil boom, and even as the depression had negative consequences worldwide in the 1930s, the major oil companies continued to see their profits rise. The Second World War also resulted in an oil boom which had positive consequences for the oil industry in Trinidad. In 1938, Trinidad was providing 44.2% of the oil in the British Empire, and this figure rose to 65% by 1946 (Brereton, 1981).

The world wars changed Trinidad and Tobago's economy from an agriculturally based one to one dominated by the oil industry, with oil accounting for 10, 50, and 80% of the exports in 1919, 1932, and 1943, respectively. Even though industries involving sugar and cocoa production continued to play an important role, and the government made heroic efforts to increase the banking and manufacturing sectors through tax-incentives and the like, Brereton (1981, p. 214) noted that by the 1960s, Trinidad had become "a classic petroleum economy, dangerously dependent on oil for export earnings and for government revenues."

Whereas Trinidad did not see the need to invest in tourism given its oil dollars, tourism became increasingly important for Tobago for a variety of reasons in the 1900s. First, the central government in Trinidad neglected Tobago prior to the late 1950s and provided little investment in for developing the infrastructure or the economy. Second, Tobago did not have oil revenues, but did have beautiful beaches, a coral reef, and other attractions that proved popular with wealthy Europeans, particularly during the winter months.

In 1962, Trinidad and Tobago was granted independence and took their place among the free nations of the world. Given the importance of oil on the world stage, Trinidad and Tobago had one of the strongest economies among the developing nations. However, in the midst of plenty there were many waiting for their share of the wealth:

> There were wide income disparities between the sectors and between the occupational groups, with employees in the oil and manufacturing sectors earning far more than their counterparts in agriculture and services. Oil still dominated exports, and manufacturing had failed to develop as an important foreign exchange earner. Further, there were few linkages between the oil and manufacturing sectors and the domestic economy, and this retarded growth; and the importation of foreign services and capital increased over this period. Unemployment and underemployment also increased, as the population continued to grow rapidly and as agriculture and oil employed decreasing numbers, while manufacturing created relatively few new jobs (Brereton, 1981, pp. 221–222).

Recent Economic Conditions in Trinidad and Tobago

The Trinidadian dependence on oil for a viable economy and Tobago's dependence on Trinidad for capital to finance the tourism industry set the stage for the economic fortunes of the country over the last two decades. The drop in oil prices in the 1980s had a tremendous negative impact on the economy of Trinidad and Tobago (Dookeran, 1998), resulting in a number of years of negative economic growth

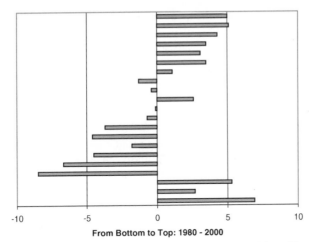

From Bottom to Top: 1980 - 2000

Fig. 1. Real GDP Growth Rates 1980–2000. *Note:* Data obtained from Theodore (1995) and World Factbooks (Central Intelligence Agency, 1999, 2000, 2001), with extrapolations for missing years.

(see Fig. 1) alongside increased unemployment and inflation rates (see Fig. 2). Between 1988 and 1995, the government devalued the dollar three times to satisfy requirements for loans from the International Monetary Fund and the World Bank. Dookeran (p. 64) argued that these actions and other reforms (e.g. privatization of state enterprises) resulted in "a successful turnaround in the performance of the Trinidad and Tobago economy" (see Figs 1 and 2) and "an increase in foreign

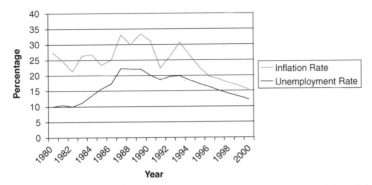

Fig. 2. Unemployment and Inflation Rates 1980–2000. *Note:* Data obtained from Table 3.2 (Central Statistical Office, 1996), Table 6.1 (UNDP, 2001), and World Factbooks (Central Intelligence Agency, 1999, 2000).

direct investment in the economy (p. 63) in the second half of the1990s. Dookeran also contended that "the lifting of exchange controls . . . [enabled] residents of Trinidad and Tobago the freedom to acquire financial assets virtually anywhere in the world" (p. 63).

Nonetheless, there were lasting negative effects on the people of Trinidad and Tobago. Consider the impact of the devaluation on the Trinidad and Tobago (TT) dollar in comparison to the United States (U.S.) dollar. In 1988, one U.S. dollar was worth approximately $2.60 TT, and in 2001, one U.S. dollar is worth $6.20 TT. Thus, an imported candy bar that had cost $1.30 TT (U.S. 50 cents) in 1988 now costs $3.10 TT, an increase of 240%. Similarly, an automobile that cost $26,000 TT ($10,000 US) now costs $62,000 TT. In actuality, the devaluations resulted in a drop in the real income and buying power of the average citizen of Trinidad and Tobago whose salary did not increase to compensate for the devaluations. As one teacher put it, "we still have middle class sentiments and want our children to take piano lessons, but we have working class incomes and can no longer afford a piano or piano lessons" (J. C. Sealey, personal communication, January 5, 2000).

With the growth in American and other foreign investment, there was also an increase in the presence of Americans and American companies in Trinidad. Companies like United Parcel Service and Federal Express are paying their drivers approximately 66% of the salaries that they would make in the United States. However, these salaries are higher than the salaries of teachers, public servants, and other individuals with degrees, leading to resentment in many individuals who were formerly members of the middle class. Further, members of the upper-middle and upper classes who had money to invest anywhere in the world as suggested by Dookeran (1998) did make such investments. The result was a growing and obvious gap between those who *have* and those who *do not have*. In 1995, a building of million dollar condominiums was sold out before completion, and there has been a growth of *gated* communities in Trinidad and Tobago. Thus, while it is accurate to say that the economy of Trinidad and Tobago has been on the upswing through the 1990s, the majority of society did not benefit from the country's economic growth; rather, the masses were subjected to and continue to experience frustration at being unable to afford previously affordable items, as well as the rage of a disillusioned and growing group of unemployable individuals who are sending the violent crime rate to new levels.

Poverty in Trinidad and Tobago

To clearly see the magnitude of a problem, one needs to have verifiable data on the problem. Unfortunately, in many developing nations including Trinidad and Tobago, data are typically not collected with the frequency and accuracy that occur in the more developed countries. There are a number of reasons for the lack of data collection. Two of the more salient, I believe are (a) a failure to understand that data are important and (b) the fear on the part of politicians that accurate data on social problems may work against them in subsequent elections. Thus, data from a variety of sources are used to estimate the scope of poverty in T & T.

POVERTY RATES

Theodore (1995) summarized a series of studies on poverty in Trinidad and Tobago conducted over the years 1981–1992, and reported poverty estimates ranging from 18 to 37% across counties. He concluded that "in Trinidad and Tobago, the evidence has shown that there has been a definite increase in the rate of poverty from 1981/1982 to 1992" (Theodore, p. 41). Recent editions of *The World Factbook* (CIA, 1999, 2000, 2001) provided a 1992 estimate of 21% of people living below the poverty line in Trinidad and Tobago, a figure that falls within the range reported by Theodore. Figure 1 indicated that 1994 was the last year of negative growth in the decade of the 1990s, however, and poverty estimates after 1994 must be examined in any current analysis of poverty in Trinidad and Tobago.

Education Level of Labor Force Entrants

One set of poverty estimates is provided by the unemployment rates, which have declined steadily since 1993 (see Fig. 2). However, there are other figures that suggest that the trends are not all positive. Figure 3 contains numbers of people in the labor force from 1995 to the first quarter of 1999 by educational

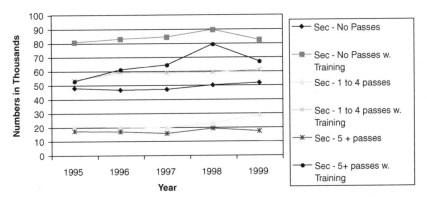

Fig. 3. Labor Force Participation Numbers in Thousands for Selected Education Levels. *Note:* Data obtained from Table 5 (Central Statistical Office, 1997).

accomplishment. These individuals attended five years of secondary schooling, and in the exam at the end of the fifth year, they obtained between zero and five or more subjects. Ideally, the graph should indicate that numbers of people with five or more subjects (with or without training) increasing, and individuals with less than five passes decreasing. However, the trend is increasing across all groups with the exception of the five or more subjects group with no training. These figures indicate that through the second half of the 1990s, increasing numbers of individuals with low skills were joining the work force. These individuals are the ones least likely to obtain jobs that pay decent wages:

> Regarding the changes in occupations from 1990 to 1997, indications are that young persons are not in significantly better positions, either financially or in terms of human resource. They may be in a worse position, as the market is demanding higher skills and increased knowledge . . . . [Further, data] for young people aged 15–19 indicated that 87.6% earned incomes under $1,300 per month [$210 USD] and 48.9% received incomes between $500 [$81 USD] and $1,299 [$210 USD] (UNDP, 2001, pp. 70–71).

Figures for the 20–24 age group are not much better with 68% of them earning under $1300 TT per month.

Recipients of Public Assistance and Food Subsidies

Although the data for children are not as recent, the trends are equally negative. Table 1 contains numbers of recipients of public assistance from 1987 to 1996. We can look at two dates as markers in discussing these results – 1989 when

Table 1. Number of Recipients of Public Assistance and Food Subsidies in Thousands.

Year	Public Assistance			Food Subsidies
	Children	Adults	Total	
1987	22.1	14.9	36.9	
1988	22.3	16.2	38.4	
1989	33.8	23.1	57.0	
1990	33.2	17.3	50.5	
1991	19.7	17.5	37.2	
1992	30.1	19.4	49.5	
1993	30.8	20.4	51.1	112.0
1994	31.0	21.3	52.3	112.1
1995	32.0	21.9	53.9	112.7
1996	33.4	14.0	47.5	118.4

Note: Data obtained from Tables 158 and 160 (Central Statistical Office, 1998a).

the first devaluation went into effect, and 1995 when the real economic growth began to be positive after a number of years of negative growth. As Table 1 indicates, between 1988 and 1989, child recipients of public assistance increased by over 11,000, a figure, which remains stable through 1996. There is a smaller increase in adult recipients of public assistance – 7,000 individuals – from 1988 to 1989. In 1995, there is no drop in the recipients of public assistance although there is a decline in adult recipients in 1996. When we look at the percentage of the population receiving public assistance over this 10-year period (see Fig. 4), the trend is increasing. Additionally, given that the number of adults receiving assistance does not decrease from 1990 to 1991, it is likely that the large drop in the child recipients of public assistance in 1991 is an artifact – perhaps the result of undercounting or misreporting. The food subsidy figures from 1993 to 1996 also indicate an increasing trend (see Table 1 and Fig. 4).

Poverty by Region of Country

As in most countries, residents of suburban and urban areas in Trinidad and Tobago tend to have higher incomes than residents of rural areas. Figure 5 contains a graph showing the 1996 mean monthly incomes of families by administrative region of the country (CSA, 1997) as well as the percentage of homes that had pipe-borne water going into the house and public sewer connections in 1990. As the figure indicates, there is a substantial relationship between mean income and access to water and sewer connections. In fact, the correlation between an area's mean income and the percentage of households with water going into the dwelling in that area is 0.89, and the correlation between income and percentage of sewer connections is 0.91. These figures tell us that poverty has a tangible impact on the lives of many T & T residents.

Impact of Poverty

Poverty would not be of tremendous concern if it did not put people, and especially children, at risk for a host of other problems. In fact, as Kozol (1992) clearly articulated, poverty is one of the most pervasive and pernicious risk factors for children in modern society. Poverty serves as a risk factor for poor health, susceptibility to diseases, low educational attainment, dropping out of school, and participation in delinquency and other criminal activity (Barrington & Hendricks, 1989; Hanson & Ginsburg, 1988; Rumberger, 1983). Poverty is such an important variable, it is often used as a marker for at-risk status in longitudinal studies of at-risk youth (e.g. Werner, 1987, 1989, 1990; Werner, Bierman & French,

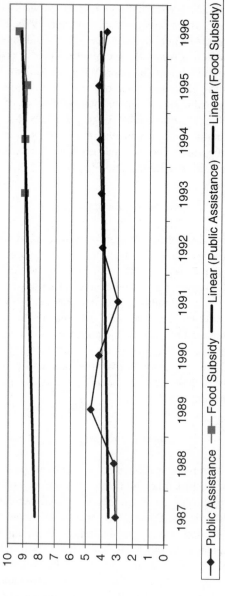

Fig. 4. Recipients of Public Assistance and Food Subsidies as a Percentage of the Population (with Trend Lines). *Note:* Data obtained from Table 158 and 160 (Central Statistical Office, 1998a).

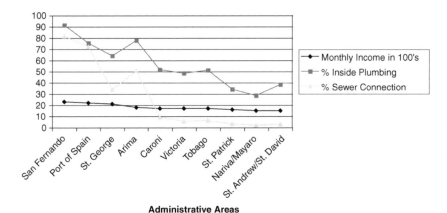

Administrative Areas

Fig. 5. Monthly Income in Hundreds of Dollars and Percentage of Households with Inside Plumbing and Sewer Connections by Administrative Region. *Note:* Data obtained from Tables 6.4 and 6.5 (Central Statistical Office, 1996) and Table 61 (Central Statistical Office, 1997).

1971; Werner & Smith, 1977, 1982). The next three sections will examine health concerns, educational concerns, and criminal activity in Trinidad and Tobago children and youth in the context of socioeconomic status (SES).

HEALTH MATTERS

Mortality Rates

As societies become more *modern*, there are generally a number of positive health correlates that occur related to better nutrition and broader access to health care. These benefits include a decrease in the general death rate, a decrease in still births, a decrease in the peri- and neo-natal death rates, and a decrease in deaths due to infectious diseases. In all of these areas, the data for Trinidad and Tobago are positive when compared with data from the 1960s and 1970s (e.g. Fig. 6). For example, although actual deaths increased from 6,956 in 1970 to 9,376 in 1996, the actual death rate decreased falling below 7% in 1974.

Mortality Among Infants and Toddlers

However, the most recently available statistics indicate that the decrease evident in long term rates is not reflected in rates over the past decade and the trend in

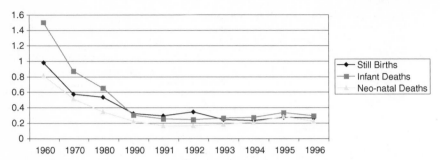

Fig. 6. Still Births, Infant Deaths and Neo-natal Deaths in Thousands (1970–1996). *Note:* Data obtained from Table 5.1 (Central Statistical Office, 1996) and Table 5.2 (UNDP, 2001).

these rates in now an increasing one. As indicated in Fig. 7, although the post neo-natal death rate and the stillbirth rate remained relatively constant from 1989 to 1996, increases in the peri- and neo-natal rates resulted in an increase in the overall infant mortality rate for this period. Moreover, infant mortality rates varied widely by administrative areas (see Table 2), in part due to the poverty index of the area and the availability of health and education services (UNDP, 2001). The tremendous fluctuation in rates within administrative areas and across the nation in a country of less than 2000 square miles and less than 1.3 million people suggests that there is no consistent health policy or health education, nor is there regular access to health care and other health-related services. Further, data on causes of death among children indicate that indicate that in 1995, 29% of child deaths were due to infectious diseases, 29% were due to cancer, and 31% were due to injury (UNDP, 2001). These are all areas where prevention and early intervention can play a major role.

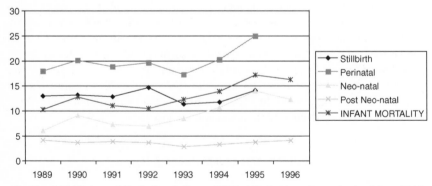

Fig. 7. Still Births and Early Death Rates (1989–1996). *Note:* Data obtained from Table 5.2 (UNDP, 2001).

Table 2. Infant Mortality Rates by Administrative Area Based on Mother's Residence.

Administrative Area	1989	1990	1991	1992
Port of Spain	12.1	10.4	9.9	16.9
San Fernando	6.8	7.9	38.3	26.4
Arima	40.7	49.0	65.7	22.6
St. George	15.5	13.9	11.2	14.9
Caroni	11.8	7.4	12.8	19.3
Nariva	10.1	12.3	14.2	14.2
Mayaro	1.0	3.0	2.0	2.0
St. Andrew/St. David	22.0	12.0	12.2	23.1
Victoria	5.0	4.7	15.6	15.9

Note: Data obtained from Table 5.3 (UNDP, 2000). Data on Tobago was not available.

Mortality Among Children and Youth

When one examines the principal causes of death by age-group (see Fig. 8 for the 1995 percentages), some harsh realities are unavoidable: (a) The number of deaths from injury for males 5 to 24 is astronomical; (b) AIDS is the third leading cause of death for males and females from 5 to 24; and (c) The rate of female deaths from AIDS is almost equal to males in the 5–14-year-old group and is higher than males in the 15–24-year-old group. Many of the injuries that lead to death occur "at home within the family unit" (UNDP, 2001, p. 59), raising important questions on types of discipline, frequency of abuse, and knowledge of parenting skills. Also as reported by UNDP, "in recent years, HIV and AIDS have reached pandemic proportions in Trinidad and Tobago" (p. 59), and one health educator estimated "that by the year 2000, 75% of Tobago's youth population would test positive for the virus" (p. 61).

The figures for AIDS transmission, especially among the young female population, highlight a number of factors related to poverty. First, there is the economic issue of sex tourism and youth prostitution. As noted earlier, Tobago is more dependent on tourism than Trinidad and the transmission rates of AIDS in Tobago are correspondingly higher. Second, there is the problem of lack of a good general education which leaves many young women with little in the way of marketable skills. Third, education around HIV transmission and the transmission of sexually transmitted diseases in general is ineffective or unavailable. Thus, the incidence of gonorrhea is also high. The lack of education also leads to the propagation of folk tales such as "sex with a virgin is a cure for AIDS," which in turn result in higher incidences of sexual contact between older males and younger

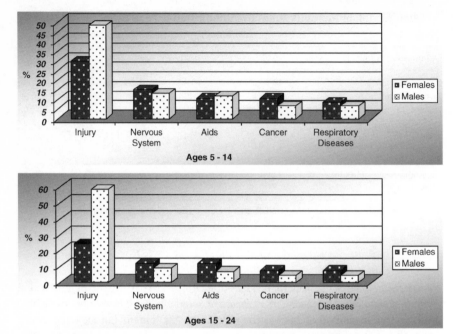

Fig. 8. Primary Causes of Deaths in 5–14 and 15–24 Year-Old Groups for 1995. *Note:* Data obtained from Tables 5.11 and 5.12 (UNDP, 2001).

females, sometimes for money, or sometimes through acts of rape in the desperate search for a cure.

Other Health Concerns

There are two other areas of health concerns with regard to children and youth in Trinidad and Tobago: teenage pregnancy and the issue of mental health. With regard to the former issue, data indicate that the percentage of teenage births has stabilized over the last seven years at about 13%, and that teenage fertility figures have dropped from 80.2% in 1985 to 46.2% in 1995 (UNDP, 2001). While these are positive indications, teenage pregnancies raise other concerns. As in many other countries, teenage pregnancy in T & T is correlated with leaving the school system early and with unstable and dysfunctional family relationships. Early pregnancy contributes to mothers remaining in poverty, and leads to additional health concerns (e.g. high blood pressure of mother, malnutrition of mother and infant, and higher incidences of congenital defects). Additionally, there are concerns about the quality of parenting and the conflicting developmental needs of adolescent mothers and their infants, concerns which can easily result in child abuse and lead to another generation of teenagers living in poverty and having children of their own.

The problem of mental health services is even more acute. To this day, the St. Ann's Hospital where mental health concerns are dealt with is commonly referred to as *The Madhouse*. Trinidad and Tobago has no assessment procedures or legal mandates to identify basic mental health problems (e.g. depression) in children and youth. A basic psychoeducational evaluation costs upwards of $3,000 and only the more affluent members of society can afford these services. There are about 35 guidance officers assigned to over 100 secondary schools, and a smaller group assigned to elementary schools with the highest rates of academic failure; thus, the majority of schools do not receive regular psychoeducational or mental health services. Further, the guidance officers have been hired into the educational system from a variety of disciplines including teaching, social work, and the probation system. Consequently, their knowledge in areas like diagnosis, assessment, and intervention is limited. The guidance officers with degrees are trained in individual and group counseling, a skill that is of limited utility when faced with severe academic, behavioral, or emotional problems. Moreover, as the gap grows between the rich and the poor in T & T, the need for mental health services for children, youth, and adults grows ever more acute:

> The demand on services is growing because of increasing drug abuse problems both at the parent and child levels, increasing referrals, and the levels of emotional trauma among children who have been witnesses to incidents such as rape or murder of one parent or another, abandonment, etc (UNDP, 2001, p. 63).

ACCESS TO EDUCATION, QUALITY OF EDUCATIONAL EXPERIENCES AND EDUCATIONAL ATTAINMENT

Trinidad and Tobago proudly boasts one of the highest literacy rates in the world. The most recent World Factbook (CIA, 2001) reported that the T & T's literacy rate – i.e. people aged 15 and over who can read and write – was 97.9% (98.8% for males and 97% for females). Unfortunately, we are not told at what level these individuals can read. As an educator and school psychologist who has worked in both Trinidad and Tobago and the United States, I believe that we really need to revisit the definition of literacy, not just for Trinidad and Tobago, but all of the countries of the world. As the data to be presented will demonstrate, the reported literacy rate may serve as a point of pride for the nation, but it does not really indicate the percentage of the population that are functionally literate. Moreover, the currently reported literacy rate provides a convenient number for governments to point to when told that there is a problem with the educational system.

ACCESS TO EDUCATION

Over the past three decades, there has been an increasing emphasis by the Ministry of Education on providing free primary and secondary education for all of the nation's students. This goal has not been fully realized at either level of schooling:

> In no year up to 1998/1999 has a net or gross enrollment ratio of 100% been registered for children aged 5 to 11+ . . . [In 1995] the number of enrolled students in the public schools from the infant level to Standard 5 was 177,651 or 79.5% of the possible 5- to 11-year-old population of 199,406 children. The private primary schools accounted for a further 7,000 students . . . and the schools with challenged children for 912 . . . these gross figures leave at least 13,800 children or 7% of the 5 to 11 cohort out of the school system (public and private) and unaccounted for (UNDP, 2001, p. 44).

Moreover, as students progress through the seven years of elementary school, *at least* an additional 3% drop out of the system (Central Statistical Office, 1998b).

The percentages of students attending secondary school are lower than the elementary school enrollment figures, primarily due to a lack of secondary school places. The secondary schools are classified into three tiers, informally: Tier 1 (assisted secondary schools or prestige schools), Tier 2 (five to seven year government schools) and Tier 3 (junior and senior secondary comprehensive schools and composite schools). Tier 3 schools were one of the most recent additions to the system and were built in the 1970s and 1980s to provide increased access to secondary education. Consequently, many of them operate on a shift system with two separate cohorts of students attending the morning and afternoon shifts, respectively. The shift system raises concerns about time spent in school and the amount of unsupervised time available to the 11- to 14-year-olds who attend these schools. On average, students with the highest scores on the secondary entrance examination are sent to the Tier 1 schools and students with the lowest scores are sent to the Tier 3 schools.

Although the addition of the Tier 3 schools resulted in a substantial increase in the number of students attending secondary schools, it did not result in universal secondary education, and the shortage of spaces in secondary school continued to grow as the population grew. Thus, the percentages of eligible students enrolled in secondary schools began to decline in the late 1980s and 1990s (see Table 3). In the 1996/1997 school year, only 73% of students who were eligible for secondary placement by age were actually enrolled in secondary schools and these figures

Table 3. Secondary School Enrollment Rates for 1990/1991 to 1993/1994 School Years.

School Year	UNDP: Ages 12–16	CSA: All Students
1990/1991	74.9	88.7
1991/1992	73.2	88.0
1992/1993	63.3	76.5
1993/1994	63.9	77.3

Note: UNDP = United Nations Development Program; CSA = Central Statistical Office. Data obtained from Table 1 (Central Statistical Office, 1998b) and Table 4.6 (UNDP, 2001).

differed across educational regions, ranging from a low of 51% in Tobago to a high of 92% in St. Patrick (*Mdn* school enrollment rate = 70%).

Quality of Educational Experiences

Although not reported in education statistics, there is a substantial correlation between parental education/income and assignment to one of the three tiers (see Fig. 9). The correlations between mean income of administrative regions and the percent of students attending Tier 1, Tier 2, and Tier 3 schools in those regions is 0.82, 0.15, and −0.35, respectively. In other words, regions with higher incomes have more Tier 1 school spaces and fewer Tier 3 school spaces and vice versa,

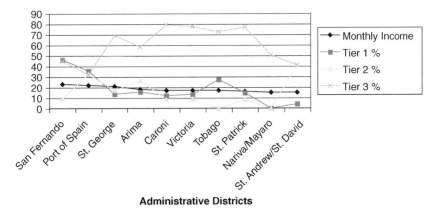

Fig. 9. Mean Monthly Income in Hundreds of Dollars and Percentages of Students Assigned to Tier 1, Tier 2, and Tier 3 Schools by Administrative Region. *Note:* Data obtained from Table 14 (Central Statistical Office, 1998b) and Table 61 (Central Statistical Office, 1997).

Table 4. Percentage of Students Enrolled in the Three School Tiers by
Administrative Area 1996/1997.

School Levels Administrative Area	Tier 1	Tier 2		Tier 3	
	Assisted Secondary	Government Secondary	Junior Secondary	Senior Secondary	Composite Schools
Port of Spain	35.7	32.5	22.8	9.0	0.0
San Fernando	46.2	8.7	18.9	26.1	0.0
Arima	15.7	26.0	0.0	58.3	0.0
St. George	13.5	17.3	39.4	25.9	3.9
Caroni	12.1	8.5	44.9	29.0	5.4
Nariva/Mayaro	0.0	0.0	21.2	24.2	5.2
St. Andrew/St. David	4.1	40.9	39.0	0.0	1.6
Victoria	13.4	8.8	34.5	31.5	11.7
St. Patrick	14.6	8.2	40.9	19.1	17.1
Tobago	27.2	0.0	44.4	0.0	28.3

Note: Data obtained from Table 24 (Central Statistical Office, 1998b).

but do not differ significantly on Tier 2 school spaces. Although the figures are
not available, it is likely that this pattern also holds within education regions, with
students from higher SES families attending higher tier schools (Table 4).

As students are assigned to school tiers on the basis of test scores, one can argue
that from a student input standpoint, the Tier 1 schools start off with an advantage.
However, this advantage is not limited to student input, but also to the teaching staff.
Due to a lack of availability of credentialled teachers – i.e. teachers with a degree
in education or a degree in their subject area and appropriate teacher training – it is
possible to teach at the secondary school level in Trinidad and Tobago with only a
university degree in a subject area or with final year high school passes (*A Levels*).
Elementary teachers require five *O Level* passes and/or a two-year diploma from
one of the teachers colleges. No education degree or teacher training is required.
Thus, teachers with subject-area degrees are often the most qualified teachers in
the secondary school system. Table 5 contains the percentages of teachers with
degrees or with some teacher training in each type of school in the system. As
is evident from the percentages reported, the Tier 1 and 2 schools which get the
students with higher achievement test scores also have the highest percentages of
teachers with university degrees.

The figures are reversed for trained teachers, but the numbers are not as positive
as they appear. When the Tier 3 schools were built, the shortage of teachers for
the secondary system became even more acute, and teachers from the elementary
system who had specialties (e.g. some training, but no credentials) in particular

Table 5. Percentages of Degreed Teachers and Trained Teachers by Type of Secondary School 1996/1997.

	Teachers with Degrees	Trained Teachers
Assisted secondary (1)	86.6	51.9
Government secondary (2)	73.6	44.8
Junior secondary (3)	43.4	60.8
Senior secondary (3)	62.0	35.2
Composite (3)	56.1	58.9

Note: Data obtained from Table 25 (Central Statistical Office, 1998b).

areas were seconded to the junior secondary system which is roughly equivalent to the middle school years in the United States, or to composite schools which include the middle school years. The majority of these teachers had no degrees, but had completed the two-year diploma, and were thus considered *trained* teachers. My aunt who had less musical training than I did 15 years ago was assigned to a junior secondary school as a music teacher. Currently, I could not get a job in a public elementary school in the U.S. on the basis of my current musical training, although I have continued to upgrade my musical skills over the last 15 years. The point is not that many of the teachers in the Tier 3 schools were incompetent; the point is that the students who have the lowest academic skills receive the teachers with the poorest knowledge base in the various subject areas.

Educational Attainment

The education system in T & T is structured after the old British model with seven years of elementary education beginning at age five, and five years of secondary education, upon successful completion of the secondary entrance examination. At the end of the five years of secondary schooling, there is another examination – the *O Level* exam originally administered by Cambridge and Oxford Universities – that qualifies the student for an additional two years of secondary education necessary for entrance into universities operating under the British model. As indicated earlier, the number of students placed in secondary schools increased dramatically when the Tier 3 schools were built. The increase was not necessarily because more students were *passing* the examination, but because there were more secondary school places available.

In an attempt to provide a high school credential indicating the attainment of basic academic skills, Trinidad and Tobago joined other islands in the formation

Table 6. Percentages of Students Passing General and Basic Proficiency
Examinations in English, Mathematics, and Integrated Science.

Subjects	1991	1992	1993	1994
English language (General)	66.1	77.3	71.3	39.7
English language (Basic)	3.2	5.8	1.5	5.2
Mathematics (General)	52.6	51.4	54.0	31.7
Mathematics (Basic)	1.5	0.6	1.6	1.6
Integrated science (General)	70.2	68.8	77.0	63.5
Integrated science (Basic)	18.3	22.3	39.8	49.5

Note: Data obtained from Table 67 (Central Statistical Office, 1998a).

of the Caribbean Examinations Council, a unit which replaced Oxford and
Cambridge Universities, and developing a two-tiered examination process. Strong
students (i.e. the majority of students at Tier 1 and 2 schools) wrote *General
Proficiency* (GP) exams whereas weaker students (i.e. the majority of students
at Tier 3 schools) wrote *Basic Proficiency* (BP) exams. Table 6 contains pass
rates in three fundamental subject areas – English Language, Mathematics, and
Science – at the GP and BP level for four academic years. The results in English
Language and Mathematics are equally abysmal. Less than 80% of the students
passed GP English Language and less than 55% passed the GP mathematics
exam. Moreover, the equivalent percentages for the BP exams are less than 6%
(English Language) and less than 2% (Mathematics). The GP Integrated Science
rates are similar to the GP English. However, the BP Science exam results are
getting better.

Why are so many students who are among the strongest academically five years
before not succeeding at the GP examinations? Is it poor teaching or something
else? Should more of these students be taking the BP exams? Further, the results of
the BP examinations in English Language and Mathematics can only be described
as criminal. The percentage of students passing the BP examinations after five
years of secondary schooling makes it clear that these students are not being
educated in their schools. The lack of education may be due to teaching, student
absences, teacher absences, or poor learning environments, but no learning is taking
place. Although student absenteeism probably plays a role, teacher absenteeism
certainly does as well. In addition to the three terms breaks in December, April,
and July/August, teachers are allowed 14 days of casual leave and 14 days of sick
leave during the academic year and there is no substitute teacher system. Thus,
when teachers are absent, no teaching occurs in their classrooms. Further, many
teachers insist on taking *their* 28 days.

Consider a school that has 10 teachers, each of whom takes all of the allowable days – this results in 280 days of no teachers in classes across a school year. When we consider that there are 4,894 teachers in Trinidad and Tobago, if only 25% of the teacher cohort takes all 28 days, the system has lost over 34,000 teaching days, and far more than 25% of the teachers take all their days. Further, the above figures do not include teachers who are tardy for classes – another epidemic in T & T – or those who are in school but choose not to go to class that day.

The system needs restructuring, and the introduction of vocational and technical subjects should be a major component of the restructuring process. However, these subjects are often considered of lesser status than the traditional academic subjects and some parents insist that their children prepare for the GP or BP exams with the disastrous consequences outlined in Table 6. Moreover, the Ministry of Education has failed to take a leadership role with regard to this issue. In 1996 and 1997, in response to the increasing numbers of students not being placed in secondary schools, the government built a few Post-Primary centers modeled after an extremely successful vocational training program (Servol). However, very few of these were built and they were not given the resources to do the job for which they were intended – i.e. give children with low academic skills functional job skills to allow them to become contributing citizens.

Subsequently, the government built two *model* schools that opened in 1999. Students who obtained the lowest scores on the secondary school entrance examination – lower than the scores of the students sent to the Tier 3 schools – were placed in these model Tier 4 schools, with standard secondary school curriculum and no vocational or technical subjects. The limited data available suggests that most of the students assigned to the model schools would qualify for special education labels (e.g. mentally retarded, behavior disordered, emotionally disturbed) in the United States. Moreover, these schools are staffed with new teachers (again, without teacher training) or teachers who have retired, and these teachers are expected to teach the regular secondary school curriculum with the assistance of a few remedial reading teachers. An assessment of three of the students at one of the model schools, albeit students who are having tremendous difficulties in school, indicated that they could not read the first sentence of a kindergarten passage. And as indicated previously, the system has no school psychologists, and the government has yet to approve the Diagnostic and Prescriptive Service (DPS) which is intended to provide academic and behavioral support for teachers and students. The DPS has been suggested since 1997.

In summary, the education system is in serious need of reform. The students who are from the most deprived backgrounds are being sent to schools where the teachers have the least knowledge, and the examination results are clearly showing that learning is not occurring.

CHILDREN, YOUTH AND CRIME

As indicated earlier, the crime rate began to increase with the devaluation of the TT dollar. This escalation has continued through the late 1990s into 2001. Moreover, "serious crimes that carry a sentence of five years or more are in the increase" and "the largest age cohort within the prison population is between the ages of 17 and 21"(UNDP, 2001, p. 77). A recent report in one of Trinidad and Tobago's daily newspapers summarized the dire situation with regard to crime in Trinidad and Tobago:

> As the country [Trinidad and Tobago] remains stuck in a political gridlock with the two main parties haggling over who should hold the reins of power, violent crime continues to spiral out of control with murders taking an unprecedented and bloody toll on an already battle-fatigued citizenry. This country now has one of the highest murder rates [presumably in the world] for the first time in over a decade. The latest crime figures show an increase in violent crime nationwide, with murders jumping to a 13-year high of 148 at week's close. The grim reality is a murder every 60 hours in a country with a population of 1.3 million. More disturbing is the average age of the vast majority of violent perpetrators: 18 to 25.... Only last month, Prime Minister and Minister of National Security Basdeo Panday conceded that crime was a battle the Government could not win (Marajh, 2001, p. 10).

The description in the preceding quotation is disturbing in any country, but especially so in a small one.

The rate of a murder every 60 hours coupled with the facts that youth make up the vast number of the violent criminals and the government believes that the problem is beyond governmental intervention (with the Police Force and Army as agents of the government) summarizes a situation that is of unparalleled severity in a nation that is relatively affluent. In the 10-year period, 1987–1996, the percentage of youth (17–21) in the prison system increased whereas the percentage of 22–26 year-olds decreased (see Fig. 10). However, these trends will eventually result in an increase in both of the age groups. Moreover, the Prime Minister's pessimistic comment on the crime situation is based, unfortunately, on the data that are currently available. As Table 7 shows, most of the crimes that were committed in 1994 through 1996 were not prosecuted in that period. Even when we acknowledge that many of people in prisons have not yet been brought to trial (UNDP, 2001), the figures on the number of crimes detected vs. the number convicted – see Fig. 11 – indicate that the majority of individuals who commit crimes have little fear of facing negative consequences for their actions.

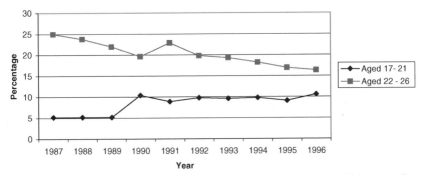

Fig. 10. Percentage of 17–21 and 22–26 Year Olds in Prison (1987–1996). *Note:* Data obtained from Table 7.3 (UNDP, 2001).

The UNDP (2001) report identified a number of characteristics of the perpetrators of crime. These characteristics included dysfunctional or unstable family lives, learning problems, low literacy and numeracy skills, undeveloped vocational and technical skills that could result in employment, and a low sense of accomplishment. To the extent that these characteristics play a *causal* role in crime, the data in Tables 1, 5 and 6, and in Figs 3 and 4 suggest that crime will continue to increase for a number of years to come.

Table 7. Crimes Committed and Percentage[a] of Crimes Prosecuted in a Three-Year Period.

Crime Type	1994	1995	1996
Murder	133 (53%)	121 66%)	107 (56%)
Wounding (felonious)	533 (49%)	501 (53%)	505 (51%)
Other crimes against the person	696 (76%)	783 (81%)	828 (77%)
Breaking and burglary	7,635 (15%)	6,542 (14%)	6,835 (15%)
Robbery	4,490 (17%)	3,858 (18%)	4,075 (21%)
Larceny	2,834 (11%)	2,781 (11%)	3,196 (12%)
Larceny in dwelling houses	367 (22%)	326 (16%)	352 (19%)
Other crimes against property	308 (42%)	335 (45%)	627 (60%)
Forgery and currency crimes	447 (91%)	396 (74%)	283 (41%)
Narcotic offenses	1,098 (99%)	1,118 (150%)	1,259 (100%)
Total major crimes[b]	18,614 (26%)	16,783 (27%)	18,093 (28%)
Total minor crimes[c]	21,176 (27%)	21,311 (36%)	19,808 (30%)

Note: Data obtained from Table 7.1 (UNDP, 2001).

[a] Percentages are in parentheses.

[b] Major crimes include crimes not listed here (e.g. Other).

[c] Minor crimes include indecent assault, possession of firearms, unlawful entry, and so on.

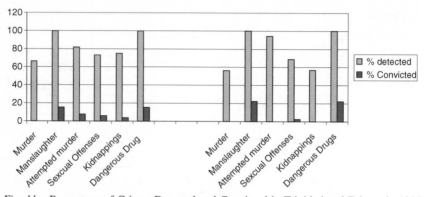

Fig. 11. Percentage of Crimes Detected and Convicted in Trinidad and Tobago in 1995 and 1996. *Note:* Data obtained from Table 7.2 (UNDP, 2001).

CONCLUSION

The conclusions on the basis of the available data are clear and stark. Although Trinidad and Tobago has had positive economic growth for much of its 40-year history, including the last seven years (see Figs 1 and 2), poverty is prevalent in the country, and is having a negative impact on children and youth in the areas of health, education, and involvement in criminal activity. The percentage of the T & T population receiving public assistance has increased over the last 14 years by at least one percentage point (see Table 1 & Fig. 4), with a corresponding increase in the number of people dependent on food subsidies from the government and the percentage of the workforce with low educational attainment (Fig. 3). No region of the country, including capital and other urban centers have 100% inside plumbing or sewer connections, and there are still several regions of the country where sewer connections and inside plumbing are available in less than 50% of homes (see Fig. 5). Eighty percent of the variance in household sewer connections and inside plumbing can be explained by mean income of the region.

From the late 1980s to early 1990s, infant mortality rates have climbed in seven of the nine administrative regions of the country. The exceptions were the Arima area where they were tremendously elevated to begin with (see Table 2 and Fig. 6), and St. George county which consists of much of the suburban regions surrounding the capital. Moreover, the Arima region still reports one of the highest infant mortality rates in the country. Health and health education remain a serious concern, with the largest proportion of deaths among children and youth being from preventable causes (see Fig. 8). Additionally, the HIV infection rate among children and youth is tremendously elevated, with females in the 15–24-year-old age group at tremendous risk.

Quality education is not available to all. Rather, there is a differentiation of education quality available dependent on the income of the family. The children of individuals with higher incomes are more likely to attend Tier 1 or prestige schools whereas the children of families with lower incomes are more likely to attend Tier 3 schools. The lack of educational equity is due, in part, to the location of prestige schools in more affluent regions and vice versa (see Table 4 and Fig. 9). Moreover, a recent set of schools which can be labeled Tier 4 have been created to absorb the students with the lowest scores in the secondary school entrance examinations. The most qualified teachers are assigned to the Tier 1 schools whereas the teachers with the least qualifications are assigned to the lower tier schools where the students have greater academic and behavioral deficiencies (see Table 5). The percentage of students passing the general proficiency examinations is low, and the percentage of students passing the basic proficiency examinations is even lower, resulting in a growing number of students leaving the secondary school system unable to read, write, or do basic arithmetic (see Table 6).

Finally, the increase in the involvement of youth in criminal activity has reached proportions that can only be described as epidemic, with the number of individuals 17–21 participating in crime increasing dramatically over the last decade (UNDP, 2001). The connection of crime to poverty and education is also evident. Eighty-three percent of convicted murderers in Trinidad and Tobago are from low SES groups, and 86% of them have a junior high education or less (Baldeosingh, 2001).

RECOMMENDATIONS

It is clear that health, education, and crime concerns about children and youth in Trinidad and Tobago reflect a lack of commitment in the midst of plenty. The critical question is what can be done to reverse these trends. Social scientists are often accused of providing simplistic solutions to complex problems, and it is clear that the problems that Trinidad and Tobago face are complex. However, I contend that the road to a solution in Trinidad and Tobago is relatively simple – i.e. simple to articulate although not simple to implement, and thus not simplistic in conception. Trinidad and Tobago's problems in education, health, crime, and other areas of social concern can be addressed, at least in part, through the utilization of four general recommendations, Each of which is discussed briefly in the following paragraphs.

Promoting Individual and Collective Accountability in the Government Sector,
with Positive and Negative Consequences for Actions

One of T & T's greatest problems is a lack of accountability for actions taken personally or professionally. The country does not have a legal system which allows for lawsuits to be easily initiated and heard by the courts. Thus, gross misconduct in public office, damage to personal property by businesses, government, or individuals, medical malpractice, and many other areas in which individuals or groups should be held accountable lead to no consequences and, thus, no incentives to improve. Lawsuits are becoming more common, but are still relatively rare and there is a standing joke in society that you can sue, but the case is unlikely to be called in your lifetime.

The public service provides another example of lack of accountability and consequences. Absenteeism and tardiness are chronic in the public sector, including the health system, the police force, the teaching service, and the public service. The lack of accountability coupled with no consequences for actions have created a system that cannot accomplish basic goals. The inability of the police force to fight crime and the poor pass rates of secondary school students must be interpreted in this context. As I pointed out to a group of teachers at a recent workshop, you cannot insist that your students are punctual if you are not in class to greet them when they arrive.

The lack of consequences has also led to a general sense of learned helplessness. In late October of 2001, I ordered six items from companies like the National Association of School Psychologists to be sent to the Central Guidance Office in Trinidad. As of the end of December, 2001, only three of the items had arrived. One arrived relatively quickly but took a month to clear customs, with conflicting instructions from the same people on different days. The second arrived in the second week in December. Three *Collect Package* cards came to the office on the same day. At the Post Office, I was rebuked for not collecting the item when I received the first card, although the cards had all arrived at the same time. At that time, I asked the clerk at the Post Office to check and see if there were other parcels waiting for me. She refused and said that if there were other parcels, I would get a card. On December 27th, I received a card dated November 27th from the Post Office, indicating that the package I collected on 12/27 had been there when the previous package had been collected. Moreover, the set of handouts in that package was no longer in the box nor the plastic wrap in which they are shipped; they were crumpled up in a post office bag. The Post Office clerk blamed the customs officials who had inspected the package and indicated that there was no one at the Post Office to whom I could complain. I confess that I would not have filed a complaint anyway, as nothing would have occurred in response to the complaint other than

Table 8. Internet Joke on the Nature of Accountability and Lack of Consequences in Trinidad and Tobago.

A man dies and goes to hell. There he finds that there is a different hell for each country. He goes first to the German hell and asks, "What do they do here?"

He is told, "First they put you in an electric chair for an hour. Then they lay you on a bed of nails for another hour. Then the German devil comes in and whips you for the rest of the day."

The man does not like the sound of that at all, so he moves on. He checks out the American hell as well as the Russian hell and many more. He discovers that they are all more or less the same as the German hell. Then he comes to the Trinidadian hell and finds that there is a very long line of people waiting to get in.

Amazed he asks, "What do they do here?"

He is told, "First they put you in an electric chair for an hour. Then they lay you on a bed of nails for another hour. Then the Trinidadian devil comes in and whips you for the rest of the day."

"But that is exactly the same as all the other hells – why are there so many people waiting to get in?"

"Because there is never any electricity, so the electric chair does not work, someone stole all the nails, and the devil used to be a public servant, so he comes in, punches his time-card and then goes back home."

the possible deliberate delaying or misplacement of the packages that I was still expecting. Although these stories are personal and anecdotal, they speak about a way of doing things that is common in Trinidad and Tobago. Table 8 contains a recent joke being circulated on the Internet on the Trinidad and Tobago character – a joke that highlights the lack of consequences in the Trinidad and Tobago system as much as the percentage of convictions reported in Fig. 10.

Emphasizing the Use of a Problem-Solving Model and Data-Based Decision Making

The use of problem-solving models is emphasized in many situations and across many domains, in part because the use of a problem-solving model encourages: (a) looking at data to help define the problem; (b) considering multiple intervention options, including costs, benefits, and feasibility; (c) developing criteria for evaluating a problem's solution; and (d) evaluating the solution's effectiveness. Problem-solving models are used in both clear-cut and ambiguous situations, and may be particularly useful in areas of public policy where there are multiple factors, multiple stakeholders, and multiple solutions. Moreover, by explicitly using a problem-solving process, many decision-making pitfalls like groupthink, use of the availability and representativeness heuristics, and mental set can be avoided. Additionally, the problem-solving model results in greater accountability and in better implementation of public policies, as individuals who are responsible for various aspects of a plan are identified and the criteria for success or lack of success are made explicit. And of course, basing decisions on sound data will result in better problem identification and problem solving.

Thinking of Public Education as Primary and Secondary Prevention Activities for Society

The benefits of primary and secondary prevention activities are well documented in most countries in the world. The low incidence of diseases like polio, smallpox, and malaria are a tribute to these types of activities, as is the decreased risk of cavities in areas where water is fluoridated. However, the concept of primary and secondary prevention is one that is not limited to the arena or public health. We can think of education in primary prevention terms. For example, based on the some of the data reported in this chapter, it is possible to argue that poverty leads to low educational attainment, which in turn leads to involvement in criminal activity. Alternatively, it can also be argued that a good education leads to well-paying jobs, and ultimately to being a productive citizen. Although a government may find it difficult to eliminate poverty directly, governments control the resources that are put into education.

From this perspective, quality education for all is a primary prevention activity which can have positive effects on the crime rate, the economy, the use of welfare, and family dysfunction. Further, education from this perspective involves more than the traditional academic subjects that are typically done in Trinidad and Tobago. This country must develop a strong vocational and technical training program (a) to supply quality technicians to the society; and (b) to provide educational options for students whose strengths are not in the traditional subjects.

I spoke to a 15-year-old young man who was unable to read a kindergarten passage and who could not verbalize the difference between a triangle and a square, although he could draw the two shapes. He became very animated when he discussed fishing – animation that we do not see from him in school or the classroom – and he was able to name a large number of varieties of fish. This young man was also able to do basic arithmetic when it was framed as buying and selling fish that he had caught. Instead of the daily failure that he experiences currently trying to do junior high work that is clearly beyond him, the young man should be involved in a supervised apprenticeship program that will allow him to pursue his interest in fishing. This program could also provide support and guidance in marketing the fish to the public and to restaurants, while teaching about resource conservation. Thus, someone who at this point is best known by all of the teaching staff at the school that he attends as the student who is often using obscene language on the sidewalk because he has been sent home yet again will actually be studying a trade that he enjoys and making a meaningful contribution to the local economy.

Nor need this type of education be limited to people of traditional school age. Last week, I visited a waterfall in Tobago with some colleagues who were visiting T & T for a few days. We hired a local guide, Dave, who was knowledgeable about the local flora and fauna to lead us to the waterfall. Dave was running his business as were the other guides with very little government involvement. These individuals are, in essence, local park rangers. However, their income is dependent on visitors choosing to hire guides – many locals do not. The trails are not as well maintained as in the U.S. national parks, nor the restroom facilities. Trinidad and Tobago has a number of wonderful areas such as the reef off the coast of Tobago, the old British forts, and a number of waterfalls and hiking trails that can be supported by the government. Regularization of fees will allow them to be self-supporting in part, and proper maintenance will encourage more local and foreign visitors. At the same time, classifying these areas as maintained recreational facilities will provide a more reliable income for the enterprising individuals who already act as guides in these places, and will allow for a systematic education of these guides on the history and geography of the sites and on the conservation of resources.

Utilizing the Skills Available from Trinidad and Tobago Nationals Who Live Abroad

Trinidad and Tobago, like many nations of the Caribbean, has a wealth of expertise available in nationals who emigrated to and were trained in North America and Europe. Many of these nationals are willing to assist in the ongoing development of T & T, and in fact, many have offered their services to the government in a variety of domains. The response to these offers varies from indifference to indignation, and most of these nationals eventually stop trying to help a country that does not appear to want their help. Some of these nationals have moved back to Trinidad and Tobago, only to leave again after dealing with the lack of accountability, the inability to get things done, and the general belief that things will not change anyway.

It is important to note here that I am not describing people who want to make Trinidad into a second England or USA. Rather, these are individuals with expertise in a particular arena, an expertise that can be applied in a Trinidad and Tobago context. Currently, Trinidad has no one who is trained in school psychology working in its education system. In one plan that I did for Trinidad and Tobago a few years ago, I suggested providing scholarships for T & T nationals to receive doctoral training in school psychology with the ultimate goal of setting up a training program at the Trinidad campus of the University of the West Indies, so that Trinidad and Tobago would become self-sustaining in this area. And that is the goal of many other nationals who would like to repay the country of their birth. However, for these types of plans to be considered and adopted, there needs to be a commitment to national development that goes beyond winning the next election. Ultimately, national development takes longer than one or two political terms of office to occur, and politicians must think of the country more than themselves to engage in long term development strategies, especially ones where the ultimate payoff does not win an election or result in your name on a plaque touting your achievements.

Closing Words

In the title, I described Trinidad and Tobago as lacking commitment in the midst of plenty. I do not believe this to be a harsh assessment. The Trinidad and Tobago economy continues to grow, even after the September 11, 2001 disaster. Given the low TT dollar in relation to the U.S. dollar, investment continues to pour into Trinidad and Tobago from the United States and other countries. However, as in the United States, the gap between those who have and those who do not have also continues to grow. Trinidad is on average 50 miles by 37 miles, and Tobago is on average 26 miles by 7.5 miles. In islands this size, those who have and those who do not have must interact much more than in a county the size of the United States. The motto of Trinidad and Tobago is "Together we aspire, Together we achieve." For Trinidad and Tobago to become more than just another developing nation, for T & T to live up to its motto, this 40-year-old nation must, individually and collectively, accept a sense of responsibility and accountability. The nation must serve all its citizens, but particularly those in economic circumstances that do not allow for options other than government-provided ones. Only then will "every creed and race find an equal place" as stated in the final lines of the Trinidad and Tobago National Anthem.

REFERENCES

Baldeosingh, K. (2001, December 23). Why people become killers? *Sunday Express*, 11.

Barrington, B. L., & Hendricks, B. (1989). Differentiating characteristics of school graduates, dropouts, and nongraduates. *Journal of Educational Research*, 82, 309–319.

Brereton, B. (1981). *A history of modern Trinidad: 1783–1962*. Exeter, NH: Heinemann Educational Books.

Central Intelligence Agency (1999). *The world factbook 1999: Trinidad and Tobago*. Retrieved from www.umsl.edu/services/govdocs/wofact99/291.htm.

Central Intelligence Agency (2000). *The world factbook 2000: Trinidad and Tobago*. Retrieved from http://www.odci.gov/cia/publications/factbook/geos/td.html.

Central Intelligence Agency (2001). *The world factbook 2001: Trinidad and Tobago*. Retrieved from http://www.cia.gov/publications/factbook/geos/td.html.

Central Statistical Office (1996). *Social indicators 1985–1992: Education, health, crime, consumption, productivity, demographic characteristics*. Port of Spain, Trinidad: Author.

Central Statistical Office (1997). *Continuous sample survey of population: Labour Force report 1996*. Port of Spain, Trinidad: Author.

Central Statistical Office (1998a). *Annual statistical digest 1996*. Port of Spain, Trinidad: Author.

Central Statistical Office (1998b). *Report on Education Statistics 1996/1997*. Port of Spain, Trinidad: Author.

De Suze, J. A. (1966). *The new Trinidad and Tobago* (formerly *Little folks' Trinidad*). Glasgow, England: Press of the Publishers.

Dookeran, W. (1998). The Trinidad and Tobago economy: Past, present and future. *Quarterly Economic Bulletin, 23*, 62–67.

Hanson, S. L., & Ginsburg, A. L. (1988). Gaining ground: Values and high school success. *American Educational Research Journal, 25*, 334–365.

Kozol, J. (1992). *Savage inequalities: Children in America's schools*. New York: HarperPerennial.

Marajh, C. (2001, December 23). Chief cop in a quandary. *Sunday Express*, 10.

Rumberger, R. W. (1983). Dropping out of high school: The influence of race, sex, and family background. *American Educational Research Journal, 20*, 199–220.

Theodore, K. (1995, March). *Poverty reduction strategies: The role of health and education – A Trinidad and Tobago perspective*. Paper presented at the Seminar on Poverty Reduction and Social Policy in the Caribbean: The Role of Health and Education, Port of Spain, Trinidad.

United Nations Development Programme (2001). *Trinidad and Tobago national human development report 2000: Youth at risk in Trinidad and Tobago*. Port of Spain, Trinidad: Author.

Werner, E. E. (1987, April). Children of the garden island. *Scientific American*, 106–111.

Werner, E. E. (1989). High-risk children in young adulthood: A longitudinal study from birth to 32 years. *American Journal of Orthopsychiatry, 59*, 72–81.

Werner, E. E. (1990). Protective factors and individual resilience. In: S. J. Meisels & J. P. Shonkoff (Eds), *Handbook of Early Childhood Intervention* (pp. 97–116). New York: Cambridge University Press.

Werner, E. E., Bierman, J., & French, F. (1971). *The children of Kauai*. Honolulu: University of Hawaii Press.

Werner, E. E., & Smith, R. S. (1977). *Kauai's children come of age*. Honolulu: University of Hawaii Press.

Werner, E. E., & Smith, R. S. (1982). *Vulnerable but invincible: A longitudinal study of resilient children and youth*. New York: McGraw-Hill.

8. THE DILEMMA OF CHILD SOLDIERING IN SUB-SAHARAN AFRICA

Kingsley Banya and Juliet Elu

INTRODUCTION

Currently, more than 300,000 children under the age of eighteen are fighting as soldiers with government armed forces and armed opposition groups in more than thirty countries worldwide. In more than eighty-five countries, hundreds of thousands more under-eighteens have been recruited into government armed forces, paramilitaries, civil militia and a wide variety of non-state armed groups. Millions of children worldwide receive military training and indoctrination in youth movements and schools. While most child soldiers are aged between fifteen and eighteen, the youngest age reported is seven (*UN Chronicle*, Winter 2000).

These statistics represent only a snapshot of the problem, as children are recruited, captured, demobilized, wounded or even killed every day. Many of today's adult soldiers started out as children, growing up in military ranks. In many countries, with inadequate systems of birth registration, age can be difficult to determine (Amnesty International, 1996, 1999).

In many countries, military training and indoctrination is provided through schools and youth movements, often as a means of bolstering defense preparedness or recruitment levels. In Iraq, thousands of children aged ten to fifteen participate in the Ashbal Saddam (Saddam Lion Cubs) youth movement formed after the 1991

'Suffer the Little Children': National and International Dimensions of Child
Poverty and Public Policy
Advances in Education in Diverse Communities: Research, Policy and Praxis, Volume 4, 177–205
Copyright © 2006 by Elsevier Ltd.
All rights of reproduction in any form reserved
ISSN: 1479-358X/doi:10.1016/S1479-358X(04)04008-2

Gulf War; training reportedly includes small-arms use, hand-to-hand combat, and infantry tactics (Human Rights Watch, 1994). In Ghana the youth movement, the Ghana National Service Scheme (GNSS) has occasionally been used by various military regimes to indoctrinate the youth (Sikah, 2000).

In the United States of America, military-run programs exist for children as young as eight. In the Young Marines, boys and girls from age eight to eighteen wear uniforms, are assigned military ranks and participate in boot camp and rifle drills. The program has over two hundred units nation-wide, with 14,865 participants in early 2001 (Amnesty International, 2001).

The problem is especially severe in developing countries, in which children constitute nearly half the population and in which children are often reared in a system that mixes war, poverty, violence, hunger, environmental degradation, and political instability. This situation happens almost every day in any of a dozen countries where young troopers have come to represent the modern-day universal soldier, i.e. a pint-sized, tireless baby Rambo who spends his or her tender years roaming the battlefields of Africa's civil wars. In the African civil wars of the last twenty years, an increasing number of combatants are as young as eight or ten, with girl fighters increasingly common. Thousands of children have been orphaned by the conflict, making them vulnerable for recruitment. Some 8000 children have been separated from their families or orphaned by civil unrests in Sub-Saharan Africa. Children are abducted and allegedly forced to torture and murder their own relatives, prior to going to other villages to slaughter others (Skinner, 1999).

Up to 10,000 children have been abducted and forced through the most brutal methods imaginable to become child soldiers and virtual slaves in northern Uganda. The children, some as young as eleven years old, have been seized over the past three years by the Lord's Resistance Army (LRA), and forced to fight the Ugandan army (Amnesty International, 1997, 1998). The Lord's Resistance Army has been wildly accused of using as its warriors children as young as eight years old who were kidnapped, tortured, raped, virtually enslaved and sometimes killed in the name of the "Holy Spirit."

In Sub-Saharan Africa for thousands of youngsters, due to circumstances beyond their control, wars have altered their view of the world. Parents and grandparents have been replaced with images of Rambo and gun-toting thugs masquerading as the local "president" and "his excellency." Children all over the continent have willingly or unwillingly exchanged their school pens and pencils for rifles and hand grenades to become the ultimate representatives of lost generations. Instead of becoming the flowers of the revolution (Machel, 1973) children have blossomed into trained killers (Skinner, 1999).

Child soldiering violates the fundamental rights of children. It exploits youth for political purposes, subjects them to slaughter and the ravages of war. Child soldiering immerses children in a system that sanctions killing (Machel, 1996). This also poses formidable security risks for others. A society that mobilizes and trains its young for war weaves violence into the fabric of life. This increases the likelihood that violence and war will be such society's future.

Based on empirical study, document analysis, interviews and observations, this qualitative chapter analyzes the widespread phenomena of child soldiers in Sub-Saharan Africa. The Chapter is divided into four main sections: why child soldiers – reasons for children in armed conflict; samples of voices of children in and out of combat, interviews, comments; efforts to combat the use of children in armed conflicts and the impact on the psychological, socio-economical, cultural and educational impact of child soldiering on children and society. This chapter ends with recommendations that call for action.

WHY CHILD SOLDIERS?

Why Sub-Saharan societies mistreat their children raises troubling questions for the contemporary world. Historically, all societies have tended to recognize that their children represent their future. In small scale societies this is quite clear since daily life readily indicates that children are the human capital that perpetuate their cultures and languages. Not to have and rear children is seen as social death in many countries. It is frequently only to save themselves by responding to major environmental or socio-cultural imperatives that societies painfully sacrifice their young. The Palestinian Intifada is one such example where hundreds of Palestinian youngsters joined their elders to fight Israel for their own state (Quota et al., 1995). Various theories have been advanced for the use of children in armed conflicts. This chapter will elaborate on some of them.

THE COMING ANARCHY THEORY

Child soldiers are the harbingers of the "coming anarchy" theory that has become fashionable among certain influential Western writers. Sierra Leone is said to be a perfect example of what is in store for Sub-Saharan Africa and the poorest lands of the developing world. According to the Kaplan thesis, overpopulation, environmental collapse, armed conflict over dwindling resources, and the spread of killer diseases will combine to push Sierra Leone and scores of African nations over the precipice into chaos (Kaplan, 1994). Kaplan's thesis was distributed by the U.S. State Department to all its embassies in developing countries. It has served to help formulate U.S. policy in Africa, despite the fact that the authors spent all of one week in the region!

There are some problems with this theory, as evident in Sierra Leone. First, it is impossible to speak of overpopulation in a territory as big as Scotland or New York State inhabited by 4.5 million people. The environment shows no sign of collapse, and Sierra Leone is hardly resource-starved. Once known as the "Land of Iron and Diamonds" it is blessed with substantial deposits of diamonds, iron ore, retile, bauxite, and gold. Although it is true that Sierra Leone is now classified as one of the world's most impoverished countries (UNDPC, 2001), it is the widespread distribution of wealth that is the main problem. Secondly, cultural identity is an essential and durable rather that context-dependent feature of social systems. Different cultures and civilizations are thereby prone to clash, be theses cultures western or African (Huntington, 1993).

Third, during the post-Cold War period the world has changed. States have lost the monopoly of military violence once underwritten by nuclear balance of terror. War equipment is cheap, and widely available to religious, cultural and criminal organizations prepared to pursue armed conflict independent of sovereign states and without reference to international opinion (Crevald, 1992).

Fourth, culture clash, resource competition and environmental breakdown provoke a rash of small, localized and essentially uncontrollable armed conflicts. Many are anarchic disputes – i.e. apolitical events indistinguishable from banditry and crime. Insulation rather than intervention is the rational response of the major powers. Lacking any Cold War roots, or evident religious or ethnic dimensions, but possessing a high quotient of apparently bizarre and random acts of violence, many perpetrated by children, this conflict is cited by Kaplan as a prime instance of the New Barbarism spun off from a falling traditional society. The arguments linking environmental determinism and cultural essentialism are hardly new. They have been regularly refuted by Africans just as quickly they spring up again. The fear of the revenge of the enslaved and dispossessed is hard to quell (Skinner, 1999).

The fatal flaw of the "coming anarchy" argument, however, is a contemporary echo of the colonial view which held that before the European powers arrived, Africa was a blank state – there was no civil society of which to speak. The human factor is completely missing in such analysis. For example, hundreds of dedicated Sierra Leoneans do not underestimate the country's terrible problems but are working for a better future. They may lose the battle to halt a future of chaos and conflict, but if they do, it will not be without a fight. How else to explain Sierra Leone's democratic elections in March 1996, when despite all predictions to the contrary, voters braved threats, random shootings, and the active hostility from both sections of the government army and the Revolutionary United Front (RUF) rebels to cast their ballots. The combination of vocal lobbying by women's groups, human rights activists, the press, and a groundswell of community support for democracy proved that Sierra Leone's supposedly mortally wounded civil society still lives. This same country is set to have elections in May 2002 despite the fact that thousands of its citizens are displaced and many more live in refugee camps.

Contrary to the new Barbarism theory, the violence of the Sierra Leone conflict is shown to be moored, culturally, in the hybrid Atlantic world of international commerce. Over many years Europeans and Americans have played a prominent and often violent part in such countries. Although a small and highly localized conflict, the war has a global range of symbolic and dramaturgical reference.(In this context dramaturgical refers to tragic comedy) The war is one of the world's first truly post-Cold War conflicts, since it owes little if anything to Super Power rivalry, and everything to the media flows and cultural hybridizations that make up globalized modernity (cf. Waters, 1995). Globalization disengagement from Africa's violence is no longer an option and as recent events have indicated, African wars have international implications far beyond the continent.

PATRON-CLIENTELISM THEORY

The modern African state is a legacy of colonial rule, not a historical evolution. The state in Africa, therefore, exists in an overdeveloped relationship with its society. This results in fragile bases of legitimacy and a political culture of ambivalence toward the propriety of impersonal rules and public purpose. From this configuration patron-clientelism has emerged as the mode of governance or neo-patrimonial rule. This theory sees development efforts as a tangible reward that the patron bestows for political royalty (Banya, 1996; Kpundeh, 1995; Reno, 1995). Long-term patterns of "primitive accumulation" of forest and mineral resources in sub-Saharan Africa have fed a modern politics dominated by patrimonial redistribution. The political elite builds support through distributing resources on a personal basis to followers. Relatively few resources are distributed according to principles of bureaucratic rationality. From the 1980s, through a combination of circumstances (oil shock, IMF conditionalities), the resources available for patrimonial redistribution in sub-Saharan went into sharp decline, a decline exacerbated by the ending of the Cold War and a general reduction and tightening up of overseas aid budgets. This crisis has severely tested the loyalty of the younger generation. Meanwhile, as a result of political machinations and resource shortages the various countries' capacity to control some of their peripheral regions were weakened. The wars in Sierra Leone, Republic of the Congo, Angola, Liberia and to a lesser extent Uganda, it can be argued, are a product of this protracted, post-colonial, crisis of patrimonialism (Murphy & Bledsoe, 1987).

Acutely aware of the extent to which power is personalized, people come to suspect that politics "feeds" on weak and defenseless persons. A critical analysis of the situation suggests that the nub of the problem is patrimonial leadership and lack of institutional continuity. This in turn is linked to short-term (unsustainable) resource extraction procedures. These short-term processes may be "primitive" but they are also procedures in which the outside world has long played a prominent part, for example the extraction of alluvia diamonds in Sierra Leone, the Republic of the Congo and Angola (Richards, 1995b, 1996b).

SOCIAL AND CULTURAL VALUE THEORY

Africa is not only the world's poorest continent but it is also its youngest. Half or more of the population of African countries are under the age of 18. For example, according to UNICEF half of the population of African countries with major problems of child soldiers, are children (Table 1).

All the above countries have different ways of socializing the young to adulthood. For example, the initiation is a central historical feature of the Sub-Saharan region; with a near universality of the male and female associations, Poro and Sande (D'Azevedo, 1962; Ferme, 1992; Gittins, 1987; Jedrej, 1976; La Fontaine, 1985; Little, 1949; Murphy, 1980; Sawyer, 1971). Initiation marked the ending of childhood and allowed for re-birth into a world of adult responsibility. The Poro "devil" seizes boys from the family home, and in symbolically breaking the family tie, opens up membership of a wider social world. The rigors of initiation create bonds among peers, life-long respect for the expertise of elders, and commitments beyond the web of kinship (Sawyer, 1972). The main concern

Table 1.   Percentage of Children in Total Population in Select Countries.

Countries	Total Population	Under 18s
Angola	11,599,000	6,049,000 (52%)
Bueundi	6,398,000	3,372,000 (53%)
Congo-Brazzaville	2,745,000	1,433,000 (52%)
Democratic Republic of Congo	48,040,000	25,934,000 (54%)
Liberia	2,467,000	1,224,000 (50%)
Rwanda	5,883,000	3,115,000 (53%)
Sierra Leone	4,200,000	2,565,000 (53%)
Somalia	10,217,000	5,533,000 (54%)
Sudan	27,899,000	13,173,000 (47%)

Sources: UNICEF (1999).

of this secret society for women is to cultivate in adult women the qualities of wifehood and motherhood. The Sande protection regulations cover the initiates during the period between their admission to the sacred bush and their official *debut*. Both "poro" and "Sande" embody the spirit of the community – powerful forces which hold the members together. Both societies are made manifest by a sense of rites and ceremonies depicting death to the early stages of life, and re-birth through resurrection to adulthood, in which each male and female member of the community must participate to be enrolled in the tribe. At the same time these rites and ceremonies having been deeply entrenched in the life of the tribe, are now thought to have been instituted in *illo tempore* by a power superior to the community. A supreme god is accordingly postulated (Harris & Sawyer, 1968).

Many commentators have noted the judicial and military aspects of Poro (Fulton, 1972; Little, 1965). Perhaps a more basic feature of initiation in Sub-Saharan African society is that it is a process for creating social bonds "from within" (Hoejbjerg, 1995). Only initiates create initiates. This gives initiation comparative advantage over means of establishing social bonds dependent on external reference. Lacking heavy weapons, both rebels and government forces have made extensive use of cultural resources in their campaigns. In particular, the rebels deploy forest knowledge in both practical and symbolic way to make coverts to their cause and demoralize opponents. By these cultural ploys, they manifest a distinctly "postmodern" awareness of modern media and the propaganda opportunities they provide. The skills on view are those of the hybrid and globalized world of Atlantic commerce rather than the "traditional" subsistence worlds of the African bush. Thus, in both Sierra Leone and Angola, the language of initiation is used to justify the attempt to rebuild society from within. Many of the child soldiers see joining the armed groups as belonging to a special group. Terrorized in the process of capture they are later treated generously by the rebels and the secrets of the movement are revealed. This process amount as to a type of initiation, for several centuries a near universal feature of forest society in the western half of West Africa.

Initiation separates young people from their immediate family and builds adult loyalties to a wider society. This creates paradoxical loyalties between hostage and captor, by the children captured by the rebels, hence the "stockholm syndrome."[1] Traditional society has taken a number of blows, first the active repression by the British colonial authorities, and since independence urbanization, the spread of Western-style education, and now the war. "Desecration of sacred shrines in the countryside, growing promiscuity among young women, and the loss of dignity and influence among community elders are shredding the social fabric" (Richards, 1996, p. 15). The damage to values is palpable.

TECHNOLOGICAL DEVELOPMENT

The rapid development of technology has added to the widespread use of child soldiers. The relatively light firearms, primarily the Ak-47 Kalashmnikov assault rifle are easy for children to handle. The proliferation of weapons, especially small arms, have made semi- automatic rifles light enough to be used and simple enough to be stripped and reassembled by a child of ten. A single pull of the trigger is enough to release a steady stream of bullets that can cause mayhem. Many of the children are no taller than the rifles they carry. Moreover, these weapons are not expensive. In many countries at war in Sub-Sahara Africa, an Ak-47 may be bought for as little as $20.00 (US). Cheap and efficient Ak-47s flood the continent (Human Rights Watch, 1995a; Machel, 1996).

Thus, so armed, child soldiers become model soldiers. They are preferred because blessed with great endurance, the ability to survive on relatively little food and water, child soldiers accept orders with few questions. This is not true of their adult counterparts. "Boy soldiers are ideal," says Dr. Nahim, a psychiatrist in Sierra Leone and chairman of a local nongovernmental organization, Children Associated with War, which helps former child soldiers return to civilian life. "They are good at taking orders, they do not have many outside responsibilities, and for many of them war becomes a game they enjoy."[2]

SURVIVAL THEORY

The overwhelming majority of child soldiers come from:

- Children separated from their families or with disrupted family backgrounds (e.g. orphans, unaccompanied children, children from single-parents families, or from families headed by children);
- Economically and socially deprived children (the poor, both rural and urban, and those without access to education, vocational training, or a reasonable standard of living);
- Other marginalized groups (e.g. street children, certain minorities, refugees and the internally displaced);
- Children from the conflict zones themselves who have experienced alienation and discrimination (UNICEF, 2001a).

Few child soldiers come from wealthy families. Typically, they are from poor and working families living in overcrowded urban slums, isolated rural villages in the war zone, or impoverished camps for those displaced by the fighting. A wide spread feeling of social exclusion feeds the child soldier phenomenon, and rebel commanders cleverly exploit it. For example, in remote corners of Sierra Leone and Liberia, they have set up video parlors powered by generators show violent action films as "First Blood" to indoctrinate young fighters. The uneducated Vietnam War veteran Rambo, who resorts to his military prowess to pay back a society that has persecuted him as a vagrant, has a powerful resonance. Many youthful combatants, lacking familial support, become brave and loyal fighters. Militia life offers the youth training and a livelihood in poor countries where educational opportunities and jobs are extremely difficult to obtain.

To prove their manhood, egged on by a culture of violence, or driven by a desire to avenge atrocities committed against their family, many children join armed groups. In the case of children who "voluntarily" join armed opposition forces in their respective countries, research conducted for the United Nations (UN) by the Quaker UN Officer in Geneva showed that the single major factor influencing child volunteers is ill-treatment of children by their families or by government troops (Brett & Mcollin, 1996).

Some children enlist "voluntarily" in order to escape the daily routine life of refugee camps. Sometimes they have nowhere else to go. They might be intoxicated by the power and prestige that a weapon can command or be searching for a sense of belonging that they can no longer find in their wartorn communities. Many of the youngsters who found themselves "on the street" in a war zone viewed the militia group as both a meal ticket and substitute education. The pay is often negligible, but weapon training provided quicker dividends than school. The AK47 brings food, clean clothes and instant adult respect. Comrades subsitute for lost family and friends (NGO's http//www.hrw.org 1998).

PROTRACTED WARS

The longer the conflict goes on, the more likely children are to be "recruited," as the shortage of manpower, due to increasing casualties and escalation of the conflict, leads to an ever more desperate search for fresh recruits to fill the ranks. When they are not specifically sought out, recruitment of underage children may occur because official procedures are not followed or because the children have no identity papers showing how old (or rather, how young) they are.

Conflicts come and go, the more protracted the armed conflict, the more likely children will participate. In recent years, large numbers of children fighting in Latin America and the Middle East region have been replaced as conflicts recede by new generations of soldiers in Africa and Asia (Human Rights Watch, 1995b). In the industrialized world, there is general trend away from conscription and towards volunteer, professional armies.

Although prevailing international law sets 15 as the minimum age for military recruitment and participation in armed conflict, there is widespread agreement that this age limit is too low and that it must be raised to 18. Although most countries prohibit recruitment and participation of under-18s, others have signaled their intention to continue to recruit 16- and/or 17-year-olds. The United States, for instance, is the country most opposed to setting 18 as the minimum age for recruitment (Amnesty International, 2000; UNICEF, 1996).[3]

In a bid to swell the ranks of its armed forces, the U.K. recently embarked on a recruitment drive of those under-eighteen years of age. If a sixteen year old is enrolled – normally for twenty-two years of service – he or she has the right to "buy out" after three years. The three year period, however, only begins to elapse upon the recruit's 18th birthday – this is known as the "five-year trap." British soldiers under the age of 18 fought – and died – in both the Falklands conflict and the Gulf War (Hetherington, 1998).

In addition to British and U.S., other countries that recruit (i.e. conscript, enlist or otherwise accepted into their armed forces) under eighteen years of age include France, Germany, Italy, Portugal, Finland, Canada, Australia and many developing countries including Angola, Burundi, Kenya, Rwanda, Uganda, Sierra Leone and Denmark Republic of Congo (Brett & Mcollin, 1996).

Other factors that have contributed to the child soldier phenomenon include but are not limited to forced recruitment, fear, and obedience. Children usually become soldiers through coercion, through forced recruitment. When national armies have a manpower shortfall, they may find it convenient not to search too closely for the accurate candidate of a conscript. In countries covered by the Machel study (1996), government forces as well as rebel forces were often equally likely to use child soldiers. In Ethiopia, for example, armed militias would surround a public area such as a marketplace, order every male to sit down and then force into a truck anyone deemed "eligible." At particular risk of abduction were teenagers who worked on the streets selling cigarettes or candy. Forced abductions, says the Machel Study, were commonly one element in a larger campaign to intimidate communities. Armed groups that abduct children for soldiering are also inclined to go on rape-and-looting rampages while in the villages (Machel, 1996).

Militias often use brutish methods to weaken resistance to forcible recruitment. Drugged on crack cocaine, marijuana, alcohol, ephedrine, amphetamines, heroin, methausphetamine, and a cocktail of local substances, including gunpowder, the youthful recruits become ferocious fighters and deploy terroristic methods apparently reflecting a knowledge of Resistencia Nacional Mocambicana (Renomo) tactics in Mozambique (Ruiz, 1992; Wilson, 1992). Thousands of children in Rwanda were forced by adults, from father and uncles to militia leaders and politicians, to participate in 1994 genocide against the minority Tutsi people.

A case study from Uganda reports that people who resisted attacks by the Lord's Resistance Army "would be cut with pangas (machetes). Quite a number of victims had their lips and ears chopped off in macabre rituals" [The same is true of the Revolutionizing United Front (RUF) in Sierra Leone]. To seal off possible avenues of resistance from the children's communities, recruiters may deliberately destroy the bonds of trust between child and community. In Mozambique, for instance, recruiters from Renamo forced boy recruits to kill someone from their own village (Ruiz, 1992).

Coercion is only the first step in a process that uses fear, brutality, and psychological manipulation to achieve high levels of obedience, converting children into killers. In many countries, child recruits are subjected to beatings, humiliation, and acts of sadism. In Liberia, government military trainers beat children with sticks or rifle butts and burned them with cigarette while verbally mocking them. Those who resisted or who attempted to escape were further brutalized or killed. A frequently used tactic is to have children learn by doing, which may mean exposing them progressively to violence, numbing them so they might someday commit acts of sadism on fellow humans (United Nations, 1996). Child recruits in Sierra Leone, for example, were forced to cut the throats of domestic animals and drink the blood (Keen, 1995).

A 14-year-old Mozambican boy, quoted by the Machel Report (1996) said of RENAMO forces: "I was told to train. I would run, do head-over-heels, and climb trees. Then they trained me to take guns apart and put them back together again for four months. Every day the same thing. When it was over they did a test. They put someone in front of me for me to kill. I killed" (Machel, 1996, p. 2).

Few constraints exist on what trainers can do to children. Because children themselves may lack the internal constraints against violence that ordinarily develop through exposure to positive role models, or the rewards for socially constructive behaviors, they blindly obey orders. Weakened psychologically and fearful of their commanders, children can become obedient killers, willing to take on the most dangerous and horrifying assignments. In countries such as Uganda, Liberia, and Sierra Leone, as child soldiers have served as executioners, and in some countries – notably in Liberia and Mozambique – they have been required to perform ritual acts of cannibalism on their victims, acts calculated to install contempt for human life (Maier, 1998).

THE VOICES OF CHILD SOLDIERS

In this section the field notes and document analysis of examples of voices of children in war are given. The identities of the children have of course been altered.

The particular country from which the voices are chosen will be indicated at the end of each.

> The best thing about the army was that they protected me from rain and cold, and I learned how to cook. But I am glad to be out. Now I can cook for myself an my friends. Maybe I can go to school and become a carpenter. I never wanted to become a soldier (UNICEF, May 1995, p. 2). Uganda (16 years old).
>
> It was terrible I was a member of the so-called "Interahamwe" militia. We were backing the army to flush out anything that resembled a Tutsi. It seemed to me that almost everyone was taking part in the fighting. While the army was busy fighting the RPF [Rwandan Patriotic Army], we people were also taking part, to make sure that the whole country was being cleansed. In Gikondo suburb (Kigali), I remember going through hundreds of dead bodies with a FAL rifle. People were crying all the time, amid heavy gunfire and mortar shells (Abayeho, 1995 p. 3) Rwanda (14 years old).
>
> I became a combatant in 1991 when I was 8 years old. I became a fighter because I felt that my friends and my parents were suffering. I joined a faction and served as a bodyguard to one of the chiefs of staff. I used an AK-47. It wasn't too heavy. I used it often, but I never killed civilians. I was often really afraid (UNICEF, 1998, p. 4) Liberia, (13 years old).
>
> I was given cigarettes and marijuana during the war, but I've changed now and I don't smoke. I don't really think about the war much now, and I don't have nightmares. I talk to counselors a lot about what happened. Now I'm learning to be a carpenter, but I first want to go back to school before starting to work (Beauchemin, E. "Child soldiers in Liberia," Radio Netherlands, updated (http://www.mw.nl/en/liberia), p. 5) Liberia (14 years old).
>
> I have no interest in going to school, Musimbi said proudly. I've fought and killed many people. I'm a soldier, it's all the experience I need.
>
> Pitman, T. "Kibumba – Child Soldiers Fight War in eastern Congo," (Reuters, 9 February 1999 p. 4). Democratic Republic of the Congo (13 years old).

Silvester, now 17, was with Burundi Hutu rebels fighting the Tutsi-dominated army when paratroopers assassinated the first democratically-elected President, Melchior Ndadaye – a Hutu in 1993. At that time he was barely 12 years old.

> It was a sudden twist of events, in our Kamenge suburb (north of the capital, Bujumbura). They (the army) has killed our President, we had to fight back. I dropped (out of) school. School was almost impossible for us, as Kamenge was almost daily rocked with heavy shelling by the army and the rebels. Soon after the attempted coup, we went on rampage destroying houses belonging to Tutsis. Most of them had already fled, knowing very well that Kamenge was no longer their place. Those who remained were slaughtered. We use to live together, but what the Army had done was unacceptable (Abayeho, 1995, p. 3) Burundi.

A nine-year-old Liberian girl – Fatu recounted this story:

> I saw 10 to 20 people shot, mostly old people who couldn't walk fast. They shot my uncle in the head and killed him. Then they made my father take his brains out and throw them into some water nearby. Then they made my father undress and have an affair with a decaying body. Then they raped my cousin who was a little girl of nine years old (UN Chronicle, 1996, p. 4) Liberia.

Abu (14 years old)

At 2 p.m., they gourge out two eyes, at 3.00 p.m. they cut off one hand, at 4 p.m, they cut off two hands, at 5 p.m. they cut off one foot and ... at 7 -p.m. it is the death which falls down (Saint Paul, 1999, p. 4) Sierra Leone.

I was walking with two girls. And they called me. I was too close to them, so I couldn't run. Even through my identification card said I was underage – and that was true – I was big, they insisted I was old enough, and they grabbed me and took me to a police station. It was full of kids. They put me in a cell with the other kids, while the cops went to get trucks. When they capture you they immediately send you to the provinces for training, far away where you don't know anyone. I was very lucky. A neighbor saw me being taken and told my mother. My uncle is a policeman, and he talked to the station commander. When the rest of the guys were loaded the trucks, my uncle got me out (New York Times, July 1998, p. 5) Angola (24 years).

The commanders ... would tell us to run straight into gunfire. The commanders would stay behind and would beat those of us who would not run forward. I remember the first time I was in the front line. The other side started firing, and the commander ordered us to run towards the bullets. I panicked. I saw others falling down dead around me. The commanders were beating us for not running, for trying to crouch down. I don't know why we were fighting ... We were just ordered to fight (Human Rights Watch, 1998b, p. 2). Uganda (16 years old).

We were given a lot of drugs to make us strong. Drugs like gunpowder in our food and cocaine. They make your heart strong, to have zeal. The drugs made me feel that I was not afraid of anything (Interviewed in Freetown, p. 4) Sierra Leone (17 years old).

I was bored in Freetown, with school. I wanted to do something exciting she indicates. Morie told me how to make my way to Daru. One of my friends had an aunt in the army who also told tier how exciting it was, so we ran off together (Interviewed in Freetown, p. 5) Sierra Leone (15 years).

Some of us were used as spies by the rebels. They sent us into the city to study ECOMOG troop movements and military strength to prepare the way for the 6 January assault, he said (Interviewed in Freetown, p. 3) Sierra Leone (13 years old).

We hid sometimes on the main road and when a car came, we killed everyone and took everything we needed. Stress appeared then in the camp. There, as women, we had to cook for the men. We were very badly treated, we were allowed to eat only the rests, we were always persecuted and hit for almost nothing. When we struck back they threatened to kill us. Even thought of escape was smothered. One day, four of us escaped from the camp. They were quickly caught, brought back and killed in front of us (Interviewed in Bo, p. 6) Sierra Leone (15 years old).

A Testimony of a Uganda Child Soldier:

They arrested a boy called Oyet who had tried to escape. They tied him and stabbed him in the back. The commander told us (new recruits) that Oyet will be hit three times and then "sent home" (killed). The commander chose one boy who was given an axe and told to hit Oyet once. Then he was told to hand over the axe to another boy who hit. And then I was given the axe ... I knew that it is my blow that sent him home. Later on, the new recruits were asked to finish off all the wounded soldiers. The commander said, 'The new recruits can now feed themselves on these two soldiers' (initiation by killing). This was my second day with the rebels ...

I heard later that two boys from my home were captured and beaten because I had escaped. One of the boys was stabbed in the hand and asked to bring the rebels to my parents' home.

> They beat my mother and brother with clubs and axes until they died. They threatened that
> they'll kill more people if I don't come back. This was told me by a boy who lived near my
> home. He told me it was my fault my mother and brother had been killed (Coalition to Stop the
> Use of Child Soldiers, 1998, p. 7) Uganda (13 years old).

Finally, a reporter for the Herald Guardian in London who was captured by the Armed Forces Revolutionary Council (ARFC) and Revolutionizing United Front (RUF) in Koidu town, testified to the role of child soldiers. Some of his captors were under ten years old and wielded guns. He said,

> There were little kids, boys, around seven, nine, twelve years old who were among the soldiers.
> They had guns and felt they had power . . . I saw girls held in vehicles ready to be transported. The
> last groups of kids I saw were held at the Branch Energy mining group office in Koidu town.
> They had 1,300–2,000 of them there. I saw them. In Koidu, the junta forces shouted for kids
> and gathered them. A soldier told me they are holding these kids as a shield in the event of an
> ECOMOG [Economic Community of West Africa (ECOWAG) Ceasefire Monitoring Group]
> attack. They also use them as soldiers, for labor, and for sexual purposes (Human Rights Watch,
> July 1998a, p. 4) Sierra Leone.

EFFORTS TO STOP USE OF CHILD SOLDIERS

A U.N. study in 1995 found that in Angola, 36% of children had accompanied and supported soldiers and 7% had fired a weapon at someone. A thousand boy soldiers fought with the Angolan government army, and Joanas Savimbi's Unita rebel movement fielded 7,000. The United Nations Children Fund (UNICEF) estimates that a quarter of all fighters in Liberia's civil war, some 2,000 soldiers are children. In Sierra Leone, the best guess of the total is 4,000, half fighting for the government and half for the rebels (Maier, 1998).

Given the worldwide phenomenon of child soldiers, what has been done to address this scourge by the international community? A brief summary of the international attempts to stop the use of child soldiers follows.

At the international level since 1946, when the organization was founded as the United Nations International Children's Emergency Fund in the aftermath of World War II – UNICEF (its full name is now the United Nations Children's Fund) has devoted special attention to the plight of children affected by armed conflicts. This role is no less relevant today, with children increasingly the first to suffer in a growing number of conflicts. In just four years, the scope of UNICEF's humanitarian activities in countries has almost quadrupled – from 15 countries in 1995 to some 55 countries in 1999. UNICEF, as an advocacy organization for children's rights has repeatedly called on all warring sides to put an end to the use of children as combatants. UNICEF has also demanded that in any future peace settlements provisions be made for children's physical and emotional welfare. Carol Bellamy, Executive Director of UNICEF, contends that, "Children should have no part in war. By making them agents of civil conflict and depriving them of their childhood, the vicious cycle of violence is perpetuated." Bellamy concludes that, "Child soldiers are a symptom of the wider problem, the complete neglect of whole generations" (gopher://gopher.unicef.org:70/11/:s596impact).

UNICEF has provided assistance for the resettlement of children soldiers all over the world For example, in Sierra Leone "more than 60% of a group of 1000 fighters" (p. 2) screened by the Disarmament, Demobilization and Resettlement Committee (DDRC) before the May 25 coup, were children. Some of these child soldiers were demobilized and encamped at Jui, about 25 miles east of Freetown. Here they received technical and vocational training in a program sponsored by the United Nations Children Fund (UNICEF). (gopher://gopher.unicef.org:70/11/:s596impact).

The use of child soldiers violates international norms. The Geneva Convention forbids the recruitment of children under fifteen as soldiers, an age that most human rights advocates consider extremely young. The UN Convention on the Rights of the Child (CRC), signed in 1989 and ratified by more than 160 nations, establishes 15 years as the minimum recruitment age (see Article 38).[4] In fact, most countries have endorsed an optional protocol (UN Commission on Human Rights) that boosts the minimum recruitment to 18 years.

Although the various UN resolutions and protocols exist, they are not enforced effectively and in some cases they are totally ignored. One way to strengthen the CRC is to pressure non-state actors to respect its provisions even though they are not signatories. If only governments adhere to the norms set by the convention, abuses of children's rights by opposition or rebel groups will continue. Pressure to adhere to the standards set by the convention may be applied to both state and non-state actors through careful monitoring by UN agencies, nation states, non-governmental organizations, and international media (Cairns, 1996).

Steps must be taken to build commitment to the CRC, the most comprehensive instrument for the protection of children's rights. Although more than 160 nations are parties to the convention, there are several noteworthy exceptions – primarily the United States, which signed it in 1995, but has not ratified it. The ratification effort in the United States has been short-circuited by questionable concerns over whether setting the minimum recruitment age at 18 would compromise national security or limit sovereignty (Maier, 1998).

KEY ORGANIZATIONAL EFFORTS

Formed in May 1998, the coalition brings together seven international non-govermentaal organizations. It works collaboratively with United Nations agencies, the Red Cross and Save the Children. They organize regional conferences in Africa, Latin America, Asia and Europe to seek to end the use of children as soldiers. The coalition is spearheading campaigns against the use of child soldiers in more than 40 countries around the world. Other organizations formed the steering committee of the coalition, which meets four times a year to agree on policy and strategy including: the African Forum on Child Welfare (AFCW); Amnesty International; Asia Coalition to Stop the Use of Child Soldiers; Christian Children's Fund; Human Rights Watch; International Federation Terre des Hommes (TDH); International Save the Children Alliance; Jesuit Refugee Service (JRS); Quaker United Nations Office; and, World Vision International.

AFRICAN FORUM ON CHILD WELFARE (AFCW)

The AFCW is a regional grouping of the International Forum for Child Welfare (IFCW), an international not-for-profit organization for cooperation and information exchange in child welfare. AFCW seeks to improve the quality of life for children and young people in the region. It ensures that services for children in need and especially those in need of special protection, and those whose rights are violated by individuals and/or States as well as non-state entities. AFCW assists governments, organizations and institutions as well as non-state entities in the region to understand the needs of children and respond appropriately.

AMNESTY INTERNATIONAL

Amnesty International is a worldwide voluntary movement that works to prevent some of the gravest violations by governments of people's fundamental human rights. The main focus of its campaign is to: free all prisoners of conscience; ensure fair and prompt trials for political prisoners; abolish the death penalty, torture and other cruel treatment of prisoners; end extra judicial executions and "disappearances" (Amnesty International, 1998).

ASIA COALITION TO STOP THE USE OF
CHILD SOLDIERS

Formed following the Asia Conference in May 2000, the aim is to prevent the use of children in conflict and respect their human rights. This is especially aimed at countries such as Sri Lanka and Myanmar, who rival parts of Africa as one of the largest recruiters of child soldiers.

CHRISTIAN CHILDREN'S FUND

Christian Children's Fund is an independent, non-governmental organization set up in 1979 (the International Year of the Child) to promote and protect the rights of the child. DCI has grown to become and international network with members in some 60 countries. It is in consultative status with the United Nations Economic and Social Council, UNICEF, UNESCO AND THE Council of Europe.

HUMAN RIGHTS WATCH

Human Rights Watch conducts regular, systematic investigations of human rights abuses is some seventy countries around the world. Human Rights Watch addresses the human rights practices of governments of all political stripes, of all geopolitical alignments, and of all ethnic and religious persuasions. Human Rights Watch defends freedom of thought and expression, due process and equal protection of the law, and a vigorous civil society; it documents and denounces murders, disappearances, torture, arbitrary imprisonment, discrimination, and other abuses of internationally recognized human rights. Its goal is to hold governments accountable if they transgress the rights of their people. (http://www.child-soldiers.org, 2001).

INTERNATIONAL FEDERATION TERRE DES HOMMES

Terre des Hommes (TDH) [translated federation of mankind] movements have as their mission to act in favor of the rights of the child and equitable development, without any discrimination based on race, religion, political opinions, culture or gender. To do so, they support development projects designed to improve the living conditions of disadvantaged children, their families and their communities. The Convention on the Rights of the Child constitutes the conceptual framework guiding TDH activities.

In their own countries and regions, the TDH movements raise funds to achieve their objectives. They also raise public awareness, including among children and youth, on the causes of underdevelopment and on the rights of the child, mainly through information campaigns. They act to mobilize the political will and advocate for appropriate governmental policies.

At international level, the International Federation Terre des Hommes (IFTDH) works in collaboration with relevant bodies of the UN system to promote and implement the rights of the child and to advocate for people-centered and equitable development (Coalition to Stop the Use of Child Soldiers, 2001b).

INTERNATIONAL SAVE THE CHILDREN ALLIANCE

Swedish Save the Children is a non-governmental organization that fights for the rights of children, in Sweden and around the world. Activities are designed to improve conditions for children at risk. The organization undertakes the following actions:

> identifying and analyzing problems and potential courses of action, that children and sponsors practical development and support programs. It also hopes to influence public opinion about plights of children.

JESUIT REFUGEE SERVICE

Jesuit Refugee Service (JRS) is an inter-national non-governmental organization with a presence in some 40 countries around the world. JRS mission is to accompany, serve and defend the rights of refugees and displaced persons. Set up in 1980, JRS is a worldwide network of associates and institutions of the Society of Jesus (Jesuits), a Catholic religious order. It serves forcible displaced persons, offering them practical and spiritual support. These include social counseling, legal representation, education programs, and community development, according to their humanitarian needs, regardless of their beliefs.

QUAKER UNITED NATIONS OFFICE, GENEVA

Quaker UN Office, Geneva, represents (together with its counterpart in New York, Friends World Committee for Consultation) the international Quaker body of the approximately 300,000 Quakers worldwide. The Geneva office was set up in 1923, and works within three broad areas of UN/international issues identified as being the essentials for a peaceful world: human rights and the protection of refugees; peace and disarmament; and trade and labor.

WORLD VISION INTERNATIONAL

World Vision is an international, Christian, child care, humanitarian assistance and development organization. Founded in 1950, it is a worldwide partnership of national entities working with communities in 106 countries to bring about transformational development. World Vision programs are community based and sustainable. The organization is also an advocate for justice and rights of children, women and the marginalized. World Vision strives for a world that no longer tolerates poverty in all of its various aspects (Coalition to Stop the Use of Child Soldiers, 2001c).

In addition to the above organizations the UN has commissioned a number of reports on child soldiers, the most important of which is the UN study led by children's rights activist Grace Machel, wife of late Simonal Machel of Mozambique – normally referred to as the "Machel study." One of the main conclusions of the study is that child soldiering is a global problem that occurs more systematically than most analysts had previously suspected. The Machel Study showed that in some countries, children constitute a significant percentage of the combatants. In Liberia, for instance, about 20% of an estimated 60,000 combatants in the civil war that began in 1989 were children. In El Salvador, children composed 30% or more of the Fuerzas Armadas de El Salvador (FAES). In Afghanistan, 10% of the Mujahadeen forces are estimated to have been children under sixteen years. In Palestine during the Intifada, nearly 80% of Palestinian children are believed to have participated in acts of political violence such as stoning Israel troops (United Nations, 1997).

The report provided impetus for many countries to take seriously the problem of child soldiers and for non-governmental organizations (NGOs) to come together to fight the evils of children bearing arms. The position of UN special representative for the various countries at war was created because of the Machel report. To better coordinate and emphasize the seriousness of the problem, a new office has been created by the Secretary General of the UN, that of the Special Representative of the Secretary-General on children and Armed conflict. Currently being occupied by Olara Otunnu, the Special Representative reports annually to the Secretary-General of the UN, on the conditions of children conflicts (United Nations, 1999).

Regional, countries, NGOs and individual efforts are been made to discourage the use of children as soldiers. In Africa, for example, in "Making the Day of the African-Child," the Secretary General of the Organisation of African Unity, Salim Ahmed Salim called for better protection of children, referring to the experiences of child slaves, soldiers and prostitutes. He stated:

With the on-going conflicts on the continent, some children are exploited to become soldiers and fight alongside the adults. As a result they are injured, killed, maimed or become permanently disabled . . . More needs to be done to protect them from the scourge of abuse and exploitation. First and foremost the children themselves should be sensitized and educated to their rights, in particular, how to protect themselves. While every effort should be deployed to eradicate child exploitation and abuse, families and communities should carry out their responsibilities of assuming that the children are cared for . . . we should also ensure that member states ratify and implement the various instruments for the protection of children (Salim, 2001, p. 1).

Although significant efforts are made to eliminate the use of child soldiers, there are still challenging issues ahead.

IMPACT ON CHILDREN

Physical

The physical and psycho-social impact of child soldiering is profound. The 1996 Machel report paints a devastating picture of the impact of armed conflict on children. According to the report, in terms of physical impact, child soldiers are treated with untold suffering and cruelty of a world increasingly "being sucked into a desolate moral vacuum. This is a space devoid of the most basic human values; a space in which children are slaughtered, raped and maimed; a space in which children are exploited as soldiers; a space, in which children are starved and exposed to extreme brutality" (Machel Report, 1996, p. 3).

Why are children so brutally exposed during modern warfare, not just accidentally, but as deliberate targets? The report points to the changing character of modern warfare, where wars are being fought not between States, but within them, and are marked by increasing brutality. In many cases, religious and ethnic affiliations are manipulated to heighten feelings of hatred or aggression – against children, as well as adults. Battles are fought from village to village and street to street. As a result, the proportion of war victims who are civilians has leapt in recent decades from 5% to over 98%, and at least half of these are children. Increasingly, children have become both targets and perpetrators of violence (Machel Report, 1996). According to the UN Special representative in the Democratic Republic of Congo, the Alliance of Democratic Forces for Liberation (AFDL) use children as soldiers citing the case of "11-years-olds carrying heavy weapons, these child soldiers, known as 'kadogos,' have been corrupted and have participated in robberies and killings. The total number of children used by Kabila as soldiers in the war against Mobutu has been estimated at up to 10,000, or possibly even more" (Braeckman, 1998). Desire Kabila led a successful revolt against the government of then Zaire under President Mobutu Sese Seko who was in power for nearly 30 years. About a year ago, Kabila was assassinated by a member of his bodyguard.

The U.S. State Department reported, in its 1998 Human Rights Report on Congo-Brazzaville that undisciplined government soldiers including "Cobra" militia forces, were responsible for summary executions and rape in response to anti-government violence during the last four months of 1998, Rebels who had attained the "age of bearing arms" were killed (Le Point, January 9, 1999).

Widely perceived to be a cheap and expendable commodity, child soldiers tend to receive little or no training before being thrust into the front line. Recently, during the border war with Eritrea in 1999–2000, Ethiopian government forces reportedly press-ganged thousands of secondary schools students from marketplaces and villages, some of whom were used in human wave attacks across minefields (Amnesty International, 2001).

Tens of thousands of children die each year as a direct result of armed violence – from knives, bullet bombs and land-mines. But millions more die from the indirect consequences of warfare – as a result, for example, of the disruption in food supplies or the destruction of health services, water systems and sanitation. In poorer countries, where children are already vulnerable to disease, the onset of armed conflict may increase death rates by 50-fold with those under five years of age placed at particular risk (UNICEF, 2000).

According to a sociologist at the University of Sierra Leone, children were not just affected by being forced to carry a gun, but the war had disrupted their lives in many ways. Not only had children witnessed the gradual collapse of basic services, but also the food distribution had been disrupted and immunization campaigns have been halted, leaving children susceptible to epidemics of measles, typhoid and whooping cough. In the country between 1992 and 2000, war caused an estimated 5,000 excess childhood deaths, above what would have normally been expected (Kamara, 1999). During the conflict in Liberia more than half the deaths in some places were caused by measles – a normally curable or preventable disease (UNICEF, 2001b).

GENDER-BASED VIOLENCE

Modern warfare increasingly wreaks havoc on the lives of women and girls, and on the health and educational services that are key to family and community survival and development.

The targeting of women and girls by armed forces exacerbates an already intolerable situation. One of the most severe problems faced by women and girls during armed conflicts is a heightened risk of rape, sexual humiliation, prostitution and other forms of gender-based violence. Women of all ages are targets, but adolescent girls are often especially vulnerable since they may be thought less likely to have sexually transmitted diseases, such as HIV/AIDS. While most victims have been girls, young boys are also raped or forced into prostitution (Wessells, 1997).

Rape and other forms of gender-based violence are also being used systematically as weapons of war. In Rwanda, between April 1994 and April 1995, more than 15,700 girls and women were raped. Yet such violence is rarely taken as seriously as it should be. Girls are at particular risk of rape, sexual slavery and abuse, although the exploitation of boys for these purposes is also reported. Concy A., a 14-year-old girl abducted from Kitgum a town in Uganda by the Lord's Resistance Army (LRA) and taken to camps in Sudan told how "we were distributed to men and I was given to a man who had just killed his woman. I was not given a gun, but I helped in the abductions and grabbing of food from villagers. Girls who refused to become LRA wives were killed in front of us to serve as a warning to the rest of us." Grace A. gave birth on open ground to a girl fathered by one of her [LRA] abductors: "I picked up a gun and strapped the baby on my back and continued to fight the government forces" (p. 3).

Even in the supposedly sophisticated armed forces of industrialized countries, young recruits especially girls are subject to hazing, harassment and abuse. In recent years, cases of bullying and humiliation of under-18 recruits in the British Army have included mock execution, forced simulation of sexual acts, regimental baths in vomit and urine and the forced ingestion of mud. In August 1997, a 17-year-old recruit to the British Army was forced to perform a sex act and was raped by a drunken instructor while she was on maneuvers. She told the judge that she "didn't shout out because he is a sergeant and a higher rank. You don't disrespect your boss." (The instructor was jailed for seven years in November 1998, p. 3.) In 1999, one school district in the U.S. State of Washington banned recruiters from schools after several Army recruiters from a local recruiting station were investigated for sexual harassment of high school girls (CSUCS, 2001, p. 4).

Even the children who escape, or are demobilized, find no easy road to civilian life. Some are branded, literally. One boy who was recently returned to his home village in the Bo district in Sierra Leone, after two years with the rebels, had RUF branded across his chest. For children involved in attacks against their own villages, return is even harder. A teacher who fostered a 15-year-old former rebel says that the boy's mother sent a letter warning her son that he would be killed if he returned home. The boy fears both the rebels, who would know him as a deserter, and villagers, who suspect him. An impossible situation!

PSYCHOLOGY

Apart from been stigmatized by the families, communities and society, as "evil" "bandits" and "Vermin" and "barbarians," child soldiers have major psychological problems.

The full psychological impact on children of participation in armed conflict, especially for those who have witnessed or committed atrocities, is only beginning to be understood. According to one 14-year-old girl abducted by the RUF in Sierra Leone in January 1999, "I've seen people get their hands cut off, a ten-year-old girl raped and then die, and so many men and women burned alive . . . So many times I just cried inside my heart because I didn't dare cry out loud. "From Algeria, one report cites boys who appeared to be around the age of 12 decapitating a 15-year-old girl and then playing 'catch' with her head" (CSUCS, 2001).

"The long periods they've spent in the authoritarian regime of military life have left them with a low regard for civilians and an inability to make their own decisions. "They will not take any orders except from their military officers"(p. 3), says Father Mick Hickey, an Irish priest who works with demobilized child soldiers in Sierra Leone. "They have a total disdain for civilian life" (p. 4). Unless they can find a place to live children often end up as delinquents – boys as armed robbers and girls as prostitutes. For these children traditional social mores have little meaning and see violence as an acceptable means of communication. "The child must be given a feeling he belongs somewhere, whether it's in the family, in the community, or some other arrangement" (p. 2), according to UNICEF's Galuma (Hodges, 1992; UNICEF, 1999, 2001c; Wessells, 1996). "The recovery of the children will be very slow and very painful" (Human Rights Watch, 1999, p. 3).

A number of NGOs have set up live-in trauma counseling centers in many countries for children who have escaped from the rebels, but the centers are stretched thin and cannot take in all of the children in need. At most of the centers, after completing a program which include counseling to help children come to terms with loss, bereavement, displacement and fear, the children must move on in order to make room for new escapees. Where they go and how they will support themselves is not followed up. Their prospects for recovery are bleak because governments are doing little to provide for the rehabilitation and reintegration into society of these children. Another issue is what the participant of youth in violent combat will mean for the future of these societies. Under what circumstances will these youngsters be able to develop the attitudes that would enable them to respect adults and themselves so as to build viable families. Data from Rwanda suggest that marriages among young people who lived in refugee camps prove disastrous. The civil war with its consequent poverty and social dislocation radically changed the young people.

PATHS TOWARD RECOVERY

Despite the daunting level of damage done to child soldiers, attempts to help them recover are underway. In Sierra Leone, school age children have participated in singing, dancing, drama and writing projects to express and ease the pain of their memories. In Liberia some traumatized young people have been trained to help care for younger children as "junior facilitators." They are able to establish rapport with their kind, and can also therapeutically share their own experiences of war. Such activities as food preparation, laundry, gardening and going to school can foster a sense of purpose, self-esteem and identity. It is essential to re-establish familiar routines of home and community life and a sense of normalcy. Programs that reflect the cultural values and traditions of the people they are intended to serve must be established. In this regard participation by local people in the design, implementation and monitoring of aid programs should be encouraged. For example, restoring spiritual harmony through traditional healing is an essential first step in helping child soldiers demobilize and integrate into their communities.

In Sub-Saharan Bantu cultures, people believe that when one kills, one is haunted by the unavenged spirits of those who were killed. A purification ceremony is performed, which involves symbolic deaths and rebirths of the child. It is a ceremony to push away the bad spirits that they might have brought back with them. During the ceremony, the child is covered with blood in an imitation of death and birth. They are re-born to the group in a reintegration process (Hoejbjerg, 1995).

It is premature and without scientific justification to assume that former child soldiers who have killed or committed other atrocities are forever "damaged goods" and beyond rehabilitation. Traditional healing methods work, in part, because they fit local beliefs.

Many humanitarian assistance and development efforts overlook traditional healing methods, which are dismissed as unscientific. Although traditional methods should not be romanticized or viewed as a panacea, they can be important tools for assisting former child combatants.

The most immediate healing steps involve demobilizing everyone under the age of 18 years. They are then reintegrated with families and communities. Assistance is provided for them in making the transition into civilian life. Effective demobilization programs provide basic needs, such as food, water, shelter, and security. This is most often accomplished by locating members of the child's immediate or extended family and then reuniting them as soon as possible. To offer opportunities for health development and life in the community, reintegration programs often attempt to place former child soldiers in schools or provide vocational training that can lead to jobs. In many of the war-torn countries of Sub-Saharan Africa, efforts are made to provide some form of training for child soldiers. In Liberia and Sierra Leone, International NGOs in collaboration with local NGOs have established tech-prep schools for child soldiers.

SCHOOLING: TEACHER EMERGENCY PACKAGE (TEP)

In addition to providing basic services such as food, water, security, health care and shelter, to children affected by war, the introduction of education comes next. Whether it be at refugees camps or internally displaced persons camps, education helps the healing process. Organized recreational and educational activities bring routing back into children's lives and help them to maintain a connection to their own socio-cultural environment. Whether formal or non-formal, schooling can re-establish a sense of normalcy in an abnormal situation, and offer alienated youth an alternative to militias, crime, delinquency or drugs. In emergency situations, schools can be one of the most valuable channels for communicating messages about the environment, nutrition, mine awareness, cholera and AIDS prevention (Richmond, 1999; UNESCO, 1999).

Schools are also places where themes such as human rights, peace and reconciliation can be broached. Such values constitute the underpinning of any subsequent program of national reconstruction. Schools can often serve as centres for relief and rehabilitation programs for the community at large. Education can offer opportunities for paid employment and provide adults with a chance to play a role in their new, albeit temporary, surroundings. This has been the case with Sierra Leone refugees in Guinea and Liberian refugees in Sierra Leone. Education also symbolizes a commitment to the future (UNESCO, 1999).

A phased approach enabling education to be introduced in the early stages of humanitarian assistance has become standard practice in emergency situations. After the collection of relevant educational data (number of children, availability of teachers, etc.), a first phase brings children together for recreation activities-games, such as songs and listening to stories. During a second phase, non-formal schooling is established on a systematic basis, often using a Teacher Emergency Package (TEP), which was first conceived by UNESCO for use in Somalia and has now been translated into several languages and culturally adapted to suit different populations (UNESCO, 1999).

Although the concept is evolving, this "school-in-a-box" or "mobile classroom" is designed for approximately eighty refugee children of primary school age and aims to teach functional literacy and numeracy. This replaces a formal graded curriculum with exams. A box typically includes slates, chalk, exercise books and pencils for students and a teacher's bag containing cloth charts (alphabet, number and multiplication), a guide outlining teaching methods, an attendance book and scrabble sets of small wooden blocks so that teachers can create language and number games (UNESCO, 1999).

TEPs are designed for a six-month learning period and act as a bridge between no schooling and a return to some form of regular schooling. After this interim period, the third phase of near-normal schooling generally begins, based on curricula and textbooks (when available) from the country of origin. An important aspect of emergency education programs is the training of teachers to recognize symptoms of trauma in children.

The concept, first clearly articulated during the experience of providing schooling to Mozambican refugees in Malawi in the 1980s, has gained growing acceptance in the 1990s. This is partly because host countries, which are too poor to absorb a large foreign influx, need to be reassured that refugees will not settle there on a permanent basis. Hence the importance of using the mother tongue as the language of instruction and using the curriculum of the country of origin. Where possible, refugee teachers should largely staff the schools (UNESCO, 1999; UNICEF, 1998).

CONCLUSION

As has been demonstrated throughout this chapter, the child soldiers problem haunting Africa are not sui generis. The manner in which the continent was integrated into the emerging world system has left many of its societies fragmented. Since decolonization began in the 1960s, not a single African country has been able to decolonize its economy. The African states were so manipulated during the Cold War that their leaders did not have the opportunity or the will to build viable societies. Almost every single case of civil war on the continent could be traced to the past and present activities of the foreigner – from the legacy of "ethnicity" to the struggle to control diamonds or oilfields. The thousands of young people who increasingly are the major participants in most African civil strife are caught up in conflicts stemming from the untidy decolonization of the continent. The small group of westernized African elites who pressured their European masters or independence failed to realize that their centuries-long exploited societies did not have the cultural, economical, political and social infrastructures to stand alone.

Finally, the Convention on the Rights of the Child optional protocol[5] raising the age of recruitment from fifteen to eighteen must be enforced. Around the world, nations that are parties to the convention must invoke it, not ignore it. They must point out the massive violations of children's rights that occur as a result of armed conflict. There must be enforcement of its basic provisions for safeguarding the physical, social and psychological integrity of children. Children must be guaranteed basic rights such as the right to education.

In order to be successful, prevention efforts need to work towards structural changes that address poverty and oppression, fundamental sources of armed conflict and of much child soldiers. Connections must also be built between children's rights, arms transfers and militarization. These issues should be dealt with as a whole, not I part. Only a holistic approach will succeed in ending child soldiering and build healthy social systems that protect children and orient them toward peace (Amnesty International, 2001).

NOTES

1. The Stockholm Syndrome: The apparent paradoxical loyalties between hostage and captor when children are captured by rebels in conflict.
2. Interview with Dr. Nahim – July 8, 1999.
3. The Defense Appropriations Authorization Act, passed by Congress and signed by the U.S. President in October 1998, includes a provision specifically encouraging the U.S. not to block 18 as the minimum age for participation in an Optional Protocol to the Convention on the Rights of the Child.
4. Convention on the Rights of the Child, Article 38 (2): "States Parties shall take all feasible measures to ensure that persons who have not attained the age of 15 years do not take a direct part in hostilities." Fifteen years is the minimum age for recruitment under international humanitarian law as reflected in Protocols I and II of 1977 to the Four Geneva Conventions of 1949.
5. The Optional Protocol to the Convention on the Rights of the Child on the involvement of children in armed conflict, adopted by the United Nations in May 2000:

- Prohibits governments and armed groups from using under-18s in hostilities;
- Bans all compulsory recruitment of under-18s;
- Raises the minimum age and requires strict safeguards for voluntary recruitment;
- Bans all forms of recruitment of under-18s by nongovernmental armed groups.

REFERENCES

Abayeho (1995). Consultant researcher, Coalition to Stop the Use of Child Soldiers.
Amnesty International (1996). *Burundi: Armed groups kill without mercy*. London: AL.
Amnesty International (1997). *Stolen children, stolen lives*. AI Index: AFR 59/02/97.
Amnesty International (1998). *Uganda: The Lord's Resistance Army enslaves children*. AL, London.
Banya, K. (1996). Cannon debate continues: Multicultural education in higher education. In: C. Ryan, L. Woods, K. McLachlan & E. J. Kaplan (Eds), *Urban Multicultural Issues* (pp. 78–89).
Braeckman, C. (1998). Les apprentis-militaires qui siuvaient Kabila sont aujord? Hui livrés à eux-màmes: Mulume, enfant-soldat du Congo, condamné àmort. *Le Soir, 15* (April).
Brett, R., & Mcollin, M. (1996). *Children: The invisible soldiers*. Stockholm: Swedish Save the Children.
Cairns, E. (1996). *Children and political violence*. Oxford: Blackwell.
Coalition to Stop the Use of Child Soldiers (1998). *Africa report* (various countries). Retrieved from http://www.child-soldiers.org/reports_africa/congo_dem_rep.html.
Coalition to Stop the Use of Child Soldiers (2001a). *Africa report* (various countries). Retrieved from http://www.child-soldiers.org/reports_africa/congo_dem_rep.html.

Coalition to Stop the Use of Child Soldiers (2001b). *Global report on child soldiers 2001 launch: Child soldiers, an overview*. London: Author.

Coalition to Stop the Use of Child Soldiers (2001c). Steering committee members – untitled document. Retrieved from http://www.child-soldiers.org/steering.html.

Crevald, M. (1992). *On future war*. London: Brasseys.

D'Azevedo, W. (1962). Some historical problems in the dileneation of a central west Atlantic region, Annals. *New York Academy of Sciences, 96*(2), 512–538.

Ferme, M. (1992). Hammocks belong to men, stools to women: Constructing and contesting gender domains in a Mende village (Sierra Leone, West Africa). Doctoral dissertation, University of Chicago.

Gittins, A. (1987). Mende religion: Aspects of belief and thought in Sierra Leone. *Studia Insitution Anthropolos, 41*. Nettetal (Germany): Steyler Verlag.

Hetherington, B. (1998). *Memorandum on the U.K. government's policy on the recruitment of young persons to the armed forces and on the engagement of young persons in armed conflict*. Peace Pledge Union, U.K.

Hodges, R. (1992). A view of psychological problems resulting from the Liberian civi conflict and recommendations for counseling and other corrective strategies. Appendix V. *A report of the round table conference on strategies and direction for the reconstruction and development of Liberia*. The New African Research & Development Agency, Monrovia.

Hoejbjerg, C. (1995). *Staging the invisible: Essays on Loma ritual and cultural knowledge*. Doctoral thesis, Institute of Anthropology, University of Copenhagen.

Human Rights Watch (1994). *Children's rights project*. New York: HRW.

Human Rights Watch (1995a). *Children in combat*. New York: HRW.

Human Rights Watch (1995b). *The scars of death: Children abducted by the Lord's Resistance Army in Uganda*. New York: HRW.

Human Rights Watch (1998a). *Sierra Leone: Sowing terror atrocities against citizens in Sierra Leone*. New York: HRW.

Human Rights Watch (1998b). *Children of Sierra Leone: Street children and child soldiers*. New York: HRW.

Human Rights Watch (1999). *More than 120,000 child soldiers fighting in Africa*. New York: HRW.

Huntington, S. (1993). The clash of civilizations? *Foreign Affairs, 72*.

Jedrej, C. (1976). Medicine, fetish, and secret society in a west African culture. *Africa, 46*, 247–257.

Kamara, S. (1999). *The health crisis in Sierra Leone*. Freetown: University of Sierra Leone Bulletin.

Kaplan, R. (1994). The coming anarchy: How scarcity, crime, overpopulation, and disease are rapidly destroying the social fabric of our planet. *Atlantic Monthly* (February), 30–76.

Keen, D. (1995, October). Sell-game: The economics of conflict in Sierra Leone. Paper presented at West Africa at War: Anarchy or Peace in Liberia and Sierra Leone? A one-day conference held at the Department of Anthropology, University College London.

Kpundeh, S. (1995). *Politics and corruption in Africa: A case study of Sierra Leone*. Larnham, MD: University Press of America.

La Fontaine, J. (1985). *Initiation: Ritual drama and secret knowledge across the world*. Harmondsworth: Penguin Books.

Little, K. (1949). The role of the secret society in cultural specialization. *American Anthropologist, 51*, 199–212.

Little, K. (1965). The political function of the Poro. Part I *Africa, 35(4)*, 349–365, Part II *Africa, 36*(1), 62–71.

Machel, G. (1996). Report of the expert of the secretary general, Grace Machel, on the impact of armed conflict on children. (Document No. A/51/306).

Machel, S. (1973). *Children: The flower of the revolution.* Speech around the country, Maputo, Mozambique.

Maier, K. (1998). The universal soldier (child soldier). *Yale Review, 86*(11), 70–93.

Murphy, W. (1980). Secret knowledge of property and power in society: Elders vs. youth. *Africa, 50*, 193–207.

Murphy, W. & Bledsoe, C. (1987). Kinship and territory in the history of a Kpelle chieftan (Liberia). In: I. Kopytoff (Ed.), *The African Frontier: The Reproduction of Traditional African Societies* (pp. 123–147). Bloomington: Indiana University Press.

Pitman, T. (1999, 9 February). Kibumba- child soldiers fight war in eastern Congo. *Reuters, Kimbumba.*

Quota, S., Punamaki, R., & el-Sarraj, E. (1995). The relations between traumatic experience, activity, and cognitive and emotional responses among Palestinian children. *International Journal of Psychology, 30*, 291–299.

Reno, W. (1995). *Corruption and state politics in Sierra Leone.* Cambridge: Cambridge University Press.

Richards, P. (1996). *Fighting for the rain forest: War, youth and resources in Sierra Leone.* Oxford: James Carrey.

Richmond, M. (1999). Schooling in times of strife. *The UNESCO Courier, 9*, 1–6.

Ruiz, H. (1992). *Uprooted Liberians: Casualties of a brutal war.* U.S. Committee for Refugees. Washington, DC.

Saint Paul, P. (1999, January). Freetown: Bienvenue en enter. *Le Figaro.*

Salim A. (2001, September). Message of the OAU secretary general on the occasion of the day of the African child. *Child Soldiers Newsletter.*

Sawyer, H. (1971). *Springs of Mende belief and conduct.* Freetown: University of Sierra Leone Press.

Sikah, V. (2000). *The Ghana National Service Scheme: Perceptions of former educational personnel, students and guardians.* Doctoral dissertation, Florida International University.

Skinner, E. (1999). Child soldiers in Africa: A disaster for future families. *International Journal on World Peace, 16*(2), 7ff.

UNDPC (2001). Human Development Index. Washington, DC: World Bank.

UNICEF (1995). The State of the World's Children 1995.

UNICEF (1996). The State of the World's Children 1996.

UNICEF (1998). The State of the World's Children 1998.

UNICEF (2001a). The State of the World's Children 2001.

UNICEF (2001b). *Voices of Youth.* Retrieved from http://www.unicef.org/vog/meeting/war/war.a-html.

UNICEF (2001c). *UNICEF-assisted programmes in the area of: Children in need of special protection.* Retrieved from http://www.unicef.org/crc/bg022.html.

United Nations (1996). Too soon for twilight, too late for dawn: The story of children caught in conflict. *UN Chronicle, 33*(4), 7–8.

Waters, J. (1995). *Globalization.* London: Routledge.

Wessells, M. (1996). Assisting Angola children impacted by war: Blending western and traditional approaches to healing. *Coordinators notebook: An international resource for early childhood development, 19.* West Springfield, MA.

Wessells, M. (1997). Child soldiers: In some places if you're as tall as a rifle, you're old enough to carry one. *Bulletin of the Atomic Scientists, 53*(6), 32–40.

Wilson, K. (1992). Cults of violence and counter-violence in Mozambique. *Journal of Southern African Studies, 18*(3), 527–582.

9. VIOLENCE, DEMOCRACY AND EDUCATION: AN ANALYTIC FRAMEWORK[☆]

Jamil Salmi

Education provides people with the keys to the world

José Martí (1853–1895).

INTRODUCTION

On October 21, 1989, the Berlin wall fell, announcing the collapse of the Soviet empire and the demise of 20th century socialism. In a much celebrated article published the same year, a senior official of the U.S. Department of State, Francis Fukuyama, announced the "end of history," celebrating "the unabashed victory of economic and political liberalism and the universalisation of Western democracy as the final form of human government."[1] Indeed, the Cold War is over and we can all rest in peace. Capitalism has prevailed and we can now use interchangeably such words as market economy, freedom and democracy.

And yet, how do we reconcile the triumph of Western liberalism with the pictures of chaos, war, crime, terror and poverty which continue to appear in the daily news? These disturbing images do not come only from the unruly former republics of the Soviet Union, the fundamentalist regime of Afghanistan, or the former fanatic

☆This article is adapted from Salmi, J. (1993). *Violence and democratic society: New approaches to human rights*. London: Zed Press.

'**Suffer the Little Children': National and International Dimensions of Child Poverty and Public Policy**
Advances in Education in Diverse Communities: Research, Policy and Praxis, Volume 4, 207–230
Copyright © 2006 by Elsevier Ltd.
All rights of reproduction in any form reserved
ISSN: 1479-358X/doi:10.1016/S1479-358X(04)04009-4

dictatorships of Saddam Hussein and Slobodan Milosevic. They originate also from the rich democratic societies of our planet. For example, in the United States, the wealthiest nation of the world, 20% of the children live in poverty, one in four children is exposed to family alcoholism, 3.5 million people are homeless, one-third of low-income families go hungry on a regular basis, 25 million adults are functionally illiterate, 44 million citizens live without health insurance, 23,000 people are murdered and 50,000 rapes are reported every year, and the country boasts the highest concentration of jailed people in the world. Are these staggering statistics just reflections of accidental events and crises, or does violence coexist, in a significant fashion, with capitalism and democracy? What role does education play in this context?

To begin to address these questions, this article is divided into three parts. First, it presents a framework, which compares and contrasts different forms of violence in a systematic way. Second, it discusses how this typology can be used along various analytical dimensions. Finally, it focuses on the complex relationship between violence and education as an illustration of how the framework can be applied to analyse issues which are not commonly looked at from a violence and human rights perspective.

THE DIFFERENT CATEGORIES OF VIOLENCE

Most people think of violence in a narrow context, equating it with images of war (as in Kosovo), murders (as in Washington, DC), or riots (as in Indonesia). But violence, defined as any act that threatens a person's physical or psychological integrity, comes in many forms. Four main analytical categories can be put forward to classify the different forms of violence that can be inflicted upon a human being:

- Direct violence;
- Indirect violence;
- Repressive violence; and
- Alienating violence.

When people write or talk about violence, it is usually *direct violence* they refer to, those physical acts that result in deliberate injury to the integrity of human life. This category includes all sorts of homicides (genocide, war crimes, massacres of civilians, murders) as well as all types of coercive or brutal actions involving physical or psychological suffering (forced removal of populations, imprisonment, kidnapping, hostage taking, forced labour, torture, rape, maltreatment, battery, female circumcision). What the Serb army and police inflicted upon the Muslim populations of Bosnia and Kosovo for the ten years is a sad illustration of this category of violence. In the 17th century, the Turks would cut out the tongue of any Armenian citizen caught speaking Armenian. Two centuries later, they took even more drastic actions when they attempted to wipe out the entire Armenian population in 1915. The conquest of the Americas, by Spanish and Portuguese colonists in Central and South America and by British settlers in North America, brought war, massacres and slavery to the Native Americans. Entire populations were decimated as the European settlers took over the land and looted the gold and silver mines of the American continent.

Indirect violence is a category intended to cover harmful, sometimes deadly situations which, though due to human intervention, do not involve a direct relationship between the victims and the institutions, population groups or individuals responsible for their plight. Two sub-categories of this type of violence need to be distinguished: violence by omission and mediated violence.

Violence by omission is defined by drawing an analogy with the legal notion of non assistance to persons in danger. In some countries, there is a legal penalty to punish citizens who refuse or neglect to help victims of accidents or aggression in need of urgent care. Addressing violence by omission requires applying, at the social or collective level, a similar notion of "criminal failure to intervene" whenever human lives are threatened by actions or phenomena whose harmful effects are technically avoidable or controllable by society. For example, some historians have accused the U.S. Government of failing to intervene early enough on behalf of the victims of the Nazi holocaust, arguing that the State Department had received sufficient information about Hitler's "final solution" as early as 1942.[2] Only in January 1944, after reading the conclusions of a secret memorandum entitled "Acquiescence of This Government in the Murder of the Jews,"[3] did President Roosevelt order the U.S. army to take immediate steps to rescue the victims of Nazi extermination plans. A book written by Richard Breitman (1999) documents a similar failing in Great Britain, where Anthony Eden's government did not react to reports of mass executions of Jews. Because of his strong anti-Semitic feelings, Anthony Eden refused to act upon the devastating information gathered by British intelligence monitoring German radio communications.

This "violence by omission" approach does not apply only to the lack of protection against physical violence, but also to the lack of protection against social violence (hunger, disease, poverty), against accidents, occupational and health hazards, and against violence resulting from natural catastrophes. In countries where resources are abundant but unequally distributed, the victims of poverty, which Mark Twain called "the greatest terror," could be regarded as experiencing violence by omission. This is certainly true in the case of mass hunger. In 1944 and 1945, for example, the French occupation forces in Indo-China contributed indirectly to the death by starvation of two million Vietnamese by denying them access to rice stocks after the crop had failed.[4]

The absence of strict gun control laws in the United States is another striking illustration of this type of indirect violence. To give just one example, in December 1998, a woman was shot dead by her ex-husband in New Jersey, even though she had obtained a restraining order from a judge because she feared for her life and the police had forced her ex-husband to surrender his gun. But the angry ex-husband needed only to drive ten miles to the neighbouring county, to walk into a store, and purchase another gun before going to kill his ex-wife. It could be argued that gun manufacturers, the U.S. Government, and perhaps, even more, Congress members bear a significant degree of responsibility in this death and the several thousand gun accidents, suicide and murders which occur every year.

The devastation of natural disasters can similarly be seen as a form of indirect violence, whenever it is recognised that human intervention could have lessened the impact of seemingly uncontrollable acts of God. For example, experts have established that the Armero catastrophe in Colombia in 1985 would not have killed as many people, had the Nevada del Ruiz volcano been carefully observed and the population evacuated before the fateful mudslide.[5] We all remember the sad eyes of Omayra, the little girl whose slow death was retransmitted by all the TV channels of the world, and who became the symbol of the 25,000 victims of this tragedy.

In contrast to violence by omission which happens in a passive way, *mediated violence* is the result of deliberate human interventions in the natural or social environment whose harmful effects are felt in an indirect and sometimes delayed way. Examples of mediated violence are all forms of ecocide involving acts of destruction or damage against our natural environment. The use of the defoliant Agent Orange in the Vietnam and Afghanistan wars by the U.S. and Soviet armies, which was primarily intended to destroy crops in enemy territory, has caused genetic malformations among babies in the infected areas and cancer among war veterans. The sale, in developing countries, of pesticides and medical products banned in the country of origin is another illustration of this type of violence.

Paradoxically, embargos against repressive regimes, motivated by generous principles of solidarity with populations suffering under a dictatorial regime, can also be a source of mediated violence. A book by the former Unicef representative in Haiti documents the terrible impact, on the children and women of that country, of the UN imposed embargo against the illegal government of General Cédras.[6] In the countryside, for example, many people died of common diseases because transport was disrupted as a result of the embargo on petrol.

Repressive violence refers to the most common forms of human rights violations, regularly documented and monitored by international NGOs like Amnesty

International or Human Rights Watch. Violations of civil rights occur whenever people are denied freedom of thought, religion, and movement, or when there is no equality before the law, including the right to a fair trial. Violations of political rights exist in countries where there is no genuine democracy, no fair elections, no freedom of speech and free association. Violations of social rights occur in countries where it is not legal to form a trade union or to go on strike.

Democracy is a fairly new phenomenon in the history of human civilisation and, until a few decades ago, repressive violence was widespread in most countries of the world. But the gradual disappearance of dictatorships in Latin America over the past twenty years, the recent abolition of apartheid in South Africa and return to civilian rule in several African countries, and the elimination of the Soviet Empire have brought about a significant reduction in the need for and reliance on repressive violence by governments. It does not mean, however, that this form of violence has vanished altogether. Repressive violence continues to be prevalent in many countries, even in the more ancient democratic societies. In Great Britain, for example, the Thatcher administration promulgated new laws in 1980 and 1982 which restricted the rights of trade unions and workers. Grave judicial errors were committed in connection with the intervention of the British army in Northern Ireland, such as the notorious case of the Guilford Four portrayed in the movie "In the Name of the Father."

The notion of *alienating violence*, which refers to the deprivation of a person's higher rights such as the right to psychological, emotional, cultural or intellectual integrity, is based on the assumption that a person's well-being does not come only from fulfilling material needs. Looking at alienating violence means paying attention to the satisfaction of such diverse non-material needs as empowerment at work or in the community, the opportunity to engage in creative activities, a young child's need for affection – some child psychologists are now talking about the crucial role of a dimension called emotional intelligence – the feeling of social and cultural belonging, etc. Examples of alienating violence are found in countries with deliberate policies of ethnocide threatening to destroy the cultural identity of an entire linguistic or religious community. In Morocco, for example, the Berber part of the population, which represents 60% of the total population, does not have official recognition at school or in the media. In several African and Latin American countries, indigenous population groups are being gradually assimilated, losing their identities as a result of discriminatory cultural policies. Racism, and any form of prejudicial practice against any particular group in society, such as homosexuals or the elderly, are other forms of alienating violence found in many places.

Freedom from fear is a key dimension in this discussion of alienating violence. The daily lives of millions of people throughout the world are affected by feelings

Table 1. Typology of Different Categories and Forms of Violence.

Perpetrator Category	Individual	Group	Firm	Government
Direct violence (deliberate injury to the integrity of human life)	X	X		X
Murder		X		X
Massacre				X
Genocide	X	X		X
Torture	X	X		X
Rape and child sex	X	X		X
Maltreatment	X	X		
Female circumcision	X	X		X
Forced resettlement		X	X	X
Kidnapping/hostage taking	X	X	X	X
Forced labour (incl. Child labour)				
Slavery				
Indirect violence (indirect violation of the right to survival)				
Violence by Omission (lack of protection against . . .)				
Poverty			X	X
Hunger			X	X
Disease			X	X
Accidents			X	X
Natural catastrophes				X
Mediated violence (harmful modifications to the environment)		X	X	X
Repressive violence (deprivation of fundamental rights)				
Civil rights		X		X
Freedom of thought		X		X
Freedom of speech		X		X
Freedom of religion				X
Right to a fair trial				X
Equality before the law				X
Freedom of movement				
Political rights				X
Freedom to vote				X
Freedom of association				X
Freedom to hold meetings				
Social rights			X	X
Freedom to go on strike			X	X
Freedom to form a union				X
Protection of private property				
Alienating violence (deprivation of higher rights)				
Alienating living/working conditions	X	X	X	X
Racism	X	X		X
Social ostracism	X	X		X
Cultural repression		X		X
Living in fear	X			X

of anxiety, apprehension and dread. This is found among communities caught up in situations of direct violence, such as war, civil strife and repression. Colombia, Northern Ireland, Lebanon, Sierra Leone, Rwanda, Bosnia and Kosovo are present-day examples. Feelings of apprehension often continue for years after the end of the conflicts, aggravated in many cases by the presence of land mines, which lie dormant in the ground in more than 70 countries and kill or maim about 26,000 people a year, mostly civilians.

People living in urban areas with high crime rates are also subject to this type of anxiety. A recent survey among inhabitants of the largest metropoles in Latin America indicates that, even in cities with relatively low levels of crime like Buenos Aires, a large proportion of people live in fear. Often, this leads to restricted mobility in terms of the times of day people can leave their houses or district and the places they can safely go to. The rapid growth of security products and services in both industrialised and developing countries is a sad illustration of the importance of this dimension of fear. In his Annual Message to Congress in 1941, President Roosevelt had mentioned "freedom from fear" as one of the four essential freedoms he wanted to preserve for the American people, together with freedom of expression, freedom of worship and freedom from want.

Table 1below summarises the main dimensions of the proposed analytical framework and indicates possible levels of responsibility.

APPLYING THE ANALYTICAL FRAMEWORK FOR VIOLENCE

How can this framework be used? Its main advantage is that it constitutes a flexible analytical tool for investigating complex situations in a systematic, thorough and objective manner. One can compare situations of violence along several dimensions, for example geographical, historical, ideological, and institutional in order to establish and study patterns of interconnections and causal relationships in a consistent way.

Along the space dimension, levels and occurrences of violence can be analysed in different countries using the same methodological approach. Linkages can be found even across national borders. For example, between the look of wonder of a European child buying her or his first electronic game and the exhaustion in the eyes of an Asian woman who spends her day assembling tiny electronic components, there is a whole set of complex economic and social relationships. In some cases, action in the name of economic development leads to both social and environmental catastrophe. Environmental specialists have explained that the impact of the October 1999 floods in India – which killed more than

17,000 people – would have been much less deadly, had the mangrove trees which had always been a natural protection against floods not been cut to set up lucrative shrimp farms geared to the export market.

Second, along the time dimension, one can look at historical patterns of violence, outlining for example the causal relationship between colonialism and the growth of the Western economies. To quote the Nobel Peace Prize winner Bishop Desmond Tutu of South Africa, "When the missionaries first came to Africa they had the Bible and we had the land. They said 'let us pray.' We closed our eyes. When we opened them, we had the Bible and they had the land."

Third, there often is a dynamic relationship between different forms of violence which can be mutually reinforcing. Recent econometric studies have shown, for example, that income inequality (indirect violence) has a significant and positive effect on the incidence of violent crimes.[7]

Fourth, the same approach can be applied to compare different realities across ideological boundaries. The typology of human rights violations can be used for capitalist and communist societies, for kingdoms and republics, for secular and fundamentalist regimes. Looking, for example, at the defunct Soviet Union through this analytical framework, it is possible to identify the main dimensions of the human cost of socialism as it functioned in that context. The history of the Soviet regime is indeed filled with tales of terror, massacres, mass executions, deportation of entire population groups, purges and concentration camps, reflecting unprecedented levels of institutionalised state terrorism.[8]

Fifth, the framework is helpful in identifying harmful situations in democratic societies where, theoretically, human rights are fully protected by the rule of law. The French Government has recently been condemned by the European Court of Justice for the use of torture by police against common criminals. Amnesty International has launched a campaign against capital punishment in the United States which is one of the few countries in the world, together with Iran, Pakistan and Somalia, where the death penalty can still apply to young people under the age of 18.

Sixth, the typology allows measurement of the respective roles and responsibilities of different institutions, from individuals to groups of people to firms to governments to multinational companies. For example, thousands of Bolivians and Paraguayans died between 1932 and 1935 because their two nations were at war; but in reality it was a war by proxy between two giant oil companies – Standard Oil of New Jersey and Shell Oil – competing for control of the Chaco oil fields at the border between the two countries.

A final observation concerning the application of the framework is that a particular occurrence of violence may fall under several categories at the same time. Slavery, for example, cuts across all four categories of violence. It encompasses the direct violence of the manhunt in West Africa, the forced voyage to America and the denial of freedom, the indirect violence of the slaves' living conditions, the repressive violence inflicted upon people who never had any rights whatsoever, and finally the alienating violence involved in uprooting Africans and plunging them in a totally foreign cultural and social environment and denying them their basic dignity as human beings. As an extreme illustration of the relationship between individual cruelty and the significance of slavery as an economic system, one can evoke a "delicate" practice used in 19th century Cuban plantations to preserve the continuity of the slave population. Before punishing a pregnant slave woman who had misbehaved in her work, a hole would be dug in the ground so that the woman could lie on her stomach and be whipped without any damage to the baby she was carrying.[9]

VIOLENCE AND EDUCATION

Can the same analytical framework be applied to the concept of education? At first sight, violence and education do not fit well together. The former refers to harmful situations,which cause people to suffer, and the latter to a positive process of intellectual and moral growth. But these two notions which, appear to belong to very separate realities have, in fact, many points of intersection. In some countries, schools are violent environments and the education process, or lack thereof, are important determinants of violence. At the same time, education can be a powerful instrument to reduce violence and improve the human rights situation in any given society.

As early as 1948, the international community decided to include in the Universal Declaration of Human Rights an article affirming that *"Education shall be free, at least in the elementary and fundamental stages."* The Declaration went on to indicate that elementary education should also be compulsory. Several other texts and legal instruments have reaffirmed the importance of this basic human right, for example, the International Covenant on Economic, Social and Cultural Rights, the 1959 Declaration of the Rights of the Child, and the 1990 Convention on the Rights of the Child ratified by 191 countries.[10]

The UNESCO Convention against Discrimination in Education has introduced a second, related dimension: equality of educational opportunities. This refers to the obligation of States to offer access to education equally to all children, regardless of differences in terms of regional, ethnic, religious, linguistic or gender background.

The third dimension of education as a human right defended by the United Nations system is the notion of freedom of choice. The International Covenant on Civil and Political Rights mentions that "The State Parties to the present Covenant undertake to have respect for the liberty of parents . . . to ensure the religious and moral education of their children in conformity with their own convictions."

To emphasise the importance attached to education as a human right, the UN Commission on Human Rights, under the authority of the Economic and Social Council, has begun to issue, since 1998, a yearly report on the degree of compliance of countries with the right to education as defined by the United Nations system. However, the content of the report reveals a relatively cautious and restricted discussion of the issues involved.[11] With regard to access and availability, the report focuses on national legislation on compulsory and free education, without reviewing actual compliance. The equality of opportunity dimension is looked at exclusively from the viewpoint of gender inequities, undoubtedly a crucial element but certainly not the only one. Unequal access deserves to be analysed as well along socio-economic, ethnic, linguistic, and religious lines. Finally, there is little consensus, among the members of the General Assembly, on considering "the choice of parents" as a fundamental human right at the same level as access to basic education. Many States view it as a Western, capitalist notion designed to legitimise existing patterns of social or racial inequality or justify the introduction of voucher systems.

To ensure a more systematic and thorough assessment of the relationship between violence and education, it is possible to apply the analytical framework presented earlier, looking at the linkages from two complementary angles: first, education as a place or a determinant of violence, and second education as an instrument to reduce societal violence.

NEGATIVE DIMENSIONS IN THE CONTEXT OF EDUCATION

To begin with direct violence, it should be noted that schools are not always the sanctuaries of peace and harmony they are expected to be. In many countries, societal violence reaches into the schools. The U.S. case is one of the most striking example in that respect.[12] In a society where gun violence has become a major public health hazard, schools are not immune from the same type of violence. In many urban schools, passing through a metal detector is the first daily "educational" experience of a student. Students are not allowed to carry a book bag to school. Police officers and dogs on patrol are part of the regular school landscape. The frequency of school massacres, such as the Stockton massacre in January 1989 or, more recently, the Columbine High School killings in Colorado in April 1999, has increased in dramatic proportion. Nine school shootings were recorded in 1999 and 2000 across the country.[13,14] A Washington Post (1999) poll of the concerns of

American people in the context of the presidential electoral campaign revealed that, out of a list of 51 problem areas, lack of safety in schools was ranked number two. Financial resources which could be used for pedagogical purposes are channelled to purchase security equipment, as exemplified by the recent decision of Montgomery County authorities in the State of Maryland to invest close to US$700,000 to install electronic monitoring equipment in all schools of the county.

The presence of guns and knives in schools is also a major preoccupation in countries going through civil war, such as Colombia or Sierra Leone. In Nicaragua, gang violence in schools has become a worrisome phenomenon and the presence of armed policemen is now indispensable to assuage the fears of parents. The University of Antioquia in Medellin, Colombia, the oldest higher education institution of the country, is increasingly under siege by armed groups from all political sides. Students live in a state of "panic and consternation."

> The main administration building has been dynamited by leftist guerillas; a respected professor, a student leader and a popular cafeteria worker have been shot to death on university grounds for political reasons; and a right-wing paramilitary group has begun to operate openly and circulate a death list of future targets.[15]

War and post-conflict situations can have other devastating effects on the school system. In 1996, 29 out of the 48 countries of Sub-Saharan Africa were affected by civil strife. In countries like Angola, Afghanistan, Bosnia, Cambodia, Croatia, Iraq, Mozambique, Nicaragua, Chechnya and Somalia, the presence of land mines in former conflict areas prevents children from getting an education because of the life-threatening danger involved in something as basic as walking from the home village to the local school. In several instances, schools have been bombed and children have died during conflicts, as has happened in Lebanon, Iraq and Bosnia during the past few years. On December 17, 1999, 20 students ages nine to 15 were wounded by shrapnel when shells fired by an Israeli-allied militia exploded in an elementary school in southern Lebanon which has been hit five times in as many years.[16] In Colombia, large numbers of school teachers and students have been threatened or killed by the various guerrilla and paramilitary groups. In the Northern Colombian province of Bolivar, 300 teachers are currently on leave with pay away from their schools of assignment because of death threats.

> In the last ten years, being a teacher in Colombia has become as dangerous as being a soldier, policeman or journalist. On average, one teacher is killed every fifteen days . . . Some teachers, who ignored the threats, have been murdered in front of their own class.[17]

Refugees and displaced persons offer another challenge to the educational authorities of the affected countries. Additional resources are needed to provide schooling in remote areas where often there are no schools. Appropriate pedagogical approaches are required to help children traumatised by their exposure to conflict situations. At the end of 1996, there were about 6.2 million refugees and internally displaced people in Sub-Saharan Africa. In Colombia again, it is estimated that up to 15% of the rural population is displaced as a result of guerrilla or paramilitary activity, which means that thousands of children are deprived from a normal school experience. As a result of the civil war in Guatemala in the early 1980s, an estimated 20% of the overall population lived as refugees in the mountain areas of the country or in neighbouring Mexico.

While less newsworthy, corporal punishment is another important dimension of direct violence which is part of the daily school experience of children in many countries, especially in the developing world. Beatings are seen in many cultures as a normal enforcement tool to motivate students to learn better, in defiance of the International Convention on the Rights of the Child, which stipulates the use of discipline appropriate with the dignity of the child. In Morocco, for example, a majority of primary school teachers work with a ruler, a stick or a piece of rubber garden hose which are generously used to hit the children.[18] The American researcher Maher, who spent a year in the Moroccan countryside, recalls that teachers usually *"shout their lesson, delivering ridicule and blows freely."*[19] As one teacher explained, *"the children have always been hit, beaten at home and in the street. If one takes up a different system in school, they become too spoilt and one cannot control them anymore. True we are taught many things at the teacher training college, everything about psychology and pedagogy, but when we arrive here, we don't know how to deal with them. Using the stick is the best way."*[20] There is an old Colombian saying to the effect that you can learn well only after a strong beating ("la letra con sangre entra"), reflecting an ancient tradition of school beatings which is still prevalent in the rural parts of the country. Corporal punishment and school bullying is also widespread in socially cohesive societies like Japan. The 1994 suicide of a 13-year-old boy, Kiyoteru Okochi, who had been repeatedly humiliated and harassed by other boys without intervention of the school authorities, brought this issue to international attention.[21] In the United Kingdom, where corporal punishment had traditionally been extensive and brutal, there have been recent efforts to reintroduce this practice in schools, despite the European Court of Human Rights' condemnation of Britain in that regard.[22]

Illiteracy, a strong factor of poverty, is one of the most debilitating forms of indirect or social violence. For the millions of girls and boys who are denied access to school, or who are rejected after only a few years, living without the capacity to read and write will be a serious handicap during their entire life. It affects their ability to find remunerated employment and become more productive if they are self-employed. Illiteracy is also potentially life-threatening because of its negative impact on the health of its victims and that of their family, especially in the case of girls and mothers who usually play the leading part in the transmission of progressive hygiene and health habits. World Bank researchers have underscored a clear correlation between girls' education and mortality rates, especially child mortality.[23]

The scores of children who are excluded from schools are usually the victims of negligent government policies which have failed to make "education for all" a real national priority. Some groups in society can be affected more than others. In many South Asian, African and Arab countries, for example, girls fare systematically worse in terms of access to school and permanence in the education system. According to UNICEF, 60% of the 130 million children aged 6–11 who are not in school throughout the world are girls. In the Caribbean region, by contrast, there is a reverse pattern of gender inequality, whereby the school performance of boys is below that of girls. In several Latin American countries, children from the indigenous populations are less likely to enter school, to stay in school, or to perform well academically than the rest of the population. In Peru, for example, Quechua children score an average of 30% lower than Spanish speakers on national tests of academic achievement.[24] In Guatemala, according to Ministry of Education statistics, the average education level of indigenous females is less than one year of formal education and the illiteracy rate is as high as 70%. By contrast, average number of school years achieved is 4.5 for the non-indigenous population, whose illiteracy rate is only 40%.

Sometimes, government negligence is compounded by deliberate discriminatory practices against "minority" groups from a social or legal standpoint. In South Africa until the early 1990s, education for the black majority was a powerful instrument of perpetuation of the unjust apartheid system. In 1970, for instance, less than 1% of the African and coloured population had finished 10 years of formal schooling, compared to 23% for the white population. In the words of the Minister of Native Affairs, "... *my department's policy is that education should stand with both feet in the reserves and have its roots in the spirit and being of Bantu society. . . There is no place for [the Bantu] in the European community above the level of certain forms of labour*"[25] Indonesia, Malaysia and Sri Lanka are other examples of countries whose education policies were purposely and systematically biased against some ethnic minorities in the form of explicit or implicit quotas. In Hungary, children of the Gypsy minority continue to be discriminated against to this day. Many rural schools are segregated, including the provision of separate toilet facilities.

The AIDS epidemic, which has reached alarming proportions in many Sub-Saharan African countries, is a strong factor of exclusion. It is estimated that there are already 4.5 million "AIDS orphans" in Eastern Africa alone. In the absence of special attention to their plight, most of these children do not have access to school or do not stay in school for long.

Illiteracy is not only a developing country's social disease. Recent surveys in industrialised nations have shown that a surprisingly high proportion of the adult population is functionally illiterate. The 1995 survey indicates that, for the adult population in the 46–55 age category, the range of functional illiteracy is between 7% (in Sweden) and 36% (in Ireland). It is as high as 25% in the United Kingdom and 21% in the US.[26] This situation is all the more worrisome as rapid technological change and the information and communication revolutions are drastically changing the content of jobs and career patterns. Lifelong education is not a luxury anymore but a necessity for survival and adaptation, but it is not accessible to the relatively large share of the population falling in this category of functionally illiterate people. UNICEF estimates that, at the eve of the new century, almost 900 million people, representing close to one sixth of humanity, were functionally illiterate.

In many developing countries, especially in the rural areas, the physical infrastructure conditions for learning available to the children are far from being adequate. Schools operate without proper sanitary infrastructure or without sufficient protection against harsh climatic conditions (rain, heat). In rural Peru, for instance, 68% of the smaller schools have no working latrines; 39% of the classrooms have no roof.[27] In Northeast Brazil, a third of all schools do not have bathrooms.[28] In some countries, for example in Trinidad and Tobago, asbestos has been used in school construction, with a significant risk of harmful exposure for the children.

School accessibility is also a factor to consider. In rural El Salvador, the number of teachers and children drowning on their way to school has increased so much, in the wake of recent floods, that it has become a national problem for the Ministry of Education.[29] In some rural areas in the Philippines, children carry ropes which are used routinely to cross rivers and avoid drowning in the daily school commute.

With respect to the "repressive violence" category, an uneducated population is fertile ground for the denial of civic and political rights. Even in countries with a long democratic tradition, the high proportion of abstentions at key political votes, for example in the U.S. or in France, could be an indicator that adult illiteracy and the lack of civic education in schools are obstacles to full participation of the majority in democratic life. Successive surveys of college freshmen in the U.S. indicate that young people are increasingly detached from political and community life.[30] In many societies, school governance, structure, organisation and pedagogical practices do not reflect the democratic ideals which could impact positively the young people educated in these schools. As two U.S. professors emphasised in a recent book on democratic schools, "the most powerful meaning of democracy is formed not in glossy political rhetoric, but in the details of everyday lives."[31]

The last category of violence, alienating violence, is particularly relevant to this review of education and human rights. In many education systems, there is a wide disconnect between the curriculum taught at school and the community it is meant to serve, as humorously illustrated by Charles Schulz and his Peanuts character.

> I learned something in school today.
> I signed up for folk guitar, computer programming, stained glass art, shoemaking and a natural foods workshop.
> I got Spelling, History, Arithmetic and two study periods.
> So what did you learn?
> I learned that what you sign up for and what you get are two different things.[32]

For millions of children, being confronted with an alien curriculum in terms of content and, sometimes, language of instruction makes for a very unsettling educational experience. The language situation in Morocco offers an interesting example of this type of challenge. As a child, the young Moroccan learns either one of three Berber dialects or Moroccan Arabic in the family and immediate community. When a child enters primary school for the first time, he/she starts to be taught in classical Arabic, an erudite written language which is linguistically distinct from the Moroccan Arabic spoken in the country. After two years, children are introduced to French which will serve as the vehicle for learning mathematics and natural sciences. During these years of acquiring basic literacy skills, the mother tongue (Berber or Moroccan Arabic) is strictly banned from the classroom. Many students end up with serious shortcomings in terms of cognitive achievement, not because of inherent intellectual deficiencies, but because they have to study in what are for them, from a purely linguistic viewpoint, two "foreign" languages.[33]

Textbooks often reflect a cultural, urban or gender bias which misrepresents minority groups or population segments with a minority status. Studies of textbooks used in Latin America have shown, for example, that black people have been systematically eliminated from any reference outside the slavery period. Moreover, when depicted, black persons are associated with negative images reflecting profound racist prejudices in society.[34] At times, the level of frustration of minority groups can be so high as to lead to extreme reactions. In Sri Lanka, for example, it appears that the violent Tamil Tigers movement started among students disenchanted with an education system which totally ignored their minority culture.

Again, this type of curriculum problem is not confined to the developing world. The progress of "creationism" in the U.S. is a striking example of biased teaching in an industrialised country. Over the past ten years, Christian fundamentalists have taken over school boards in many districts or counties and successfully removed any reference to Darwin and evolutionism from the biology curriculum in high schools.[35] The August 1999 decision of the Kansas board of education to eliminate, from State education standards, references to Darwinism and to scientific accounts of the origin of the universe and the Earth which conflict with the biblical version of creation, has revived the national debate and raised the spectre of censorship.[36] As a result of the Kansas board decision, zealous librarians in religious schools have torn out the section on Charles Darwin in books about great scientists and labelled "dangerous" biology books with the following warning:

Teacher beware: This book contains evolutionary statements. Use material carefully.[37]

Another important dimension of alienating violence is the culture of fear prevailing in many school systems where tests and exams have become an end in themselves. When the purpose of each school cycle is solely to prepare for the next cycle, the anxiety to pass replaces the pleasure of learning. Intense competition, starting sometimes as early as in kindergarten, is associated with the dread of failure and engenders worrisome phenomena. Widespread cheating has been documented in several developing countries, for example Pakistan and Bangladesh.[38] Even in the United States, a recent survey among Duke University students revealed that close to half acknowledged some degree of high school cheating.[39] Child suicides occur in closely knit cultures where school failure brings humiliation for the child and disgrace to the family, like in Japan and Hong Kong. One of the most dramatic and extreme illustrations of the weight of social pressure was the recent murder of a two-year-old toddler in Tokyo, whose only "sin" was to be selected by lottery for admission to a prestigious kindergarten. He was strangled by an envious neighbourhood mother whose own child had not been accepted.[40] Also, as a result of the prevailing physical violence in inner city U.S. schools, in European schools in low income suburbs, and more generally in societies torn by civil war, teachers live in fear of being victimised by aggression from unruly students.

Finally, it is worth mentioning that, as in any other situation of violence, the different dimensions of the relationship between violence and education can be mutually reinforcing. In Jamaica and Colombia, for example, failure at school and growing unemployment lead young males into a vicious cycle of drug abuse and street violence.

EDUCATION AS A POSITIVE FACTOR

Education makes a people easy to lead, but difficult to drive; easy to govern but impossible to enslave

Henry, Baron Brougham (1778–1868).

Fortunately, the relationship between violence and education is not always harmful, quite the opposite. On the positive side, education is an important instrument to overcome violence and improve respect for human rights. In societies where direct violence is or was pervasive until recently, for example in countries torn by civil war like Sierra Leone and Colombia, in post-conflict nations such as Mozambique and El Salvador, or in post-apartheid countries like South Africa and Namibia, political and civic leaders have emphasised the need to make schools violence-free and to promote peace education, as a key channel for changing the value system and bringing up generations of young people able to coexist in a more peaceable fashion. In Namibia, for example, corporal punishment has been eliminated at the end of the apartheid period and school discipline is now based on a non-violent approach called "discipline from within."

Ongoing experiences of education for peace and human rights in Colombia offer rays of hope in an otherwise discouraging situation of widespread violence. In the Northern Province of Bolivar, for instance, the Convivial Schools program ("Escuelas Territorios de Convivencia Social") has adapted the traditional local figure of the "palabrero" or mediator, prevalent among the Indigenous population, to train a network of negotiators chosen among students, parents, teachers and school administrators, whose role is to promote peaceful modes of conflict resolution in the school and the community. Set in a region of acute violence where three different guerilla groups, various squads of paramilitary terrorists, drug lords and the national army have been actively fighting and terrorising the civilian population for two decades, the program has begun to transform the culture of schools in a more democratic way and to shield them relatively from the surrounding violence, even achieving the safe release of teachers kidnapped by the guerilla or the paramilitary.

In countries with repressive political systems, universities have often provided a forum for voicing criticism on important political and social issues. In many parts of the world, authoritarian governments have been seriously challenged by student protests, as illustrated by the Tianamen Square events in China (1989), or even overthrown, for instance in Thailand (1974) and Korea (1987).

Providing education helps young people acquire the fundamental skills and values needed to find productive employment, be able to adjust to changing labour market requirements over their lifetime, and live a politically, socially and culturally meaningful life. Higher levels of education also result in better health and longer life expectancy. Girls' education, in particular, has high individual and social health benefits. More educated mothers maintain better hygiene and feeding habits in their household; resulting in lower infant mortality. Educated teenagers are less at risk of adolescent pregnancy and sexually transmitted diseases. Girls' education also helps reduce fertility rates.

... In Brazil, illiterate women have an average of 6.5 children, whereas those with secondary education have 2.5 children. In the Southern Indian state of Kerala, where literacy is universal, the infant mortality rate is the lowest in the entire developing world – and the fertility rate is the lowest in India.[41]

Experiences throughout the world demonstrate that programs specifically dedicated to those children who have been excluded from the education system for one reason or another can have very positive results. The BRAC schools in Bangladesh, to give just one example, have been successfully offering quality education to a growing number of children from low income families, with a special emphasis on girls and disadvantaged children. In addition, in any society, keeping children in school is also the best way to eliminate child labour and the sexual exploitation of children.

As discussed earlier, transforming schools into settings which are free from physical violence is a fundamental requirement. But it is equally important to eliminate dimensions of indirect violence in schools by offering to all children a healthy school environment which entails, at a minimum, provision of potable water, decent sanitary facilities and a safe building.

Finally, several channels can be used to make the formal education experience of children in schools more meaningful, with the purpose of reducing alienating violence. In several countries, far-reaching innovations have been introduced to transform the curriculum and improve pedagogical practices so as to provide underprivileged groups with a more empowering education. *Escuela Nueva*, for instance, is an interactive teaching and learning approach which stimulates learning among peers and the development of democratic behaviours in multigrade schools. Started in Colombia in the 1980s, it has been successfully adapted in other countries, including Guatemala and Honduras. The EDUCO movement in El Salvador, which began as a grassroots initiative at the end of the civil war in 1992, has brought about an active involvement of the communities in the operation of schools in the poorest districts of the country. The City of Emmaus School in Northeast Brazil is designed as a new form of education for street children, giving them the opportunity to learn to live as independent and responsible citizens.

For many children from linguistic minorities, access to bilingual education is an important factor to assure a meaningful school experience and increase their chances of academic success. In Latin America, the education authorities in Ecuador, Bolivia, Mexico and Guatemala have taken the lead in developing and implementing bilingual programs with appropriate education materials, adapted pedagogical practices and qualified teachers.

With respect to the teaching of tolerance, a pioneering programme in Southern California has had a remarkable impact at San Clemente High School, where inter-ethnic tensions among whites, Latinos, Blacks and Asian Americans had led to

Table 2. Violence and Education: A Typology.

Manifestation Category	Negative Dimensions in the Context of Education	Education as Positive Factor
Direct violence (deliberate injury to the integrity of human life)	Effects of violent conflicts . . . Land mines . . . Bombing . . . Threats, kidnappings, murders Weapons in schools Corporal punishment Failure suicides	Education for peace Weapon-free schools Banishment of corporal punishment
Indirect violence (indirect violation of the right to survival) Violence by omission	Illiteracy Inequities of access and achievement . . . Gender . . . Socio-economic groups . . . Ethnic groups . . . Linguistic groups . . . Religious groups	Education for all Equality of opportunity Including the excluded (minorities, refugees, displaced children) Education for life
Mediated violence	Inadequate Infrastructure . . . Lack of basic hygiene . . . Exposure to rain and heat . . . Asbestos	Adequate infrastructure . . . Potable water and latrines . . . Protection from rain and heat . . . Harmless construction materials
Repressive violence (deprivation of fundamental political rights)	Absence of democracy in schools Lack of education for democracy	Democratic practices in schools at all levels Education for democracy (civic education, recognition of equal rights and freedoms)
Alienating violence (deprivation of higher rights)	Foreign/biased curriculum and textbooks (history, biology, etc.) Foreign language Alienating pedagogical practices Harassment Examinations as negative incentive	Appropriate curriculum Education for tolerance and cultural diversity Use of mother tongue or bilinguilism Pedagogical practices for intellectual and emotional growth Harassment-free schools

serious incidents in the early 1990s. A course where students are taught to identify and reject all forms of prejudice and racism – not just ethnic discrimination – has significantly modified the social climate on campus.[42] Similarly, the Givat Gonen school in Israel, located in a district characterised by high levels of criminality and antagonism between Jewish and Arab youths, has pioneered an "education for peace" program which has successfully integrated children from the two communities.

Table 2 below summarises this discussion of the relationships between violence and education with a typology of the role played by education from both a negative and a positive perspective.

CONCLUSION

To understand fully the role of violence and the related extent of harm inflicted upon various population groups or individuals in a democratic society, or in any society for that matter, two things are required. One needs first to conduct a systematic analysis of the different forms of violence existing in that society. Second, on the basis of this analysis, one must try to establish the patterns and relationships linking these manifestations of violence to the prevailing economic, social and political power structures, in order to establish accountability. The framework outlined in these pages is offered as a tool to facilitate this type of analysis.

This paper was guided by the assumption that violence is a multifaceted phenomenon associated with specific causes and responsible people or institutions. The paper also reflects a strong belief in the existence of universal human rights and the premise that the different forms of violence mentioned to in the article are sources of harm or suffering regardless of the type of society and culture one lives in and no matter one's own individual characteristics. Whether Chinese or Swiss, Muslim or Jew, man or woman, situations such as torture, hunger, illiteracy, lack of political freedom, living in fear, and lack of self-determination are hurtful. The degree of tolerance towards various manifestations of harm may differ from one person to the other, and from one culture to the other, but there are common experiences of oppression, suffering and alienation which affect all human beings alike.

Education's place in the study of human rights violations is particularly important because of its potential role as either a negative or a positive factor with strong multiplier effects in each case. As discussed in this paper, the possibility to enjoy an education and the quality of that educational experience bear on all four forms of violence. This was illustrated in a dramatic way by the anguished cry for help message left behind by the two Guinean teenagers who were found dead in

July 1999, after hiding in the landing gear bay of a Sabena aeroplane which flew from Conakry to Brussels. Their letter, addressed to the "Excellencies and officials of Europe," is self-explanatory:

> ... We suffer enormously in Africa. Help us. We lack rights as children. We have war and illness, we lack food ... We have schools, but we lack education ... [43]

NOTES

1. Fukuyama, F. (1989, Summer). The end of history. *National Interest*, No. 16.
2. Morse, A. (1967). *While six million died*. New York: Ace Publishing Corporation.
3. Breitman, R. (1999). *Official secrets: What the Nazis planned, what the British and Americans knew*. London: Penguin Books.
4. Reported in: Zinn, H. (1980). *A people's history of the United States*. London: Longman, 461.
5. Vanhecke, C. (1985). Armero ne devait pas être détruite. In: *Le Monde* (30 November).
6. Gibbons, E. (1999). *Sanctions in Haiti: Human rights and democracy under assault*. Washington, DC: CSIS Press.
7. Fajnzylber, P., Lederman, D., & Loayza, N. (1999, November). Inequality and violent crime, unpublished paper. Washington, DC: World Bank.
8. See for example Heller, M., and A. Nekrich (1986). Utopia in Power: *The History of the Soviet Union from 1917 to the Present*. New York: Summit Books. Conquest, R. (1973). *The Great Terror: Stalin's Purge of the Thirties* (Rev. ed.). New York. Conquest, R. (1979). *Kolmya: The Arctic Death Camps*. Oxford: Oxford University Press. Medvedev, R. (1976). *Let History Judge*. Nottingham: Spokesmann Books. Carrère d'Encausse, H. (1978). *L'Empire Eclaté*. Paris: Flammarion.
9. Reported in Galeano, E. (1981). *Les veines ouvertes de l'Amérique latine*. Paris: Editions Plon, 119.
10. Only two countries have not ratified the Convention on the Rights of the Child to this day: Somalia and the U.S.
11. Preliminary Report of the Special Rapporteur on the right to education, Ms. Katarina Tomasevski, submitted in accordance with Commission on Human Rights resolution 1998/33. United Nations, Economic and Social Council, document E/CN.4/1999/49.
12. See for example Salmi, J. (1992, April). "L'Amérique malade des armes à feu." *Le Monde Diplomatique*.
13. Pressley, S. A. (2000, 3 January). Year of Mass Shootings Leaves Scar on U.S. *The Washington Post*.
14. What worries Americans. *The Washington Post* (7 November 1999).
15. Rohter, L. (1999, 29 December). College students warily live, learn in war's shadow. *The Miami Herald*.
16. Mantash, A. (1999, 17 December). Children hurt in S. Lebanon militia attack. *The Washington Post*.
17. Restrepo, J. D. (1991). "Ser maestro: un peligro mortal [Risking your life to be a teacher], *Educación y Cultura*. FECODE, Santafé de Bogotá, Colombia, no. 24, p. 8. Quoted in Camargo Abello M. (1997, September). "Are the seeds of violence sown in schools?", *Prospects*. UNESCO: Paris, *XXVII*(3).

18. Salmi, J. (1981). *Educational crisis and social reproduction: The political economy of schooling in Morocco.* University of Sussex: Unpublished Ph. D. thesis.

19. Maher, V. (1974). *Women and property in Morocco.* Boston: Cambridge University Press, 81.

20. Belarbi, A. (1976). *Les relations enseignants/enseignés dans la classe.* University of Paris, unpublished thesis, 49.

21. Hirsh, M., & Takayama, H. (1994). The other side of paradise. *Newsweek* (19 December), 37.

22. Parker-Jenkins, M. (1997, September). Sparing the rod: Schools, discipline and children's rights in multicultural Britain. Paper presented at the Conference of the South African Education Law and Policy Association. Stellenbosh, South Africa.

23. Hill, M. A., & King, E. M. (1995). Women's education and economic wellbeing. *Feminist Economics, 1*(2). London: Routledge.

24. The World Bank (1999). Peru – Education at a crossroads: Challenges and opportunities for the 21st century. Washington, DC, Report No. 19066-PE, Vol. 1, p. 38.

25. Quoted in Troup, F. (1976). *Forbidden pastures: Education under apartheid.* London: International Defence & Aid Fund, p. 4.

26. OECD (1995). *Literacy Skills In The Knowledge Society.* Paris: OECD, table 1.6 page xx.

27. The World Bank (1999). Peru – Education at a crossroads: Challenges and opportunities for the 21st century. Washington, DC, Report No. 19066-PE, Vol. 2, p. 101.

28. Waiselfisz, J. (1999, November). Ambientes Escolares. Unpublished document. Ministry of Education.

29. Interview with the Minister of Education, October 4, 1999.

30. Referred to in *Infobrief* (1998). Alexandria, Va: Association for Supervision and Curriculum Development, Issue 13, June 1998, p. 2.

31. Apple, M. W., & Beane, J. A. (1995). *Democratic schools.* Alexandria, Va: Association for Supervision and Curriculum Development, p. 103).

32. Quoted in Reimer, E. (1971). *School is Dead: An Essay on Alternatives in Education.* Harmondsworth: Penguin Books, p. 22.

33. Salmi, J. (1987). Language and schooling in Morocco. *International Journal of Educational Development, 7*(1), 21–31.

34. Arenas, A. (1999). Education of people of African descent in Latin America and the Caribbean. In: A. A. Kwame & H. L. Gates (Eds), *Encarta Africana.* Redwood, WA: Microsoft Corporation.

35. Mathews, J. (1996, 8 April). Creationism makes a comeback. *The Washington Post.*

36. Keller, B., & Coles, A. D. (1999, 8 September). Kansas evolution controversy gives rise to national debate. *Education Week.*

37. Rosin, H. (1999, 5 October). Creationism, coming to life in Suburbia. *The Washington Post.*

38. Greaney, V., & Kellaghan, T. (1996). The integrity of public examinations in developing countries. In: H. Goldstein & T. Lewis (Eds), *Assessment: Problems, Developments and Statistical Issues*(pp. 167–188). Chichester: Wiley.

39. Raspberry, R. (1999, 23 November). Their cheating hearts. *The Washington Post.*

40. Tolbert, K. (1999). In Japan, education is deadly serious. *The Washington Post* (27 November).

41. UNICEF (1999). *The state of the world's children 1999*. New York, pp. 7–8. Based on UNESCO 1995 data.
42. Smith, H. (1999, 18 September). Before the violence breaks out. *The Washington Post*. Washington, DC.
43. Quoted in Hoagland, J. (1999). Help us. *The Washington Post*. Washington, DC, 22 August 1999, page B7.

REFERENCES

Apple, M. W., & Beane, J. A. (1995). *Democratic schools*. Alexandria, Va: Association for Supervision and Curriculum Development (p. 103).

Arenas, A. (1999). Education of people of African descent in Latin America and the Caribbean. In: A. A. Kwame & H. L. Gates (Eds), *Encarta Africana*. Redwood, WA: Microsoft Corporation.

Belarbi, A. (1976). *Les relations enseignants/enseignés dans la classe*. University of Paris, unpublished Thesis (p. 49).

Breitman, R. (1999). Official secrets: *What the Nazis planned, what the British and Americans knew*. London: Penguin Books.

Camargo Abello, M. (1997). Are the seeds of violence sown in schools? *Prospects*. UNESCO: Paris (Vol. XXVII, No. 3, September).

Carrère d'Encausse, H. (1978). *L'Empire Eclaté*. Paris: Flammarion.

Conquest, R. (1979). *Kolmya: The Arctic death camps*. Oxford: Oxford University Press.

Conquest, R. (1973). *The great terror: Stalin's purge of the thirties* (Rev. ed.). New York.

Fajnzylber, P., Lederman, D., & Loayza, N. (1999, November). *Inequality and violent crime*. Unpublished paper. Washington, DC: World Bank.

Fukuyama, F. (1989). The end of history. *National Interest* (16).

Galeano, E. (1981). *Les veines ouvertes de l'Amérique latine*. Paris: Editions Plon (p. 119).

Gibbons, E. (1999). *Sanctions in Haiti: Human rights and democracy under assault*. Washington, DC: CSIS Press.

Greaney, V., & Kellaghan, T. (1996). The Integrity of public examinations in developing countries. In: H. Goldstein & T. Lewis (Eds), *Assessment: Problems, Developments and Statistical Issues* (pp. 167–188). Chichester: Wiley.

Heller, M., & Nekrich, A. (1986). *Utopia in power. The history of the Soviet Union from 1917 to the present*. New York: Summit Books.

Hill, M. A., & King, E. M. (1995). Women's education and economic wellbeing. *Feminist Economics*, *1*(2). London: Routledge.

Hirsh, M., & Takayama, H. (1994). The other side of paradise. *Newsweek* (19 December), 37.

Hoagland, J. (1999). Help us. *The Washington Post*. Washington, DC. 22 August 1999, p. B7.

Infobrief (1998, June). Alexandria, Va: Association for Supervision and Curriculum Development (Issue 13), p. 2.

Keller, B., & Coles, A. D. (1999, 8 September). Kansas evolution controversy gives rise to national debate. *Education Week*.

Maher, V. (1974). *Women and property in Morocco* (p. 81). Boston: Cambridge University Press.

Mantash, A. (1999, 17 December). Children hurt in S. Lebanon Militia Attack. *The Washington Post*.

Mathews, J. (1996). Creationism makes a comeback. *The Washington Post* (8 April). Medvedev, R. (1976). *Let history judge*. Nottingham: Spokesmann Books.

Morse, A. (1967). *While six million died*. New York: Ace Publishing Corporation.

OECD (1995). *Literacy skills in the knowledge society*. Paris: OECD, table 1.6 page xx.

Parker-Jenkins, M. (1997, September). Sparing the rod: Schools, discipline and children's rights in multicultural Britain. Paper presented at the Conference of the South African Education Law and Policy Association. Stellenbosh, South Africa.

Preliminary Report of the Special Rapporteur on the right to education, Ms. Katarina Tomasevski, submitted in accordance with Commission on Human Rights resolution 1998/33. United Nations, Economic and Social Council, document E/CN.4/1999/49.

Pressley, S. A. (2000, 3 January). Year of mass shootings leaves scar on U.S. *The Washington Post*.

Raspberry, R. (1999, 23 November). Their cheating hearts. *The Washington Post*.

Reimer, E. (1971). *School is dead: An essay on alternatives in education* (p. 22). Harmondsworth: Penguin Books.

Restrepo, J. D. (1991). Ser maestro: un peligro mortal [Risking your life to be a teacher]. *Educación y Cultura*. FECODE, Santafé de Bogotá, Colombia (No. 24, p. 8).

Rohter, L. (1999, 29 December). College students warily live, learn in war's shadow. *The Miami Herald*.

Rosin, H. (1999, 5 October). Creationism, coming to life in Suburbia. *The Washington Post*.

Salmi, J. (1981). *Educational crisis and social reproduction: The political economy of schooling in Morocco*. University of Sussex: Unpublished Ph.D. thesis.

Salmi, J. (1987). Language and schooling in Morocco. *International Journal of Educational Development*, 7(1), 21–31.

Salmi, J. (1992, April). L'Amérique malade des armes à feu. *Le Monde Diplomatique*.

Salmi, J. (1993). *Violence and democratic society: New approaches to human rights*. London: Zed Press.

Smith, H. (1999, 18 September). Before the violence breaks out. *The Washington Post*. Washington, DC.

The World Bank (1999). Peru – education at a crossroads: Challenges and opportunities for the 21st century. Washington, DC: Report No. 19066-PE (Vol. 1, p. 38).

Tolbert, K. (1999, 27 November). In Japan, education is deadly serious. *The Washington Post*.

Troup, F. (1976). *Forbidden pastures: Education under apartheid*. London: International Defence & Aid Fund (p. 4).

UNICEF (1999). *The state of the world's children 1999*. New York (pp. 7–8). Based on UNESCO 1995 data.

Vanhecke, C. (1985, 30 November). Armero ne devait pas être détruite. *Le Monde*.

Waiselfisz, J. (1999, November). *Ambientes Escolares*. Unpublished document. Ministry of Education.

What Worries Americans (1999, 7 November). *The Washington Post*.

Zinn, H. (1980). *A people's history of the United States* (p. 461). London: Longman.

10. THE REACH AND POSSIBILITIES OF EDUCATIONAL REFORM FOR THE RURAL POOR IN MEXICO

Maria Teresa Tatto

INTRODUCTION

After Jomtien[1] under the goal of providing "education for all" a great number of countries made a strong commitment to extend the benefits of education to the poorest sectors of their population. Efforts have been made in the following years to fulfill this promise. But the issues associated with understanding and addressing disadvantaged populations are multiple and complex. Moreover the strategies followed by a number of countries have been framed under structural assumptions inherently limiting and undermining the intentions of the policies that gave them origin. Seeking to understand the challenges and complexities of change in these contexts, I analyze Mexico's assumptions framing educational policy toward the rural and indigenous poor.[2] I argue that a number of initiatives may fail to fully address the needs of these populations due to the assumptions underlying these policies which end up resting agency to the poor, their children, and to their teachers and schools. After describing the theoretical framework used in this chapter and providing a brief description of Mexico's political economy, I examine Mexico's past and current government policies toward the poor and look at the spaces that have opened up for innovation due to growing relationships with the global economy and the global community and to relationships between

'Suffer the Little Children': National and International Dimensions of Child
Poverty and Public Policy
Advances in Education in Diverse Communities: Research, Policy and Praxis, Volume 4, 231–252
Copyright © 2006 by Elsevier Ltd.
All rights of reproduction in any form reserved
ISSN: 1479-358X/doi:10.1016/S1479-358X(04)04010-0

Mexico's central and local governments. I suggest that *compulsory* early childhood education is one obvious avenue (complementing policies such as Federalizacion and teacher education) to correct centuries of injustice and neglect. I discuss the implications of this analysis within the context of the current decentralization movement and the growing discontent among the rural poor.

THEORETICAL FRAMEWORK

A post structural critique of the policies directed at the education of the rural/indigenous poor in Mexico is appropriate at this time as new initiatives continue to emerge as a result of national educational reform movements sweeping the nation. While the reform promises change and community-based decision making, the traditionally centralized system of governance in Mexico continues to reinforce a top-down educational model based on past assumptions of how people learn and what knowledge is to be valued. Although the traditional model of Mexican education may have proven adequate for a particular portion of the population in an specific social and political moment, it has remained inadequate for those who have been kept at the periphery of social and economic development (Latapi, 1996).

Historically, policies directed at providing education for the rural poor have been bounded by a number of enduring policy dilemmas: (a) attention to the education of those in more urbanized areas at the expense of the education of the rural poor where emphasis has been on access rather than on quality and relevance; (b) the pursuit of "mass schooling" strategies (e.g. age graded classrooms, teacher centered instruction, discipline-structured curriculum, mandated schooling to begin at age six) at the expense of models tailored to serve the needs of specific poor and/or rural communities; and (c) the dominance of the hierarchical power structure in schools permeating all levels of education, from the Secretariat of Public Education (SEP) to supervisors, principals, teachers and pupils and their families at the expense of bottom up participation.

The existence of such historical dilemmas raise questions for current practices: (a) how do historical and power conditions underlying policies for the education of the rural and indigenous poor have shaped current thought and innovative efforts in rural education (e.g. the development of a bilingual curriculum for teachers and their students, the legitimization of one-room multi-grade classrooms as strong vehicles for learning, the development of strategies to support teachers' instruction in one-room schools with multiple grades, and the design of better opportunities to learn for pupils)? (b) given the prior history of educational neglect among the rural and indigenous population (Kobayashi, 1992; Loyo, 1992; Martinez Jimenez,

1992; Miranda, 1968; Vazquez de Knauth, 1992), what circumstances make it now possible to move to a different model of schooling in rural areas if at all? (c) what conditions seem to support challenges to traditional structures? And conversely, what conditions seem to reinforce and reproduce traditional structures?

The examination of these questions point to the fact that Mexico's reforms to the education of the poor have and continue to operate against a background of "inherited tradition"[3] that limit what can be accomplished vis-à-vis the particular needs of poor rural children, their teachers, and their families. A transformation of this situation would require responses based on visions of what is "beautiful, good, and true instead of fixed, structured, moral or objective certainties" (Cherryholmes, 1988, p. 151). Transforming the quality and relevance of the education of the poor may require the development of a new language and set of norms to establish a dialogue on these issues and to act upon them.

POVERTY IN MEXICO

Poverty among Mexico's rural and indigenous population is acute and pervasive. In spite of the reduction of the proportion of Mexicans who live in rural areas since the 1940s by almost half, in 1992 about 30% of Mexico's close to 90,000,000 inhabitants lived in rural areas of whom close to half were indigenous groups. As of 1992, a large number of inhabitants in rural areas suffered high levels of malnutrition and infant mortality, more than 50% of its inhabitants lacked decent housing, and close to 75% of the rural population older than 15 years old had not finished primary school. In 2000, statistical sources indicated improvement in primary and secondary school attendance and completion.[4] The same statistics however indicate that in recent years the percentage of children in the age range between 12 and 17 are increasingly combining school and work, and consequently fewer children are attending school on a full-time basis (Robles-Vasquez & Abler, 2000).

About a third of the poorest people in Mexico is concentrated in three states of Mexico's southwest: Chiapas, Guerrero and Oaxaca; in these states about 80% of the population live in marginal conditions and is economically dependent of agriculture. Many of these communities lack electricity, drainage and potable water, phone lines are few and unreliable and roads are few effectively isolating more than 7 million people. The mean salary for those dedicated to agriculture and husbandry is well below the average of other economic activities, in addition only a third of the economically active population perceives a salary and for half of them the salary is below the minimum legally required. The per capita income is three times lower than the national average and between 30 and 40% of the population lack health and education services. Regarding education, children are lagging behind and there is high inequality in responding to the demands for education. In these areas student retention is very low across the different education levels as is the achievement level among those who manage to stay at school. Another layer of complexity is added by the variety of indigenous people living in Mexico. At least 9% of the Mexican people has as a mother tongue one of the 56 indigenous languages spoken in Mexico. The number of people who speak these languages vary widely, for instance Nahuatl is spoken by about 1 million 400 thousand inhabitants older than 5 years of age compared with Papago spoken by only 236 people according to the 1980 census. Also according to this census five languages are spoken by more than 60% of those who speak indigenous languages; these are: Nahuatl, Maya, Zapoteco, Mixteco and Otomi. The indigenous population in Mexico during this century has grown from two to eight millions, the largest in the American continent. They are also the population group who live in conditions of high marginalization in both rural areas as well as in the greater Mexico City area (estimated to be close to a million).

EDUCATING THE RURAL POOR: RECENT POLICY RESPONSES

The general tone of the 1995–2000 *Educational Development Plan* was one of educational equity and indicated the need to pay special attention to rural and indigenous communities where marginalization and poverty tend to predominate.

A number of policies have been put in place over the last decade to facilitate what is seen as fundamental changes in the current state of education for the poor. One of these changes concerns the context in which educational equity is to be achieved and has been defined as *educational federalism* or decentralization. Decentralization is a movement to reorganize the Mexican educational system in the hopes of increasing its efficiency and a more just distribution of resources. This movement gained momentum in the early 1990s as part of the National Agreement to Modernize Mexico's Basic Education. In 1992 the Federal Government transferred to the states the systems of preschool, primary, secondary, special education and teacher training. This decentralization movement was to encourage local governments to strengthen decision making capacity, to build linkages between local authorities and communities, and to distribute resources to the localities. The major goal of the decentralization reform was to give responsibility for the delivery of basic and normal education to the states and as a consequence bring decision making and planning closer to rural and other marginal zones.[5]

Nevertheless the central SEP, located in the capital, still maintains core functions such as setting national curriculum guidelines, controlling the evaluation and examinations systems, and regulating the flow of resources to the states claiming that doing so insures equity. The fiscal Coordination Law published in the *Official Gazette of the Federation* on December 20, 1997 established that each state government will receive directly most of the federal resources allocated to basic education, and that the use and distribution of these resources is under the sole jurisdiction of the state governments.

In addition to decentralizing the educational system, The National Agreement to Modernize Education included provisions for the development of the *Programa de Desarrollo Educativo* (PDE or Education Development Program) which began in 1995. This program included a number of strategies to improve the quality of education and to promote equity as part of its compensatory policy: (a) the reformulation of teaching methods, curricular content and materials; (b) the formation, upgrading and improvement of teachers; (c) the provision of infrastructure and educational materials (including the *rincones de lectura* or reading corners); and (d) the production and distribution of free textbooks for all basic levels of education; among others. Arguably the program called for a higher degree of integration among communities, teachers and school administrators to facilitate actions and planning that would better suit the local environment. According to the reform rhetoric, the implementation of these strategies would improve the coverage, efficiency, and quality of education in the country and specifically for the rural poor.[6]

WHAT THE REFORM HAS AND HAS NOT ACCOMPLISHED AND WHY

The stability and effectiveness of the educational reform in Mexico needs to be discussed within the economic context of a variable economy resulting in declining and standards of living, and high rates of inflation incomes since 1980 caused in part by a significant drop in world oil prices and a large external debt. After a short recovery at the end of 1994, Mexico had another severe economic crisis this time as a result of the government's decision to devalue the peso and move to a free-floating exchange rate regime. A number of factors have been suggested to help explain the later crisis such as the global economic crisis created by speculation in the international financial market, mistakes in the planning and internal management of the economy, the lack of efficiency and solvency of some members of the public and private sectors, and the insufficiency of social programs. It was not until 1998 that the country was able to recover part of its stability and growth.

Faced with this crisis the Mexican government in the early 1990s, launched as part of the Solidarity Program the "National Modernization Program for the Rural Poor." Preceded in April 1989 by the National Justice Commission for Mexico's Indigenous Peoples whose principal task was to study the possibility to reform the Constitution to create the juridical instruments to correct injustices and to promote the development of Mexico's indigenous people. After broad public consultation in the months of October and December of 1989 with indigenous representatives from the different regions and with more than 2000 presentations, documents and technical opinions president Salinas de Gortari proposed adding to the Constitution Article 4 stating: "The Mexican nation is pluricultural a characteristic sustained in its indigenous peoples. The law will protect and promote the development of their language, culture, uses, costumes, resources and specific forms of social organization and will guarantee to its members the effective access to the juridical system of the State. The agrarian judicial processes of which they may be part will take into account their juridical practices and costumes in the terms established by the law" (SEP, 1993).

In spite of the crisis, important changes in educational policy have occurred since the early 1980s with steady advances in access to education and in the elimination of illiteracy among the Mexican population. In 1943 of 5,022,422 children (6–14 years old) only 2,352,502 were enrolled in schools attended by 48,817 teachers, while 2,669,920 were unable to enroll in any kind of school. In 1992 of a population of 12,772,000 children 100% enrolled in first level education (primary education with a duration of six years with 94% reaching 2nd grade and 84% 5th grade due to repetition. In secondary level education (2 cycles of 3 years each) of a population of 12,159,000 in 1992 only 46% enrolled. The teacher student ratio is for pre-primary of 25:1, for first level (or primary) 30:1 and for second level 17:1. The number of illiterates in 1995 was 6,246,000 and the total estimated adult literacy rate was 10.4 with almost 4 points higher for women than for men. In 1992 Mexico had a total of 88,187,000 inhabitants 26% lived in rural areas (UNESCO, 1995, pp. 119–145). In addition during this period important institutions were created to deal more directly and effectively with issues of poverty such as El Instituto Nacional Indigenista, la Direccion General de Educacion Indigena (DGEI) part of the Sub-Secretaria de Educacion Basica y Normal under SEP, and CONAFE or *Consejo Nacional de Fomento Educativo* (National Council to Promote Education) created in the 1970s, to advance education in disadvantaged regions. Importantly, in 1993 Mexico increased the compulsory schooling age from grade six to grade nine (elementary education 1–6 has been free and compulsory since 1934). At the same time however between 1982 and 1986 real public expenditures on education per capita fell by more than 50% (Robles-Vazquez, 2000). Although public expenditures in education have increased, several generations of school children have been affected by low educational resources.

In spite of these and other actions taken by the government, conditions for the rural poor remained unequal compared with the rest of the population. The end of 1994 was marked in Mexico by the uprisings in a remote Indian village in the southwestern state of Chiapas almost six years to the date in which President Salinas de Gortari established as a first act of his government the National Solidarity Program to bring about the welfare of the poorest citizens of Mexico.[7] But *solidarity* was soon in crisis – in part due to the economic adjustment policies imposed by the international monetary fund (IMF) – creating tension between the liberals and the neo-liberals who wished to maintain the old 70-year one party ideology. This tension had the effect of breaking the hegemony of the PRI (Partido Revolucionario Institucional) – until then maintained since the post-revolutionary period – and marked the beginning of a strong democratic movement which in turn has strengthen political representation of once repressed voices including those of the rural and indigenous poor. The breakdown of the PRI, which has been seen since the revolution of 1910 as equivalent to the government, has damaged its legitimacy and thus weakened the government's capacity to fulfill the promises made in the past to the poorest sector of the population.

The Chiapas upraising not only shook the assumptions of the government's modernization project whose major concern at that point was globalization and economic competition but made clear that the pledge of the Solidarity Program had fallen short of its promises. The national impact of the "Zapatista Movement," as it is known, was to put into question the whole idea of modernization by recasting traditional indigenous values and moving forward the cause of regional autonomy. From the educational point of view this meant rethinking very seriously the traditional ideas about the poor, of indigenous people, the aims and means of education, the values it was to promote, and the legitimacy of alternative implementation venues.

Within this context, however, many issues directly affecting the education of the poor have remained ignored. The education for the rural and indigenous poor still uses as a frame of reference the structure of a general educational system designed to address the needs of a middle class and the ladino or majority population. This situation creates a number of discrepancies with the particular needs of rural children: (a) although rural children could greatly benefit from early childhood education when this possibility exists in the rural areas it is optional, loosely organized, under-resourced, lacking in serious academic content, and it is only available to and only for 4 to 5 year old children; (b) mandatory primary education officially starts at the age of 6 assuming that all should complete it by the age of

12 but due to repetition children who have not dropped out by then do not finish until age 14; (c) the lower secondary system has been mandatory since 1983 last 3 years and includes an academic and a vocational track which may or many not correspond to the needs of those in rural areas; and (d) the telesecundaria has proven an effective learning method for remote areas but it has failed to reach many as drop out problems actually seem to occur for the most part in the lower grades.

RESTRUCTURING POLICY: FEDERALIZATION

One of the most important policy instrument through which the Educational Development Plan had proposed to promote equality among the poorest sectors of the populations was the Federalization of the educational system. The major assumption behind federalization is that bringing power and resources closer to the people for whom the services are intended would increase their efficiency and relevance. The model of "federalizacion" or decentralization adopted by Mexico follows that of Maddick in his classic work *Decentralization, Democracy and Development* (1963, cited by Street, 1992, p. 60). Maddick's model assigns a specific function for each level of government, the model is layered and top down as the resources move from top to bottom. Each level is expected to provide material support, technical assistance and manpower to the inferior levels. The central levels retain accountability functions such as evaluation, and supervision while the local governments manage the operational level supported by the people who receive the policies. This policy can be criticized post-structurally as it provides that the degree to which the center exerts control over the periphery should be inversely proportional to the maturity of the local governments to manage their own affairs effectively (Street, 1992, p. 60). By this mere principle the policy subverts its argued raison d'être, that is, increased equity, capacity, and relevance as those entities that are in most need of resources (e.g. where the indigenous and rural poor are located) are the less likely to get them.

Manifestation of the inequalities exacerbated by the federalization policy are already evident in Mexico as in the years since the decentralization reform was declared as "accomplished" (in 1993) those local governments who had reached a high level of sophistication previous to the reform have taken the lead not only in the educational but in the political arena as well. The most disadvantaged regions such as municipalities in Chiapas, Guerrero and Oaxaca find themselves at a greater disadvantage even in comparison with their situation before the reform (Schmelkes, 1997).

TEACHER POLICY: THE NEW ROLE OF THE TEACHER AND THE REFORMED SYSTEM OF TEACHER DEVELOPMENT

As in the past, the reform rhetoric places the teachers and school administrators as the most important elements in the process of change. Indeed one of the most important declared goals of the PDE is teacher development. Congruent with this intention efforts have been made to provide inservice preparation to teachers of marginal populations not only through "compensatory programs" but also through the development of the "pedagogical networks" which are expected to serve as infrastructures to support teachers much in the way the "misiones culturales" did in the mid 1900s. More recently the most important institution educating preservice teachers, the Normal de Maestros, has announced its intention to reform its study programs "to eliminate redundancy and to align them with current research on teaching and learning." The reform of the Normales however is mostly symbolic as in contrast with a number of Latin American countries who have moved teacher education to the universities such as Chile, Mexico has decided to leave the Normales as the "centers of higher education" for teachers – that is, as they were. A review of the "Plan de Estudios" (Study Plan) published by SEP in 1997 reveals that teachers will continue to receive a diluted curriculum and poor preparation in the subject matters, and that program personnel will for the most part remain the same (SEP, 1997).[8]

Inservice teachers have received materials designed to support the "new teaching" advocated by the reform. Many of these materials are characterized by a constructivist philosophy based on Piaget's thinking – although Bloom's taxonomy and ideas have also maintained their presence in the curriculum. Reformers have sought to restructure schools and have called for collaborative work among teachers within and across schools in the same regions. Teachers and administrators are expected to develop plans for classroom and school improvement. The relatively new career ladder or "the carrera magisterial" system designed as part of this reform movement is used as an incentive to encourage teachers to undertake this demanding change agenda.

In spite of this vigorous reform program little seems to have changed in the rural classroom.[9] As in the past, teachers continue to be excluded from participating in the conceptualization and development of educational policy. The importance attributed to rural teachers is still circumscribed to the classroom and limited to the implementation of policies handed down by others. Although recently all teachers have been encouraged to participate in their school's decision making through the "technical councils" their role is still confined within the SEP's and

SNTE's hierarchical structure. This situation is exacerbated for rural teachers who rarely participate in a technical council and depend mostly on the district supervisor as their only source for guidance. Thus the influence of rural and indigenous teachers in decision making – if any – occurs usually through the interpretation that others make of teachers and their students' needs. It is no wonder – as we will see later on – that after attempting to follow the reform guidelines, teachers go back to their old and tried ways, as the initial impulse and support for change metamorphoses into confusion and solitude. Failure to implement the reform is seen by the government as teacher resistance and/or incompetence but rarely as the result of the poor conceptualization of the policy or even less, as a result of structural constraints present in the classroom and/or schools.

In a previous article I documented the difficulties Mexican teachers are having in implementing the kind of teaching asked of them (see Tatto, 1999a, b, c). The reform does not only ask that teachers implement a new curriculum but also to change their teaching to make it more participatory, and action oriented. Teachers are expected to construct with the students a conducive learning environment and new ways to learn without enough preparation and with little to no support – a situation that closely parallels past reforms. Teaching in the way proposed by the reform entails deep changes in teachers' ways of knowing, thinking and acting, changes that cannot be produced after admittedly high quality but short, massive courses. The outcomes of the well conceptualized but hurriedly implemented methods to educate teachers through in service courses with little to no follow-up, may have grave consequences for teaching and learning in rural Mexico. From the teacher's perspective the new reform which attempted to follow a constructivist philosophy is now understood among many "as a way to allow children to do nothing and as an excuse for teachers who rather be 'lazy' than teach" (SEP Education Officer, personal communication, June 1999).

But while the government's efforts to encourage teacher development may have failed to move in the direction expected by the reform, it has created spaces for teachers to begin to think and talk about their roles and the possibilities for change within the rural school context (Tatto, 1999c). In addition and perhaps stimulated by the decentralization movement the national teachers union, SNTE which lost some of its power as it also "became decentralized" has begun to reconstruct a new role in the area of teacher development, especially that of teachers working with the rural poor. A number of scholars have documented efforts by the teacher union to support and orient teachers in the complex process of educational reform sweeping the country (Loyo, 1999; Street, 1999).

CURRICULAR POLICY: THE REFORMULATION OF TEACHING METHODS, EDUCATIONAL CONTENT AND MATERIALS

The education of teachers needs to be explored simultaneously with the development of new curricular materials, as the later is usually a justification for the former in the Mexican policy context. Congruent with the goal to modernize education and the development of cognitive needs deemed necessary for a global economy, the PDE argued for a curriculum that would promote critical thinking among all pupils and more independent learning. The aims of the curricular reform begun in 1992 were ambitious. The curricular design used a multi-theoretical frame of reference including the thinking of Piaget, Vygotsky, Cole, Ausubel, Mayer, Anderson, Norman, Rumlhart and Minsky among others (Moreno et al., 1994, p. 106). The curricular reform intended to transform in its entirety México's basic education (both rural and urban), including the curricular contents, teaching methods, school organization, social participation and school connections with the community. It aimed to transform teaching to a more conceptual level, to open the space for developing collaborative structures of authority within and across the schools, and to increase relevance by becoming a more integral part of the community. Knowledge that was considered essential in the new curriculum was that of the disciplines: reading, writing, and mathematics followed by the natural and social sciences, including aspects such as health, nutrition, environment awareness and protection, and issues related to work, ethics, and creativity. The curriculum also included national culture, history, and values education. The 1993–1994 curriculum provided the normative criteria that shaped study programs and textbooks and required the implementation of inservice teacher education programs and the development of teacher guides for elementary school teachers, to be used in conjunction with the educational programs and textbooks. The teacher guides presented information about basic curricular contents, suggested activities, and attempted to capture "the accumulated wisdom" of the Mexican elementary school by using case studies and raising issues derived from teachers' and students' varied classroom experience. The guides were designed to offer a set of strategies and didactic resources that teachers could use on a day-to-day basis. A central resource for curriculum implementation, and the backbone of the reform, were the national textbooks. The textbooks which were changed to reflect the, more conceptual, curriculum were printed in Spanish for the majority population and in Nahuatl, Maya, Zapoteca, Mixteco and Otomi for the indigenous population. All the textbooks are centrally distributed free to all the population enrolled in the

Table 1.   Distribution of Free Textbooks (1997–1998).

Level	Number of Copies
Pre-school	
Books for pupils	2,300,000
Books for parents	2,300,000
Primary	
Textbooks	112,700,000
"Get to know our Constitution"	8,200,000
Primary for indigenous people	941,550
Subtotal pre school, primary and primary indigenous	126,441,550
Secondary	
Technical general	2,000,000
T. V. secondary	7,600,000
Subtotal basic education	136,041,550
Books for teachers (primary and secondary)	7,000,000
Total	143,041,550

Source: Comisión Nacional de Libros de Texto Gratuitos, SEP, 1997.

first six grades of basic education and also to secondary education (technical and secondary via television). The following table shows the text distribution effort of the government (Table 1).

These are no doubt impressive efforts, the impact of which will not be known for several years. A number of considerations are important however. The first is that in spite of the sophisticated curriculum design used and the effort spent in redesigning and distributing textbooks, these met with considerable rejection by teachers – indeed in 1993 a disgruntled group of teachers in the southern state of Michoacan literally burned the books in the middle of the town's plaza in protest against the Modernization program imposed on teachers by the then Salinas government (SEP officer, personal communication, 1993). In several schools I visited during that time, teachers had not open the boxes sent by the SEP and one teacher intimated that she asked her students to buy textbooks other than SEP's as she considered the later difficult to use (the books she liked included pages of worksheets per lesson which reinforced her traditional style and sabotaged the SEP's intentions to introduce a problem solving oriented text) (Teacher Interview, 1994). The second is that for those teachers who began to use the texts these became teaching prescriptions, rigid structures that must be followed – just as previous books have been used.[10] The lack of guidance and support in the classroom as teachers begin to know the textbooks and to decide whether they will "stick with them" is crucial. A number of teachers I interviewed argued the books were difficult to understand and follow, and that older methods worked better (Teacher Interview, 1994). Other teachers seemed to be using the textbooks successfully and referred to their in-service courses as the resource that helped them move toward a different way of (thinking about) teaching. It is, interestingly enough, those teachers I observed in rural areas, teaching in one room schools with three grades at a time (or what is called a multigrade school or one room schools with multiple grades) who seemed to be better at adopting the goals of the reform to their classroom.

COMPULSORY EARLY CHILDHOOD EDUCATION: A POLICY WHOSE TIME HAS COME?

Empirical support for the contribution of early childhood education to future education and well being is definitive but scarce and can be found in at least two important areas: its contribution to the cognitive and social development of individuals specially those considered as disadvantaged, and its contribution to school retention and completion (thus higher productivity levels) vis-à-vis individuals' early incorporation to the labor market (IEA Pre-primary Project, 2003; Olmsted & Montie, 2001; Olmsted & Weikart, 1989).

There is growing evidence that as Mexican children mature, their school involvement decreases while their involvement in work activities increase (Post, 2000; Robles-Vazquez & Abler, 2000). Although the rates at which this happens varies, poor rural children seem to be the most affected as ENIGH data suggests (e.g. more poor students had to work in 1996 than four years earlier). In addition unpaid, domestic responsibilities for Mexican girls seem to be a major reason they don't go to secondary school.[11] Since 1980 enrollment, attendance, school progress, and other educational indicators have generally improved for Mexican children less than 12 years old, but actual school attendance and time spent in school and work among Mexican children aged 12–17 provides an strong argument to "front-load" education at an early age (Post, 2000; Robles-Vazquez & Abler, 2000). According to Knaul and Parker (1998) the labor force participation rate among children younger than 12 is below 3 or 4%. Thus the years from 3 to 12 should be seen as prime learning time. Even if common wisdom suggests that poverty is a cause of low school participation and early incorporation into the labor force, recent research suggest that poverty has only a small impact. Instead, a careful econometric analysis by Robles-Vasquez and Abler (2000) shows that, the largest impact on the probability of being a full time student are age and education:[12]

An increase in the child's age by one year leads to a reduction in the probability of being a
full time student ranging from about one-tenth to about one-fifth . . . .. Holding age constant, an
increase in the child's number of years of schooling leads to an increase in the probability of
being a full time student . . . household income has an impact on child labor force participation,
but the impact is very small (pp. 9–11).

The situation is more alarming if one looks at the average number of hours children
work. According to data from ENIGH in 1996 the average number of hours worked
per week among poor children of ages 12–14 was about 33% for urban boys and 29
for urban girls, 33 for rural boys and 30 for rural girls; among children of 15–17
years of age the average number of hours per week was 41 for urban boys and
girls, 39 for rural boys and 37 for rural girls. Earnings by these children accounted
for about one-fifth of total family income in 1996 with larger earnings brought by
older children (Robles-Vazquez & Abler, 2000).

Research on the contributions of early childhood education to cognitive and
social development argues that good quality early childhood education (3–5)
improves children's abilities to be successful at school, and to pursue studies
longer than children who do not participate in such programs (Berrueta-Clement
et al., 1994; Karweit, 1989). In addition research documents that disadvantaged
children who attend early childhood education seem to have lower rates of
delinquency than those who do not (Karweit, 1989). The preschool programs
that have been proven successful in rigorous longitudinal studies such as the Perry
Preschool in Ypsilanti, Michigan for disadvantaged children, programs described
in the international and longitudinal IEA Pre-primary project of the High Scope
Foundation, Head Start in the U.S., and Montessori all used well conceptualized,
highly integrated, very structured, coherent approaches to preschool education.
Unfortunately longitudinal research in early childhood education in Mexico is just
beginning. In order to implement policies such as this, Mexican educators will
need to begin their own empirical investigations as what strategies would work for
poor rural children.

DISCUSSION

The term poor is defined by the dictionaries as "having little or no money, goods,
or other means of support; as dependent upon charity or public support; lacking in
skill, ability or training; deficient in moral excellence, cowardly, abject or mean."
The word is also synonymous with "needy, indigent, destitute. Poor is the simple
term for the conditions of lacking means to obtain the comforts of life."

Implicit in this definition is the sense that being poor represents a lack in a
number of areas on the individual, but it rarely reflects on the societal conditions

that allow for poverty to exist or on the power mechanisms that help shape how we think and act toward the poor in relation to ourselves. As Cherryholmes argues (1999) power materializes in "asymmetrical relationships by which some people are rewarded and indulged, and others are deprived and sanctioned [...] power circulates in the transactions that constitute these relationships, and social institutions are shaped when these relationships become sedimented and routinized – they often look as natural as trees and rocks" (Cherryholmes, *Reading Pragmatism*, p. 16).

Indeed the definition of the poor and the discursive practices a population uses, will shape policies directed toward the poor. Education policy in Mexico as elsewhere in the world has undeniably disadvantaged the poor for centuries by rewarding the rich and depriving the poor. Recently in Mexico, however, the discourse has shifted in part due to the commitments made after Jomtien to educate the rural poor, in part due to the mobilization of the poor in the most marginalized states, in part due to pressure exerted by Mexican educators, intellectuals and scholars, and in part to the work of international organisms. The result of this shift is the recognition and legitimization of the rural indigenous population's costumes, traditions and language to the point of changing the laws in the Constitution to acknowledge Mexico's indigenous diversity; this is a step that begins to pave a new way of thinking about the indigenous poor in Mexico. Indeed, discursive practices are not purely and simply ways of producing discourse. They are embodied in technical processes, in institutions, in patterns for general behavior, in forms for transmission and diffusion, and in pedagogical forms which, at once, impose and maintain them (Foucault, *Language, counter-memory, practice*, 1980, p. 200).

The dramatically different discourse regarding the rural poor in Mexico has made possible the creation of institutions to study and address the specific issues related to their education and other social and economical needs. It has also made possible to develop a policy of bilingual education responsible for the development of a whole curriculum and textbooks in several indigenous languages; and the creation and support of compensatory programs. Yet after almost ten years of these policies the census still tells a sad story:

According to the XI Population Census, in 1990 there were in Mexico 1,441,277 indigenous people between 5 and 14 years old. Among them only 66.7% attended schools. In general terms, a very small proportion of the students that begin the first grade of primary education finish their studies in six years. In 1985–1986 160,396 children enrolled in first grade at the end of the cycle in 1990–1991 only 40,911 passed six grade. This is only 25.5% of those who began primary education six years before in contrast with a national percentage of 56.4% (World Education Data, UNESCO, 1998).

Paradoxically, the very policies that seem so promising for the future reduction of inequities and in helping communities shape their own education agenda, also seem to have the capacity to exacerbate disparities:

(a) The policy of decentralization has increased inequalities between developed and underdeveloped regions. Indeed power still remains at the center and rural communities attempts at developing social capital are seen with suspicion and resentment;

(b) Education policy makers insist in applying urban models to rural problems. Would it not be possible to begin educating children of the rural poor to learn arithmetic and reading at age of 3 or 4 using pedagogy that has proven appropriate for young children lacking in social and cultural capital? One needs to question the logic of following a uniform model of schooling across the country if rural children tend to drop out generally after 3rd grade (why not then begin formal schooling three years early?). Assuming that all children should begin "formal" schooling at age 6, benefits only those who will be able to complete elementary schooling. When so many children cannot finish sixth grade even in the urban areas we have a big problem which may indeed begin in the early years. Again the problem here seems to be structuralist-rooted assumptions about when schooling should begin and what knowledge is valued and for whom;

(c) Although the EDP strongly suggests children should attend preschool education, it has not yet been made mandatory. In one of the best researched books produced by PARE in 1994 *Analisis curricular de la educacion primaria*, a citation by Bruner (1972, in Moreno, Pulido & Ruiz, 1994, p. 49) justifies this possibility:

> ... any subject can be effectively thought in an intellectually honest manner, to any child in any phase of development. This is a daring hypothesis, and also essential, when thinking about the nature of a study plan. There are no tests that challenge this hypothesis, and there are a number of confirming tests that supports it.

Indeed, by the age of six, and even before children enter first grade they should be able to read and understand important mathematical concepts. One only needs to enter a Montessori classroom to see children of 3, 4 and 5 years of age engaged in serious intellectual learning for hours following their own inner habits of mind that have been formed day after day of consistent and disciplined interaction between teachers, students and subject matters. Possibly part of the reason for the lack of a mandatory pre-school education dedicated to teach sound subject matter to children of the rural poor in an honest intellectual manner is the unwillingness by the Mexican government – and I would argue many governments everywhere – to take young children seriously and invest heavily in their education. The following

Table 2. Ordinary Public Expenses Allocated to Elementary Education
by Grade (%).

Año	Pre-primaria	1er Grado	2do Grado	3er Grado	Sin Distribución
1990	5.6	26.7	29.6	16.5	21.6
1991	–	–	–	–	–
1992	–	–	–	–	–
1993	6.4	30.8	25.9	13.7	23.3
1994	–	–	–	–	–
1995	–	–	–	–	–

Source: Anuario Estadístico de la UNESCO, 1996 (gastos del Ministerio de Educación solamente);
[–] no available data.

table shows the distributions of resources across the first four years of elementary education were the expenses in 1st and 2nd grades are approximately five times larger than those in pre-school (Table 2).

This pattern of investment goes against what current research on children's cognitive development demonstrate: that important learning occurs between the ages of 3 and 6 with another major learning period between the ages of 6 and 8 (Bruner, 1972, in Pulido & Ruiz, 1994).

Current government policy for preschool children mandates education *through play* and new products have been developed to complement it: the *Material para Actividades y Juegos Educativos* (or material for educational activities and play) accompanied by a guide to the teacher and one to parents explaining the importance of preschool education.[13] It is still an empirical question how well do these policies reach indigenous and poor children. The stated educational goal at this level is limited to "finding a balance between oral expression, mathematical reasoning, and observation and reflection on nature." Research is needed to understand how to adjust preschool education to the needs of young children in rural areas and according to current thinking on child cognition and development. Old and new thinking about early age learning calls for the introduction of strategies to develop habits of mind (e.g. perseverance, disciplined thinking, independence in learning), and genuine learning of subject matter such as reading, and basic arithmetic (adding, subtracting, multiplication and division) as avenues to enable young children to become independent learners and critical thinkers. Young indigenous children represent the highest growth in enrollment at the preschool level. In 1996–1997 there was an increment of 3.6% compared with the previous cycle reaching a total enrollment of 280,675 pupils indicating the willingness and interest of these communities to have young children attend school at an early age. Mexican policy has yet to respond in kind to this interest by making preschool education for the rural poor compulsory and well resourced.

(d) Poor rural children encounter not only impoverished classrooms but also un-trained teachers. The traditional model of schooling still dominates in these classrooms and the balance of power and authority still favors the didactic model of teaching. An alternative model tried in rural areas in some countries in Latin America seeks to enable pupils to learn independently and for themselves, with each other and their teacher as is the case of Colombia's Escuela Nueva.

(e) Multigrade schools in rural areas may provide the solution to the inflexibility in structure and teaching methods so frequently found in traditional schools in either urban or rural areas in the world. Organically emerging from the community itself, the multigrade classroom include children of different ages in the same learning space. Managed appropriately the structure of the multigrade classroom has the potential to change not only the traditional balance of power in the classroom, which typically advantages the teacher and the more advanced students, but also its learning dynamics allowing young and older children to learn to work independently and in groups. In the multigrade classrooms I visited in Mexico – teachers and pupils engaged in group work and in academic related dialogue rarely seen in richer and larger schools (Tatto, 1997). These findings are also confirmed by ongoing research in multigrade classrooms (Little, 1999). Policy makers' structuralist assumptions however make it difficult for these environments to reach their full potential. The curriculum still attempts to keep distinctions across grades and insists in making teachers the center of learning instead of letting children learn from the materials, their classmates and indeed their teachers. Multigrade classrooms are as a consequence seen – under a deficit model – as a drawback rather than as a viable and real alternative to traditional and often inefficient models of schooling for rural areas:

> Attention to multigrade groups represents difficulty and overloading to the teacher who has to attend several groups of different grades at the same time . . . and has to function as a principal/administrator . . . this makes it difficult to offer a quality education for all the children" (Manejo de grupos multigrado PARE, documento al docente, p. 25).

Still teachers have to function according to the structure provided by SEP, even if it does not make sense or fails to adjust to the context where the teacher is engaged. Innovative, teachers have been seen – in the case of Mexico – as reluctant collaborators with the federal and local governments in the move toward its modernization strategy. Moreover, teachers as well as children have only been seen as objects in the policy discourse.

In sum, structuralist thinking strongly permeates the political discourse and shapes the education policies for the rural poor in Mexico. The Mexican government needs to evaluate and rethink its policies regarding education for the rural poor, specifically the structure and content of the curriculum for the first years of basic education, the preparation of teachers, and the structure of schooling. International experiences in educating the children of the poor underline the urgent need to carefully study the possibility of instituting mandatory preschool education for the rural poor in Mexico in order to increase poor children's personal capital – that is their intellectual and emotional capital – before it is too late. I argue that increasing poor rural children's personal capital via effective early education (using approaches such as those recommended by Montessori and Piaget among others) may be the only way to counteract the pervasive effects of growing up poor in rural Mexico. Policies that shape educational opportunities for the rural poor have been historically an area of ideological and political contestation where the poor has rarely entered in the policy discourse. This is a situation that needs to change.

NOTES

1. In 1990, an important conference, titled the World Conference on Education for All (WCEFA), was convened in Jomtien, Thailand by the World Bank, UNESCO, UNICEF and UNDP. The conference brought together some 1500 people representing 155 governments, 33 intergovernmental bodies, and 125 non-governmental organizations (NGOs), institutes, and foundations. Organised in response to the widespread concern over the deterioration of education systems during the 1980s, the Conference concluded with the unanimous adoption of the "World Declaration on Education for All" and endorsed a "Framework for Action to Meet Basic Learning Needs." Through these two texts, the world community renewed its commitment to ensuring the rights of all people to education and knowledge (World Declaration on Education for All, March 1990).

2. I use elements of poststructuralism as a framework for analysis. Structuralism is defined by Cheryholmes as a systematic way of thinking about whole processes and institutions whereby each part of a system defines and is defined by other parts. Poststructuralist thought attacks structuralist assumptions and the arguments built upon them and points out their weaknesses, the most important is that these subvert themselves and fail to deliver on their promises (1988, pp. 13–14). I use the term rural poor to encompass all those who make their living in areas with less than 2500 inhabitants (this is according to Mexico's official definition of "rural"). The term includes peasants or campesinos, "hired hands" or jornaleros, indigenous peoples, and other disadvantaged groups.

3. This is a term coined by Wittgenstein and quoted by Putnam (1983, p. 240) (in Cherryholmes, 1988, p. 151).

4. Instituto Nacional de Estadistica, Geografia e Informatica (INEGI) (1999). Encuesta Nacional de Empleo (1991–1997). Instituto Nacional de Estadistica, Geografia e Informatica (INEGI) (1995). Perfil educativo del la poblacion Mexicana, Vol. 4. INEGI is the Mexican organization responsible for integrating at a national level, the systems of information and statistics and geography in Mexico in addition to promoting and orienting the development of national information in the country.

5. According to the article #37 of the Law for General Education in Mexico, basic education includes preschool (for children aged 4 and 5), elementary and more recently secondary education. Only elementary and secondary education are compulsory. The national average of children served by preschool education was 69.5% for the school year 1999–2000. The largest number of children served are in the states of Baja California Sur with 92% and Colima with 88.4. One of the lowest is the Estado de México with 52.2 in spite of registering significant investment in education.

6. The Plan de Desarrollo Educativo or PDE intended through these normative arrangements to give more independence to principals and supervisors to make decisions. As these new expectations demand more qualifications for school administrators a framework of support, incentives, training, guidance, and monitoring was also envisioned as part of the program. Regarding teacher education and support, the PDE stated as a priority the formation and upgrading of teachers via the reform of the Normales de Maestros the primary preservice teacher education institutions, incentives to encourage existing teachers to learn and adopt new teaching methods and to engage in further specialization. Strategies for improving teachers' status included the introduction of the *carrera magisterial* (a career ladder), and increasing recognition of the importance of teachers' social role. The development of new materials and new in-the-classroom-libraries (or rincones de lectura) were expected to increase, especially in the rural areas, the population's ability to read and write and the capacity to solve mathematical problems. According to the PDE emphasis was to be given not only to the accumulation of formal knowledge but also to value formation such as the generation of self-esteem, respect and citizenship. In addition, the program proposed the revision and distribution of free national textbooks including special versions for the indigenous population; the extension of the school calendar as well as its adaptation according to local conditions such as weather and harvest periods in the rural areas; the elimination of tedious and repetitive teaching practices; and allowing extra time for arts and sports.

7. This is a situation that currently "haunts" current Mexican President Vicente Fox's government notwithstanding his initial promise to solve the "Chiapas crisis" as soon as he took power (in December 2000).

8. An innovation is that teacher candidates will spend a year in the classroom before they graduate under the guidance of inservice teachers and program personnel, but given the poor condition of Mexican schools, inservice teacher's current overload, and lack of experience or preparation as mentors, the success of this approach remains an empirical question.

9. Changes at a different level are impressive though they do not necessarily reflect an increase in the quality of teaching and learning. These changes do reflect advances in access to educational services (such as the significant reduction in illiteracy in the past years, the number of schools created for indigenous populations, the number of textbooks that have been distributed to these populations, among others).

10. This "common" reaction to reform, in which teachers apply or use resources in a mechanical manner (whether texts or teaching pedagogies) is according to Hall and Loucks (1977) a stage in a process of teacher development. Achieving technical mastery in the specific texts/pedagogies along with follow-up seems to facilitate teachers moving out of mechanical responses to more reflective thoughtful ones.

11. This is a problem that has been widely recognized in Mexico and the government has developed a program for targeted scholarship programs (such as PROGRESA) which aim to

compensate girls for domestic work. This is yet another argument to provide early childhood education to poor girls PROGRESA (Programa de Educación Salud y Alimentación de Mexico. http://www.ifpri.org/themes/progresa.htm).

12. Other variables included in the econometric model were: year in which the data was collected, children's wage, age, education, number of siblings, relationship with the head of the household, number of children at different ages, gender and age of head of household, whether the head of household is working, absent or working on a unsalaried job, household income, assets (e.g. refrigerator), enterprises, and home production technology, the median number of students per school in the household's community, and regional variables.

13. Preschool education in Mexico is under the SEP for rural and urban areas, and for indigenous populations under the Dirección General de Educación Indígena (DGEI, 1993a, b) taught by bilingual teachers who know the respective languages. Another modality is offered through *cursos communitarios* (community courses) coordinated by CONAFE (Consejo Nacional de Fomento Educativo) and is given to localities that have no elementary schools and have more than 35 school-age children. *Cursos comunitarios* are taught by secondary school graduates who receive training as instructors and are paid by the community, which also provides food and housing.

REFERENCES

Berrueta-Clement, J. R., Schweinhart, L. J., Barnett, W. S., Epstein, A. S., & Weikart, D. P. (1994). Changed lives: The effects of the Perry Preschool program on youths through age 19. *Monographs of the High/Scope Educational Research Foundation, 8.*

Cherryholmes, C. (1988). *Power and critricism: Postructural investigations in education.* New York: Teacher College Press.

Cherryholmes, C. (1999). *Reading pragmatism.* New York: Teachers College Press.

DGEI (1993a). *El bilingualismo en la practica docente indigena.* Mexico, D.F.: Subsecretaria de Educacion Basica, SEP.

DGEI (Direccion General de Educación Indígena) (1993b). *El bilingualismo en la practica docente indigena.* Programa para Abitir el Rezago Educativo. Mexico, D.F.: Subsecretaria de Educacion Publica.

Hall, S., & Loucks, S. (1977). A developmental model for determining whether the treatment is actually implemented. *American Educational Research Journal, 14,* 263–276.

IEA Pre-primary Project (2003). *High scope foundation.* Ypsilanti, Michigan. http://www.highscope. org/Research/iea.htm [consulted October, 18, 2004].

Instituto Nacional de Estadistica, Geografia e Informatica (INEGI) (1995). *Perfil educativo de la población Mexicana.* Mexico City: INEGI.

Instituto Nacional de Estadistica, Geografia e Informatica (INEGI) (1999). *Encuesta Nacional de Empleo (1991–1997).* Mexico City: INEGI. http://www.inegi.gob.mx/inegi/default.asp [consulted 10/18/2004].

Karweit, N. (1989). Effective preschool programs for students at risk. In: R. Slavin, K. Karweit & N. Madden (Eds), *Effective Programs for Students at Risk* (pp. 75–102). Needham, MA: Allyn & Bacon.

Kazuhiro Kobayashi, J. M. (1992). La conquista educativa de los hijos de Asis. In: J. Z. Vazquez de Knauth (Ed.), *La Educacion en la Historia de Mexico* (pp. 1–28). Mexico, D.F.: El Colegio de Mexico.

Loyo, A. (1999, April 14–18). The voice of basic education teachers in Mexico. Paper presented at the annual meeting of the Comparative International Education Society, Toronto, Canada.

Loyo, E. (1992). Lectura para el pueblo, 1921–1940. In: J. Z. Vazquez de Knauth (Ed.), *La Educacion en la Historia de Mexico* (pp. 243–290). Mexico, D.F.: El Colegio de Mexico.

Martinez Jimenez, A. (1992). La educacion elemental en el Porfiriato. In: J. Z. Vazquez de Knauth (Ed.), *La Educacion en la Historia de Mexico* (pp. 105–143). Mexico, D.F.: El Colegio de Mexico.

Miranda, B. A. (1968). *La evolucion de Mexico.* Mexico, D.F.: Editorial Herrero.

Moreno, F. X., Pulido, O. R. I., & Ruiz, N. C. (1994). *Analisis curricular para la educacion primaria.* Mexico, D.F.: Secretaria de Educacion Publica and Universidad Pedagogica Nacional (PARE).

Oficial Gazette of the Federation (1997, December). www.oecd.org/dataoecd/.

Olmsted, P. P., & Montie, J. (Eds) (2001). *Early childhood settings in 15 countries: What are their structural characteristics?* Ypsilanti, MI: High/Scope Press.

Olmsted, P. P., & Weikart, D. P. (Eds) (1989). *How nations serve young children: Profiles of child care and education in 14 countries.* Ypsilanti, MI: High/Scope Press.

SEP Education Officer, personal verbal communication (1999, June). Conference on Teachers in Latin America: New Perspectives on their development and performance San Jose, Costa Rica, Organized by the World Bank.

Street, S. (1992). *Maestros en movimiento. Transformacion en la burocracia estatal (1978–1982).* Mexico, D.F.: CIESAS.

Street, S. (1999, April 14–18). Teachers' work and democratic struggle in Mexico. The challenge to neoliberal policy. Paper presented at the annual meeting of the Comparative International Education Society, Toronto, Canada.

Tatto, M. T. (1997). Reconstructing teacher education for a global community. *International Journal of Educational Development, 17*(4), 405–415.

Tatto, M. T. (1999a). Improving teacher education in rural México: The challenges and tensions of constructivist reform. *Teaching and Teacher Education, 15*(1), 15–35.

Tatto, M. T. (1999b). Mejorando la educacion de maestros rurales en Mexico: Las tensiones y retos de la reforma constructivista, *Revista Mexicana de Investigacion Educativa* (Translation, in press).

Tatto, M. T. (1999c). Education reform and state power in México: The paradoxes of decentralization. *Comparative Education Review* (in press to appear in August 1999).

Vazquez de Knauth, J. Z (1992). La Republica restaurada y la educacion. In: J. Z. Vazquez de Knauth (Ed.), *La Educacion en la Historia de Mexico* (pp. 93–104). Mexico, D.F.: El Colegio de Mexico.

World Declaration on Education for All (1990). Meeting Basic Needs. Jomtien, Thailand. http://www.globalmarch.org/gaw/Jomtien.html.

World Education Data, UNESCO (1998).

11. POVERTY AND EDUCATION: BRAZIL'S SEARCH FOR VIABLE SOLUTIONS?

Francis Musa Boakari*

ABSTRACT

Though poverty is one of the consequences of the lack of education, this latter can be the solution to poverty, particularly when children and youngsters are prioritized in school. And in the fight against inequality, education for the development of human beings is the key, especially if we want to save children and adolescents in order to guarantee the future.

INTRODUCTION

In the last few decades, Brazil's more positive characteristics have been most specially overshadowed by its historically pervasive social inequalities. And during the past decade, it has prominently shown itself as a rather puzzling case of social and economic development. While consistently being listed among the world's ten largest economies, the country continues to figure markedly as one of the three worst distributors of wealth. As commonly held among nationals, the country

*The author, originally from Sierra Leone, West Africa, is professor at the Universidade Federal do Piauí, Northeastern Brazil, and presently teaches at the University of the Incarnate Word, San Antonio, Texas, USA.

'Suffer the Little Children': National and International Dimensions of Child
Poverty and Public Policy
Advances in Education in Diverse Communities: Research, Policy and Praxis, Volume 4, 253–294
Copyright © 2006 by Elsevier Ltd.
All rights of reproduction in any form reserved
ISSN: 1479-358X/doi:10.1016/S1479-358X(04)04011-2

is doing very well, but the people continue to get poorer. With the more recent neo-liberal government policies and the pressures of globalization, this situation has tended to become worse. How do we explain why national wealth fails to get transformed into social goods and services that meet the basic needs of most of the people in the nation?[1] What are some of the outcomes of this in human terms?

The most dramatic consequences are the large contingents of children and adolescents whose needs have not really been attended to. In a society where more than one-half of the economically active population finds itself below the poverty line, and more than one-third of the families live in misery, members of future generations tend to suffer the most. For example, since the 1970's, data from the *Instituto Brasileiro de Geografia e Estatística* (IBGE) – National Institute of Geography and Statistics, have consistently shown that the general population has increasingly become poorer,[2] and that the number of children without guaranteed support systems[3] has even grown at a larger rate. Whereas three decades ago, the problem of abandoned children and adolescents[4] was basically restricted to large metropolitan areas, this "unwanted segment"[5] of Brazilian society, has called for particular attention since the 1980's as it's members are found in even smaller towns. In its diverse manifestations, the question of abandoned children and adolescents apparently became a concern, not only because of its magnitude, but even more so because of increased international pressures that could no longer be overlooked in the 1980s.

In 1989, the International Convention on the Rights of the Child (CRC) was ratified by the United Nations and signed by 145 countries. Brazil was one of the signatories. The big break provided by this document was the recognition that every child and adolescent had a right to social well-being; that attendance to the basic needs of children was not a question of welfare or philanthropy, but of justice which the state, society and family had obligations to guarantee and defend. According to the pledges of the CRC, among other rights, children the world over were to be: protected against degrading-inhuman treatment, free to enjoy civil rights, provided with adequate educational, health and living conditions. They were also to be protected from all forms of social, economic and cultural exploitation. Children gained the right to be children, and society was required to respect this condition.

International agencies continued to contribute to the effective implementation of those rights defined by the 1989 Convention. The International Labor Organization drafted a new convention seeking to abolish all forms of "extreme" and hazardous child-adolescent labor in 1998. In the same year, the United Nations Children's Fund (UNICEF), established a Child Protection unit with the responsibility of protecting the rights of children and adolescents. International and National

Non-Governmental Organizations, like Human Rights Watch and *Missão Criança* (Children's Mission), apart from their more traditional goals of seeking the well-being of the child, have also continued to contribute in diverse ways so as to emphasize the centrality of children's rights.

One of the direct results of the CRC was that Brazil went ahead to promulgate a code specifically directed to protecting young members of society. The Statute of the Child and Adolescent (*Estatuto da Criança e do Adolescente* – ECA) was promulgated in 1990. For the first time in Brazil's history, there was official recognition of the child as a person, with individual rights that the state and society had to protect in all circumstances and from all, including the child's own family.[6]

At the same time, there has been an explosion in the number of institutions, both private and non-profit, which assume as their *raison d'être*, the total and complete care for children, especially the homeless and the poor. In one of the largest municipal districts, Rio de Janeiro, a survey conducted in 1990 verified the existence of more than 500 agencies working in the areas of child protection and well-being. These included public, private, non-governmental and church institutions, which predominantly provided day-care centers, boarding facilities and social assistance.[7]

With such efforts, it would be expected that the general situation of poor children and adolescents would be better. However, this does not seem to be the case. From every-day-lived experiences and even official data, what is easily evident are the consequences of an inability (absence of political will power?) to solve the problem of this important segment of the population. Apparently, the general public, high government officials and public administrators have yet to assimilate the urgent need to pay more attention to the children of today in order to build a more democratic country and humane society. To face these challenges more realistically, systematic reforms and monitoring policies in the areas of child poverty (outcomes of adult poverty) and education, might hold the key.

The underpinning question here is the search for explanations as to how poverty relates to education, and how such relationship has nourished Brazil's social maladies, especially those that victimize children and adolescents the most. We will examine how the state seems to have understood and consequently dealt with the consequences of the double-edged-sword relationship between these two phenomena.

In order to fully appreciate the relevance of the present discussion, we must keep in mind that poverty most affects children and adolescents. As the prime targets of poverty, any treatment of this social malady also relates to them. With this understanding, we would like to tackle some of the questions that follow. How best can this phenomenon be explained? What are some of its dimensions in very practical terms? How is poverty related to social inequality? As a social problem, how does it fit into the structural framework of a developing country like Brazil? And by extension, how do these issues interact with education as schooling, especially at the elementary level?

DEFINING POVERTY AND SOCIAL INEQUALITY

Poverty is a historic phenomenon which affects more than one-third of the population of Latin America today. It should be understood as a condition, which goes far beyond income though both are related. Income level is one of the determinants of poverty.[8] Nonetheless, this latter is more complex. It involves factors related to cultural, psychological, economic and social structures, standards and expectations. In its more objective definition, poverty refers to that condition which prevents people from gaining access to primary goods and services necessary to satisfy basic human needs.[9]

To be poor is to be deprived of social goods-services in the areas of food supply, health, education, infra-structure and culture.[10] To live in poverty or be impoverished, is to be without access to items in these areas. It can also entail being forced to utilize very few or very low quality products and inefficient services in these same sectors of modern life. Accordingly, poor people face food shortages and low diets. And if fortunate, they might study in schools that are poor, receive medical attention in hospitals that are poorly equipped and staffed, live in places prone to health hazards and reside in make-shift shelters. In this same vein, we could include the absence of or insignificant levels of political participation and the consciousness of being a citizen. Finally, poverty is highly related to a person's chances of making individual and/or collective choices in society. In this sense, conditions of poverty have to do with an absence of those capacities necessary for one's well-being. These capacities include a balanced dosage of knowledge, social capital and financial resources.[11]

A concept very closely related to, but distinct from poverty, is that of social inequality. The latter refers to the relative amount of material possessions and social positions of individuals and/or the groups they belong to. While poverty is a measure of social well-being, inequality measures the equity of the distributive structure of wealth and social goods. It evaluates how equitable the distribution of social goods-services-positions and cultural capital are in a particular society at a specific time in history.

One of the central services included in defining individual well-being is access to formal education of quality which allows for relevant learning opportunities and assures positive classroom performance by all participants.[12] Because of the advantages of a good education, educational services of quality are dependent upon poverty levels and have much to do with social inequality in its diverse manifestations. With regard to formal education, some considerations need to be made.[13]

First, in most societies today, the schooling experience is considered a *sine qua non* condition for adequate social participation and subsequent reduction of social inequalities. The belief that school knowledge (certificates?) does indeed make a difference in one's chances in life is still largely shared by many. As such, though many criticize school, the majority in society still make enormous sacrifices to have offspring attend those schools believed to potentially increase the range of social opportunities for children when they reach adulthood. Though educational researchers do not tire to warn us of the pitfalls of our schools, most have only gone so far as to suggest internal (curricular and pedagogical) modifications, and not their elimination.[14]

Second, schooling is the educational component in the construction of the knowledge base necessary for competing, with more realistic chances of being successful in a highly competitive social environment. Maybe schools do not necessarily teach what one might need on a particular job or in specific everyday social interactions. However, the contents of the "hidden" curriculum do prepare, to a large extent, for assuming different kinds of responsibilities in life. Schools transmit values, beliefs and behavioral tools needed in life. The fact that there are very few successful persons who do not have the schooling experience (and certificates?), does add weight to this argument. Schools might not guarantee success in life. However, without acquiring those experiences peculiar to them, one's chances for success and well-being would be drastically reduced.

Finally, since education is necessary for the well-being of people and poverty hinders access to good schools, it contributes to social inequality. The socially privileged who have more access to better schools and can afford to perform well, more easily guarantee that their privileges are maintained. For those who already live in conditions of poverty, the contrary mostly holds true. Such poor individuals would most likely be very disadvantaged, politically dominated and socially excluded. They would also suffer the most from economic exploitation and cultural marginalization. Accordingly, while education might help create socioeconomic opportunities and allow for some social mobility, it is also important for the maintenance of political power by certain groups and individuals in society.[15]

Basically, we try to emphasize that education (as schooling) and poverty (in its diverse dimensions), have interdependent relationships. While the former serves as a central determinant for preventing poverty, this in turn serves as an important factor in determining how and to what extent individuals and groups interact with education. School attainment does intervene through diverse mechanisms to reduce and control poverty levels. At the same time, poverty plays a vital role in determining educational access and performance. The complexity, not only of the intervening variables between poverty and education, but even more importantly, of the sociopolitical, economic and cultural outcomes and implications cannot be neglected, especially in a relatively rich (but socially very poor) country like Brazil.

In the next few pages, with the objective of showing the configurations of social inequality in Brazil, we will try to present some data about the general situation of poverty and then further along, educational data will be presented. Attempts will be made to discuss, explain and contextualize how poverty in Brazil continues to shape the educational map, and consequently, the distribution of social resources. Some recent attempts to reduce poverty and improve school performance would be discussed to make the case that pervasive poverty and poor educational performance have causes which are intrinsic to Brazil's social history, administrative practices, hegemonic strategies, political arrangements and cultural expectations.

In discussing poverty and education, the focus of attention will indirectly rest upon those Brazilian children and adolescents who are underprivileged and excluded. Since their families, when fortunate to have any, live in poverty, one of the direct consequences of the social inequality of which they are victims, involves access to schools that would offer them those educational opportunities they need in order to have a childhood as well as an adolescence they deserve as citizens, and consequently be able to perform well as students. Our discussion begins with the incongruities between national economic growth and persisting social inequalities despite expenditures in the social area. Investments in social programs should be viewed from the perspective of both their effectiveness in reducing social inequality, and how these affect the lives of the poor, especially the young.

SOCIAL INEQUALITY AND PUBLIC INVESTMENTS

Brazil has not been very successful in distributing national wealth. For example, in 1983, 1985, 1987, 1989, 1992 and 1995, the richest 1% of the population respectively controlled 14.0, 14.1, 14.5, 17.3, 13.7 and 13.9% of the nation's wealth. During these same years, the poorest 40% of Brazilians respectively possessed only 8.5, 8.0, 7.7, 6.9, 9.8, and 8.9% of this wealth (IBGE/PNAD, 1995).[16] These values indicate two tendencies which describe the social gaps between rich and poor. In the first place, there has been very little variation between the participation rates over the years. The differences between the groups are almost equal over the years – 8.5% compared to 14.0% in 1983, and 8.9% compared to 13.9% in 1995. During this period, the largest single difference of 10.4% was in

1989, and the lowest (5.0%) in 1995. In other words, in more than a decade, access to and appropriation of the national wealth remained basically unchanged for both the poor and the rich.[17]

This same set of data shows that while the average per capita income for the richest 1% of Brazilian households was over twenty Minimum Salaries,[18] for the poorest 40%, this amount was about one-half the value of this monthly income. Similarly, whereas the richest households could boast of about 3.8 persons, the poorest households had more than five members on average. The more affluent families had stronger buying power to satisfy the needs of less people, while the poorest households earned much less to spend on more people. This unbalance has and continues to have widespread social repercussions, most especially on children in these latter circumstances.

Table 1 points to two basic points. First, that the poorest 40% of the population lives in very precarious conditions. Their access to "healthy drinking water"[19] is only about 71.3% against 98.5% for the most affluent group. The same trend holds with regard to adequate waste disposal – 58.4% against 97.2%. When we consider number of years of study, the quantity of fourteen year-olds and under who work and female-headed households, the discrepancies are once again evident. Second, whereas data referring to positive conditions are high for the affluent, the opposite holds for the poor. This situation may not be unique to Brazil. However, what cannot be mistaken are the enormous gaps between the two groups.

This picture becomes even clearer when we divide the poor into the poorest 20 and 40% of households among the population. According to data from the IBGE/PNAD (1995), the former receives an average of about 0.34% of the MMS and the poorest 40%, 0.52% of this amount on average. (For the rest of the population, this average value rises to 1.74 minimum salaries.) Both groups have

Table 1. Characteristics of Households With Children of 14 and Below.

Characteristics of Households	Richest 1%	Poorest 40%
(1) Average household income per capita in minimum salaries	22.3	0.5
(2) Participation in total of national wealth (%)	9.9	12.2
(3) Inadequate water-supply system (%)	1.5	28.7
(4) Precarious sewage disposal system (%)	2.8	41.6
(5) Female headed household (%)	8.6	20.8
(6) Children, 14 and below in female headed households (%)	7.1	19.1
(7) Head of household below age 30 (%)	4.7	22.3
(8) Head of household with less than 4 years of schooling (%)	0.9	52.0
(9) Child workers of 10–14 years (%)	2.3	13.9
(10) Children 7–14 years out of school (%)	0.7	11.5

Source: IBGE/PNAD (1995).

about five persons in a household. Among the poorest 20% of households, about 36.7% have inadequate water and 45.2% do not have adequate waste disposal systems. This group also has more households headed by females (23%), and about 59.3% did not finish the first four grades of elementary school. About 14.4% of the children 10–14 years, worked outside the home, and 14.1% of school-aged children were also out of school in 1995.[20]

This situation assumes its real dimensions when these data of unequal access are presented in another format by dividing the poor into the two categories, poor and indigent. Data since 1977 from the *Instituto de Pesquisas Econômicas Aplicadas* – IPEA (Institute of Applied Economic Research), show that in the past thirty years, the deprivation differentials between these groups have varied little when we consider what percentage of the MMS each group received between 1977 and 1998 (Table 2). There have been fluctuations, in fact several of them. However, two features remain unchanged – the high levels of social injustice wherein about one-third (50.1 million) and (21.4 million) one-fifth of the total Brazilian population of 152 million inhabitants in 1998, were in conditions of poverty and indigence respectively.

Another indistinguishable characteristic of Brazilian social inequality has remained the incapacity (political unwillingness?) to transfer national wealth to the poor and miserable. In the periods 1985–1986, and 1994–1996 when economic reforms significantly reduced inflation rates and some kind of social equity seemed possible, no real differences seemed to have occurred in the numbers of indigents and poor people. This can be evidenced from the fact that soon after these periods, the rate of inequality resumed its regular distinctive pattern. In more than two decades, this pattern has been maintained in the country as the results from comparing data of 1977 with those of 1997 from Table 2 would confirm. Reforms which somewhat stabilized the economy have not been enough to bring about viable changes neither in the general structure of wealth distribution nor in the access to social goods and basic services.

Table 2. Poverty and Indigence – Earnings in MMS Values.

Year	1977	1978	1979	1981	1982	1983	1984	1985	1986	1987
Poor (%)	39.6	42.6	38.8	43.1	43.1	51.0	50.4	43.5	28.2	40.8
Indigent (%)	16.8	20.7	15.9	18.8	19.4	25.0	23.6	19.2	09.8	18.5

Year	1988	1989	1990	1992	1993	1995	1996	1997	1998	
Poor (%)	45.3	42.9	43.8	40.8	41.7	33.9	33.5	33.9	32.7	
Indigent (%)	22.1	20.7	21.3	19.3	19.5	14.6	15.0	14.8	13.9	

Source: IPEA (1998).

Between 1975 and 1998, the per capita income in Brazil increased from about US\$3.464–US\$4.509.[21] During this period, earnings per capita were US\$4.253 in 1980, US\$4.039 in 1990, and US\$ 4.078 in 1995. As we can see, some monetary gains were made on a global basis as income levels improved in more than a thousand U.S. dollars. These increases were not uniform. For example, while between 1975 and 1980, there was a positive change to the effect of more than US\$700, between 1980 and 1990, there was a loss of more than US\$200. The small gains between 1990 and 1995 were followed by a sizeable upward trend (US\$431) between this latter year and 1998.

These gains do not seem to have been invested in goods and services to meet basic social needs. Rather, some other consumer items whose imported technologies and parts consumed the gains as they were prioritized. For instance, whereas in 1990, 65 of every 1000 inhabitants owned telephone lines, in 1996/1998 this number increased to 121. Growth was also evidenced regarding ownership of television sets – 213 per 1000 inhabitants in 1990 and 316 in every 1000 in 1996/1998. Other consumer items included computers whose ownership increased from only about three in every thousand Brazilians in 1990, to more than 316 per 1000 in 1998.[22] While the affluent seemed to have purchased luxury goods and conspicuous consumer products, and those with low incomes acquired basic items of modern consumption, large numbers of families, and most especially their children, continued to struggle to satisfy basic natural and social needs.

How can we summarize this set of information in terms of social equity and human development? Analyses of data from the IPEA (1998) indicate that the Gini index (where 1.00 means the most inequality possible, and zero absolute equality), was about 0.605 in 1993. In 1998, it improved to 0.601. In other words, despite some strides toward degree of equality. The country was still far from being an island of socioeconomic equality as data from Tables 1 and 2 cogently demonstrate.

Furthermore, based on data till 1997 and 1998,[23] the United Nations Development Program (UNDP) reported that Brazil showed some positive signs of social progress, as measured by the Index of Human Development (IHD),[24] when its 1997 and 1999 world rankings (79th and 74th) were compared with those of countries like Saudi Arabia (78th and 75th), Iran (95th and 97th), China (98th and 99th), South Africa (101st and 103rd) and Egypt (120th and 119th). Nonetheless, it's rank did not compare favorably to those of such countries like – Ireland (20th and 18th), Argentina (39th and 35th), Chile (34th and 38th) and Uruguay (40th and 39th). Moreover, while the IHD for Brazil was only 0.747 in 1998, it was 0.881 for Argentina and 0.764 for Colombia, countries whose economies are much smaller than the Brazilian (UN Human Development Report, 2000).

Though the Brazilian IHD underwent some change, the same could not be said of the Index of Human Poverty (IHP).[25] As we saw above, Brazil's world ranking on the IHD scale improved somewhat between 1997 and 1999. On the other hand, on the IHP scale, the country went from the 19th to the 21st position, meaning that social inequalities increased.

Further examination of IHD scores in the past thirty years helps put this situation into a better perspective. Since 1975, the Brazilian index of human development has suffered only marginal changes. This rather positive trend remains on the macro-level. For the common citizen, these improvements remained unknown and unfelt. The IHD which was 0.639 in 1975, improved to 0.747 in 1998; making a difference of 0.108 points, twenty-three years later. In the intervening period, the indices were as follows: 1980 – 0.674; 1985 – 0.687; 1990 – 0.706; 1995 – 0.728 and 1997 – 0.739. At this rate, the country would only achieve a value of about 0.855, still a long way from the Israeli situation today of 0.883, in the year 2023. The growth or improvement rates indicated by these values merely go to show how seriously skewed the historical structure of wealth distribution continues to be. More poverty and indigence have been produced over these years, as have the suffering and exclusion of children-adolescents become even worse.

More children, even as young as four and five, have lost their childhood years. Many continue to become domestic helpers. Even larger numbers are forced to work for long hours, generally during the whole week, under unsafe and unhealthy conditions in order to help with the domestic budget. That is, just to survive and assist family members to do the same, they have to work for ever longer hours daily. For most, this serves as the determinant factor for doing poorly in school, or even for dropping out altogether.[26]

SOCIAL PROGRAM EXPENDITURES

Understanding social spending as expenditure in education, culture, housing, urban development, health, sanitation, environmental protection, labor, assistance and social welfare, it is possible to see how the state has spent in these areas over the past few years.

Tables 1 and 2 above try to show that economic growth has not been transformed into social well-being and improved conditions of life for most of the population, though state spending in the social sector quantitatively increased.[27] Whereas in 1987 it accounted for about 4% of GNP, it rose gradually to 9% two years later. Due to an economic crisis in 1991 and 1992, these values were reduced to 6.5%. However, in 1993/94, social investments resumed their growth tendency and reached 11%. In 1995, these investments rose to over 12% of GNP.[28] Such values may be impressive. However, compared to a country like Chile, which spent about 9.3% of its GNP on health services alone in 1993, it becomes clear that Brazil still has much to do in the area of financial transfer to the social sector.

According to information from the SIAFI, in 1987 the map of government social spending was drawn up like this: 48% for education and culture; 32.8% for housing and urban development; 14.6% for health and sanitation; 2.5% for welfare and 1.9% for labor. In 1995, some changes took place – educational spending was reduced by about 10.5%; housing/urban improvements surged to 65.9% and health/sanitation increased to 18.5% of the total investment in the social sector.

The expanding trend in direct government social spending was not repeated in those programs whose specific target group was composed of children and adolescents (0–18 years). These investments rather suffered a decrease between 1987 and 1995. Whereas they had accounted for about 70% of the total spending on this population in 1987, funding fell to about 34.5% in 1995. Since then, through several sub-programs, administrative mechanisms and budgetary adjustments,[29] there have been serious attempts to recuperate the historic losses in these vital sectors for national construction and social development.

Considering the structure of income gaps and the composition of the different income levels of Brazilian households, it becomes evident that, like in other countries, the economically underprivileged do not only have the most children, but also pay dearest for inefficient public policies and poorly administered social spending. In general terms, Brazil does not do poorly because, though below what good reason would demand, it invests a reasonable amount of its GNP in social investments. However, so far, these investments do not seem to show consistent positive returns.

A UNICEF publication had the following to say:

> ... while general government social spending per capita showed increasing tendencies between 1987 and 1995, expenditures on child-related programs was reduced in about 10 ... 57% of the poor are children and adolescents between the ages of zero and seventeen, ... this shows that poverty affects this segment of the population to a much larger extent. ... It was evident that both the general social spending and expenditures on child-adolescent programs were neither sufficient to guarantee a reduction in inequalities, nor to create more viable opportunities for the socially unprotected ... sheer increase in volume of spending is not enough to reduce poverty and to improve upon the quality of life that would be considered acceptable for citizens (UNICEF, op. cit., 1998, p. 55).

These observations are very important in any attempt to try to understand how poverty remains intricately related to the general structure of Brazilian public policies, and how social areas suffer consequences of administrative inefficiency and other historical factors which predominantly victimize more children and adolescents the most. One crucial area in which these consequences are evident is that of education.[30] In the next few pages, we will present information related to the efficiency of the educational system in order to see how schools, especially public institutions, have responded to government policies in the last few decades. Examination of rates of illiteracy, school failure, drop-out, and age-grade distortions, would indicate how effectively education is being used to indirectly reduce social gaps by investing in the future.

Like in the general area of social programs, the problem does not seem to be an insufficiency of investments. Rather, it seems there are systemic difficulties with how to assure that investments help effectuate changes in teaching-learning relationships so as to make the system more efficient, and contribute more positively to social mobility. When administrative loopholes begin to be taken care of, it seems student performance would undergo positive changes. The educational data we present, mainly those from the late 1990s, tend to support this position. However, it would still remain to be verified whether this educational improvement would be lasting, and even more importantly, if it would eventually and systematically translate into some social mobility for the poorest of Brazil's children and adolescents.

EFFICIENCY OF BRAZIL'S EDUCATIONAL SYSTEM IN QUESTION

The educational situation in Brazil remains problematic as can be imagined from the discussions about the historic unequal nature of wealth distribution in the country. Educational reform strategies which resulted from the International Convention of Children's Rights (1989) and the Jomtien Declaration of Education For All in 1990 which were ratified by the government, served as incentives for changes.[31] In 1990, the *Estatuto da Criança e do Adolescente* – ECA (Statute for the Child and Adolescent) was promulgated. In conjunction with the 1988 Constitution, it helped transform formal education into an individual social right for all, and re-emphasized the obligatory nature of basic elementary schooling for all children. As a citizen's right, the State and even parents, could be legally taken to account for the provision of the best services possible in this area, assuring that they perform well. From the nominal school attendance obligation stipulated in official documents of the past, children, adolescents, parents/guardians and the state were transformed into agents responsible for education. School access, quality, attendance, performance and positive learning experiences for citizenship formation became the watch words in the educational sector. How have these expectations been fulfilled will be part of our discussion here.

As we saw above, federal expenditures in the educational sector suffered some reductions after 1990. However, constitutional changes through the LDB and the

FUNDEF laws had also mandated federal, state and municipal governments to spend specific percentages of annual budgets on their school systems.[32] In this way, any real losses were to be made up for through these new sources of public funds for schools. The federal government remained primarily responsible for providing free higher public education. Private institutions at all educational levels also continued to provide services for those who could pay their highly competitive tuition and fees.[33]

An examination of the general educational situation in the country does give an idea of how the system has responded to various strategies over the years. It is important to note that the data presented describe a situation that is gradually improving, but still far from ideal.

Illiteracy rates over the last many years indicate a very problematic educational reality (Table 3). These rates improved from 64.9% in 1920 to 25.4% in 1980 and decreased further to 15.6% in 1995. Projections for 1996 on paint an even more positive scenario. Though these improvements need to be recognized, the persisting high illiteracy levels definitely have many repercussions in all areas of national life. Apart from the concrete and potential losses in human, technological and economic resources which would affect the younger generations much more adversely, we must also remember the debilitating effects of illiteracy on parenting in today's world.

The decreasing tendency in the illiteracy rates can also be observed when we look at the age cohorts and their performance on the literacy index for 1980,

Table 3. Illiteracy Among Population of 15 and Older.

Years	Illiteracy (%)
1920	64.9
1940	56.0
1950	50.5
1960	39.6
1970	33.6
1980	25.4
1991	20.1
1992	17.2
1993	16.4
1995	15.6
1996[a]	14.7
1999	13.3
2000	11.0

Source: IBGE/PNAD (1920–2000).

[a]The values from 1996 on are estimates based on the reduction (−6%) achieved between 1995 and 1996.

Table 4.   Illiteracy Among Cohorts of 15 Years and Above.

Cohorts (Years)	1980 (%)	1991 (%)	1996 (%)
15–19	16.5	12.1	6.0
20–24	15.6	12.2	7.1
25–29	18.0	12.7	8.1
30–39	24.0	15.3	10.2
40–49	30.8	23.8	15.5
50 and above	43.9	38.3	31.5

Source: IBGE/PNAD (1996).

1991 and 1996 (Table 4). For these years, among members of the 15–19 age group, and those in the 20–24 years range, the rates say much about the success rates of educational policies since the 1970s. Whether these successes have been transformed into gains which have narrowed social gaps may not be difficult to say. At the same time, the most economically active, 19–49 years, who were in their best reproductive years and parents to most of the school-aged children, still boasted of illiteracy rates that could have hampered social mobility, widened social gaps and strengthened practices contrary to the social interests of children and youngsters. Between ages 40 and 49 as well as 50 and over, the rates are much higher; a pointer to failed educational strategies and inefficient literacy programs in the past.

Data from Table 5 point to an inverse relationship between adult illiteracy and school attendance over the past four decades. Whereas in 1960 adult illiteracy was 39.5% and school attendance 49.3%, this situation is radically reversed in 1996 where we have 96.1% of school-aged children in school and only 14.7% of adult illiterates. Such a tendency shows that the historic problem of adult illiteracy

Table 5.   Rates of Adult Illiteracy and School Enrollment of 7–14 Year Olds.

Rates	Years				
	1960 (%)	1970 (%)	1980 (%)	1991 (%)	1996 (%)
Adult illiteracy	39.5	33.6	25.5	20.1	14.7
School attendance	49.3	67.1	81.1	91.6	96.1

Note: MEC (Federal Ministry of Education), *INEP* (Institute of Educational Research), *SEEC* (Secretariat for Basic Education) and *IBGE* (Brazilian Institute of Geography and Statistics). For more details about these data, consult Maria Helena Guimarães de Castro and Áurea Maria Queiroz Davanzo (1999, pp. 69–90).
Source: MEC/INEP/SEEC/IBGE (1999).

began receiving some attention in the 1990s, especially through increased school enrollments in both regular and special educational programs.

Projections in 1998 by INEP indicated that adult illiteracy would be about 11% in 2000, 10.1% in 2001, 6.5% in 2005, 3.7% in 2008, 1.9% in 2010, and reaching 0.1% only in 2012. Nevertheless, there is still enough cause for alarm. Apart from the limitations placed on a growing democracy with so many adult illiterates, more efficient use of social goods and services could also be impaired because simple user instructions fail to be correctly interpreted.

As if these were not enough, neighboring countries like Paraguay, Argentina and Uruguay, regional market competitors, respectively boasted of 8.0, 4.0 and 3.0% illiteracy rates in 1996. These challenges in an even more competitive market could negatively affect the country's capacity to invest in long-term programs, especially in areas vital for socially reaching the young.

Table 6 tries to show that on the average, increasing numbers of Brazilians of ten years and above are spending more time in school. When the 1981–1996 data are compared, this tendency becomes evident as those with no study or less than one of school become fewer. Those with eight years or more of study have remarkably increased, and in a gradual manner. Those in the one to three years group have decreased, as more of the four to seven years group has increased. In other words, increasingly more Brazilians have begun to spend more time in school. Nevertheless, this latter group calls attention as it concentrates the largest number of persons ten years and older in the country. In 1981 they formed only 32.0% and in 1996, the group had grown to 35.1%. This group might be pointing to one of the persistent problems of the educational system – large numbers of young people apparently do not study much beyond the first four grades of elementary school.

Table 6. Years of Study Among Population of 10 and Older.

Years of Study	Years				
	1981 (%)	1986 (%)	1990 (%)	1995 (%)	1996 (%)
No study or less than one year	23.1	20.0	18.1	16.2	13.6
1–3 years	26.5	24.3	22.9	21.1	21.5
4–7 years	32.0	33.2	33.9	34.8	35.1
8 years or more	18.3	22.3	25.0	27.7	28.9
No response	0.1	0.2	0.1	0.2	0.9
Total	100	100	100	100	100

Source: IBGE/PNAD (1996).

Table 7.   Enrollment for Grades I–IV and V–VIII – 1975/1997.

Years (1975/1997)	Enrollments	
	Grades I–IV (%)	Grades V–VIII (%)
1975	71.2	28.8
1978	71.1	28.9
1979	70.9	29.1
1980	71.2	28.8
1984	70.6	29.4
1985	70.0	30.0
1988	69.1	30.9
1989	68.4	31.6
1993	64.8	35.2
1996	60.4	39.6
1997	60.1	39.9

Source: MEC/INEP/SEEC (1998).

The fact that about one-third of those ten years and older do not even complete elementary school in a country where more than 10% remains illiterate, should be alarming for two reasons. The older illiterates are poor and already socially excluded. Besides, the youth who have few years of study are potential illiterates who might suffer the consequences of this condition in the future. The offspring of the members of both groups may also be potentially condemned to share in the same fate of impoverishment as their parents.

The situation depicted in Table 6 above becomes clearer when one studies Table 7 below which presents enrollment data between 1975 and 1997 for grades I–IV and V–VIII.[34] This table is important because of one central reason. While the enrollment rates drop for the basic cycle of elementary school, they gradually rise for the upper cycle, from grade V to grade VIII. For example, if we consider a student who was in the first grade in 1980, in 1984 this student should be studying in the fifth grade. However, at this point we observe that in 1985 student enrollment was only 30.0% for the higher level of elementary school. This same pattern is maintained for the whole period covered by the data presented. Though these differences have been reduced gradually, the data from 1997 is still alarming. Almost 40% of the children registered in 1991, had dropped off or were still in classrooms of the basic cycle. This might explain why this system loses more than one-half of its first graders even before completing elementary school. In earlier periods, these losses were even larger since less than 20% of elementary school children went on to high school.[35]

So as to observe these data from another perspective, we will examine the age/grade discrepancy rates between 1982 and 1996 (Table 8). These data exhibit a

Table 8. Age-Grade Discrepancy Rates in Elementary Schools.

Years	Grade Cohorts (%)							
	1st Grade	2nd Grade	3rd Grade	4th Grade	5th Grade	6th Grade	7th Grade	Total
1982	71.9	76.5	77.2	76.6	80.4	80.2	79.8	76.2
1991	59.5	62.6	63.3	62.7	70.2	68.6	67.4	64.1
1996	40.0	44.1	46.4	46.6	55.6	53.2	49.2	47.0

Source: MEC/INEP/SEEC (1997).

decreasing pattern, but older students studying in grades lower than the normal age equivalence, continues to be a hurdle for the improvement of elementary schools in the country. Claims that these older students are school returnees, resuming school after a stint in the work force, neither justifies nor reduces the negative effects of this problem.

The question of age-grade discrepancy negatively affects the productivity of the school system. Under normal circumstances, children between the ages of seven and eight should be in the First grade; nine and ten in the Third; eleven and twelve in the Fifth; thirteen and fourteen in the seventh and fourteen to fifteen, in the eighth. As we can see from Table 8, there are considerable proportions of older students studying in grades disproportionate to their biological ages. The rates presented with regards to grades I, IV, V and VII need more careful attention because of the strategic points they occupy in elementary education. While first grade is the entry point in the system, grades IV and V are turning points which determine a student's performance at this level of the schooling experience. Grade IV is the last year of the basic cycle, a transition phase between the two levels. The fifth grade is the entry point into the senior years at the elementary level. The significant "losses" and levels of failure in grades considered crucial for school success, cannot be easily overlooked if the system is to improve its performance and productivity levels.

In 1982, the gross rate of age-grade distortion was about 76.2%. Nonetheless, these proportions have gradually begun to improve – 64.1% in 1991 and only 47.0% in 1996. However, this remains a worrisome situation since it means that almost one-half of the system's participants were above the ideal ages for the grades in which they studied as late as 1996. This issue assumes further importance when we remember that older students in lower grades cost more to the system. They tend to do more poorly than their younger class-mates, and are relatively more prone to drop out. Generally, they need more resources in order to do well at school.[36]

Another dimension of the age-grade discrepancy which increases educational costs is related to the average number of grades concluded and the mean number

Table 9. Elementary Enrollment by Administrative System – 1975–1997.

Years	Federal (%)	State (%)	Municipal (%)	Private (%)
1975	0.6	56.0	30.4	12.9
1980	0.7	52.8	33.6	12.8
1985	0.5	57.2	30.2	12.1
1989	0.5	57.2	29.8	12.5
1991	0.3	57.2	30.0	12.4
1996	0.1	55.7	33.0	11.2
1997	0.1	52.9	36.3	10.7

Source: MEC/INEP/SEEC (1998).

of years it takes to do so. According to simulated data from MEC/INEP (1996), it took about 8.8 years to complete an average of 5.71 grades of study in 1985; 9.32 years to complete 6.16 grades in 1990. In 1993, it was 6.55 grades during 9.65 years. But in 1995, it took about 9.69 years to complete 6.77 grades on average, almost three additional years of educational costs. Such data help highlight the pernicious nature of the age-grade distortion, both as an individual saga and a collective problem which is concentrated in the public schools.[37]

The increasingly important position of municipal elementary school system is being confirmed by the information in Table 9 where enrollments in these schools increased from 30.4% in 1975 to about 36.3% in 1997.[38] The jump between 1996 (33.0%) and 1997 (36.3%) compared to the gradual change between 1991 and 1996 can be best explained by the use of state run propaganda urging parents to send children to school, as well as special campaign drives urging to comply with the demands of the Constitution and Law No. 9394/96. The behavior of municipal school enrollment figures, compared to the decreasing percentage points with regard to the other educational systems,[39] is also further confirmation that some changes were being implemented. How these changes might have influenced the general academic performance of the whole system will be observed next in Table 10.

From the total average of end-of-year approvals, the national system reports a steady improvement. From an average of 61 percentage points of student approval in 1988, this amount rose to 73.0% in 1996. The schools from each of the individual administrative bodies (federal, state, municipal and private), confirmed this improvement trend. For instance, whereas the federally supported schools showed approval ratings of 61.5% in 1988, the system raised its performance level to 75.9% in 1996. Similarly, the state, municipal and private schools followed suit. Increasingly more students were approved each year between 1988 and 1996. The largest increase in percentage points occurred in the federal school system which

Table 10.   Rates of Elementary School System Performance.

	Years (%)	Federal (%)	State (%)	Municipal (%)	Private (%)	Total Av. (%)
Rates of approval	1988	61.5	59.2	56.5	80.1	61.0
	1995	77.9	72.3	63.9	83.5	70.9
	1996	75.9	73.2	66.9	90.3	73.0
Rates of retention – repetition	1988	24.4	18.5	23.4	11.2	19.1
	1995	12.8	15.7	19.1	7.6	15.8
	1996	9.9	13.1	18.3	6.8	14.1
Dropout rates	1988	14.0	22.3	20.0	8.7	19.9
	1995	9.3	12.0	17.1	8.9	13.3
	1996	14.2	13.7	14.8	2.9	12.9

Source: MEC/INEP/SEEC (1997).

reported a difference of 14.4% between 1988 and 1996. Closely following behind was the state educational system with a difference of 14.0%. The municipal and private schools also reported differences of 10.4 and 10.2% respectively.[40]

Continued observation of Table 10 indicates that retention (grade repetition) rates were falling in all four systems. On the average, the whole educational system reported a decrease from 19.1% in 1988 to 14.1% in 1996. The federal system reported the highest decrease (14.5%) in retention over the period covered. The considerable decrease in the number of schools directly administered by the federal government, and the accompanying reduced enrollments could be responsible for making the system more efficient.

Though not as markedly as the federally administered schools, the other systems also reported downward trends in retention rates. As we have observed above, such positive records could have everything to do with those changes implemented in the mid-1990s. More recent data is needed in order to confirm the reliability of these decreasing patterns in the number of students retained at the end of the academic year.

Student retention rates, no matter how high or low, are always significant since they are burdensome to any educational system. Apart from directly increasing educational costs, retention rates have more damaging effects on the system and on those students who fail at the of the school year. As a whole, retention overburdens the system, leading to larger class sizes and higher student-teacher ratios. Also, those students who get retained, especially the multiple-retained, might find it more convenient to drop out of school in order to preserve their self-esteem. Besides, such students might receive pressure from family and friends to drop out in order to "find something more useful to do in life."[41]

As Table 10 shows again, there is a general reduction in dropout rates across the national system, decreasing from 19.9% in 1988 to 12.9% in 1996. Within the individual systems, the same pattern is maintained. The performance of the municipal school system is much better than that of the others. What might also call attention is the fact that both for the federal and state systems, the retention rates reported for 1995 are lower than those of 1996. If this situation cannot be explained by problems in data collection, then we can forward that adaptations were being made to accommodate for the introduction of institutional changes. What has happened in years subsequent to 1996 remains to be seen.

Close observation of these data forces a return to the municipal system which exhibited the largest percentage in system-loss regarding repetition and dropout rates. Whereas the net student loss for the private schools was around 9.7; 26.8 and 24.1% for the state and federal governments systems respectively, the municipal schools reported a 33.1% loss. This contradictory situation (higher enrollment and larger student drop out) can be explained by the fact that the greater majority of these schools are located in the interior while the federal and state governments' schools are mainly found in larger towns and cities.[42] In these cities, generally the administrative, political and business centers, more investments are made in education because of contingent political and social pressures. Moreover, in the smaller towns in the interior, with large numbers of illiterates coupled with little or no control by the authorities, most children and adolescents have to "help" on the farm and/or "assist" with domestic chores. These responsibilities negatively compete with school attendance and academic performance. The municipal schools and the performance levels of their students point to these problems which are historic.[43]

On an overall basis, Table 11 would indicate that between 1984 and 1996, the productivity of the elementary system was most concentrated in the state administered schools, as these schools also accounted for the largest number of

Table 11. Elementary Graduation by Administrative Systems – 1984/1996.

Years	Federal (%)	State (%)	Municipal (%)	Private (%)
1984	0.7	65.5	11.0	22.8
1986	0.8	65.0	11.3	22.9
1987	0.7	64.3	11.2	23.7
1988	0.6	65.0	11.5	22.9
1990	0.5	65.1	11.7	22.7
1995	0.2	66.4	14.6	18.7
1996	0.2	66.1	15.4	18.3

Source: MEC/INEP/SEEC (1997).

students at this educational level. As observed from Table 9 above, while the municipal schools grew in number and in enrollment, they were also able to produce more elementary school graduates. Variations between graduating students in each system accompanied the enrollment patterns described earlier. This can be seen particularly in the private schools where graduation rates decreased as did enrollment figures. Whether graduating figures say anything about instructional quality and academic standards is an important preoccupation which is not being considered here.

Another aspect of the educational situation under discussion, especially pertaining to the productivity and quality of the system, has much to do with the level of teacher qualification. Whereas in the urban centers, most teachers have the minimum teaching credentials required by law, in the interior the contrary is more frequent.[44]

The situation between 1975 and 1996 depicted in Table 12, is an indication of the low level of teacher qualification in elementary/high schools in Brazil. Data show that the problem is gradually being resolved. However, in 1975, there were about 12.1% of elementary faculty who had not even finished elementary school. In the same year, only about 28.5% of all elementary/high school teachers had college degrees. About ten years later, only 6.1% had completed elementary school, 45.1% had high school certificates and 40.5% had gone through college/university. About eleven years later, we still had 4.6% who had not finished elementary school, and only 47.2 and 43.8% respectively had high school and college diplomas. In over twenty years, the qualification of teachers very gradually improved, and continues

Table 12. Elementary Teacher Qualification Levels.

Years	Elementary Incomplete (%)	Elementary Complete (%)	High School Complete (%)	College Degree (%)
1975	12.1	13.2	46.2	28.5
1980	12.8	9.9	43.7	33.5
1985	8.3	6.1	45.1	40.5
1989	6.5	6.0	47.4	40.2
1991	5.6	5.2	48.2	41.0
1996	4.6	4.4	47.2	43.8

Note: The information bases for these data do not specify the areas of college/university studies. However, it can be assumed that four years of academic experience in an institution of higher education helps prepare for teaching at either the elementary or high school levels much more than merely six or seven years of elementary schooling. The problem extends to even the high schools where it is still possible to find persons with elementary school credentials acting as teachers, especially in the poorest parts of the poorer North and Northeastern Regions.
Source: MEC/INEP/SEEC (1997).

to get better. However, the system still had more than one-half of the elementary or high school teaching staff without the minimum qualification, as regulated by the LDB.

Data from INEP in 2000, showed that over 48% of elementary/high school teachers were still without university training. This situation begins to assume its real dimensions when, according to the same data sources above, only about 60% of teachers in private schools had university training, against less than 50% in the public school system. With unqualified teachers in private schools, nationally synonymous with higher educational standards, the situation in those schools historically believed to offer less efficient services, would be anyone's guess.[45]

Since the implementation of FUNDEF in 1998, based upon the demands of the LDB, some programs are being implemented in order to qualify and re-qualify elementary school faculty in-service. Gradually, it is expected that teachers at other levels would follow suit. Some of the programs, with funds from FUNDEF, include *Proformação*, a training program which uses distance learning methods to reach all teachers. At the same time, special university courses are being specifically organized for these untrained teachers all over the country. Other modalities of training programs are Pedagogical Workshops, special seminars and thematic activities organized by State and Municipal Educational Secretariats. Most of these training programs are conducted during week-ends with monitors and specialists from the education secretariats.

Capping these reform efforts is the requirement that 60% of all FUNDEF resources be used for elementary teacher training and faculty salary improvement. Until a few years back, there were teachers, especially in the interior, and more specially the untrained, who earned less than US$20 monthly. Nowadays, over 90% of all public elementary teachers earn at least the Minimum Monthly Salary. Accordingly, these educational professionals have begun to be qualified more relevantly, and are receiving the financial reward their profession deserves.[46]

We have presented data to support the argument that during several decades, the Brazilian schooling system, instead of serving as a social door-opener for the poor, allied itself with established societal structure, and thus contributed to the unequal distributive pattern of social goods and services till the early 1990s. Public schools with their sufferable performance records, did not seem successful in systematically contributing to social mobility for large segments of poor youth and children. Nonetheless, since about the mid-1990s, we began to notice some signs of change. Though the real effects of these reforms might still take some time to appear, they have helped build some trust in public schools and strengthened positive expectations among the poor. So as to place into a better perspective, the case of child poverty and the educational drama of the underprivileged, we will now briefly mention some of these reform efforts.[47]

CHILDREN, POVERTY AND EDUCATION: RELATIONSHIPS IN SEARCH OF EXPLANATIONS

Recent changes mostly gradually introduced after 1996 and mainly in elementary education, have been effectively related to the questions of access, performance, curriculum content, financing, and administration.[48] These modifications are being implemented through the following mechanisms:

(1) Legislative measures – the LDB stipulates fundamental norms for administering, funding, teaching, evaluating and developing educational institutions with emphasis on local municipal control (municipalization);

(2) Decentralization – especially the change from direct federal funding to indirect financing through the State and Municipal Educational Agencies. Resources being transferred directly to the schools (more local governance);

(3) Community participation – organization of school councils with teacher, parent and administrative representatives, coupled with the election of school principals to control and monitor finances, curricular and routine administrative matters;

(4) Curricular contents – through the *Paramêtros Curriculares Nacionais*, PCN – (Nacional Curriculum Parameters), subject matter, pedagogical strategies[49] and conceptions of classroom evaluation are gradually being adopted and adapted to regional and local conditions for adequately training students as citizens;

(5) Text-books – centralized ministerial control of content matter through evaluations of adequacy by national specialists and more agility in distribution to all public schools;

(6) School television – the use of modules in daily programming aimed at teacher-training and for serving as a supplementary teaching aid for the children;

(7) School lunch program – all children in public schools receive free lunch (for many, the only guaranteed daily meal); and

(8) Systematic evaluations – through the *Sistema Nacional de Avaliação de Educação Básic*, SAEB (National Evaluation System of Basic Education), students in Grades IV and VIII of elementary school and Grade III of high school are tested bi-annually in Mathematics, Sciences and Portuguese in order to measure the system's efficiency.

Results of the SAEB have been elucidative about the effectiveness of these reforms. If what these tests indicate is anything to go by, we can say that Brazilian education still has a long journey up-hill in order to become a more efficient system for adequately educating all children and helping reduce social gaps.

Outcomes of tests conducted in 1995, 1997 and 1999 indicated that those of 1999 were the worst.[50] Though some States demonstrated improvement tendencies, on the national level, the general situation was a disaster. Just to cite an example, whereas high school students had attained an approval index of 290 in 1997 on the Mathematics test, this dropped to 267 in 1999. In the case of Portuguese for grade VIII, the decrease was from 256 to 233 points. Such results could just be indicating that the system was still getting adjusted to the changes. However, they could also be calling attention to the possibility that the reforms implemented so far have failed. Only further SAEB tests and other kinds of evaluations can help advance this debate.

Though the SAEB is a system's evaluation instrument and not necessarily a student's performance tool, these latest results force us to ask some questions, since good schools are believed to be those learning institutions which get students to learn adequately, and do well on tests. Can we expect students to perform well in an inefficient school system? Can educational reforms really function in the absence of political will power and changed social-cultural attitudes, belief systems and behaviors? Since schools in the final analyses fundamentally deal with people, could reforms that do not affect cultural values and social practices not be doomed to frustrate expectations? How do all these related to poverty and social inequality? As a final observation in this regard, good schools are those learning institutions, which get students to learn adequately and do well on tests.

CHILDREN, POVERTY, SOCIAL GAPS AND EDUCATIONAL PERFORMANCE

Data related to income distribution consistently showed that the historic gaps between the "haves" and "have-nots" in Brazil basically remained unchanged, and indicated possibilities for continuity. This becomes more evident when we consider that the state seems to have so far failed to really begin to address the underlying causes. Public expenditures which target poverty reduction remain to be sources of uncertainties because of political practices (clientage and patronage systems) and administrative styles[51] which mostly penalize the poor. In a scenario where large segments of households, especially those with the most children, are the poorest, these future adults would carry the largest of the burdens of poverty. Social indicators showed that poor families have access to deficient social services, and the many children they tend to have grow up in environments that are richest in negative social indicators.

As a way out of such conditions, these families, generally with poor and illiterate adult members, place high expectations on the power of schooling. They do not measure sacrifices to send their children to school. However, since schools basically serve as a mechanism for social selection, political exclusion, economic marginalization and dominant cultural reproduction, children from poor backgrounds, most of whom attend public schools, are generally those who are selected against.

In the realm of enrollments, there was a disproportionate concentration of students in the public schools compared to those in private schools. Unlike other societies where social selection through the schooling process operates through such mechanisms as differentiating public financing schemes, special programs and organizational structures,[52] in Brazil, this selection is determined by whether a child goes to a private or public institution. While private schools are better equipped with qualified and better-paid teachers, working with students in highly-motivating environments, poor children study in the poorer public schools best known for their predominating low expectations, deficiencies and negative performance records. Apart from studying in institutions, which are poor and enveloped in a different culture, underprivileged children also have to face other problems inherent to school as an institution.

In addition to the general situation mentioned above, the internal workings of the school, the hidden curriculum, prejudices, self-fulfilling prophecies and low expectations regarding students from poor backgrounds work together to "expel" such students from school. These are the students who fail at the end of the year, repeat grades several times and study in classes with much younger colleagues.

According to Ogbu (1987),[53] the existence of systematic and historic discriminatory practices against social minorities turns them into a "castelike" underprivileged and impoverished group. By extension, we can contend that the Brazilian poor and indigent who have suffered from continuous differentiating public policies in the social areas also become more impoverished, and worse still, fatalistic. This world-view which gets transferred to children and adolescents from this background, negatively affects their school performance since they believe that even doing well at school will not help change their chances in life.[54]

The negative attitudes developed and transformed into discriminatory behaviors by school teachers in public schools is also sustained by these professional's interpretation of the contextual reality of underprivileged students. Basing themselves upon past experiences, these teachers claim to know who the ideal student is. And using this "knowledge" as a reference, they define poor children and adolescents as inherently different and far from being ideal students. These teachers adjust their levels of expectation so as to accommodate such students presumed to have lower cognitive abilities. Concomitantly, more time is spent on discipline rather than teaching. Teachers also interact less with members of this group. Learning activities, which involve these students are also developed more slowly and with little or no interest by teachers.[55]

These hindrances operate interdependently against school success among the poor. Dependent upon contextual factors, one element or the other may be more determinant. The more consistent negative results of school performance as shown in the data above, could be attesting to this, while calling attention to some other considerations about poverty among children and adolescents in Brazil today.[56]

The interactive nature of the deterrents to better school performance at the elementary level jeopardizes the whole educational system, and consequently asphyxiates social mobility, perpetuates impoverishment and naturalizes existing social inequalities. In this flow of negative educational-societal variables, whose interactions castigate children and youth the most, public policy solutions need to be interactive too. But have they been interactive in Brazil? With this understanding, we will briefly present three recent federal programs, which exemplify Brazil's official perspective of poverty as a social problem.

The *Bolsa Renda* (Family allowance) is a monthly payment from the federal government in the value of about one-third the Minimum Salary to poor and indigent families in the poorest regions of the country. As a compensatory program, its main objective is to guarantee some minimum monthly income to alleviate the effects of increased poverty especially during the annual draught period in these subsistence farming areas. Prospective beneficiaries are selected based upon household income levels.

Those families that earn less than half the Minimum Salary qualify for this benefit, though priority is given to those with young school children who have to continue attending school. However, the selective process is conducted by municipal agents since this level of government is responsible for registering and forwarding the names of qualified families to the Federal Ministry for Land Reform that pays out the benefits.

Another program, the *Bolsa Escola* ((School Grant), initially introduced in some municipalities in the mid-1990s,[57] had as its target population, families with children in elementary school. Priority was given to at-risk students, especially those with poor academic records. Children who were in grades lower than their age equivalence were also included in this group. The amounts paid out to the families of the students selected, varied from one place to the other. While the wealthier municipal governments paid the value of the Minimum Salary, some paid varying percentages of this amount. No matter what the final value was, all the programs developed so far have received positive ratings.

In return for the financial benefit, three basic conditions were always established – that the children attend school, maintain at least average grades in all subjects, and guarantee that the benefit was paid to the mother.[58] A fourth condition, which was not applied in all municipalities, was that the parents had to prove that they were either actively in search of a job, or were at least undergoing training for this purpose. The purpose of this last requirement was to maintain the program's feature as supplementary source of family income. Positive evaluations of these experiences have recently led the federal government to adopt this program at the national level.

Studies conducted to evaluate programs in Brasília and Recife,[59] concluded that the School Grant invariably helped maintain students in school, and emphasized the central role of teachers in this accomplishment. The programs were also believed to have helped reduce drop-out and failure rates, as school performance and levels of "wanting to study" increased. After receiving the benefit, some adult family members returned to the labor force, thus making the grant the supplementary income it was intended to be. Whether this increased income will disqualify the children from continuing in the program is an issue that needs to be resolved.

More recently, the federal government through the Ministry of Education, adopted this program, and a federal version is still being implemented all over the country. While payment is deposited directly in an account in the mother's name, there is a limit of three children per family. Moreover, the value of the benefit has been drastically reduced to about 8% of the Minimum Salary.

In even more recent times (summer of 2001), the *Programa Federal de Bolsa Alimentação* (Federal Food Grant Program)[60] was introduced, initially in those regions with high levels of poverty and indigence. It is also a targeted group program, which selects the poorest of pregnant women and mothers with children of six and below. Beneficiaries receive about 8% of the Minimum Salary monthly, and are obliged to have pregnancy check-ups, vaccinate their children and keep the necessary records.

These programs demonstrate a concerted federal effort to fight against poverty and poor school performance, particularly among students in elementary school. While there is one program that attempts to combat poverty among adults, there is the other which assists school children, and still another which offers monetary assistance so that healthier children will be born and remain healthy until they enter school at seven. Households that qualify for any of these programs, or even for all, would seem to have much better life conditions. But do such programs really help redistribute social wealth more equitably, make families less dependent upon government hand-outs, or are they mere stop-gap transitory propaganda tactics motivated by political circumstances?[61]

Notwithstanding the questionable nature of the declared objectives of these programs, there are some inherent problems which question their effectiveness in the fight against poverty, low school performance and social inequalities.

The fact that each of the programs pre-defines its target group is seen as an impediment to achieving the declared objectives of poverty alleviation and social participation, in a country where over 20 million of its 170 million inhabitants face chronic poverty. As it can be imagined, the largest segment of this group is formed by children and adolescents. Pre-defining program participants is exclusionary,[62] no matter what the technical or political explanations would be. Besides, there could be problems regarding the selection processes themselves. How efficient could a selection process, based upon income levels, be in areas where most workers are found in the informal and agricultural sectors, in a society where clientage and patronage rules abound?

Another dimension of this problem concerns the principle of universality, which seems to be disregarded in the selective processes which determine who participates in the programs. This neglect is even more serious when we remember that the objectives of these programs are to guarantee some regular household income and contribute to better schooling for poor children and adolescents. By adopting practices that are not all-inclusive, those families and children who are not chosen are discriminated against, even though they may be as deserving as those selected. Since it seems qualifying conditions prioritize the worst cases of poverty and school performance, would these selection criteria not reinforce dependency while they discourage self-help behaviors?

Other concerns related to these programs involve their temporary and complementary features. It is customary that such programs last as long as the political mandates of their creators. Discontinuity turns out to be a recurrent bedfellow. Besides, except for isolated cases, like those of the *Bolsa Escola* in Brasília and Recife, consistent and continuous program monitoring and evaluation are not common practices in these parts. In addition, beliefs and practices that hold the state to be a bad spender, an irrational administrator and unaccountable boss, reduce the efficiency, efficacy and effectiveness of social programs.

Closely related to these elements are the exorbitant costs involved in social spending because many public administrators and politicians still have immense difficulties in working with public funds solely for the public interest; acquiring social goods and services that effectively reach the poor and the most vulnerable.[63]

Another hindrance to program success is the diversified manner in which they are implemented. Despite the interdependent nature of the problems they seek to solve, program development is basically unconsolidated, extremely sectorial. As such, the problems are treated like independent realities belonging to separate spheres of government and the bureaucratic machinery. In a way, the three federal programs presented above serve as good examples of this political and administrative model, in which each program is planned, coordinated and financed by a different ministry. Though fundamentally welfare mechanisms, the ministry of social welfare has nothing to do with them. Segmentation of public policy efforts, instead of explicitly focused strategies concentrated into a centralized umbrella program, seemingly continues to negatively influence returns from social investments.

Critical considerations like the above have led some to claim that these programs, maybe with the exception of the School Grant, with their relatively insignificant monetary benefits, do not really target the eradication of poverty or the reduction of social inequalities. Rather, they are meant to merely mitigate hunger, the ugliest of the effects of these social maladies. Consequently, as claims go, social equity and justice are not concerns in the kind of public policy agenda Brazil has been known for. Economists like Amélia Cohn,[64] have summed up their concerns in the following question: for how much longer can Brazil, and other Latin American democracies, resist change by supporting pressures that arise from social inequalities that are historic, un-waning and cultural?

Concrete answers to questions like the above are deemed more urgent, when we remember that social policies in the last few decades have been mostly dictated by political ideologies and little interest in realistic nation building. In conjunction with market trends, they have prioritized economics at the cost of more widespread social development that focuses on people, with special concerns for the poor of today and those who might live in poverty tomorrow, if this situation remains unchanged. Fluctuating tendencies in social spending and short-lived programs, especially those whose targeted beneficiaries are the poor and their poorer offspring, is just one of the consequences of the development model we are analyzing.

Poverty and social inequalities affect adults, but their most long-lasting victims are the young. When the consequences of poverty are tackled squarely by avoiding program pitfalls as those mentioned above, because strengthened by a burning political will and a national drive for real change, then children from impoverished families might begin to hope for a brighter future. Good sense and an unwavering recognition of the urgent need for viable poverty eradication programming, would demand that the problem of poverty, whose diverse manifestations include continued impoverishment, persistent social gaps and an inefficient school system, be accepted as a national problem. Without this acceptance and the adoption of social spending strategies that are more inclusive, continuous and integrated, Brazil might continue to be a wealthy nation of mostly impoverished families.

This position might be better understood when we reflect upon the words of Darcy Ribeiro, one of this country's most ardently constructive critics. In his last book in which he discusses Brazil, he understood the country's problems in these words:[65]

> What is bad here, the real determinant factor for our backwardness is the organizational structure of this society which operates against the people's interests, a people that have been drained of life in order to serve outside interests that go against their own welfare. In this country, there has never been, and there continues not to be, people who are free, with liberty to captain their destiny in the quest for prosperity. What we have been, and continue to be, are a bunch of exploited workers, humiliated and offended by a dominant minority, incredibly efficient in formulating and maintaining a project for its very own prosperousness and well-being. At the same time, this select group, is always ready to crush whatever threats there may be for reforms that might affect the status quo (this author's free translation).

NOTES

1. In a rather instigating manner, Cristovam Buarque, discusses some of the recent roots of the problem of social apartheid in *O que é apartação?* (1993). In *O Colapso da Modernidade Brasileira e uma Propósta Alternativa* (1991), this author argues that Brazil's clear division along social-economic lines has created a distinguished group of privileged and non-privileged Brazilians; "haves" and "have nots." More historical explanations for Brazil's social inequalities can be found in Caio Prado Júnior (1987), Darcy Ribeiro (1995).

Two contributing explanatory factors which these latter authors have emphasized are those of racial/ethnic differentiating treatments and regional discriminatory practices which have always penalized the Northeastern region. It is no coincidence that large segments of Brazilian blacks live in this region. In the present text, these variables will remain untouched since they cannot be given the space and attention they deserve. In this and other texts, one can only really begin to understand Brazil when its racial heritage of Portuguese, Indian and African elements are kept as a backdrop of its everyday reality and future prospects.

2. We should observe that between 1994 and 1996, there was some reprieve to this tendency because of a stabilized economy with the introduction of a new currency, the *Real*. This did not only help re-organize the hyper-inflationary economy, but was instrumental in transferring money to the poor, mainly through increased direct buying power, government savings for investments in the social sector and some control over international debt payments.

3. Historically in Brazilian culture, as still evidenced in some circles, a child is only really an individual when he/she has an adult as primary reference. Without such a social reference, the young individual becomes a *menor* (a minor, a non-person), and thus without rights. He/She is culturally invisible, though socially active. *Menor* as a label is mostly applied to poor children-adolescents. For further discussion of issues related to these *menores* (minors), see especially – Ivete Ribeiro (Org.) (1982), Carlos Alberto Luppi (1987), Irene Rizzini (1994).

4. We are referring here both to children whose "homes are the streets," *meninos/meninas de rua* (street living and working boys/girls), and those who still maintain some kind of family ties, *meninos/meninas na rua* (street working boys/girls). Generally, these latter go to

work on the streets but regularly return to some adult's place they call "home." Despite some important differences between these two groups, in the final analyses, they form Brazil's marginalized young population. They are the direct results of exclusionary social policies which lead to rural-urban migration, ever-expanding shanty towns (*favelas*), unemployment, underemployment, uprooted families, child labor and violence.

Fundamentally, these children/adolescents do not differ in their degree of exclusion. They are poor, extensively exploited, unprotected, victims of unscrupulous adults and out of school. Apart from publications by international agencies like UNICEF (1997), some national researchers have studied this phenomenon in its diverse dimensions. To cite some examples – Irene Rizzini et al. (1986); Irene Rizzini and Thomas Sanders (1987 – mimeo). Rosilene Alvim and Lícia (1988), Sónia Altoe (1990), Mary Del Priore (Org.) (1999); Irandi Pereira, Maria do Carmo B. Carvalho et al. (1994).

5. See especially Rizzini, op. cit. (1986).

6. See especially *O Estatuto da Criança e do Adolescente* (1990), José de Sousa Matins (1991) and Maria del Priore (1999).

7. Irene Rizzini and Flávio B. Wiik (1990). This study showed that one of the main problems of work in this area is the lack of a general coordination. As such, rehabilitation activities tend to overlap and are mainly cost ineffective. Also debilitating are administrative rivalries, unlimited unaccountability and conservative working philosophies.

8. Income levels are generally related to poverty, as a condition which interferes in one's ability to have access to basic social goods and services. However, since income is only a means to the acquisition of such items, there is no guarantee that people with high incomes would automatically invest in these goods and not in more luxury and conspicuous consumer products. There are several sociocultural determinants involved in this relationship that is more complex than we are ready to admit sometimes.

9. It is not uncommon for researchers to base themselves on more human development factors to define basic social needs. The adoption of the Human Development Index (HDI) is proof of this growing tendency. The HDI measures nutritional level and conditions of clothing, housing, water; sewage system, security, access to health care, education, cultural goods-services and others. As a corollary, there must be accessible transportation. Adequate facilitators and ecological conditions are priority needs, to guarantee full use of the services listed above so that people can perform those activities considered absolute necessities to achieve individual well-being, collective development and social integration. See R. Katzman (1989).

10. This systemic comprehension of poverty, combining economic indicators and sociocultural factors, is discussed in H. Tolosa (1991) and Sônia Rocha (1990). Also see next footnote.

11. Augusto de Franco, former Director of Brazil's Central Bank, discusses Brazilian poverty along these lines. In his analysis of Amartya Sen's *Development as Liberty*, he sustains that Brazil's vulnerabilities, discriminations and exclusions, are produced and reproduced because of insufficient development. He continues that poverty is a political and institutional problem. Accordingly, in order to combat poverty, "there is a need to simultaneously invest in all those factors which affect development, and not merely in the economic sector . . . reuniting political conditions in order to implement such an agenda" (p. 3). On the individual level, this argument underlines the idea that poverty "goes far beyond individual income levels." Cf. http://www.saturno.no.com.br/notitia/leitura/pdf/franco_gustavo.pdf, accessed August 30, 2001. Also see Amartya Sen (1987).

12. About the importance of education as determinant of social exclusion, see especially P. Battos, D. de los Rios and F. Torche (1996), World Bank (1995).

13. The array of arguments on which the considerations and comments below are based can be found in publications related to education as schooling and society. A rather dated publication, Jerome Karabel and A. H. Halsey (1977), contains a good example of the kinds of basic ideas that continue to preoccupy educational researchers, policy makers and decision-making agents the world over. The titles of the book's chapters give a better idea of what we are talking about – "Education and social structure"; "Education and social selection"; "Education, "Human Capital" and the labor market"; "The politics of education"; "Cultural reproduction and the transmission of knowledge" and "Social transformation and educational change." In this and similar texts, the main questions concern the advantages and challenges of schools, school and social mobility, perspectives and problems of educational reform and education and politics. An idea dear to these discussions is that education shares an interdependent relationship with other social factors and society itself; that while education is determined, it is also a social determinant. The validity of this claim lies in the fact that education has overwhelmingly become a major player in determining social progress and individual well-being.

14. For a good example see: *Brasil: Parâmetros Curriculares Nacionais* (1997), a multi-volume publication which offers a national curriculum guide based upon the principles of respect for local conditions/experiencies, transversality and pluri-culturalism.

15. Paulo Freire's work focused on Popular Education as instrument for social liberation and self-emancipation; consciousness-raising and political involvement-action. In books like – *Pedagogy of the Oppressed* (1970); *Educação como Liberdade* (1985a); *The Politics of Education: Culture, Power and Liberation* (1985b) and *Educação como Prática de Liberdade* (20th ed.) (1991), he explained and defended this alternative/complementary kind of education. Freire's position becomes better appreciated against the background of Brazilian society which was very rural at the time he elaborated his principal works. Popular Education is fundamentally political as it emphasizes the importance of "education" (abilities to read and understand one's world so as to have the opportunity of choosing to become actively involved or not) for social change, development and collective well-being.

16. These are data from the *Pesquisa Nacional por Amostragem de Domicílios* – PNAD (National Household Survey), an organ of the IBGE. In combination with data from other research institutes, it's research findings are normally employed in defining public policies and determining investments.

17. Between 1964 and 1985, Brazil was ruled by the military. However, since 1985, civilian governments have ruled the country. The fact that the picture of wealth distribution has remained markedly unchanged, points to the need to look to other factors, and not the political regime, for explanations.

In the past few years, Brazil's economic performance has not been very different from past periods. Though hyper-inflation was controlled between 1994 and 1998, the savings were not consistently transformed into social services and/or redistributive programs, the most efficient mechanism through which the poor can participate in the economy. Since about the early 1990s, this failure has led to an increase in "social nobodies," the extremely marginalized, some of whom have formed local and national groups. Cogent examples are the *Movimento Nacional de Meninos e Meninas de Rua* – MNMMR (The National Movement for Street Boys and Girls) and the *Movimento Sem Terra* – MST (Movement for the Land-less). Other groups, not as well organized are the *Sem Teto* (Roofless), *Sem Emprego* (Unemployed), *Sem Saúde* (Without Health).

18. The value of the national Minimum Monthly Salary (MMS) normally gets readjusted, at least once a year, in order to make up for losses due to inflation and other facts that cause economic erosion of individual income. To have an idea, the minimum salary of R$100 in 1995, was equivalent to US$100. However, though this value has been raised to R$180 (since about May, 2001), its buying power in August 2001 is only about US$70. It is worth noting that the real (R$) maintained parity with the U.S. dollar from about 1994 till January, 1999. Presently, August 2001, the exchange rate is one US$ dollar to R$2.50.

19. We prefer this expression to the more commonly used "drinking water" so as to remind the reader of it's contextual relativity. For instance, water drunk in very poor rural areas or urban slums, may be considered unfit. However, it is "drinking water" because compared to other possibilities, a very likely one being the complete absence of alternative sources, it is relatively healthier and satisfies the thirsty.

20. The equivalence in these last two values are not coincidental. Children who work, especially outside the home, are also most likely to be out of school in order to increase working time and supposedly earn more.

21. These dollar values refer to the exchange rates in effect in 1995 when there was parity between the U.S. dollar and the Brazilian *Real*. In Brazil's rather unstable economy, this rate remains highly volatile. For example, in 1999, the national per capita income was reduced to US$3.230, though the value in *Real* was about R$5.861. In 1998, before the currency devaluation the following year, this would have been equivalent to about US$4.700. These currency fluctuations need to be taken into consideration when comparisons are made with other economies. Most important however, is that internal comparisons would remain valid since the local market remained based upon the *Real*.

22. Though the Federal Government has a program through which many public schools have been equipped with computer technology and internet access, without mentioning that most of the different kinds of private schools have boasted of these signs of modern educational consumption, among the general population, less than half of 1% has access to these modern communication technologies. Low income levels and high illiteracy rates can also help explain this situation, and remind us of the effects on children.

23. Data till 1997 and then till 1998, helped produce the UN Human Development Reports for 1999 and 2000 respectively. In 1999, Brazil occupied the 74th position; a slight improvement over its 79th ranking of 1997. The IHD for 2000 was 0.747, still far from that of a country like Cyprus with an index of 0.886.

24. The IHD measures the quality of life in a determined country. As a rejection of the more traditional economically oriented method of measuring poverty, this scale emphasizes elements like health care, life expectancy, adult literacy and school enrollment. According to Amartya Sen, Nobel Laureate and one of the creators of the IHD, a nation's development, as a social and human factor, should never be unilaterally measured through economic performance on the macro-level. For the IHD, what is important is how effectively positive economic performance gets transformed into products and programs that guarantee social well-being by providing basic services of quality for the needy.

25. The IHP, another World Bank scale, measures how effectively national economic growth affects people's lives and offers equity in opportunities. It's calculation is based on the following variables: life expectancy, adult illiteracy, healthy drinking water, health and waste disposal services, the weight of children of five and below, and the comparative

incomes of the poorest 20% and most affluent 20% of the national population. As a composite index, the IHP has more effective explaining power, especially with regard to social and human factors in a highly dependent market economy like that of Brazil.

Brazil's 21st ranking on the IHP with a score of 15.6% among developing countries in 2000, based on data from the previous year, contrasts with its 19th position with a score of 15.8% in 1999. However, contrary to the IHD, a higher ranking on the IHP signifies poorer performance levels regarding the delivery of basic goods and services; i.e. higher poverty levels among the population. Though the richest country in Latin America, about twelve neighboring countries show data considered much more positive when compared with the Brazilian performance. These countries deliver better social products, services and conditions of life than does Brazil. Accordingly, their offspring would be better-cared-for, schooled, cured and protected.

Questions of reliability and fidedignidade may be warranted because of the numberless difficulties involved in data gathering and compilation in a country like Brazil. The fact that data come from different sources, governmental and non-governmental, only increase the reliability concerns. Nevertheless, despite differences in numerical values, all data about Brazil consistently point in one direction – the country's very poor showing in wealth distribution, when compared to its overall economic weight as measured by such indices as GNP, market size and per capita income.

26. For some relevant discussion about the dimension and problematic of child labor in Brazil, see – R. P. de Barros et al. (1994) and L. M. Miller (1994). Though child labor may be considered a serious social problem, we must not forget that there are sectors of society and even some international groups that prefer to emphasize its social contributions as integral part of the socialization and learning process for these children as future adults. About this position, especially in Latin America, see Jo Boyden (1999). And for a more general discussion of the issues, consult William E. Myers (2000).

27. Over the last years, problems of how to effectively measure official budget and spending have been mitigated. With the taxation and budgetary modifications implemented since the Constitution of 1988, it has gradually become viable to realistically examine how and where governments have spent financial resources. With the centralization of most of such expenses in the General Federal Budget (*Orçamento Geral da União* – OGU) and the creation of the *Sistema Integrado de Acompanhamento Financeiro* – SIAFI (Integrated Monitoring System of Public Spending), it has become possible to follow up on government expenditures.

These calculations were also made difficult because of the country's hyper-inflationary economy. Before the stability measures in 1994, currencies were frequently changed. From 1986 till today, Brazil has had five currencies with corresponding devaluations. These have been the following currencies: 1986–1989, the *Cruzado*; 1989–1990, the *Cruzado Novo*; 1990–1993. the *Cruzeiro*; 1993–1994, the *Cruzeiro Real*, and since 1994, the *Real* which maintained parity with the U.S. dollar till 1999.

28. UNICEF (1998, pp. 13–108).

29. Owing to the 1988 Federal Constitution, whose main characteristic has been the decentralization of programs since the 1990s, most federal funding has gone directly to specific projects in specific municipalities with this latter administrative structure having the responsibility for planning, implementation, control and evaluation. In the last decade, most public programs in health, education, sanitation, housing, urban development, security and child-adolescent development have been administered in this fashion. On the whole,

due to the novelty of the experience and a culture of non-evaluation of programs, the results of such measures are still to be objectively evaluated. Nevertheless, studies conducted so far point to two fundamental changes: more accountability and greater popular participation. If anything else, in a historically dominant culture with administrative practices that are not known for their transparency and broad public interest, these trends are important social victories. Some studies which have dealt with Brazil's heritage in public administration and recent changes include: Victor N. Leal (1975), Simon Schwartzman (1982), Marcos P. D. Lanna (1995), Olavo B. Lima Júnior (1997), B. Geddes and A. R. Neto (1992) and Marcos Otávio Bezerra (1999). For more general aspects of this problem, see A. Strickon and S. Greenfield (1972).

30. Emphasizing education is not an attempt to minimize the importance of such areas as health, food, sanitation and housing in any conscientious public policy strategies to reduce social inequities. We consider education to have a pivotal role in this task, however. Though all levels of the schooling process are crucial in this regard, the state has underscored elementary education, with the apparent presumption that apart from its leading role in gaining access to higher educational levels, elementary teaching and learning are vital factors in adequately preparing man-power since their effectiveness fundamentally attacks illiteracy, and this could open doors for greater participation as citizens.

31. Credit should also be given to the democratization movement orchestrated by organized social groups including unions of civil servants, teachers and other workers in the 1980s. These groups pushed for realistic changes regarding education as a constitutional right, and went further to demand that schools be made to respond more fully to the country's needs and realities.

32. With the creation of the *Fundo Nacional de Desenvolvimento Educacional*, FNDE – (National Funding for Educational Development) in 1968, it became possible to obtain funds, though always fraught with high levels of unpredictability, for the maintenance and development of Basic Education by providing funds for school lunch program, libraries, text books, health and transportation. However, these failed to really impact upon the schools because administrative, political and cultural barriers to the rational application of public funds were not removed. This situation had to change in order to guarantee that educational funds were spent on matters that were *directly related* to teaching, learning, school infra-structure, equipment and personnel.

Subsequently, a constitutional amendment to the 1988 Constitution (Law no. 9492 promulgated in 1996 with implementation from 1998 to 2007), stipulated that while the federal government was primarily responsible for financing higher education, the individual states had as their main responsibilities elementary and high schools. The municipal governments had the obligation of investing the most in elementary and kindergarten education. Federal and state governments had to spend no less than 18% of tax funds on education. Municipal governments were mandated to spend at least 25% of these same funds on schools. For the implementation of this law, a special funding system was introduced so as to prioritize elementary education, understood as the most crucial level in the schooling process.

Initially called *Fundão* (Big Funds), the *Fundo de Desenvolvimento do Ensino Fundamental e Valorização do Magistério* – FUNDEF (Funds for the Development of Elementary Schools and the Valuation of Teachers) made it possible to divide all educational spending this way – elementary education 75%, pre-schools 12%, high schools 11 and 2% for higher education. These funds originated from 78% of all educational resources from the municipalities, 75% of funds from the states and 7% of federal money. Of the remainder of the federal funds for education, 69% went to higher education, 22% to high schools, and only 1% to pre-schools. The emphasis on elementary education cannot be mistaken *Folha de São Paulo, Cotidiano* (February 1, 1998, pp. 3–6). See specially Arts. 208, 212, 213 and 242 of the 1988 Brazilian Constitution. Also see, Art. 68 of the *Lei de Diretrizes e Bases da Educação Nacional* – LDBN (Law for the Directives and Bases of National Education) and the explanations presented in Paulo Nathaniel Pereira de Souza and Eurides Brito da Silva (1997).

Legally (thus ideally), public funds should be spent on public schools. However, due to constitutional loopholes, political interests and other legal mechanisms, these funds are also spent on private schools which formally claim to be "non-profiting institutions for the public interest." In a society where there are difficulties as to differences between private and public property, private and public interests, this type of contradiction has not been easy to correct. See especially, Marilena Chaui (1991).

33. Between the late 1970s and early 1990s, there was an ever-growing number of private educational institutions, especially from kindergarten to high school. In some states, this growth was more than 100%. Confessional schools have not grown at the same pace. Nevertheless, most children and adolescents still study in public schools.

34. Elementary education is divided into two levels, one basic and an upper level. Normally, both last four years each. High school lasts three years, and university education has a duration of four years.

35. The Age-Grade discrepancy can be understood as an "institutional invitation" for the student to withdraw from the system. Especially in the case of students with experiences of multiple-failures and grade repetition, the irremediable effects on their self-esteem could serve as incentive to drop out; a fate which many poor students share, and for which many continue to be blamed.

36. It is good to realize that this problem is not restricted to Brazilian schools. In fact, it may be universal, as observed by Benigno E. Aguirre and Roberto J. Vichot (1998, pp. 118–138); see p. 130. These researchers state – "It is reasonable to expect a positive correlation between the percentage of student dropouts and the percentage of students repeating the grade. Indeed, in Cuba, the United States, and other countries, grade repeaters tend to drop out more often, especially in the later grades, because they older than other students and have more problems adjusting to school as well as other difficulties."

37. In more recent times, some specific programs are being developed for recuperating those students most victimized by age-grade distortions. Two of the most common are the *classes de aceleração* (accelerated classes) and the change from the grade (vertical placement) system wherein cognitive skills are treated in a hierarchical manner. A more circular pedagogical system, organized in cognitive-skill blocks during the basic cycle of elementary schooling, is being gradually adopted in many schools. This arrangement makes it possible for students to spend more than one academic year learning basic reading and writing skills. Efficiently developed, most of the students acquire these basic skills adequately. This enables them to advance with fewer difficulties within the system. A question which still needs answers is whether such students attain more success rates throughout the elementary school years.

38. Data of 1998 from MEC/INEP/SEEC indicate that between 1975 and 1997, municipal elementary schools increased from 60.8 to 69.6%. During the same period, federal and state elementary schools were gradually reduced. The FUNDEF has no provisions for

building new schools since these are considered enough. Where logistical problems exist regarding attendance, student transportation is generally provided.

39. Studies conducted under the auspices of UNICEF-Brazil found that private schools were decreasing gradually as more parents opted for the municipal schools which had begun to show signs of educational quality since the mid-1990s. See for example, Francis Musa Boakari and Roberto M. Gurgel Rocha (1999, pp. 23–54).

40. As we examine these success rates, another problem termed "illiteracy in the classroom," seems to continuously hamper the general performance of the educational system. This has been. It consists of that situation wherein students demonstrate incapacity to read or write at levels corresponding to their age-grade level of study. The PNAD of 1996 pointed to these percentages among: 7 year olds – 5.8%; ages 8 and 9 – 8.6%; ages 10 and 11 – 3.6% and 12 year olds – 0.9%. See *Folha de São Paulo Cotidiano*, (February 1, 1998, pp. 01 ff.). In other words, about 8.6% of the students in the second and third grades did not know how to read and write. How then could they follow what teachers were teaching? And what of those illiterates (0.9%) in the 5th or 6th grades? Such information point to the necessity for adopting more systemic perspectives and critical attitudes in interpreting social data from/about a country like Brazil.

41. The cultural, political, historic, social and contextual meanings and subsequent policy implications of the problem of working children are complex because of the diverse interests on the part of government, parents, international agencies, NGOs, social movements, and the children/youth themselves. For an appropriate discussion of how most of these social subjects interact, see David Post and Riho Sakurai (2001, pp. 8–10).

42. According to data from MEC/INEP/SEEC (1998), in 1975, 75.9% of all elementary schools were located in the rural areas. In 1989 and 1991, 75.4 and 72.9% of these establishments were still in the interior. Only since about 1996 (68.5%) and 1997 (66.8%) did this concentration begin to suffer some reduction. Because of more recent budgetary reforms which have assigned more funds to elementary school education, state governments have begun to compete with municipal administrators for students since financial transfers are positively related to enrollment figures. This can also be positive in the fight against school repetition and dropout since students need to be maintained within the system in order to maintain budget volumes. The possibility that such a solution is really a problem in disguise, is another question.

43. In no way are we trying to unilaterally claim that the problem of poor school enrollment of many school-aged children who have to work with their families is restricted to the rural, non-urban areas. The same problem exists in the urban centers. Nevertheless, whereas in the interior there are limited opportunities for studying outside the regular system, in the towns, supplementary educational programs like the *Ensino Supletivo* (Supplementary Schooling) and *Ensino Noturno* (Night School), help these child-adolescent workers continue their studies. Their performance levels show that many do not do as well as their counterparts in the more regular school system. However, we may argue that some schooling is still better than none.

44. The question of unqualified teachers in Brazil is not new. The minimum requirement for teaching the first four Grades of elementary school is a basic teaching certificate, earned after three years in a Normal School (Basic Teacher Qualification Institution) upon completion of the eighth grade. A college diploma is necessary to teach at the higher levels of elementary and in high schools. Whilst there are teachers without these minimum qualifications teaching at one level or the other, there are those teaching professionals who

have college degrees but lack teaching certificates. All are classified as *professores leigos* (unqualified teachers). In the municipal schools in the interior, large contingents of such teachers are still found.

45. Private schools in Brazil are believed to be better than the public schools. Though there are no consistent studies attesting to this, two supporting arguments are often presented. First, at the university entrance exams, insignificant numbers of public school graduates attain success. Second, there is a general belief that "that which is public, is everybody's. And being everybody's, no-one really takes care of it, and consequently, its services are very inefficient." Public schools do not escape this line of thinking. Owing to the strength of mechanisms constructed from social representations, such beliefs have easily become self-reproducing and tend to affect negatively, teachers, students and parents who have a stake in public schools. Poor teacher qualification in such a context only aggravates the negativity of an already discredited system which is the only alternative for the poor who want to study.

46. Apart from its financial stipulations, the FUNDEF also emphasizes the concrete universalization of high quality elementary education, so as to improve upon the other levels of the educational system. Moreover, the LDB (Law No. 9394/1996) helped define Brazil's educational objectives, established necessary norms, defined financial resource distribution ratios and offered orientations about school administration.

It is essential to remember that teachers' cheap salaries and consequent low social status, have not been historically inviting to highly motivated students. As such, teaching has been a second or even far-third professional choice among in-going university students. There are expectations that with these reforms, more competent professionals will be trained, and that teaching would once again assume its social importance.

47. Though referring to reform attempts in an earlier period which had not attained their declared objectives principally because of the wide gap between policy discourse and implementation, it would be enlightening to read – Francis Musa Boakari (1994).

48. These efforts to improve elementary instruction and performance, raise questions about the needs of public pre- and high schools. Since 2000, curricular modifications and teacher qualification strategies are being implemented to improve upon both the academic and technical streams of high school education. Nevertheless, pre-schools have so far not received any particular attention. Would this neglect be affirming that children who depend upon public funds for schooling, can begin elementary school already school-prepared? Could it also mean that kindergarten experience is not necessary for successful elementary school performance? Issues such as these are still in debate.

49. The PCNs for the first cycle of elementary education (grades I–IV) were first published in 1996 and later distributed to most public schools. Since then, other volumes have been published for the upper cycle of elementary and high schools. The idea of the PCNs is to offer guide-lines about the contents of the curriculum and teacher practices. Based on the idea of a transversal curriculum, the "suggestion" is to include discussions about health, cultural pluralism, the environment, sexual education and ethics into the more traditional school subjects in such a way as to emphasize the universal nature of problems and the local dimensions/implications/manifestations of these same questions. The basic and explicit intention is to make the school experience more useful for students' daily activities as citizens. Though there are critical analyses of the PCNs, we cannot fail to recognize their contributions in giving some basic orientations for making schools more responsive to the real needs of students as active agents in the teaching-learning process. There are problems

regarding the implementation of the recommendations from the PCNs with the most serious being the inadequate training of teachers in the how, why, when and for what to use these orientations. Apparently, these are being gradually solved, especially with the involvement of teacher-education institutions in using the PCNs as integral course material.

50. See especially INEP/MEC (1998) and *Informações Educacionais do Estado do Piauí* (1999).

51. E. Gellner and J. Waterbury (1977) and Marcos P. D. Lanna (1995) are two essential works which treat the question of how certain political practices create insurmountable barriers to effective public policy implementation in favor of the excluded.

52. For some understanding of this situation, Jonathan Kozol's (1991) would be good reading. The strategies may be different, but the outcomes are basically comparable to the situation in Brazil.

53. J. Ogbu has treated the problem of self-discriminatory attitudes and practices among minority students in school. He has tried to adopt more systemic treatments of the problems related to this group, and for the present discussion, this approach throws some light upon the complex issues involved. See John U. Ogbu (1987, pp. 312–335).

54. The classic work of Paul Willis explaining how school helps working class students exclude themselves from pursuing higher educational attainment goals, and consequently become excluded as their parents, is an important contribution in this discussion. Paul Willis (1977).

55. To understand how this mechanism operates in the U.S., see W. A. Firestone and S. Rosenblum (1988, pp. 285–299).

56. Amélia Cohn (2000) argues that the historic nature of poverty in Brazil points to two causes, one traditional and the other, more modern market forces. These factors have led to "... a process whereby poverty is naturalized, and treated like a fatality which has resulted from globalization, an external force to our reality, and thus outside national and governmental control" (p. 10). According to her, this understanding still serves as incentive for social policies which merely try to combat poverty, and do not really focus on its eradication.

57. The first municipalities that implemented this program were Campinas in São Paulo, Brasília in Distrito Federal and Recife in Pernambuco. Many others have copied this program outright, or at least had something very similar being developed. See Sílvio Rocha Sant'Ana and Andréa Moraes (1997). Also see, http://www.saturno.no.com.br/notitia/, accessed August 29, 2001.

58. This condition was established because it was believed that mothers were more responsible in taking care of their young children and adolescents. Some of the cultural implications of this criterion in a male-dominated society, do not seem to have so far impeded the smooth-running of these programs. Officially recognizing the important role of women in the household has so far turned out to be a positive contribution too. See Lena Lavinas (Coord.) (2000).

59. See note 50 above.

60. This program which pays out money, is different from other welfare programs in Brazil, which donate food items and/or meals. Both strategies have advantages and disadvantages as discussed by: Peter Rossi (1998), James C. Ohls and Harold Beebout (1993).

61. The use of social spending, normally accompanied by widespread campaign to boost government support, especially in pre-electoral periods, is a phenomenon that comes to mind here since 2002 is an election year. See a study of the politics of targeted social spending in Mexico, Indonesia and Ghana – Kimberly Niles (1999).

62. See Lena Lavinas (www.no.com.br – accessed in July 2001). She argues that these programs are exclusionary, and therefore discriminatory, even though we can call this "positive discrimination."

63. See Luis Henrique Amaral (2001). He argues that though "there is still lots of work to be done, presently, both society and public institutions are making the action of corrupt officials more difficult" (p. 42).

64. See Amélia Cohn, op. cit. (2000), Emir Sader and Pablo Gentili (1999), and M. C. Tavares and J. L. Fiori (1993).

65. Darcy Ribeiro (1995, p. 446).

REFERENCES

Aguirre, B. E., & Vichot, R. J. (1998). The reliability of Cuba's educational statistics. *Comparative Education Review, 42*(2), 118–138.

Altoe, S. (1990). *Infancias perdidas*. Rio de Janeiro: Shanon.

Alvim, R. A., & Lícia, P. V. (1988). *Infancia e Sociedade no Brasil: Uma Análise da Literatura*. Rio de Janeiros: ABIB, ANPOCS.

Amaral, L. H. (2001). O Brasil no Caminho da Mudança. *Veja* (August 1), 42–43.

Anonymous (1990). *O Estatuto da Crianca e do Adolescente*. Brasilia: Congresso Nacional.

Bank, W. (1995). *Brazil: A poverty assessment* (World Bank Report, N 14323-Br). Washington, DC.

Battos, P., de los Rios, D., & Torche, F. (1996). *Lecturas sobre la Esclusao Social*. Santiago: International Labor Organization.

Bezerra, M. O. (1999). Em Nome das "Bases": Politica, Favor e Dependencia Pessoal. In: R. Dumara (Ed.), *Nucleo de Antoropologia da Politica*.

Boakari, F. M. (1994). Educational system reform as legitimation for continuity: The case of Brazil. In: A. Yogev & V. D. Rust (Eds), *International Perspectives on Educationa and Society: Educational Reform in International Perspctive* (pp. 109–133). Greenwich: JAI Press.

Boakari, F. M., & Rocha, R. M. G. (1999). *A Educação no Piauí*. Brasília: UNICEF, MEC/FUNDESCOLA, Banco Mundial.UNDIME.

Boyden, J. (1999). *A time for play and a time for school – the results of a survey of practitioners, advocates and other experts on childhood and children's work*. Stockholm: Rada Barnen.

Buarque, C. (1991). *O Colapso de Modernidade Brasileira e uma Prosposta Alternativa*. Rio de Jeneiro: Paz e Terra.

Buarque, C. (1993). *O que e apartação?* Sao Paulo: Brasiliense.

Chaui, M. (1991). *Conformismo e Resistência: Aspectos da Cultura Polular no Brasil*. Sao Paulo: Brasiliense.

Cohn, A. (2000). Gastos sociais e políticas sociais nos anos 90: Do padrão histórico de proteção social brasileiro. Paper presented at the XXIV Encontro Anual da ANPOCS, Caxambu.

de Barros, R. P. et al. (1994). Is poverty the main cause of child work in urban Brazil? *Series Seminarios: IPEA, 13*(94).

de Castro, M. H. G., & Davanzo, A. M. Q. (Eds) (1999). *Situação da educação básic no Brasil*. Brasilia: Instituto Nacional de Estudos e Pesquisas Educacionais – INEP.

de Franco, A. (2001). [http://www.saturno.no.com.br/notitia/leitura/pdf/franco_gustavo.pdf].

de Souza, P. N. P., & de Silva, E. B. (1997). *Como Entender e Aplicar a Nova LDB*. Sao Paulo: Pioneira.

Del Priore, M. (1999). *Historia das Criancas no Brasil*. Sao Paulo: Contexto.

Firestone, W. A., & Rosenblum, S. (1988). Building commitment in Urban High Schools. *Educational Evaluation and Policy Analysis, 10*(4), 285–299.

Freire, P. (1970). *Pedagogy of the oppressed*. New York: Seabury.

Freire, P. (1985a). *Educação como liberdade*. Sao Paulo: Brasiliense.

Freire, P. (1985b). *The politics of education: Culture, power and liberation*. New York: Bergin & Garvin.

Freire, P. (1991). *Educação como Prática de Liberdade* (20th ed.). Sao Paulo: Paz e Terra.

Geddes, B., & Neto, A. R. (1992). Institutional sources of corruption in Brazil. *Third World Quarterly, 13*(4), 15–21.

Gellner, E., & Waterbury, J. (Eds) (1977). *Patrons and clients in Mediterranean societies*. London: Duckworth.

INEP/MEC (1998). *Primerio Relatório do SAEB/97*. Brasilia: MEC.

Karabel, J., & Halsey, A. H. (1977). *Power and ideology in education*. New York: Oxford University Press.

Katzman, R. (1989). *La Heterogeneidade de la Pobreza: El Caso de Montevideo*. Rivista de la CEPAL, no. 37. Santiago.

Kozol, J. (1991). *Savage inequalities: Children in America's schools*. New York: Crown.

Lanna, M. P. D. (1995a). *A divida divina. Troca e Patronagem no Nordeste Brasileiro*. Campinas: UNICAMP.

Lanna, M. P. D. (1995b). *A Divida Divina: Troca e Patronagem no Nordeste Brasileiro*. Campinas: UNICAMP.

Lavinas, L. (2000). *Avaliação do Programa Bolsa-Escola de Recife: Relatório Final*. Brasilia: Convenio ILO-Banco Mundial/ANPEX-IPEA.

Lavinas, L. (2001). *Combinado Compensatorio e Redistributivo: O Desafio das Politicas Sociais no Brasil* (www.no.com.br).

Leal, V. N. (1975). *Coronelismo, Enxada e Voto*. Sao Paulo: Alfa-Omega.

Lima, O. B. J. (1997). *Instituicoes Politicas Democraticas: O Segredo da Legitimidade*. Rio de Janeiro: Jorge Zahar Editor.

Luppi, C. A. (1987). *Malditos Frutos do Noso Ventre*. Sao Paulo: Icone.

Matins, J. d. S. (1991). *O Massacre dos Inocentes: A Criança e a Infância no Brasil*. Sao Paulo: Hucitec.

MEC (1999). *Informacoes Educacionais do Estado do Piaui*. Brasilia: MEC.

Miller, L. M. (1994). Condições de Trabalho da Criança e do Adolescente Urbanos. *Anais do III Encontro Nacional de Estudos do Trabalho*. Rio de Janeiro: ABET.

Myers, W. E. (2000). *Educating children who work*. New York: Save the Children Alliance.

Niles, K. (1999). Economic adjustment and targeted social spending: The role of political institutions. Working Paper, The World Bank, Washington, DC.

Ogbu, J. (1987). Variability in minority school performance: A problem in search of an explanation. *Anthropology and Educational Quarterly, 18*, 312–335.

Ohls, J. C., & Beebout, H. (1993). *The food stamps program – Design, tradeoffs, policy and impacts*. Washington, DC: A Mathematica Policy Research Institute.

Pereira, I., Carvalho, M. d. C. B. et al. (1994). *Trabalho Infantil: Mitos e Dilemas*. Sao Paulo: Editora Forja.

Post, D., & Sakurai, R. (2001). The impact of global politics on child labor in Mexico: What role for the ILO, UNICEF, and international advocacy. Paper presented at the CIES Annual Conference, Washington, DC.

Prado, C. J. (1987). *A Formação do Brasil Contemporâneo*. Sao Paulo: Brasiliense.

Ribeiro, D. (1995). *O Povo Brasileiro: A Formação e o Sentido do Brasil*. Sao Paulo: Companhia das Letras.

Ribeiro, I. (1982). *Menor e Sociedade*. Rio de Janeiro: IUPERJ.

Rizzini, I. (1994). Brazil: A new concept of childhood. In: C. S. Blanc (Ed.), *Urban Children in Distress: Global Predicaments and Innovative Strategies*. Florene: UNICEF.

Rizzini, I. et al. (1986). *A Geração da Rua: Um Estado sobre as Crianças Marginalizadas no Rio de Janeiro*. Rio de Janeiro: CESME/USU.

Rizzini, I., & Sanders, T. (1987). Brazil's street children: Misconceptions and reality. Paper presented at the International Symposium on Mobile Youth-Work, Esslingen, Germany.

Rizzini, I., & Wiik, F. B. (1990). *O que o Rio tem feito por suas Crianças*. Rio de Janeiro: A4maos.

Rocha, S. (1990). Pobreza – Renda e Indicadores Sociais como Criterios Complementares. *Planejamento e Politicas Públicas*, no. 4. Rio de Janeiro.

Rossi, P. (1998). *Feeding the Poor – Assessing federal food aid*. Washington, DC: AEI Press.

Sader, E., & Gentili, P. (1999). *Pos-Neoliberalism II: Que Estado para que Democracia?* Petropolis: Vozes.

Sant'Ana, S. R., & Moraes, A. (1997). *Avaliação do Programa Bolsa-Escola do GDF* (http://www. saturno.no.com.br/notitia/). Fundação Grupo Esquel Brasil.

Schwartzman, S. (1982). *Bases do Autoritarismo Brasileiro*. Rio de Janeiro: Editora Campus.

Secretaria de Ensino Fundmental (1997). *Brasil: Parametros Curriculares Nacionais*. Brasilia: MEC.

Sen, A. (1987). *The standard of living*. Cambridge: Cambridge University Press.

Strickon, A., & Greenfield, S. (1972). *Structure and process in Latin America: Patronage, clientage and power systems*. Albuquerque: University of Mexico Press.

Tavares, M. C., & Fiori, J. L. (1993). *Desajuste Global e Modernizacao Conservadora*. Rio de Janeiro: Paz e Terra.

Tolosa, H. (1991). Pobreza no Brisil: Uma Avaliação dos Anon 80. In: *A Questão Sociale do Brasil*. Sao Paulo: Nobel.

UNICEF (1997). *Situacao Mundial da Infancia*. Brasilia: UNICEF.

UNICEF (1998). *A Infancia Brasileira nos Anos 90*. Brasilia: UNICEF.

Willis, P. (1977). *Learning to labor: How working class kids get working class jobs*. New York: Columbia University Press.

12. SMALL HANDS: GLOBAL DIMENSIONS OF CHILD LABOR AND EXPLOITATION

Carol Camp Yeakey and Judith Brooks Buck

> With economic globalization tying national economies more closely together, awareness of the incidence of child labor in third World nations is growing rapidly in the industrialized countries, as Northern consumers respond with discomfort to reports showing that the clothes they wear and the toys with which their children play are made by child workers.
>
> Weissman, R. (1997). Stolen Youth, Brutalized Children,
Globalization and the Campaign to End Child Labor, p. 10.
>
> In the fields, the United States is like a developing country.
>
> <div align="right">Human Rights Watch (2000). <i>Fingers to the Bone</i>, United
States Failure to Protect Child Farmworkers, p. 2.</div>

The term child labor conjures up visions of Charles Dickens and of soot laden workhouses in Victorian London or, in America, pictures of children in the early 1900s sorting coal in the mines of Pennsylvania and West Virginia. While the exploitation of child labor is both an urban and rural phenomenon, the common thread is poverty. Economic globalization is the newest factor contributing to the rapid growth of child labor which is also caused by cultural and religious traditions, discrimination and employers' desire for cheap and docile labor. Debt bondage of children, prostitution, domestic help and commercial agriculture work are some of the more common forms of child labor. Reports are emerging of children working in the export-oriented sectors giving evidence of market globalization, wherein transnational companies shift their manufacturing to nations which have

'Suffer the Little Children': National and International Dimensions of Child
Poverty and Public Policy
Advances in Education in Diverse Communities: Research, Policy and Praxis, Volume 4, 295–305
Copyright © 2006 by Elsevier Ltd.
All rights of reproduction in any form reserved
ISSN: 1479-358X/doi:10.1016/S1479-358X(04)04012-4

the cheapest labor costs (Barber, 1996; Lechner & Boli, 2000; Stiglitz, 2002). It is the purpose of this research to examine the issue of child labor and, in so doing, examine some of the implications of economic globalization on child labor across the globe.

How does one define child labor? Not all child labor is as repugnant as the most hazardous and exploitative forms. Even the most ardent anti-child labor advocates recognize that appropriate work tasks may teach children skills and responsibility, and bind families together to contribute to family incomes. According to UNICEF criteria, child labor is inappropriate if it involves: full-time work at too early an age; excessive hours spent working; work that exerts undue physical, social or psychological stress; work that entails inadequate pay and too much responsibility; work that impedes access to education; work that undermines children's dignity and self-esteem, such as slavery or bonded labor and sexual exploitation; and, work that is detrimental to a child's full social and psychological development (UNICEF, 2002).

With economic globalization tying national economies more closely together, awareness of the incidence of child labor in Third World nations is growing rapidly in industrialized countries, as Northern consumers respond with discomfort to reports showing that they may be enjoying the fruits of exploitative child labor. At the same time, the globalization process which is spurring the new Northern awareness of child labor, is putting strains on the economies and social structures of countries in the global South – and, in many ways, intensifying the problem of child labor.

FORCED LABOR AND HAZARDOUS CONDITIONS

Approximately 120 million children under the age of 14 labor full time, according to recent estimates by the International Labor Organization (ILO) (U.S. Department of Labor, 2002, 2001; UNICEF, 2000). If those for whom work is a secondary activity are included, the number of working children rises to 250 million. The majority of child laborers live in Asia, although Africa has a higher rate of child labor. The ILO estimates that 40% of African children between the ages of five and fourteen years of age, work. (U.S. Department of Labor, 2002, 2001) Although the majority of the 120 million full time working children labor in the commercial agricultural sector, child labor is not confined to any particular economic sector. Children work as domestic servants, in mining, as divers in deep-sea fishing, in construction, as prostitutes, in toy, shoe and garment factories, as cigarette makers, as rug weavers, in charcoal making, in glass and ceramics factories, as sports equipment and surgical instrument makers, in the match and fireworks industries and in many other jobs.

Moreover, child labor does not affect all children uniformly. While boys are more likely to be employed in wage-earning jobs, girls work more often in the family home or as domestic servants in the homes of others, often without pay. The nature of such work often results in girls being undercounted in child labor statistics (Statistics on Working Children, 2001). Certain children may also face greater risks than others. Working children under the age of twelve years and working girls are among the most vulnerable (International Program on the Elimination of Child Labor (IPEC) at a Glance, 1995, 2001).

The most appalling circumstances of child labor involves forced labor and children working in hazardous conditions. The most common form of forced child labor is debt bondage, a practice by which parents pledge their children's work to pay off debts (U.S. Department of Labor, 2001). The debts are often miniscule, but the children may work for their entire childhood – indeed for their entire lives – to pay them off because of fraudulent accounting mechanisms employed by debt holders. Debt bondage and other forms of forced child labor are most pervasive in India, Pakistan and Nepal, where they are supported by longstanding traditions and cultural biases against castes or minority ethnic groups.

Both bonded and unbonded child laborers are frequently employed in shockingly brutal and hazardous conditions. Consider the following examples highlighted by child labor activists in recent years (Save The Children Fund, 2000; U.S. Department of Labor, 2002, 2001; Weissman, 1997):

- Children in the Asian rug industry often work in cramped quarters, hovering over their work in poorly lit rooms. They frequently develop spinal deformities from persistent crouching; weakened eyesight; and respiratory ailments from chronic exposure to dust and wool fluff in poorly ventilated quarters. Many of the child laborers receive no wages at all. Carpet weaving is among the industries employing a high proportion of bonded child laborers. Bonded children in the Asian rug industry toil in the most horrifying conditions, working up to 20 hours a day, every day, and living and working in the same small, damp room. Labor Department statistics suggest that child rug weavers may number as many as 150,000 in Nepal, one million in Pakistan and 400,000 in India.
- Hundreds of children in Colombia work in labor intensive coal mines. With low and narrow passageways, the mine owners – often parents of the workers – view children as ideally sized to slip through tunnels and pick at small coal exposures. Hunched over and straining for breath, the boys carry heavy sacks of coal on their backs. They are exposed to high levels of dust, risking permanent lung damage and disease.
- In Cambodia, children work in brick-making factories, where they generally work barehanded, and often barefoot. The children are regularly cut by the bricks

and often drop them on their hands or feet. Some of the children work with heavy machinery; and, many of them suffer severe cuts to their hands and fingers on the machines. More than half of the child brick workers interviewed for a study by the Asian American Free Labor Institute (AAFLI) indicated they were in debt to their employer. The high incidence of injury and the substantial debts notwithstanding, AAFLI found, the children's biggest complaint was fatigue.

- Trafficking in young girls sold into prostitution is on the rise, especially along the Burma-to-Thailand, Nepal-to-India, Vietnam-to-Cambodia and internal Thai routes. Other important routes include: from Latin America to Europe and the Middle East; from Belarus, Russia and the Ukraine to Hungary, Poland and the Baltic states or to Western Europe; from the Philippines and Thailand to Australia, New Zealand and Taiwan; and from Southeast Asia to Hawaii and Japan. Girls are often sold into prostitution by their parents. They are moved from rural to urban areas, or to new countries altogether, where they face a life of exceptional violence and danger. Customers and brothel operators frequently rape and subject young girls to extreme forms of physical and psychological abuse. The girls are at high risk of contracting AIDS and other sexually transmitted diseases, and of having unwanted and early pregnancies.

- About 27 million people worldwide are bought and sold, held captive, brutalized and exploited for profit (Cockburn, 2003; Warren, 2003). They are known as 21st century slaves. The mix of total domination and economic exploitation defines modern slaveholding. Slaves today are controlled not by legal ownership, but by what is called "the final authority of violence." While slavery is illegal across the globe, the following countries were known to have trafficked human beings last year: Albania, Angola, Armenia, Austria, Bahrain, Bangladesh, Belarus, Belgium, Belize, Benin, Bolivia, Bosnia and Herzegovina, Brazil, Brunei, Bulgaria, Burkina Faso, Burundi, Cambodia, Cameroon, Canada, China, Colombia, Costa Rica, Croatia, Cuba, Czech Republic Democratic Republic of the Congo, Denmark, Dominican Republic, El Salvador, Equatorial Guinea, Estonia, Ethiopia, Finland, France, Gabon, Gambia, Georgia, Germany, Ghana, Greece, Guatemala, Haiti, Honduras, Hungary, India, Indonesia, Israel, Italy, Ivory Coast, Jamaica, Japan, Kazakhstan, Kenya, Kuwait, Kyrgyzstan, Laos, Latvia, Lebanon, Liberia, Lithuania, Macedonia, Malawi, Malaysia, Mali, Mauritius, Mexico, Moldova, Morocco, Mozambique, Myanmar, Nepal, Netherlands, Nicaragua, Niger, Nigeria, North Korea, Norway, Pakistan, Philippines, Poland, Portugal, Qatar, Romania, Russia, Rwanda, Saudi Arabia, Senegal, Serbia and Montenegro, Sierra Leone, Slovakia, Slovenia, South Africa, South Korea, Spain, Sri Lanka, Sudan, Suriname, Sweden, Switzerland, Taiwan, Tajikistan, Tanzania, Thailand, Togo, Turkey, Uganda, Ukraine, United Arab Emirates, United Kingdom, United States, Uzbekistan, Venezuela,

Vietnam, Zambia, and Zimbabwe (Cockburn, 2003, p. 12). The estimated contribution of slavery to the global economy is $13 billion dollars.

• Visions of pastoral serenity notwithstanding, commercial agriculture work is as difficult and dangerous as any. For children, the physical demands of cutting, harvesting and hoeing on poorly mechanized farms or plantations can be overwhelming. In Brazil's sugar plantations, for example, children cut cane with machetes, a punishing task putting them at constant risk of mutilation. According to UNICEF, child workers involved in commercial agriculture make up a third of the workforce in some areas and are involved in over 40% of the work related accidents (Human Rights Watch, 2000; UNICEF, 1997). Pesticides pose another serious danger to children working on plantations. With the excessive use of pesticides, children are especially susceptible to pesticide exposure-related disease and death because of their developmental stage. A recent ILO report concludes that in rural areas, more children die of exposure to pesticides than from the most common childhood diseases put together (Human Rights Watch, 2000).

Let us now turn to child labor as practiced in the industrialized United States.

THE U.S. EXPERIENCE IN PERSPECTIVE

In 1916, U.S. President Woodrow Wilson signed into law an act regulating the use of child labor in industry. The Supreme Court of the United States struck down the law in 1918, but in 1938, with adoption of the Fair Labor Standards Act, the United States banned the use of child labor altogether. While the ban still suffers from serious enforcement problems, the widely held belief is that the widespread use of child labor in the United States has been effectively eradicated.

Most Americans believe that exploitative child labor is a problem mainly of the developing world and that if it exists at all in the U.S., it is an isolated phenomenon found only at the far fringes of society, affecting highly marginalized groups such as migrant farmworker children, the children of deaf Mexicans in New York City who sell trinkets on the subways, or workers from Thailand imprisoned in a factory in California. Unfortunately, this view is far from accurate. Child labor – in both its legal and illegal forms-is widespread in the U.S. (Cockburn, 2003; Human Rights Watch, 2000). Modern child labor has positive as well as negative aspects. On the plus side, legal work such as babysitting, grocery bagging, lawn work, and odd jobs can encourage the development of discipline, teach a child or teen the meaning of money, and provide valuable role models. But on the negative side, exploitative and illegal child labor is as tragic now as it was 100 years ago.

One just needs to know where to look. Across the U.S., child labor accounts for more than 20,000 workers compensation claims, 200,000 injuries, thousands of cases of permanent disability, and more than 70 deaths per year (Landrigan & McCammon, 1997). Agriculture and newspaper delivery are the two most hazardous areas of employment for children and adolescents. Poverty, massive immigration and relaxation in enforcement of federal child labor law are the three factors principally responsible for the last two decades resurgence of child labor in the U.S.

No one knows how many adolescents work in agriculture in the United States. Farmworkers aged seventeen and younger – all considered children under U.S. and international law – can be found working all across the country (Human Rights Watch, 2000). Particularly large populations of farmworkers live and work in California, Texas, Florida, Washington and Arizona. Migrant streams travel up each year through the Midwest, the eastern seaboard and into New York. Virtually no state in the U.S. is without child labor in agriculture, and certainly no state is without its fruits, as the produce that is harvested and picked by youngsters' hands, may travel thousands of miles to grocery store shelves. Farmworkers in the U.S. include both migrant and seasonal agricultural workers. Migrant workers are those whose work requires them to be absent overnight from their permanent place of residence. In practice, many may be absent from their permanent homes for months at a time. Seasonal agricultural workers are those whose work does not require an overnight absence from their permanent residences.

In the U.S., children come to agriculture at varying ages. Reports of children as young as four or five working alongside their parents are not uncommon (Human Rights Watch, 2000). Full time agricultural work, whether during school vacations and weekends or year-round, usually begins in early adolescence. Twelve hour days are routine, as are six and seven-day work weeks. During peak harvesting seasons, children may work fourteen, sixteen, or even eighteen hours a day, seven days a week. Whether paid by the hour or on the basis of piece rates, child laborers are not paid overtime wages – since U.S.the law does not require it. Health and safety risks include, in addition to exposure to pesticides, the lack of adherence to minimal sanitation requirements; lack of toilet and hand washing facilities; and, lack of drinking water. The foregoing does not even consider work related illnesses due to hazardous conditions and work related injuries due to hazardous equipment. The special risks to farmworker girls is particularly compelling, for they are exceptionally vulnerable to sexual harassment and assault.

Child labor in less severe conditions can also be brutal and interfere with children's physical, intellectual and emotional development. "The physical harm is ... the easiest to see," explains UNICEF's *The State of the World's Children (1997).* "Carrying heavy loads or sitting for long periods in unnatural positions can permanently disable growing bodies," by stunting physical stature by up to 30% of biological potential (p. 12). "Children are also vulnerable psychologically," the report continues. "They can suffer devastating psychological damage from being in an environment in which they are demeaned or oppressed" (p. 12).

SEARCHING FOR CAUSES

Poverty and child labor are intertwined. Brutalized child laborers are almost exclusively poor. Children typically work to earn money for their families or to help pay off family debts. Wealthier families do not need or permit their children to labor at the expense of education and physical, intellectual and emotional development. But poverty is not, by itself the cause of child labor. The fact that rates of child labor vary dramatically between countries of similar levels of economic development proves this point most clearly. In China, for example, there has been little child labor in recent decades, according to U.S. diplomatic sources. Even though extremely poor until recent years, China made a political decision to puts its children in school, rather than on the work rolls. Similarly, Kerala State, in India, the country most famous for abuse of child labor, has virtually abolished child labor (Multinational Monitor, 1995). The lesson that emerges from the China and Kerala examples is that child labor can only exist where it is treated as politically and culturally acceptable.

Many countries have strong traditions of tolerating child labor and these traditions often combine with prejudices against ostracized and undervalued populations. The result is widespread child labor among certain poor ethnic groups. Similarly, discriminatory attitudes toward women and girls may undergird parents' willingness to send their daughters off to prostitution, or to be domestic servants. Where education is compulsory, available and understood to be relevant, child labor rates decline. "Education is one of the keys that will unlock the prison cell of hazardous labor in which so many children are confined," UNICEF, 2000, p. 55). On the demand side, research shows that many children are hired because they are more easily exploited than adults (U.S. Department of Labor (2001, 2002). Employers prefer children because they are docile, incapable of collective bargaining and willing to work to support their family or simply to survive.

Since England's industrialization, employers have justified their reliance on child labor by claiming children offer unique skills – "nimble fingers" – in certain areas. But the ILO reports that its research in hazardous industries in India, and elsewhere, including carpet making, glass factories, mining, lock making and gem polishing, has shown this argument to be entirely fallacious. Even in the hand-knotting of carpets, which calls for considerable dexterity, an empirical study of over 2,000 weavers found that children were no more likely than adults to make the finest knots," (Human Rights Watch, 1996, p. 44).

GLOBALIZATION AND CHILD LABOR

All of these factors – poverty, cultural traditions, prejudice against ethnic, religious or racial groups, discrimination against girls, inadequate access to education and employer desires for cheap and docile labor – have existed for centuries. What is new in the child labor equation is economic globalization. The most obvious contribution globalization is making to the increase in child labor is its intensification of price competition for global consumer markets. As competitors in the global market look for ways to lower costs, exploitative child labor provides the solution by which cost containment can take place, amidst a submissive and docile workforce. In the absence of law enforcement, an unregulated industry continues unabated.

This unregulated competition is responsible in significant part for children sewing garments in Haiti, Guatemala and Honduras for labels and retailers such as Disney, Kathie Lee Gifford and Wal-Mart and Phillips-Van Heusen, or children making toys for sale in the U.S. market (U.S. Department of Labor, 1995, 2000). The foregoing instances of child labor have received the greatest attention in the United States in recent years. Even in China, where child labor has long been minimized, there are reports that child labor is increasing rapidly in the low-wage export industries of the Pearl River Delta in the southeast.

The number of children working in the export-oriented sectors of the economy is small in proportional terms, however. The U.S. Department of Labor (2002, 2001) estimates child labor in the export sector at approximately 5%, although international price competition – including goods sold domestically in competition with foreign imports and as inputs for products to be exported – may raise the proportion somewhat.

There are other, less obvious, but still important ways that globalization is contributing to an increase in child labor. Cheap agricultural exports to the Third World and promotion of export-oriented agriculture in developing countries have rocked the social structure in rural communities across the globe. Relying on violence, coercion or sometimes impersonal market forces, plantation owners have ejected many rural families from their land, depriving them of their livelihood and leaving them with narrow economic options. Some have taken work on plantations, where children are likely to be employed as well; some move to urban slums, where children may search for jobs to support their family; and, some send their children to urban areas to earn cash to support their families.

In Brazil, reports the U.S. Department of Labor (2002, 2001), the agricultural sector underwent a major transformation in the 1980s. Large-scale plantations became increasingly mechanized and export-oriented, and land became concentrated in the hands of large agricultural businesses. Both resident workers on plantations and small farmers expelled from their land joined the ranks of migrant and temporary workers that became known as "boias-frias" or "volantes." Because the earnings of many families diminished considerably, they increasingly employed children to bolster family income. Today, child "boias-frias" and "volantes" comprise a large number of Brazil's child workers (Buckley, 2000).

In Southeast Asia, urbanization and impoverishment of rural economies are important factors encouraging families to sell their girls into prostitution (Cockburn, 2003; Warren, 2003). The rise in child prostitution is also linked to the growth of international sex tourism, another global industry as well as a particularly unsavory manifestation of globalization.

At the macro- economic level, the International Monetary Fund (IMF) and World Bank's imposition of structural adjustment policies on Third World economies has strengthened many of the trends contributing to child labor (UNICEF, 2000). As a condition for receiving further loans, the IMF and World Bank instruct indebted Third World countries to promote exports and cut government spending. In many cases, governments pressed by the IMF and World Bank to reduce spending have reduced expenditures for education, as well. In recent years, however, the World Bank, in particular, has recognized the importance of education and health care, and has urged governments to maintain programs in these areas as investments in human capital. The World Bank has also encouraged governments to charge students for attending school, or for books and supplies – a so-called cost-recovery approach. However, such an approach may be self-defeating for even small fees prevent poor families from sending some or all of their children to school, and those unable to afford school, frequently choose work over school.

The Myth of Inevitability

Given the multiple overlapping causes of child labor, no single approach will end the scourge. Most serious analysts agree that complementary approaches are needed. Yet, it is a widely held belief that child labor is an inevitable consequence of poverty: that is, child labor is a necessary first step to help countries develop economically. On the other hand, the economic growth and prosperity of a nation are key to eliminating child labor.

The pertinent fact is that child labor perpetuates poverty, generates it and regenerates it. Children who work become sickly adults and a drain on national economies. With little if any education, they are less productive workers as adults. Simply put, children fill jobs that adults would otherwise occupy. In every country with high rates of child labor, there is a severe unemployment problem, with adults' skills, creativity and labor wasted. Conscious and purposeful intervention is needed to make meaningful inroads in eradicating child labor.

Some Third World non-governmental groups have taken direct action in workplaces, conducting raids to rescue bonded and forced child laborers (Weissman, 1997). While these raids cannot directly reach a significant proportion of child laborers, they have focused attention on the issue. The experience of these groups has also revealed the importance of establishing rehabilitative programs for children removed from brutal laboring conditions. Such children need access to educational facilities, physical treatment and psychological counseling. Third world national governments have the most important role to play in eliminating child labor. They must first create national laws banning the use of child labor, and then enforce those laws. In addition, governments must ban the use of child labor, provide quality universal education for children and, ensure that cultural traditions and prejudices are not allowed to override national commitments to child-free workplaces, in the quest for human rights and human dignity.

Most countries have chosen not to crack down on child labor, but there are increasing possibilities to bring pressure to bear on those who do not act on their own. With national economies becoming more interwoven, the children stitching clothes in Haiti or India or Thailand are more likely than ever before, exporting such goods to the United States, Germany, or other industrialized country consumers. This fact, alone, gives industrialized governments and consumers the power to influence Third world country child labor practices. As Northern consumers have expressed increasing concern about the conditions under which the products they buy are made, many corporations have adopted codes of conduct for their overseas operations and especially for overseas contractors. For example, the U.S. Department of Labor's (2002) survey of major garment manufacturers, designers and retailers found that many had adopted codes of conduct with provisions specifically prohibiting the use of child labor in the manufacture of goods they imported. These corporate codes may have little effect, however, because they are not only poorly monitored, but virtually none of the codes call for independent monitoring.

A potentially more reliable means of purging goods made with child labor from international commerce are labeling programs. The most prominent child labor related labeling scheme is the Rugmark program, an international project which certifies carpets are made without use of child labor. Not all internationally traded goods lend themselves to labeling, however. Despite Rugmark's considerable success, the delays in getting the program off the ground and the voluntary nature of the program suggest the labeling approach will not be a comprehensive solution to child labor, even in international markets.

In conclusion, it is clear that a comprehensive approach to abolishing child labor will require not only intervention by industrialized country consumers and governments, but strong political commitments by governments in the developed and developing world. Whether countries can muster that political commitment in an era when the pressures of globalization are exacerbating the conditions leading to the use of exploitative child labor, remains to be seen.

REFERENCES

Barber, B. R. (1996). *Jihad vs. McWorld*. New York: Ballantine.

Buckley, S. (March 16, 2000). The littlest labors: In a wealthier world, children still hard at work. *Washington Post*, Al.

Cockburn, A. (2003). 21st century slaves. *National Geographic, 204*(3), 2–29.

Human Rights Watch (2000). *Fingers to the bone. United States failure to protect child farmworkers*. New York, NY: Human Rights Watch.

Human Rights Watch (1996). The small hands of slavery: Bonded child labor in India. http://www.hrw.org/hrw/reports/1996/India3.htm.

International Program on the Elimination of Child Labor (IPEC) at a Glance (2001). http://www.ilo.org/public/english/standards/ipec/about/implementation/ipec.htm.

International Program on the Elimination of Child Labor (IPEC) at a Glance (July/August 1995). Kerala state: A social justice model. *Multinational Monitor* (pp. 37–49).

Landrigan, P. J., & McCammon, J. B. (1997, November/December). Child labor. *Public Health Reports* (pp. 466–473).

Lechner, F. J., & Boli, J. (2000). *The globalization reader*. Oxford, England: Blackwell.

Save the Children Fund (2000). Small hands, children in the working world. Working Paper No. 16. United Kingdom: Save the Children Fund.

Statistics on Working Children (2001). http://www.ilo.org/public/english/standards/ipec/simpoc/stats/child/stats.htm.

Stiglitz, J. E. (2002). *Globalization and Its discontents*. New York: W. W. Norton.

United Nations Children's Fund (UNICEF) (1997). *The state of the world's children*. New York, NY: United Nation's Children's Fund.

United Nations Children's Fund (UNICEF) (2002). *The state of the world's children*. New York, NY: United Nation's Children's Fund.

U.S. Department of Labor (1995). *By the sweat and toil of children: Consumer labels and child labor*. Washington, DC: U.S.DOL.

U.S. Department of Labor (2000). *By the sweat and toil of children: An economic consideration of child labor*. Washington, DC: USDOL.

U.S. Department of Labor (2001). *Findings on the worst forms of child labor*. Washington, DC: U.S. Deparment of Labor, Bureau of International Labor Affairs.

U.S. Department of Labor (2002). *Advancing the campaign against child labor. Efforts at the country level*. Washington, DC: U.S. Department of Labor, Bureau of International Labor Affairs.

Warren, L. (2003, September). Inhuman profit. *National Geographic, 204*(3), 26–29.

Weissman, R. (1997, January/February). Stolen youth, brutalized children, globalization and the campaign to end child labor. *Multinational Monitor* (pp. 10–16).

13. CHILD PROTECTION AND SURVIVAL IN SOUTHERN AFRICA: FOCUS ON CHILD WELFARE POLICY IN NAMIBIA

Rodney K. Hopson

INTRODUCTION: INHERITING A LEGACY OF DESTRUCTION AND DESOLATION

The impact of apartheid, destabilization, and warfare in southern Africa has especially taken a severe and unimaginable toll on the future and life chances of children in the region. Prior to 1990 when a series of significant events changed the social and economic landscape of the sub-continent, a number of disturbing profiles and trends pointed to a desolate situation for children and women by most child welfare, household, poverty, education, and health indicators. As a result of massive underdevelopment compounded by war and economic destabilization for decades, only aggravated by colonialism and post-colonial policies, the health and welfare of children in southern Africa had reached tragic proportions.

A 1989 report for United Nations Children's Fund (UNICEF) described how children fell victim to brutal holocausts which had become synonymous with southern Africa (Asrat et al., 1989). It depicted a region where the plights of children were unparalleled anywhere else in the world. Of a population of some 3.5 million children in the then nine country Southern African Development

'Suffer the Little Children': National and International Dimensions of Child
Poverty and Public Policy
Advances in Education in Diverse Communities: Research, Policy and Praxis, Volume 4, 307–334
Copyright © 2006 by Elsevier Ltd.
All rights of reproduction in any form reserved
ISSN: 1479-358X/doi:10.1016/S1479-358X(04)04013-6

Co-ordination Community (SADC),[1] 750,000 died before 5 years of age, a fifth of which were attributed to the impact of conflict. In particular, two countries then on the eve of widespread changes stood out: Angola and Mozambique where over 11 million people in both countries had been driven from their homes at least once, according to conservative estimates, nearly half of the population being refugees in their own countries. Of the over 1 million people killed directly or indirectly in the 1980s due to open warfare between the governments and rebels, women and children were the primary victims to mass murder, rape, arson, and other destructible conflicts. An estimated 850,000 infants and children perished as a result, totaling more than the number of U.S. soldiers lost in wars since 1776.

The susceptibility of children to social and economic destruction is evident in broad terms when one recognizes the snowballing effect of forced migration, mass armed destruction and conflict. As evident of this utter destruction and desolation, child health, malnutrition, and mortality were directly affected and revealed broader ramifications on nutrition and food security for these children, their education and literacy, and household incomes of poor and vulnerable groups. The result of profound social and economic decline throughout the 1980s adversely affected the situation of children in most southern African countries where some twenty-five children every hour were dying from effects and after-effects of war in the region and another twenty suffered as victims of economic pressures, of basic social service deterioration, and of food scarcities (Balch et al., 1995) (Fig. 1).

Whereas this legacy of apartheid, destabilization, and warfare has shaped most of the latter part of the 20th century, the cusp of the 20th and 21st century has brought dramatic sociopolitical and economic transformation in the sub-region of the continent. Winds of change throughout southern Africa manifest among nearly all countries in the region. Most notably since 1990, the process of peace and reconciliation has spread throughout, with independence in Namibia, democratic elections in Mozambique, multi-party electoral systems in Lesotho, Malawi, and Zambia, and the elimination of apartheid in South Africa (Balch et al., 1995). The prospects for a healthy, productive, and prosperous southern Africa in the new millennium, for the first time in decades, not only seem doable and hopeful, the social change apparent has gained momentum in recent years. While successes in terms of child protection, survival and development are apparent from examples of priorities to the eradication of poverty, empowerment and participation of children and women across sectors, and attention to pressing issues that affect children, insurmountable challenges, however, remain in the region as a result of the destructive and debilitating legacy of profound social and economic deprivation caused by decades of apartheid and destabilization.

As the sub-region braces itself for peace and national reconciliation, it is necessary to give analysis to impending issues that protect the survival and

Economic costs of Destabilization	USD, in millions
Direct war damage	1, 610
Extra defence spending	3, 060
Higher transport, energy costs	970
Smuggling/looting	190
Refugees (including internal displaced persons)	660
Export loss	230
Boycotts, embargoes	260
Loss of existing production	800
Lost economic growth	2, 000
Trading arrangements	340
TOTAL (1980–1984)	**10, 120**
1985	7, 000
1986	8, 000
1987	9, 000
1988	10, 000
TOTAL	**44, 120**

Fig. 1. SADCC Estimate of Economic Costs of Sestabilization, 1980–1988. *Note:* The macro-economic costs of wars in southern Africa largely include destruction of assets, enforced military expenditure, higher transport costs, lost output, and need for relief and survival support to refugees and displaced person. Figures above reflect estimates based on totaling particular costs and the economic growth loses resulting from reduced investment as taken from the then-Southern African Development Co-ordination Conference figures in 1985. The estimates and increases from 1985 relate to escalation of conflict, the rising defence expenditures, cumulative output losses, and inflation. *Source:* Asrat et al. (1989).

development of its children. This chapter provides a discussion of child welfare in southern Africa, especially amidst the context of post-apartheid nation states in the region. In keeping with the aim of the book, this chapter examines a plethora of issues that inhibit childrens' chances as well as the contexts in which poverty occur for the southern African child. It is worth noting that whereas apartheid was directly "administered" in only two countries of the region: Namibia and South Africa, the indirect implications to apartheid had far-reaching implications to the entire sub-continent.

The aim of the paper is not to limit discussion on the countries where apartheid was carried out in the rule of law, but to extend analysis of child poverty and policy where policies of destabilization of the region were suffered by all. This is not a comprehensive analysis applicable to the whole southern African region largely due to incredibly diverse historical processes of colonialist and capitalist relations; rather, the aim of this essay is to present a general analysis of comparable social and economic life transformations whereby common trends and patterns are identified.

Additionally, in examining the general social welfare of children in the sub-region of the continent it goes without stating that that policies that relate to child protection, survival and development can not be totally isolated from the status and protection of women; hence key issues that relate to women's rights and their status find their way into the analysis of this paper. Still, efforts will be made to single out the issues that relate to child policy and welfare in the southern Africa.

In particular, the paper will focus on the Republic of Namibia as an example, one that is characterized by both its legacy of destruction due to apartheid as well as opportunity for hope and national reconciliation promoted during the first ten years of independence. In the Namibian case study, illustrations of governmental and non-governmental decision-making around child welfare during its first eleven years of independence reveal how this one country addresses the topics of child protection, survival, and development. By illustrating the case study of Namibia in the context of the larger region, attention is paid to the educational, social, legal, political, and economic realities of this country and the critical issues that face Namibian children in their development and social change within this fledgling democracy. One could argue that focus on this previous decade may not necessarily depict a true evaluation of the events to occur, considering longer periods of apartheid and colonialism; nevertheless, the aim of the paper is to generally reflect and give thought to the critical issues that face this post-apartheid nation within a more revealing context of southern Africa and continent.

CONCEPTUALIZING CHILD PROTECTION IN GLOBAL PERSPECTIVE

Violence, exploitation, and abuse of children represent a global phenomena, hardly restricted to the southern part of Africa. It is estimated that in the decade of the

1990s, an estimated 2 million children were killed in armed conflict and three times that number have been wounded or disabled as a result of this conflict, including over a third of those people maimed or killed by landmines each year. Regarding exploitation, nearly one million children enter the global sex market each year and some 250 million children between the ages of 5 and 14 in developing countries work full or part time (UNICEF, 2000a). These statistics which describe the pervasive nature of child abuse, violence, and exploitation by themselves reveal little about the interrelated conditions which emanate in global contexts. A complex interplay of socioeconomic, political, legal, and cultural forces contribute to child violence, exploitation, and abuse and must be analyzed if particular conditions related to child protection are understood and proper interventions are designed.

Considering economic conditions, child protection issues are inextricably linked with structural and poverty situations in developing countries. For instance, poverty levels in developing countries have risen and the gap between rich and poor is increasing as a result of globalization of the world economy and structural adjustment programs. As a consequence to governments in developing countries who attempt to keep up with economic global demands, their own commitment and ability to provide safety nets for their own citizens is severely strained. A lack of a developing countries' governments to meet the social welfare needs of its citizens at a structural level compounds at the household level where families find themselves unable to provide basic necessities, encouraging commercial exploitation of children through labor or sex and who are furthermore more vulnerable to military recruitment and organized crime in urban areas (UNICEF, 2000a) (Fig. 2).

The collapse of nation states in Europe and Africa have brought with it rampant violence within and sometimes beyond the borders of the conflicting areas. Control mechanisms usually stable during times of peace experience disintegration from violence and economic disruption. Significant fundamental political change in some cases or little change in others, inevitably lead to a breakdown of social systems. The severity of the breakdown may result in widespread unemployment, aggravating the political life of certain groups who may turn to violence in defense of their own rights. Children and youth, traditionally the most vulnerable to risk taking, suffer for lack of full participation in society as well as access to adequate political and religious outlets, only further aggravating the tendency to violence.

Cultural norms also play a role in understanding the context for lack of child protection in nation states around the globe. The physical abuse and chastisement of children and women may not only be culturally acceptable in some societies, so too is child marriage, child labor or domestic work to support family economic means. Related to cultural norms are religious practices that may condone violence and child sexual exploitation.

Recruitment by force (press-ganged, kidnapped, conscription....)

Economic reasons to join guarantees meals, medial attention

Participation of children as soldiers (or in supporting roles)

Threat of rape and sexual humiliation as weapon of war

Sexual exploitation and gender-based violence

Prostitution in exchange for food, shelter, safety

Physical and health dangers due to flight

Population movements and refugee children

Emotional and developmental issues related to family separation

Compounding and Interlinking Problems of Children at Risk of Armed Conflict

Destroying of schools and school networks

Education

Lower quality of education due to fleeing teachers, lack of funding, administrative support

Greater spread of sexually transmitted diseases

Health and nutrition

Inadequate attention to reproductive health services and water/sanitation systems

Disintegration of Families

Interruption of food supplies and destruction of food crops/ agriculture systems

Fig. 2.   Compounding and Interlinking Problems of Children at Risk of Armed Conflict. *Source:* Adapted from UN General Assembly, 1996.

Though international human rights laws allow individuals the right to be free from violence, exploitation, and abuse, significant ramifications occur when international legal standards are not integrated at a domestic level which may be due to lack of political will or political support, political or economic corruption which undermines the rule of flaw, and particular interests of the political elite. The further lack of confidence by the civil society to insist on protection of human rights has a compounding effect on the sociolegal conditions of child protection in respective nation states.

A discussion and debate on conceptualizing child protection can not occur without treatment to the challenges of globalization. The effect of globalization potentially influences all of the interlinking and associated conditions which threaten or ensure child protection, survival, and development. It is interesting to note that efforts to rid many African countries of colonialism during the 1960s and 1970s were stalled as problems of economic dependency in the 1970s and 1980s led to the inability of the state to provide welfare services to the larger populace (Olukoshi & Laakso, 1996).

In plain terms, post-colonial Africa's entrée into the international economic market had its ebbs and flows. With the hope of nation-building at independence, most African governments benefited from post-colonial economic booms and implemented top-down approaches aimed at vigorous social and economic modernization campaigns. Engulfed by the larger international economic environment, African governments too fell victim to global recession in the 1980s and shifting economic policies all over the world. Laakso and Olukoshi describe the shift from welfarist principles to neo-liberal principles that placed "greater weight on market forces and the struggle against inflation whilst simultaneously downgrading the Keynesian goal of full employment and the role of the state in the economy" (1996, p. 17). This ideology, as they explain, not only fed into the process of globalization strengthened by the collapse of the Soviet bloc, the disintegration of the Soviet Union and the adoption of market-based economic reforms by former socialist states of eastern Europe, the free-market agenda lay feed for the development of and exacerbation of the debt crisis promulgated by the International Monetary Fund (IMF) and the World Bank. The results of the structural adjustment and donor-led initiatives underpin an integral part of the dynamic crisis in post-colonial Africa, largely manifest in deepening social fragmentation, inequality, and divisions among class lines and disillusionment with independence.

Complex too are the positions of children related to the concept of the child's best interest relative to the changing economic and social transformations that have permeated Africa. As Rwezaura documents (1994), the changing context of Africa in regards to the introduction of colonial rule and the penetration of capitalist relations has had a tremendous impact on the status and welfare of children. For instance, the use of bridewealth (though many African societies have a specific name for it, such as lobola, bogadi, or bohali as it is known in areas of the southern sub-continent) marriage payments in traditional African societies where transfer of resources are used to validate marriage and symbolize the husband's families possession of all the wife bears and owns, has taken on new economic and social character (from livestock to the use of cash, as marriage payment). While the transformation of bridewealth had direct implications to the authority of elders who were responsible for initiating the process of marriage and narrowing the obligation to pay for one's marriage, the corresponding impact on children was as obvious. Among the consequences of the transformation of bridewealth were most notably changing notions of how courts settle disputes in handling child-rearing and maintenance debts from fathers as well as the shifting balance of power and authority in marriage relationships from the community to the family. Rwezaura illustrates how the growing conflicts over scarce resources became linked with competition over childrens' rights:

> As husbands struggled to raise the necessary resources to marry, they began to feel entitled to exercise authority over their wives as well as over their children. This authority was given blessing by the colonial state which began to order husbands to meet the cost of child rearing. Besides the obvious inclination for men to maximize returns from a marriage relationship, there was also the problem created by the weakening of kinship ties which created insecurity and thus motivated men to expand their immediate families by having more children (pp. 99–100).

The trend has been, in a changing context of sub-Saharan Africa, as noted by Rwezaura, for capitalist relations to penetrate traditional systems and reinforce an ethos of individualism. That is, the inevitable change of traditional marriage systems which served to link and maintain social cohesion between two groups or families was transformed as the cost of marriages became more concentrated in single families or on individual males. This effect would change not only husband's relationships in the household and their own expectations of their role as provider and head of the household but the role of the state too would witness changing roles and expectations in postcolonial sub-Saharan Africa. The State, in Rwezaura's analysis, while being concerned with protecting childrens' interests, is however not able to provide the necessary economic capacity to support families, further shifting the concept of the best interest of the child to be equated more to material needs and interests rather than traditional notions of community and extended family participation. In cases where children are most at-risk of living under extreme living conditions in the case of war, economic deprivation, and disease, a further burden is placed on the family and the general society.

ISSUES AFFECTING CHILD LIFE CHANCES IN THE CONTEXT OF SOUTHERN AFRICA

A constellation of issues portray the grave situation that affect children in the southern African region. Rather than focus on one, this section offers a view of several impending issues that affect child life chances; in this manner, one observes the compounding and complex result of apartheid, destabilization, and warfare on health, education, poverty and general social and economic neglect.

The Legacy of Apartheid in Health

The legacy of apartheid in the health can be portrayed a number of ways. Most notably, access to quality health care services and the increasing alarm to HIV/AIDS are perhaps the most critical concerns relative to the legacy of apartheid and destabilization in the health sector.

The characteristic of inequality of access to services due to public and legal apartheid has most clearly left a detrimental impact on the life chances of children. The fragmentation of basic health services and widespread disparity between those living within homelands or Bantustans and those living outside these self-governing states were markedly clear in South Africa, for instance. The challenges pertaining to child health and nutrition in the KwaZulu Natal Province are among the most severe in the country where over half of these children live in poverty, nearly 40% have vitamin A deficiency, and one quarter of the children in rural areas are stunted (UNICEF, 1998).

McKerrow and Fincham describe these marked differences in quality of health care in one health ward within the KwaZulu Natal Province as a result of the unequal allocation of resources and disproportionate cycles of violence associated with the struggle against apartheid (1995). Their case study suggests that these inequalities in health were most revealed by the unavailability of health care due to the increase in political violence; that is, as social and political unrest increased during an eight year period between the mid 1980s to mid 1990s, public health residential clinic hours of operation diminished significantly. Opened for a 24 hour period 90% in 1986, the health care clinics not only did not remain open for a 24 hour period by 1993, they operated eight hours per day nearly 75% of the time and the rest of the time they remain closed. As expected, patient attendance during this same period showed similar drastic decreases at clinics in the region, due to the reduction of services caused by decrease of clinics and clinic hours of operation. Consequently, the violence and lack of quality basic health services had consequences to the children in the health ward, as their health and nutritional status decreased, resources to address the totality of their handicaps were limited, and the number of abandoned and orphaned children rose.

Severely complicating the issue and challenge of reconstructing child welfare and health is the HIV/AIDS pandemic in the region. A number of reports depict the state of the HIV/AIDS pandemic in sub-Saharan Africa, especially in southern Africa during the last decade (Green et al., 1991; GRN/UNICEF, 2000; Moeti, 1995; NIEP, 1995; UNICEF, 2000b; USAID, 2001). In one year – 1998, two million people died as a result of AIDS compared to an estimated 200,000 as a result of armed conflict. Its impact over this last decade, in fact, is greater than the combined destruction of the continent's wars. Throughout the sub-Saharan region, some 22 million people are currently infected with HIV (two-thirds of the total global population of HIV-infected men and women), as the pandemic annihilates entire families, villages, professions, and age groups. In particular, the disease has preyed on young and poor girls and women, only contributing to the socioeconomic devastation of the region. Of the nine countries with the highest adult HIV/AIDS prevalence, the southern African region is by far disproportionately affected compared to the rest of the continent, as depicted in Fig. 3.

In Zambia which now has one of the highest HIV infection rates on the African continent, the catastrophy of the disease accounts for over a third of a million children who have lost at least one parent to AIDS. Life expectancy, over the last ten years has dropped by ten years to forty years of age and child mortality rates are rising to levels not seen for thirty years. The combining effect of the country's social and economic decline has only provided opportunity for AIDS to flourish, where some 70,000 formal sector jobs were lost in the early to mid 1990s and resources to combat the disease are severely constrained by foreign debt which accounts for more than the Zambian Government's health and education budget combined (UNICEF, 2000b).

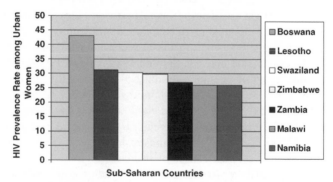

Fig. 3. Highest Median HIV Prevalence Rate Among Sub-Saharan Urban Women in Antenatal Care Clinics. *Source:* UNAIDS, 2000.

In highlighting the growing crisis facing countries largely believed to have suffered the least from the impact of apartheid and destabilization in the sub-region, namely in Swaziland and Botswana, Moeti portrays how rural and urban districts of these two countries have witnessed rapid increases in HIV seroprevalence in the early to mid 1990s.[2] That the countries neighboring South Africa have been affected by the complex socioeconomic problems caused by apartheid and destabilization is especially evident in the spread of HIV. Moeti further describes a number of social factors, specifically extreme population mobility, the dispersal of communities and families, and subsequent breakdown within traditional networks and institutions due to a century of male migrant labor which further encouraged multi-partner sexual behavior, a deterioration of social norms and male responsibility in community and family welfare matters. Exacerbated by extreme disparate levels of poverty among women and women-headed households whose strategies for economic survival often depend on multiple partners and prostitution and largely unchecked HIV incidence data where full-scale civil wars pervade like in Angola and Mozambique, the legacy of apartheid and destabilization on HIV will be realized for decades to come.

These HIV/AIDS challenges place a particular and cumbersome burden on children. Two implications pose increasing alarms, namely AIDS-related illnesses and a growing number of children left without adequate care as a result of AIDS in the southern African region. AIDS-related illnesses, according to Moeti (1995), are primary causes of death in children under five years of age, overtaking malaria and diarrheal diseases as the number one killer. To make matters worse are increasing accounts in South Africa of child abandonment cases in hospitals by parents and families of children with HIV-related diseases, hundreds of thousands of children orphaned by AIDS, and an escalating number of child-headed households in more and more communities in the sub-region. A signal for troubling times ahead in the region, children orphaned due to AIDS face unique circumstances only now being realized, due to a combination of characteristics, namely the huge scale of the problem, a weakened social and economic AIDS infrastructure responsible for combating the disease at governmental and nongovernmental levels, less than adequate social support systems, and socio-cultural stigmas related to the disease (UNAIDS/UNICEF, 1998).

The Legacy of Apartheid in Education

Just as historical and structural inequalities persisted in health, the specter of apartheid and regional destabilization were profound in education where gross disparities existed between race, province, and class, especially in South Africa (Chisolm & Motala, 1995; Junabhai, 1995; UNICEF/NCRC, 1993). Inherent in the context of the legacy of apartheid existed complex patterns of disparity manifest in drop out rates, low teacher qualifications and overcrowded classrooms at all educational levels – primary, secondary, and tertiary (Cross & Chisolm, 1990; Unterhalter, 1991). Like in health, issues of accessibility, quality, equity, and democracy consisted of the major stumbling blocks in education.

The result of massive migration into urban areas and development of informal settlements of South Africa due to apartheid contributed to little or no provision for schooling for large numbers of children. Reporting findings from educational research in the country, Chisolm and Motala show that while primary school enrollments were relatively high, as were the numbers of potential children at primary school age and of all ages not at school (1995). Levels of disparity and inequity were particularly acute when comparing between black and white schooling, evident in disproportionality of children of school-going age not in school and of children who reach senior secondary classes, the time it requires to complete different phases of school, high teacher pupil ratios, curricular and pedagogical materials and practices, and inequities in the structural financing of an ethnically fragmented educational system.

The result of one United Nations Children's Fund/National Child Rights Committee situation analysis of children in education and development on the eve of the eradication of legislative apartheid in South Africa reports that the most disadvantaged and marginalized in South African society had the least access to education. That is, while a quarter of the population of those classified as African had no schooling, lowest levels of primary and secondary school attainment were likely to be African or colored and living in white designated rural areas and in homelands. In cases where children and youth are resident on white farms, these children generally not only start school at a later age, child labor is common practice and children tend to be poorly nourished, contributing to farm schools believed to be the worst off in the educational system with highest drop out rates and the worst facilities. Further, services for children with special needs in the self-governing territories and the independent homelands were grossly under-resourced with 80% of the total special student population being African but with only 20% of the children having access to these services, compared to whites with 8.5% of the student population receiving 40% of special education benefits (UNICEF/NCRC, 1993).

The educational apartheid in South Africa extended beyond its borders, creating a spiraling influence on other nation states. Simão documents the spillover effect in Angola, for instance, where the human, material, and financial resources of war and armed conflict have obstructed attendance and matriculation in schools, largely attributed to the South African government's financial and material support of the armed opposition, the National Union for the Total Independence of Angola

(UNITA) (1995). The massive destruction of economic and social infrastructures was clearly visible in education, where the destruction of schools buildings and the august exodus of rural populations to urban areas were characteristic of the 1980s and 1990s.

The effect the war had on children who would suffer from the increases in pressure in urban schools and general lack of attention given to them has contributed to the loss of basic educational rights for most. Where education following independence in Angola witnessed rapid expansion in primary school enrollment and all levels of basic education, this expansion was not matched by similar expansions in educational infrastructure (i.e. procurement of buildings, hiring of teachers, etc . . .) and various teacher improvements. By the 1990–1991 academic year, as a result of these pressures on the educational system, over half of potential school-going children were excluded from school because of a shortage of places and large-scale population displacement due to the political instability of the country. As Simão further notes, of the total number of five year old children, only a fifth could find places in school, compared to nearly six of the ten at the primary school level, only worsening to over 95% of children who have no place in schools between grades five and eight. The catastrophic situation, compounded by full-scale civil war throughout much of the country, reveals a potential trend where Angolan youth, as an example of the wider influence of apartheid in the southern Africa region, will be condemned to illiteracy and insufficient education throughout their school-going ages.

The Legacy of Poverty, Neglect, and Economic Dependency

The southern African regions' picture, leading up to 1990, has been a predictable one in terms of consequences to poverty and neglect. With the exception of two countries: Botswana and Zimbabwe, where relatively good economic and budgetary growth has simultaneously existed with an emphasis on family needs, other southern African nations strained by comparison. While war has contributed most dramatically and terribly on the situation of children in the region, other dynamics play a debilitating role.

A 1991 UNICEF report documents the extremely harsh economic environment that was characteristic of the 1980s for nearly all of the nation states in southern Africa (Green et al., 1991). Here, the authors attribute the declining purchasing power of the SADC countries and increasing regional external debt as contributing to the decline of the region. As examples, they cite the diminished expectation of the coffee and copper exports which surged during the 1970s but followed with dramatic slumps over the next two decades and the irreversible external debt in

Tanzania, Mozambique, Zambia, and Malawi which ballooned to over $25 billion by the 1990s.

As if external economic pressures are not enough, every state in the region had experienced the effects of drought which severely limited food production in the respective countries. The drought-stricken harvests over substantial areas of Mozambique, Tanzania, Malawi, and Botswana have further exacerbated the problems of financing imports of food, drugs and vaccines, and of sustaining national budget expenditures in health, education, water, drought relief, and supplementary feeding (UNICEF, 1989).

The consequence of harsh economic conditions and impoverishment among a large segment of the population has significantly increased participation of children in the labor force, with the displacement and vulnerability of many households in the case of war, declining household incomes and employment and food production significantly and inevitably affecting the vulnerability of children. Where dire economic circumstances dictate in the sub-region, the likelihood of households to encourage children to work in low-income formal employment, in early-entry informal sector activities, or in communal areas is obvious where in many southern African countries, one-half of the population is below 15 years of age. Mhone suggests the reinforcing and complex trends that pervade households where children have become necessary victims of the labor force; they have "emerged as a exploitable labor resource because of pressures at the household level, and because the opportunity cost of their use as labor appears low, both for the households and the employers, no matter how erroneous such a view may be in the long term" (1995, p. 173).

CHILD PROTECTION, SURVIVAL AND DEVELOPMENT IN POST-APARTHEID NAMIBIA

Namibia lies on the southwest coast of Africa, sharing the boundaries with Angola, Zambia, Botswana, and South Africa. With a highly varied geo-physical setting, it is one of the most a sparsely populated countries in the world. The 12th largest country in sub-Saharan Africa, Namibia's base population is small with an estimated 1.6 million people. This figure includes a 100% population increase over a twenty-year period between 1970 and 1991. Other notable characteristics of the population include the following: in 1991, nearly three-fourths (72%) of the population resided in rural areas, 42% of the population were made up of children aged 0–14, and over half of the population were women (UN, 1999).

Namibia is inhabited by different ethnic groups. Indigenous groups include Ovambo, Herero, Damara, Nama, Kavango, Caprivi, San, Tswana, and Baster

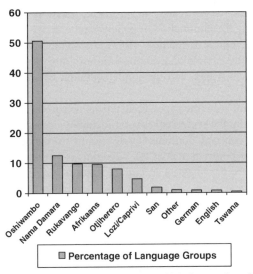

Fig. 4. Population in Namibia by Language Group, 1991. *Source:* Population and Housing Census, 1991 in UNDP, 1999.

groups and a small but economically influential group of Germans, Afrikaaners, and other whites of European descent make up the predominant population. The following figure depicts the distribution of the population by language spoken at home, estimated shortly after independence (Fig. 4).

After 106 years of German and South African rule, Namibia inherited a multitude of consequences due to apartheid imposed by South Africa, none more pronounced than a devastating war in the northern part of the country which inevitably left major obstacles to child life, health, and welfare systems at independence. The pre-independence period was typified by German rule marked by the extermination of over two-thirds of the population of central and southern Namibia on one hand, and South African rule which extended the systematic alienation of land and formalized discrimination into apartheid, on the other. The backdrop of colonial history and armed conflict's disruption on child life was apparent at the founding of the new republic as over 300,000 Namibians were displaced in their own country due to a contract labour system, and another 40,000–100,000 were in exile abroad (of a total population of roughly one and a half million), all further consequences to the legacy of apartheid in the country.[3]

Inherent in the South West African People's Organization (SWAPO), the former liberation movement turned ruling party's strategy and objectives for socio-economic and educational development were the eventual address of regional inequalities, political oppression, and a disintegrated system of social welfare systems, including the elimination of policies and practices of the previous South African colonial regime (Mbamba, 1982). As such, a main goal has been to integrate fragmented homeland administrations into united ones, preservation of civil and human rights, and the implementation of social welfare programs (Tapscott, 1999).

This section concludes the paper, focusing on the current context of independent Namibia, especially the social and economic duality in regards to the provision of resources in the country. It continues by discussing the major actions taken around child welfare and policy issues at the governmental level as well as issues and obstacles facing the life chances and future status of children following ten years of independence.

ONE NAMIBIA, TWO NATIONS

The context of children in the Republic of Namibia is characterized by severe social and economic disparities, largely due to the impact of apartheid, destabilization, and warfare for decades prior to independence in 1990. This legacy of intense child disruption revealed some alarming statistics relative to health and nutrition, household food security, water and sanitation, and basic educational services (Asrat et al., 1989).

One picture of independent Namibia shows a country of great duality and contrast. The almost century of colonial rule clearly benefited the white minority, 5% of the population who controlled about three-fourths of the Gross Domestic Product, earning very high incomes in multinational mining corporations and as settler farmers. In contrast are the black majority who live on very low incomes, notably as communal farmers. The restrictive laws and policies of the previous colonial Afrikaner administration, geared at preventing the majority population from reaping social and economic rewards, disenfranchised black Namibians in all sociopolitical and economic areas of life (Smith, 1986). The situation facing children at independence was characterized by homelessness on the part of those who were in exile, displaced families as a result of the war, unequal distribution of wealth and poverty between blacks and whites, poor basic education and health services due to the fragmented delivery, and low expenditure per capita compared to the privileged white minority (Ithana, 1990).

The disjointed and unequal nature of education was evident for the black population at independence with inadequate schools, ill-prepared teachers, and insufficient teaching materials in the education sector and the lack of primary health care services, inadequate hospitals, and a very small number of doctors in the health sector. Consequently, the most important factor affecting children at independence was alleviating the severe inequality of access to basic social services and productive resources which resulted in blacks being excluded from high-skilled employment and agricultural extension and credit services. Further, the infant mortality rates of 160:1000 were similar to those rates in southern Angola, among the world's worst, a typical situation of the negative impact of war on preventative health services in the sub-region (Morgan, 1990).

When comparing selected quality of life indicators for black Namibians, white Namibians, and black Namibians in exile, it is clear that the social and human costs of apartheid, destabilization in the region, and warfare had a particularly detrimental affect on the majority of black Namibians who stayed in the country during the conflict and occupation prior to the 1990s if one considers life expectancy, infant mortality rates, and other quality of life indicators like those in Fig. 5.[4]

These indicators, revealing as they are, however, only tell part of the story of exiles located outside of the country and a portion of a larger story relative to the socioeconomic obstacles that were present at independence in Namibia.

Another picture of independent Namibia shows a country that has made great strides in the survival and welfare development of children in a few years. The immediate aftermath of independence was characterized by extended services and concerted efforts to expand social welfare to all sectors of the population, from an increase in the number of schools to the provision of safety nets for poor rural households. A number of important strides have occurred in post-apartheid Namibia as they pertain to children's social welfare, namely, the ratification of the UN Convention on the Rights of the Child and subsequent monitoring, over 90% primary school enrollment for school age-going children, an increasing (albeit inconsistent) Human Development Index, and increased access to basic health and educational services. Still, however, major challenges remain that portray Namibia as two nations within one due to the disparate nature of the situation affecting children who seem to be facing both first world and third world scenarios as they relate to their protection, survival, and development.

The third world picture of Namibia is one that re-portrays the scene prior to independence: highest levels of under-nutrition in the world among countries where Gross National Product per capita exceeds USD $1,000 per year, one of the most dualistic economies of the world where the richest 10% of the society receive 65% of income and wealth, and poverty in Namibia correlate highly where one lives and one's home language. Even with an increase of small pockets of wealthy individuals, some of them forming a new black elite, the disparities between language and ethnic groups inherited at independence have remained still a decade later (Fig. 6).

Being white and belonging to either German, English or Afrikaner language groups allow one to enjoy standards of the first world, whereas the majority

	Black Namibians in country	White Namibians in country	Black Namibians in Angola
Population (millions)	1.5	0.1	0.075
Under 5 mortality (per 1,000 births)	235–300	30	70
Infant mortality (per 1,000 births)	175–200	21	50
Access to health services (%)	60	100	100
Access to safe water (%)	33	100	75
Primary school enrollment (%)	60–75	100	100
Adult (over 15) literacy (%)	30	100	75
Life expectancy at birth	40–43	69	NA

Fig. 5. Comparison of Quality of Life Indicators of Namibians, 1986. *Source:* Asrat et al. (1989, p. 63).

Highest Population	Highest Population of "No Educational Attainment"	Highest Human Development Index[6]	Lowest Human Poverty Index[7]
Oshiwambo	San	German	English
Nama Damara	Otjiherero	English	German
Rukavango	Rukavango	Afrikaans	Afrikaans
Afrikaans	Caprivi	Tswana	Tswana
Otjiherero	Oshiwambo	Otjiherero	Lozi/Caprivi
Lozi/Caprivi	Nama/Damara	Oshiwambo	Nama Damara
San	Tswana	Lozi/Caprivi	Otjiherero
German	Afrikaans	Nama Damara	Oshiwambo
English	German	Rukavango	Rukavango
Tswana	English	San	San

Fig. 6. Rank Order of Selected Social and Educational Indicators by Language Group in Namibia. *Note:* Human Development Index (HDI) is calculated in terms of purchasing power parity (PPP) in U.S. dollars and measures progress in development. It includes three components: longevity, knowledge, and access to resources. Human Poverty Index (HPI) is a measure of deprivation. It measures the proportion of the population being deprived of certain elements of life. The main three dimensions of HPI include longevity, knowledge, and decent standard of living. *Source:* Adapted from UN, 1999.

of the indigenous black population is poor and less educated (GRN/UNICEF, 1999). Furthermore, despite reprioritized public expenditures which have increased spending in social service sectors and directed to poverty programs, the second five years of independence depicts a sizeable proportion of the population, generally children, who remain poor and appear to be worsening as the years progress (Tapscott, 1999).

Child Policy and Welfare Decision-Making in Independent Namibia

Since independence, a considerable amount of development and decision-making has focused on the need to improve child welfare systems and policies at the legislative, programmatic, and community level in the country. The major actions on the rights and welfare of children have come about following the ratification of the UN Convention on the Rights of Children which is generally described as an international "Bill of Rights" for children. Its 54 articles covering civil, economic, social, and political rights of children remain the barometer by which the Namibian Government has made decisions regarding the progress of child protection, survival, and development in the country. Hailed among the first African countries to sign and ratify the Convention on the Rights of the Child (CRC), the nascent republic at independence made considerable strides to gear specific activities to improving child welfare within the country.

As ratifying country of CRC, the Namibian government made an international commitment to invest in children's health, nutrition, and education as foundation for national development. One of the first tasks, as a result, was the development of a yearly Programme of Action for Children which would serve as an inter-ministerial technical committee to develop strategies for the completion of the CRC goals and focus on several problems by sub-committee that were inherited at the dawn of the new republic, namely primary health care; nutrition and household food security; water and sanitation; early childhood development, basic education and literacy; advancement of women; and children in especially difficult circumstances. For each problem area, a plan of action was coordinated inter-ministerially with necessary resources and responsible agencies, including a strategy for operation and necessary monitoring mechanisms in the coverage of each programme (Republic of Namibia, 1991). The development of the National Programme of Action (NPA) for Children in Namibia had a far-reaching impact, fostering broad-based collaboration and intersectoral support. The cooperation in Namibia by different Government and public sector institutions was particularly important during the radical restructuring that occurred shortly after Independence as the NPA development process helped civil servants better determine their assignments relative to other institutions and participate in a wider development endeavor focused on Government social programming (Adkisson & Hogan, 1994).

Considerable decisions were made to revisit the legislation that affected and impacted the state of child welfare and status in the post-apartheid nation to craft child-centered legislation consistent with the new constitution and the CRC. One of the first efforts was made to revisit the Children's Act of 1960, outdated legislation inherited from South Africa and the most comprehensive existing laws on children in the country. Among the necessary areas of the 1960 Act that needed revisiting included the authoritative and prescriptive role of the State, the fragmented and discriminatory nature of resources as a result of the apartheid legacy in interventions for white and black children, and the minimal role of the father in the care and maintenance of child interests and needs. As custodian for all child protection issues in the country, the Directorate of Social Services within the Ministry of Health and Social Services has played a key role in the introduction of the Child Care and Protection and Children's Status bill which served to replace the 1960 Act. The spirit of the bill generally speak to identification of mechanisms that address the best interest of children in Namibia in the case of alternative care needed, issues of inheritance, and the status of children in families. More specifically, the combined bills address the need to limiting the role of the state as a watchdog, to provide a more empowering role of parents, including a more accessible role of the father, and more prevention measures to assist and work with families that are in need. Inherent in the passage of the two acts is the overriding standard for the interpretation of the new laws consistent with Article 3 of the CRC and the development of an inter-ministerial Child Welfare Advisory Council designed to coordinate and monitor the functions of this legislation and a Children's Ombudsperson (Coetzee-Masabane, 2001; GRN/UNICEF, 2000; UNICEF, 1995). Other acts, implemented and proposed, are several that pertain to issues of child protection, survival, and development, including the Rape Act of 2000, a juvenile justice bill in early stages of being drafted as a layman's bill for approval to the Cabinet committee, pending Maintenance legislation which assists individuals in obtaining provision for basic needs of life from persons who are legally liable to maintain them, and drafting of juvenile justice legislation which aims to change the way young offenders are handled within the legal system.

Other efforts in the health sector concentrated on shifting resources to disadvantaged persons, focusing on preventive care, provision of clinics, and an overall strengthening of the health services delivery area at the rural and district levels. A testament to the amount of governmental resources was the increase of 15% of government spending for health expenditure in the first decade of independence and the substantial allocation of health resources to primary health care, all designed to contribute to the Ministry of Health and Social Services' then objective of "Health For All Namibians By 2000" reform process. Besides primary health programmes, health systems benefited from the extended coverage of policies, strategies, and plans for every major public health problem in Namibia (UNICEF, 1999).

Despite the efforts in the health sector to develop new policy frameworks, namely "Towards Achieving Health and Social Being For All Namibians" aimed at equity, accessibility and affordability, community involvement, and intersectoral collaboration (MoHSS, 1998), the policy reforms have not kept pace with implementation and monitoring expectations. Whereas the delay in the passing of key legislation related to child welfare threatens to derail important interventions and transformations being proposed by the Namibian government, the preparation of legislation relative to the status of children in Namibia has faced more complicated sociopolitical and sociolegal issues considering that the iterations of the current draft have been under discussion since 1991. To compound matters, limited staff and training continue to be impediments in the passing of this important legislation. Even with the confirmation of the Government's address to rights to women and monitoring vehicles underway through the Convention on the Elimination of All Forms of Discrimination Against Women (CEDAW), current laws, customs and practices limit the full realization of equal and equitable status paid to women, an even more urgent call to exercise full attention to children and women rights issues in the post-independent Namibian context.

Furthermore, the objective of addressing issues of health inequities have not reached all and raising the health profile in Namibia has not kept pace with its hope. Considering Namibia's GNP level and expectations of similar countries at a middle income level, the country's health profile and health statistics do not differ from other sub-Saharan countries when comparing the majority of Namibians. Major challenges remain in improving the allocation of capital and human resources for primary health care and decentralization, addressing the regional, urban/rural, and ethnic group divides as well as improving the efficiency and quality of health care in the country, primarily the result of the legacy of apartheid (UNICEF, 1999; GRN/UNICEF, 2000).

A number of recent reports document that HIV/AIDS has become the principal public health problem in Namibia. Namibia finds itself among countries with the highest prevalence of HIV infection in the world, becoming the principal cause of death in the country for all age groups. In 1999, The reported number of deaths from HIV/AIDS accounted for nearly one-fourth of all reported deaths and nearly one-half of deaths in the age group of 15–49 years (MoHSS, 2001). It has now become the leading cause of death in the country, ranking fifth for children under 13 and sixth for children under one year where over 3000 HIV-positive children are born each year in Namibia. Poverty implications of the HIV/AIDS epidemic appear greater in the northern areas of the country where three-fourths of the population of those infected are located and HIV prevalence among pregnant women is disproportionately high in four urban areas of the country: Katima Mulilo (33%), Windhoek (31%), Oshakati (28%), and Walvis Bay (28%) (MoHSS, 2001; UNICEF, 1997). Contributing to the high HIV prevalence in the country are contributing factors, such as physical and sexual abuse, unfriendly and non-existent adolescent health services, lack of voluntary or confidential counseling and testing or availability of anti-retroviral drugs, a minimal number of civil society organizations helping AIDS infected and affected, and already stressed family resources to assist those affected and infected by AIDS (GRN/UNICEF, 2000). Its consequences to the Namibian society, however do not end at the public health sector, but extend to education and training and the general social and economic development of this young democracy (UNDP, 1997) (Fig. 7).

Year	Direct Medical Costs	Support to People with AIDS (proposed disability allowances)	Value of Productive Years Foregone	Total Direct and Indirect Costs	Gross Domestic Product	Direct and Indirect Costs As% of GDP
1996	21.6		407.8	429.4	$13, 593	3.2%
1997	34.2	14.6	615.8	664.6	$14, 273	4.6%
1998	47.4	20.1	1, 016.6	1, 084.1	$14, 986	7.2%
1999	64.6	27.7	1, 415.9	1, 507.5	$15, 736	9.6%
2000	89.3	37.7	1, 903.3	2, 030.3	$16, 522	12.3%
2001	127.7	55.4	2, 648.1	2, 831.2	$17, 348	16.3%
Total	384.8	154.8	8, 007.5	8, 592.3		

Fig. 7. Projected Costs of HIV/AIDS on Human Development in Namibia, 1996–2001 (Constant 1996 N$ Millions). *Note:* These costs were based on the then current scenario of rapidly increasing rates of HIV/AIDS infection. *Source:* UNDP, 1997.

In the education sector like the health sector, wide-ranging decisions at independence, most notably a considerable emphasis was placed on improvement of the education system with the main goal of meeting basic learning needs of all children and youth in the country (Fig. 8).

Where health expenditures rose following independence, so have education expenditures by 28% to account for currently 25% of the total government budget, nearly 10% of GNP. Including other social services (education, health, issues that pertain to women and child welfare), this sector accounts for over 40% of the

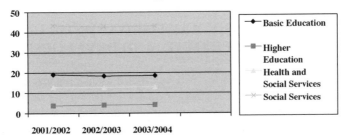

Fig. 8. Percent of Social Service Expenditures on Total Budget, 2001/2002 – 2003/2004. *Note:* The Social Services sector includes the following Governmental Ministries: Health and Social Services, Women Affairs and Child Welfare, Basic Education, Culture, and Sport, and Higher Education, Training, and Employment. *Source:* Republic of Namibia, 2001.

total budget. Noticeable government interventions paid to education consisted of increasing numbers of schools and school enrollment rates at all levels of education, especially at the senior secondary level whose enrollment rates were three times higher than in 1990 near the end of the decade (UN, 1999).

The goal of "Education for All" as promoted by the then Ministry of Education and Culture had promised to address the historical legacy of apartheid and decolonization which limited most Namibians to only primary education and a general segregated and unequal system that only emphasized basic literacy and numeracy (MEC, 1993). The fact that the areas of access and quality are posing the most serious challenges to current education in Namibia suggests that the problems inherited prior to independence continue to lag, most evident in lack of infrastructure, insufficient funding and lack of trained manpower – especially in the northern regions of the country (MBESC, 2001; UN, 1999). Contrary to constitutional provisions and compliance to national and international standards and benchmarks (i.e. the Labour Act of 1992 and the CRC), a large percentage of working children is a cautionary signal that the educational rights of some children are being compromised (MoL, 2000).

Recent efforts, such as the recent First National Conference on Orphans and Other Vulnerable Children in Namibia and the upcoming programme strategy for cooperation between the Government of Namibia and UNICEF, to focus on educationally marginalized children who are peculiar difficulty in accessing basic education (e.g children of farm workers, those in remote rural areas like San and Ovahimba, in squatter areas and resettlement camps, or who face physical or mental handicaps) are particularly timely (GRN/UNICEF, 2000; MBESC, 2000), potentially pointing to ways to target specific educational and institutional interventions at most needed populations and to address disparities between an educated rich and uneducated poor in Namibia.

CONCLUSION: THE WAY FORWARD FOR CHILD PROTECTION, SURVIVAL, AND DEVELOPMENT

The independence of Namibia in 1990 was hailed as harbinger for democracy and national reconciliation in southern Africa, considering the regions history and legacy of apartheid, destabilization, and war. The new beginning was characterized by the establishment of a new constitution forged through inter-party consensus and subsequent multi-party political systems, a separation of power, free and fair elections, real parliamentary powers, respected rule of law, and other important conditions of democracy (Marshall, 1998), including several independent institutions (most notably, an Ombudsperson and Auditor General).

During the first several years following Namibia's independence, a number of achievements were evident throughout sectors pertaining to social welfare and human development in the country. The promises to accessible, unfragmented, and equitable solutions in health and education were laudable in their attempt to address systemic inequalities largely on the basis of race and ethnicity in the country.

Some social and political scientists, however, have been critical of building capacity to organize and sustain policies geared for the poor, enabling poor and disadvantaged populations, and ensuring democratic social welfare for all in Namibia (Tapscott, 1999). The issues that relate to the general social welfare of the citizenry are not detached but are inextricably linked. The test for an independent and post-apartheid Namibia lies in the ability to still perpetuate its hopes and aspirations a decade ago. To do so would certainly put it as an example for other countries to follow in the region and on the larger continent.

NOTES

1. SADC (formerly the Southern African Development Co-ordination Conference – SADCC) now contains fourteen countries. In addition to the inclusion of Namibia and South Africa, pursuant their independence and abolishment of public and legislative apartheid in 1990 and 1994, respectively, the other member countries include: Angola, Botswana, the Democratic Republic of Congo, Lesotho, Madagascar, Malawi, Mauritius, Seychelles, Swaziland, Tanzania, Zambia, and Zimbabwe.

2. Though Moeti describes these two countries in the southern part of the continent has having a "window of opportunity" in regards to the HIV/AIDS pandemic, the author does not necessarily suggest why this apparent window of opportunity was averted when taking the disease into account. He does hint that the extreme income distribution differentials may be one explanation in Botswana, especially affecting women and women-headed households who are most likely to face poverty in the country.

3. The higher figure estimate, though documented by some authors prior to independence (cf. Asrat et al., 1989) is believed to be inflated. A more realistic number of exiles abroad who actually returned were closer to between 40,000–50,000 around 1990.

4. While Asrat et al.'s figures tell one story, this is not to suggest that all black Namibians in exile did not have social and economic hardships as a result of their displacement from their own country. When considering quality of life indicators, according to Asrat et al. (1989) the assumption is that those in exile, although their data is limited to exiles in Angola, were living at higher standards of living than those within the country.

ACKNOWLEDGMENTS

I would like to especially thank Lavinia Shikongo of UNICEF-Namibia and Petronella Coetzee-Masabane, of the Ministry of Health and Social Services for their comments on an earlier draft of this paper and their invaluable assistance on a number of matters related to the paper. Additionally, I extend gratitude to Rina de la Cruz of UNICEF-Namibia Resource Centre and Randolph Mouton of the Social Impact Assessment and Policy Analysis Corporation for their help in locating materials and resources.

REFERENCES

Adkisson, S., & Hogan, H. (1994). *The development and decentralization of the national programme of action for children in Namibia.* Innocenti Occasional Papers – Decentralization and Local Governance Series, Number 13. Florence: UNICEF International Child Development Centre.

Asrat, D., Covadia, H., Green, R. H., Maurás, M., Morgan, R., Ramphele, M., Reynolds, P., & Wilson, F. (1989). *Children on the front line: The impact of apartheid, destabilization, and warfare on children in Southern and South Africa.* NY: UNICEF.

Balch, J., Johnson, P., & Morgan, R. (1995). Apartheid and destablization in Southern Africa: The legacy for children and the challenges ahead. In: J. Balch, P. Johnson & R. Morgan (Eds), *Transcending the Legacy: Children in the New Southern Africa.* NY: Africa-European Institute/Southern Africa Research and Documentation Centre/United Nations Children's Fund.

Chisolm, L., & Motala, S. (1995). Education for all: The challenge of educational development in South Africa. In: J. Balch, P. Johnson & R. Morgan (Eds), *Transcending the Legacy: Children in the New Southern Africa* (pp. 41–53). NY: Africa-European Institute/Southern Africa Research and Documentation Centre/United Nations Children's Fund.

Coetzee-Masabane, P. (2001). Interview, Deputy Director: Social Welfare Services, Ministry of Health and Social Services (3 May).

Cross, M., & Chisolm, L. (1990). The roots of segregated schooling in twentieth century South Africa. In: N. Mokubung (Ed.), *Pedagogy of Domination: Toward a Democratic Education in South Africa* (pp. 43–74). Trenton, NJ: Africa World Press.

Government of the Republic of Namibia/United Nations Children's Fund (1999). *Mid term review.* Windhoek: GRN/UNICEF.

Government of the Republic of Namibia/United Nations Children's Fund (2000). *Strategy for the GRN-UNICEF Programme of Co-operation, 2002–2005.* Windhoek: GRN/UNICEF.

Green, R. H., Morgan, R., & Davids, C. (1991). *Children on the front line: From wartime survival to postwar rehabilitation and renewed development in Southern Africa.* NY: UNICEF.

Ithana, P. (1990). The situation of children and women in Namibia. *Child Survival on the Frontline: How to Counter the Effects on Children of Destabilisation* Conference Report. Harare: African-European Institute/Association of West European Parliamentarians for Action Against Apartheid (pp. 37–38).

Junabhai, C. C. (1995). 'NPA for children' in the New South Africa: Opportunities for implementing the health and nutritional goals. In: J. Balch, P. Johnson & R. Morgan (Eds), *Transcending the Legacy: Children in the New Southern Africa* (pp. 92–104). NY: Africa-European Institute/Southern Africa Research and Documentation Centre/United Nations Children's Fund.

Laakso, L., & Olukoshi, A. O. (1996). The crisis of the post-colonial nation-state project in Africa. In: A. O. Olukoshi & L. Laakso (Eds), *Challenges to the Nation-State in Africa* (pp. 7–37). Uppsala: Nordiska Afrikainstitutet.

Marshall, G. (1998). *Dictionary of sociology.* Oxford: Oxford University Press.

Mbamba, A. M. (1982). *Primary education for an independent Namibia: Planning in a situation of uncertainty and unstability*. Stockholm: University of Stockholm.

McKerrow, N., & Fincham, R. (1995). Combatting the legacy of apartheid in health: Edendale in KwaZulu/Natal, South Africa. In: J. Balch, P. Johnson & R. Morgan (Eds), *Transcending the Legacy: Children in the New Southern Africa* (pp. 113–119). NY: Africa-European Institute/Southern Africa Research and Documentation Centre/United Nations Children's Fund.

Mhone, G. C. Z. (1995). Child labor in Southern Africa: Work and work-related activities. In: J. Balch, P. Johnson & R. Morgan (Eds), *Transcending the Legacy: Children in the New Southern Africa* (pp. 170–176). NY: Africa-European Institute/Southern Africa Research and Documentation Centre/United Nations Children's Fund.

Ministry of Basic Education, Sport and Culture (2000). *National policy options for educationally marginalised children*. Windhoek: Author.

Ministry of Basic Education, Sport and Culture (2001). *Strategic Plan 2001–2006*. Windhoek: Author.

Ministry of Education and Culture (1993). *Toward education for all: A development brief for education, culture, and training*. Windhoek: Gamsberg Macmillan.

Ministry of Health and Social Services (1998). *Towards achieving health and social well being for all Namibians: A policy framework*. Windhoek: Author.

Ministry of Health and Social Services (2001). *Report of the 2000 HIV Sentinel Sero Survey*. Windhoek: Directorate of Primary Health Care and Nursing Services/National AIDS Co-ordination Programme.

Ministry of Labour (2000). *Namibia child activities survey 1999: Report of analysis*. Windhoek: Author.

Moeti, M. R. (1995). HIV/AIDS: A challenge to post-apartheid reconstruction in Southern Africa. In: J. Balch, P. Johnson & R. Morgan (Eds), *Transcending the Legacy: Children in the New Southern Africa* (pp. 77–82). NY: Africa-European Institute/Southern Africa Research and Documentation Centre/United Nations Children's Fund.

Morgan, R. (1990). Destabilisation, warfare, and economic recession: Effects on children in Southern Africa and some UNICEF responses. *Child Survival on the Frontline: How to Counter the Effects on Children of Destabilisation*. Conference Report. Harare: African-European Institute/Association of West European Parliamentarians for Action Against Apartheid.

National Institute for Economic Policy (1995). *Children, poverty, and disparity reduction: Towards fulfilling the rights of South Africa's children 1995*. Johannesburg: Author.

Republic of Namibia (1991). *National programme of action for the children of Namibia*. Windhoek: Author.

Rwezaura, B. (1994). The concept of the child's best interests in the changing economic and social context of Sub-Saharan Africa. In: P. Alston (Ed.), *The Best Interests of the Child: Reconciling Culture and Human Rights* (pp. 82–116). Oxford: Oxford University Press.

Simão, P. (1995). Education in Angola in the post-apartheid era: Overcoming physical and spiritual destruction. In: J. Balch, P. Johnson & R. Morgan (Eds), *Transcending the Legacy: Children in the New Southern Africa* (pp. 61–66). NY: Africa-European Institute/Southern Africa Research and Documentation Centre/United Nations Children's Fund.

Smith, S. (1986). *Namibia: A violation of trust*. Oxford: Oxfam.

Tapscott, C. (1999). *An assessment of governance in Namibia*. Cape Town: Department for International Development – Southern Africa.

United Nations (1999). *Common country assessment of Namibia*. Windhoek: United Nations System in Namibia.

United Nations AIDS (2000). *Report on the global HIV/AIDS epidemic*. Geneva: Joint United Nations Programme on HIV/AIDS.

United Nations AIDS/United Nations Children's Fund (1998). *Children orphaned by AIDS: Front line responses from Eastern and Southern Africa*. NY: UNICEF.

United Nations Children's Fund (1995). *Children in Namibia: Reaching towards the rights of every child*. Windhoek: University of Namibia/Legal Assistance Centre/UNICEF.

United Nations Children's Fund (1997). *Annual report, 1997*. Windhoek: United Nations.

United Nations Children's Fund (1998). *The state of the world's children 1998*. Oxford: Oxford University Press.

United Nations Children's Fund (2000a). *Towards a new global agenda for children in the 21st century: Child protection*. NY: UNICEF Programme Division, 2000a.

United Nations Children's Fund (2000b). *The state of the world's children 2000*. Oxford: Oxford University Press.

United Nations Children's Fund/National Children's Rights Committee (1993). *Children and women in South Africa: A situation analysis*. Johannesburg: UNICEF/NCRC.

United Nations Development Programme (1997). *Namibia human development report, 1997*. Windhoek: Author.

United Nations General Assembly (1996). *Promotion and protection of the rights of children*. Report of the Expert of the Secretary-General, Ms. Graça Machel, A/51/306. NY: Author.

United States Agency for International Development (2001). *Background paper on children affected by AIDS in Zimbabwe*. Harare, Zimbabwe.

Unterhalter, E. (1991). Changing aspects of reformism in Bantu education, 1953–1989. In: E. Unterhalter, H. Wolpe, T. Botha, S. Badat, T. Dlamini & B. Khotseng (Eds), *Apartheid Education and Popular Struggles* (pp. 35–72). Johannesburg: Ravan Press.

14. THE HEALTH AND COGNITIVE CONSEQUENCES OF INTERNATIONAL CHILD POVERTY

Jeanita W. Richardson

> The world has failed 'deplorably' to ensure children's right to health care, education and protection from violence ... 1 in 3 children suffers from malnutrition, 1 in 4 has never been immunized against disease and 1 in 5 has never attended school.
> UN Secretary General Kofi Annan (as cited in DeYoung & Lynch, 2002 p. A18).

INTRODUCTION

UN Secretary General Kofi Annan in the opening quote reminds us that despite the medical and public health gains of recent decades, benefits have not accrued to the most vulnerable of citizens, children (DeYoung & Lynch, 2002). For decades research has quantified the links between poverty, ill-health and the global burdens imposed by disease. Yet, the distribution of poverty and disease has changed little over the last thirty years, continuing to be concentrated among poor children in both emerging and developed nations (Bellamy, 1999; Brundtland, 1999). Fundamentally, the complex web of poverty relegates youth to a lifetime of suffering because of the relationships between and among resources, health and neurological development.

'Suffer the Little Children': National and International Dimensions of Child
Poverty and Public Policy
Advances in Education in Diverse Communities: Research, Policy and Praxis, Volume 4, 335–358
Copyright © 2006 by Elsevier Ltd.
All rights of reproduction in any form reserved
ISSN: 1479-358X/doi:10.1016/S1479-358X(04)04014-8

This chapter discusses the role of poverty in persistent health and cognitive risk in economically deprived children. More specifically, by calling attention to malnutrition and its role in worsening the effects of infectious disease, as well as absorption of toxic chemicals, this examination also reveals much about poverty's role in perpetuating poor health and visa versa. The health prospects of infants and children are particularly vulnerable to dimensions of depravity because of their low threshold for irreversible damage (Bartlett et al., 1999; World Resources Institute, 1999). Youth are also most apt to suffer from a combination of agents that diminish health, physical environments and mental facilities (Guo & Harris, 2000; UNICEF, 2002a). Consequently, isolated evaluations of economic deprivation, poor health and/or cognitive development do not adequately address the interdependence of prevailing risk factors. If the tragic cycle of poor health and poverty is ever to be broken, the connection between family health and economic stability must be tackled by policymakers and implementation bodies (Millen et al., 2000a).

No single group could possibly direct the fundamental changes in perception and practice required to achieve social, health and economic parity for poor children. Public health networks, national and international governmental agencies, nongovernmental agencies (NGOs) and the research community each play a pivotal role in the development and implementation of strategies designed to mitigate the short- and long-term consequences of child poverty. However, until meaningful and sustainable collaborations are forged, impoverished youth throughout the world will continue to subsist rather than flourish (Bartlett et al., 1999; Millen et al., 2000a).

Half of the world's poor are children (Guo & Harris, 2000). Each year eleven million youth under five die of preventable or treatable diseases. Helpless to rectify their status, 150 million children in emerging nations suffer from malnutrition (UNICEF, 2003). Long before many youngsters have an opportunity to live or exercise their intellectual prowess, predominant killers (malnutrition, pneumonia, diarrhea, malaria, measles and HIV/AIDS) rob them and rob us of their potential contributions (Brundtland, 1999; UNICEF, 2001, 2002a; World Health Organization, 2001). Whether the result of benign neglect, insufficient resources or inadequate healthcare networks, the consequences are the same, poor children lack access to the support systems necessary to ensure their healthy arrival to adulthood (Bellamy, 1999).

While the primary foci of this discussion are the relationships among disease, malnutrition and toxic chemical exposure in children, one cannot disentangle the health of children from their mothers. Throughout the world, women tend to earn less than men contributing to the disproportionate representation of female-headed households among the ranks of the poor (Bartlett et al., 1999). Mothers with inadequate diets experience depleted health resources and are incapable of providing nutrients optimizing fetal development. If maternal malnutrition persists after birth, nutrients normally passed from mother to child as a function of breastfeeding are unavailable. During both of these periods (prenatal development and infancy) neurological development is at its height and influences lifelong cognitive capacity (Bartlett et al., 1999; UNICEF, 2001).

The implications of the mother/child health relationship do not disappear after birth or early childhood, but rather persist into adulthood. Maternal health and nutrition together set the stage for healthy starts to life or conversely a lifetime of health battles, thereby confirming the strong correlation between a women's well-being and the well-being of her children (Bartlett et al., 1999; Harper & Marcus, 1999). Deadly interactions between inadequate resources, disease and the poor health of mothers, account for 97% of the premature deaths of children under five born in emerging nations. Tragically, most of these deaths are preventable (Millen et al., 2000b).

For purposes of clarification, terms commonly used in discussions of childhood maturation, such as growth, development, learning and cognition have been defined. These terms refer to distinct but inter-related processes. Growth tends to apply to an increase in physical size. Development is a more inclusive term including growth and also the intellectual and emotional changes that take place in an organized and integrated manner. Learning is the acquisition of skills that are heavily dependent upon interactions between neurological and physical development, as well as, environmental stimuli (Bartlett et al., 1999). Finally, cognition, "processes of the mind such as perceiving, thinking, or remembering" (Schettler et al., 2000 p. 34), is influenced by the complex interactions between genetics, physical environments, nutrition and social interaction. Because neurological development does not take place uniformly throughout the brain and some brain regions control particular functions, the timing of hindrances to the sensitive progression of neurological maturation can result in diminished capacity.

Malnutrition is an antagonist to child health because whether caused by insufficient food or inadequate nutrition, it increases the probability that otherwise benign illnesses will become fatal. Diets may include ample calories without providing satisfactory levels of proteins and micronutrients, the absence of which compromise immune systems and neurological development. Further, cultural factors have been known to contribute to malnutrition in children. For example, in some cases it is common for men to eat first, leaving little for women and children. Food insecurity (the irregularity of meals and/or inadequate nutritious diets) also heightens the toxicity of some chemicals because nutritional deficits can increase absorption rates. Malnourished children tend also to be at great risk of experiencing stunted growth, developmental deficiencies and a lack of energy to interact with their environment, an essential exchange enhancing cognition and learning (Bartlett et al., 1999).

The tragedy of lost potential is worsened by the lopsided distribution of health services. As per the World Health Organization (WHO);

> Never have so many had such broad and advanced access to healthcare. But never have so many been denied access to health. The developing world carries 90% of the disease burden, yet poorer countries have access to only 10% of the resources that go to health (Millen et al., 2000b, p. 4).

As per Dr. Gro Harlem Brundtland, former director-general of WHO, 30% of the world's population have no access to public health systems at all (Foreign Policy, 2002). Many childhood diseases that have long been responsive to vaccines, cures and treatments continue to reap havoc upon impoverished communities and in conjunction with malnutrition continue to convert relatively harmless maladies, such as measles, into fatal diseases.

Not only has there been a concentration of health benefits among the privileged few, there have concurrently been deleterious health consequences engendered by the practices of some Transnational Corporations (TNCs). TNCs for purposes of this chapter are corporations that market and produce their products in many countries concurrently while claiming resident status in countries providing low wage workers and the most beneficial tax and trade policies (Millen & Holtz, 2000).

Population health is not often included in discussion of transnational corporations and economic expansion. Presumptions about unilateral benefits accruing to individuals within nations as a result of globalized economies sound promising. On the contrary however, data reveal that one consequence of corporate practice has been exponential growth in the numbers of poor persons particularly in emerging nations (Millen et al., 2000b). For example, exposure to toxic substances produced in some TNCs can create occupational hazards harming not only workers, but also their families and the communities in which they live (Millen & Holtz, 2000). Children, in this scenario are more susceptible to the negative effects of toxic chemicals than adults because of size, their proximity to the ground where chemicals settle, and their rapid physical and neurological developmental stages.

According to representatives from WHO and UNICEF, two of the most significant contributors to inadequate interventions on behalf of the world's children are politics and the income gap between the rich and poor within and between nations (Foreign Policy, 2002; UNICEF, 2003). Restated, impoverished children are utterly subject to politics and the fickle nature of public opinion, fluctuating national and international resources and a multitude of social and economic policies.

THE POLITICS OF HEALTH

The worth adults place on children is evident in the policies implemented and the resources designated to ensure health and well-being. As aptly put by Audrey Cheynut of Monaco, a youth representative at the United Nations General Assembly Special Session on Children, "We (the children of the world) are not the sources of problems . . . We are not expenses; we are investments" (as cited in UNICEF, 2002b, p. 3). Unfortunately, the investment value of the poor rises and falls (Kozol, 2001).

Many definitions of politics circulate, however, for purposes of this examination, a useful definition highlighting the predicament of destitute children was proposed by Colmers (2002), who identified politics as decisions determining, "who gets what, when, where, how and why" (p. 1217). Poor children are subject to politics by virtue of the fact that they are at the mercy of adults who assign value to their well-being and determine the distribution of limited assets.

The relationship between income disparities and politics endures at least in part because income gaps between and within nations are influenced by explicit and implicit policies. As per Nobel Laureate Amartya Sen, the "quality of life in societies depends to a large extent on social policies and public action" (Kawachi et al., 1999, p. xxix). Policies, as defined by Dunn (1994), are the collective actions and inactions of bodies designed to address social problems. Prevailing inequalities mirror societal priorities, which are reflected in public policy choices (Kawachi & Wilkinson, 1999). Given this frame of reference, it should be no surprise that without demonstrative political will and a long-term commitment to devote necessary resources, the health challenges of politically and socially disenfranchised populations remain unresolved (Garrett, 2000). More specific to this discussion, because health systems are primarily governed and resourced by political bodies, beneficiaries of services reap the attendant advantages and disadvantages of policy-makers' priorities.

Analyses of public health policies have quantified the direct correlation not only between health, politics and poverty, but also the health consequences of income polarization between the rich and poor (Garrett, 2000). One theory attempting to explain why some populations are more apt to suffer from the ills of poor health than others is the Relative Income Hypothesis (RIH), developed by Richard G. Wilkinson in 1984. This theory sheds light on how the health prospects for poor children in developed nations such as the United States are relatively as dismal as poor children in developing nations (Kawachi & Wilkinson, 1999; Rainwater & Smeeding, 1997).

As articulated by Kawachi et al. (1999), Wilkinson's theory posits that an, "individual's health is affected not only by their own level of income, but also by the scale of inequality in society as a whole" (p. xvi). Paraphrased, the wider the disparities in income within or between nations' populations (relative income) the greater the health differences. As the income gap widens, policy preferences tend to shift away from more egalitarian health systems to a more individualistic focus (Wilkinson, 1999b). This is precisely why the United States' public health system with all its innovative medical technology fails be rated as one of the best in the world. According to the WHO, despite its wealth and advanced treatment protocols forty million persons in the United States have no access to health care and those numbers continue to rise. Conversely, nations with a more equitable distribution of care are rated as the world's best public health systems, e.g. France, Italy, and San Marino (Foreign Policy, 2002).

According to Wilkinson's RIH theory, even when funds are plentiful and resources could be distributed to meet the health needs of the poor, policies and services reflect the opposite trend. The greater the economic gap between the few who have acquired wealth and those who struggle for survival, the greater the likelihood economically deprived children will suffer from inadequate health care. These tendencies according to the theory also hold true when comparing the accumulated wealth between nations. Risk for families is further heightened if women lack political and/or economic status because the absence of status can equate to poverty (Wilkinson, 1999a).

Theoretical presumptions of RIH can be validated with even a cursory survey of children in the United States. In the U.S., 17% of all children suffer from poverty and malnutrition. Thirty-six percent of the total population of African American children live in poverty (Federal Interagency Forum on Child and Family Statistics, 2000). Sixty percent of the children that die in America between the ages of one to four (1–4) are African American. On virtually every federal indices of childhood well-being, the gap between the health of poor children (especially poor African American children) and the rest of the nation's youth has prevailed or widened over the last thirty years (Federal Interagency Forum on Child and Family Statistics, 2001; Kawachi et al., 1997; Richardson, 2002).

If the U.S. has not resolved health parity issues within her borders she would predictably lack the effectiveness her wealth and expertise might suggest when intervening in the affairs of emerging nations. In a global application of RIH, the vast economic divide between developing and industrialized nations portend public policy's persistent failures relative to remediating health disparities.

Dr. Brundtland, lends credence to Wilkinson's premise that politics and income distribution influence the health prospects particularly of the poor. In an interview with Foreign Policy Magazine, she states;

When you see how different the health systems are around the world, you see how much the health sector reflects the political and economic system of each country . . . on the more political front (one sees the struggle to) finance healthcare or what part of the GDP (Gross Domestic Product) should go to health – all of these issues are deeply political (Foreign Policy, 2002, p. 26).

Dr. Brundtland goes on to say that one of the most significant challenges to nations concerned with reforming health systems is how to pay for it and how to distribute the costs of health though the population. Policy-makers in this context find themselves in a precarious position because to reduce poverty substantive investments must be made to health systems and these outlays compete for limited funding with other social and economic development expenditures (Foreign Policy, 2002). Theoretical suppositions such as RIH help explain how income, politics, poverty and sickness are related, however no matter how astute considered in isolation they fail to expose the personal and poignant day-to-day suffering of children.

THE HEALTH AND COGNITIVE CONSEQUENCES OF CHILDHOOD POVERTY

Staggering numbers of persons live in poverty and experience the health and cognitive consequences induced by subsistence. Over one billion people are unable to secure adequate housing, nutritious food and health care. One billion persons support their families on less than $1US per day (Macfarlane et al., 2000; World Resources Institute, 1999). Over three billion men, women and children living in emerging nations have no access to sanitation facilities; more than one billion do not have access to clean and safe drinking water; at least 600 million urban citizens in Africa, Asia, and Latin America live in life threatening toxic homes and neighborhoods; and, over 50% of individuals living in the 46 poorest countries have no access to modern healthcare facilities. Since poor children live with poor adults or alone, they are most often subjected to the same circumstances as their caregivers. Should poor children survive, through no fault of their own they also become complicit in the economic insecurity of their family because of the care they require and the high costs associated with medical treatment (Bartlett et al., 1999).

The longer children live in poverty the lower their educational achievement and the slower their general maturation processes not necessarily because of innate deficits, but because of preventable diseases, toxic exposure and malnutrition (Guo & Harris, 2000). Even short bouts of poverty at critical junctures, can permanently

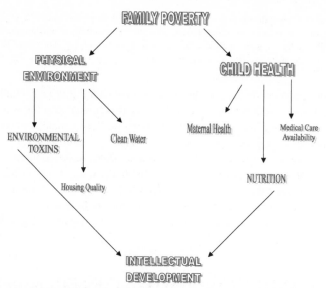

Fig. 1. Poverty and Intellectual Development. *Note:* Adapted from Guo and Harris (2000). (Environmental toxins and nutrition are highlighted as two foci of this essay, not necessarily because they are deemed more dangerous than other factors.)

diminish cognitive capacity. For example, the period before birth until age two is considered the most important as it relates to prospects for long-term health and cognitive development (Bartlett et al., 1999). Figure 1 provides a diagram of some of the poverty-related factors that can result in a reduction in intellectual potential.

There are many factors that hinder normal intellectual maturation, only a few of which are displayed in Fig. 1. The availability of water free of toxins and other contaminants; homes that adequately shelter children from physical elements; nutritious diets; and, freedom from air-, water- or land-born chemicals are vital if physical environments are to facilitate normal growth and development. The absence of any of the above-mentioned conditions reduces the chance that genetically-determined intellect can be maximized in adulthood. In other words, a child may be born with normal intellectual/cognitive capacity that is destroyed because of conditions after birth (Guo & Harris, 2000).

Any impediment to the normal sequence of development before the age of five can potentially yield irreversible damage (Schettler et al., 2000). When a baby is born, nearly 100 billion neurons in the brain become heavily influenced by diet, sensory experiences and physical environments (Nash, 1997). After birth, the evolving brain in infants and young children directs change in vision, emotional control, ways of responding, language and cognitive skills. The most critical periods relative to the maturation of vision, emotional control, language and the foundations of neurological development typically occur between birth and two years of age. Precursors to social and cognitive skills peak between the age of three and five (UNICEF, 2001). Consequently, first as a fetus and then as a young child, every touch, meal, breath, and interaction influences the development of billions of neurons and neurological networks (Begley, 1997; Schettler et al., 2000; UNICEF, 2001).

In an effort to highlight some of the complex interactions that place disproportionate burdens on youth the influence of malnutrition; infectious diseases such as measles, acute respiratory infections (ARIs), human immunodeficiency virus and acquired immunodeficiency syndrome (HIV/AIDS) and environmental toxins will be discussed. Malnutrition is of particular importance because it weakens the immune system making children more susceptible to disease and the adverse affects of toxic environments. The AIDS epidemic arguably may not be caused by poverty, but treatment options, adequate diets and information about transmission behaviors are severely constrained if fiscal resources are absent. As such, HIV and AIDS merit consideration in this examination of infectious diseases in children because of its disproportionate impact on poor populations. Given the complementary relationship between malnutrition, infectious diseases, HIV/AIDS and toxic chemicals, questions whether children will arrive to healthy adulthoods are not contrived, but grounded in alarming trends.

HUNGER AND CHILD HEALTH

Poverty is deemed the major contributor to childhood malnutrition and malnutrition is the major cause of child mortality and diminished intellectual capacity. Food insecurity can result in or increase the likelihood that children will be underweight, experience stunted growth, respiratory infections and infectious diseases. If children survive, malnutrition creates a vicious cycle of illness that saps their strength increasing the chances that they not have the energy to interact in meaningful ways with their environment thus reducing learning capacity (UNICEF, 2002a). The combination of inadequate diet and exposure to preventable diseases is the most common cause of premature death.

The numbers of children paying the price for malnutrition are astronomical. Of the 31,000 children under five who die daily, over 50% perish because of the deadly combination of chronic malnutrition and impaired immune systems (Begley, 1997; Millen et al., 2000b; Schettler et al., 2000; UNICEF, 2001). Figure 2 identifies some of the long and short-term effects of malnutrition.

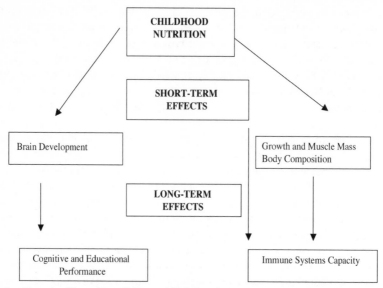

Fig. 2. Short- and Long Term Effects of Childhood Nutrition. *Note:* Adapted from: Mendez and Adair (1999), Schettler et. al (2000), UNICEF (2001), Wauben and Wainwright (1999), World Resources Institute (1999), Zander (1989).

It is difficult to predict how individual children will react to short-term food insecurity. Effects of long-term or poorly timed short-term deficits in diet may range from minimal to life threatening hindrances to brain development, depressed immune systems and stunted growth. The complex interactions between environment and genetic predisposition also make it difficult to definitively predict the precise intellectual and health effects of poverty on each child. What has become generally accepted is the role of nutrients on neurochemistry and neurological development at critical stages and concern that certain types and times of exposure will likely result in more serious effects (Schettler et al., 2000; UNICEF, 2002a; Wauben & Wainwright, 1999).

While child hunger is evident throughout the world, the greatest concentration of malnutrition is found in emerging nations. Approximately 828 million people in emerging nations battle malnutrition (Millen et al., 2000b). Figure 3 reflects the distribution of 150 million malnourished children as of 2001 (UNICEF, 2002a).

Over 50% (78 million) of the children suffering from food insecurity in the emerging nations depicted in Fig. 3 live in South Asia. Thirty-two million children are malnourished in Sub-Saharan Africa; twenty-seven million are hungry in the East Asia/Pacific region; seven million the Middle East and Northern Africa; four

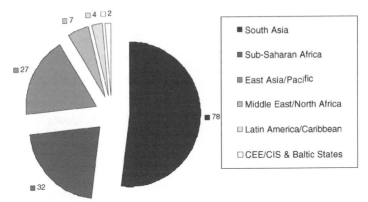

Fig. 3. 150 Million Malnourished Children in Developing Countries as of 2001 (Numbers in Millions). *Note:* Adapted from: UNICEF (2002a).

million in Latin America and the Caribbean and in Central & Eastern Europe (CEE), in the Commonwealth of Independent States (CIS) and the Baltic states there are two million starving children (UNICEF, 2002a).

Progress was made in the 1990s reducing the number of hungry youth from 174 million to 150 million. However, improvements bring little comfort to those whose struggle persists. As noted eloquently by one Zambian mother, "If you are a mother . . . you don't know what suffering is until you have watched your babies go hungry. I have suffered many times" (as cited in Jeter, 2002, p. A11).

Hunger in and of itself evokes specific vitamin and mineral deficiencies associated with health and neurological risks. For example, Vitamin A is essential for immune system functioning. Over 100 million of the world's children under the age of five are Vitamin A deficient making them vulnerable to blindness, death, and a host of other childhood diseases such as measles, malaria and diarrhea. Pregnant women deficient in Vitamin A risk dying during pregnancy and childbirth, having anemia and experiencing compromised immune systems making women and their offspring more susceptible to infection. The risk of mortality from childhood ailments such as measles increases by 25% if youth have a Vitamin A deficiency (Brundtland, 1999; UNICEF, 2002a).

Iodine deficiencies are the world's leading cause of preventable impaired psychomotor development and mental retardation in children under five. In women iodine deficiencies contribute to the numbers of stillbirths and miscarriages (UNICEF, 2002a). Figure 4 reveals the widespread nature of iodine deficiencies.

Goiters are the most obvious sign of iodine insufficiency. Salt iodization has been found the most effective strategy to reduce health-related risks because it is

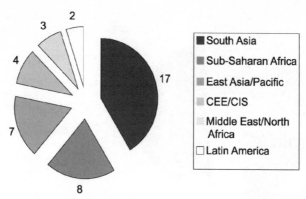

Fig. 4. Iodine Deficient Newborns (in millions). *Note:* Adapted from: UNICEF (2002a).

an inexpensive process and salt is widely consumed. Even in light of impressive gains, there are thirty-five (35) countries where less than 50% of the population have access to iodized salt and forty-one (41) million babies remain subject to the consequences of deficiencies. South Asia (seventeen million), Sub-Saharan Africa (eight million) and the East Asia/Pacific region (seven million) experience the greatest incidents of iodine deficiency (UNICEF, 2002a).

Other food related nutrients can also impact the health and neurological development of children. Proteins and carbohydrates aid in the synthesis of serotonin, which influences behavior and spatial memory. Fatty acids are linked to memory. Deficits in zinc, may impair learning because of its relationship to physical activity and memory functions. Anemia or deficiencies in iron have been linked with cognitive deficits, motor impairment and susceptibility to the harmful effects of environmental toxins (Schettler et al., 2000; Wadsworth, 2001; Wauben & Wainwright, 1999).

As stated earlier, one should not consider childhood health issues in the absence of mothers' health. Well-nourished women are more apt to give birth to healthy resilient babies poised to develop normally both physically and mentally (Bartlett et al., 1999; UNICEF, 2001). Conversely, mothers in poor health or with insufficient diets experience increased risk of giving birth to under-weight infants. To be considered low birthweight infants must weigh 2,500 grams or less at birth. Figure 5 reveals the millions of low birthweight babies by region.

Health-related consequences of low birth weight are considerable. Babies in this category experience an increased risk of dying in the early months of life. Muscle and immune systems are impaired, cognitive abilities are diminished and the risk of contracting and dying from infectious diseases rise. As per recent estimates, nearly 18 million babies are born underweight principally in developing nations and

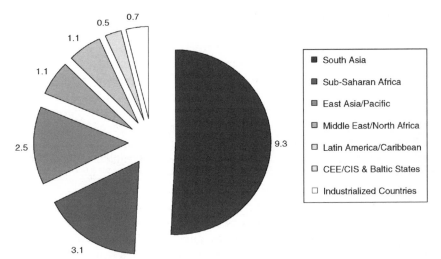

Fig. 5. Low Birthweight Babies (in millions). *Note:* Adapted from: UNICEF (2002a).

approximately half were born in South Asia. These estimates are apt to be highly underreported because weight at birth is not consistently assessed and reported in all nations (UNICEF, 2002a). Malnutrition's influence does not end with vitamin deficiencies. The indirect costs of food insecurity are also evident in the HIV/AIDS pandemic and other infectious disease susceptibility.

INFECTIOUS DISEASES AND CHILDHOOD RISK

The human immunodeficiency virus (HIV) is the virus that causes the acquired immunodeficiency syndrome (AIDS). This deadly virus can be passed by pregnant women to their unborn children, in breastmilk and through blood-to-blood and sexual contact. HIV/AIDS impact on society works with a reverse Darwinian vengeance, it takes the lives of "fit" adults leaving behind vulnerable children ill-equipped to care for themselves (Collic et al., 2001). By the end of 2001, there were 40 million documented cases of individuals infected by human immunodeficiency virus (HIV). Over 95% of persons currently infected live in emerging nations, 18.5 million were women and three million were children under the age of fifteen (UNICEF, 2001). Again there is evidence of the disproportionate impact of diminished health in women. The rise in infected women has a destabilizing effect on local economies because women do most of the subsistence farming, food preparation, educating the young and are caregivers of family members in many cultures (Brown, 2002d).

AIDS though widespread has not yet reached its saturation point. In Brazil, the numbers of women suffering from AIDS increased ten fold during the 1990s (Faiola, 2002). While pandemic in Africa, HIV/AIDS is spreading rapidly in other nations, such as the former Soviet Central Asian countries and Eastern Europe. China, India and Indonesia, all of which are on the brink of catastrophic outbreaks (Brown, 2002b). India is second to South Africa in the number of citizens infected with HIV in the world (Constable, 2002). The resulting dire projections of AIDS related deaths over the next twenty years exceeds 68 million people (Brown, 2002b). As it relates to children, it has been estimated that four children every minute become infected with HIV (UNICEF, 2003).

The World Health Organization (WHO) estimates that nearly six million people in the poorest countries are showing AIDS-related symptoms that could be mitigated with antiretroviral treatment, yet, only 730,000 of the 40 million people believed infected with HIV throughout the world are currently being treated with life extending drugs. Only 30,000 infected persons are being treated with these drugs on the continent of Africa (Brown, 2002a). In Jamaica, the drugs necessary to keep the virus under control cost $1,100 per month. One treatment costs more than the annual income of many persons (Collic et al., 2001). To impoverished adults and children throughout the world the costs of life extending treatments are beyond their grasp.

Passing the HIV virus to children is often the result of mother-to-child transmission. Infants can contract the deadly virus at birth or as a function of being breastfed. There are drug treatments that hold the promise of reducing mother-to-child transmission, but they are expensive. The cost for the AZT regimen is $1,045 per case in the United States. Trials are under way to identify less expensive interventions, however, as yet they are largely unavailable (The World Bank, 2003). Mothers with no viable alternatives breastfeed their children even in light of the risks because this is the only source of food for infants.

The prevalence of AIDS has cascading effects on children even if not infected with the deadly virus. For example, when poor families assume the care of orphaned children the increased financial burden drives families deeper into poverty. Fees for school are cut because children are needed to work and contribute to sustenance. Unfortunately, keeping children out of school only increases the likelihood that they will remain poor because they do not gain marketable skills. Many children do not have anyone to assume care after the death of parents and as a result are relegated to support themselves as best they can. Currently, there are nearly 108 million documented orphans from all causes in Africa, Asia, Latin America and the Caribbean of which 12% (nearly 13 million) were orphaned by AIDS. By 2010, it is anticipated nine out of ten orphans in Zimbabwe alone (21% of Zimbabwe's children) will be AIDS orphans (Brown, 2002c).

Another example of the relationship of HIV/AIDS to poverty and the life prospects of children can be found in a study conducted by the University of the West Indies. In the Caribbean, there are at least 390,000 Caribbean adults and children infected with HIV. Eighty-seven percent of the HIV cases in the Caribbean come from the island Hispaniola, where both the Dominican Republic and Haiti are located. Orphaned children must seek their own sustenance making them vulnerable to sexual predators and consequently HIV. In Haiti as in other nations it is not uncommon that children band together in gangs for purposes of survival since orphanages have reached capacity. There are an estimated 11,000 street children orphaned by AIDS in Jamaica alone. By the end of 1999, it was estimated that the number of AIDS orphans exceeded 85,000 in the Caribbean (Collic et al., 2001). Poverty in the case of HIV/AIDS and other infectious diseases proves disastrous for children resulting in thousands of avoidable childhood cases proliferated because of an absence of support networks.

Diarrhea, measles, malaria, polio and respiratory infections are each tied to the availability of safe and clean water, adequate sanitation, nourishing diets and immunizations. Contaminated water is associated with the spread of dysentery, cholera and diarrhea. Inadequate sanitation facilities have been blamed for over two million deaths per year, of primarily children under the age of five. Risks associated with water and sanitation are linked to broader socio-economic and environmental factors to include the corporate disposal of toxic chemicals and agricultural run-off (UNICEF, 2002a). Each of the aforementioned illnesses continues to place poor children more than any other group at risk. As noted earlier, children tend to succumb to multiple assaults on health as opposed to singular causes. Malnutrition is associated with one-half of all deaths in children, which makes it difficult to isolate primary causes of death. However, whether primary or secondary in nature, "normal" childhood diseases are fatal most often when poor children are hungry. Figure 6 illustrates the most common causes of death in children under five.

Over two million children under the age of five die from diarrhea annually. Many diarrhea-related mortalities are associated with dehydration. Rehydration therapy works well to restore lost electrolytes (sodium, potassium and bicarbonate), however, treatment has to be accessible and affordable. The most successful disease interventions have been those applying multiple strategies such as, immunizations, a safe water supply, adequate sanitation and nutrition in concert (UNICEF, 2002a). Despite the success of holistic approaches, singular treatment options are often the only ones available for ailing children, if healthcare is accessible at all.

Malaria's symptoms are caused by a parasite that is transmitted by the Anopheles mosquito. The mosquito thrives in pools of water in warm humid climates. Once

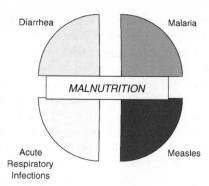

Fig. 6.   "Normal" Childhood Diseases with Abnormal Consequences. *Note:* Adapted from:
UNICEF (2002a).

in the bloodstream infected persons become ill within 7–21 days with a range
of symptoms including fever, drowsiness, painful joints, vomiting, headaches,
diarrhea and in severe cases convulsions and coma. Combination drug treatments
at symptom onset is most effective because increasingly the parasites are resistant
to the historic remedy of chloroquinine alone (UNICEF, 2002a). Again, access to
health professionals and appropriate treatment can make the difference between
life and death.

Measles is most effectively controlled with at least one dose of a vaccine, yet,
measles remains endemic in Africa, Asia and parts of Europe because of the costs
associated with the vaccine. Rarely fatal in healthy children, measles symptoms
are a rash and fever. Measles is highly contagious because it can be spread through
coughing or direct contact with infected secretions. Childhood measles fatality
rates in emerging nations are 300 times higher than those in industrialized nations.
Children with deficiencies of Vitamin A, and weakened by inadequate diets are
much more likely to perish (UNICEF, 2002a).

In the case of acute respiratory infections (ARIs), the conditions and chemicals
known to exacerbate breathing distress have been linked to the practices of some
TNCs. Acute respiratory infections, primarily pneumonia, are the leading causes of
death in youth under five reflected in Fig. 6 (World Health Organization Division of
Child Health and Development, 1998). Pneumonia is caused by a virus or bacteria
and is particularly dangerous to individuals with suppressed immune systems. One
of the reasons children are at increased risk of respiratory maladies is because their
metabolic rates are faster than adults. Children actually breath twice as much air
per pound of body weight as adults. Toddlers walk and play closer to the ground
where dust (and toxic dust) concentrations tend to be higher, which intensifies the
severity of respiratory maladies such as pneumonia or asthma (World Resources

Institute, 1999). ARIs, like measles, malaria and HIV/AIDS when experienced concomitantly with malnutrition increases the likelihood that normal childhood diseases yield abnormal results, premature death.

TOXIC CHEMICALS AND CHILD HEALTH

Attracting TNCs as a means of enhancing economic development in emerging nations exacts a high environmental price. Profit-making ventures such as transnational corporations seek to maximize returns on investments and operations. Relative to child health issues, practices designed to keep operational costs low can be the very factors placing poor workers' health and the health of their families and communities in jeopardy. Poisoning of land, air and water supplies can result because many emerging nations lack the systemic networks, expertise and resources to implement and enforce environmental protection policies. Toxic exposure associated with TNCs is also related to the aggressive importation of toxic waste from industrialized nations, such as the United States. As a result, the risk that toxic chemical release will be unchecked and unresolved increases in the same countries shouldering the burden of substantive numbers of poor families (Millen & Holtz, 2000).

Toxins released into the land, water or air do not remain where they are deposited, but rather leach into water supplies, are taken up into the food chain, settle in soil and are carried by wind far from their point source. Developmental neurotoxicants have been defined as chemicals that hinder the normal development of the brain and hormonal systems more markedly in infants and young children than in adults. Some of the most potent neurotoxicants are lead, mercury, dioxins, polychlorinated biphenyls (PCBs) and dichlorodiphenyl trichloroethane (DDT) (Schettler et al., 2000). This is not to say that adults are immune from negative health consequences of contact with neurotoxicants, but rather, because of their size and respiratory rate, children are more vulnerable to harm than adults (Schettler et al., 2000; World Resources Institute, 1999).

Developmental neurotoxins can be transmitted to children through the air, water, physical contact or from their mothers. For example, lead is retained in the bones for nearly 25 years. Pregnant women can pass this retained lead to their unborn children (Richardson, 2002). PCBs and DDTs are synthetic chemicals that tend to be commercially used in the electrical industry and agriculture, which can be passed to children, who are breastfed by exposed women. Both chemicals because of their environmental mobility have contaminated fish and ground water supplies. PCBs can also be passed from mother to child during gestation (Schettler et al., 2000). Toxic chemicals particularly PCBs and DDTs are also known to increase the risk of spontaneous abortions, miscarriages fertility problems, cancer and birth abnormalities (Millen & Holtz, 2000).

Since the time between exposure and the latent effects of neurotoxicant exposure might be years, it is difficult to draw cause and effect relationships in the traditional scientific sense (Schettler et al., 2000). However, there have been decades of research generally accepted in the medical and public health community which link certain chemicals, to negative cognitive, behavioral and learning consequences in children. Multiple causation, (i.e. interaction between chemicals, malnutrition, environmental and genetic factors) is the most likely cause of reduced intellectual capacity. At the nexus of poverty and health we again find poor families.

Consider the plight of families in the rural Peruvian town of Ilo. Daily over 2,000 tons of sulfur dioxide are emitted from the copper smelters in Southern Peru Copper, an American-owned TNC. Plant emissions exceed United States legal limits by ten times resulting in sustained air pollution and damage to crop production. Farmers have complained of premature vegetation death and severely reduced crop yield to no avail. Decreased food production has propelled families into poverty who were formerly self sufficient adding to the ranks of the poor. Emissions from the corporation's mining plant have also had a negative impact on human health. Respiratory ailments, chronic coughing and cancer are some of the common maladies that can be traced to prevailing corporate practices (Millen & Holtz, 2000).

In Bhopal, India the residual (or by-product) metals released in the extraction of zinc from batteries discarded in the United States and Europe are toxic metal dust, lead, zinc, copper and aluminum. After the extraction process metal wastes are dumped in open areas. As per Greenpeace, 450 tons of lead are annually disposed in the community surrounding the Bharat Zinc plant a TNC (Millen & Holtz, 2000). Lead is known to cause neuropsychiatric, metabolic, and neurological disorders particularly in children (Millen & Holtz, 2000; Schettler et al., 2000).

Along the U.S.–Mexican border there is a class of workers called maquiladora. Maquiladoras work in companies encouraged to establish manufacturing plants to promote Mexico's economic development thorough implementation of the North American Free Trade Agreement (NAFTA). As families migrate from other parts of Mexico to work as maquiladoras, the environmentally insensitive practices of many companies in the region have resulted in a dangerous distribution of toxins in broad populations. In the lower Rio Grande Valley, high levels of lead, mercury, chromium and nickel were identified in the water supply and in sewer lines for example (Brenner et al., 2000). Cognitive and developmental costs to disadvantaged youth like those living in Ilo, Bhopal and the Rio Grande Valley are considerable.

Table 1. The Relationship Between Neurotoxicants and Developmental Deficiencies.

TOXIN	POTENTIAL DEVELOPMENTAL DEFICIENCIES
Lead	Visual-motor and visual-spatial integration
	Attention Deficits
	IQ Deficits
	Aggression
	Impulsivity
Mercury	Mental retardation
	Visual disturbances
	Language and attention deficiencies
	Memory impairment
Manganese	Hyperactivity
	Learning disabilities
Dioxins and PCBs	Learning disabilities
	Hyperactivity
	IQ deficits

Source: Adapted from: Mendez and Adair (1999), Richardson (2002), Schettler et al. (2000), Wauben and Wainwright (1999), World Resources Institute (1999).

Table 1 highlights some of the potential deficiencies resulting from childhood exposure to the most potent neurotoxicant metals (lead, mercury and manganese) and pesticides (dioxins and PCB).

In the case of lead, exposure to small amounts during infancy or early childhood are associated with attention deficit disorders, lowered IQ, and aggression. Mercury exposure can cause mental retardation, and visual disturbances, as well as, memory language and attention impairments. Manganese has been identified as a potential cause of hyperactivity and learning disabilities. Dioxins and PCBs are linked with attention deficits and a host of learning disabilities (Schettler et al., 2000).

While Table 1 admittedly provides a cursory list, one can see even here that the health prospects of poor children are inextricably linked to their ability to learn particularly when combined with the effects of malnutrition noted in Table 2 .

Here are a few examples of how malnutrition and disease can diminish potential. Mental retardation, linguistic impairments, and visual disturbances can all be precipitated by exposure to mercury and lead. Motor and social impairment can be caused by anemia or exposure to lead. Dioxins, PCBs and lead are known to reduce the IQ of children. Short attention spans and hyperactivity, an inability to control oneself and a tendency to fidget incessantly, are characteristics considered both behavioral and cognitive in nature. Hyperactivity might be the result of a

Table 2.

Symptoms	Possible Cause
Motor Impairment and Stunted Growth	Malnutrition
	Toxic Chemical Exposure
Visual Impairment	Malnutrition
	Toxic Chemical Exposure
Cognitive Deficits (e.g. mental retardation, lost I. Q., memory deficiencies)	Malnutrition
	Toxic Chemical Exposure
Compromised Immune Systems	Malnutrition
	Infectious Disease Exposure

Source: Adapted from: Richardson (2002), Schettler et al. (2000).

manganese deficiency or exposure to lead, dioxins or PCBs. Protein, carbohydrate, zinc, iron and mercury deficiencies are related to poor memory. Reading disabilities are associated with lead exposure. Thus, the relationship between the health of young children and the ways in which poor health robs children of their genetic predisposition to learn and grow is a cost of poverty.

REFLECTIONS: POOR CHILDREN, POOR HEALTH & COGNITIVE CONSQUENCES

> We cannot waste our precious children. Not another one, not another day. It is long past time for us to act on their behalf.
>
> Nelson Mandela and Graca Machel (as cited in UNICEF, 2002b).

Discussions in this chapter only tap the surface of not only the health disparities experienced by impoverished youth, but also our collective inertia to act on their behalf. It would appear based on our actions and inactions that poor children are "damaged goods" unworthy of investment. Poverty in the 21st century continues to diminish the prospects of millions of children. Challenges facing policymakers are formidable because poverty and ill-health, particularly in children, are inextricably linked. In the absence of concerted and comprehensive intervention on their behalf, innocents will continue to personify the tragedy of the income gap between the poor and the rich and should they survive perpetuate that legacy of curtailed potential to their children (Rainwater & Smeeding, 1997).

The etiology of subsistence differs within and between nations, but the price of potential forever lost is high, too high for any country (Millen et al., 2000a). As policy makers deliberate relative to, "who gets what, when, where, how and why" (Colmers, 2002, p. 1217), children are dying. Risks disproportionately experienced by poor infants and youth provide compelling evidence of suffering painting a dismal picture of persistent linkages between health, hunger and political and economic forces just as the Relative Income Hypothesis would predict.

So much childhood misery is preventable. The ultimate paradox is that suffering associated with poverty and vulnerability flourishes concurrently with unparalleled medical advancements and wealth. Medical innovations and care benefit precious few, while the absolute number of persons living in abject poverty without access to any healthcare continues to rise (Millen et al., 2000). To reduce poverty investments must be made to ensure health (Foreign Policy, 2002). Struggles to reconcile the many dimensions of poverty must take into account the short-and long-term consequences of eroding health in youth and the pervasive economic ramifications poor health plays in nuclear family and broader social and economic networks. Consider a study conducted by the University of the West Indies. Researchers determined that there has been a 5% reduction in Trinidad's and Jamaica's gross national product as a result of AIDS-related deaths. As infected individuals become ill they lose jobs and consequently families' resources are depleted because of the need for medical care and issues attendant to mortality, such as the care of orphaned children (Collic et al., 2001).

Much progress has been made to improve the health prospects of children around the world but there is yet much to be done. One way to construct adequate and sustainable interventions on behalf of poor children and their families is to cease defining health issues in narrow apolitical terms. Assessments of poverty and health should consider national and international dimensions of income disparity and politics because both influence health-related systems.

Child poverty does not have to equal poor health. It is possible to meet the needs of poor children as exhibited by countries with the longest life expectancies and most equitable distribution of health. These nations are not the wealthiest, but rather those with the narrowest gap in national incomes, supporting Wilkinson's RIH theory. For example, the life expectancy of individuals in China, Bangladesh, and certain regions of India are higher than African Americans living in Harlem (Lynch et al., 1999). One reason the United States consistently ranks lower than her income might suggest lies in the income gap between the wealthy and the poor in the United States, which continues to widen (World Resources Institute, 1999).

"These are dangerous times for the well-being of the world," in the words of Dr. Gro Brundtland, outgoing Director General of the World Health Organization (as cited in Murray & Lopez, 2002, p. 3). We bury untold potential in the bodies of children and youth who disproportionately suffer from the costs of being poor. The fundamental questions for advocacy groups and governments are how many surviving children will emerge from childhood with their intellectual capacity in tact; and what can be done to curb the tide of lost potential? Given the distribution of malnutrition, environmental toxins, and preventable infectious diseases drastic measures are required if children are to be saved.

Children of poverty are in particular need our protection from the variables that diminish their health and learning capacity because their families do not command the resources to do so. As noted throughout this chapter, impoverished youngsters are more apt to be born under-weight, be malnourished, suffer from HIV/AIDS, chronic illnesses and exposure to environmental toxins. We do well to remember that consequences of poverty markers do not disappear after birth or early childhood, but rather persist well into adulthood (Schettler et al., 2000).

If one considers the deleterious impact of poverty in the context of child developmental stages, one can begin to perceive a more comprehensive cost of poverty. While genes pre-dispose children to certain traits and behaviors, the influence of health and environmental factors cannot be denied. Effective investments in children require holistic collaborative approaches addressing the complex dimensions of child poverty. The absence of integrated interventions will continue to severely damage capacity, creating an attendant loss for all of the world's citizens (UNICEF, 2002a).

The responsibility for protecting children is more than a nuclear family or national responsibility. It is a challenge of global proportion. That poverty has been designated the greatest thief of our young reflects the absence of a collective appreciation of the potential of each child. Investing in the health and well-being of the world's children is not a choice, it must be a global priority. As a result, Nelson Mandela and Graca Machel's words resonate with the call of this author to actively intervene on behalf of the neediest of the world's youth;

> We cannot waste our precious children. Not another one, not another day. It is long past time for us to act on their behalf.
>
> Nelson Mandela and Graca Machel (as cited in UNICEF, 2002b).

REFERENCES

Bartlett, S., Hart, T., Satterthwaite, D., De La Barra, X., & Missair, A. (1999). *Cities for children: Children's rights, poverty and urban management.* London: Earthscan Publications.

Begley, S. (1997). How to build a baby's brain. *Newsweek Special Issue* (Spring/Summer), pp. 28–32.

Bellamy, C. (1999). The roll of the dice. *The Progress of Nations 1999* (pp. 1–6). New York: UNICEF.

Brenner, J., Ross, J., Simmons, J., & Zaidi, S. (2000). Neoliberal trade and investment and the health of Maquiladora workers on the U.S.–Mexico border. In: J. Y. Kim, J. V. Millen, A. Irwin & J. Gershman (Eds), *Dying for Growth: Global Inequality and the Health of the Poor* (pp. 261–290). Monroe: Common Courage Press.

Brown, D. (2002a, July 7). Conferees call for new AIDS alliance. *The Washington Post*, A13.

Brown, D. (2002b, July 3). Report on AIDS offers dire prognosis. *The Washington Post*, A3.

Brown, D. (2002c, July 11). Report: Number of AIDS orphans to rise. *The Washington Post*, A14.

Brown, D. (2002d, November 27). Women now half of HIV infections. *The Washington Post*, A1, A12.

Brundtland, G. H. (1999). *Breaking the poverty cycle: Investing in early childhood* (press release). Geneva: World Health Organization.

Collic, T., Salcedo, M., & Bauza, V. (2001, June 10). Witness to an epidemic: AIDS in the Caribbean. *South Florida Sun-Sentinel*, 1–24.

Colmers, J. (2002). Why "government, politics, and law"? *American Journal of Public Health*, *92*(8), 1217.

Constable, P. (2002, March 7). Poverty, prejudice India's AIDS fight. *The Washington Post*, A1, A18.

DeYoung, K., & Lynch, C. (2002, May 9). War of word at youth summit. *The Washington Post*, A18.

Dunn, W. N. (1994). *Public policy analysis: An introduction*. Englewood Cliffs, NJ: Prentice-Hall.

Faiola, A. (2002, September 30). Brazilian women ravaged by AIDS. *The Washington Post*, A34.

Federal Interagency Forum on Child and Family Statistics (2000). *America's children: Key national indicators of well-being, 2000*. Washington, DC: U.S. Government Printing Office.

Federal Interagency Forum on Child and Family Statistics (2001). *America's children: Key national indicators of well-being, 2001*. Washington, DC: U.S. Government Printing Office.

Foreign Policy (2002, January/February). Stopping the next global epidemic: An interview with Gro Harlem Brundtland. *Foreign Policy*, 24–36.

Garrett, L. (2000). *Betrayal of trust: The collapse of global public health*. New York: Hyperion.

Guo, G., & Harris, K. M. (2000). The mechanisms mediating the effects of poverty on children's intellectual development. *Demography*, *37*(4), 431–447.

Harper, C., & Marcus, R. (1999). *Child poverty in Sub-Saharan Africa* (Background Paper). New York: Save the Children Fund and The World Bank.

Jeter, J. (2002, February 19). Less Than $1 Lets A Family of 6 Live. *The Washington Post*, A1, A11.

Kawachi, I., Kennedy, B. P., Lochner, K., & Prothrow-Stith, D. (1997). Social capital, income inequality, and mortality. *American Journal of Public Health*, *87*(9), 1491–1498.

Kawachi, I., & Wilkinson, R. G. (1999). Health and social cohesion. In: I. Kawachi, B. P. Kennedy & R. G. Wilkinson (Eds), *The Society and Population Health Reader: Income Inequality and Health* (pp. 195–201). New York: New Press.

Kawachi, I., Wilkinson, R. G., & Kennedy, B. P. (1999). Introduction. In: I. Kawachi, B. P. Kennedy & R. G. Wilkinson (Eds), *The Society and Population Health Reader: Income Inequality and Health* (pp. xi–xxxvi). New York: New Press.

Kozol, J. (2001). *Ordinary resurrections: Children in the years of hope*. New York: HarperCollins.

Lynch, J. W., Kaplan, G. A., Pamuk, E. R., Cohen, R. D., Heck, K. E., Balfour, J. L., & Yen, I. H. (1999). Income inequality and mortality in metropolitan areas of the United States. In: I. Kawachi, B. P. Kennedy & R. G. Wilkinson (Eds), *The Society and Population Health Reader: Income Inequality and Health* (pp. 69–81). New York: New Press.

Macfarlane, S., Racelis, M., & Muli-Musiime, F. (2000). Public health in developing countries. *The Lancet*, *356*(9232), 841–846.

Mendez, M. A., & Adair, L. A. (1999). Severity and timing of stunting in the first two years of life affect performance on cognitive tests in late childhood. *The Journal of Nutrition*, *129*(8), 1555–1562.

Millen, J. V., & Holtz, T. H. (2000). Dying for growth, Part I: Transnational corporations and the health of the poor. In: J. Y. Kim, J. V. Millen, A. Irwin & J. Gershman (Eds), *Dying for Growth: Global Inequality and the Health of the Poor* (pp. 177–224). Monroe: Common Courage Press.

Millen, J. V., Irwin, A., & Kim, J. Y. (2000a). Conclusion: Pessimism of the intellect, optimism of the will. In: J. Y. Kim, J. V. Millen, A. Irwin & J. Gershman (Eds), *Dying for Growth: Global Inequality and the Health of the Poor* (pp. 382–390). Monroe: Common Courage Press.

Millen, J. V., Irwin, A., & Kim, J. Y. (2000b). Introduction: What is growing? Who is dying? In: J. Y. Kim, J. V. Millen, A. Irwin & J. Gershman (Eds), *Dying for Growth: Global Inequality and the Health of the Poor* (pp. 3–10). Monroe: Common Courage Press.

Murray, C., & Lopez, A. (2002). *The World health report 2002: Reducing risks, promoting health life.* Geneva: World Health Organization.

Nash, J. M. (1997). Fertile minds. *Time* (February 3), 48–56.

Rainwater, L., & Smeeding, R. M. (1997). Doing poorly: The real income of American children in comparative perspective. In: J. H. Skolnick & E. Currie (Eds), *Crisis in American Institutions* (10th ed., pp. 105–114). NY: Addison-Wesley.

Richardson, J. W. (2002). Poor, powerless and poisoned: The social injustice of childhood lead poisoning. *Journal of Children & Poverty, 8*(2), 141–158.

Schettler, T., Stein, J., Reich, R., Valenti, M., & Wallinga, D. (2000). *In harm's way: Toxic threats to child development* (http://igc.org/psr). Boston: Greater Boston Physicians for Social Responsibility.

The World Bank (2003, March 2). *Preventing mother-to-child transmission.* http://www/worldbank.org/aids-econ/arv/conf-aids-4/box4–6.htm.

UNICEF (2001). *The state of the world's children 2001.* New York: UNICEF and the United Nations.

UNICEF (2002a, February 22). *Statistical data,* (www.childinfo.org/). UNICEF.

UNICEF (2002b, February 22). *United Nations special session on children.* www.unicef.org/specialsession/about/index/html. UNICEF.

UNICEF (2003). Building a world fit for children. Paper presented at the United Nations General Assembly Special Session on Children, New York.

Wadsworth, M. (2001). Early life. In: M. Marmot & R. G. Wilkinson (Eds), *Social Determinants of Health* (pp. 44–63). Oxford: Oxford University Press.

Wauben, P. M., & Wainwright, P. E. (1999). The influence of neonatal nutrition on behavioral development: A critical appraisal. *Nutritional Reviews, 57*(2), 35–44.

Wilkinson, R. G. (1999a). The culture of inequality. In: I. Kawachi, B. P. Kennedy & R. G. Wilkinson (Eds), *The Society and Population Health Reader: Income Inequality and Health* (pp. 492–498). New York: New Press.

Wilkinson, R. G. (1999b). The epidemiological transition: From material scarcity to social disadvantage. In: I. Kawachi, B. P. Kennedy & R. G. Wilkinson (Eds), *The Society and Population Health Reader: Income Inequality and Health* (pp. 36–46). New York: New Press.

World Health Organization (2001, http://www.who.int/child-adolescent-health/NEWS/news_main.htm). *News and Events: Efforts to Improve Child and Adolescent Health and Development* (September–October) (2001, November 21).

World Health Organization Division of Child Health and Development (1998). *Reducing mortality from major killers of children* (Fact Sheet http://www.who.int/inf-fs/en/gsct178.html). Geneva: World Health Organization.

World Resources Institute (1999). *Linking environment and health: Poverty, health and the environment.* Washington, DC: World Resource Institute.

Zander, J. W. V. (1989). *Human development* (4th ed.). New York: McGraw-Hill.

15. JUVENILE INSTITUTIONALIZATION PRACTICES IN INDIA: A STUDY OF TWO INSTITUTIONS IN MADRAS

Sesha Kethineni and Tricia Klosky

INTRODUCTION

How delinquent, dependent/neglected, and abused children are treated by criminal justice agencies is a concern that crosses geographical boundaries. Do the courts sentence juveniles too leniently or, conversely, too harshly? Around the world some of the most serious questions involve the placement of juveniles in penal institutions. There are some clearly recognized problems. First, many countries still house delinquents and non-delinquent children in the same institutions, despite nation-wide reforms or legislation specifically prohibiting such practices. Second, many juveniles, regardless of their status, are held in jails and detention facilities built or administered for adult populations that greatly outnumber the younger inmates. Third, efforts at reform, while ambitious, have been ineffective in changing objectionable practices and/or aiding children in need. Fourth, left unresolved is the question as to whether the problems noted above in developed countries are present to a greater or lesser degree in developing countries.

'Suffer the Little Children': National and International Dimensions of Child
Poverty and Public Policy
Advances in Education in Diverse Communities: Research, Policy and Praxis, Volume 4, 359–384
Copyright © 2006 by Elsevier Ltd.
All rights of reproduction in any form reserved
ISSN: 1479-358X/doi:10.1016/S1479-358X(04)04015-X

A developing country such as India contends with many issues noted above, as well as other problems that are culture specific. India's ability to wrestle with the range of problems is complicated, even compromised, by over population, poverty, high rates of illiteracy, and traditional prejudices along gender, caste, and religious lines. Government resources had the priority target of providing basic necessities for day-to-day survival for years after the 1947 independence from Great Britain. Juvenile crime and victimization were low priorities until recently, as the country was reorganized politically and developed its infrastructure.

But more than relative political and economic stability has led Indian leaders to address the problems of children. That same development has led to an increase in migration of children from rural to urban areas in search of employment. Tragically so many of those children have become street children and/or abandoned children, a vast majority of whom have ended-up as delinquent or abused. Initial government efforts were aimed at restructuring that internal migration by creating cottage industries and encouraging children fourteen and under to attend schools. Those efforts too often failed, as children continued to leave their rural homes. Restructuring aside, employers have remained eager to exploit vulnerable children as the cheapest pool of available labor.

Public concern about the treatment of children has led to many legislative reforms. These came with the Juvenile Justice Act of 1986 and other special acts directed at providing care, protection, rehabilitation, and reintegration of juveniles. This chapter first addresses the status of children in terms of child protection, child victimization, and child criminality. Second, it examines the legislative efforts at protecting, prosecuting, and providing treatment in institutional settings.

Third, the practices and procedures of the juvenile justice system are examined for one particular state. The data were collected in the city of Madras, capital of Tamil Nadu, for the years 1985–1996. Two juvenile institutions, one male and one female, were selected. The institutional records for a total of 965 juveniles were examined, of which 907 were males and 58 were females. Lastly, our findings for this one state were compared with official records maintained for the entire country.

STATUS OF CHILDREN IN INDIA

India, whose independence is relatively new, has not prospered the way other, more established countries have. To complicate the matters further, over 40% of India's one billion people live in extreme poverty. The problems of over-population, poverty, and lack of resources have impacted the lives of children. Female infanticide, although outlawed, is still practiced. With parental life spans cut short by disease, malnutrition, and accidents, thousands of children are orphaned at very young ages. The same malnutrition and diseases which cut down the life span of

Table 1. Laws Protecting Children in India.

The Factories Act, 1948 (Amended in 1954)	Restricted the maximum hours of work Raised the minimum age of employment to 14 years Provided training for children who used machines Provided medical examinations of young persons Created punishment for employers who violated the law
Hindu Adoption and Maintenance Act, 1956	Made adoption equally available for males and females Provided for maintenance of legitimate or illegitimate minor children
Hindu Minority and Guardianship Act, 1956	Set requirements for the legal guardianship of minors
Probation of Offender Act, 1958	Placed restrictions on the imprisonment of young offenders
Child Marriage Restraint Act 1929 (Amended in 1979)	Fixed minimum age of marriage for boys 21 and for girls 18
Children (Pledging of Labour) Act, 1933	Prohibited pledging of children under age 14 by parents in return for compensation
Child Labour (Prohibition and Regulation Act), 1986	Prohibited children less than 14 years of age from employment Created facilities for welfare and rehabilitation of young persons in employment
Prenatal Diagnostic Technique Act, 1994	Regulated prevention and misuse of prenatal diagnostic to prevent infanticide of female fetus

Source: Shardha, N. K. (1988).

their parents even more insidiously attack the children whose physical and mental growth are stunted. India had passed many laws intended to protect the children who were destitute, neglected, abused, or delinquent.

Legislations Protecting Children

There are several significant pieces of legislation directed specifically at protecting children from violence, abuse, and neglect (see Table 1). These include the Factories Act, (1954), the Hindu Adoption and Maintenance Act (1956), Hindu Minority and Guardianship Act (1956), the Probation of Offenders Act (1958), the Child Marriage Restraint Act of 1929 (Amended in 1979), the Child Labour (Prohibition and Regulation) Act (1986), and the Prenatal Diagnostic Technique (Regulation, Prevention, & Misuse) Act (1994). Specific laws were also passed to protect children against bonded labor and dangerous jobs. These laws include Children (Pledging of Labour) Act (1933) and the Child Labour (Prohibition and Regulation) Act (1986).

Some of these laws date back to British rule when India was a colony. Since gaining independence in 1947, the Government of India has revised some laws, as well as passed new ones to provide help for children in need of care, protection, and treatment. While some of those laws were considered viable, many were found to be ineffective in protecting children. Factors such as over population, extreme poverty, culture, and politics often presented barriers to the enforcement of those laws. For example, child labour laws are often unenforceable due to economic realities of family survival. Also laws protecting children from infanticide fail because of low social position of females in Indian society.

Child Labor

In 1933, the British Parliament passed the Children (Pledging of Labour) Act, which imposed punishments on employers who used children as bonded laborers (Kundu & Kundu, 1990). More than four decades later, the Indian Parliament passed the Child Bonded Labor System Act (1976), which formally ended forced labor. The Child Labour (Prohibition and Regulation) Act of 1986 further prohibits employment of children in hazardous occupations. Under the Indian Constitution, Article 24, children below fourteen years of age are prohibited from being employed in any factory or any work setting outside the home. Article 39 further protects children from being employed at an early age in dangerous occupations wherever located (Badiwala, 1998).

Despite legislative initiatives to protect children against the rigors of employment, many poor families send their children to work at very young ages to provide vital portions of the shared incomes. Children's wages may mean the difference between starvation and eviction on one hand and survival and shelter on the other. A study by Mehra-Kerpelman (1996) found that a single child's income ranged from 34 to 37% of the average total income for any household sending a child out to work. A majority of the working children are concentrated in rural areas. Although no accurate statistics are available, the Indian Planning Commission in 1983 estimated 17.3 million children working in the age group of 5–14 and 15.7 million 10–14 years of age alone (Kundu & Kundu, 1990). UNICEF cites even more recent figures ranging from 75 to 90 million child laborers under the age of fourteen (Human Rights Watch, 1996, p. 122). Other studies place the number of bonded child laborers at approximately one million (International Labour Organization, 1992, p. 15).

Many of these children work in service industries such as restaurants, pick rags, sell goods on the streets and in small shops, or are employed in hazardous industries. The hazardous industries include fireworks and matchbox units, glass factories, and stone quarries or crushing/sorting facilities. For example, fire works factories in Sivakasi in Ramnathapuram district in Tamil Nadu (southern part of India) employ approximately 45,000 children. The glass factories of Ferozabad in Uttar Pradesh (central part of India) are estimated to employ more than 45,000 children. A large number of children work in stone industries in Jaipur, lock making in Aligarh, slate-quarrying industry in Markapur (Andhra Pradesh) and Mandsaur (Madhya Pradesh), and carpet making in Jammu and Kashmir (Ahuja, 1992; Chockalingam, 1998). Many claim that without their children's earnings already subsistence living standard would decline even further. Generally poor families believe that their children are better off learning a trade rather than going to school because jobs for high school only graduates are risky propositions (Badiwala, 1998; Parker et al., 1998). Overall, India contributes to one-fourth of the world's working children and a third of Asia's children.

Besides poverty, religious beliefs may contribute to increased child labor. Many believe an individual's life course is divinely predetermined by placement in a particular family at birth. For example, the Hindu religion has traditionally divided people into castes. People have certain roles and occupations based on their castes. Lower caste status makes it difficult for individuals to get education or obtain decent employment (Nangia, 1987; Parker et al., 1998). Children from these families are told from an early age that they should be content with their inferior position. Those who choose to defy tradition find themselves ostracized by family members and kept from upward mobility by the prejudices of other castes or classes. Those prejudices exist, in spite of official efforts to break down caste distinctions. University and public employment quotas, for example, seem to have limited effects.

Although poverty has shaped the size and nature of child labor, the status of the national school system reinforces the practice. A lack of quality schools and expenses associated with sending children to schools leave some with little to do but work (Badiwala, 1998). Some families exchange their children's labor for money in the form of loans. Bonded children may only be released from their servitude after the loans are paid off in full. Children who do not have families or come from families that cannot support them, sometimes end up as destitute, victim, or worse, criminals (Chokalingam, 1998). Those children often end up either in the custody of the state or they become ripe for victimization and exploitation.

Laws Protecting Children from Criminal Victimization

In addition to the above child protection laws, there have been legal provisions concerning the criminal victimization of children as early as the Indian Penal Code (1860) and the Indian Evidence Act (1872). In the subsequent century and a half, various state and local, as well as national, laws were passed and implemented. Those measures also provide rights and benefits to children in the areas of education, property, health, housing, and other basic needs (Menon, 1990). The Indian Penal Code and state and local laws such as the Immoral Traffic (Prevention) Act of 1986 have provisions for protection of children against victimization.

A common form of victimization that children experience in India is rape. In 1998, children accounted for 27% of all rape victims. The share of child rape victims to the overall rape victims has shown a slight decrease from 1994 (30.2%) to 1998 (27%). Children below 10 years represented 15.4% ($N = 626$) of all child rape victims ($N = 4059$) in 1998. A majority of rape victims were between 10 and 16 years of age ($N = 3433$, 84.6%) for the same year. Even though the percentage of child rape victims to the overall rape victims slightly declined from 1994 (30.2%) to 1998 (27%), still a large number of child rape victims were below 10 years of age (see Table 2).

These figures raise some interesting questions. First, was it a coincidence that the number of rape victimizations were stable over the years, or was it a function of police arrest practices. Second, were victims and their families so reluctant to report, or were the police willing to report or deal with a token number of cases? Or were these figures the result of both tendencies?

In addition to victims of rape, other children were kidnapped and abducted, sold or bought as prostitutes, or abandoned (see Table 3). Commercial sexual

Table 2. Victims of Child Rape by Age Groups from 1994–1998.

Year	Age Group				Total
	Below 10 Years		10–16 Years		
	No	Percent	No	Percent	
1994	727	18.2	3259	81.8	3986
1995	747	18.4	3320	81.6	4067
1996	608	14.9	3475	85.1	4083
1997	770	17.4	3644	82.6	4414
1998	626	15.4	3433	84.6	4059

Source: National Crime Records Bureau (2000). *Crime in India.*

Table 3. Common Offenses Against Children from 1994–1998.

Type of Victimization	Years					Percent Variation 1998 Over 1997
	1994	1995	1996	1997	1998	
Child rape	3986	4067	4083	4414	4059	−8.0
Kidnapping & abduction	864	726	571	620	699	12.7
Procuration of minor girls	206	107	94	87	171	96.6
Selling of girls for prostitution	34	17	6	9	11	22.2
Buying of girls for prostitution	4	19	22	13	13	0.0
Abetment of suicide	7	9	11	13	28	115.4
Exposure and abandonment	491	570	554	582	575	−1.2
Infanticide	131	139	113	107	114	6.5
Foeticide	45	38	39	57	62	8.8
Child Marriage Restraint Act	53	57	89	78	56	−28.2

Source: National Crime Records Bureau (2000).

exploitation of young girls continues to increase despite laws prohibiting such a trade (Rastogi, 1998).

In other cases both poor and wealthy families often abort pregnancies when they find out that they will have girls or kill them right after birth (infanticide). In India, girls are often considered as an economic burden to their families as parents may have to pay money and goods to bridegrooms at the time of marriage. More often girls are taught to be dependent on others, while boys are encouraged to be independent achievers. Young girls are protected by their fathers, married women are sheltered by their husbands, and older women are provided for by their eldest sons (Kethineni & Klosky, 2000). Thus, women are never free to make their own choices and must rely upon males in their lives for protection and survival (Ismail, 1990).

Males in general are valued more than females as potential wage earner. Females, on the other hand, represent an economic burden for many families, as they have to pay dowries to get their daughters married. As a result, female children are more likely to fall prey to infanticide, abuse, or neglect than to become delinquents.

Criminal Laws and Legislations Relating to Children

As India was a British colony until 1947, British laws were originally applicable in India (Sarkar, 1987). The first laws to recognize the special status for juveniles in India had come in the form of the Apprentice Act (1850), the Indian Penal Code (1860), the Code of Criminal Procedure (1861), and the Reformatory Act (1870). These laws were closely related with similar laws in Great Britain (Sarkar, 1987).

The Apprentice Act (1850) dealt with children between the ages of 10 and 18 years who were either destitute or had committed petty offenses. Those who were tried and convicted under the Act were sent as apprentices to employers. The Indian government modified the Act in 1961, enabling children to undergo training to secure employment as adults.

The Indian Penal Code of 1860 recognized the special status of children in setting age limitations for criminal responsibility. The Code presumed that those below seven years of age were not responsible for their actions, while children between 7 years and 12 years might be convicted if they had attained sufficient maturity to understand the nature of their actions. The Code of Criminal Procedure of 1861 allowed separate trials of persons under age 15 and their confinement in reformatories or placement on probation. With the enactment of these laws penal philosophy regarding the treatment of juveniles changed from punishment to reformation.

This separate treatment of juveniles was bolstered by the Reformatory School Act of 1870, which solely dealt with the treatment of young offenders. It allowed boys under 15 who had been sentenced to transportation or imprisonment to be placed in reformatories up to the age of 18. Boys over 14 years of age were released on license if they could obtain employment. The Act, however, did not contain provisions for the establishment of such facilities for destitute male youth. Most glaringly, there were no facilities for female youth, whether criminal or destitute. In essence, these reforms were meant for male delinquents (Sharma, 1996).

The first attempt at removing children from adult institutions came with the Indian Jail Committee (1919) that recommended enactment of a special children act, establishment of juvenile courts, and separate institutions for children. Prior to 1919 juveniles were supposed to be housed in separate reformatories, the provincial governments were never strictly enforced that regulation. As the country was still under British rule, and divided into princely states and other units, it could not enact a uniform juvenile legislation for the entire country. The responsibility to enact separate legislation relating to juveniles, however, was vested with individual provincial governments.

The Madras Children Act (1920) was the earliest comprehensive delinquency law passed by a provincial government. This Act made provisions for the custody, trial, and punishment of youthful offenders and the protection of children and young persons. The law did not use the term "delinquent," instead defined a "child" as anyone under the age of fourteen and a "young person" as someone between the age of fourteen and sixteen. A "youthful" offender was anyone under sixteen years of age convicted of an offense punishable with imprisonment or transportation (Sarkar, 1987; Sharma, 1996). The law also included various non-offenders such as dependent/neglected and destitute children. Although the Madras Children Act was passed in 1920, it took the provincial government of Madras almost 20 years to set up a separate juvenile court. During this time, two other provinces, Bengal and Bombay, passed their own children acts. Apart from these three provinces, other areas have either did not have separate legislation for juveniles or did not enforce any existing legislation to the fullest extent until independence.

By 1986, almost all states have passed Children Acts. Since these acts were inconsistent in terms of definition of delinquency, court procedures, and institutionalization of delinquents, the Government of India felt a need for uniform children act that could be applied throughout the country. In 1986, the central (federal) government passed the comprehensive, uniform Juvenile Justice Act. This Act provided for the care, protection, and treatment of delinquent, dependent, and neglected children. This Act is considered model social legislation intended to provide care, protection, treatment, development, and rehabilitation of neglected and delinquent juveniles. Crucially the act outlines separate procedures for handling offenders and non-offenders. Juvenile courts have been set-up to deal with delinquents, and juvenile welfare boards have been established to handle neglected juveniles.

OFFICIAL JUVENILE CRIME STATISTICS IN INDIA

Crimes Under the Indian Penal Code

According to the Ministry of Home Affairs estimates in 1998, as many as 9,339 cases under the Indian Penal Code (IPC) were registered against juveniles. That is an increase of 18.1% over 1997 (see Table 4). The 1998 crime statistics are the most recent data available at the time of this study.

Increases in arrests from 1997 to 1998 were found for rape (19%), kidnapping and abduction of women and girls (179%), dacoity or gang robbery (75%), preparation for dacoity (100%), dowry death (59.2%), cruelty by husbands and relatives (61%), sexual harassment (48%), and other IPC (26.3%) crimes. Significant decreases were found in murder (20.6%), culpable homicide not amounting to murder or manslaughter (12%), kidnapping and abduction of others (20.8%), cheating or fraud (23.3%), counterfeiting (100%) and arson (35%).

When compared to the 1988 figures, the share of juvenile crimes in the overall crimes under the IPC declined from 1.7% in 1988 to 0.5% in 1997 and 1998. This decline occurred despite an increase in the overall population from 796,600,000 to 970,900,000, an increase of 174,300,000 (National Crime Records Bureau, 2000).

Table 4.   Juveniles Apprehended Under the IPC.

Type of Crime	1998	Percent Change From 1997 to 1998
Murder	251	−20.6
Attempt to commit murder	161	9.5
Culpable homicide/not murder	22	−12.0
Rape	194	19.0
Kidnapping & abduction	153	112.5
Women & girls	134	179.2
Of others	19	−20.8
Dacoity	35	75.0
Preparation for dacoity	2	100.0
Robbery	53	6.0
Burglary	1293	11.3
Theft	2152	9.0
Riots	574	11.9
Criminal breach of trust	19	18.8
Cheating	33	−23.3
Arson	26	−35
Hurt	1642	32.2
Dowry death	78	59.2
Molestation	138	5.3
Sexual harassment	37	48.0
Cruelty by husband and relative	248	61.0
Other crimes	2228	26.3
Total	9145	18.1

Source: National Crime Records Bureau (2000).

Offenses Under Special and Local Laws

Arrests for juvenile crimes under Special and Local Laws (SLL) underwent an increase of 36.2% from 1997 to 1998 (see Table 5). These SLL were passed based on changing social needs and many are similar to mala prohibita laws. The SLL increases were most noticeable under the Gambling Act, Prohibition Act, and Immoral Traffic Prevention Act. The gambling-related arrests increased 185.6% from 1997 to 1998. Offenses such as prostitution that fall under the Immoral Traffic Act increased by 172.3% from 1997 to 1998. Juvenile arrests under the Prohibition Act increased 763.8% from 1997 to 1998 (National Crime Records Bureau, 2000). The Prohibition Act prohibits the manufacture, transportation, and sale of alcohol without permit. Decreases in arrests were recorded for offenses under the Arms Act (55.4%), the Excise Act (42%), and the Indian Railways Act (42.3%).

Table 5. Juvenile Apprehended Under the Special and Local Laws.

Type of SLL Crime	1998	Percent Change From 1997 to 1998
Arms Act	45	−55.4
Narcotic Drugs & Psychotropic Substances Act	18	63.6
Gambling Act	277	185.6
Excise Act	128	−42
Prohibition Act	1313	763.8
Immoral Traffic Act	226	172.3
Indian Railways Act	15	−42.3
Registration of Foreigners Act	15	−16.7
Protection of Civil Rights Act	3	−50.0
Indian Passport Act	5	−37.5
Essential Commodities Act	1	−50
Dowry Prohibition Act	4	33.3
Child Marriage Restraint Act	3	200.0
Schedule Caste/Schedule Tribe Prevention of Atrocities Act	16	6.7
Forest Act	5	0.0
Other SLL Crimes	3936	7.2
Total cognizable under SLL	6005	36.2

Source: National Crime Records Bureau (2000).

Overall Juvenile Arrests by Gender

When gender differences in arrests were compared, more boys than girls were involved in various crimes (see Table 6). Girls were represented more than boys under the offense categories of kidnapping and abduction, dowry death, cruelty by relatives, Registration of Foreigners Act, Immoral Traffic Prevention Act (prostitution), Dowry Prohibition Act, and the Indian Passport Act. In some cases, young girls are forced to participate with other, older family members in harassing new brides for money. If the female victims or their families complain about such

Table 6. Juveniles Apprehended Under the IPC and SLL Crimes by Gender.

Year	Boys		Girls		Total
	Frequency	Percent	Frequency	Percent	
1997	14282	80.3	3514	19.7	17796
1998	14005	73.9	4959	26.1	18964

Source: National Crime Records Bureau (2000).

Table 7.   Juveniles Apprehended Under the IPC and SLL Crimes by Age
Groups.

Year	7–11 Years		12–15 Years		16–18 Years		Overall Age Groups
	Frequency	Percent	Frequency	Percent	Frequency	Percent	
1997	2747	15.4	12171	68.4	2878	16.2	17796
1998	3327	17.5	11570	61.0	4067	21.4	18964
Percent change 1998 over 1997		21.1		−4.9		41.3	6.6

Source: National Crime Records Bureau (2000).

harassment by the husbands' families, police tend to arrests as many members as possible before starting the investigation. These blanket arrests explain why so many girls were apprehended under those acts.

Overall Juvenile Arrests by Age Groups

The next table represents juveniles by age group arrested in 1998. Juveniles in the 12–15 year age group were more likely to be apprehended under IPC and SLL crimes (61%) compared to the other age groups (see Table 7). The arrests for juveniles in the age groups of 7–11 and 16–18 increased 21.1 and 41.3% respectively in 1998 over figures for 1997. In contrast, the arrest figures for the 12–15 year age group declined by 4.9% from 1997 to1998 (National Crime Records Bureau, 2000).

Socioeconomic Characteristics of Arrested Juveniles

Official records indicate that almost three-fourths of juveniles arrested in 1998 had a primary education (i.e. equivalent to grade school in the U.S.). Less than one-fourth (22.5%) had surpassed primary education levels (see Table 8). Further, 78.7% of juveniles came from low to lower middle-class families with incomes ranging from Rs. 0–1000 (one thousand rupees is equivalent to $22 per month). Less than 10% come from upper-middle to upper class families (National Crime Records Bureau, 2000).

   As far as family structure is concerned, three-fourths were living with one or two parents at the time of arrest, less than one fourth were living with guardians,

Table 8. Number and Percent of Education, Income, and Family Background of Arrested Juveniles in 1998.

Juvenile Attributes	Number	Percent
Level of education		
Illiterates	7230	38.1
Primary	7460	39.3
Above Primary but below Higher Secondary	3500	18.5
Higher Secondary	774	4.1
Total	18964	100.0
Level of income		
Low (up to Rs. 500 per month)	9886	52.1
Lower/middle (Rs. 501–1000 per month)	5048	26.6
Middle (Rs. 1001–2000 per month)	2725	14.4
Upper middle (Rs. 2001–3000 per month)	1019	5.4
Upper (above Rs. 3000 per month)	286	1.5
Total	18964	100.0
Family background		
Living with parent(s)	13835	73.0
Living with guardian(s)	4137	21.8
Homeless	992	5.2
Total	18964	100.0

Source: National Crime Records Bureau (2000).

and only one twentieth were considered homeless. In general the data suggest that juveniles who were arrested come from poor families with little or no education.

Offenses Under Special and Local Laws in Tamil Nadu

Juvenile arrests under IPC for the state of Tamil Nadu, the research site for the study, ranked 7th in the country (National Crime Records Bureau, 2000). Out of the total juvenile arrests under IPC for 1998 (11,982), Tamil Nadu accounted for 4.2% (502). In contrast, arrests for SLL crimes accounted for 48.4% (3,380). Furthermore, Tamil Nadu had the highest number of juvenile arrests in the age groups of 7 and 11years (1,648) and 12 and 15 years (1,513). These figures suggest that law enforcement in Tamil Nadu enforces local laws more stringently in comparison to other states.

JUVENILE COURT PROCESSING AND INSTITUTIONALIZATION

Juvenile Courts Under the JJA

The juvenile court bench is composed of Judicial or Metropolitan Magistrates, one of whom is appointed as a Principal Magistrate. The ultimate decision of how many magistrates to appoint is left up to the individual states. Any state wishing to establish a separate juvenile court must also have an honorary panel of two social workers, one of whom has to be a female. States that do not have a separate juvenile court are required to have Metropolitan or Judicial Magistrates preside over juvenile cases in separate physical settings. However, these trials are conducted in criminal court houses. These magistrates are required to have special training with or knowledge of juvenile issues.

Children who are neglected and dependent come before the Juvenile Welfare Boards. Each board consists of a chairperson and as many other members as the states see fit to appoint. Similarly to the juvenile court personnel, one member must be a female. Cases are to be decided on a case-by-case basis in a manner that is informal, non-punitive, and non-judicial in nature. Generally, dispositions include placing juveniles with guardians or "fit institutions," such as Juvenile Homes.

Juvenile Institutionalization Under the JJA

A central part of the Act was to ensure that children were not institutionalized along with adults either before or after trial. Terms such as lock-up, confinement, detention, and remand have been replaced with more treatment-oriented terms, such as protection, reception, and treatment (Mookerjee, 1989). Specifically, three separate types of institutions were created to accomplish this goal: Observation Homes (pre-trial detention centers), Special Homes (facilities for adjudicated delinquents) and Juvenile Homes (residences for neglected children). The Act explicitly prohibits housing juveniles who are awaiting trial in police lock-ups or jails (Menon, 1990). Juveniles arrested or brought before the Court or the Juvenile Welfare Board are to be housed in Observation Homes prior to their determination of status. Where no such facility exists, the local government can designate any other place as a temporary holding facility (Mitra, 1988). Although the maximum length of stays in Observation Homes are not listed in the Act, Observations Homes are supposed to serve as temporary holding facilities while awaiting trial or determination by the Welfare Board. According to Pawar (1993), observation homes process as many as 40,000 juveniles annually.

All Observation Homes must provide a basic standard of care (medical, food and board, and education) as well as occupational training. In addition, juveniles' family backgrounds, scholastic aptitudes, psychological make-ups are assessed to diagnose the juveniles needs.

The Observation Home where pre-trial detainees are held facing problems of security in the form of escapes and discipline. Because of recent escapes in the center, the administration decided to lock-up all children from morning to night without even providing proper recreation. The room where male children were housed resembled a small dormitory with very little space. The children eat, play, bathe, and sleep in this dormitory. Instead of increasing staff to monitor children, they decided to secure the place by keeping the kids in one room.

Demographic information on gender, age, education, religion, and place of residence was collected. Other variables included were type of offense, length of detention, length of time between admissions and the court orders, number of cases transferred from other schools, number of escapes, and number of escapees rearrested.

In many cases these facilities are overcrowded with staff who are overworked and under-trained. Furthermore, the facilities are often in poor condition and do not meet minimum standards of detention. As a result, they are ill-equipped to meet the basic individual needs of juveniles (Pawar, 1993).

Nor are individual rights being protected. Article 21 of the Indian constitution states that no person should be deprived of life or personal liberty except according to procedures established by law. A newspaper exposé found that children who were in observation homes had no right to appellate review of their placement (Van Bueren, 1999). Furthermore, juveniles were often not provided with copies of the rules governing their detention and a written description of their rights. Many children housed in these facilities stay there without knowing the purpose and the length of their institutionalizations (Pawar, 1993).

One significant focus of this Act is to segregate offenders from non-offenders by creating separate facilities. Juvenile offenders are housed in Special Homes, while neglected/dependent children are sent to Juvenile Homes. The period of detention in Special Homes should not exceed three years for juvenile males over age 14 and juvenile females over 16 years of age. In all other cases, juveniles may be housed in Special Homes until they reach the age of majority.

Juveniles in Special Homes should be provided with accommodation, maintenance, education, vocational training, rehabilitation, character development, and training in order to foster reformation (Mitra, 1988). Of all the juveniles arrested and brought to court ($N = 18,964$) in 1998, only 9.2% ($N = 1751$) were sent to

Table 9.   Dispositions Received by Arrested Juveniles in 1998.

Type of Disposition	Number	Percent
Sent to home after admonition	2620	13.8
Release on probation/placed in care of parents	3889	20.5
Released on probation/placed in care of fit institution	829	4.4
Sent to special homes	1751	9.2
Fine	908	4.8
Acquitted/otherwise disposed off	2107	11.1
Pending disposal	6860	36.2
Totals	18964	100.0

Source: National Crime Records Bureau (2000).

Special Homes and less than 5% ($N = 829$) were referred to fit or similar institutions (National Crime Records Bureau, 2000). Many of those are released to the care of parents and placed on probation (see Table 9).

Neglected juveniles may be sent to Juvenile Homes until they cease to be juveniles (i.e. 16 for boys and 18 for girls). The Board may extend the period of stay for up to age 18 for boys and 20 for girls. Similar to Special Homes, these homes provide for care, education, vocational training, and character development. However, unlike delinquent juveniles, neglected children were given special training. Lawmakers believed that neglected children are particularly vulnerable to exploitation or abuse by adults for prostitution or crime. The Act stipulates that Juvenile Homes take different approaches in insulating neglected/dependent children against these dangers. They specifically focus on preventing victimization. It is unfortunate that similar protection is not offered to delinquent children, as many of them come from backgrounds similar to those of neglected/dependent children. The same dangers are present, but legislators believed that neglected children are more deserving of protection (Pawar, 1993).

The progress of juveniles, whether sent to Special Homes or Juvenile Homes, is periodically assessed. After serving two-thirds of their sentences, their cases are reviewed and juveniles are released on license. Juveniles released on license must meet the conditions set forth by the judge or face further prosecution. Aftercare, on the other hand, occurs after juveniles have served their sentences and they are not under court or formal supervision. While on statutory or aftercare license, juveniles are directed by probation officers toward reintegration into their communities. If juveniles have no home to return to, they may be referred to Aftercare Homes for assistance and possible accommodation (Janeksela, 1991).

Aftercare Homes are supposed to provide opportunities for future employment and skills to adjust to life outside the institutional settings. While these homes are intended to accomplish the above tasks, in reality they faced several obstacles in rehabilitating juveniles (Pawar, 1993). First, many of these facilities have faced antiquated equipment, crumbling buildings, and limited maintenance services. Second, rehabilitative efforts are often hampered by non-cooperation by family members and the public at large. Third, many of these institutions lack resources for assisting juveniles in finding future employment such as employment counselors and ties to the community. Finally, these facilities must operate in the face of a government that would rather react to the delinquency problem than prevent it by providing delinquency prevention programs.

Juveniles who are released to Aftercare Homes could benefit from an untapped resource – Juvenile Guidance Bureaus. The prevention programs offered at Juvenile Guidance Bureaus can be extended or adapted to offender populations in Aftercare Homes to prevent or limit recidivism. These Bureaus offer counseling and therapy; diagnostic services to schools, teachers, and parents; and services to find the best placement alternatives for special need juveniles. There is no uniformity in the number and scope of the programs offered among bureaus. Further, no systematic information is available regarding their overall functioning and effectiveness (Pawar, 1993, p. 57).

According to Janeksela (1991), the problems with aftercare services stem from several conditions. First, scant resources often lead to offenders and non-offenders being housed together under one roof. Second, many judges base dispositions on offenders' personalities, as they appear in court hearings rather than through testimony of experts, and the needs of correctional institutions that house juveniles, rather than the needs of offenders. Third, police officers often determine the ages of offenders without hard evidence from experts (i.e. medical doctors and psychologists). Finally, the expertise of social workers and other mental health professionals is not sought in judicial decision-making process.

SUPREME COURT DECISIONS AFFECTING JUVENILE INSTITUTIONALIZATION PRACTICES

As the JJA (1986) prohibits detention of children in adult jails and prisons, many lawsuits contesting such detentions have been filed since the Act's passage. The most noteworthy cases reaching the Supreme Court were brought by the public interest groups. In *Supreme Court Legal Aid Committee v. Union of India and others* (1985), a writ petition was filed requesting relief for delinquent children detained in jails and also for a report as to the fulfillment of the Act's conditions. Specifically the establishment of juvenile courts, observation homes, special homes, and juvenile homes. All the District Judges in the entire country were ordered to supply the particulars of juveniles who were awaiting trials as well as those convicted juveniles who were housed in adult jails. The number of juveniles detained in adult jails from various states ranged from 30 to 437. Some of those states took initiatives and release or transferred children from jails to appropriate institutions.

In a subsequent case, *Sheela Barse v. Union of India* (1986), a social worker and a freelance journalist filed a public interest lawsuit in the Supreme Court challenging the appalling conditions of jails in which children were detained. The suit requested the production of information on children detained in jails, on the existence of juvenile courts, and special schools. In addition, the suit asked the Court for a direction as to the proper care of children and a direction to the State Legal Aid Board to appoint a counsel to ensure free legal representation for juveniles accused of committing crimes.

The Supreme Court commended the litigants for bringing the matter to the attention of the Court. They then directed every district and session court judge to visit jails in his/her area once every two months, keep track of children detained in jails, and inform a higher court as to their findings. The Court also directed the State Legal Aid Board to provide legal advice to children who are pre-trial detainees in prisons/jails (Van Bueren, 1999).

THE CURRENT STUDY

Up to this point, the discussion has focused on various issues relating to children and institutionalization of children in India. The data reported thus far have come from official national sources. Official statistics paint a picture of delinquency and institutionalization that may not carry over to individual states. In order to understand the dynamics of juvenile institutionalization, data were collected from two juvenile institutions in one state, Tamil Nadu, in southern India. The data from these two institutions will be compared with national statistics in order to understand similarities and differences.

Research Methodology

The data on a total of 965 cases were collected in Madras, the capital of Tamil Nadu over a period of six months. Tamil Nadu is one of the largest states in India with a population of 55,859,000. The State comprises 17% of India's total population of 966,783,171. Madras, one of the major cities in the southern part of India, has a population of 4,428,900 (Government of India, 1999).

Madras is a multilingual city populated primarily by people who speak Tamil as their principal language, followed by Telugu (5%). It is similar to the country as a whole in terms of religious distribution with 80% Hindu, 14% Muslim, 2.4% Christian, and 3.6% in other religious groups (3.6%).

The data were collected from two Special Homes, one for males and one for females. Prior to passage of the JJA, these homes were referred to as Approved Schools for Boys and Girls. Permission to collect the data was obtained from the Chief Metropolitan Magistrate, the Tamil Nadu Ministry of Social Welfare, and the Superintendent from each of the two institutions.

Data pertaining to juveniles sentenced to these schools from 1985 through 1996 were collected over a period of six months. The process resulted in a total of 965 cases, of which 907 were males and the remaining 58 were females.

The Special Home for males in Madras is relatively large in comparison to the female facility. Perhaps because of its smaller, more manageable inmates, the female Special Home seems to provide a greater variety of vocational programs than its counterpart. In other words, staff at the female home can spend more time on programming, rather than facility management or security. Furthermore, female delinquents are allowed to mix more freely with female non-offenders, except for separate housing arrangements at night than in the male home.

Demographic Characteristics

Gender

Of all the juveniles sentenced to Madras juveniles Special Homes from 1985 through 1996, almost 95% were male while the remaining 5% were female. Girls are much less likely come to the attention of the juvenile justice system for several reasons. First, families maintain strict supervision over their young daughters. Girls are not given the same amount of freedom as boys. Second, Indian communities are very cohesive and, as such, exercise informal social control over the girls. Parents are not the only adults who supervise and punish neighborhood children. Third, police officers and judges are less stringent with females and more likely to act in a fatherly or paternalistic manner. Girls then are either monitored so closely by their families and their communities that they do not generally commit juvenile offenses, or those who do frequently find the cases against them dismissed by juvenile justice officials. When females are institutionalized, it is often at an older age because their families, as well as communities feel less responsible for older females.

In contrast, male children are more likely to be institutionalized for several reasons. First, they have more freedom and more opportunities to commit crimes. When they commit crimes, they are more likely to do so in a public place. Second, they tend to participate in more serious offenses than females because they have been socialized to take more risks. Third, male children may have to steal or beg to support their families because their youth is no bar to the expectation that they are to be wage earners. Male children are often the sole breadwinners for their families as early as age seven, which puts them at even greater risk for criminal behavior.

Age

The age of male institutionalized juveniles in the study ranged from under one year to eighteen, with an average age of 13 years. Madras was one of the states that prior to the JJA sent neglected/dependent children to the same institutions. Yet, even after the JJA was passed, occasionally younger juveniles who were either destitute or neglected were housed in facilities designed for delinquents, for lack of other housing placements. From 1985 through 1996, twenty-five (2.78%) out of 904 male juveniles were under the age of six.

The age of institutionalized females ranged between seven and 18 years, with an average age of 14 years (see Table 10). Unlike male juveniles, there were no females under the age of seven. The youngest girls are least likely to be allowed to roam freely on the streets where they are visible and picked up by the police. Above the age of six, youth, even female youth, begin to appear on the streets.

Religion

The majority of male juveniles were Hindus (90.5%), followed by Muslims (6.2%) and Christians (3.3%), reflecting the distribution of religious affiliations in the region. Of the females, 94% were Hindu, 3.4% were Muslim, and 1.7% were Christian.

Education

The educational level of males ranged from no education to 11 years of school, with a mean of 4.4 years of school. A quarter of male juveniles ($N = 217$, 24.1%)

Table 10. Distribution of Age by Gender.

Age Groups	Males		Females	
	Frequency	Valid Percent	Frequency	Valid Percent
Under 1	1	0.1	0	0
1–5	24	2.6	0	0
6–10	133	14.7	5	8.8
11–15	598	66.2	32	56.1
15 and above	148	16.4	20	35.1
Total	904	100.0	57	100

Note: Due to missing data, the total *N* is not equal to 907.

had no formal education, suggesting that many of these male juveniles were from poor families who could not afford to send their children to school. The situation may well have been even grimmer for females as to educational background. There was not a single notation of female inmates' formal educational level. At least two assumptions can be drawn. Either all females had never been to school. Or officials believed education was of little or no consequence for females.

Place of Residence
Two fifths of male juveniles ($N = 370$, 40.8%) came from towns, almost similar % ($N = 336$, 37%) were from cities. Less than one fifth ($N = 116$, 17.7%) of male juveniles had come from villages and a very small% ($N = 14$, 1.5%) came from out-of-state. As far as females were concerned, a majority ($N = 27$, 61.4%) had come from towns, followed by cities ($N = 15$, 34.1%) and out-of-state ($N = 2.4.5\%$).

TYPE OF OFFENSES COMMITTED BY INSTITUTIONALIZED JUVENILES BY GENDER

Although theft was the most common offense for both males (37%) and females (50%), major gender differences were found in the number of neglect cases and drug offenses. While 38.2% ($N = 338$) males were sent to an institution for being neglected or dependent, only one female was housed in an institution for being neglected (see Table 11). Furthermore, 22.5% of the institutionalized females were involved in drug offenses, while no institutionalized males were involved in drug offenses. Females are often used as drug peddlers because they are less likely to raise suspicion.

Institutionalized male juveniles are reported as having committed a majority of offenses alone, while 18.5% ($n = 168$) of them committed offenses with others. Similarly, females committed the majority of offenses (77.6%, $n = 45$) alone, while 22.4% ($n = 13$) committed offenses with others (see Table 12).

Of the 965 total incarcerated juveniles, 140 (15.4%) males and 8 (13.8%) females escaped during their confinement. The institutional records indicate that out of 140 male escapees, 100 (71.4%) escaped alone, while the remaining 40 (28.6%) joined others in their escapes. All of the female escapees acted alone (see Table 13).

Length of Stay in Male and Female Institutions

The length of detention in Special Homes for males ranged from one day to 4,380 days, with an average of 947 days. Only one male neglected juvenile stayed the

Table 11.   Number and Percent of Type of Offenses Committed by Gender.

Type of Offense	Males		Females	
	Frequency	Valid Percent	Frequency	Valid Percent
Offense against persons				
Murder	25	2.8	4	6.9
Rape	3	0.3	0	0
Resist arrest	5	0.6	0	0
Criminal intimidation	0	0	1	1.7
Possession of weapon	0	0	1	1.7
Kidnapping	0	0	2	3.4
Offenses against property				
Theft	327	37.0	29	50.0
Burglary	136	15.4	0	0
Criminal damage to property	1	0.1	0	0
Unlawful possession of railway property	29	3.3	0	0
Ordinance offenses				
Liquor violations	13	1.5	0	0
Prostitution	0	0	3	5.2
Drugs	0	0	13	22.5
City Police Act	7	0.8	4	6.9
Neglect/dependent	338	38.2	1	1.7
Total	884	100.0	58	100.0

Note: Due to missing data, the total N is not equal to 907.

longest (4,380 days) as he was admitted when he was only a year old. Females, on the other hand, stayed anywhere between 9 days to 4,380 days, with an average of 1462 days. As far as the location and the physical conditions are concerned, significant differences were found. While the female facility is located in the city,

Table 12.   Number and Percent of Offenses Committed Alone and with Others.

Alone/Others	Gender			
	Males		Females	
	Frequency	Percent	Frequency	Percent
Alone	739	81.5	45	77.6
With others	168	18.5	13	22.4
Total	907	100.0	58	100.0

Table 13. Number and Percent of Types of Escapes by Gender.

Type of Escape	Gender			
	Males		Females	
	Frequency	Percent	Frequency	Percent
Alone	100	71.4	8	100.0
With others	40	28.6	0	0.0
Totals	140	100.0	8	100.0

the male home was built on the outskirts of the city. Furthermore, the male facility was in a dilapidated condition, while the female facility was relatively new when this researcher visited both facilities.

CONCLUSION AND DISCUSSION

In recent years, the Government of India has taken steps to protect the status of children and improve the juvenile justice system. One effort designed to help street children provides training and assistance so that they can be self-sufficient by legitimate means. This is being accomplished with the cooperation of voluntary organizations separately from institutional settings. The members of these organizations are largely social workers, educators, and communication specialists. Funding for these projects comes from foreign and local donors, as well as federal government. Such efforts could curtail exploitation by employers and further reduce the number of street children in institutions (Hassen, 2001).

Criminal victimization continues to be a major concern for the country, especially child rape and infanticide. Both of these crimes against children stem from either economic or cultural pressures. Girls in India are often used as prostitutes to provide income for their families' survival or, worse yet, put to death for being economic burdens. The Indian multi-party politics and a bloated bureaucracy have left scarce funding for prevention programs – whether aimed at delinquency, neglect, or dependency.

With prevention programs largely ignored, stillborn, or abandoned, more recent government efforts have targeted juveniles after they have committed crimes or become neglected. Even there the government's hand had been forced by litigation filed by public interest groups contesting the status of juveniles in Indian jails, Supreme Court rulings, and international laws for the protection of children. Early these groups or factors were primarily responsible for the enactment of

JJA, which formally created a separate system for juveniles. Passed by the Indian Parliament, the JJA has yet to reach full implementation. Many states still are non-compliant by either not creating separate courts or housing juvenile offenders and non-offenders in the same facilities. Still worse, housing juveniles in adult jails continues. As a result of this range of non-compliance, the Supreme Court issued orders requiring district-level magistrates to expeditiously investigate and report the detention of juveniles in adult jails. These orders have led many states to release juveniles from adult facilities or transfer them to appropriate institutions.

Another legislative change came into effect in the year 2000. The President of India signed the Juvenile Justice (Care and Protection of Children) Bill to: (1) bring the juvenile law in conformity with the United Nations Convention on the rights of children; (2) ensure a uniform age of 18 years for both boys and girls; (3) to emphasize a speedy disposal of cases by the courts and welfare boards; (4) designate the role of the Government as a facilitator of change rather than an enforcer; (5) encourage voluntary organizations and grass-roots organizations to take active part in helping children; (5) create special police units, which will be trained in handling juveniles with an humanitarian approach; and (7) increase accessibility for juveniles by establishing a juvenile justice board and a child welfare committee in each state (India, 2001, p. 1).

Currently, the juvenile justice system is still undergoing change and reform. In order for the system to work effectively and efficiently, enforcement and periodic monitoring mechanisms to assess compliance with the Act must be put into place. The results from the Madras study indicate that neglected juveniles are still housed along with delinquent children. Although some of the neglected children were referred to the Special Home prior to the JJA, a vast majority of them were sent to these homes after the passage of the Act. This means that neglected juveniles are still being placed with delinquent juveniles despite the fact that the Act prohibits the practice.

Another aspect of the Act seems to be undermined by the realities of the juvenile justice system. Although the Act prohibits incarcerative sentences for juvenile in adult jails/prisons, the practice still continues today. It is not unusual to find juveniles being housed side-by-side with adult criminals, especially in states that have yet to build facilities since 1986. The Act was intended to prevent juveniles from being compromised by the problem associated with the adult system.

The most Supreme Court cases since 1987 on juvenile justice have focused on pre-adjudication detention and conditions of confinement. Pretrial detention in observation homes, however short, is crucial because it compromises juveniles' rehabilitation or well-being (Pawar, 1993). The law still allows for children accused of crimes and those who are the products of neglect and dependency are kept in the same observation homes. In these homes, there is no special consideration for age or seriousness of crime. Therefore, young, impressionable dependent children could be influenced by older, more experienced delinquent children. Currently there are not even mechanisms in place to determine the extent of the problem, much less alleviate it.

Reform should concentrate on improving the juvenile justice system's functions all the way from arrest to disposition. First, police officers should be required to seek expert opinions before ascertaining age. Second, although media outlets are supposed to be given only very limited access to juveniles who have been apprehended, quite often reporters and institutional officials ignore those rules. The government should enforce strict compliance with existing laws prohibiting such actions. Third, each state must create a separate juvenile court headed by judges trained specifically in juvenile matters. Quite often judges who are awaiting promotion to higher positions are placed as juvenile court judges in the interim. There is no stability in judicial decision-making. In Madras, for example, a well-intended but untrained judge in juvenile affairs was heading the court on a part-time basis. In order for the juvenile court to be consistent, there needs to be consistency on the bench.

Fourth, the government should require juvenile court attorneys to undergo special training in juvenile laws, as well as procedures. Prosecutors and defense attorneys should have special knowledge of the juvenile court and should work together in the best interests of the children.

Finally, research in this area is scant primarily because of the limited access to the data. Courts have outdated or no technology to keep accurate, complete records. Any data have to be manually collected. Future research should include a qualitative component so that problems that are not addressed in quantitative research can be tapped through interviews of juvenile justice professionals. For example, how many see their careers continuing in the field of juvenile justice? What are their social and educational backgrounds? What legal and managerial changes would they suggest? If national and state governments continue to pass reforms without providing the resources to ensure their implementation, these professionals, if they truly are professionals, will continue to shoulder the burdens of caring for the youths. One is left with a lingering question – just how far, in reality, has the juvenile justice come in the fifty years since the independence?

REFERENCES

Ahuja, R. (1992). *Social problems in India*. New Delhi: Rawat Publications.

Badiwala, M. (1998). *Child labour in India: Causes, governmental policies and the role of education*. [On-line]. Available: wysiwyg://10/http://www.geocities.com/CollegePark/Library/9175/inquiry1.htm.

Chockalingam (1998). Criminological developments in India with a special focus on marginal criminality. In: E. W. Plywaczwski (Ed.), *Current Problems of the Penal Law and Criminology* (pp. 115–134). Bialysto, Poland: Temida2.

Government of India (1999). *India*. [On-line]. Available: http:/www.madras.com.

Hassen, F. (2001, April 6). Street children project lauded at world summit. *India Abroad*, 10.

Human Rights Watch (1996). *The small hands of slavery: Bonded child labor in India*. New York: Author.

India: President's nod for two bills (2001, January 10). *The Hindu*. LEXIS.NEXIS. Academic Universe. http://web.lexis-nexis.com/universe/doc. . .1&_md5=13eefadec078c2427d5a265d49d444cfd.

International Labour Organization (1992). *World labor report*. Geneva: Author.

Ismail, R. (1990). India's girl child: Daughter of denial. In: S. C. Batia (Ed.), *Children in India* (pp. 7–11). New Delhi: Development Communication Group.

Janeksela, G. M. (1991). Descriptive analysis of five juvenile justice systems: United States, Scotland, England, India, and South Africa. *International Review of Modern Sociology*, *21*(1), 1–19.

Kethineni, S., & Klosky, T. (2000). The impact of juvenile justice reforms in India. *International Journal of Offender Therapy and Comparative Criminology*, *44*(3), 312–325.

Kundu, U., & Kundu, C. L. (1990). Child labor and education. In: S. C. Batia (Ed.), *Children in India* (pp. 12–18). New Delhi: Development Communication Group.

Mehra-Kerpelman, K. (1996). Children at work: How many and where? *World of Work*, *15*, 8–9.

Menon, N. R. M. (1990). Law, policy and enforcement. In: S. C. Batia (Ed.), *Children in India* (pp. 19–46). New Delhi: Development Communication Group.

Mitra, M. L. (1988). *Juvenile delinquency and Indian justice system*. New Delhi: Deep and Deep Publications.

Mookerjee, A. (1989). *Juvenile justice: An in-depth study on matter relating to children*. Calcutta: S. C. Sarkar & Sons.

Nangia, P. (1987). *Child labour: Case-effect syndrome*. New Delhi: Janak Publisher.

National Crime Records Bureau (2000). *Crime in India*. New Delhi: Government of India, Ministry of Home Affairs.

Parker, D. L., Engfer, L., & Conrow, R. (1998). *Stolen dreams*. Minneapolis, MN: Lerner Publication.

Pawar, M. S. (1993). Rehabilitation of juvenile delinquents in India. *Indian Journal of Social Science*, *6*(1), 41–64.

Rastogi, V. (1998). Preserving children's rights: The challenges of eradicating child sexual exploitation in Thailand and India. *Suffolk Transnational Law Review*, *22*, 259–282.

Sarkar, C. (1987). *Juvenile delinquency in India: An etiological analysis*. Delhi: Daya Publishing House.

Shardha, N. K. (1988). *The legal, economic and social status of the Indian child*. New Delhi: National Book Organization.

Sharma, D. D. (1996). *Young delinquents in India*. Jaipur, India: Printwell.

Sheela Barse v. Union of India, AIR 1986 SC 1773, AIR 1988 SC 656.

The Supreme Legal Aid Committee v. Union of India and others, Criminal Writ Petition. No. 1451 of 1985. AIR 1989 Supreme Court 1278.

Van Bueren, G. (1999). International Perspectives on adolescents' competence and culpability: A curious case of isolationism: America and international child criminal justice. *Quinnipiac Law Review*, *18*, 451–464.

16. CHILD POVERTY IN SIERRA LEONE: VIGNETTES FROM THE LEONENET STREET CHILDREN'S PROJECT

Samuel Hinton[*]

INTRODUCTION

This article is divided into seven sections randomly organized to address specific issues related to poor and destitute children in Sierra Leone. The contents are primarily flavored by the work and implementation dynamics of a small non-profit organization trying to make a dent in the welfare and upkeep of some of Sierra Leone's poor children. Sometimes the activities of our organization also touch the lives of adults, particularly when these adults are so poor that they are unable to provide for themselves and their children. The first section gives an introduction. The second section describes the country in geographical, educational, and socio-economic contexts. The third provides snapshots or vignettes of what it means to be poor and the realities of working among the poor in Sierra Leone. In the fourth section, we discuss the nature of child poverty in the country. Section five discusses probable contributions made by the state towards child poverty in Sierra Leone. Section six narrates the nature of the work done by the Leonenet Street Children

[*]Samuel Hinton is Founder/President of the Leonenet Street Children Project. Pinkie McCann-Willis became the first volunteer country Director in 1996.

'Suffer the Little Children': National and International Dimensions of Child
Poverty and Public Policy
Advances in Education in Diverse Communities: Research, Policy and Praxis, Volume 4, 385–405
Copyright © 2006 by Elsevier Ltd.
All rights of reproduction in any form reserved
ISSN: 1479-358X/doi:10.1016/S1479-358X(04)04016-1

Table 1. Infant Mortality, Gross National Product and Life Expectancy at Birth.

Country	Under 5 Mortality Rank	Infant mortality Rate (Under 1)		Total Population (Thousands)	GNP Per Capita (USS)	Life Expectancy at Birth (Years)
		1960	1998	1998		
Ethiopia	18	173	145	59,649	110	37
Rwanda	21	143	81	6,604	210	41
Uganda	35	133	84	20,554	330	40
Congo	47	133	81	2,785	670	49
Sudan	43	290	157	28,282	290	55
Liberia	6			2,666	490	48
Sierra Leone	1	222	182	4,568	160	38

Source: UNICEF, State of the World's Children 2000.

Project.[1] Recommendations are made in section seven on what needs to be done to ameliorate the situation.

Three tables are provided to supplement the information in the narrative. Each table contains information on countries, which had been affected by war, or violent crisis so that the reader could make comparisons based on the listed indicators. Table 1. presents data collected by the United Nations International Children's Fund (UNICEF) on under-5 infant mortality rate, infant mortality rate under 1, total population in thousands, gross national product, and life expectancy after birth. Comparison data for six African countries are listed.

Table 2 presents data collected by the World Bank to indicate average percentage growth rate and school enrollment statistics for six African countries and Sierra

Table 2. Average Annual Percentage Growth and School Enrollment.

Country	Average Percent Growth 1986–1996	School Enrollment			
		Primary		Secondary	
		1980	1992–1998	1980	1992–1998
Ethiopia	1.0	51	67	11	19
Rwanda	1.4	59	80	–	41
Uganda	1.7	44	36	46	17
Congo	–	48	–	22	–
Sudan	1.7	105	90	16	29
Liberia	−0.5	46	60	11	16
Sierra Leone	−0.3	52	–	14	–

Source: World Bank (1997). *African Development Indicators.*

Table 3. Refugees From Selected African Countries.

Country	Refugees	Asylum Seekers	Internally Displaced	Total Population of Concern
Ethiopia	257,700	2,010	14,1600	274,310
Rwanda	34,000	1,770	49,200	711,470
Uganda	218,200	180	–	219,580
Congo	39,900	220	–	117,620
Sudan	319,000	–	–	319,260
Liberia	96,300	30	90,600	597,530
Sierra Leone	6,600	–		704,730

Source: UNHCR *(1999). *Statistical Overview*. United Nations High Commission For Refugees.

Leone. Table 3. charts the number of refugees, asylum seekers, internally displaced persons, and the total population of concern to the United Nations High Commission For Refugees.

SIERRA LEONE IN CONTEXT

Sierra Leone is a merger of the former British Crown Colony – Freetown, and the former British Protectorate of Sierra Leone. The two regions were amalgamated in 1961 into the independent country of Sierra Leone. The land mass encompasses an area of 27,000 square miles (73,000 square kilometers), roughly equivalent to the State of South Carolina, USA. Sierra Leone lies between the seventh and tenth parallels of north latitude and is approximately bisected by the meridian at twelve degrees west longitude. Annual average temperature is about 80 degrees Fahrenheit, except between November and February when a cold dry wind (harmattan) lowers temperatures to the mid-fifties. There are two distinct seasons consisting of a dry period, which lasts from November to April, and a rainy stretch extending from May to October. Average yearly rainfall is about 89 inches resulting in considerable soil erosion in deforested areas.

Before the war the Sierra Leone economy was mainly fueled by exports of diamonds, bauxite, cocoa, coffee, palm kernels, and corn. The GDP per capita was $159 per year before the war. Seventy-five percent of the population is living below the poverty line. Adult illiteracy is 67%, and adult life expectancy is 39 years for men, and 36 years for women. Sierra Leone is a complex country to understand because of the myriad problems associated with its development or underdevelopment and the many players, national and international contributing to such complexity. A country rich in minerals such as gold, diamonds, and iron-ore is mismanaged for over thirty years by an unscrupulous kleptocracy of civil and military governments to the extent that it became one of the poorest countries in the world.

Sierra Leone is at the bottom of the United Nations Development Programme's 2000 annual report on human development in the world. The population is 4.8 million, of which 1.4–2 million people are displaced or are refugees. Population density is 275 persons per square kilometer (before the war), which started in 1989. Among Ethnic groups, 30% are Temne, 30% Mende, and 39% others. English is the official language but Mende, Temne, and Krio are widely spoken local languages.

The mining industry, financed and operated by expatriate companies, accounted for more than 60% of the gross domestic product from the beginning of the First World War to the late 1960s. While the mining of iron ore did not significantly affect migration, the diamond industry contributed to a phenomenal shift in population – from the rural farm communities to the "urbanized mining areas." While the towns in the diamond regions suffered from inflation, overpopulation, health, and sanitation problems, the rural diamond fields attracted thousands of young unemployed eager to get rich quickly. However, this was an idealized hope which many could not fulfill, and in the quest of which some found a more degrading life consisting of violence and crime.

Illicit Mining and Armed Gangs

Widespread illicit mining by armed organized bands, from the early 1950s to the late 1960s introduced an element of conflict between the miners and the then colonial government. These irritations became persistent and triggered wide social and economic problems which post-independence governments were often unable to contain. Among the principal issues proving worrisome to the governments of the post-independence period was the maintenance of private "armies" by diamond dealers. These groups were well-trained and equipped with arms and ammunition. They also presented the problem of defying government forces and posing a threat to law and order in those areas. Later, in the 1990s, these armed groups offered a springboard for "rebel" conscription of militias.

An inflationary spiral, begun as a result of "too much money chasing too few goods" in the late 1950s and 1960s. Government spending after independence was increased and this affected the cost of living in these areas. Much of the available government money spent on development projects was borrowed from international monetary institutions such as the International Monetary Fund and the World Bank. A substantial amount came from loans made available by developed countries of the West. There was and still is also considerable indebtedness to more advanced Eastern European countries, such as the U.S.S.R. and Czechoslovakia. Repayment of a substantial foreign debt became an added problem of development because it depleted the amount of liquid assets available for immediate use.

For example, in 1976–1977, Le.33.6M (thirty-three point six million) were paid out in maintenance of debts by the country. As oil prices continued to climb and the developed countries kept asking for more money for their industrial products, the general world economic outlook for the 1980s became gloomy. Sierra Leone did not expect to come out of its economic stagnation unless valuable minerals, such as offshore oil or alluvial gold, were discovered and utilized. This decade also ushered in an increase of poverty because of the impact of structural adjustment programs (SAP) imposed by the International Monetary Fund (IMF) and the World Bank. The SAPs included mandates to the government to reduce expenditures, especially in social spending; cut or contain wages; privatize state enterprises and deregulate the economy; eliminate or reduce protection for the domestic market; place fewer restrictions on the operations of foreign investors; and devalue the currency.

Structural adjustment significantly reduced the growth rate and produced rising unemployment, reduced social spending, reduced consumption and low output. Further IMF and World Bank loans were directed to repaying external debts and nothing else. This decapitalization brought neither growth, nor debt relief. It brought institutionalized economic stagnation and intensified poverty. High unemployment rates particularly among the youth, civil war, and environmental degradation became prevalent.

Pro and anti-government troops were notorious for burning farms, houses, and government offices. Schools and other educational institutions were frequently razed. Even hospitals, churches, and mosques were not spared the rage and viciousness of these groups. Such destruction translated to the displacement of large masses of the population. These groups can only be sustained by nature – forest animals and reptiles, trees, shrubs, and grasses. Large tracks of land are used for the resettlement of large numbers of refugees regardless of whether such land is fertile or useful to sustain such numbers.

Economic Stagnation and Decline

In the 1990s Sierra Leone was plunged into armed conflict. The Revolutionary United Front (RUF) declared war on the All People's Congress Party government of President Joseph Momoh. The government was unable to contain it because of limited funds and also because members of the government's military forces were undisciplined, reluctant and unprepared to fight a war of attrition. Unfortunately for the general populace, both the Revolutionary United Front and government forces attacked and pillaged towns and villages, and committed human rights atrocities such as rape, mutilation and murder against innocent civilians. The leader of the RUF and some of its leaders were accused of plotting to overthrow the government and were detained at the time of this writing.

The Sierra Leone Government and the Revolutionary United Front signed a peace treaty in Lome, Togo in 1999.[2] The Leader of the rebel movement was co-opted into the government and made head of the countrys mineral resources, a vice-presidential position. Other rebel leaders were given Cabinet positions in the government. The United Nations approved an 11,000 man peace-keeping force to monitor and implement the peace. Slow progress was reported because of the mutual suspicion and insincerity of warring factions and the lukewarm response of the international community to contribute the necessary funds. The United Nations has contributed an 11,000 peacekeeping force, and efforts are underway to find a peaceful solution to the crisis by both sides.

VIGNETTES

Future generations of national and international volunteers will need some basis for anchoring their commitment to help build a peaceful, stable, and reconciled country. A description of some of our experiences and events will provide an informational smorgasbord for the reader. We begin this section with a definition of "contextual vignettes" and proceed with a rationale for their use. To do this, we borrowed two terms from educational psychology, namely, "mental associationism" and "apperception." These constructs provide some justification for using contextual vignettes, sketches from past, and recent Sierra Leonean experiences, to add perspective to the work of the Leonenet Street Children Project.

One definition of "context" is the set of circumstances or facts that surround a particular event.[3] A definition of "vignette" as a short, graceful, literary sketch, a brief, quietly touching or appealing scene or episode in a play, movie or the like,"[4] will be adopted in this article. Contextual vignettes are intended to provide thresholds of consciousness with regard to the reality of poverty among children in Sierra Leone.

The significance of contextual vignettes is that relevant bits of information will help readers to better understand the topic at hand through the dynamic of "mental associationism" usually termed "apperception." Apperception[5] is idea-centered learning. An idea is apperceived when it appears in consciousness and is assimilated to other conscious ideas. Thus, apperception is a process of new ideas associating themselves to old ones. This linking of old ideas and sketches to new ones helps to give a better perspective to a topic such as child poverty in Sierra Leone.

"Associationism" is a general psychological concept within which is assumed the process of learning.[6] It is one of the combining irreducible elements. In recall, we connect ideas or actions simply because they were connected in our earlier experiences with them. There are two broad types of associationisms: (1) early mental associationisms, which focus upon the ideas in a mind; and (2) more modern physicalistic stimulus-response associationisms which focus upon formation of connections, either between cells in a brain and peripheral nervous systems or between organic responses and environmental stimuli. The method of studying human beings within a framework of an associationism is analytic or reductionistic; learnings are reduced to their component structural parts. The basic elements that are associated may be mental, physical, or a combination of both. But in apperception, the associated elements are completely mental and constitute the structures of minds. Whereas mental discipline implies that a mind is a substance, apperception implies that it is a structure. The following vignettes are provided to acquaint the reader with pertinent issues related to helping poor children in Sierra Leone. We hope that they will heighten the reader's level of consciousness on the realities of poverty among children in Sierra Leone.

First encounter

I was walking down a major street in the center of Freetown, the capital of Sierra Leone. Freetown used to have a population of 150,000 before the war, which began in 1989. In 1996 the population was close to one million. I was surrounded by children, boys and girls, some as young as four and others as old as 16. They wore an assortment of shaggy, dirty t-shirts, dresses, and shorts. These children were unwashed and unkempt. Some of them had protruding stomachs and the color of their hair had turned brown. Some looked ill and deprived of sleep.

They all extended their arms while one said "Papa, please give me some money;" "please Sir, give me some money." I reached into my pocket for some small paper currency and gave to two of the smallest outstretched hands. They said "thank you" and as I turned my back to leave, a fresh set of children suddenly appeared with the same requests for help. Within fifteen minutes, the bevy of young, poor innocent bright brown eyes surrounded me with shriveling outstretched hands. I walked away as fast as I could but my conscience was bothered that I was not able to give to all who had asked.

I wondered, what would become of thousands of children in similar circumstances that will not get a solitary meal because they were not lucky enough to come across a stranger from overseas who took pity on them. I wondered why the local adults who see them everyday chase them away or just ignore their pleas. I wondered why their parents, and their government had abandoned them to the streets. I wondered, I wondered . . . .[7]

Government Wharf

The headquarters of the Sierra Leone telecommunications agency is located in Freetown in an area commonly known as "government wharf". I went there to make a long distance call to the United States in one of the available telephone booths. At the entrance to the agency, I was surrounded by five disabled boys ages 6 to 13, each in a wheel-chair. One said "hello sir" and indicated that he wanted to start a conversation. I stopped, introduced myself and asked them their names. Issa, Mamadu, Joseph, Sorie, and Kamanda engaged me in a chat.

They each told me what part of the country they came from and the circumstances that led to their disability. Some had war-related injuries and others were polio or spina-bifida victims. They all now live in a shelter for disabled boys supported by funds coming from overseas. However, they were half clothed, unwashed and unkempt, and I believed that they did not receive adequate care. They said that they were hungry. Yes, they received one meal a day, but there were no planned recreational or educational activities for them. They were encouraged to go out in the street and beg. They usually do this in twos or threes. There is a little security in numbers. I promised to return the next day with some gifts because I did not have enough money in my pocket to give to all five. I returned home asking "why."[8]

City Hall

A group of young boys were playing street soccer in front of the Freetown City Hall. I stopped to watch and started to inwardly cheer the side I wanted to win. During half- time I conversed with Abdul, a sprightly 16 year old. His body was glistening with perspiration and he looked like a healthy lad. I asked where he was from and he responded "Makeni" a northern large city. Abdul recounted that he was a refugee in Freetown who ran away from rebel attacks on his hometown. He indicated that the other boys in the street soccer game shared similar fates although they came from different parts of the country.

They were supposedly being taken care of in a shelter program sponsored by the Freetown City Council with funds from an organization in the United States. I asked to take a look at his sleeping quarters and he pointed to the cement sidewalk. Apparently, these boys were fed lunch and dinner, but were not allowed to sleep in the building. They each had a mat and some had blankets for cover. At night, the office and building were locked up and the boys must find a place to sleep on their own. They were prey for sex-perverts, thieves, and all sorts of evildoers.[9]

Answer to Prayer

"Dear Florence. You are an answer to prayer. Thank you so much for your very welcome donation to our project. Since the January 6th rebel incursion, we have seen the number of single parent families increase dramatically. One 19-year-old mother, displaced here from Makeni is living at the National stadium. She gave birth on April 28th by 'C' section to twins. Rebels shot her husband in Makeni and she does not know whether he is alive or dead. She also does not know the whereabouts of their 3-year-old son.

Social Welfare referred her to us and due to the complication of her surgery she was unable to care or nurse the babies, so we have been caring for them at our foster home. We assisted her to find medical help, and gave her a small sum of money for daily sustenance. With your generous donation we will be able to help her on the road to a better life for her and her children."[10]

Death of Kadiatu

"I am sorry to report the death of Kadiatu, the disabled 9-year-old girl who was temporarily staying at the foster-home. As you would recall, she was very ill, and there was a report to social services that her family was abusing her. The family believed that she was possessed by the devil. To cut a long story short, she was removed from the home by social services, but no shelter will take her, so they asked us to let her stay temporarily.

Last night, I took her home with me. After I had given her a bath, she exhaled her last breath in my arms and expired. I am very overwhelmed by this experience. However, her body looked so satisfied and peaceful, that I thought that it was her time to go to a better place because there was nothing positive around here that she could look up to except us. The local Imam performed a simple but very dignified funeral – her body was bathed and oiled, and wrapped in a white cloth. The Imam and mourners were very respectful of the dead body and treated it with great dignity. I am so tired, I have to go to bed now."[11]

Corpse in a Cardboard Box

"You remember the six year old boy Lamin whom we were caring for because the mother was shot and the father did not have a job and could not care for his son? The father had asked to keep him – did not give a reason. Several weeks passed, and we believed that both of them were doing well. There was no communication from the father and we thought all was well.

This afternoon, we heard a knock on the door. When we opened it, there was this man standing with a cardboard box in his hand. It was Salifu. He looked aged and very distraught. He came inside, put the cardboard box on the floor and started sobbing. About five minutes passed before we learned what had happened. Inside the cardboard box was the body of Lamin. Apparently, his dad had not bought the medicine we gave him money to buy and the boy had suddenly died that afternoon. In desperation, Salifu put his body in a cardboard box and boarded a "poda-poda" (commercial privately owned mini-bus). We arranged for Lamin's funeral and he has since been given a decent Muslim funeral."[12]

Foster-Home Placements

"Plans are under way with the cooperation of Ministry of Social Welfare to consult with SOS Children's Village in Lumley for permanent placement of (5) of the children. These children are Daniella (the new baby), Junior John and Tony who are both severely developmentally delayed, and the Sankoh twins who came to the center in April. This has been decided since the Center is not a long term residential programme and lacks the facilities for long-term care of the 'handicapped' children. SOS Children's Village has special care facilities for handicapped orphan children including a medical clinic and meetings are planned to discuss this proposal. It is highly unlikely that foster families can be found to foster these children. One potential foster family is under consideration for Daniella, however her medical condition may make it impossible for the family to be approved."[13]

Reunification

"Reunification is still planned for Fatmata Kanu whose family is in Bo-Waterside, Liberia and Mariama Sannoh and her baby Pinkie2 in Kenema. These reunifications have been planned for the last several months, however due to the lack of security on the roads, reunification has been postponed."[14]

Education

"Assessment is currently ongoing to locate a new Primary School for the children. Emmett Primary School where they are now going is overcrowded and running two shifts. Primary two class has 125 students and the performance of the LSCP students is declining. One school, which is being considered, is in Malamar, which is close to the Center, however it is not within walking distance, but with the leased vehicles it will be possible for the children to be transported to school if this is the one chosen."[15]

Health matters

"The month of May saw the start of the rainy season. During May and June many of the children had colds and malaria. Starting in June, LSCP has been able to reduce the cost of medical care for the children using UNICEF referrals to the Marie Stopes Medical Center. All the babies have also had their Polio and regular childhood vaccinations (Maklets). In order to reduce the cases of malaria, it is necessary to complete the screening of all the windows at the center. At the end of June, it was reported to the Center that the step-mother of Sahr Kabia passed away during childbirth. The baby also died two days later. Sahr has been greatly affected by this sad situation."[16]

Safety and Security

"During April and May, there were several reports of intruders into the compound at the center. It is necessary to rebuild the part of the compound wall that is missing to enhance security at the center. Interim Care Center Staff: A new staff member has been hired in the month of June to assist with the laundry and ironing, particularly with all the diapers for the babies. The current total of staff is now four. The Center Manager has been attending meetings with the country director regarding child violence and also is continuing monitoring of the babies not living at the center. The addition of the vehicle, which is allowing easier access to medical, and physical therapy appointments have directly facilitated this."[17]

Donations

"Dear Shinewater Church Congregation, Nigel, Sandy, Nancy et al.: On Friday afternoon, 30th March, Leonenet Street Children Project (LSCP) here in Freetown, Sierra Leone, received your donation of 888,500 Leones. On behalf of LSCP, I want to thank you for your donation and good wishes. This will go a long way to helping the child victims of the war here in Freetown.

Our latest addition to the LSCP family, is one little girl who appears to be about 8 years old. She was found in the bush in a town called Masiaka, which is about 38 miles out of Freetown, by some of the UN military forces. She appears to be a polio victim since she cannot walk, and also cannot talk. The United Nations Military Observers took her to the ministry of Social Welfare who then deposited her at the Remand Home. This is a facility for juvenile offenders of the law who are awaiting trial.

She had been there about two weeks, when the United Nations Children Fund (UNICEF) called to advise we should check out the situation. Upon arriving at the Remand Home, we found her locked in a room, with the windows closed. She was sitting on the concrete floor wearing a urine soaked ragged t-shirt and sitting in a pile of urine/faeces. The smell was overpowering. We cleaned her up as best we could and brought her back to our Interim Care Center where I am happy to report she is in a much better situation."[18]

Inquiry

". . . my name is David Holmes, and I am a teacher at Cowichan Secondary School in Duncan, British Columbia, Canada. I have been surfing the Net, looking for anyone and everyone who might be able to help us. My students and I have begun a project to bring Maria tu Kamara and her sister Adaman from Sierra Leone to Duncan. We have established the Kamara Trust Account with a local bank and are about to begin the process of raising as much money as we can to accomplish our goal. If we are as successful as we hope, the potential is $C50,000.

With this we hope to fly the girls to Canada, provide them with medical help, especially prostheses (both girls were mutilated by rebels in Port Loko, Maria losing both hands and part of a forearm, and Adaman losing one arm and part of the other hand), and with a home if they wish to stay here. We have already received offers of foster care, and we are receiving donations as a result of media coverage in the last week. We are new at this sort of thing, and I happened on a description of the Leonenet Street Children's Project while surfing for information. The girls are currently in an amputee camp near Freetown and we are in touch with World Vision who run the camps. Is there any advice you can give us? I realize that the immigration laws are different in the U.S. – in our province no-one under 19 is considered a refugee! You would, however, have information on the kinds of things we will need to prepare for if, as we hope, the girls come to us. I would be grateful for anything you can tell me."[19]

Child prostitution

Adama is 15 years old. Two years ago armed men looted everything in her home, raped her and set the house on fire with her mother inside. Adama survived because she summoned the courage to run even though hails of bullets were trailing her. She mourns her mother's death and bears the emotional scar of rape and is now living in a refugee camp in Freetown.

She spends her days cooking, fetching water, braiding other girls' hair, and cleaning up her tent. At night, she goes to a major tourist hotel to trade sexual favors for money. She has never used a condom because the men do not want to use it. She has never been to a clinic. When asked if she is not worried about contacting Aids/HIV, she just shrugged her shoulders. There are hundreds and thousands of Adamas. Prostitution by boys under 18 is also rampant in the big cities in Sierra Leone.[20]

POVERTY

Poverty in Sierra Leone among children is the result of many factors. The deplorable socio-economic conditions in Sierra Leone were partly the result of colonial mis-management during over 150 years of British rule. The situation was aggravated after independence in 1961 by the greed, mismanagement, and apathy of governments led by indigenous Sierra Leoneans. War, killings, mutilation and destruction from 1989–1999 exacerbated the situation. Caulker (2000) indicated that people in Freetown, the capital were "scratching a living out of nothing."[21] Burchall (2000)[22] stated that in countries such as Sierra Leone people live in absolute poverty and that children die everyday from poverty related diseases.

Strikingly enough, poor people do not sit down and wallow in self-pity because of two reasons. They want to be productive, and if they do not get up and go, others will perceive them as lazy or unambitious. Extremely poor people including children in the towns and cities find a way to earn money legitimately. Some sell items such as fruits and, used clothing, cooking implements, books, etc. Many of these entrepreneurs can only afford to peddle a few items at a time.

Peddlers walk all day under the blazing sun or the heavy rain and depend on the very erratic earnings of their self-employment. Garbage dumps in poor countries are "workplaces" for extremely poor children and adults. They forage these dumps all day long sometimes with their bare hands, in the hope of extricating something of perceived value. An old plastic bottle, a discarded cooking utensil, a broken tin-lamp. They use considerable ingenuity and creativity to "recycle" these items and then sell them for a small sum that could provide a meal for a day. Street children do not worry about contracting diseases from these dumps.

Sierra Leone does not have a compulsory education law; therefore there are no consequences when children do not go to school. Education is valued by society but street children are hesitant to go to community schools for fear that they will be discriminated against by teachers and students. In December 2000, the Sierra Leone government announced that it intends to provide free primary education for all children effective September 2001. Whether the government has the financial capacity and moral tenacity to implement this edict is another story.

This is a very positive sign for education and development for Sierra Leone street children who brave the stench and filth and accidents such as cutting their feet on broken bottles, or getting stuck by sharp objects in garbage dumps. When injured in this way, they ignore it because they cannot afford first-aid. Of course, their injuries sometimes become infected, and open sores develop. However, they have to plod on. Young people sleep on bare pavements in front of bars, churches, government buildings, or stores. Some sleep in open-air stadiums or fields. Many sleep in shacks made from discarded card boxes, strips of plastic material, and some sticks. Poverty is an incurable disease for hundreds of thousands of Sierra Leonean children.

THE GOVERNMENT'S PROBABLE CONTRIBUTION TO CHILD POVERTY

Poverty is a relative concept. It is difficult to explain poverty in Sierra Leone to people who are poor in the United States of America or in the United Kingdom. Poverty is not the same to people in each of these countries. Poverty generally concerns income and assets but it is about much else. It concerns health, life-expectancy, diet, shelter, education, security, access to vital resources and other aspects of living standards.[23] In some way, the types of government that these countries have and the attitudes of government officials trigger levels of poverty. The extent to which democracy is entrenched in a country's government also affects the levels of poverty experienced by its citizens.

Democracy is not just about the right to vote in a government – important as that is. It is about a whole set of rights which citizens must be afforded if a government is to be open, accountable and participatory. These rights include freedom of speech; an independent press; freedom to associate, for example, in trade unions or pressure groups; access to state information, particularly about specific state plans for those directly affected by them and the right to be consulted in such decisions; and freedom from discrimination, whether on grounds of sex, race or creed.[24]

Poverty among children in Sierra Leone is accelerated by the negligence, connivance, incompetence, or apathy of the state. Politicians or military rulers can be well described as "suspended in mid-air above society," Hyden (1993).[25] Because of this the government of Sierra Leone lacks an effective directive capacity. Personal aggrandizement appears to be high on the list of most public officials. Competent and honest civil servants quickly become demoralized by graft, fraud and theft of public property Sanbrook (1985).[26]

The state is weak and fragile, and those in power are primarily concerned with their own survival. Politicians and civil servants give these twin concerns more priority than economic development or the welfare of poor men, women, and children. There is more attention paid to a cult of personality of the head of state than for anything else. The utterances and appearances of the head of state, politicians and civil servants dominate the news every day, and every hour. Patrimonial rule is sometimes seen as inevitable under the circumstances. Nevertheless, the state has extensive responsibilities for a wide range of tasks.

The state is responsible for overseeing activities related to the public and the private sectors. Large-scale sector agencies are usually termed "parastatals." So, the state has a hand in the running of public corporations in areas such as telecommunications, electricity, energy, agricultural produce, road construction, fisheries, and mining. Because the state has a patrimonial leader, it is difficult for professionals to do their jobs independently and efficiently. The patrimonial leader dispenses personal favors in order to acquire loyalty and support. He therefore appoints cronies to boards of major corporations and to high professional positions in these agencies. In situations such as these professional efficiency and transparency are compromised.

The following are consequences of the above scenarios. The state becomes engaged in unproductive and inappropriate spending. Corruption and nepotism are encouraged to flourish. Ordinary citizens are forced to make extra payments to public officials to get services for which these officials have already received salaries. Sometimes, public officials complain that they do not regularly receive their salaries for several months. While, this may be the case, it is very common for all officials, those who receive monthly official checks, and those who do not, to charge ordinary citizens extra in order to perform legitimate services.

Another problem is nepotism, in which government jobs are distributed among the family and friends of officers of the government. This process becomes worrisome particularly when kinsfolk appointed under nepotism are not qualified for the positions to which they are appointed. All of the above problems add up to state inefficiency and a slowdown, complete standstill, or downward spiral of economic development.

Governmental negligence, connivance, incompetence, or apathy affect the whole population. When personal aggrandizement takes center stage at the expense of concern and responsibility of national constituencies, poverty and underdevelopment will reign. When ordinary citizens do not have champions of their social and economic welfare, poverty develops. Because children do not form a political constituency, they receive only ceremonial attention from the state. Child abuse and neglect occur more frequently in populations in which the parents themselves had been abused and neglected. More importantly, children are at risk in a society in which there are few consequences to those who abuse them. The staggering numbers of street and runaway children in Sierra Leone are the result of overt and covert governmental, parental and societal abuse and neglect. The plight of Sierra Leone's poor children is shamefully real, and these children need champions and advocates both inside and outside of the country.

The Nature of Poverty

The United Nations Development Programme[27] stated in 1997 that "if income is not the sum total of well-being, lack of income cannot be the sum total of poverty. Human poverty does not focus on what people do or do not have, but also on what they can or cannot do. It is deprivation in the most essential capabilities of life, including leading a long and healthy life, being knowledgeable, having adequate economic provisioning and participating fully in the life of the community."

An alternative way of looking at poverty is to use the Human Poverty Index. Indicators of this index include the following: deprivation of a long and healthy life, as measured by the percentage of people not expected to survive age 40; deprivation in knowledge, as measured by adult literacy; deprivation in economic provisioning, from private and public income, as measured by the percentage of people lacking access to safe water and the percentage of children under five who are moderately or severely underweight.

Perhaps the most troubling indicator is that pertaining to child malnutrition. Long-term, malnutrition of children under five who are underweight (having low weight for their age) is a perennial problem. Short-term, especially in crisis situations such as war, the troubling indicator is that of "child-wasting," children with low weight for their height. All of these factors put together paint a grim picture of children who are liable to die before age 5 or 15.

Judged by any, or all of the above criteria, Sierra Leone would qualify as one of the least developed or one of the poorest countries in the world. Arnold (2000)[28] believed that many African wars were unashamedly about the control of the state' resources. In Sierra Leone, the war is about who controls the diamond fields. He raised issues about military and political power that are relevant in Sierra Leone with regard to addressing issues of war and poverty. Among the issues are – the proper uses of democracy, and the ability and will to resolve political issues amicably. He observed that in Sierra Leone, the events of the 1990s were a mixture of warlordism and greed and the breakdown of state structures.

Mugyeni (2001)[29] stated that "conflict contributed to debt, but by the same token unsustainable debt posed an ongoing and insidious threat to the well-being and security of millions of people in the developing world. Scarce national resources are siphoned away from poverty alleviation to purchase arms and service the debt, enriching the creditors of the affluent Western world. At least 20% of the most heavily indebted poor countries (HPICS) transfer more than one-fifth of their revenues to creditors in the developed world every year."[30]

THE LEONENET STREET CHLDREN PROJECT

The Project is a non-profit, non-stock organization registered in the United States with the Internal Revenue Service and the office of the Secretary Of State, Commonwealth of Kentucky respectively. We are registered in Sierra Leone as a non-governmental organization (NGO) under the Ministry of Economic Planning and Development and the Ministry of Children and Gender Affairs respectively. Our work centers on foster-care, teenage-mother and child welfare and education, advocacy, and outreach. We also collaborate with government agencies and non-governmental organizations to provide one-time or short-term emergency aid to destitute children and families. The project was started in the hope that it would provide a model that will help the country to develop a national child-care program that will rehabilitate children through community foster-care. This model concentrates on the needs of the whole child (emotional, social, intellectual, physical and creative).

The Sierra Leone Street Children Committee, an off-shoot of the Child Protection Committee provided the following definition for street children: "a boy or girl below eighteen years of age who has dropped out of the nurturing environment of the family, lives in/on the streets without any care and fends for himself/herself to meet basic needs "Street Children" for lack of a better term come from a variety of groups including the homeless, neglected and abandoned." There are children from indigent families, runaways and orphans, and there are some in camps for persons displaced by war who need to be included in the definition. Some children panhandle as a way of generating income. All street children share the scourge of poverty. They live dangerous and risky lives and are usually used and abused by unscrupulous adults. Many qualify for full Foster-care until age 18 or reunification with their family or relatives as long as they fully comply with LSCP rules and regulations.

The Leonenet Street Children Project (LSCP) provides foster-care for orphaned and homeless child-victims of the civil war in Sierra Leone. LSCP advocates a national foster-care policy to forestall a burgeoning street (neglected, abandoned, and abused) children crisis. We collaborate with NGO's and agencies doing relief work and engage in outreach and referral services helping children. The process of soliciting funds in the United States and Europe for the Project is a slow and frustrating one. Donor fatigue is affecting small organizations such as ours even with our effectiveness in the frontline and our low overhead.

It appears as if larger international organizations are more effective in securing large governmental and foundation grants to help the poor in Sierra Leone. They have more funds to advertise what they do and attract more donors. Donors usually assume that funds given to large aid organizations will trickle down to smaller ones, or to the poorest of the poor. Our experience has been the opposite. There are children and families who never benefit from the activities of large non-governmental organizations and this is the clientele that we mostly serve.

Large aid organizations have to project an image and maintain a posture. Their personnel from the developed countries are paid well and offered perks which sometimes seem exorbitant to the governments and peoples of the countries they work in. Hancock (1989)[31] attacked this life style in a best-seller and accused the personnel of large international aid organizations of self-serving behavior, arrogance, paternalism, moral cowardice, and mendacity.

There is a dearth of work of genuine volunteers in smaller aid organizations who undergo deprivations just as their clients do. They live modestly, provide services voluntarily, and live on financial assistance provided by relatives, friends and religious organizations from their home country. Many of them depend on public transportation, and work irregular hours to help the poor. They all go beyond the call of duty to help poor men, women, and children. These are the volunteers of the ilk of Mother Theresa who are humane, nurturing, modest, and caring. There are many of them in Sierra Leone and LSCP volunteers and personnel are proud to be counted among their number.

The lavish life style and flaunting of wealth by some personnel associated with these large organizations appears to have created ill-will between them and the Sierra Leone government. In 2000, the government of Sierra Leone passed legislation that will regulate all non-governmental organizations. Ironically, the richer ones can easily meet the new registration charges imposed on NGO's. They have the resources to pay any costs. Smaller NGO's such as ours have to sacrifice sparse resources to meet new governmental demands. LSCP is working to comply with re-registration procedures, although this will take away funds earmarked for direct services to poor children.[32] We will continue to collaborate with the Sierra Leone government and other NGO's to alleviate the sufferings of the poor.

Activities

Foster-Care: Sponsorships of children in foster-care and providing food, clothing, shelter, medical and education assistance for children in the Capital Freetown. These children range in ages from newborn to 18 years. Eighteen years may be considered an adult, but in a country ravaged by war since they were 8 years old, we considered necessary to extend consideration to these young people who may need some help. Additional education fees were provided for children in the northern town of Port Lokko. Interim Care Center. This is a residential facility providing care for separated, abandoned children, small babies and children with special needs. We worked in the area of juvenile justice. The Children in Conflict with the Law (CCL) program provides monitoring and advocacy for children detained in Police stations in the Western Area. Field workers for child protection monitored cases and visited juvenile offenders twice a day.

In the area of vocational training we provided combination skills training and day care for child mothers. These programs were located in Kissy, east of Freetown and in Port Lokko in the north. Teen mothers received training in soap making, tailoring, hand sewing, and bread and cake making. Lectures were given on nutrition, reproductive health, child care, and basic literacy/numeracy. Social integration skills were learned through conflict resolution exercises, discussions, and debates. A community Child Protection Committee comprising elders, leaders, and parents was formed. Community involvement included participation in recreational gardening and soccer activities.

The Project collaborated in the provision of educational workshops. We collaborated with World Vision to present a workshop on "Community Capacity Building." The fifty-seven participants came from several villages in the Freetown peninsula. Many of the ideas generated in this workshop have been used for community development. For example, one village group used what they learned from the workshop to organize a maintenance project to re-pave an access road.

The promotion and development of the human resource capacity of staff is important to the Leonenet Street Children Project. Our staff capacity grew to 26 in 2000. The majority were temporary contractors hired to deliver relevant services. Our staff participated in training and development workshops in topics such as first-Aid, computer basics, driver education, psycho-social and counseling techniques, conventions on the rights of the child, non-governmental education code of conduct, and project planning and management.

Our work may fall under the area of "poverty alleviation." The Leonenet Street Children Project directly assisted a total of 612 infants, homeless children, teen mothers, and community leaders during the year 2000. However, there is a multiplier effect when material and developmental aid is provided that could not be effectively calculated. We suggest that if the benefits of our direct efforts extend to distant extended family members and friends, we would could have easily and positive touched the lives of over a thousand people in any one year.

POVERTY ALLEVIATION

Poverty alleviation may cushion the impact of poverty for a short while. What is preferred in the long run for a poor country such as Sierra Leone is poverty eradication. Combs and Ahmed (1974)[33] suggested long-range rural development as one of the answers. Rural development does not just address agricultural and economic growth, but also balanced social and economic development. The goals must be the generation of new employment, more equitable access to arable land, more equitable distribution of widespread improvement in health, nutrition, and housing. It should also include the provision of the promise of education and giving voice to all rural people in shaping the decisions and actions that affect their lives (p. 13).

Clark (1991) introduced the principle of "just development" in poverty eradication. "Just development is about attacking the web of forces that cause poverty. This demands that equity, democracy and social justice be paramount objectives, alongside the need for economic growth. It must enable the weaker members of society to improve their situation by providing the social services they need and by enabling them to acquire the assets and to improve the productivity of those assets. It must combat the vulnerability and isolation. It must ensure the sustainable use of natural resources and combat exploitation, particularly the oppression of women. And it must make the institutions of society accountable to the people."[34] The ingredients of a just development according to him could be remembered in the acronym DEPENDS:

- development of infrastructure
- economic growth
- poverty alleviation
- equity
- natural resource base protection
- democracy
- social justice.

We agree with Clark that a concerted effort of international financial agencies, governments, non-governmental agencies, religious groups, and the people should work together to making Sierra Leone a decent place to live and work. An elaboration of this theme could be better left to other writers.

CONCLUSIONS

The central focus of this article was the condition of poverty among children in the West African country of Sierra Leone. We explained the geographical, educational, and socio-economic contexts that influenced contemporary socio-economic developments in the country. Next, we presented snapshots of what it means to be poor and the realities of working among the poor in "Vignettes." The nature of child poverty in the country and governmental ineffectiveness and disinterestedness were perceived to be partial reasons for the level of child poverty in Sierra Leone.

We discussed the work of a small non-profit organization and its mission, goals and activities in this poor country. Ironically, the Leonenet Street Children Project is struggling to raise funds to help poor children at a time when the perception is that all non-governmental organizations are rich, and extravagant. Our experiences mirror the reality faced by a sample of poor Sierra Leone children, their relatives and other agencies. There is a considerable amount of work to be done to narrate, document, and arrest various degrees of poverty among child populations such as – ex-child combatants, children in refugee camps, and children attending school in formal classrooms. Work also has to be done to solve problems associated with the care of throwaway babies, the teenage mothers who were raped, and severely disabled infants and children.

To a large extent, child poverty is a residue of adult poverty. Job creation for a majority of Sierra Leonean adults is necessary to lower the incidence of child poverty. Sierra Leone has abundant rich land in the rural areas and farming is the general avocation of the majority of the population. Ten years of war helped to displace large numbers of men, women and children. The government's work and that of international donor work should be basically directed toward resettlement, reconstruction, rehabilitation, and job creation and training in the agricultural sector.

The traumas associated with the war affect hundreds of thousands of men women and children. Mentally traumatized children whose conditions were triggered by the ravages of war, or who experienced violent situations need to be counseled and rehabilitated. The condition of ex-child combatants who participated in vicious acts under duress, coercion and brainwashing should be assessed. Depression and mental illnesses associated with these conditions will make it impossible for these children to become productive, well-adjusted adults. If this cycle is allowed to continue, several will become unproductive mentally ill adults whose children will be poor, ill-nurtured, uneducated and probably violent. We believe that all children and adults who suffered and were traumatized by violence should receive counseling assistance subsidized by the state. So far, very little has been done to facilitate mental health and counseling programs in the community and the schools.

We have barely scratched the surface by translating our perception of child poverty and the herculean task of responding to and abating it in Sierra Leone. We encourage further work on child poverty in Sierra Leone by those who directly work with Sierra Leonean children on some of the areas mentioned above.

NOTES

1. The Leonenet Street Children Project is a non-governmental organization (NGO) incorporated in the United States of America by Sierra Leone expatriates and friends of the country.

2. Signed. The peace agreement between the Sierra Leone government and the Revolutionary United Front of Sierra Leone to end the country's eight-year civil war was signed in Lome, Togo on July 7 1999 but not implemented. Both sides blame the other.

3. See Random House College Dictionary (1991, p. 294).

4. *ibid.*, p. 1486.

5. See Morris and Shermis (1999, p. 33).

6. *Ibid.*

7. Samuel Hinton (1996). The following vignettes were provided from experience in Freetown, Sierra Leone.

8. *Ibid.* (1996).

9. *Ibid.* (1998).

10. Pinkie McCann-Willis (2000). The following vignettes were provided by Ms. McCann.

11. *Ibid*

12. *Ibid.*

13. *Ibid.*

14. *Ibid.*

15. *Ibid.*

16. *Ibid.*

17. *Ibid.*

18. *Ibid.*

19. Inquiry letter from a Canadian school teacher (April 2001).

20. Self-report. Freetown, June 1997.

21. Elaine Caulker (2000, p. 11).

22. John Burchall (2000, p. 24).

23. Clark (1990, p. 11).

24. *Ibid.*, p. 14.

25. Hyden (1993).

26. Sandbrook (1985).

27. United Nations Development Programme Report (2000).

28. Arnold (2000, pp. 9–11).

29. Mugyeni (2000, pp. 12–14).

30. *Ibid.*
31. Hancock (1974).
32. Government of Sierra Leone (2000, August).
33. Combs and Manzoor (1974).
34. Clark (1991, p. 23).

REFERENCES

Arnold, G. (2000, December 4–10). So many wars in Africa. *West Africa*, 9–11.

Burchall, J. (2000, June 19–25). Children can lead the way. *West Africa*, 24.

Caulker, E. (2000, July 31–August 7). A traumatized City. *West Africa*, 11.

Clark, J. (1990). *Democratizing development: The role of voluntary organizations*. Hartford, CT: Kumarian Press.

Clark, J. (1991). *Democratizing development: The role of voluntary organizations*. West Hartford, CT: Kumara Press.

Combs, P. H., & Manzoor, A. (1974). *Attacking rural poverty: How non-formal education can help*. Baltimore: Johns Hopkins University Press.

Government of Sierra Leone (2000). *Policy regulations on the operations of non-governmental organizations*.

Hancock, G. (1974). *Lords of poverty: The power, prestige, and corruption of the international aid business*. Atlantic Monthly Press.

Hyden, G. (1993). *No shortcuts to progress*. London: Heinemann/Berkeley: University of California Press.

Morris, L. B., & Shermis, S. S. (1999). *Learning theories for teachers* (6th ed.). New York: Longman.

Mugyeni, F. (2000, December 4–10). The arms trade and African conflicts. *West Africa*, 12–14.

Sandbrook, R. (1985). *The politics of Africa's economic stagnation*. Cambridge: Cambridge University Press.

UNICEF (2000). *State of the world's children 2000*.

United Nations (2000). *United Nations development programme report*.

United Nations High Commission For Refugees (1999). *Statistical overview*.

World Bank (1997). *African development indicators*.

17. STOLEN CHILDHOOD: CULTURAL CONSTRUCTIONS OF "UNMARRIED" PREGNANCY IN BANGLADESH

Margot Wilson

... we had a very premature infant girl born to a 10 or 11 year old a week ago ... the mother has no breast development and no pubic hair so, of course, no milk. I took her to the hospital at 3:30 AM Sunday morning and the baby was born about 15 minutes after we arrived. Such a tiny little thing ...

... the hospitals are so bad that the girls wait until the last minute to tell you they're in labour and we've delivered three here. I helped with the one this week ... by the time the doctor got here it was all over but she had to do some internal stitching ....

... some of these girls are as young as 11–13 years. We have had six caesarians due to very young underdeveloped mothers and the babies not having room to turn ... had a little 12 year old give birth to a $6\frac{1}{2}$ month baby girl yesterday, but she only lived a few hours as only weighed about $1\frac{1}{2}$ lbs ....

... by the end of January, we had 14 cases and have had 91 cases to date (November). Some of these have been so young and we have had a lot of heartaches ... some days we seem to take two steps forward and four back ....

... one little girl came in ... deaf and dumb, we thought ... seven months pregnant ... and the cutest thing you ever saw. Said with her hands that the man of the house she was working in tied her hands behind her back, gagged her and then raped her. The doctor doubts she's even 12 and she's never had a period. She had a caesarian and had a beautiful baby boy that we then lost

'Suffer the Little Children': National and International Dimensions of Child
Poverty and Public Policy
Advances in Education in Diverse Communities: Research, Policy and Praxis, Volume 4, 407–432
ISSN: 1479-358X/doi:10.1016/S1479-358X(04)04017-3

to tetanus. Even with the extra trauma of losing the baby, this little 12 year old started to talk, very softly at first, and is now jabbering a mile a minute . . . (we) think she was so traumatized that . . . she just stopped talking . . .

. . . it is not easy because in so many ways they are children, with children . . . .

(excerpts from the correspondence of Betty Steinkrauss Brown, Director, CTRDW).

INTRODUCTION

The Centre for Training and Rehabilitation of Destitute Women (CTRDW, also the Centre throughout) is a euphemistic name for a shelter for abandoned pregnant women and their infants in Dhaka, Bangladesh. Seventeen percent of the women admitted to CTRDW over an eight year period (1981–1989) are very young teenagers (15 years of age and under) who have sustained unmarried, and therefore unwanted, pregnancies. It is with these young mothers that this paper is concerned. The circumstances under which these young women find themselves both pregnant and abandoned by their families are culturally constructed. The data presented here are taken from CTRDW admission records, life histories taken by the CTRDW Social Worker, interviews with the Director, Betty Steinkrauss Brown, and her extensive correspondence with her family in Canada.[1] Betty is a Canadian woman who originally went to Bangladesh is 1977 to administer the Families for Children (FFC) orphanage in Dhaka.

CTRDW grew out of her experiences in the orphanage. Not all of the children admitted to FFC were orphans *per se*. Many were the abandoned infants of unmarried women. Betty was well aware that accepting these children, especially those of very young teenage mothers, only addressed half of the problem. At the same time, Dhaka University School of Social Welfare fieldworkers discovered that as many as eight unmarried teenage women were attempting suicide each month, in one district of Bangladesh alone, as a direct result of sustaining unwanted pregnancies. Abandoned and desperate, these young women were seeking 2nd and 3rd trimester abortions at family planning clinics. On being refused, they attempted to take their own lives. Many were successful. Originally, Social Welfare simply asked Betty to take some of the very youngest mothers into the orphanage and support and protect them in the final months of their pregnancies. Betty readily agreed. Then in August 1981, the Government of Bangladesh held a one-day workshop to identify pressing social problems. Betty argued for recognition of and immediate action on this particular issue. Collaborating with University faculty, she proposed to establish a shelter specifically supporting young unmarried, pregnant women. She received Government of Bangladesh approval but since these were, and remain, extremely sensitive issues in Bangladesh, Betty was required to mask the actual situation of the women needing support and to refrain from mentioning the specific services provided. The emphasis was placed on training and rehabilitation and no mention was made of either "moral danger"[2] or unmarried pregnancy, hence the euphemistic name for the Centre.

"Unmarried" is a term rigorously endorsed by CTRDW to refer not only to the marital status of the mother but also to the pregnancy and the infant born of that pregnancy. In this way, unmarried becomes a shorthand for "out of wedlock" mothers, pregnancies and infants. Once when I used the word "illegitimate" in conversation, CTRDW personnel immediately corrected me, arguing strenuously that no one has the right to judge another person, to label them as "legitimate" or not. In Bangladeshi parlance, the English word illegitimate is closer in meaning to unlawful. "Illegal" is another term in common usage to describe out of wedlock pregnancies, see for example the case histories of Masuda, Jacinta and Momtaj below. Since the women who sustain unmarried pregnancies and their children are severely judged by Bangladeshi cultural standards, the use of the term "unmarried" reflects an ideological shift from judgment (and blaming) of the victims to empathy and support. For these reasons, I have used the term unmarried throughout the discussion that follows.

The CTRDW provides a place where women can live out the term of their pregnancy while receiving training in the use of production equipment for the garment industry. Training includes pattern drawing, cutting, sewing and the use of all types of garment production equipment. CTRDW personnel have established contacts with local garment factories and, if a woman completes her training successfully, she may find employment in factories known to the Centre where hopefully they will be relatively more protected and less exploited than if they returned to domestic duties or took up other jobs. Nevertheless, workers of both sexes are routinely exploited in garment industries throughout the developing world as a result of long hours, poor working conditions, low wages, forced overtime and no job security (see Amin et al., 1998; Kibria, 1995; Rahman, 1989 for discussions of the situation in Bangladesh). Women also receive "life skills" training, which includes money management, functional literacy, numeracy, human and legal rights, gender training, human sexuality, birth control, personal hygiene, nutrition and health. The intent, then, is to provide shelter and safety during the final months of their pregnancy, empower these women with basic skills and knowledge and help them to reenter society following their delivery. A 24 hour day care centre provides an opportunity for mothers to keep their infants, if they wish. Alternatively, if a young mother decides to relinquish her child, CTRDW seeks to place these children in approved foster homes.[3] I have discussed the mother's decision-making about relinquishing their infants elsewhere (Wilson-Moore, 1999).

The data presented here are delineated by Betty's approximately eight year tenure at CTRDW (December 1981–January 1990) as this represents a time of consistent philosophical and administrative decision-making. At the end of January 1990, the programme was turned over to Bangladeshi administration with the result that many aspects of the programme changed (see Wilson-Moore, 1995 for a discussion of some of these changes). It bears remarking, however, that although the data set employed here is more than 10 years old, more recently conducted interviews with several of the Bangladeshi Directors of CTRDW and with the Director of the donor organization indicate that the patterns reflected by this data set remain representative of CTRDW experience up to the present time.

During this eight year period, 420 women were admitted to the Centre. Of these, 70 (17%) are 15 years of age or under and unmarried. All are abandoned by their families and/or employers. Children having children, I will characterize their abandonment in terms of the social, economic and cultural contexts in which it occurs. In the sections that follow, I describe the circumstances under which they became pregnant, who are the "fathers," why they were abandoned, where they went after they left the CTRDW and what happened to their babies. Many had been working as domestic servants, often from a very young age. In the final analysis, therefore, poverty, as much as sexual exploitation, prescribe lost childhoods for these young women.

CHILDREN HAVING CHILDREN

While 70 women 15 years old and younger were admitted to CTRDW, it is important to remark that only half of these are 15 years old; the other half range in age from 10 to 14. The very young age of many of these teenage mothers and their concomitant physical immaturity result in a number of serious problems at the time of their delivery, such as the need for caesarian sections, prolonged and difficult labours, premature births, low birth weight and stillborn infants and neonatal deaths. Pre-delivery problems include poor general health, poor nutrition, anaemia, no prenatal care, and psychological problems, as the opening quotes indicate (Table 1).

Fifty (72%) of these teenagers were already working outside the home at the time of their pregnancy, all but one as domestic servants. Data regarding the age at which they began working are available for 44 of these women; 17 (39%) began working between the ages of 5 and 9 years, 15 (34%) between 10 and 12 years and 12 (27%) between 13 and 15 years. In contrast to women working as servants, 16 women (24%) defined themselves as "daughters" living at home

Table 1. Age.

Age	Frequency	Percent	Cumulative Percent
10 years	1	1.4	1.4
12 years	5	7.1	8.6
13 years	13	22.9	31.4
14 years	16	18.6	50.0
15 years	35	50.0	100.0
Total	70	100.0	

Table 2. Occupation.

Occupation	Frequency	Percent	Cumulative Percent
Servant	49	70.0	70.0
Daughter	16	22.9	92.9
Jute worker	1	1.4	94.3
Student	3	4.3	98.6
Beggar	1	1.4	100.0
Total	70		

when they became pregnant. 3 women (4%) report that they were students at the time their pregnancy occurred and 1 woman was working as a beggar (1%) (see Table 2).

I have discussed differences in the pregnancy experience of servants and daughters in more detail elsewhere (Wilson-Moore, 1996), but in essence, daughters are much less likely to sustain unmarried pregnancies, but those who do are more apt to have had incestuous relations with male family members. Servant women, on the other hand, are far more vulnerable to sustaining unwanted pregnancies from male colleagues, visitors or other males in the home where they work or, indeed, from the employer himself. The largest individual source of unwanted pregnancies (31.4%) is neighbours, although employers, their sons, brothers and friends account for 24.3% of unwanted pregnancies in the sample. 14.3% are the result of sexual relations with relatives and 12.9% result from liaisons with other males (see Table 3).

PROMISES, POWER AND EXPLOITATION

What makes the relationship between these variables more poignant is the relatively large proportion of these women who have been working as domestic servants,

Table 3. Who is the Father.

Father	Frequency	Percent	Cumulative Percent
Unknown	4	5.7	5.7
Colleague	8	11.4	17.1
Neighbour	22	31.4	48.5
Employer's	17	24.3	72.8
Friend	3	4.3	
Brother	2	2.9	
Son	7	10.0	
Himself	4	5.7	
Tenant	1	1.4	
Relatives	10	14.3	87.1
Brother-in-law	4	5.7	
Cousin	2	2.9	
Step-father	2	2.9	
Step-grandfather	1	1.4	
Unspecified	1	1.4	
Others	9	12.9	100.0
Passerby	4	5.7	
Uncle's employee	1	1.4	
Tenant	2	2.9	
Boyfriend	1	1.4	
Fiancé	1	1.4	
Total	70	100.0	

many from a very young age. That the man responsible for the pregnancy is someone for whom she works and with whom she may have grown up is especially insidious. The opportunity for employers (or other males in the employer's household) to take advantage of young servant women is enormous. To whom can they complain and how many are willing to jeopardize their jobs? Similarly, neighbours take advantage of young women who have grown up next door and relatives enter into incestuous relationships with women who have grown up in their family compounds. In cases such as these, the issue of consent is difficult to ascertain. Indeed, it is questionable whether some of the youngest women understand enough to be able to consent to sexual congress at all. Men coerce and manipulate young vulnerable women, offering compensation in the form of special attention, small gifts and promises of marriage.

It is remarkable that only 2 of 70 women (2.9%) claimed their lovers as a fiancé and/or boyfriend; only 1 reports that she was paid to engage in sexual relations (see Table 4). By contrast, 38 (54.3%) believed that their partner had promised to

Table 4. How Became Pregnant.

Reason	Frequency	Percent	Cumulative Percent
Marriage promise	38	54.3	54.3
Ignorance	13	18.6	72.9
Sexual abuse/Rape	13	18.6	91.5
Consent	2	2.9	94.4
Paid	1	1.4	95.8
Not pregnant	3	4.3	100.0
Total	70	100.0	

marry them. The popularity and relative success of this common ruse for motivating young women to engage in premarital sex is substantiated by these data (see Aziz & Maloney, 1985 for similar findings). Thirteen women (19.4%) cited ignorance as the primary reason for their pregnancy. Women in Bangladesh are routinely denied information about human sexuality until after marriage in the mistaken belief that the less they know, the less apt they will be to "get into trouble." Indeed, some researchers (Maloney et al., 1981) report that women are expected to learn about sex from their husbands following marriage. Nevertheless, women (regardless of their age) are held responsible for controlling not only their own sexuality but the sexuality of the men around them as well. This is especially true in the case of unmarried pregnancies where the responsibility, and blame, for the pregnancy are routinely placed squarely on the woman. Men quickly and easily extricate themselves from the situation by tendering a public apology, occasionally paying a small fine and/or arranging a marriage to another woman whose reputation has not been impugned, if they are not already married. When young women are made responsible without having sufficient information with which to make appropriate decisions, it is surprising that there are not more unwanted pregnancies.

Further, believing that their partners would marry them appears as another form of, if not ignorance, at least naïveté. By definition these young teenage women are naïve; indeed, their unsophisticated lack of experience is what makes them so appealing and vulnerable in the first place. They are easily duped and relatives, neighbours and employers can easily take advantage of them. Furthermore, given the wide disparity in socio-economic status between many of them and their lovers – at least in situations of servant women and employers or employer's sons, brothers and friends – the possibility of such a marriage is extremely remote. Similarly, 14 women (20%) knew that their lovers were already married. Nevertheless, many of these young women were seduced (literally) by promises of marriage. Far from their natal homes and families, lonely and suffering from lack of affection, women working as domestic servants easily succumb to promises, not only of marriage, but of small attentions, gifts or cash.

The result, then, is that promises of marriage (or of small gifts or attentions) by sophisticated men entice young naïve women to enter into risky sexual relationships. Similarly, coercion by men in positions of power may motivate vulnerable women to engage in premarital liaisons. Subsequent pregnancies and failure of men to take responsibility for their actions are tantamount to sexual exploitation. Thus, some 92% of the pregnancies in this sample result from some form of sexual exploitation.

CULTURAL CONTEXT

The data presented here delineate the ways in which patriarchal attitudes toward women generally and toward young unmarried women in particular predispose them to sexual exploitation. Similarly, bleak economic circumstances result in women leaving their families, often from a very young age, to work for wages. The result is often an unmarried pregnancy and abandonment. There can be no denying that opportunity plays a large role in unwanted pregnancy. Young women in public places routinely become targets for the attentions of the males who "see" them. This is true in the case of domestic servants who rarely have a private place to call their own and are routinely "seen" by household males. If they are required to do the family marketing or other errands, they may also come into the view of other males outside of the household. This is also true for female students who go out to school, a commonly cited reason for not educating daughters beyond the primary level. Other unmarried women (for example, daughters) may undertake domestic duties for their natal families, which place them where they can be "seen" by males related, or unrelated.

Cultural myths abound regarding the irresistible allure of nubile young women (actually, any woman) and the helplessness of men in the face of that allure. Even occasional fulfillment of these myths, reinforces and substantiates Bangladeshi preferences for not educating girls, early marriages for daughters and the seclusion of women within the household. Thus, family honour is literally embodied in the sexual behaviour of the females of the household, especially the young unmarried ones; in the cases of daughters and students, the honour is that of their own family, while in the case of servant women, the risk extends to the family for whom they work as well. It is not surprising, therefore, that unmarried pregnancies precipitate immediate expulsion of the woman from the household. Unswerving commitment to the honour of the family is the culturally appropriate (and accepted) response in such circumstances and the woman, especially a young teenage woman, falls victim to family honour in the face of social sanction. These young women routinely find themselves with no means of support, nowhere to go and little understanding of their situation or even how it came about.

Sixty-eight of 70 women (97%) indicated that their pregnancy, suspected pregnancy or birth of an out of wedlock child was the primary impetus to their abandonment. Only one woman claimed that she was not abandoned, but left of her own volition. Fifty-eight (83%) came to CTRDW seeking shelter, safety and/or medical care. 10 (14%) requested abortions and 2 women (3%) sought to abandon a child already born to them. 66 of 70 women (94.3%) were pregnant when they arrived at CTRDW, 60% already 5 months or more into their pregnancy – well past the time for a safe abortion. Three women were found to be not pregnant when tested and 3 arrived with newborn infants.

LIFE AFTER CTRDW

What happens to these young women and where do they go after they leave CTRDW? Thirty-five (50%) returned to their villages and/or family. Thirteen (18.6%) returned to their employers. Another 13 (18.6%) joined the CTRDW training programme. The remaining 9 (13%) transferred to other health/support facilities such as hospitals, the Families for Children orphanage, World Vision and the Bottomly Home for Girls.

And, what of their infants? Seven (11.9%) women left CTRDW prior to delivery, 3 were not pregnant and one mother left without her child. Of 59 infants, 10 (17%) were stillborn or died neonatally; 7 (11.9%) were discharged with their mothers; and the majority, 42 (71%), were abandoned to CTRDW. That 17% of the infants died or were stillborn is a poignant testimony to the physiological problems inherent in pregnancies among very young, physically immature women. These problems are further complicated by the need to hide their pregnancies for as long as possible. The results include poor prenatal nutrition, little or no prenatal medical care, prolonged and obstructed labours, caesarian sections, extensive episiotomies and premature births. Although the majority of women delivered their babies in hospital, as one excerpt above indicates, some women chose to hide their labours for as long as possible in order to avoid going to hospital. This is partly a reflection of the conditions in the hospital delivery wards. But, it is also a response to the judgmental attitudes and punitive treatment unmarried mothers routinely receive at the hands of nursing and medical staff, which mirror those of society generally (Table 5).

Table 5.   Where Did They Go.

Mothers	Freq.	Percent	Cum. Percent	Babies	Freq.	Percent	Cum. Percent
Village/Family	35	50.0	50.0	With Mother	7	11.9	11.9
Employer	13	18.6	68.6	Died/Stillborn	10	17.0	28.9
Training Programme	13	18.6	87.2	Abandoned	42	71.1	100.0
Other facilities	9	12.8	100.0				
Total	70	100.0			59	100.0	

CASE HISTORIES

A series of short case histories are presented in this section. Originally, a 20% sample of all CTRDW admission records was randomly selected for analysis. For the purposes of this paper, I have extracted from that sample those case histories specific for unmarried women 15 years of age and under. These 17 histories comprise a sub-set of the 70 cases discussed in the sections above, a 24% sample. These histories help to contextualize the circumstances within which unmarried pregnancies occurred for these young women. Further, they provide a human face for the numerical data presented above. The naïveté of young women and their susceptibility to manipulation and exploitation by men emerge clearly in these cases. The final discussion draws together the common themes of these histories. The interviews were originally conducted in *Bangla* by the CTRDW social worker. They were later translated into English by the same social worker and the author. I have minimally edited the translations in order to preserve the texture of the stories and the language used to tell them. Some of these histories are more detailed than others but together they provide a finely drawn portrait of the experiences of these very young mothers.

Salihma

Salihma arrived at the gate in a very ragged and poor condition. She is about 10 or 11 years old and said she had lived in the home of Deputy Superintendent of Police since she was very young. The son of the house made her pregnant but when it became apparent she was pregnant, she was thrown out. She had been on the street for some time before finding her way to the CTRDW. She is a very good girl and after two months, she is doing very well in the embroidery programme and is a very willing worker. A month later, she is sent on trial to the house of a local doctor to work as an *ayah* on trial. A month later, she is doing very well at her job and would like to keep child but her position (as a single mother) is very difficult. Two weeks later the child was released with Salihma.

Shulota

Shulota is 13 years. She is the second oldest of two brothers and three sisters. Shulota's father is a poor man who works as a day labourer for other farmers in the village where her parents live. His daily income is only 20 *taka* (about 80¢) but there are 6 members in his family. Shulota was reading in class VII (this is quite an accomplishment for a village girl), but now she is pregnant. Her uncle's employee raped her. Her father and uncle tried to get her an abortion but failed. Shulota's parents and uncle were frustrated; they don't know what to do about Shulota. They discussed the matter with some people and they heard about the activities of CTRDW and decided to come here. Shulota came with her uncle on 13th of May and now she lives here. After her baby was born, she abandoned it to the Centre and went back to live in the village.

Hosneara

Hosneara is 13 years old. She is the youngest of 2 brothers and sisters. She is deaf and dumb and abnormal (mentally challenged). When she was 12 years old, she ran away from home. Nobody knew where she went. After 7 or 8 months, Hosneara came back home on her own. She was on the street. Her mother worked as a maidservant. Her father is a rickshaw puller. He does not live with the mother. He does not look after them (does not support them). Hosneara became pregnant, her mother couldn't understand. After 2 or 3 months, Hosneara does not take food (eat), vomits and feels sleepy much of the time. Then her mother understood that she is pregnant. Her mother didn't ask anything about the pregnancy because Hosneara can't speak. Her mother took her to Dhaka Medical College for a checkup and tried to get an abortion. But it was too late. Then her mother brought her back from the hospital. Her mother was so worried; now what will she do? They lived in a slum area and everybody noticed about her pregnancy. One of the CTRDW trainees lives in the same area and she brought Hosneara to the Centre where she is now staying. She is 5 months pregnant. A few days later, Hosneara went into labour and blood was coming out. We sent her to Dhaka Medical College hospital. After two days, she had a stillborn baby but the baby's size was bigger (than expected). She was probably more than 5 months pregnant. But she was not so upset and doesn't look sick. A few days later, her mother came to take Hosneara back.

Asma

Asma is 13 years old. When she was very young, her father died. Asma's mother worked as a maidservant. When Asma was 10 or 11 years old, her mother came to Dhaka with her and took a job at a hospital as a sweeper. When Asma was 12 years old she took a maidservant job. Asma was not a smart girl. Her housemaster's son gave her some money and told her to make a sexual relationship with him. Asma didn't understand, she took the money and made a sexual relationship with him. When her menses had stopped for 3 months and she was feeling very weak and nauseous, then Asma told to her mother about what had happened. Asma's mother took her to the hospital for a checkup and discovered that she is pregnant. Her mother was upset because she was so young. Then her mother contacted a nurse to arrange for an abortion. But, it was too late. Then Asma's mother took her to Missionaries of Charity for help. Then two sisters of Missionaries of Charity brought her to the Centre. Asma couldn't say how many months she is pregnant. She might be 6 or 7 months pregnant.

She had a boy that was fostered soon after his birth. Asma is staying at the Centre and is breastfeeding another baby. When her breast milk is finished, then she will go back to her mother.

Renu

Renu is only 13 years old. When she was 3 years old, she came to an orphanage because her mother died and her father was a day labourer. Who will look after the child? Renu was at the orphanage for 11 years. She was reading in Class 10. Renu went to her village home during the last Ramzan holidays and after one month she came back to the orphanage. When she came back at the orphanage, nobody knew that she was pregnant. After one month she came here (CTRDW) and the nurse in charge found that Renu is pregnant. When she asked how she became pregnant, Renu confessed. When she was in her village, she made a sexual relationship with her cousin. He promised to marry her but when her father heard she is pregnant, he was so upset and angry with her. Her father said to her "I will not take any responsibility for this daughter." Renu's position was so helpless and it looks very bad for the orphanage. Then the Director of the orphanage contacted us and brought her to the Centre. She is now 6 months pregnant.

She had a baby boy and was released to the Director of the orphanage. Again, Renu will start her studies. They are hoping she will appear for the Secondary School Certificate examination next year.

Tashlima

Taslima's parents are both alive. She has 1 brother and 5 sisters. Her father used to work in a shop selling perfume and her mother works as a maidservant. She used to work in her father's boss's house as a maidservant. That man's brother told her that he will marry her and one day he got married with her (this was likely a ceremony contrived to trick Taslima, certainly the rest of the story indicates that the marriage was not sanctioned by either family). And after some time she became pregnant by that man. When it had come to the brother's notice, he sent back his brother to Madras in India. He never came back again. She lived with a paternal cousin in Dacca for one month and then she somehow came to Missionaries of Charity.

Taslima is now taking training here. She was a problem before but now she has adjusted to the situation here. Now she can sign her name. She is in *nakshi katha* (traditional embroidery). She is doing well in this. After having the child she wants to see her mother in the village. She is really intelligent. She loves her child and does not care about what sex it is. If she were capable, she would not give the child up for adoption.

Beauty

Beauty is about 14 years old. She was referred by Holy Family Hospital because she is carrying an unmarried pregnancy. She became helpless and shelterless, along with her pregnancy. Her family could not shelter her because of social custom. She has two sisters and one brother. She is the eldest of them. Her father had been working in the Court as a *muhuri* (messenger). Her father's economic condition was not good because he could not work regularly. Sometimes, her maternal grandparents supported them financially.

That's why one day Beauty went to visit her paternal aunt's house for some days. Her aunt had a son and he (the cousin) was characterless. According to Beauty's version, he convinced her to make a sexual relationship without marriage. Though at first she did not agree to that proposal, her cousin made a sexual relationship by force with her in secret. In this way, her cousin made sexual intercourse with her for four or five days. After coming home again, she told her mother about her cousin's conduct. But, her mother did not believe it. After six months, when Beauty's pregnancy became apparent, her mother came to Dhaka to do an abortion. After coming to Dhaka, her mother told about her condition to her aunt. Then her aunt brought her to Holy Family Hospital for an abortion, but the doctor refused to do an abortion and sent them to the CTRDW to overcome their problem. At that time she was carrying a 6 month pregnancy.

She gave birth to a male child at Dhaka Medical College Hospital. It was a normal delivery, but unfortunately the baby died a few days later. She was released to her maternal aunt and went back to her family.

Masuda

Masuda is 14 years old. She has 4 brothers and sisters. Masuda is the second of her family. Masuda's family was very poor, that's why her father did not look after them properly. When Masuda was 12 years old she came to Dhaka with her neighbour to find a job. She worked as a maidservant. When she was 13 years old she had a sexual relationship with the housemaster's son. This boy was a college student. When Masuda was about 3 months pregnant, everybody noticed and the housemaster threw her out from their house. Then Masuda came to Azimpur to find a maidservant job. She told them "I am married and my husband left." Masuda worked in the second house for 5 months. When the housemaster realized that this was an illegal pregnancy, he was very upset and wanted to send her to her village. But Masuda would not agree to go back to her village. Then the housemaster brought her to the Dhaka Medical College hospital for treatment and explained her position to the doctor who referred her to the Department of Social Welfare. Then they referred her to our Centre for rehabilitation. Masuda is 8 months pregnant. Masuda is very upset about her situation. When I (social worker) interviewed her, she was crying and saying, "how will I go back to my parents because I am an unmarried girl?" Masuda gave birth to a baby girl but because she is an unmarried girl, she couldn't keep her baby. She loves her baby, but two weeks later Masuda abandoned her baby and she went to our training programme.

Nazma

Nazma is 14 years old. She has 3 brothers and sisters. Nazma is the youngest. When Nazma was 13 years old, her family promised to marry her to a neighbour cousin. He was a serviceman (he has a wage job). His family also agreed to the marriage. After 5 or 6 months, they made a sexual relationship before marriage and Nazma became pregnant. When Nazma was 2 months pregnant, she told to her future husband. But he refused her and ran away. His family also moved their house. When Nazma told her family, her family tried to find out where that man had gone, but they couldn't find him. Nazma's position was desperate. Nazma's brother wanted to take her to Dhaka Medical College hospital for an abortion, but Nazma did not agree. After that, they were very worried about the girl because it was a matter of prestige. Then Nazma's brother talked with a lady who was a staff member of the New Life Centre. This lady knew about our organization. Then she brought Nazma to our Centre. Now Nazma is $3\frac{1}{2}$ months pregnant. She is a very young girl. After 3 days Nazma said, "I don't want to stay here. I want to do an abortion." We said to her, "you are so young. It is very risky for you." We tried to motivate her to stay here. Then, the next afternoon Nazma ran away from our Centre.

Moina

Moina has a fair complexion and is a good-looking girl. She has got good health and clear, intelligent eyes. When she came, she sat and then started crying. I had to wait for some time and then I started questioning her. She has parents and some brothers and sisters. Her two sisters are married. The younger brothers and sisters are studying in the school. She does not read or write. She has got an idea that if she studies, she falls sick. The village people say that she has some evil spirit on her. For the first day it was enough, so I let her go and take rest.

Moina is too much attached to her brother-in-law. She always talks about her brother-in-law but she never talks about her father. She does not want to go to her father but to her brother-in-law. I sent her to the adult literacy training class. She studied there but did not feel bad. The teacher was praising her that she did well in her study. But she did not study at her own house. This day also Moina did not like to talk about her pregnancy.

Moina can write her name and the Bengali alphabets; however, she does not like to do routine work in the house. One point she sticks on, that is, she wants to see her brother-in-law but not her sister, not even her two nephews. Moina is really very sharp. Within a very short time she has learned to stitch *nakshi katha* (traditional embroidery). She has got a new *katha* and independently she is stitching it. Also, she picks up studies quickly. I said, "Now you tell me what happened to you that you became pregnant. How did it happened?" She kept quiet and said, "I will tell you later."

Moina hesitated at first and then again she lied. She told that it was a evil spirit who came to her at night, she dreamed it and next month she became pregnant. I helped her to understand that a girl cannot become pregnant unless a man comes to her. It took one hour and then she confessed that it was a boy in the village. He raped her. She agreed that her parents know about it. She gave birth to a son. After she gave birth she was crazy to go home. Within this time (at CTRDW), she learned a lot so that she can earn money. Her parents are capable enough to look after her and settle her to a good life.

The child is the problem because it was born out of wedlock, which is a great social stigma in our society. Her father was informed to take her home. It is our first concern to rehabilitate her to her own family with some training that she can earn and feed herself. She is very much sensitive about her brother-in-law. Some of the girls told that it was his son she was carrying. But she was furious about the story. It seems that she was raped by her cousins who had given her sedaxin (sleeping tablets). Only her parents and her brother-in-law know about her pregnancy. They want her back in the family. The brother-in-law brought her from their village home when she was $3\frac{1}{2}$ months pregnant. Menstrual Regulation (M. R. is in essence a suction abortion available up to 8 weeks gestation) clinics were tried but M. R. was refused because she was then over 4 months. A man in the staff quarter knew of this Centre and accompanied the brother-in-law to this place. Her brother-in-law is keeping in touch and will take responsibility when she returns back home.

Jacinta

Jacinta is 15 years old. She has three brothers and sisters. Jacinta is the youngest. Her father is old. Jacinta's brother-in-law lived in their house and made an affair with her. When Jacinta became pregnant, her brother in-law ran away from their house. Jacinta's neighbour and relatives began to notice when she was seven months pregnant. Jacinta is helpless and her elder brother brought her to the Missionaries of Charity. They brought her to our Centre.

Jacinta had a baby girl but she was confused about her baby because this baby is illegal. She loves her baby and she has a lot of affection for her baby. After three months, her brother didn't come to take her. Then Jacinta thought, I will keep the baby and I will take training. She was discharged with the baby and joined our training programme. She tried to keep her baby but our society is very strict. That's why she couldn't keep the baby. Then, she abandoned the baby to the Centre. Now she is working at the Bottomly home.

Kodeza

Kodeza is 15 years old. She has no brother or sister. When she was very young her parents died. Kodeza was raised by her neighbour aunt. When she was 14 years old, Kodeza fell in love with her aunt's brother. Kodeza called him uncle. Her boyfriend was a student. He wanted to marry her. After a few months they made a sexual relationship and she became pregnant. When Kodeza was five months pregnant everybody noticed and her lover refused her. Then her aunt brought her to Dhaka. Kodeza stayed for three months at the aunt's sister's house. They were very worried for Kodeza. They heard from a doctor about our organization. Then they came to our Centre. Now Kodeza is staying at our Centre. She is eight months pregnant. She is very upset for this situation.

Kodeza gave birth to a baby girl. She has a lot of affection for her baby but this baby is illegal. She is confused about her baby. She is saying, "I want to keep my baby." But our society is very difficult. Then Kodeza told to me, "Again, I will think." Later, she was crying and saying, "I will try to keep my baby. If I can not manage the baby, I will abandon the baby." After one month she talked with me again. She told me, "I like to go my village with the baby" and she left a few days later with the baby. Then we heard Kodeza is working in garment factory.

Berusu

Berusu is 15 years old. She has two brothers and sisters. She is the eldest of her family. Berusu's father is a day labourer. Their economic condition was very bad. That's why Berusu also went to do a maidservant job when she was only 11 years old. The people in the house where Berusu worked were Muslim. But Berusu was Christian. She works very nicely, that's why everybody likes her. When Berusu was 13 years old, she fell in love with the son in the house. For one year, they made a sexual relationship and Berusu became pregnant. When everybody noticed, then the boy tried to marry her. But he couldn't because Berusu was Christian and the boy was Muslim. Even the economic condition between them was that of lord and slave. They faced many problems. That's why the boy couldn't marry her. Berusu's father was so upset because she was an unmarried Christian girl. His position was desperate. What he will do? Her father contacted the Father of the (local) Catholic Church. Then they wrote a letter to our organization. Berusu's cousin brought her to our Centre. When I was talking with her, she was crying. She was saying to me, "I still love him." I was very upset because she was very young. Now Berusu is staying inside and everyday she is going to our training programme.

She had a baby boy. When she first came to our Centre, she told us, "I will not keep the baby. Because if I try to keep the baby, our society will never allow me." But after the baby was born, her mind changed. She wanted to keep the baby. She loves him very much. But when she thought very deeply, she told me, "I will not keep the baby. Very soon I would like to go back home." I (the social worker) wrote a letter to the Catholic Church. They are coming very soon to take her back to her home. Berusu went back to her village. She abandoned her baby.

Momtaj

Momtaj is 15 years old. She has only one brother. When Momtaj was nine years old her parents died. She didn't want to stay with her brother because her brother was young. Who will look after both of them? When Momtaj was 10 years old, she came to Dhaka with her neighbour. She worked in Dhaka as a maidservant. When Momtaj was 14 years old she fell in love with a shopkeeper. He wanted to marry her. After six months they made a sexual relationship and she became pregnant. When Momtaj became pregnant, she told her boyfriend. He told her, "Don't be nervous. I will marry to you after two months. I have to contact your brother and my family. Otherwise, I will not marry to you." Momtaj waited up to one month, but he didn't contact his family about the marriage. When Momtaj was five months pregnant, her boyfriend left her. He never came back to see her. Momtaj came away to another area because everybody knew about her illegal relationship. Again, she started a maidservant job. She told everybody, "When I was three months pregnant, my husband left me." Momtaj couldn't go back to her brother because if her brother heard about her illegal relationship, he will hit her and all of the village people would know.

When Momtaj was nine months pregnant, she couldn't work properly any more. The housemistress didn't keep her. Momtaj's position was desperate. Where could she go? One of the production girls told to her about our organization. Then Momtaj came to our Centre at night, by herself. She is nine months pregnant.

She had a baby girl and after the baby was born, she told me, "I will leave the baby. Otherwise, where will I go with the baby? I will leave the baby here and I will go back to my village." Then she changed her mind. She told me, "I would like to keep the baby and I will join the training programme. I don't want to go back to the village." She joined the training programme and is keeping her baby in the daycare.

Amiron

Amiron is 15 years old. She came here with a lady who was her neighbour. Amiron is nine months pregnant. She has three brothers and sisters. Amiron is the second. Her father died three years ago. Her father was a day labourer. Their economic condition was not good. After her father died, Amiron came to Dhaka along with her family. At that time, she was 11 years old. Her mother worked as a maidservant, her two brothers sell pins and Amiron works as a maidservant here and there. When Amiron was 14 years old, she fell in love with a rickshaw puller who lived beside her home. He wanted to marry her. For six or seven months, they made a sexual relationship and she became pregnant. Her menses stopped from two months and she felt very weak, still Amiron didn't understand that she was pregnant. When she told to the rickshaw puller about her problem, he understood but he said to Amiron, "No problem, I will take care." When Amiron was 4 months pregnant, the rickshaw puller ran away from the area. Then Amiron's mother understood, she is pregnant. What will she do? Her mother didn't know. Then they moved from that area and came to live in another slum area. Her mother told to everybody, "My daughter's husband left her, when she was four months pregnant." When Amiron was nine months pregnant, her mother took her to a mother and child health clinic for an anti-natal checkup and she explained her position. Then her mother sent her with one lady to our Centre. She had a baby by caesarian. Now she is in hospital. She came back from the hospital a few days later. She will abandon the baby here (to CTRDW) and will go back to her village. She abandoned the baby and went back with her brother to her village. The baby died of asthma.

Shokina

Shokina is 15 years old. She has two sisters. Shokina is the second one. When Shokina was nine years old, her father died. Her father was a day labourer. Their economic condition was not good. That's why Shokina went to find a maidservant job. In the village she didn't get any job. Then Shokina came to Dhaka and worked as a maidservant. At that time she was 13 years old. Where she was working, the housemistress was so nice to her. But after 1 or $1\frac{1}{2}$ years, she made a sexual relationship with the son of housemaster. Nobody knew about it and she became pregnant. When she was 3 or 4 months' pregnant, she advised the housemistress that she doesn't feel very well and that her menses have stopped. When her housemistress discovered that Shokina became pregnant by her son, she was so upset. But she couldn't say anything to her son because of their prestige. The housemistress told Shokina to leave their home. Shokina couldn't go back to her village. She was rounding here and there. When she was 9 months pregnant, water (edema) has come to her leg and body. Her position was very bad. Then one of the sisters of Thomas's church picked her up from the street and took her to their church. But in this position, what could they do? Then they took her to Missionaries of Charity. They didn't take her but referred her to our Centre. Now Shokina is nine months pregnant.

She had a baby girl. Now Shokina is thinking, she will abandon the baby here and will go back to her home district. A few days later, she abandoned the child to the Centre and she went back to the village.

Salma

Salma is 15 years old. She has two brothers and sisters. Salma is the second. Her father was a day labourer. When Salma was seven years old, her father died. Her mother raised her. When Salma was 13 years old, she has been sick and the doctor found she has diabetes. Then Salma took a maidservant job in a foreigner's home. She was working there and was getting treatment from the foreigner. The foreigner is a doctor in a village health clinic. But before one year, Salma fell in love with a man who does work with the foreigner as a helper. Then they made a sexual relationship. The man was married but Salma didn't know until after she became pregnant. It wasn't possible to marry him. Then Salma went back to her home when she was four months pregnant. She didn't say anything to her mother. Again, Salma had got sick and went back to the same doctor. The doctor arranged for her admission to Dhaka Diabetic Hospital and they found she is pregnant. Then the foreigner contacted the Centre and brought her here. Now Salma is six months pregnant.

She had a baby girl. She has diabetes and she has got eye problems. She couldn't take any training. She tried but couldn't catch up. Now she plans to leave the baby and go back to her parents. Salma went back to her village without the baby.

CASE HISTORY THEMES

Poverty and Child Mothers

In 13 of 17 case histories, poverty is a major influence. For nine of these women, poverty provides the impetus for their joining the workforce as servants, a primary prerequisite in their becoming pregnant (see particularly those seven cases where the man responsible for the pregnancy is another member of the household in which she works). For four women, the death of their fathers or both parents resulted in economic (and social) vulnerability. For Renu, the death of her mother resulted in her placement in an orphanage at a very young age. Similarly, since Beauty's father was unable to work regularly due to poor health, he could not provide properly for the family. Taslima's history appears, on the surface, to be an exception to this pattern. Both of her parents are alive and both are employed. Nevertheless, she was working as a maidservant in the house of her father's boss when she became pregnant, which suggests that the family was in need of additional income. Hosneara's family also survives in difficult economic circumstances (the father does not support them) and although her inability to communicate prevented her from working, it did not prevent her from running away from home or protect her from sustaining an unwanted pregnancy. It merely leaves many of the details of her experience a mystery.

It is important to remark at this juncture that these are, for the most part, the experiences of poor women who come from the lowest economic classes. They, therefore, cannot be taken to represent the experiences of women from more affluent families who may have other options available to them. These options include abortions (even second and third trimester abortions which are available, although illegal, at very expensive private clinics where the fee for services increases exponentially with the length of gestation), visits to distant relatives (possibly even overseas) and hastily arranged marriages.

The case histories of Moina, Jacinta and Kodeza demonstrate the risk of sexual liaisons with males within the family – Moina and Jacinta apparently with their sisters' husbands and Kodeza with her "uncle." In all three cases, it is unusual for such a man to be living in the family. Traditionally, Bangladesh is a patrilineal and patrilocal society. That is, kinship is traced through the male line and married couples live with the husband's family. Thus, a brother would not normally live with his adult sister, as in the case of Kodeza's "neighbour aunt." Similarly, it is highly unusual for Moina's and Jacinta's brothers-in-law to reside with them, especially since the parents in both cases are still alive. Indeed, in Bangladesh a somewhat derogatory term, *"dulu bhai,"* refers specifically to this unusual eventuality. One cannot help but wonder if this situation – a sexual relationship between brothers-in-law and younger sisters-in-law – isn't exactly why this particular familial configuration is considered inappropriate.

All of the women portrayed in these case histories are very young. Seven are 15 years of age and 10 are between 10 and 14 years old. No apparent relationship exists between teenage pregnancy and birth order: two are the eldest; three are the youngest; six are middle children; two have siblings but their birth order is unknown; three are only children. However, a relationship does seem to exist between education and unmarried pregnancy. Only two women went to school: Shulota, who was reading in grade 7, and Renu, who was reading in grade 10 in the orphanage, at the time of their pregnancies. Moina can read and write but claims that "if she studies, she falls sick." The remaining 13 women did not attend school. Lack of education is related to unmarried pregnancy in this sample; however, lack of education for these particular women is also closely related to poverty. Women who live in poverty are forced into early wage labour, which precludes going to school.

Abortion, Abandonment and Finding CTRDW

Eight of the men responsible for the pregnancies were living and/or working in the house where the woman was working: five are the sons of the women's employer, one is the brother of the employer, one is the woman's uncle's employee and one is another employee. Two cousins are responsible for pregnancies, as are two brothers-in-law. In Moina's case, this is questionable as she tells so many different stories that it is difficult to discern which story is true. In Kodeza's case, the responsible man is her "uncle," in Amiron's a rickshaw puller and Momtaj's a shopkeeper. The man is unknown in Hosneara's case as she is unable to say.

Eight servant women entered into sexual relationships with men in the house. Of these, only Asma was paid to engage in sexual intercourse. Shulota and Beauty were raped or forced, while promises of marriage motivated 7 others to engage in premarital sexual liaisons. Both Momtaj's and Amiron's lovers, on learning about the pregnancy, promised that they would "take care" but eventually abandoned them. A marriage had been arranged for Nazma who became pregnant following premarital sex with her fiancé. She too was abandoned when the pregnancy became known. Even Taslima, who believed that she was married, was abandoned once she became pregnant. Marriage in Bangladesh is a social contract and without the sanction of the family, it is not considered legal. Thus, Taslima's marriage was contrived to convince her to enter into a sexual relation with her "husband." That he was sent back to India and that she had no claim on his family for support indicates that the family had not sanctioned the match.

All 17 women claim to have been abandoned as a direct result of their pregnancies. Six report that they attempted to secure abortions (one in the guise of Menstrual Regulation), but all failed because they were too far advanced in their pregnancies. Nazma refused to have an abortion at first but later said that she wanted one and left the CTRDW ostensibly to procure one. Salihma and Momtaj found their own way to CTRDW, Momtaj under cover of night. Asma, Taslima, Jacinta and Shokina were referred from Missionaries of Charity. Renu was brought by the Director of the orphanage where she lived. Masuda was referred from New Life Centre, Beauty from Holy Family Hospital and Berusu from the Catholic Church. Salihma, Shokina, Masuda and Momtaj had been expelled from their place of employment due to their pregnancies. Indeed, Salihma and Shokina had been living on the street for some time before finding their way to CTRDW. By contrast, most of the others were brought to CTRDW, usually by their family members and sometimes by their employers. This seems to indicate that families and/or employers may be willing to help very young, unmarried women find shelter provided the pregnancy can be hidden and no loss of prestige occurs. In many of these cases, the families were also willing to take the woman back after the birth provided the infant was relinquished.

Social Sancion and Lack of Responsibility

Social custom, loss of prestige and negative sanctions for women and families as a result of unmarried pregnancies are mentioned frequently in the histories. 12 cases specifically mention issues of social custom or loss of family honour. In 4 cases, the family is reported to be worried, frustrated, upset and/or angry with the woman. For example, Momtaj fears that "if her brother heard about her illegal relationship, he will hit her and all the village people would know." In 4 cases (Hosneara, Masuda, Kodeza and Berusu), that "everybody noticed" about the pregnancy is cited as the primary reason for moving away and/or expelling the woman from her home. In Taslima's case, the man responsible was sent away, while the men responsible for the pregnancies of Jacinta, Momtaj and Amiron ran away, leaving these women to fend for themselves. Similarly, the lovers of Nazma and Kodeza "refused" them once a pregnancy had occurred. These are all examples of negative sentiments that surround unmarried pregnancy and the ways in which men are able to avoid taking responsibility for their actions. 6 women specifically mention social sanctions that prevent them from keeping their babies, although in the end, 3 women (Salihma, Momtaj and Kodeza) decide to retain custody of their infants and leave CTRDW with them. Masuda, Jacinta, Kodeza and Momtaj all use the terminology "illegal" to describe their relationships, pregnancies and infants. This single word reflects the extent of negative social sentiment and explains why these women have been fired from their jobs, why they cannot go back to their families and why the child must be abandoned.

After the birth of their infants, Salihma, Jacinta and Kodeza began new jobs. Masuda and Momtaj joined the CTRDW training programme. Nazma left the Centre before delivering her baby, ostensibly to acquire an abortion. Renu returned to the orphanage where she had grown up to continue her schooling. Asma stayed at CTRDW to nurse other infants after her own had been fostered. The remaining nine women returned to their families and villages. Only three women left CTRDW with their infants, while nine abandoned them to CTRDW. One child was stillborn, one died neonatally and one baby died later from medical problems.

Relinquishing a Child

The decision to abandon a child is a very difficult one, even when the mothers are well aware that their child will never be accepted by their families or by society at large. Momtaj's decision-making clearly demonstrates the dilemma of the relinquishing mother.

"I will leave the baby. Otherwise where will I go with the baby? I will leave the baby here and I will go back to my village." Then she changed her mind. She told me, "I would like to keep the baby and I will join the training programme. I don't want to go back to the village."

Masuda asks, "how will I go back to my parents because I am an unmarried girl" and Taslima asserts that "if she were capable, she would not give the child up for adoption." Similarly, Jacinta is

> confused about her baby because this baby is illegal. She loves her baby and she has a lot of affection for her baby. After three months, her brother didn't come to take her. Then Jacinta thought, I will keep the baby and I will take training. She was discharged with the baby and joined our training programme. She tried to keep her baby but our society is very strict. That's why she couldn't keep the baby. Then she abandoned the baby to the Centre.

Finally, Kodeza cries and says,

> Again, I will think . . . I will try to keep my baby. If I can not manage the baby, I will abandon the baby . . . I would like to go my village with the baby.

In the end, we hear that Kodeza is working in a garment factory. We do not know what relationship (if any) she has been able to establish with her family. In Momtaj's case, we know that she has had to separate herself from her village home in order to keep her infant. For Masuda, Jacinta and Taslima, the prospect of being permanently separated from their families and sanctioned by society is too weighty; they relinquish their infants.

Religion

The importance of religious belief is explicated in Berusu's case. Because she is Christian and her lover is Muslim, their union is unacceptable to the family, regardless of the commitment or emotions of the individuals involved. Even the discrepancy in their economic positions, "that of lord and slave," emphasizes the economic and social impossibility of such a match. Again, marriage as a socially sanctioned contract between families is emphasized. The wishes of the marriage partners are not important. Since only socially sanctioned unions are "legal," Berusu finds herself with few options. Abandoned by her lover and unable to return to her natal home, she must also decide to relinquish her infant.

> She was crying (and) saying to me, "I still love him (her lover)." I was very upset because she was very young. . . .. When she first came to our Centre, she told us, "I will not keep the baby. Because if I try to keep the baby, our society never will allow me." But after the baby was born, her mind changed. She wanted to keep the baby. She loves him very much. But when she thought very deeply, she told me, "I will not keep the baby. Very soon I would like to go back home" . . . Berusu went back to her village. She abandoned her baby.

CONCLUSION

The CTRDW shelters abandoned women and their newborn children. The very youngest of these women are children themselves, ranging in age from 10 to 15 years. The circumstances under which they have sustained unmarried pregnancies and are subsequently abandoned by their families are culturally constructed. Society not only holds these women responsible for their predicament but judges and punishes them harshly, while at the same time allowing the men responsible to shirk their responsibility through apologies, running away and hiding behind the "prestige" of their families. The discussion above characterizes abandonment in terms of the social, economic and cultural contexts in which these young women live and work. Economic constraints in their natal families require that many young women seek wage labour outside the family, often as domestic servants. For the women in this sample, such employment predisposes them to sexual exploitation, unmarried pregnancies and consequent abandonment. For a minority of others, unsanctioned sexual relations with male relatives result in similar outcomes. For all of these women, then, childhood represents a dangerous time where economic vulnerability and social and sexual naïveté place them at considerable risk for unmarried pregnancy and abandonment.

NOTES

1. Three years of research (1992–1995) were funded by the Social Sciences and Humanities Research Council of Canada.
2. Another common euphemism used throughout Bangladesh to refer to a range of situations including premarital sex (consensual or otherwise) and unmarried pregnancy.
3. The adoption laws were suspended in 1982 and to date there is no religious or legal allowance for Bangladeshi families to adopt children. Families can obtain guardianship and custody orders through the courts in a form of permanent fosterage.

REFERENCES

Amin, S., Diamond, I., & Naved, R. T. (1998). Transition to adulthood of female garment-factory workers in Bangladesh. *Studies in Family Planning, 29*(2), 185–200.
Aziz, K. M., & Maloney, C. (1985). *Life stages, gender and fertility in Bangladesh.* Dhaka: International Centre for Diarrhoeal Disease Research, Bangladesh.
Kibria, N. (1995). Culture, social class and income control in the lives of women garment workers in Bangladesh. *Gender and Society, 9,* 289–309.
Maloney, C., Aziz, K. M., & Sarkar, P. C. (1981). *Beliefs and fertility in Bangladesh.* Dacca: International Centre for Diarrhoeal Disease Research, Bangladesh.

Rahman, M. (1989). Job stress, satisfaction and mental health of factory workers in Bangladesh. *Work Stress*, *3*(2), 155–162.

Wilson-Moore, M. (1995). Ruin or metamorphosis: Interpreting change in the context of nationalizing development programs. *Canadian Journal of Development Studies*, *16*(3), 455–467.

Wilson-Moore, M. (1996). Servants and daughters: Out of wedlock pregnancy and abandonment of women in Bangladesh. *Human Organization*, *55*(2), 170–177.

Wilson-Moore, M. (1999). Take this child: Why women abandon their infants in Bangladesh. *Journal of Comparative Family Studies*, *30*(4), 687–702.

18. THE WORLD BANK, NGOS AND THE STATE OF DEVELOPMENT IN SUB-SAHARAN AFRICA: IMPLICATIONS FOR ALLEVIATING POVERTY AND ADVANCING SOCIETAL REFORM

Kingsley Banya

There is much truth in saying that development – at least in the monopolistic, formulaic, foreign-dominated, arrogant, and failed form that we have known – is largely a matter of poor people in rich countries giving money to rich people in poor countries (Caulfield, 1996, p. 338).

INTRODUCTION

Virtually, all countries in sub-Saharan Africa (perhaps with the exception of South Africa) have still not achieved the economic, social and political self-sufficiency that the pioneers of decolonization had envisaged by the closing years of the millennium. Despite the active presence of the World Bank (WB) and non-governmental organizations (NGOs) on the sub-region development scene, initial gains immediately after colonial rule have disappeared, resulting in economic and social stagnation and, in extreme cases, disintegration (Sierra Leone, Democratic

'Suffer the Little Children': National and International Dimensions of Child
Poverty and Public Policy
Advances in Education in Diverse Communities: Research, Policy and Praxis, Volume 4, 433–475
Copyright © 2006 by Elsevier Ltd.
All rights of reproduction in any form reserved
ISSN: 1479-358X/doi:10.1016/S1479-358X(04)04018-5

Republic of Congo and Liberia). According to the United Nations Development Program (UNDP) (1996, 2000) in many post-colonial countries, real per capita Gross Domestic Product (GDP) has fallen and welfare gains achieved since independence in areas like food consumption, health and education have declined. As a whole, in sub-Saharan Africa, per capita incomes dropped by 21% in real terms between 1981 and 1989.[1] Madagascar and Mali now have per capita incomes of $799 and $753, down from $1,258 and $898 twenty-five years ago. In 16 other sub-Saharan countries per capita incomes were also lower in 1999 than in 1975.[2] Nearly one-quarter of the world's population, but nearly 42% of the population of sub-Saharan Africa, live on less than $1 a day. Levels of inequality have also increased dramatically worldwide. This phenomenon is vividly reflected in the well-known graphic presentation of the UNDP (1992) in Fig. 1.

Figure 1 illustrates that 83% of the world's income is concentrated among 20% of the population, while 60% of the population survives with less than 6% of the world's income. The phenomenon of 358 billionaires, whose combined wealth equals the per capita income of 45% of the world's population (some 2.4 billion people) exemplifies this aberration, especially as the world moves toward greater interdependence and democratic coexistence with globalization.[3] In the last 30 years, while the overall income of the poorest populations of the world (some 20%) dropped from 2.3 to 1.4%, the income of the wealthiest (some 20%) increased from 70 to 83% (UNDP, 1996). The most recent human development report (UNDP, 2004) indicated that the richest fifth of the world's people consumes 89% of all goods and services, while the poorest fifth consumes just 1.3%.

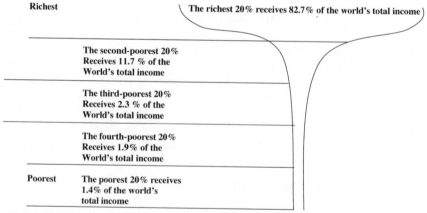

Fig. 1. World Population Income Distribution. *Note:* World population classified according to income. *Source:* UNDP (1992) *Human Development* Report. New York: Oxford University Press, p. 400.

It is in this context that this chapter discusses the roles of the WB and NGOs in sub-Saharan African development. The argument made in this chapter is that poverty, conditionalities, high indebtedness, and illiteracy affect children far more than adults. Children are the ultimate losers in the maldevelopment of the region. The empirical research on which this paper is based was part of a longitudinal study conducted in West Africa for the past seven years, with periodic visits to various countries in the region. An in-depth study was done in fall 2000 and during sabbatical in spring/summer 2001. A follow-up visit is planned for the summer of 2004.

The chapter draws on interviews as well as published documents and project assessment and is divided into three major parts: Part one provides a brief history and critical analysis of the development and purported roles of each institution – the World Bank and NGOs. Part two analyzes the relations between recipient countries and provides examples of conditionalities affecting select projects. Part three examines the impact of the two institutions on the region. The chapter concludes with a plea to reconceptualize development in light of the creation of the New Partnership for Africa's Development (NEPAD).

THE EVOLUTION OF THE WORLD BANK, NGOS AND CRITIQUES OF DEVELOPMENT

The World Bank

The World Bank (formally, the International Bank for Reconstruction and Development, or IBRD) was established at the Bretton Woods Conference in 1944 to help stabilize and rebuild economies ravaged by World War II (Morris, 1997). This is articulated by the Bank's Articles of Agreement as one of its primary purposes to assist in: "the reconstruction and development of territories of members by facilitating the investment of capital for productive purposes, including the restoration of economies destroyed or disrupted by war, the reconversion of productive facilities to peacetime needs and the encouragement of the development of productive facilities and resources in less developed countries" (World Bank, 1945).

The Bank consists of five agencies under the presidency of one individual. The President is a citizen of the Bank's largest shareholder member, which, from the Bank's inception, is and has been the United States. The position is elected by member nations in accordance with their purchased voting rights for a renewable term of five years.[4] Similarly, the Managing Director of the International Monetary Fund (IMF) is always a European appointee. The Bank is owned by its member nations, each purchasing shares of the Bank as a requisite for membership (World Bank, 1999). The developed economies of the West, of course, control the Bank, since they have the largest shares. The United States is the largest Bank shareholder, with 14.96% of the total votes in the Bank. Japan is the second largest shareholder with 10.73%, Germany is the third largest with 7.03% and France is fourth with 4.26%. Seven other nations hold between 2 and 4% of the voting rights for a total of 19.31% between them, and 149 nations hold the remaining 43.71%. A great majority of the latter group of nations hold less than one-third of 1% of the Bank's voting rights (World Bank, 1999).

It should be pointed out that none of the Western countries have fully paid up the value of their shares. Instead, rich countries have happily loaded new responsibilities onto the World Bank, knowing they will not have to foot the bill, which instead is paid by middle-income borrowers through higher interest margins. Meanwhile, the need to generate increasing income to pay for higher administrative costs explains why the Bank must continue lending large sums to middle-income countries to support often questionable development programs (Fidler, 2001).

The imbalance of Bank shares has led to the Bank endorsing the largest shareholders' economic and social policies for borrower nations' reform. Borrower nations are compelled to accept the conditions imposed by the Bank in order that they may receive much needed financial assistance, when in fact the conditions encouraged by the Bank (channeled from the majority shareholders) are ill-fitted to serve the borrower nations' economic, social and cultural needs. This phenomenon is further discussed in the chapter.

The various five agencies of the Bank include: The International Bank for Reconstruction and Development (IBRD) established in 1945, which provides loans to middle income nations and poorer nations whose credit is deemed adequate. The loans, which represent approximately 75% of the Bank's annual lending,[5] are primarily funded by the IBRD's sale of AAA-rated bonds to institutional and private investors in international markets. The IBRD has earned a positive net income every year for the last 51 years, though it is not designed as a profit-making organization (World Bank, 1999). The International Development Association (IDA), established in 1960, provides interest-free loans (termed "credits") to nations who qualify based on per capita income.[6] The loans are made only to the governments of the borrower nations. The borrower nations pay a fee of less than 1% to cover administrative costs. These loans, which represent the other 25% of Bank lending, are funded primarily by the contributions donated from both industrial and developing member nations (World Bank, 1999). The International Finance Corporation (IFC), established in 1956, provides technical assistance and advice to governments and businesses, and supports developing nations' business ventures with loans and equity financing. This financial support is provided by the IFC in conjunction with private venture capital investors (World Bank, 1999). The Multilateral Investment Guarantee Agency (MIGA), established in 1988, both assists in developing nations' promotion of business investment opportunities and provides guarantees to foreign nations who invest in a developing nation's business venture against loss, if the loss is caused by "non-commercial risks." The MIGA is funded by member capital (World Bank, 1999). The International Centre for Settlement of Investment Disputes (ICSID), established in 1966, operates to arbitrate investment disputes that arise between investor nations and the "investee" nations (Government of Canada, 1983).

The Bank shifted its focus to an emphasis on aiding developing nations when other measures were implemented to attend to Europe's financial troubles (Johnston, 2000). It should be noted that each of the five agencies of the Bank were established at the behest of the dominant Western nations, with little, if any, input from the developing nations (Kapstein, 1998/1999). At the creation of the World Bank, many of the countries in sub-Saharan Africa were under colonial regimes. The various agencies of the Bank are disproportionately influenced or manipulated by the Western elite economic institutions and have been characterized as agents of global capital (Greider, 2000).

The Bank's project loans are supposed to benefit the citizens of the recipient countries, which are made at favorable rates of interest. In theory, the Bank's policies are considered to be among the most comprehensive in the world. The policies require Bank staff and borrowers to consult with and provide information to local communities; carefully assess and minimize the risks (economic, social, and environmental) associated with projects; avoid displacement of people and ensure that displaced persons improve or at least restore their standard of living; and, respect the rights and vulnerabilities of indigenous peoples. The policies provide qualitative benchmarks against which project design and performance can be measured, and they should help guide the transition of Bank activities toward sustainable development (World Bank, 1997). The World Bank (2000) claims to contribute to the reduction of poverty and improved living standards in developing countries.

However, the Bank deals primarily with the political and economic elites of those countries, with little direct attention to the perspectives and needs of indigenous peoples, a practice for which it has been criticized by U.S. senators and officials (Caulfield, 1996; Rich, 1994). For example, former U.S. Treasury Secretary O'Neill (2001) criticized the Bank, "The world Bank Group alone has lent $470 billion since its inception and $225 billion in just the last decade. Visit some of the poorest nations in the world, and you'll see that we have little to show for it. It's time for a new approach to eliminating poverty" (Fidler, p. 45). O'Neill characterized the Bank's work as excessively diffuse, reasserting that the Bank should focus strictly on projects that "raise productivity or raise income per capita" (p. 45). The Bank has had a record of lending money to ruthless military dictatorships (engaged in murder and torture), after having denied loans to democratic governments overthrown by the military (Rich, 1994). Similarly, the Bank favors strong dictatorships over struggling democracies because it believes that the former are more able to introduce and see through the unpopular reforms its loans require (Caulfield, 1996). Borrowers of money from the World Bank typically are political elites of developing countries, and their cronies, although the repayment of the debt becomes the responsibility of people in these countries, most of who do not benefit from the loans.[7] Thus, the privileged benefit disproportionately from dealing with the World Bank, relative to the poor.[8] Today the Bank is a large, international operation with over 10,000 employees, 180 member states, and annual loans of some $300 billion (Finnegan, 2000).

Non-Governmental Organizations (NGOs) are the next foci for our analysis.

NGOs

With increased diversity and complexity of activities, substantial levels of financing and growing levels of external support and internal legitimacy, the proliferation of external non-governmental organizations and Southern volunteer development organizations has become one of the key new factors on the African development scene (Banya & Elu, 1997). There is a tremendous variation in the use of the term non-governmental organization. A broad definition would include every organization in civil society that is not part of government – for example political groups, labor and trade unions, and religious bodies. A narrower and perhaps more precise definition, derived from everyday usage, "refers to a specific type of organization working in the field of "development" – one which works with people to help them improve their social and economic situation and prospects" (Commonwealth Foundation, 1991, p. 24). The World Bank (1989) seems to use a narrower definition when it defines non-governmental organizations as "private organizations that pursue activities to relieve suffering, promote the interest of the poor, protect the environment or undertake community development" (p. 1). In this chapter, non-governmental organizations are defined by their key characteristics: voluntary, independent, not-for-profit and altruistic.

Voluntary
Non-governmental organizations are formed voluntarily; there is nothing in the legal or statutory framework of any country which requires them to be formed or which prevents them from being formed. There is an element of voluntary participation in the organization, whether in the form of small numbers of board members or large numbers of members of beneficiaries giving their time voluntarily (Commonwealth Foundation, 1995).

Independent

Within the laws of society, NGOs are controlled by those who have formed them or by boards of management responsible for control and management (UNDP, 1993).

Not-for-Profit

NGOs are not for personal, private profit or gain, although they may have employees, like other enterprises, who are paid for what they do. But in NGOs the employers or members of boards of management are not paid for the work they perform on boards, except for reimbursement for expenses they incur in the course of performing their duties. They can engage in revenue-generating activities but do not, however, distribute profits, surplus or dividends to shareholders or members like other corporations.

Altruistic

The aims of NGOs are to improve the circumstances and prospects of disadvantaged people who are unable to realize their potential or achieve their full rights in society, whether through direct or indirect forms of actions. They are to act on concerns and issues which are detrimental to the well-being, circumstances or prospects of people or society as a whole (Tandon, 1989).

These four characteristics are the litmus test for any NGO, irrespective of location. Some examples of NGOs include: non-profit consulting firms, health committees, squatters' associations, peasant leagues, village water associations, women's associations, mosque committees, environmental advocacy groups, human rights groups, youth clubs, legal aid societies, service clubs (such as Rotary) and local development associations (Banya & Elu, 1999). It should be noted that NGOs have no formalized legal status with regard to inter-governmental organizations (IGOs) or governments, and therefore the IGOs and governments are free to adopt a position they deem appropriate regarding their relationship to NGOs.

There are various reasons for the formation of non-governmental organizations. Some exist to serve those who cannot help themselves. Some provide services. Others offer mutual support, engage in public education and advocacy or provide charity. Some are concerned only with local issues. Others are oriented to national or international concerns. Some, such as Amnesty International and the American Civil Liberties Union, perform watchdog functions. And some other reasons for the proliferation of NGOS include the growing interest among agencies and national governments in strengthening the developmental roles of institutions outside the public sector and the demonstrated capacity of some NGOs to reach the poor more effectively than public agencies. In addition, a sharp decline in public development resources has necessitated a search by governments for more cost-effective alternatives to conventional public services and development programs. Because NGOs based in the industrial countries mobilize US$6 billion a year in development resources from private sources and manage another US$3.5 billion from official aid agencies (OECD, 1999), their role in development efforts has become critical. It has also been realized that some NGOs are sophisticated and influential organizations able to carry out programs on a national scale, and to influence national policies and institutions. The growth of power, external support and legitimacy for NGO involvement makes them worthy of being understood in their complexity and diversity. Major development financial institutions, such as the World Bank, IMF, the African Development Bank and host governments, are increasingly focusing on the issue of involvement of Northern and Southern NGOs in development (Edwards & Hulme, 1995). This phenomenon will be critically examined in the analysis of development.

Despite the recent focus on NGOs as "agents of change" and advocates for the poor, these were not the original roles of NGOs immediately after independence for most countries in sub-Saharan Africa. Notwithstanding NGOs' early allegiance to the idea of development, official development agencies remained largely unenthusiastic about their work. In the view of organizations like USAID, the UN and the World Bank, development was the business of the state and NGOs stood somewhere on the extreme margins of the field. While international NGOs were allowed to run their projects in Africa, this freedom was conditional, based on an unspoken assumption that they accepted or did not comment on the manner in which the state exercised its power. This arrangement suited official agencies, since key among the implicit goals of development in the Cold War era was the co-optation of post-colonial government to the economic and military agendas of Western powers. Consequently, the role of NGOs in the early post-independence period remained marginal. While they carried out "projects" providing services in peripheral areas that the state was disinclined to reach, the bulk of social services were provided by the state under its social contract with the people (Manji, 2000; Manji & O'Coill, 2002).

The work of NGOs was limited to project work where they focused the attention of "the poor" on finding participatory means for coping with the present rather than seeking justice for past crimes against them (Yamamori, 1996). Like their missionary predecessors, they offered to the poor, blessings in the future (albeit on earth rather than in heaven).[9] In their local offices they established the same racial divisions of labor and low salaries for local staff as had been customary among their missionary predecessors. The White expatriate, the technical expert, was usually the head of the local office. Militant at home about parity in salary scales within their home organizations, the northern NGOs in Africa came armed with a baggage full of reasons (usually transported in a four-wheel-drive vehicle) as to why local staff should not be paid at the same rates (Suzuki, 1998).

The emergence of neo-liberalism as the dominant political-economic ideology of the West, epitomized by the policies of former Prime Minister Margaret Thatcher of the United Kingdom and former President Ronald Reagan of the United States gave resurgence to NGOs. The major tenets of this ideology included the following:

(1) The self-interested individual: a view of individuals as economically self-interested subjects. In this perspective the individual was represented as a rational optimizer and the best judge of his/her own interests and needs.
(2) Free market economics: the best way to allocate resources and opportunities is through the market. The market is both a more efficient mechanism and a morally superior mechanism.
(3) A commitment to laissez-faire: because the free market is a self-regulating order it regulates itself better than the government or any other outside force. In this, neo-liberals show a distinct distrust of governmental power and seek to limit state power within a negative conception, limiting its role to the protection of individual rights.
(4) A commitment to free trade: involving the abolition of tariffs or subsidies, or any form of state-imposed protection or support, as well as the maintenance of floating exchange rates and "open" economies (Peters & Olissen, 2004).

A corollary of neo-liberalism is globalization. Globalization has many dimensions, but the following are most pertinent to this chapter:

(1) The growing global dominance and reach of neo-liberalism and a free-market capitalist system that disproportionately benefits wealthy and powerful organizations and individuals;
(2) The increasing vulnerability of indigenous people with a traditional way of life to the forces of globalized capitalism;
(3) The growing influence and impact of international financial institutions (such as the World Bank), and the related relative decline of power of local or state-based institutions; and
(4) The non-democratic operation of international financial institutions, taking the form of globalization from above instead of globalization from below (Friedrichs & Friedrichs, 2002; Greider, 1997).

Thus, according to the neo-liberal consensus, seen through globalization, the most important function of economic policy is to safeguard the "right" of a minority to accumulate profits at the highest rate possible (euphemistically referred to as "growth"). Only when this freedom is unrestricted, it is said, will others in society benefit from any associated spin-offs (the trickle-down effect). The purpose of "development" is, therefore, to guarantee "growth" so that ultimately other freedoms can be enjoyed at some indeterminate time in the future. State expenditure, according to this dogma, should be directed toward creating an enabling environment for "growth" and not "wasted" on the provision of public services that, in any case, can ultimately be provided "more efficiently" by private enterprise (Manji & O'Coill, 2002).

It is in this atmosphere that the Bank and other "development" agencies have embraced NGOs. For example, in spite of an absence of a legal obligation to work with NGOs, large inter-governmental organizations such as the Bank and the United Nations have accepted the establishment of working relationships with various NGOs. Schoener (1997) has studied the relationship between the United Nations and various NGOs, and finds that NGOs are "widely recognized by UN committees and programs as vital to UN work" (p. 550). Schoener attributes the United Nations' perception of NGOs' value to the "NGOs' freely offered assistance, which has made them virtually indispensable to the UN. In particular, their 'expertise, diplomatic skills, good relationships and contacts, and a clear vision about objectives' have proven useful" (Schoener, p. 550) to the United Nations.

In the last decade, the Bank has increased its use of NGO assistance in its development projects. Twenty-eight percent of its projects in the period 1987–1996 involved the participation of NGOs in some fashion; that percentage increased to 52% in the Bank's 1999 fiscal year (World Bank, 1999). Currently, the percentage has increased to 70%. The Bank states that:

> Involvement is sought at all phases of the Bank's work – planning and design of projects, implementation, and impact evaluation – because participation improves the quality, effectiveness, and sustainability of development activities. NGOs and other civil society groups play an increasingly critical role in ensuring that Bank-supported projects are participatory in nature, through both their own involvement and their ability to reach out to other stakeholders – especially poor and excluded communities (World Bank, 1999, p. 45).

In an effort to maximize the assistance offered by NGOs, the Bank has developed a team to monitor interaction between the Bank and NGOs. Specifically, the purpose of the team is to identify "examples of best practice, Bank-NGO collaboration, coordinate approaches to collaboration in policy dialogue and operations, and improve knowledge of NGOs and civil society by sharing and disseminating experience" (World Bank, 1999, p. 140). The team works in cooperation with the Bank's NGO Working Group, which, as part of the NGO-World Bank Committee meets twice a year with Bank management with the goal of strengthening Bank-NGO cooperation. According to the Bank, the Bank provides funding for NGOs in developing nations through the Bank's Small Grants Program (World Bank, 2004).

Though this is most certainly one way for the Bank to demonstrate its support of NGO existence, the funding connection between the Bank and the Bank-funded NGO impedes NGO independence from the Bank. NGO independence from the governments and International Governmental Organizations (IGOs) to which they report is important to the NGOs' ability to freely opine about the information they provide.

The close collaboration between the Bank and NGOs has not, however, pleased many of the borrowing governments. They complain that it is inappropriate for the World Bank to anoint non-elected, self-styled representatives of civil society to interfere in Bank programs. "I am deeply troubled by the distance the Bank has gone in democratic countries toward engagement with groups other than governments in designing projects," (Fidler, 2001, p. 46) lamented Larry Summers, the former U.S. Treasury secretary and currently president of Harvard University, at a private retreat of Bank country directors in May 2001. He indicated that there was little evidence that giving weight to local communities – in World Bank jargon, "empowerment" – resulted in improved decision making. "I am concerned," he said, "that the move toward empowerment, rather than an economic approach, is standing in some ways for a reduced emphasis on the analytic element in the Bank's work. If that is so, it seems to be a troubling development" (Fidler, 2001, p. 45). He further elaborates that "If you are a development organization, you really cannot be in bad grace with the principal carriers of moral energy around development," (p. 45) he said at the country retreat he attended in May 2001. Yet it would be "inimical to the goal of progress and the goal of reducing poverty around the world" if the views of NGOs and other campaigning groups guided policy. "I think it would be a great tragedy in terms of the Bank's potential contribution to reducing global poverty" (Fidler, 2001, p. 45).

Other critics charge that, under pressure from NGOs and other interest groups, the Bank has surrendered its intellectual integrity, rushing to embrace the latest fads in development thinking regardless of their substantive merit. No initiatives embody this trend better than the Comprehensive Development Framework (CDF), the World Faiths Development Dialogue, and the Global Development Gateway, launched in January 1999. According to the Bank, the CDF is a "holistic, long-term, and country-owned approach that focuses on building stronger participation and partnerships to reduce poverty" (World Bank, 1999, p. 101). The holistic approach reflects the understanding that there is no simple, single element to successful development strategies.

According to Bank documents, the CDF helps establish development priorities based on the principles of country ownership and partnership and with a focus on results and a comprehensive and long-term perspective. The Bank recognizes it does not have the resources to deal with every issue raised by the CDF, so it develops a Country Assistance Strategy aimed at intervening where the institution's expertise and comparative advantage are greatest.

For many of the Bank's critics, the CDF is not a solution to the World Bank's lack of focus but rather a good example of the problem. One former World Bank official calls the CDF "a cruel joke." (Lomax, 2001) The newsletter of the Bank's staff associate quoted one staff member as describing a new Strategic Framework Paper, published this year and meant to provide new direction for the Bank's development efforts, as "confusing, meaningless and stuffed with every cliché that has been uttered in the last two years . . . holistic, empowerment, ownership, even core competencies" (Fidler, p. 45). Critics charge that the CDF represents a capitulation to NGOs.

The World Faiths Development Dialogue brings together various religious leaders from around the world with the bank and other development institutions in order to "catalyze the active coordinated engagement of the world's faiths in the development process" (Fidler, 2001, p. 47). The dialogue, which World Bank officials now liken to George Herbert Walker Bush's initiative to use faith-based organizations as instruments of social welfare, has cost the World Bank up to $1 million annually, according to Devesh Kapur, a political scientist at Harvard University and coauthor of the official history of the World Bank.

The Global Development Gateway is an attempt to encourage new economy ideas in developing countries and create online portals for information on national-level economic development and reforms. Of the Gateway, Levinson cautioned, "To carry the IT revolution to [African countries] instead of teaching them how to reap better crops is a grave mistake. The mistake will make them poorer compared to the rest of the world" (Levinson, 1999, p. 4). Even NGOs and activist groups such as the Bretton Woods Project have criticized the Gateway, assailing it as a "major land grab on the Internet" that seeks to "gain more control over what analysis and opinions on development topics are deemed relevant and sound . . . . Many grassroots and campaign-oriented sites will be weeded out" (Levinson, 1999, p. 6).

Our next focus of critical analysis is the concept of development.

Development

For decades, the notion of "development" has been a focus of heated debate, more particularly in terms of its effect on those it purports to develop (Burkey, 1993; Escobar, 1995; Myers, 1999). Since World War II, there have been efforts to not only define what development is about, but also its viability and effects in relation to poverty alleviation. As a result, there has been a growing scrutiny and re-examination of how the process of development ultimately benefits the intended beneficiaries. For example, the Bank's interpretation of the term "development" was, until the 1990s, that of economic growth. This was in response to "the failure of economic growth to adequately address the problems of the poor." (World Bank, 1989, p. 16) The Bank "began broadening its understanding of which activities were included within the scope of its mandate by focusing more directly on poverty alleviation and basic human needs" (World Bank, 1989, p. 16). From the 1960s until now, the Bank has added "policy based lending, environmental concerns, gender issues, governance, economic transformation and private sector development to its repertoire of appropriate operations" (World Bank, 2004, p. 4).

Development is based on the premise that certain peoples and societies are less developed than others and that those who are more developed (i.e. more modern) have the expertise (knowledge) to help the less developed achieve modernity. This concept is a linear Western definition of modernity and the rationale for the development enterprise since the 1940s (Parport & Marchand, 1995). This definition of development has recently been challenged by scholars using post-modern critiques of modernity, Western universalism and dualist/binary thinking. Indeed some scholars are taking the development debate in a new direction (Crush, 1994; DuBois, 1991; Edwards, 1989; Escobar, 1992; Ferguson, 1990; Goetz, 1991; Johnston, 1991; Mathur, 1989; Pieterse, 1992). Recognizing the relationship between language and power, they have questioned the language/discourse of development, particularly the (re)representation of the South/Third World as the impoverished, backward "other" in need of salvation from the developed North/First World. This dualist construction, they point out, has reinforced the authority of Northern development agencies and specialists, whether mainstream or alternative, and provided the rationale for development policies and practices that are designed to incorporate the Southern nations into a Northern-dominated world. This approach, they argue, is no longer appropriate in an increasingly complex and interrelated world. Indeed, similar thoughts had already emerged from the "impoverished" South (Bratton, 1998).

Deconstructing Development

There are many views about the meaning of development (see for example Peet & Hartwick, 1999; Simon, 1999; Thomas, 2000), which have ultimately resulted in a wide rang e of nomenclature. The emphasis, however, has been on "well-being for all" humans (Chambers, 1997, p. 9) and, as Simons (1999, p. 2) puts it, "enhancing individual and collective quality of life" in an empowering and sustainable way. Martinussen (1997) argues that development should be viewed as the history of each and every culture in the world. He sees development as "a culturally grounded process where objectives cannot be formulated by outsiders – where North/Western researchers or decision makers cannot define what is development outside their own culture sphere" (p. 450). He contends that nobody has the right to prescribe the meaning except those who live in the culture. Martinussen's argument bears some resemblance to Yamarori et al.'s (1996) understanding that effective development entails "development of indigenous cultures and as a process of change rather than a specified level of achievement" (p. 124). Yamarori and his colleagues further maintain that for development to be effective, not only should the beneficiaries "participate" but they should also be part of the process with an ultimate goal of achieving "sustainability" (p. 125).

Escobar (1995) notes that development as a concept was a post-cursory to World War II. He views development as "a response to the problematization of poverty" (p. 44) that occurred during this period, but not a natural process of knowledge leading to the discovery of the problems. According to Escobar (1995), development was a discursive process governed by modernization thinking and premised on the belief that development was poised to occur if capacity investment was increased. This resulted in the construction of the world of "haves" and "have-nots." Those who were perceived as not having the capital investment were branded as underdeveloped (Sachs, 1992).

Modernization theories of development have occupied the development space and continue in a more subtle form through development agencies that claim to foster and deliver the promises of development. Isbister (1991) observes that modernization theories mainly "focus upon deficiencies in the poor countries – the absence of democratic institutions, of capital, of technology, of initiative, and then speculate upon ways of repairing these deficiencies" (p. 33). Modernization protagonists view underdeveloped countries as being held back by traditional society, and thus perceived as stagnant and static. Modernization scholar, Burkey (1993), strongly believes that the cure for this stagnation and backwardness is to embrace the social, cultural, and economic systems of the developed countries. Underdeveloped countries have to emulate more or less every aspect of the Western thinking and "doing" in order to achieve a growth-based innovation, which is viewed by these developed countries as essential to development in general. According to Isbister (1991), "modernizationists see the underdeveloped world achieving optimal development through transforming itself from tradition to modernity, that is to say, to follow in the footsteps of the new developed countries" (p. 38).

While elements of the developed world continue to try to make the underdeveloped world "like them" there are important challenges to modernization theory of development. In the words of Sachs:

> The idea of development stands like a ruin in the intellectual landscape. Delusions and disappointment, failures and crimes have been steady companions of development and they tell a common story; it did not work . . . But above all, the hopes and desires which made the idea fly, are now exhausted; development has grown obsolete (1992, p. 1).

Sachs' (1992) observation sums up the picture of not only development but also modernization theories as claiming to have the solutions of underdevelopment. In their rush to "help" ideas of development have collapsed virtually all the indigenous infrastructure that had been emblems of cohesion and a means of sub-Saharan African survival; for example, traditional secret societies for boys and girls. Commenting on the World Summit on Social Development held in Copenhagen in March 1995 (on the question of why development should be rejected by the poor) Kleinscmidt shares similar sentiments to Sachs and states, "thus as the issues facing the summit were concerned, the assembled leaders acknowledged that modern development has resulted in poverty, unemployment and disintegration of social structures" (Kleinschmidt, 1996, p. 1).

For a long time immediately after colonialism, there was a romanticism among Western NGOs to "bring development to the people in the newly independent countries in sub-Saharan Africa (Tucker, 1999, p. 7). As Thomas and Allen (2000, p. 210) observed, "Development NGOs mostly began as charitable organizations, often running very localized projects, and are often evaluated against goals such as their direct impact on rural poverty. It is relatively recently that such NGOs have broadened their activities to include attempts at policy influence or advocacy at both international and national levels." However, the dominant discourse of development was framed not in the language of emancipation or justice, but with the vocabulary of charity, technical expertise, neutrality, and a deep paternalism that was its syntax (participatory development was put in the mix for flavor)!

As with the racist ideologies of the past, the discourse of development continued to define non-Western people in terms of their perceived divergence from the cultural standards of the West, and it reproduced the social hierarchies that had prevailed between both groups under colonialism. On this basis, the so-called "developing world" and its inhabitants were (and still are) described only in terms of what they are not. They are chaotic not ordered, traditional not modern, corrupt not honest, underdeveloped not developed, irrational not rational, lacking in all of those things the West presumes itself to be. White Westerners were still represented as the bearers of "civilization" and were to act as the exclusive agents of development, while Black, post-colonial "others" were still seen as uncivilized and unenlightened, destined to be development's exclusive objects (Esteva, 1996; Korten, 1987; Manji & O'Coill, 2002; Smillie, 1995; Sogge, 2002; Tucker, 1999; Tvedt, 1998).

CONDITIONALITIES IN THE EDUCATION SECTOR

In this section we examine the Bank's conditionalities on the education sector in the region. In particular, we analyze World Bank policy towards higher education, and textbook production. The role of NGOs in certain social programs in the region are also examined.

The United Nations designated the period of 1960–1970, the Development Decade for Developing Countries, during which concentrated efforts would be made "to lessen the gap, to speed up the process of modernization, to release the majority of mankind from crippling poverty, to mitigate the tension and hostility which must flow from the world's vast inequalities in wealth" (Harbinson & Myers, 1964, p. 50). Economists and other social scientists had realized by then the close links or reciprocal relationships between education and development. Educational systems would produce people with the knowledge, skills, attitudes, and values that not only were favorable to economic and social development, but also were a sine-qua-non for the process of national integration. In the social science literature of the 1960s, higher education was presented as being crucial to creating a modern policy through political socialization, political recruitment and political integration. Universities were viewed as especially important for elite recruitment and national integration for "the bureaucracy remains overwhelmingly dominant" (Coleman, 1965, p. 28). The most influential studies demonstrated the productivity raising effects of investments in higher education (e.g. Schultz, 1960, 1963) and showed that the magnitude of effects increased with educational level (e.g. Renshaw, 1960). "The building of modern nations," wrote Harbison and Myers, "depends upon the development of people and organization of human activity. Capital, natural resources, foreign aid, and international trade, of course, play important roles in economic growth, but none is more important than manpower" (1964, p. 6). The authors further pointed out, "If a country is unable to develop its human resources, it cannot build anything else, whether it be a modern political system, a sense of national unity, or a prosperous economy" (p. V). This was the official thinking of the World Bank, bilateral assistance, and was vigorously prescribed for African Studies as policy for economic development. Manpower planning connected development theories emphasizing the importance of human capital to specific educational investments (Harbinson & Myers, 1964). Recent developments in the theory of economic growth continue to identify investment in education as a key element of economic growth (Barro, 2000; McMahon, 1999). This was the age of foreign educational assistance. Assistance for foreign training and institutional development was sought to rectify the situation, often accompanied by the transfer of the institutional training models of the donor country.

Without significant reform, questions were being raised about the wisdom of investing so much of state resources on education, and, in particular on higher education. As the economies of sub-Saharan African countries went into a tailspin in the late 1980s following the oil shock and subsequent woes of the late 1980s, reducing public expenditures as dictated by the World Bank became the key to national economic growth. In this context, four main effects of the general recession can be discerned: (a) reduction in international trade; (b) spiraling debt; (c) the growth of conditionality; and (d) reduction in developing assistance (Banya, 1991).

International Trade

Because of the economic recession experienced in the industrialized countries in the 1980s, the demand for imports from primary producers declined considerably. For example, the fall in the price of Sierra Leone's cash crops, especially that of cocoa and coffee, has adversely affected the country. The smuggling of cash crops to neighboring countries like Guinea and Liberia, where producers are paid sometimes twice what they would get in Sierra Leone, has worsened the situation. In 1993, commodity prices reached their lowest value since 1945 and, coupled with the decline of diamond prices, which range from $2,500 to $1,200 resulted in the worst terms of trade the country has ever experienced.[9] Similar stories abound in the sub-region.

Spiraling Debt

The high interest rates (10–18%) on existing loans from industrialized countries and international financial institutions, like the IMF, as well as the need to continuously finance current expenditure and development programs externally, have substantially increased the debt burden of the countries in sub-Saharan Africa. At last reporting, the external debt of the region was well over 1.5 billion (UN, 2003). This has exacerbated the shortage of foreign exchange. The cost of importing energy and reductions in export earnings have resulted in pressure on the balance of payments. In order to avoid fiscal crisis, the countries in the region have had to reschedule the debts to ease the payment burden. But, since new loans have had to be taken at a higher interest rate, loan repayments have pre-empted even larger proportions of expenditures, with adverse effects on all social programs.

It is worth noting that at independence many of the countries in the sub-region had relatively low debt burdens. For example Kenya, at independence in the 1960s, had a debt of only $29 million which the World Bank arranged to ensure that departing British colonists were paid for land originally stolen from the indigenous population (Leys, 1975). Today, Kenya's debt burden is in the billions. The interest payments on debts, alone, substantially reduce the GDP of many countries in the region. Debt rescheduling and our-right calls for cancellation of debts have become the hallmark of economic debates between the developed and developing countries as well as international financial institutions (Leys, 1994).

Conditionality

All countries in sub-Saharan Africa, and indeed all developing countries, have been forced to accept imposed conditions to qualify for loans. Part of one such condition is tighter control over public sector spending as well as an emphasis on balancing current accounts. The change in the external climate for loans and development assistance is a reflection of the shift in the political emphasis of industrialized countries, especially the United States and European Union countries, what has been referred to earlier as neo-liberalism. More and more emphasis is being placed on "getting the prices right" through market mechanisms. The International Monetary Fund (IMF) and other international institutions, reflecting this change in policy, attached the reduction of public expenditure and the commitment to a free market as the conditions for major loans and structural adjustment programs.[10] An example of policy-based lending is the Bank's funding of financial sector adjustment loans which originally were intended to effect reform in the borrower nation's financial sector. The purpose of the policy-based loans has been extended over time to include, *inter alia*:

> reform of the civil service; reform of the management of public sector enterprises; legal and judicial reform; family planning; improving the quality of education and the equity of access to primary education; reform of universities; land tilting and registration reform; programs to ensure that vulnerable groups such as women, children, indigenous people, and other minorities get access to health, education, and other Bank funded programs (Bradlow, 1996, p. 6).

Lending objectives for the Bank's 1999 fiscal year further illustrate the Bank's role as social governor. These objectives include, "focus on AIDS prevention, especially on the poor and high-risk groups; eradicate malaria; remote health systems reform to address needs of the poor; pursue solutions for child labor; eliminate malnutrition; improve access to credit, especially for poor women; reintegrate ex-soldiers into home communities, and provide assistance to veterans" (World Bank, 1999, p. 9).

This is the central tenet of the neo-liberal philosophy referred to in the first section of the paper. The IMF seal of approval is necessary before private and government creditors give additional credits (Banya, 2001). When faced with the problem of cuts in expenditures, the question becomes what sector has to be cut and by how much. As UNICEF observed . . . "what types of public expenditure are cut (armaments, health, food subsides, etc.) is a matter of choice. Clearly, the severity of the consequences for social equity and child welfare depends on the nature of the choice made" (UNICEF, 1997, p. 10).

Because education consumes a large proportion of the national budget, it is an easy target for cuts in fiscally troubled times, and, given limited room for maneuver, the governments in West Africa had very few choices to make. Countries, in order simply to survive, have had to make decisions, which are driven by the international money markets, including regional power-houses Nigeria and Côte D' Ivoire. For example, in Francophone West Africa, the effective devaluation of French franc by 50% was carried out without any input from those countries. The French and World Bank wanted the devaluation, so it happened. Some of the conditionalities imposed on borrowing countries include user fees.

User Fees

In keeping with the current vogue among developed countries and international development agencies to put greater stress on the market place, there has been a recent upsurge of interest in the implementing schemes of "cost recovery" and "user cost changes" in the social services. Higher education is one such area. As the population ages and the social demand for education continues to be buoyant, charging user fees for higher education will become necessary. As outlined further below, according to the Bank the present situation whereby a good number of university students hardly pay for their education, is inherently unfair to the poor and the uneducated. Equity necessitates the imposition of user fees. The Bank, argues that those who need a university degree should pay for that privilege and *not* the State. Such readjustment of education finances may lead to university students' anarchistic demonstrations and interruption of classes. The phenomenon of student strikes and riots over stipends for living expenses are well known in West Africa. Almost all countries in the region have had similar experiences, including Nigeria, when universities were closed indefinitely in the early 1990s. As it has been observed by one of its most respected economists, William Easterly, the IMF and World Bank had, during the last decade, given 36 poor countries 10 or more loans each, with conditions attached. "The growth rate of income per person of the typical member of this group during the past two decades was zero," he wrote in the *Financial Times* (2001, p. 40).

Development Assistance

Because of worldwide recession, donors have become unwilling to maintain past levels of Official Development Assistance (ODA). For example, the Organization of Petroleum Exporting Countries (OPEC) contributions to ODA shrank from $9,690 million in 1999 to $6,000 million by 1997. Total British aid to developing countries declined from $2,156 million in 1979 to $1,601 million by 1994 (Organization for Economic Cooperation and Development-OECD, 1998). It seems that the world is suffering from donor fatigue.

Since most external financing for educational development is provided by bilateral arrangements, any change in this type of aid adversely affects a country. OECD (1997) aid declined from $5,494 million in 1990 to $1,800 million by 1997, representing a drop of more than 17%. This condition had an adverse effect on many developing countries including sub-Saharan Africa. External aid is essential to the education sector, especially where there are foreign exchange shortages and a lack of expertise and training opportunities within the country. This is true in the case of countries that depend heavily, if not solely, on external donors for scholarships to train personnel. This devaluation of their various currencies has made sponsoring overseas scholarships impossible. In the absence of any inter-African training programs, external aid becomes indeed significant. The effect of the economic crisis on higher education quality and relevance has already been documented (Banya, 2001; Banya & Elu, 1997; Buchert, 1995; Johnston, 1998; King, 1991; Muyanda-Mutebi, 1993; Namuddu, 1991; Ocitti, 1990, 1991; OECD, 2002; World Bank, 1994, 2000; UNDP, 2002).

Bank Recommendations to Close Universities

At a meeting with African vice-chancellors in Harare, Zimbabwe in 1986, the World Bank argued that higher education in Africa was a luxury and that most African countries were better off closing the universities at home and training graduates overseas. Hinchliffe (1989) set out the terms of reference for the dialogue in an analysis of African higher education: social demand for higher education was increased at a time when the labor market for graduates was weakening; unit costs of higher education were too high by comparison to costs elsewhere; the internal efficiency of institutions was too low; and savings in expenditures for higher education should be made through increased student contributions. These findings were elaborated in the World Bank's 1988 policy paper in African education and became the basis of its policy dialogue with African governments. Governments were enjoined to limit or moderate enrollment increases by reducing or freezing student intake, to contain costs by lowering expenditures for academic and non-academic staff and student support and by rationalizing programs of study, and finally, to recover costs through charging tuition, raising fees and initiating student loan schemes. This argument, as will be later demonstrated, was based on false premises. Donors increasingly moved "upstream" into influencing policies affecting the higher education subsector and "downstream" into program and research funding affecting training and the activities of staff.

Recognizing that its call for a closure of universities was politically unsustainable, the Bank subsequently modified its stand, calling for universities in Africa to be trimmed and restructured to produce only those skills which the market demands. This policy was advocated for university restructuring in Nigeria in the late 1980s (Mamdani, 1993). Governments in developing countries were pressured for years by the World Bank and other aid agencies to cut spending on higher education and to reallocate their meager resources to primary and secondary schools. At the same time, donors shifted their givens to meet the Bank's view. For example, the British government issued a White Paper proposing a shift "from helping universities to helping with vocational training and other aspects of education which are closer to the grass roots" (Coleman & Court, 1993, p. 18). In the same year, the Rockefeller Foundation began phasing out support for university development in African, Asian, and Latin American countries, an activity in which it had been a leader for almost half a century. The Bank's policy was a clear contradiction of the Bank's own early policy on loans to primary schools.

Immediately after independence (early 1960s) for most countries in the region, the Bank's policy was that other sub-sectors of education were more potent in terms of economic development than the primary education sector. It further assumed that it was inappropriate for the Bank to finance school expansion resulting from population growth (Jones, 1992). Generally, there is a preference among donors for capital-intensive and foreign-intensive projects that are limited in number, scope and in geographical spread. Primary education projects do not satisfy these conditions. This is due to the fact that primary schools are highly dispersed with little or no room for hiring of expatriates. The foreign exchange requirement of primary education projects is much lower than that of other higher levels of education. Consequently, there was the prohibition by the World Bank on primary education lending between 1963 and 1970 (Babalola et al., 2000).

The primary education policy was again reversed in the 1990s. During this period there was a drastic shift in the position of the Bank with respect to primary education loans. Based upon rate-of-return data (Psacharopoulos & Woodhall, 1985) that saw primary education investments as one of the highest yielding of all development investments, the Bank accepted UPE as a matter of high priority. Consequently, World Bank lending for primary education projects during fiscal

1992–1994 and fiscal 1995–1997 exceeded lending for other types of education projects (World Bank, 1997).

Textbook Project

One of the projects that the Bank financed in the late 1980s and early 1990s was textbook production for primary education.[11] The loan for $90 million was more than the cumulative value of the Bank's lending to education in Sierra Leone prior to 1990. However, the large volume of this loan should not be misinterpreted to mean a high level of Bank's commitment to primary education. The execution of the project left a lot to be desired.[12] The textbooks were never provided on time! Logically, the Bank has to devote considerable sums of loan monies to this project since the foreign-exchange components of primary education projects are customarily low, usually confined to capital works, equipment, fellowship and technical assistance (Jones, 1992).

From the borrowers' perspective, the best indicator of project effectiveness is the impact of the book project on the quality of instruction and student enrollment. An assessment of the project indicates that the impact was minimal. Though proportions of the loans (74.75%) had gone to the procurement of books, the textbooks for primaries two to six were not available for pupil use. The primary one books which were available were not utilized in most schools as of 1998 since parents refused to pay the prescribed twenty Leones (local currency) per book (Banya & Elu, 2001). Yet, the World Bank was interested neither in financing the distribution aspect of the book project nor in its formative evaluation, which could have helped in identifying areas where corrective actions could have been needed.

Recent Bank Policy Changes: Higher Education

As part of the recent policy changes at the Bank in 1997, in collaboration with UNESCO, a Task Force on Higher Education and Society was convened. After extensive deliberations, the Task Force report, *Higher Education and Developing Countries: Peril and Promise* was published in March 2000. The six Chapters cover some of the issues discussed earlier in this paper including: "long-standing problems and new realities higher education faces; public interest in higher education; improving standards of governance; technology and better science education; diversification of higher education; and innovative general education curricula" (World Bank, 2000, p. 11). It is worth noting in particular, the report's condemnation of earlier efforts to restrict higher education as indicated:

Since the 1980s, many national governments and international donors have assigned higher education a relatively low priority. Narrow – and, in our view, misleading – economic analysis has contributed to the view that public investment in universities and colleges brings meager returns compared to investment in primary and secondary schools, and that higher education magnifies income inequality ... As a result, higher education systems in developing countries are under great strain. They are chronically under-funded, but face escalating demand ... (World Bank, 2000, p. 12).

The report continued that:

... Higher education is in a perilous state in many, if not most, developing countries. With a few notable exceptions, it is under-funded by governments and donors. As a result, quality is low and often deteriorating, while access remains limited. The focus on primary education is important, but an approach that pursues primary education alone will leave societies dangerously unprepared for survival in tomorrow's world (World Bank, 2000, p. 19).

Indeed, the Bank itself has acknowledged that:

Knowledge is critical for development, because everything we do depends on knowledge. Simply to live, we must transform the resources into the things we need, and that takes knowledge. If we want to live better tomorrow than today, if we want to raise our living standards as a household or as a country and improve our health, better educate our children, and preserve our common environment, we must do more than just simply transform resources, for resources are scarce. We must use those resources in ways that generate ever-higher returns to our efforts and investments. That, too, takes knowledge, and in ever-greater proportion to our resources (World Development Report, 1999, p. 41).

The people are perhaps the continent's most valuable resource. Development of high caliber managers and an efficient work force is a challenge that Africans must meet to maintain competitiveness. This challenge can only be successful if institutions of higher education are fully funded and supported by the people.

IMPACT OF DEVELOPMENT

It is becoming increasingly clear that development in sub-Saharan Africa has failed. With few exceptions (Botswana, South Africa and Mauritania), various efforts over the years to pull Africa from the brink of economic stagnation and collapse through several Western initiated and sponsored programs and projects have failed. The accelerated development in the immediate post-independence era in most African countries has stagnated and despondency has replaced hope as various countries strive to come to terms with the issues of globalization.

In this section we provide evidence of this belief through analysis of various indicators of development, in particular the amounts of debt burden, project failures, and imposed conditionalities that weaken the state authority in developing countries and the disbursement of aid are critically examined.

External Debt

Sub-Saharan Africa's debt burden stands at $300 billion, up from $10 billion in 1990, and the sheer weight of debt repayment is encouraging capital flight and thus strangulating development. The debt represents, on average, about three times the value of the region's exports of goods and services. Africa's crippling debt burden is a major impediment to growth. Some of the domestic resources needed for Africa's development could be forthcoming if substantial efforts were made to solve Africa's debt burden (Nyikuli, 1999).

According to the World Bank's 2004 World Debt Tables, the ratio of debts to exports declined for developing countries as a group, from 163% in 1994 to 150% in 1995. On the contrary, debt indicators in sub-Saharan Africa depict the continued deterioration of various economies. In spite of debt servicing, the total debt stock continues to rise. There was a continued increase in Africa's debt to export ratio to 270%. According to the United Nations Conference on Trade and Development's (UNCTAD) 1998 report, the debilitating debt overhang that has afflicted many African countries "deters public investment in physical and human infrastructure as well as growth enhancing current spending on health and education" (p. 14). Table 1 provides a random example of the debt burden on select countries in the region.

Table 1 clearly indicates that the debt burden has increased every year for the past ten years or more. It is worth noting that even in the cases where the Bank and IMF have selected countries as models of cooperation with conditionalities imposed by them, those countries have not fared any better with their debt burden, for example, Ghana and Uganda. At the onset of the adjustment program in 1983, the total external debt of Ghana was $1.17 billion. This had increased to $6.4 billion by the end of 1997 (Boato-Arthur, 1999). Just five years after the implementation of structural adjustment, the total debt service as a percentage of the export of goods and services increased by over 100% from 30.5 to 62.8% (Elu, 2000). By 1999, some 40% of state revenues currently need to be used exclusively for interest payments.[13]

The debt overhang has equally mortgaged Africa's future (Campbell, 1989). Debt payments always imply some level of trade-offs with investments in several sectors. Apart from South Africa, all African countries spend more on debt repayments than on health. In addition, the entire annual health budget is less than $10 per person in most African countries (Manji, 1998). No matter what Africans do, especially cutting down spending in the midst of frustrating and appalling social conditions, external debts are still on the increase. Loans contracted are utilized to service external debt, i.e. keep up with payments of interest and amortization.

In 1996, the World Bank and IMF designated 41 countries as heavily indebted poor countries (HIPCs) that lack the capacity to repay their debts. The total external

Table 1. External Debt – Random Sampling of Sub-Saharan Countries.

	Total External Debt $ Millions		Long Term Debt $ Millions		Total IBRD Loans and IDA Credits		Public and Publicly Guaranteed Debt $ Millions		Use of IMF Credit $ Millions	
	1990	2002	1990	2002	1990	2002	1990	2002	1990	2002
Angola	8,594	10,134	7,605	8,883	7,605	8,883	0	265	3,083	14,340
Benin	1,294	1,843	1,218	1,690	1,218	1,690	326	654	18	73
Gabon	3,983	3,533	3,150	3,231	3,150	3,231	69	50	140	67
Gambia	369	573	308	504	305	504	102	195	45	32
Ghana	3,837	7,338	2,772	6,382	2,740	6,129	1,423	3,476	6	143
Guinea	2,476	3,401	2,253	2,972	2,253	2,972	420	1,096	52	139
Kenya	7,058	6,031	5,641	5,188	4,761	5,139	2,056	2,460	482	88
Malawi	1,558	2,912	1,385	2,688	1,382	2,688	854	1,773	115	95
Mali	2,468	2,803	2,337	2,487	2,337	2,487	498	1,134	69	166
Senegal	3,736	3,918	3,000	3,372	2,940	3,339	835	1,578	314	253
Sierra Leone	1,196	1,448	940	1,262	940	1,262	92	479	108	169
Tanzania	6,459	7,244	5,799	6,201	5,787	6,182	1,493	2,874	140	400
Uganda	2,583	4,100	2,160	3,690	2,160	3,690	969	2,576	282	257
Zambia	6,916	5,969	4,554	4,846	4,552	4,737	813	2,155	949	1,015
Zimbabwe	3,247	4,066	2,649	3,269	2,464	3,123	449	871	7	280
Sub-Saharan Africa	176,826	210,350	149,632	174,229	144,355	161,681	24,916	42,089	6,612	7,009

Source: UNDP (2004, p. 245).

debt of such countries from public or official sources, increased from $55 billion in 1980 to $183 billion in 1990 and to $215 billion by the end of 1995. Out of the 41 HIPCs, 32 are in sub-Saharan Africa. Of the 32 HIPCs in sub-Saharan Africa, 26 are within the UNDP's lowest human development category. An initiative to accelerate Africa's development, especially in the classified heavily indebted poor countries, was put in place (see Table 2).

The key features of the HIPCs initiative are: progressive degrees of debt forgiveness, moratorium on interest payments, and extension of maturity. According to the World Bank, the aim of the HIPC initiative is to enable beneficiary countries to exit the rescheduling process and maintain sustainable levels of debt. The impact of this is that so long as indebted countries are able to obtain loans to service their debts (interest and amortization) the debts are deemed to be sustainable. It does not matter whether by such debt servicing other socially degrading conditions are being perpetuated or entrenched in the host country.

In practice, HIPC's initiative has not benefited the recipient states as indicated by the Bank itself. For example, Mozambique joined the IMF/Bank structural adjustment program in 1984. New loans were contracted. However, by the early 1990s, Mozambique had become one of the poorest countries in the world with a per capita income of less than $100. By 1997, Mozambique's debt was more than $7 billion. Between 1994 and 1997, debt service payments amounted to $113 per annum. Yet Mozambique was only paying 30% of debt actually due. Meanwhile Mozambique was expending only $100 million on health and education (Hanlon, 1998).

The HIPC initiative has been no palliative to Mozambique. As Hanlon (1998) points out, "the pre-HIPC average debt service payment (1995–1997) was $113 million per year, and the post HIPC debt service (1998–2002) [sic.] was also $113 million per year" (p. 30). The contention by the World Bank, therefore, that HIPC "would free budgetary resources" and broaden the scope of development efforts by countries in that category has been proved wrong in the case of Mozambique. Similar stories abound for several countries in the region.

Aid

Although bilateral aid and development assistance programs have helped the region in some ways, it is however obvious that many years of aid to sub-Saharan Africa have failed to achieve sustainable development. There are several reasons for this state of affairs, among which is the misidentification of needs and poor project design and implementation. More often than not, development projects are conceived in the West and executed in the South by their agents – Northern NGOs, with very little impact, if any, from the South (Banya & Elu, 1999).

Table 2. HIPC Initiative: Committed Debt Relief and Outlook 1/(Status as of February 2004) (in Millions of U.S. dollars, in National Poverty Variables (NPV) terms in the year of the decision point).

	Reduction in NPV Terms			Nominal Debt Service Relief			Date of Approval
	Original HIPC Initiative	Enhanced HIPC Initiative	Total	Original HIPC Initiative	Enhanced HIPC Initiative	Total	
Countries that have reached their completion points (10)							
Total	3,118	9,113	12,231	6,364	14,184	20,548	
Benin	0	265	265	0	460	460	March 2003
Bolivia	448	854	1,302	760	1,300	2,060	June 2001
Burkina Faso 2/	229	324	553	400	530	930	April 2002
Guyana	256	335	591	634	719	1,353	December 2003
Mali	121	417	539	220	675	895	March 2003
Mauritania	0	622	622	0	1,100	1,100	June 2002
Mozambique	1,717	306	2,023	3,700	600	4,300	September 2001
Nicaragua	0	3,308	3,308	0	4,500	4,500	January 2004
Tanzania	0	2,026	2,026	0	300	3,000	November 2001
Uganda	347	656	1,003	650	1,300	1,950	May 2000
Countries in the interim period (17)							
Total	0	18,900	18,900	0	30,909	30,909	
Cameroon	0	1,260	1,260	0	2000	2,000	October 2000
Chad	0	170	170	0	260	260	May 2001
Congo, Dem. Rep.	0	6,311	6,311	0	10,389	10,389	July 2003
Ethiopia	0	1,275	1,275	0	1930	1,930	November 2001
Gambia	0	67	67	0	90	90	December 2000
Ghana	0	2,186	2,186	0	3,700	3,700	February 2002
Guinea	0	545	545	0	800	800	December 2000
Guinea-Bissau	0	416	416	0	790	790	December 2000
Honduras	0	556	556	0	900	900	July 2000
Madagascar	0	814	814	0	1,500	1,500	December 2000

Table 2. *(Continued)*

	Reduction in NPV Terms			Nominal Debt Service Relief			Date of Approval
	Original HIPC Initiative	Enhanced HIPC Initiative	Total	Original HIPC Initiative	Enhanced HIPC Initiative	Total	
Malawi	0	643	643	0	1,000	1,000	December 2000
Niger	0	521	521	0	900	900	December 2000
Rwanda	0	452	452	0	800	800	December 2000
São Tomé & Principe	0	97	97	0	200	200	December 2000
Senegal	0	488	488	0	850	850	June 2000
Sierra Leone	0	600	600	0	950	950	March 2002
Zambia	0	2,499	2,499	0	3,850	3,850	December 2000
Countries still to be considered (11)							
Côte d'Ivoire 3/	345		345	800		800	
Burundi							
Central African Republic							
Comoros							
Congo, Rep. Of							
Lao PDR							
Liberia							
Myanmar							
Somalia							
Sudan							
Togo							
Memorandum item: Total debt relief committed for 27 countries	3,118	28,013	31,131	6,364	45,093	51,457	

Sources: HIPC country documents; and World Bank and IMF staff estimates (World Bank, 2004, p. 249).

1 Committed debt relief under the assumption of full participation of the creditors.

2 The assistance under the enhanced HIPC Initiative includes the topping up with the NPV calculated in the year of the completion point.

3 Côte d'Ivoire reached its decision point under the original-HIPC Initiative in 1998, but did not reach its completion point under the original HIPC, nor has it reached its decision point under the enhanced HIPC. The amounts of debt relief shown are only indicative of debt relief under the original HIPC Initiative, based on a preliminary document issued.

Non-governmental organizations have often been used to attempt to transfer cultural awareness and to promote values, social contracts and political alignments centered on and patterned after countries that provide funding and technical assistance. There are widely held beliefs that Northern NGOs are fomenters of revolution or destabilizing forces (DuBois, 1991). Although these organizations in their own public pronouncements and self-image belie the claim of fomenters of revolution, over a period of time, with their diverse political and social origins, they have accommodated this role. Whatever political persuasion, whether of the left or the right, the NGOs are generally alike, and at home and abroad they are often handmaidens of the governments they presumably seek to change or redirect in the longer run. For example, Johnston (1991) notes that there is a contrast between NGO's manifest objectives of development promotion and disaster relief and their latent objectives of fundamental social and political change. While it is important in itself, and not a new insight to note this, it is important to highlight the power of the manifest objectives, which allow for the preservation of the nexus between the various actors. NGO's honor the manifest objectives enough, and these connect powerfully to public values.

By highlighting their manifest objectives, the non-governmental organizations can count on the goodwill and a reservoir of public sympathy and support in helping poor people and societies respond to crisis, adjust to or recover from disaster. However, NGO's either do not stay long enough or provide adequate resources to sustain long-term assistance that makes lasting structural changes. Thus, in the public credo and debate, both governments and NGOs have to continue to stress their short-term relief functions, which leaves intact perceptions of people in developing countries – especially sub-Saharan Africa – as marginal and pitiful, rather than the long-term development aspects which would promote the region's emergence into real actor status in the world, a status which Western societies in general are not ready to promote (Nindi, 1990).

Table 3 Indicates that many of the countries in the region depend heavily on foreign aid to balance their budgets and indeed, run their governments. The dependence on aid has serious implications for recipient countries' sovereignty. Figure 2 shows the world-wide allocation of aid, a topic we shall discuss shortly.

Aid is today being used as part of the conditionalities of international financial institutions. For the international distribution of aid dollars in the year 2000, see Fig. 2.

There is a linkage between external aid and debt service repayments. In 1990, debt repayments in sub-Saharan Africa amounted to $10 billion. This constituted 59% of total aid disbursements. The pattern continues and by 1995 total debt servicing amounted to 57% of total aid inflows – $10.6 billion to $18.5 billion (Riddell, 1999). Aid is largely used to offset part of accumulated debts. Servicing

Table 3. Aid Dependency.

| | Net Official Development Assistance or Official Aid $ Millions | | Aid Per Capita $ | | Aid Dependency Ratios | | | | | | | |
| | | | | | Aid as $ of GNI (Gross National Income) | | Aid as % of Gross Capital Formation | | Aid as % of Imports of Goods and Services | | Aid as % of Central Government Expenditures | |
	1997	2002	1997	2002	1997	2002	1997	2002	1997	2002	1997	2002
Angola	355	421	31	32	5.5	4.3	18.2	11.6	5.7	4.5		
Benin	221	220	38	34	10.4	8.3	55.7	45.9	27.8	26.3		
Gabon	39	72	33	55	0.8	1.7	2.4	5.1	1.4	2.5		
Gambia	39	61	33	44	9.7	17.3	55.1	79.0	13.2			
Ghana	494	653	27	32	7.3	10.8	28.9	53.8	17.7	18.6		
Guinea	381	250	55	32	10.4	7.9	42.7	46.4	39.9	23.2		
Kenya	448	393	16	13	4.3	3.2	27.1	23.5	11.1	10.3	17.2	
Malawi	344	377	36	35	13.8	20.2	111.3	160.0	35.9	44.9		
Senegal	423	449	48	46	9.8	9.2	54.2	45.3	24.8	19.9	50.5	41.0
Sierra Leone	119	353	25	68	14.3	47.0	278.9	514.7			81.3	
Tanzania	945	1,233	30	35	12.5	13.2	82.5	78.7	44.4	53.3		
Uganda	813	638	38	26	13.0	11.2	77.2	50.7	46.0	35.4		
Zambia	610	641	66	63	16.5	18.1	107.0	99.4	37.3	36.6		65.5
Zimbabwe	336	201	28	15	4.2	18.1	22.0	29.2			11.1	
Sub-Saharan Africa	14,976	19,406	24	28	4.5	6.3	24.5	32.2	12.4	15.3		

Source: UNDP (2004, p. 249).

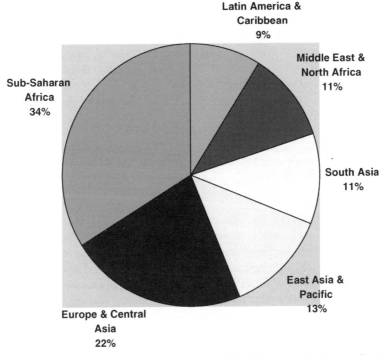

Fig. 2. Where did Aid Go in 2002? East Asia and Pacific has received a smaller share of total net aid flows, declining from 16 to 13%, while flows to Europe and Central Asia increased from 16 to 22%. *Source:* Organization for Economic Cooperation and Development (OECD), *Development Assistance Committee Report*: Paris, OECD. p. 41.

external debts at such high rates by states in serious economic crisis undermines efforts at sustainable development. Almost all donors have adopted one form or the other of tied aid. Tied aid forces recipients to purchase capital goods from donor markets. In some instances, technical experts from donor countries who could be provided by recipient countries are attached to various projects to be paid from the loan contracted for a particular project. There are many linkages between the heavy debt repayment, the persistence of unemployment and poverty in sub-Saharan Africa.

Poverty

Despite four decades of development assistance, poverty is on the rise in the sub-region. Even in countries of relative success stories, poverty is still a major issue

(Cash & Sanchez, 2003). For example, Uganda is strongly supported by aid. The country has also achieved appreciable growth in terms of macroeconomic indicators. But about 40% of the population lives in absolute poverty. Similarly, 67% of Zambians are living in poverty and the rates of unemployment have risen from around 82% in 1989 to about 88% in 1996 (Riddell, 1999). The high unemployment rate accounts for the growing levels of poverty. In 1997, the International Labor Organization (ILO) and United Nations Development Program (UNDP) observed:

> The proportion of the population living in poverty is increasing and is projected to rise from about 48% in the early 1990s to about 50% by the end of this decade. Africa is the only region in which the proportion of the population living under poverty . . . is projected to increase (ILO/UNDP, 1997, p. 46).

Deteriorating economies and the accompanying unemployment situation has led to very high incidence of poverty across the continent. This explains why approximately 70% of employment in Africa occur in the informal sector. According to ILO/UNDP, urban unemployment has increased to over 30% in the past decade and half. The ILO/UNDP projects urban unemployment to reach 50% in the year 2010. It is in this context of abject poverty that children are raised, hence their susceptibility to armed thugs who can provide some semblance of care and concern for them.

Figure 3 indicates that despite the infusion of billions of dollars of aid money, Sub-Sahara Africa still suffers death from diseases far more than any other region in the world. Children, of course, suffer disproportionately more in such poor situations than adults (WHO, 2000).

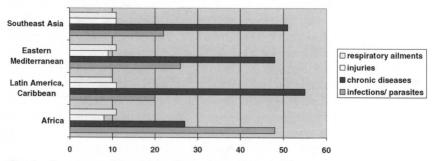

Fig. 3. Percentage of Deaths by Cause Among populations with high mortality rates (2000). *Source:* World Health Organization, *World Health Statistics* (2000). Geneva, p. 65.

The Loss of State Authority

The lesson of history indicates that strong states played a pivotal role in the industrial development of Europe, Japan and quite recently, Southeast Asia. The major economic reconstructions of the twentieth century were undertaken by interventionist states, such as Europe and the United States after World War II. Thus, the essence of a developmentalist state cannot be ignored. The strong private sector driven development of the Newly Industrializing Countries (NICs) had full support of the state. The World Bank (1997) stated as such: "An effective state is vital for the provision of goods and services – and rules and institutions that allow markets to flourish and people to live healthier and happier lives. Without it, sustainable development both economical and social, is impossible" (p. 1). Yet the Bank and others have sought to reverse this fundamental fact in the case of Africa. The conditionalities attached to their lending, especially microeconomic deregulation, tend to undermine the pre-eminence of the state in development. A state with diminished capabilities cannot play a developmentalist role.

The advent of globalization has done incalculable harm to state autonomy and the capacity of the state to make rational choices. Before globalization assumed its current form, foreign aid was in most cases tied to the procurement of equipment at higher than normal prices from donor firms (tied aid). Such tied aid has resulted in substantial gains for donor corporations, but at a great loss to African countries because the value of real aid is reduced by such higher than normal prices. Globalization has aggravated the problems associated with aid. In addition to the existing conditions, a more intrusive conditionality – that of sale of state assets – is imposed. Recipients of such assistance are, therefore, under pressure – selling of state assets and the procurement of equipment from donor nations at the same time. A further paradox is that divested assets are, more often than not, purchased by foreigners because most indigenous entrepreneurs may not have the resources to buy such assets.

The issue is compounded by the Western powers' insistence on acquiring immunities from debtor nations. The United States' Foreign Sovereign Immunities Act and the United Kingdom's State Immunities Act enable borrowers to use the U.S. and U.K. courts, respectively, as a commitment vehicle for repaying debts (Bulow, 2002). These laws forced developing countries to wave immunity when they borrow money from abroad. This means that the courts in debtor nations have no jurisdiction over foreign lenders and thus a country's foreign assets could be taken without any input from local court systems. Thus, less regulation of foreign capital by debtor countries was established. To further tighten the screws, after the success of Canada's Foreign Investment Review (CFIR) Act by the General Agreement on Trade and Traffic (GATT) in 1984, the U.S. with the support of the EU and Japan sought to use the Uruguay rounds of negotiations to create a regime of rules and principles that restricted host countries' right to regulate foreign capital (Wirth, 1994). Trade Related Investment Measures (TRIMs) was born and it limited the sovereign rights of countries to regulate foreign capital. A long-standing GATT principle allowed the regulation of foreign capital by host countries but TRIMs undermined that. The Multilateral Agreement on Investments (MAI) is meant, more or less, to tighten the rule of foreign capital. But for the stiff opposition by the Third World, led by India, Malaysia, Indonesia and member of Southern African Development Cooperation (SADC) at the Singapore meeting of WTO Trade Ministers, MAI would have been passed.

An MAI for African states would have far-reaching consequences, including:

> African countries will have no control whatsoever on how foreign capital comes into the country and how and in what sectors it operates. There will be no obligation on it to transfer technology, none to hire local workers at managerial or lower levels, none to purchase from local sources, none to fix a certain percentage of its production to local or external markets. Foreign capital will have better than "national treatment" when it comes to externalizing their profits...MAI would outlaw policies of indigenization of the economy...for that would constitute treating foreign capital differently from national capital (Tandon, 1997, p. 6).

Non-State Actors

Through neo-liberal orthodoxy, policy making in most developing countries has become the "preserve" of external actors. Bush and Szeftel (1997) aptly point out the wide array of external influences on economic decision making over the last two decades. The uncontrolled deregulation of markets and prices as well as the liberalization of trade has been the handiwork of economists and experts of the International Financial Institutions (IFIs). Over the years, IMF economists that are either supplied or imposed on cash-strapped African countries "have been setting budgets, determining fiscal policy, setting exchange rates and planning privatization measures . . . Economists seconded from the IMF and World Bank to African finance, development planning and trade ministries have long been setting government targets and hence national priorities" (Bush & Szeftel, 1997, p. 297). The main role of the state, namely the provision of strategic direction for economic development has been completely taken over by the IFIs and other foreign technical experts. With their number country missions, project overseers, economists in the budget units of finance ministries, experts placed in central banks, and privatization agencies, the IFIs and especially the IMF have not only supplanted sate power, but have also "become, if not the state then at least a large part of it" (Bush & Szeftel,

1997 p. 297). The irony is that such actors are accountable only to their external constituents.

One serious effect of the role of such external interference is that, in most cases, experts are imposed without vetting, and at the extreme end, programs are written and imposed without any inputs of officials of poor recipient countries. Experts, therefore, stay at their respective posts for over a decade without training any local personnel. Even though they are not accountable to African leaders such leaders are often blamed when policies go wrong (Bush & Szeftel, 1997).

In the current economic situation, it is now clear that the states in sub-Saharan Africa have lost their sovereignty to international financial institutions and their powerful financiers, the U.S. and other capitalist Western countries. The state in sub-Saharan has become almost an empty shell in economic terms, since all economic policies have to be vetted by outsiders before implementation.

SUMMARY

For the past three decades, 1970s, 1980s and 1990s, the International Financial Institutions (IFI – World Bank and IMF) have imposed various policies on developing countries, especially in sub-Saharan Africa ostensibly to reduce poverty and stimulate economic growth. As outlined in this chapter, all such policies have failed as indicated by the level of poverty, indebtedness, and heavy dependence on foreign aid of countries in the region by the early 2000s. An example of a failed policy is that of the structural adjustment programs (SAPs). In the 1980s and 1990s governments in sub-region hit by the debt crisis were required by the World Bank and the International Monetary fund to implement SAPs in order for existing loans to be rescheduled and new loans/grants to be given. SAPs were packages of policy reforms that aimed to achieve macro-economic stability and export led growth, on the assumption that this would reduce poverty. SAP involved structural policy reforms such as the privatization of state owned enterprises, removal of subsidies for domestic industry, agriculture and liberalization of international trade through the reduction/removal of import duties. SAPs also included monetary reforms such as currency devaluation, liberalization of the financial sector, and tightened fiscal discipline through, for example, public sector wage cuts or introduction of user fees for health and education service (Elu, 2000).

However, after three decades of practicing structural adjustment, the programs resulted in limited economic growth, increased income inequalities and in some cases reduced access to health care and education for the vast majority of the population (World Bank, 2003). Designed in Washington, the programs undermined national ownership of policy making, through adopting externally imposed reforms. As outlined in the chapter, SAPs were a failure as economic growth in many countries in sub-Saharan Africa stalled and in certain states disintegrated. A recent (2004) World Economic Forum (WEF) report indicated that income per head has fallen by 11% in the sub-region since 1974 (WEF, 2003).

By the late 1990s there was a global outcry over the devastating effects of poor country debt and over the failure of SAPs to reduce poverty (Elu, 2000; Riddell, 1992, 1999). The World Bank and the International Monetary Fund moved away from SAPs and adopted a new approach – Poverty Reduction Strategy Papers (PRSPs). Under this new approach national governments are to develop their own national poverty reduction strategy as the basis for accessing lending and aid grants from international donors. On paper, one of the key elements of PRSP is "national ownership." For a PRSP to be nationally owned strategies are to be developed with broad-based participation from civil society.

In practice, PRSP is an externally imposed requirement that governments must produce to access financing and which the World Bank has to approve. It is paradoxical to call PRSP country-driven when governments have chosen policies the IFIs will approve rather than making policy choices based on the views put forward by citizens (Sutton, 1996).

PRSP contents reflect the dominance of IFI policy prescriptions instead of the priorities of the poor. Policies opposed by the poor (such as user fees for education and healthcare) are common, while policies the poor want are not included (free schooling and health care). The World Bank/IMF guidelines for writing the PRSP are considered to have strong neo-liberal assumptions resulting in neo-liberal policy recommendations. This coupled with the need for IFI approval, gives the IFIs inordinate power over the contents of national PRSPs.

Despite the macro policy contents of PRSPs, in essence the same discredited structural adjustment policies are being re-imposed. International Financial Institutions continue to be unwilling to seek or consider policy alternatives and continue to assume that structural adjustment policies automatically contribute to poverty reduction without thorough analysis of the likely poverty effect at country level. The promised reduction in conditionalities has not been forthcoming.

The insufficiency of debt relief coupled with inadequate development assistance and the unreliability of both debt relief and aid flows renders the planning and implementation of PRSPs difficult. The debt relief currently being supplied through HIPC is insufficient to enable the required levels of growth and reduce poverty. After receiving debt relief most HIPC countries will continue to have unsustainable external debt whilst increasing their internal debt as illustrated in Table 1. Donors however, continue to use the debt sustainability approach rather than working for debt cancellation.

Unpredictable aid transfers also lead to programs not being implemented Fig. 11 indicates the new pattern of aid flow. During the 1990s, aid to Africa fell by a third, from $17bn at the start of the decade to $12bn at the end (Lusekelo, 2004). Uncertainty over and fluctuations in donor fulfillment of pledges renders planning extremely difficult, yet there are no sanctions on donors who default or delay payment. Women, children, indigenous groups and those infected or affected by HIV/AIDS are often disproportionately hit by the negative social impacts of economic policies. Despite this their situations are not considered neither are special measures targeted at them under PRSPs. In the end, countries in sub-Saharan Africa have replaced one set of conditionalities for another, without any improvement in living conditions for women, the poor, the elderly and children. As stated by the former United Kingdom (U.K.) International Development Minister, Clare Short, "Africa is the poorest continent and it's getting poorer."[13]

CONCLUSION

The dawn of the 21st century finds sub-Saharan Africa at a crisis point in its economic and political development. The challenges facing the region are multifaceted. Saddled by heavy external debt and imposed conditionalities, the very existence of state sovereignty is at stake. As outlined in the chapter, external help/aid has in many instances exacerbated the economic backwardness of the region. The intrusive reach of donors into all aspects of life in the region is militating against the development of the region. The very existence of donor agencies in the region after nearly four decades of formal independence speaks volumes. With only few exceptions, the countries in sub-Saharan Africa have either deteriorated or are stagnant economically. If the billions of dollars spent on developmental assistance were meant to pull the region out of poverty, and hence develop, the result has been abysmal failure. Africans need to rethink the whole concept development in their own terms. What is needed is an African renaissance based on African context and sense of destiny. However, the presence of globalization may make such reflections almost impossible. Despite rhetoric to the contrary, it is not in the interest of the West to see sub-Saharan Africa develop as it is currently being promoted by NEPAD. This is a sad commentary on the state of affairs in the current world order.

NOTES

1. United Nations Development Program: Human Development Report – 1996 (Oxford: UNDP, 1996, pp. 2–10).

2. United Nations Development Program: Human Development Report – 2001 (Oxford: UNDP, 2001, pp.1–8).

3. Forbes Magazine, "The Economic Effects of Globalization" July 1994 and "Globalization and Trade" July 1996.

4. The current President, James Wolfensohn, was reappointed through January 2005.

5. IBRD loans are made to borrower nations whose average annual per capita income exceeds 895 U.S. dollars, sometimes in conjunction with IDA interest-free loans. When a borrower's average annual per capita income approaches $5,500 the borrower starts to "graduate" from IBD lending.

6. To meet borrowing eligibility requirements, a potential borrower nation's per capita income must not exceed 1,506 U.S. dollars per year. However, the reality is that nations who received IDA loans have average annual per capita incomes of less than $895. Those with per capita incomes that exceed that amount generally receive a mix of IBRD and IDA interest-free loans.

7. As Noam Chomsky (2001, p. 29) has observed, "debt is not valid if it's essentially imposed by force. The Third World debt is odious debt."

8. Interview with a senior lecturer, Freetown, Sierra Leone, June 2003.

9. The Structural Adjustment Program (SAP) was initiated by the IMF/World bank to correct the structural defects of most of the developing economies that applied for the IMF loans. Conditions for obtaining a loan from the IMF include reducing public expenditure and also devaluing currencies. These measures have had a negative impact on every government institution, including education. The implementation of the SAP had devastating effects on public expenditure on education, the purchasing power of teachers, quality of education, access to education, and the gender gap in the provision of education, as well as adversely affecting social institutions such as health, welfare, etc.

10. See UNICEF (1993) analysis of impact of SAP on developing countries. It seems that most often programs dealing with social welfare of children are first to be terminated.

11. Indonesia III was the first World Bank Project to support book production for the use of primary school pupils in Indonesia. The cost structure of the Sierra Leone Project closely reflected that of the Indonesia Project. The World Bank started granting loans to primary education in 1970 and started the Indonesia Project in 1973. Because it was a successful experiment, the World Bank adopted the project as a model after which other subsequent projects would be based. Since 1973, the World Bank has gradually shifted from civil works such as construction of schools, colleges and administrative buildings to input financing designed to improve the quality and the administration of education in general and primary education specifically. The tilt is now towards aid for textbooks, teacher training, laboratory equipment, learning assessments, examination systems, educational administration, technical assistance, and research.

12. Interview with a senior Bank of Sierra Leone officer, Freetown, Sierra Leone, June 2001.

13. Interview with Clare Short, BBC London, England; June 2, 2004.

REFERENCES

Babalola, J., Sikwibele, A., & Suleiman, A. (2000). Education as aid by the World Bank: A critical analysis of post-independence projects in Nigeria. *Journal of Third World Studies, 18*(1).

Banya, K. (1991). Economic decline and the education system: The case of Sierra Leone. *Compare*, *21*(2), 127–141.

Banya, K. (2001). The challenges of financing higher education in Sub-Saharan Africa. *World Studies in Education*, *2*, 53–80.

Banya, K., & Elu, J. (1997). The crisis of higher education in sub-Saharan Africa: The continuing search for relevance. *Journal of Higher Education Policy and Management*, *19*(2), 127–141.

Banya, K., & Elu, J. (1999). 'Non-governmental organizations as partners in Africa: A cultural analysis of North-South relations. In: L. Buchento & K. King (Eds), *Changing International Aid to Education* (pp. 182–206). UNESCO/Norrage.

Banya, K., & Elu, J. (2001). The World Bank and financing higher education in sub-Saharan Africa. *Higher Education*, *42*, 1–34.

Barro, R. (2000). *The contribution of education to economic growth*. Proceedings of the OECD Quebec Conference, March 2000, Quebec, Canada.

Boato-Arthur, F. (1999). Ghana: Structural adjustment, democratization, and the politics of continuity. *African Studies Review*, *42*(2).

Bradlow, D. (1996). The World Bank, the IMF, and human rights. *Transnational Law and Contemporary Problems*, *42*, 521–524.

Bratton, M. (1998). *Poverty, organization and policy: Towards a voice for Africa's rural poor*. Paper proposed for a colloquium on the changing nature of Third World poverty. A Policy Perspective, Michigan State University, Michigan.

Buchert, L. (Ed.) (1995). *Learning from experience; Police and practices in aid to higher education*. ESSO paperback No. 24: Hague: ESSO 9–17.

Bulow, J. (2002) First world governments and third world debts. *Brookings Papers on Economic Activity*, 227–255.

Burkey, S. (1993). People first: A guide to self-reliant, participatory rural development. London: Zed Books.

Bush, R., & Szeftel, M. (1997). Commentary. *Review of African Political Economy*, *24*(73), 307–310.

Campbell, B. (1989). Indebtedness in Africa: Consequence, cause or symptom of the crisis? In: B. Ouimode (Ed.), *The IMF, the World Bank, and the African debt: The Social and Political Impact*. London: Zed Books.

Cash, K., & Sanchez, D. (2003). Reducing poverty or repeating mistakes. Retrieved www.eurodad.org/articles/defacult.aspx? ID?

Caulfield, C. (1996). *Masters of illusion: The World Bank and the poverty of nations*. New York: Henry Holt & Company.

Chambers, R. (1997). *Whose reality counts? Putting the first last*. London: Intermediate Technology Publications.

Chomsky, N. (2001). "Talking 'anarchy" with Chomsky. *The Nation* (April 24), 28–30.

Coleman, J. (1965). *Education and political development*. Princeton, NJ: Princeton University Press.

Coleman, J., & Court, D. (1993). *The development of universities in the third world: The Rockefeller foundation*. Oxford: Pergamon.

Commonwealth Foundation (1991). *Report of the first Commonwealth non-governmental organization forum*. London.

Commonwealth Foundation (1995). *Non-governmental organization: Guidelines for good policy and practice*. London.

Crush, J. (Ed.) (1994). *Development discourse*. London: Routledge.

DuBois, M. (1991). The governance of the Third World: A Foucaldian perspective on power relations in development. *Alternatives*, *16*(1), 1–30.

Easterly, W. (2001). The debt crisis in developing countries. *Financial Time* (May 6).

Edwards, M. (1989). The irrelevance of development studies. *Third World Quarterly, 11*(1), 116–135.

Edwards, M., & Hulme, D. (Eds) (1995). *Non-governmental organizations: Performance and accountability beyond the magic bullet*. London: Earthscan.

Elu, J. (2000). The impact of ten years of IMF (SAP) reform: The case of sub-Saharan Africa. *World Studies in Education, 1*(1), 41–59.

Escobar, A. (1992). Imagining a post-development era? Critical thought, development and social movements. *Social Text, 31/32*, 20–56.

Escobar, A. (1995). *Encountering development: The making and unmaking of the Third World*. Princeton, NJ: Princeton University Press.

Esteva, G. (1996). Development. In: W. Sachs (Ed.), *The Development Dictionary: A Guide to Knowledge as Power*. London: Zed Books.

Ferguson, J. (1990). Feminism, postmodernism, and the critique of modernity. *Cultural Critique*, 33–56.

Fidler, S. (2001). Who is minding the bank. *Foreign Policy*, 40–48.

Finnegan, W. (2000). After Seattle. *The New Yorker* (April 17).

Friedrichs, D., & Friedrichs, J. (2002). The World Bank and crimes of globalization: A case study. *Social Justice, 29*(1).

Goetz, J. (1991). *Gender and intercultural relations*. Bloomington, IN: Indiana University Press.

Government of Canada (1983). *Foreign Investment Review Act*. Ottowa, Canada

Greider, W. (1997). *One world, ready or not: The mystic logic of global capitalism*. A Touchstone Book.

Greider, W. (2000). Global agenda. *The Nation*, 11–16 (January 31).

Hanlon, J. (1998). African debt hoax. *Review of African Political Economy, 25*(77), 487–492.

Harbinson, F., & Myers, C. (1964). *Education, manpower and economic growth*. New York: McGraw-Hill.

Hinchliffe, K. (1989). *Higher education in sub-Saharan Africa*. The World Bank, discussion paper. Washington, DC: World Bank

ILO/UNDP (1997). *Jobs for Africa*. Geneva: ILO.

ILO/UNDP (1997) *Key Indicators of the Labor Market*. Geneva: ILO

Isbister, J. (1991). *Promises never kept: The betrayal of social change in the Third World*. West Hartford, CT: Kumarian Press.

Johnston, B. (1991). The world food equation: Interrelations among development, employment and food. *Journal of Economic Literature, 22*, 531–574.

Johnston, B (2000). The World Bank does not provide effective development programs. *World Development, 16*.

Johnston, D. (1998). The financing and management of higher education: A status report on world wide reform. UNESCO World Conference on Higher Education, Paris UNESCO 5–9.

Jones, P. (1992). World Bank financing of education: Lending, learning and development. London: Routledge.

Kapstein, E. (1998/1999). A global Third way: Social justice and the world economy. *World Policy Journal, 15*, 23–35.

King, K. (1991). *Aid and education in the developing world*. Hong Kong: Longman.

Kleinschmidt, H. (1996). Policy making from the bottom up: Beyond development slogans. Paper presented at the Third African Regional Meeting of the NGO Working Group on the World Bank. Johannesburg, South Africa.

Korten, D. (1987). Third generation of NGO strategies: A key to people-centered development. *World Development, 15*.

Levinson, M. (1999). Who's in change here? *Dissent, 46*(4), 21–23.

Leys, C. (1975). *Underdevelopment in Kenya: The political economy of neo-colonialism, 1964–1971.* London: Heineman.

Leys, C. (1994). Confronting the Africa tragedy. *New Left Review, 204.*

Lomax, R. (2001). The World Bank: Some reflection. Presentation at the Bank's Governor's Meeting, Washington, DC.

Lusekelo, A. (2004). Africa's war on terror targets poverty. Retrieved http://newsvote.bbc.co.uk/ mpapps/pagebooks/print/news/bbc.co.uk/2/hi/business/2797405.

Mamdani, M. (1993). University crisis and reform: A reflection on the African experience. *Review of African Political Economy, 58*, 7–19.

Manji, F. (1998). The depoliticization of poverty. In: D. Eade (Ed.), *Development and Rights.* London: Oxford University Press.

Manji, F. (2000). Collaboration with the south: Agents of aid or solidarity? In: D. Eade (Ed.), *Development, NGOs and Civil Society: Selected Essays from Development in Practice.* Oxford: Oxfam Publications.

Manji, F., & O'Coill, C. (2002). The missionary position: NGOs and development in Africa. *International Affairs, 78*(4), 587–599.

Martinussen, J. (1997). *Society, state and market: A guide to competing theories of development.* London: Zed Books.

Mathur, G. (1989). The current impasse in development thinking: The metaphysics of power. *Alternatives, 14*, 463–479.

McMahon, W. (1999). *Education and development: Measuring the social benefits.* Oxford: Oxford University Press.

Muyanda-Mulebi, P., & Yiga Matovo, M. (Eds) (1993). *Educational research for development in Africa.* Dakar: UNESCO-BREDA/ASESP.

Myers, B. (1999). Walking with the poor. *Principles and practices of transformative development.* New York: Orbis Books.

Namuddu, K. (1991). Educational research priorities in Sub-Saharan Africa. In: G. Miron & K. Sorenson (Eds), *Strengthening Educational Research in Developing Countries.* Paris, UNESCO/ILE 37–73.

Nindi, B. (1990). Experts, donors, ruling elites and the Africa poor: Expert planning, policy formulation and implementation – A critique. *Journal of Eastern African Research and Development, 20*, 41–67.

Nyikuli, P. (1999). Unlocking Africa's potential: Some factors affecting economic development and investment in sub-Saharan Africa. *Law and Policy in International Business, 30*(4), 623–636.

Ocitti, J. (1990). Indigenous education for today, the necessity of the useless. *Adult Education and Development, 35*, 347–357.

OECD (1999). *Development cooperation.* Paris: OECD.

OECD (2002). Development assistance committee report. Paris: OECD.

O'Neill, P. (2001). Alleviating poverty: The World Bank policy. Paper presented at the Chicago Board of Trade Meeting. Chicago, IL.

Parport, J., & Marchand, M. (1995). Exploding the canon: An introduction/conclusion. In: M. Marchand & J. Parport (Eds), *Feminism/Postmodernism/Development.* London: Routledge.

Peet, R., & Hartwick, E. (1999). *Theories of development.* New York: Guilford Press.

Pieterse, J. (1992). Emancipations modern and post-modern. *Development and Change, 23*(3), 5–41.

Peters & Olissen (2004). Neoliberalism, higher education and the knowledge economy: From the free market to knowledge capitalism. Paper presented at the Society for Research into Higher Education Conference. Royal Halloway, London

Psacharopoulos, G., & Woodhall, M. (1985). *Education for development: An analysis of investment choices*. Washington, DC: World Bank.

Renshaw, E. (1960). Estimating the returns to education. *Review of Economics and Statistics, 42*, 318–324.

Rich, B. (1994). Mortgaging the Earth: The World Bank, environmental impoverishment, and the crisis of development. Boston: Beacon Press.

Riddell, B. (1992). Things fall apart again: Structural adjustment programs in Sub-Saharan Africa. *The Journal of Modern African Studies, 39*(1).

Riddell, C. (1999). The end of foreign aid to Africa? Concerns about donor policies. *African Affairs, 98*, 309.

Sachs, W. (1992). Introduction. In: W. Sachs (Ed.), *The Development Dictionary: A Guide to Knowledge as Power*. London: Zed Books.

Schoener, W. (1997) Non-governmental organizations and global activism: Legal and informal approaches. *Journal of Global Study*, 537–538.

Schultz, T. (1960). Capital formation by education. *Journal of Political Economy, 68*(6), 571–583.

Schultz, T. (1963). *The economic value of education*. New York: Columbia University Press.

Simon, D. (1999). Development revisited: Thinking about, practicing and teaching development after the Cold War. In: D. Simon & A. Marman (Eds), *Development as Theory and Practice*. Boston: Addison Wesley/Longman.

Smillie, I. (1995). The alms bazaar: Altruism under fire – non-profit organizations and international development. London: Intermediate Technology Publications.

Sogge, D. (2002). *Give and take: What's the matter with foreign aid?* London: Zed Books.

Summer, L. (2001). The World Bank: Some reflection. Cited by S. Fiedley in: *Foreign Policy* (pp. 40–45).

Sutton, P. (1996). The south in the global political economy. *New Political Economy, 1*(3), 2.

Suzuki, N. (1998). *Inside NGOs: Learning to manage conflict between headquarters and field offices*. London: Intermediate Technology Publications.

Tandon, R. (1989). Non-governmental organizations-government relations: Westview a source of life or a kiss of death? New Delhi: Society for Participatory Research in Asia (PRIA).

Thomas, A. (2000). Meanings and views of development. In: T. Allen & A. Thomas (Eds), *Poverty and Development into the 21st Century*. Oxford: Oxford University Press.

Thomas, A., & Allen, T. (2000). *Agencies of development in poverty*. Oxford: Oxford University Press.

Tucker, V. (1999). The myth of development: A critique of a Eurocentric discourse. In: R. Muuck & D. O'Hearn (Eds), *Critical Development Theory: Contributions to a New Paradigm*. London: Zed Books.

Tvedt, T. (1998). *Angels of mercy or development diplomats? NGOs and foreign aid*. Trenton, NJ: African World Press.

UNCTAD (1998). *Handbook of international trade development statistics*. Geneva.

UNDP (1992). *Human development report*. New York: Oxford University Press.

UNDP (1993). *Human development report*. New York: Oxford University Press.

UNDP (1996). *Human development report*. New York: Oxford University Press.

UNDP (2002). *Human development report*. New York: Oxford University Press.

UNDP (2004). *Human development report*. New York: Oxford University Press.

UNICEF (1997). *The state of the world's children*. New York: Oxford University Press

United Nations (2003). *Human development index*. New York: United Nations.

WEF (2003). Africa's Tragic Economic Record at http://news.bbc.co.uk/2/hi/business/5768609.stm.

WHO (2000). *World health statistics*. Geneva.

Wirth, D. (1994). The United States and the World Bank: Constructive reforms or fly in the functional ointment? *Michigan Journal of International Law*, 687–701.

World Bank (1945). *Articles of agreement*. Washington, DC: World Bank.

World Bank (1989). Educational development in Thailand: The role of World Bank lending. Washington, DC: World Bank.

World Bank (1989). *Sub-Saharan Africa: From crisis to sustainable growth*. Washington, DC: World Bank.

World Bank (1994). *Higher education: The lessons of experience*. Washington, DC: World Bank.

World Bank (1997). *World development report, 1997*. New York: Oxford University Press.

World Bank (1999a). *Annual report*. Washington, DC: World Bank.

World Bank (1999b). *World development report*. New York: Oxford University Press.

World Bank (2000). *Higher education and developing countries. Peril and promise*. Washington, DC: World Bank.

World Bank (2003). *World development report, 2003*. New York: Oxford University Press.

World Bank (2004). *Human development index*. Washington, DC: World Bank.

Yamamori, T. (Ed.) (1996). *Serving with the poor in Africa: Cases in holistic ministry*. Monrovia, CA: Missions Advanced Research and Communication Center.

19. DEFEATING THE TRENDS: IN SEARCH OF A BETTER FUTURE

Ximena de la Barra

My dear young people: I see the light in your eyes, the energy of your bodies and the hope that
is in your spirit. I know it is you, not I, who will make the future. It is you, not I, who will fix
our wrongs and carry forward all that is right in the world.

Nelson Mandela, Former President of South Africa

INTRODUCTION

At the turn of the century, the developing world is experiencing the largest-ever
generation of children and youth. Around 1 billion people – one out of every six
on the planet – are between 10 and 19 years of age, 85% of them in developing
countries. Because of the considerable drop in fertility rates, in the next 15–20
years, the children of today will constitute the largest generation-ever of active
population. This is perhaps the greatest opportunity the world cannot afford to
miss. This paper claims that the trends keeping the majority of the children in
poverty and limiting their development are not irreversible, that the world has
enough information, technology and financial resources to defeat these trends.

Should we only decide to defeat the current negative trends and provide the
children of today all the opportunities for their full development, the active
population of tomorrow would be placed in a position to fulfill their own aspirations
and see their human rights complied with. They would also be able to provide the
world with their imagination, creative energy and skills to ensure the basis for the

'Suffer the Little Children': National and International Dimensions of Child
Poverty and Public Policy
Advances in Education in Diverse Communities: Research, Policy and Praxis, Volume 4, 477–495
Copyright © 2006 by Elsevier Ltd.
All rights of reproduction in any form reserved
ISSN: 1479-358X/doi:10.1016/S1479-358X(04)04013-6

future development of the whole of humanity. What is lacking, is the collective will to do so. In order for this potential to materialize, public policies should be specifically oriented to reverse the current trends that are denying poor children their most basic rights and their ability to develop to their fullest potential. Rather than keeping children in poverty and deprived of opportunities, public policies need to be reoriented in order to develop them into the healthy educated, happy and productive citizens of the near future. If humanity has been disregarding these negative trends before, this is the single most important moment in history to wake up, give up our share of power and collectively take advantage of this window of development opportunity, while fulfilling child rights.

THE FUTURE OF HUMANITY IS LINKED TO THAT OF THE CHILDREN OF TODAY

The Convention of the Rights of the Child, ratified by all but two countries in the world (the United States of America and Somalia) consolidates the position of children and adolescents as subjects of rights rather than objects of compassion. It also places families and States in a position of responsibility towards them, and gears adults to visualize them in relation to their potential, rather that to the demands they pose on society (United Nations, 1989). On the one hand, it forces us to recognize that we have not done enough to improve their present situation by complying with their rights. On the other, it forces us to understand that they are also our future and that they are the main source of inspiration, innovation and creative strength, of generation of new values, and of new dreams with which to build a prosperous and humane society. It places the present generations of adults in a position to be the enablers of our own solutions and of the future, which is no other than children themselves.

The Demographic Bonus

At the turn of the century, the developing world is experiencing the largest-ever generation of children and youth. Over 2 billion people – one out of every three on the planet – are under 18 years of age, and over 600 thousand – one in every 10 – are under five, 90% of them in developing countries (UNICEF, 2001). The legacy of high fertility rates prevailing in the past and the progress achieved in reducing mortality rates account for this high proportion of children and adolescents. The considerable decrease in fertility rates will mean that in one generation, children of today will constitute the biggest proportion of active population in the history of humanity (UNFPA, 2002). Never before and never again will humanity be offered this demographic opportunity, the opportunity of having a greater share of active population to make themselves responsible for the needs and rights of the population as a whole. This demographic reality could – in the near future – constitute one of the most important assets which humanity could rely on to ensure a future of prosperity, and justice.

This demographic phenomena called the demographic bonus, happens only once in the history of mankind and constitutes a unique opportunity in terms of creative and productive capacity at the level of society but also reduces the dependency weight over each active individual. This means that there will be a surplus to invest in education and health and continue increasing the development potential of society (UNFPA, 1998). These investments will stimulate economic development and will contribute to maintain it once these opportunities are no longer there. Therefore, a clear understanding of this situation and the political will to make good use of this opportunity, can have a long-standing positive effect on society as a whole. Additionally, guaranteeing child rights at present means increasing equity, diminishing injustice and social segregation, and therefore, building peace for the future.

In order to grasp this opportunity, it is necessary to invest in the current generation of children and adolescents now. Otherwise, that potential capability will not be developed and humanity will have missed this unique chance for a better future (UNFPA, 1998). By redirecting $70 to $80 billion a year in a global economy that is more than $30 trillion, the world could universally ensure basic services that respond to children's most immediate needs (UNICEF, 2000). Moreover, should humanity not invest in its children and youth now, this would lead to a crisis of wasted human potential that would immediately impact children and adolescents now with vicious severity, and which would have extended negative consequences on society in the future.

CURRENT NEGATIVE TRENDS CAN AND SHOULD BE CONFRONTED

There is no reason why we should subject ourselves to the negative effects of the current trends and passively witness the destruction of the future. "It is possible to achieve high levels of social development even without thriving economies if the right priorities are set and the political will is strong" (Lewis, 1997, p. ii). There is an urgent need to understand the consequences of the current development model over human health and wellbeing and over the environment and, to change current allocation and consumption patterns, distributing resources with justice.

The Rise of Inequality, the Most Negative of Trends

Society has been pursuing a growth oriented development model under the argument that the benefits of growth would eventually trickle down to all. Multinational Financial Institutions such as the World Bank, regional banks, the International Monetary Fund, and the World Trade Organization have engendered this model and have utilized their power through conditionalities embedded in financial negotiations, to impose it. Conditionalities that used to relate to the realm of economics and trade, impacting social policy indirectly, gradually expanded into the imposition of regressive social policy as well. This neo-liberal model is actually missing demographic opportunities and severely violating social and economic rights. It has brought about technological and scientific development but as it benefits an ever decreasing share of the population, it has also brought about injustice and social and ethical regression. Not only it is not reducing poverty, it is increasing disparities.

Experience shows that the model is so focussed on stabilizing banks and currencies, enhancing south–north financial flows, opening new markets for industrialized countries products, and benefiting transnational corporations, that it is blind to the social costs of its actions. Structural adjustments imposed on countries have translated in reduced public expenditure on health and education. External debt payments and military expenditures have taken precedence over social service public expenditure. In a recent press conference, World Bank President James Wolfensohn stated that the world spends less in development now than 40 years ago. He also stated that spending a trillion dollars in defense, military expenditure has become 20 times the amount spent trying to give hope to people (Wolfensohn, 2004). Imposed privatization, cost recovery and elimination of universal basic subsidies have placed additional limitations on the poor in accessing quality basic services. Moreover, reality has proven this model wrong, since it has not reduced poverty, and disparities of all nature have continued to increase. Social impacts are such, that mainstream neo-liberal thinking is now increasingly being questioned. Dissident voices have been gathering a strong momentum. The 2001 Latin American Parliament Summit held in Caracas, Venezuela in July 2001, denounced – once again – the negative social impacts of the external debt crisis, and considered posing the matter to the International Court of Justice.

Pope John Paul II is currently heading a strong international movement denouncing the current development model demanding debt relief to poorer countries, elimination of trade barriers to developing countries products and more official development assistance to countries in need (John Paul II, 1999). As broadly reported by the media, he has demanded the G-8 Group of industrialized countries to listen to the clamor of poor countries. The award of the 1998 Nobel Prize in Economics to Amartya Sen – a welfare economist rather than a monetarist economist, as were those awarded in previous years – seems to reinforce this surprising official dissidence to mainstream thinking. Moreover, civil society is increasingly organizing and making itself heard with strength, both nationally and internationally, against these economic policy impositions.

Powerful voices, including those powerful enough to have contributed to the imposition of this damaging development model, are now questioning it publicly (Wolfensohn, 1998). The World Bank is now acknowledging the fact that economic growth can not reduce poverty by itself and that it is the quality of growth rather than the quantity of growth that matters most (World Bank, 2000). Joseph Stiglitz, former World Bank Vice President, 2002 Nobel Laureate in Economics has recognized that the most successful countries have been those that did not follow the Washington Consensus prescriptions (Stiglitz, 2003).

Mark Malloch Brown, the United Nations Development Programme Administrator has stated that data has destroyed the myth imposed by the Washington Consensus that when abiding by its prescriptions on liberalizing the economy, reigning macroeconomic policy and cutting public expenditure, economic growth would follow. The great decade announced as the decade of economic reform, market liberalization, integration of world markets, and all those other good things, he stated, has ended with a significant group of countries in a worse situation and with an increased number of poor than a decade ago (Mark Malloch Brown, 2003).

More recently, the World Bank has acknowledged that growth alone will not be enough to reach the Millennium Goals (World Bank, 2004) that the international community has committed itself to attain by 2015 in order to promote human wellbeing that entails dignity, freedom and equality for all people. However, in spite of this new rhetoric, the same medicine continues to be fed to very sick patients. The impositions on the Argentinean people during their latest financial crisis are a vivid example of this paradox. Their current struggle to change the rules of the game constitutes a source for inspiration.

In effect, the current neo-liberal, growth and export oriented macroeconomic model is not eradicating poverty (Mehrotra & Jolly, 1997). On the contrary, it is increasingly exacerbating political, economic and social exclusion of the majority of the population. Growth fosters poverty and disparities as cheap labor, the absence of social benefits, the destruction of labor organizations and the relinquishment of environmental management are instrumental to this model (de la Barra, 1997). The ratio of the income of the top 20% of the population to that of the poorest 20% rose from 30 to 1 in 1960 to 61 to 1 in 1991 and to a new high of 82 to 1 in 1995, which means disparities are not only increasing, but that the gap between the "haves" and the "have nots" is accelerating (UNDP, 1999, 2000, 2001). Latest data gathered by the UNDP show that the richest 5% of the world's people receive 114 times the income of the poorest 5%. The richest 1% receives as much as the poorest 57% and the 25 million richest Americans have as much income as almost 2 billion of the world's poorest people. (UNDP, 2003).

The social impact of this disastrous development approach has meant that at the turn of the century, 2.8 billion people, almost half of humanity live in poverty with less than US$2 a day. Of these, 1.2 billion live extreme poverty with less than US$1 a day. More than half of the poor are children and more than 30,000 of them die each day of preventable causes. Also, more that 500,000 women die each year due to causes related to pregnancies or child birth and 14,000 additional people are infected daily with HIV/AIDS. (UNDP, 2003).

According to analysis undertaken by Giovanni Andrea Cornia of the University of Florence with a group of researchers, the last 20 years have been characterized by an increase in the number of poor children, and by a slower and increasingly more unequal distribution of gains in child wellbeing. Some regions (Easter(n) Europe, the former Soviet Union and Sub-Saharan Africa), countries within regions and people within countries (poor children, people in rural areas, children of mothers with no education) have been left behind during the recent drive towards the global economy (Cornia, 2001). This may suggest that recent improvements in child well-being have mainly benefited the middle and high income groups and that disadvantaged groups have benefited less or have deteriorated.

Recent UNICEF research, could confirm the previous assumption when stating that the average rate of infant child mortality has decreased in most of the countries with the exception of the African countries affected by HIV-AIDS. However, in all the cases where the overall average improved, the improvement of the top quintile was greater than the bottom. This also means that in some countries that are close to reaching or have reached the goal of reduction in U5MR set by the World Summit for Children, the poor are far from achieving that objective. Researchers have also recently documented that the possibility of death before reaching five years of age was three times greater among children born in families in the bottom quintile than in those families in the top. Similar findings are documented for antenatal care and delivery attendance. (UNICEF, 2001).

To make matters worse, foreign debt of developing countries, initially acquired in order to raise out of poverty, which was 800 billion in 1983 (UNDP, 2000), now amounts to more than 2.5 trillion dollars (Joint BIS-IMF-OCD-WB Statistics on External Debt) and is limiting the ability to invest in children. A UNICEF study involving 27 developing countries indicates that only nine of them manage to spend more in basic social services than in servicing the external debt. Twelve of the African countries included in the study allocate twice as many resources to debt service than to basic social services expenditure. These services, including primary health care, reproductive health, nutrition, water and sanitation, are crucial if survival and development rights of children are going to be complied with, if poverty is going to be eradicated and if disparities are going to be reversed (UNICEF, 1999).

Tendencies in the last ten years show that 54 countries have diminished their per capita income even though in some of them economic growth was experienced. In 34 countries, life expectancy has decreased. In 21 countries, hunger is on the rise. In 14 countries, under five mortality has increased and in 12 countries primary school enrolment has decreased. (UNDP, 2003). With a longer perspective, available figures speak clearly. In the second half of the 20th century, in pursuit of economic growth, the world economy expanded five fold, international trade expanded 12 fold, international – mostly speculative financial flows – expanded between 25 and 30 fold, but disparities were exacerbated and are now three times more acute (UNDP, 1997, 1998, 1999, 2000).

Simultaneously, due to the loss of balance between human activities and the environment, ecosystems have deteriorated to an alarming point. At the turn of the century, per capita water availability is less than half of what it was 50 years ago and chemical pesticides, fertilizers and human excrements increasingly contaminate it. The air is increasingly polluted, causing at least 50% of respiratory infections, as well as many other diseases. We are burning five times more fossil fuels, and increasing carbon dioxide emissions, fourfold. Urbanization has increased from 17% of the world population to 50%, yet per capita infrastructure investment has decreased. Cement use has expanded four times and built areas are limiting the earth's natural drainage capabilities. Vegetation, which constitutes the water regulatory mechanism of the planet, has been lost and global warming is threatening our future. In the last 25 years, the earth has lost 1/3 of its natural resources in terms of forests, and both sweet water and marine species (UNDP, 1998, and WRI, 1998). Increased environmental risk is therefore, yet another consequence of the development model, which compounded with increased human vulnerabilities, lay the ground for increased frequency and intensity of misnamed natural disasters.

Both Governments and Markets are Failing Poor Children

The worsening of national economic conditions in favor of global economic interests, increase pressure on the young to start working earlier, to work longer hours and to work longer into old age. The consequences are unemployed or underemployed adults vs. alarming increases in child labor, neglected children and frustrated childhood, weakening the structure and capabilities of families which constitute the basic socio-economic unit, the primary institution and the best environment for protecting and promoting the rights and well-being of children. The survival of nurturing families strongly depends on their capability to sustain themselves without undermining family life. The macro social and economic system that values individualism, competitiveness and aggressiveness is destroying the micro-family system and contradicting its natural values of affection, solidarity and belonging. In other words, *the system is denying children and their parents, the right to happiness.*

Some 250 million children between the ages of 5 and 14 work in developing countries, 120, million of which are working full time, 50–60 million of which work in hazardous conditions, 61% of them in Asia and 32% in Africa (ILO, 2002). Children are employed because they are easier to exploit and they can be paid less. Poverty begets child labor, begets lack of education, begets poverty and lack of fulfillment of personal aspirations as well as aspirations of a significant contribution to society. Children are exploited by adults not only as child laborers. Child trafficking has become a billion-dollar-a-year business, with an estimated 1.2 million children falling victim annually and an estimated 300 thousand children are thought to have been coerced into military service, whether as soldiers, porters, messengers, cooks or sex slaves, with 120 thousand in Africa alone (ILO, 2002).

When families are unable to provide adequately for their children, States have the moral and legal obligation to support and assist them, as stated by the Convention of the Rights of the Child. Yet, structural adjustment policies transfer government functions to the market, limiting subsidies to the poor and reducing public expenditure – especially social expenditure – enhancing debt repayment capabilities at the cost of investment in human development. Exactly the opposite of what Governments have committed to when ratifying the Convention of the Rights of the Child.

Ill-conceived processes of decentralization have transferred the responsibility of social policy to local governments without transferring the necessary technical or financial resources, thereby increasing not only social disparities but also territorial disparities. Unregulated privatization of public services, and transfer of public services to transnational corporations, has not meant increases in efficiency and declines in fees as expected. Privatized services ignore the demands of the poor, excluding them by imposing unrealistic service charges that they cannot afford. In a context of acute inequities, the poor are unable to compete in the market on equal standing, nor to generate reasonable incomes which would allow them to counteract the absence of the public sector in the provision of services.

To add insult to injury, the owners of capital, natural resources and of technology, in their search for maximum profit at minimum cost, employ those who only have their effort to sell and pay them the lowest possible wages. Low wages not only perpetuate poverty but also limit the viability of families and make them incapable of supporting the development of their children (ILO, 1999).

Even though life expectancy has increased, and infant mortality, decreased considerably, still each year about 11 million children die before the age of five, mostly from preventable causes. 2.5 million die of diarrhea alone, which could be prevented in an 80% with investment in water and sanitation (Minujin & Delamonica, 2001). Some 100 million children are not in primary school, the majority of them, 60%, are girls. About 150 million children are severely malnourished. As a result of this childhood deprivation, close to half a million adult women are stunted. More than 15 million girls aged 15–19 give birth each year, exposing themselves and their babies to a much greater than average risk of maternal death as well as of child morbidity and mortality. Each year, humanity looses over 500 thousand women during childbirth, almost all of them in the developing world, most of them, preventable deaths (UNICEF, 1997–2002).

Additionally, researchers analyzing the impact of the most recent financial crisis on children – Mexico, Russia, Indonesia, Thailand, Brazil, Ecuador, and Argentina – coincide in stating that the negative effects on children as a consequence of financial crisis persist even after recovery. They also claim that children suffer irreversible damage during economic recessions because they are more exposed to malnutrition, may be taken out of school, or enter hazardous jobs. Lack of safety nets and slow or inappropriate government responses to frequent financial crisis – pivoting around large fiscal cuts, without undertaking special action to protect children, have exacerbated the severity of child impact.

Lack of Governance at National Level is Compounded with the Lack of Governance at Global Level

Global governance exercised over national governments on economic and social policy, by multilateral banks and trade organizations and agreements, have not attempted to reach the transnational corporations with policy impositions. A trend to open markets and to compete for foreign investment has been imposed on developing countries. Lack of regulations over the global financial markets has allowed an unprecedented flow of financial resources encountering no barriers, changing directions at the flash of lightning, seeking increased speculative opportunities, leaving behind a trail of distress in national, local and family economies. The same absence of barriers operates for the flows and of non-renewable natural resources from the weak to the powerful and for the reverse flows of dangerous waste. None of these resource flows are regulated or taxed in order to counteract the damage. The only flows that are sometimes savagely contained are the flows of people seeking opportunities outside of their national boundaries.

Technological advance, concentrated in a few private transnational hands, rather than becoming the engines of social transformation have become a vehicle of labor exploitation, social exclusion and environmental devastation. Moreover, there has not been an equal rhythm in capabilities for the adoption of measures to reduce waste nor to recycle the valuable resources that waste – including human excrements – contain, and in so doing to re-establish a balance between human activity and the environment. Globalization, growth of industrial production and growth in publicity has generated new consumption patterns in those who benefit from the fruits of development, which has meant growth in the production of waste and contaminants. There has been no global attempt to tax neither damaging consumption nor the companies that promote it.

Privatized state utilities in the hands of unregulated transnational monopolies providing water, sanitation, electricity and telephone services in developing countries charge high prices and exclude poorest consumers. A similar situation can be observed in the equally imposed health reforms that have created dual health services and eliminated solidarity mechanisms in developing countries. Transnational managed health care corporations have creamed the solvent market in populous developing countries, siphoning revenues from private insurance holders and government subsidies, leaving the poor, the chronically ill and the elderly to be cared for in decapitalized public services of very poor quality.

Some governments are now adopting precipitated decisions to "dollarize" their economies, relinquishing their economic management through monetary policies, in favor of the United States Federal Reserve Board. The ability of governments to regulate the most negative aspects of market economies and of speculative investment flows, or even to determine social policy independently, has become highly questionable.

Decreased Expenditure on Children

Both families and governments share the responsibility in financing the needs and rights of children. Economic and employment policies determine salaries and enable families in this role. Fiscal and budgetary policies, additionally to economic and social policies, enable governments to comply with this legal and moral obligation that they have acquired regarding children. Economic and fiscal policies determine the overall funding capabilities of a government, whereas, social policy and budget allocation policies determine the funding that is directed towards children. This means, that all of the above are the tools society has available to invest in children and in the future of society.

As has already been discussed, existing economic policies are not enabling families. Unemployment, employment instability, lack of means of production, absence of land redistribution, lack of creditability, low wages as a result of competition for foreign investment, informal sector predominance, lack of social benefits, elevated user fees for basic services, regressive tax systems and loss of labor organizations with negotiation capabilities, are among the many factors determining family limitations regarding their children.

On the one hand, debt service, military expenditures, privatization of public enterprises and liberal tax reforms which are so lenient with capital whether national or transnational, are eroding funding sources for national public budgets and shrinking social public expenditure more than any other public budgetary segment. On the other hand, imposed neoliberal policies are forcing governments to slash social sector expenditures first, and among them, those that benefit children directly. Moreover, in times of financial crisis and budgetary contractions, social spending rather than being protected or even increased to help counteract other negative effects of this crisis, is being severely reduced.

In this context, development goals are not being met. If progress does not accelerate, it will take more than 100 years for some regions to achieve some of the Millennium Development Goals (UNICEF, 2004). UNICEF and ECLAC have estimated the potential for fulfilling the goals that have been established for the children of Latin America, estimating the need for additional investment in the areas of early childhood education, primary education, secondary education, infant maternal care, infant care, HIV/AIDS, water and sanitation. With great differences between countries, in an optimistic growth scenario equivalent to that of the 1990s, compliance with those goals would annually require a 50% increase over the historical level in average regional investment per child. In other words, if average expenditure in the above mentioned areas has been U.S. $0.70 per child per day, it needs to be increased to U.S. $1.05. Furthermore, it was estimated that in a pessimistic zero growth scenario, the increase in average regional investment per child would need to reach 30% above that of the optimistic scenario (ECLAC-UNICEF-SECIB, 2003).

Additionally, international development assistance funds supporting social services are also contracting. Governments have agreed to allocate 0.7 of their gross national product to official development assistance. That agreement has not been complied with- the current average is barely over 0.2 ranging from over 0.7% in most Northern European countries, with Denmark at the top with 1.06%, to less than 0.1% in the case of the United States. Development assistance continues its diminishing trend and its trend towards giving priority to other sectors not directly related to children, as are basic social services. (UNICEF, 2002) Moreover, a large share of this assistance is tied to commercial or political interests of the donor countries.

We are Unwilling to Act on Our Past Lessons or to Achieve the Goals we have Established

We organize and participate in a myriad of international conferences that come to similar conclusions and establish common goals for humanity. Each conference extends the deadlines to meet the same unmet goals. For example, goals that were set in 1978 in the Primary Health Care Conference in Alma Ata, such as attaining health, water and sanitation for all in the year 1990 had to be set once again for the year 2000 by the World Summit for Children in 1990, the Earth Summit in 1992, the Social Summit in 1995, the City Summit in 1996, the Millennium Summit in 2000, among others. Most recently, they had to be extended once again by the 2002 United Nations Special Session on Children.

Goals established for children for the year 2000 at the World Summit for Children in 1990 were also not met and were revised at the 2002 United Nations Special Session for Children. What is surprising is that new goals are perhaps more realistic, but they also mean that governments have lowered their aspirations towards children. The global situation, according to UNICEF most recent figures (UNICEF, 2002) is as follows:

- The goal of 33% reduction in infant and under five mortality for year 2000 was not met. The world achieved only a 14% reduction with 3 million fewer child deaths. A new goal has been established for 2010 that is a further 33% reduction, in pursuit of the goal of reducing it by two thirds by 2015.
- The year 2000 goal of reducing severe and moderate under five malnutrition by 50% was also not met. Only a 17% reduction was achieved. In spite of this low level of achievement, the goal for 2010 is more lenient, aiming for only a 33% reduction with special attention to children under two.
- The goal set for year 2000 for safe drinking water was universal access. Coverage that was 79% in 1990 increased by 3–82% by year 2000. The new goal for 2010 has given up on universal coverage and is only a 33% reduction of those without access.
- A similar situation happens with the year 2000 goal of universal access to sanitary means of excreta disposal. The 1990 coverage of 55% of the population increased by 5–60% coverage in year 2000. In this case, again the goal is only a 33%

reduction of those without access that abandons the aim of universal coverage for many decades to come.

- In education, the goal for year 2000 was universal access to primary education and completion of primary education by 80% of children. The trend has been of an increase in coverage from 78 to 82% and a narrowing of the gender gap. The new goals are the elimination of gender disparities in primary and secondary education by 2005, a 50% reduction of children not in school by 2010, and a net primary school enrolment of at least 90%. Again, governments are setting the mark lower than before.
- The goal with the worst performance was the 1990 goal of 50% reduction in maternal mortality by year 2000. There has been no advance in this matter. 515,000 women die every year as a result of pregnancy and childbirth, 400 maternal deaths per 100,000 live births. There has been a small increase in the percentage of births attended by skilled personnel in only 53 countries where maternal mortality is generally less severe. The new goal for 2010 is only a 33% reduction, in pursuit of the goal of reducing it by three quarters by 2015. This means that governments are not willing to act forcefully upon this glaring injustice.

Figures mentioned above are global averages and hide great disparities among regions, countries and within countries. The HIV/AIDS epidemics threaten the gains in some areas like infant and child survival, especially in Sub Saharan Africa. Additionally, new challenges regarding child wellbeing have emerged and serious violations to child rights have become evident, for which no goals had been established before and that have been incorporated as goals in 2002. Among them, the right to identity (name and nationality) without which it is extremely difficult to have access to social services and other benefits; the eradication of sexual exploitation of children; the eradication of child labor; the eradication of violence against children within homes and communities; the prevention of HIV-AIDS and early pregnancies; early childhood integrated development; sexual education, etc. While goals are extremely useful to monitor progress, the real objective is to reach the universal coverage of children under 18 without any type of discrimination.

Progress in life expectancy, reduction of child and infant mortality, and good intentions of the international institutions involved must be acknowledged, however, more than the establishment of goals and cajoling governments to meet those goals must be done. The underlying causes of this failure, as have been exposed above, must be addressed. One of the main unresolved issues is the need to invest more in children. Unfortunately, institutions are weaker than, and are being weakened by the international financial institutions and other transnational interests that flourish from global lack of governance and deregulation.

IN THE SEARCH OF A BETTER FUTURE

Trends are Reversible Only as Long as There is the Collective Will to Do So

Yet trends have to be reversed because the current development path is destructive to humanity. Progress is possible in the presence of strong political will, when strong alliances are forged and the moral frameworks of social justice and human rights guide action. Existing universal human rights instruments provide us with the moral and legal obligation to do so. Human development and human rights are mutually reinforcing and help to secure the well-being and dignity of all people, enhancing self-respect, respect towards others, social cohesion and peace.

A development agenda that will redress disparities and eliminate exclusions will require a new type of public policy, a change in institutions and a change in values. Action directed at changing the current structure of power will be necessary at all levels, from the global to the local community level, as well as to the family level, in order to eradicate the profound causes impeding well-being and preventing their effects. "To radically improve our governance capabilities and the way we interact with each other, has become a matter of survival" (Dowbor, 1998, p. 408).

The Resources that Could Reverse this Situation Exist

The resources are there. What we lack is the collective will to reverse the current investment priorities. A world that is spending 780 billion in military expenditure and 400 billion in drugs, can surely find the necessary 6 billion to meet the goal of basic education for all, the 9 billion to meet the goal of water and sanitation for all, the 13 billion to close the gap in access to health and nutrition (UNDP, 1998).

As James Grant, the former UNICEF Executive Director stated: "The problem is not that we have tried to eradicate global poverty and failed; it is that no serious and concerted attempt has ever been made" (Grant, 1993, p. 2). Development assistance should increase to the internationally agreed levels. Additional sources of revenue at a global level could come from taxation on arms sales, on excessive revenues from corporations profiting from children, and on transnational flows of speculative capital, pollution and of nonrenewable resources or, from socially responsible enterprises. At national government level, additional sources of funding could come from progressive tax systems and improved budget allocations. At family level, from putting children first in the household budget but more importantly from free and universal access to basic services for children that would liberate family income for other necessities such as food and clothing, and from fair labor remuneration.

A New Type of Human Rights-Based Public Policy

A new type of public policy that will recognize children to be a collective responsibility as well as of their individual families, needs to be developed: Policies that will firmly establish that children have a legal claim on the attention and resources of their societies and their governments. Policies with an economic base that will guarantee the realization of social rights by making available the necessary resources and by promoting the conditions that will enable families – all families – to care for their children. Policies favoring legislative and institutional change compatible with the human rights instruments in force. Policies enabling both governments at all levels, and communities and their organizations to work in partnership. Policies that will redirect technological advance towards human development. Policies that will allow poor children, youth and their families to be active participants in the processes that involve them, rather than the passive and dependent objects of social policy, and at the same time, that will increase public interest to issues related to them.

The Convention of the Rights of the Child commits society to recognize that children under 18 have the right to their wellbeing, transforming public policy from a mere assistance directed to those in need, to a public policy which guarantees rights by changing the social structures which impede them. Additionally, the Convention establishes some key principles which can contribute to the eradication of poverty and disparities in society: the principle of non discrimination, the principle of indivisibility of rights and the right of the child to free expression and to have their opinions listened to and taken into account.

The consideration of these principles implies the decision to develop inclusive societies based on values of solidarity and shared responsibility rather than individualism, where needs are considered rights and where the concept of expansion of citizenship includes both civil and political rights as well as social and economic rights. There is a global agreement that there is no human right which is more important than others are and that none of them can be fully complied with unless all of them are complied with simultaneously. There is not only interdependence among rights, there is also a synergistic relation among them. Economic, social and cultural rights create the conditions for the full compliance of civil and political rights, and vice versa.

Social Policy, including policies affecting children directly, need to be understood in the context of the prevailing economic policies. For example, poverty reduction cannot be limited to changes in public spending. All aspects of policy – ranging from stabilization to structural reforms – have to be included in this equation (UNICEF, 1999). Those concerned with the wellbeing of children should not fall into the mistake of directing their efforts only to change social policy. There is an urgent need to understand the linkages among economic and social policies. Additionally, there is a need to broaden concerns towards fiscal and budgetary policies. How the State collects revenues and spends them can not continue limiting the capabilities to look after children in the way that governments have agreed to, when ratifying the Convention of the Rights of the Child. Moreover, social policy needs to be backed by sound economic, fiscal and budgetary policies not only so that the State can spend more in basic social services but also so that families can have employment and better incomes, to enable them to care for their children.

Rather than addressing poverty alleviation, we need to aim for poverty eradication There is an urgent need to orient Public Policy to redress disparities in accordance with the human rights principle of non-discrimination. We need to recognize that while we concentrate on the poor, we run the risk of ignoring the problems of society as a whole that is precisely where the problems of the poor originate. As long as the structural roots of poverty remain untouched, compensating for poverty or alleviating poverty are impossible propositions. Rather than directing compensatory action towards the symptoms that are increasing at the same rate poverty and disparities are increasing, we need to redirect our efforts to their underlying causes, in order to avoid becoming increasingly ineffective and unsustainable.

Understanding and acting against the political, economic and cultural causes which impedes child wellbeing needs to become a collective responsibility. Gro Bruntland, the former World Health Organization Executive Director has stated: "It is also necessary to remind presidents, prime ministers and finance ministers that they are the real health ministers. Their decisions are fundamental to the wellbeing of their people" (Bruntland, 1998).

A New Type of Governance Instruments

Even though technology and the economy have evolved speedily, institutional change has lagged behind. This new type of human rights based policy needs to be supported by legislative, judicial, fiscal, institutional and budgetary reforms consistent with the new realities. A global constitutional and judicial framework based on universal human rights instruments that would supersede economic and political interests and that would guarantee supranational citizenship is needed. So are strong regulatory capabilities in order to counteract the deficiencies of the global market and its negative impacts over the most vulnerable. A global regulatory and, taxing system should be established on those entities that are the causes of global vulnerability, instability and ever-deepening crisis. A taxing system is needed, that will provide global funds to redress the wrongs which some impose on others.

This strengthened global governance system needs to be interconnected with an equally strong local governance system that will more directly articulate local interests and identities to national and global policies. This will allow for a more transparent social control; will provide permanent and universal social security arrangements which will ensure preventive safety nets at all times; will strengthen participation opportunities, including the involvement of trade unions and community organizations; will effectively regulate privatized utilities or revert them to the public sector, especially those directly serving children; and will also legitimize action at central and supranational level. In sum, global governance that will distribute resources aiming at reverting disparities, especially focusing on child well-being, and that will manage the global environment wisely and equitably, is our only alternative.

Enhanced Democracies

We should aim at improving democracies in order to ensure government will respond to collective interests, promoting inclusiveness so that nobody is left behind, impeding the negative impacts of the media and private finance in electoral processes, transforming representative democracies in participatory democracies. Beyond universal voting rights, democracy must also mean equally sharing the fruits of development and making human rights a reality. This implies strong government role in crisis prevention, in redistribution and in the protection of the vulnerable. We also need to extend the democratic enhancement to international institutions, especially financial and trade institutions, extending voting rights to developing countries beyond those that are already in place in United Nations organizations with the exception of the Security Council. What needs to be sought are democratically established macroeconomic policies to serve the many and not only the few, and that are child-friendly, including fair trade systems to benefit the developing countries and not only the industrialized countries and the transnational corporations.

Change in Values

New social values need to be developed, promoting solidarity rather than competitiveness, ending the search of supremacy of one country over others; of capital over labor; of one gender over the other; of one race and culture over others; of one age group over others. A change in values is needed, from individualism searching to maximize personal gains in the shortest period of time, to social responsibility with the present as well as the future. We should aim for a cultural change that not only serves children, but that necessarily originates with children. In sum, a change in values which will ensure the right to happiness.

Halting the destructive road through which we are speeding, and advancing instead through this new path, we run a better chance of defeating the current trends, ensuring not only our survival, but also our development. Our ultimate objective, rather than accumulating financial wealth, should be to develop more humane, sustainable and just societies. Celebrating the new millennium is the perfect opportunity to get started, before it is too late.

Starting with children today is the only possible beginning.

REFERENCES

Bruntland, G. H. (1998). World Health Organization Executive Director, speech delivered at the World Bank (18 March). http://www.who.org.

Cornia, G. A. (2001). Harnessing globalization for children, Working Paper, UNICEF Innocenti Research Centre, Florence, Italy.

de la Barra, X. (1997). *Do poor urban children matter? The urban age.* Washington, DC: World Bank.

Dowbor, L. (1998). *A reproducao social: Propostas para uma gestao descentralizada.* Editora Vozes, Petropolis, Brazil.

ECLAC, UNICEF, SECIB (2003). Investments needed to achieve the goals set for children in the Ibero-American process, ECLAC, UNICEF, SECIB, Panama.

Grant, J. (1993). As quoted in page 2 in Children in Jeopardy, UNICEF, 1999, New York, USA.

International Labour Organization (1999). *The world of work.* Geneva http://www.ilo.org.

International Labour Organization (2002). *A future without child labour.* Geneva: ILO.

Lewis, S. (1997). *Foreword to development with a human face.* In: S. Mehrotra & R. Jolly (Eds). Oxford, United Kingdom: Clarendon Press.

Malloch Brown, M. (UNDP Administrator) (2003). Address at the Inter-Parliamentary Union Conference, Santiago, Chile.

Mehrotra, S., & Jolly, R. (1997). *Development with a human face.* Oxford, United Kingdom: Clarendon Press.

Minujin, A., & Delamonica, E. (2001). Mind the gap, child mortality inequities and globalization. Innocenti Working Paper, UNICEF Innocenti Research Centre, Florence, Italy.

Pope John Paul III (1999). Exhortación Apostólica Postsinodal Ecclessia in América (Mexico), http://www.catholicpages.com.

UNICEF, The Progress of the Nations (1997, 1998, 1999, 2000). UNICEF, New York, USA (annual reports).

UNICEF, Children in Jeopardy (1999). UNICEF, New York, USA.

UNICEF (2001). Children inequality matters. UNICEF Innocenti Research Centre, Florence Italy.

UNICEF, The State of The World's Children (2000, 2001, 2002, 2003, 2004). UNICEF, New York, USA (annual reports).

UNFPA, The State of the World Population (1998, 2002). UNFPA, New York, USA http://www.unfpa.org (annual reports).

UNDP, Human Development Report (1997, 1998, 1999, 2000, 2001, 2002, 2003). Oxford University Press, New York, USA (annual reports).

United Nations, General Assembly Resolution 44/25 (1989).

Wolfensohn, J. D. (1998). The other crisis, address to the Board of Governors (http://www.worldbank.org).

Wolfensohn, J. D. (2004). World Bank condemns defense spending. *The Guardian/UK* (14 February).

World Bank (2000). *Report on poverty.* New York: Oxford University Press. http://www.worldbank.org.

World Bank (2004). *World Development Report, 2000–2001.* New York: Oxford University Press.

World Resources Institute (1998). *World resources, a guide to the global environment, 1998–1999.* New York: Oxford University Press.

Subject Index